HARR

"Pardon My French!"

POCKET
SLANG
DICTIONARY

English-French / French-English

HARRAP

First published in Great Britain in 1998
by Chambers Harrap Publishers Ltd
7 Hopetoun Crescent
Edinburgh EH7 4AY
Great Britain

ISBN 0245 50344 7 (France)
ISBN 0245 60638 6 (UK)

Reprinted 1998

Dépôt légal : février 1998

Typeset by Chambers Harrap Publishers Ltd, Edinburgh
Printed and bound in Great Britain by
Caledonian International Book Manufacturing Ltd, Glasgow

Project Editors / Rédacteurs
Georges Pilard   Anna Stevenson

with / avec
Laurence Larroche

American English Consultant / Spécialiste de l'anglais américain
Dr Jonathan E. Lighter

Publishing Manager / Direction éditoriale
Patrick White

Pre-press Controller / Composition
Sharon McTeir

Trademarks

Words considered to be trademarks have been designated in this dictionary by the symbol ®. However, no judgement is implied concerning the legal status of any trademark by virtue of the presence or absence of such a symbol.

Marques déposées

Les termes considérés comme des marques déposées sont signalés dans ce dictionnaire par le symbole ®. Cependant la présence ou l'absence de ce symbole ne constitue nullement une indication quant à la valeur juridique de ces termes.

Preface

Harrap has a long-standing reputation for giving excellent coverage of slang and colloquial language in all its dictionaries. Indeed, we are the only major dictionary publisher to publish a bilingual dictionary devoted entirely to this type of language. This book represents a continuation of that tradition, but takes a completely fresh look at the slang used as we move towards a new millennium. Since slang is a particularly productive and fast-growing area of language, we have had to be very selective in writing this dictionary. We do not claim to have compiled an exhaustive and comprehensive record of French and English slang. Rather, we have endeavoured to present a collection of the most common slang words and expressions heard in French- and English-speaking countries today. We have also included many humorous and colourful expressions, including popular catchphrases, which might usually be considered beyond the scope of such a small book. We encourage you to browse, to explore the more colourful side of the French language, and to revel in the rich exuberance of language at its most fun.

What is slang?

It should be easy for lexicographers to define the term "slang". A closer examination, however, shows that the word is used to refer to several different types of language. For example, "slang" is often used to refer to the sort of language used within particular social or professional groups, such as soldiers, criminals or even dentists. The function of this kind of slang is usually to reinforce group identity. These in-group terms, often called "jargon", have been deliberately excluded from these pages except when they have gained common currency. What is in this book represents our broader definition of slang, namely a wide range of non-standard language, from the colloquial to the vulgar - the language heard or used by us all every day in informal contexts.

Labelling

Despite the recent rise of political correctness, people are still using vulgar, racist, sexist and blasphemous language. Our extensive system of labelling those terms which are most likely to shock or offend should enable the reader to avoid making any embarrassing faux pas.

Although certain areas like sex, drugs, drunkenness, bodily functions and racism are particularly rich in slang expressions in both languages, there are nonetheless several areas where one language has generated more slang terms than the other. French, for example, seems to have a slang word for practically every mundane item from coffee (**kawa** or **caoua**) to dictionaries (**dico**), not forgetting old favourites like **boulot** (work/job). Where possible, a translation is given which matches the register (level of informality) of the source expression, but where there is no slang equivalent, as is the case for the above examples, a neutral translation has been given, followed by the symbol ◻ .

The inclusion of a headword or expression in this slang dictionary implies that it is, by definition, familiar and should not be used in a formal context. There are, however, different degrees of informality, and these are clearly indicated. The symbol [!] denotes that the word or expression may cause offence and should be used with care. The symbol [!!] is reserved for vulgar and taboo words and phrases which will shock in most contexts. You should use these items with the greatest caution. We hope that these warning signs will help you to pick your way safely through the slang minefield.

Extra help

Sometimes translations are not enough on their own to render the full meaning of a word or expression. Therefore additional information is given at many entries in the form of usage notes. We hope you will find these enlightening and entertaining. They cover the following areas:

▶ Thematic panels giving explanations and examples of the different varieties of slang [**verlan**, **javanais**, **rhyming slang**, **Black American slang**]. There is also a panel explaining the typical patterns used in that most pure and visceral type of slang - insults [see the panel at **insultes** on the French side for examples of French insults];

▶ Fuller explanations of the subtleties of racist and homophobic terms [**Rital**, **Espingouin**, **Paki**, **queer**];

▶ Interesting etymologies [**bidochon**, **Château-Lapompe**, **cowabunga**, **not!**];

▶ Productive suffixes and prefixes [**-aille**, **archi-**, **-ard**, **-arama**, **-ville**, **mega-**];

▶ Explanations of set phrases that are hard to translate [**faire avancer le schmilblick**, **as the actress said to the bishop**, **beam me up Scotty!**];

▶ Cultural items that need fuller explanations [**BCBG**, **NAP**, **new lad**, **new man**, **Essex girl**, **trainspotter**].

Our friends across the pond

Although British slang is becoming increasingly Americanized through the influence of the media, many terms remain typically British or North American. These are clearly indicated with the geographical labels *Br* and *Am*, both at headword and at translation level. Our American consultant, Dr Jonathan E. Lighter of the University of Tennessee, has systematically verified all American material and has provided hundreds of new headwords. As author of the *Random House Historical Dictionary of American Slang*, Dr Lighter is a renowned specialist in North American slang, and we owe him a great debt of thanks for his invaluable contribution to this dictionary.

Préface

Les dictionnaires Harrap se sont toujours distingués par la place qu'ils accordent à l'argot et à la langue parlée en général. De toutes les grandes maisons d'édition, Harrap est la seule à publier un dictionnaire bilingue entièrement consacré à cet aspect de la langue. Le présent ouvrage privilégie particulièrement l'argot tel qu'on l'utilise en cette fin de millénaire. La partie français/anglais contient une part importante d'argot traditionnel ayant toujours cours aujourd'hui, ainsi que de nombreux termes de ce nouveau type d'argot que l'on appelle généralement argot des banlieues ou des cités.

La langue verte est une langue foisonnante, en constante évolution; de nouveaux termes, de nouvelles expressions apparaissent sans cesse et nous avons donc dû nous montrer sélectifs au moment d'établir notre nomenclature. Plutôt que de prétendre à l'exhaustivité, nous nous sommes efforcés de rassembler dans notre dictionnaire les mots et expressions argotiques les plus communément utilisés aujourd'hui dans les pays francophones et anglophones. Figurent également de nombreuses expressions humoristiques et pittoresques, ainsi qu'un grand nombre de formules popularisées par le cinéma et la télévision qui font partie intégrante de la langue parlée et qui posent souvent de gros problèmes de compréhension au locuteur étranger. Nous encourageons le lecteur à parcourir cet ouvrage pour le plaisir, pour découvrir une langue pleine de vitalité où l'humour règne en maître.

Qu'entend-on par argot?

Il n'est pas inutile de s'arrêter un instant sur la signification du mot ''argot'' car ce terme recouvre plusieurs réalités linguistiques bien différentes. Pour certains puristes l'argot désigne exclusivement la langue de la pègre (c'est ''l'argot des vrais de vrais'' d'Auguste Le Breton). Pour d'autres, l'argot est un jargon propre à un métier (le plus connu étant le *loucherbem* ou ''argot des bouchers'', aujourd'hui tombé en désuétude). Dans les deux cas, l'utilisation d'un jargon spécifique sert à renforcer la cohésion d'un groupe donné. Ce type d'argot ne nous intéresse que dans la mesure où il perd sa fonction purement cryptique pour être absorbé par la langue populaire. Notre ouvrage est donc un dictionnaire d'argot au sens le plus large du terme: un dictionnaire du français et de l'anglais non conventionnels, dont le registre s'étend du familier au très vulgaire.

Les indications d'usage

Malgré l'apparition du "politiquement correct", nombre de termes et expressions vulgaires, racistes et sexistes ont toujours cours. Des indicateurs d'usage éviteront au lecteur de se placer dans des situations embarrassantes en utilisant à son insu des mots qui ne manqueraient pas de choquer.

Les domaines les plus riches en termes argotiques sont peu ou prou les mêmes en anglais et en français: le sexe, le corps, la drogue, l'ivresse et le racisme sont particulièrement bien représentés dans les deux langues. Cela ne signifie pas que chaque terme dispose de son équivalent exact dans l'autre langue. L'argot et le slang ne coïncident pas en tous points. De nombreux termes de "rhyming slang", par exemple, n'ont pas d'équivalents argotiques en français; c'est le cas de **apples and pears** (escalier) et de **adam and eve** (croire). Il existe également des concepts qui ne peuvent pas être rendus de façon familière en français; c'est le cas de l'un des sens de l'adjectif **straight**, par exemple, que nous avons du nous résoudre à traduire par "conventionnel".

Nous nous sommes efforcés, dans nos traductions, de respecter le niveau de langue des mots et expressions de la langue source. Cependant, lorsque ceci s'est avéré impossible, nous avons indiqué que la traduction donnée est neutre en lui accolant le symbole ▫.

Ceci étant un dictionnaire d'argot, le fait même qu'un terme (ou une expression) y soit traité est le signe qu'il appartient à la langue familière, et qu'il ne doit donc pas être utilisé dans un contexte neutre. Il existe cependant différents registres au sein de la langue familière, que nous avons choisi d'indiquer de la façon suivante: le symbole ⚠ indique qu'un mot ou expression risque de choquer et doit être utilisé(e) avec circonspection; le symbole ⚠⚠ est réservé aux termes et expressions vulgaires ou tabou. Les termes accompagnés de ce symbole doivent être utilisés avec la plus grande prudence. Nous espérons que ces indications vous aideront à éviter les principales embûches qui jalonnent la route de l'apprenti argotier.

Pour aider l'utilisateur

Il arrive qu'une simple traduction ne suffise pas à rendre fidèlement les subtilités ou parfois même le sens d'un mot ou d'une expression. C'est pourquoi de nombreuses entrées sont dotées de notes d'usage qui fournissent un complément d'information à l'utilisateur. Nous espérons que vous trouverez ces notes à la fois instructives et distrayantes. Elles comportent les éléments suivants:

▶ des encadrés sur les différentes variétés d'argot (**rhyming slang, Black American slang, verlan, javanais**). Vous trouverez également un tableau sur les différentes façons d'insulter son prochain dans la langue de Shakespeare (voir le tableau **insults** dans la partie anglais/français du dictionnaire);

▶ des compléments d'information expliquant les nuances d'usage de différents termes racistes, xénophobes ou insultants pour les homosexuels [**Paki, queer, Rital, Espingouin**];

▶ des explications sur certaines étymologies intéressantes [**cowabunga, not!, bidochon, Château-Lapompe**];

▶ des préfixes et des suffixes particulièrement générateurs [**mega-, -arama, -ville, archi-, -aille, -ard**];

▶ des explications sur des expressions et des formules toutes faites posant des problèmes de traduction parti-culiers [**as the actress said to the bishop, beam me up Scotty!, faire avancer le schmilblick**];

▶ des explications sur certains termes indissociables d'un contexte culturel ou social donné. (L'anglais britannique abonde en termes désignant des archétypes sociaux tels que **new lad, new man, Essex girl, trainspotter**).

L'argot américain

Bien que l'argot britannique subisse l'influence toujours croissante de l'anglais parlé aux États-Unis (principalement par le biais des médias), il existe de nombreux termes et expressions qui n'ont cours que d'un côté ou de l'autre de l'Atlantique. Ces termes sont précédés de la mention *Br* (britannique) et *Am* (américain); ces indications figurent aussi bien du côté anglais/français que dans les traductions de la partie français/anglais. Notre spécialiste en américanismes, le Professeur Jonathan E. Lighter, de l'Université du Tennessee, a vérifié tous les termes d'argot américain qui figurent dans cet ouvrage et a suggéré l'inclusion de centaines de nouvelles entrées et expressions. Le Professeur Lighter, auteur du *Random House Historical Dictionary of American Slang*, est l'un des grands spécialistes actuels de l'argot nord-américain.

Symboles Phonétiques de l'Anglais

Consonnes

[b]	bimbo	['bɪmbəʊ]
[d]	dishy	['dɪʃɪ]
[dʒ]	ginormous	[dʒaɪˈnɔːməs];
	jiffy	['dʒɪfɪ]
[f]	flunk	[flʌŋk]
[g]	gaga	['gɑːgɑː]
[h]	hunky	['hʌŋkɪ]
[j]	yonks	[jɒŋks]
[k]	conk	[kɒŋk]
[l]	legless	['leglɪs]
[m]	manky	['mæŋkɪ]
[n]	naff	[næf]
[ŋ]	banger	['bæŋə(r)]
[p]	prat	[præt]
[r]	reefer	['riːfə(r)]
[(r)]	(seulement prononcé en cas de liaison avec le mot suivant) rotter	['rɒtə(r)]
[s]	scran	[skræn]
[ʃ]	shooter	['ʃuːtə(r)]
[t]	tenner	['tenə(r)]
[tʃ]	chow	[tʃaʊ]
[θ]	thicko	['θɪkəʊ]
[ð]	brother	['brʌðə(r)]
[v]	vibes	[vaɪbz]
[w]	wacko	['wækəʊ]
[z]	zilch	[zɪltʃ]
[ʒ]	casual	['kæʒʊəl]

Voyelles

[æ]	slammer	['slæmə(r)]
[ɑː]	barf	[bɑːf]
[e]	preggers	['pregəz]
[ɜ]	hurl	[hɜːl]
[ə]	gotcha	['gɒtʃə]
[iː]	geek	[giːk]
[ɪ]	dippy	['dɪpɪ]
[ɒ]	pong	[pɒŋ]
[ɔː]	awewome	['ɔːsəm]
[ʊ]	footie	['fʊtɪ]
[uː]	loony	['luːnɪ]
[ʌ]	junkie	['dʒʌŋkɪ]

Diphtongues

[aɪ]	wino	['waɪnəʊ]
[aʊ]	lousy	['laʊzɪ]
[eə]	yeah	[jeə]
[eɪ]	flake	[fleɪk]
[əʊ]	loaded	['ləʊdɪd]
[ɪə]	weirdo	['wɪədəʊ]
[ɔɪ]	boyf	[bɔɪf]

French Phonetic Symbols

Consonants

[b] bagnole [baɲɔl]
[d] draguer [drage]
[f] frangin [frãʒɛ̃]
[g] greluche [grǝlyʃ]
[ʒ] gerber [ʒɛrbe]
[k] costaud [kɔsto]
[l] larguer [large]
[m] mioche [mjɔʃ]
[n] nul [nyl]
[ŋ] feeling [filiŋ]
[ɲ] guignol [giɲɔl]
[p] pépé [pepe]
[r] reum [rœm]
[s] speeder [spide]
[ʃ] chiper [ʃipe]
[t] taré [tare]
[v] vachement [vaʃmã]
[z] zonard [zonar]

Vowels

[a] aprème [aprɛm]
[ɑ] pâlichon [pɑliʃɔ̃]
[e] bourré [bure]
[ǝ] peler [pǝle]
[ø] dégueulasse [degølas]
[œ] gueule [gœl]
[ɛ] craignos [krɛɲos]
[i] nippes [nip]
[ɔ] hosto [ɔsto]
[o] dope [dop]
[u] roupiller [rupije]
[y] nunuche [nynyʃ]
[ã] lambin [lãbɛ̃]
[ɛ̃] joint [ʒwɛ̃]
[ɔ̃] défoncé [defɔ̃se]
[œ̃] parfum [parfœ̃]

Semi-vowels

[w] boîte [bwat]
[j] flicaille [flikaj]
[ɥ] puissant [pɥisã]

Labels

Indications d'Usage

English	Symbol	Français
gloss	=	glose
[introduces a brief explanation]		[introduit une explication]
cultural equivalent	≃	équivalent culturel
[introduces a translation which has a roughly equivalent status in the target language]		[introduit une traduction dont les connotations dans la langue cible sont comparables]
very familiar	!	très familier
vulgar	!!	vulgaire
neutral translation	▫	traduction neutre
abbreviation	*abbr, abrév*	abréviation
adjective	*adj*	adjectif
adverb	*adv*	adverbe
American English	*Am*	anglais d'Amérique du Nord
auxiliary	*aux*	auxiliaire
British English	*Br*	anglais britannique
Canadian French	*Can*	canadianisme
exclamation	*exclam*	exclamation
feminine	*f*	féminin
humorous	*Hum*	humoristique
offensive	*Injurieux*	injurieux
[denotes a racist or homophobic term]		[signale un terme raciste, xénophobe ou insultant pour les homosexuels]
invariable	*inv*	invariable
ironic	*ironic, ironique*	ironique
masculine	*m*	masculin
modal auxiliary verb	*modal aux v*	auxiliaire modal
noun	*n*	nom
feminine noun	*nf*	nom féminin
feminine plural noun	*nfpl*	nom féminin pluriel
masculine noun	*nm*	nom masculin
masculine and feminine noun (same form for both genders)	*nmf*	nom masculin et féminin (formes identiques)
masculine and feminine noun (different form in the feminine)	*nm,f*	nom masculin et féminin (formes différentes)
masculine plural noun	*nmpl*	nom masculin pluriel
Black American English	*Noir Am*	anglais noir américain
plural noun	*npl*	nom pluriel
proper noun	*npr*	nom propre

offensive	*Offensive*	injurieux
[denotes a racist or homophobic term]		[signale un terme raciste, xénophobe ou insultant pour les homosexuels]
pejorative	*Pej, Péj*	péjoratif
prefix	*prefix, préfixe*	préfixe
preposition	*prep, prép*	préposition
pronoun	*pron*	pronom
registered trademark	®	marque déposée
something	*qch*	quelque chose
somebody	*qn*	quelqu'un
somebody	*sb*	quelqu'un
something	*sth*	quelque chose
suffix	*suffix, suffixe*	suffixe
Swiss French	*Suisse*	helvétisme
verb	*v.*	verbe
intransitive verb	*vi*	verbe intransitif
impersonal verb	*v imp*	verbe impersonnel
reflexive verb	*vpr*	verbe pronominal
transitive verb	*vt*	verbe transitif
inseparable transitive verb	*vt insép*	verbe transitif à particule inséparable
[phrasal verb where the verb and the adverb or preposition cannot be separated, eg **bunk off**; he **bunked off** school]		[par exemple: **bunk off** (sécher); he **bunked off** school (il a séché les cours)]
separable transitive verb	*vt sép*	verbe transitif à particule séparable
[phrasal verb where the verb and the adverb or preposition can be separated, eg **chuck** in; he **chucked** his job **in** or he **chucked in** his job]		[par exemple: **chuck in** (plaquer); he **chucked** his job **in** ou he **chucked in** his job (il a plaqué son travail)]

English-French
Anglais-Français

A

AC/DC [eɪsiː'diːsiː] *adj (bisexual)* à voile et à vapeur, bi

ace [eɪs] **1** *adj (excellent)* super, génial **2** *vt Am* **to ace an exam** réussir un examen les doigts dans le nez

aces ['eɪsəs] *adj Am (excellent)* super, génial

acid ['æsɪd] *n (LSD)* acide *m*; **to drop acid** prendre de l'acide; **acid house** *(music)* acid house *f*

acidhead ['æsɪdhed] *n* **to be an acidhead** consommer beaucoup de LSD □

act [ækt] *n* **(a) to get one's act together** se prendre en main □ **(b)** *Am* **to queer the act** tout faire foirer
▶ *voir aussi* **riot**

actress ['æktrɪs] *n Br Hum* **he's got a huge one… as the actress said to the bishop** il en a une énorme, si j'ose dire…

"As the actress said to the bishop" est une formule humoristique prononcée lorsque l'on se rend compte que ce qui vient d'être dit peut être interprété de façon grivoise.

adam ['ædəm] *n (ecstasy)* ecstasy □ *f*, exta *f*

adam and eve ['ædəmən'iːv] *vt Br (rhyming slang* **believe***)* croire □; **would you adam and eve it!** tu te rends compte?

aggro ['ægrəʊ] *n Br (abrév* **aggravation***) (violence)* castagne *f*; *(hassle)* problèmes □ *mpl*; **my Mum's giving me so much aggro at the moment** ma mère est toujours sur mon dos en ce moment

aid [eɪd] *n* **what's that in aid of?** pourquoi t'as fait/dit ça, exactement?

airhead ['eəhed] *n* = jolie nana pas très futée

alky ['ælkɪ] *n* **(a)** *(abrév* **alcoholic***)* alcolo *mf*, poivrot(e) *m,f* **(b)** *Am (abrév* **alcohol***)* gnôle *f*

all [ɔːl] *adv* **(a) the team was all over the place** l'équipe a joué n'importe comment □; **at the interview he was all over the place** *or* **shop** il a complètement foiré son entretien; **he was pretending to be sober but he was all over the place** il était visiblement complètement bourré même s'il faisait tout son possible pour le dissimuler
(b) he's not all there il n'a pas toute sa tête
(c) she was all over him at the party elle l'a dragué tout le temps qu'a duré la soirée; *Hum* **he was all over her like a rash** *or* **a cheap suit** il l'a draguée de façon flagrante

all right [ɔːl'raɪt] **1** *adj* **an "I'm all right Jack" attitude** un comportement du style "moi d'abord, les autres ensuite" **2** *exclam* **(a)** *(as greeting)* salut, ça va? **(b)** *(in approval)* super!, cool!
▶ *voir aussi* **bit**

ambulance chaser ['æmbjʊlənst-ʃeɪsə(r)] *n Am Péj* = avocat qui ne s'occupe que d'affaires de demandes de dommages et intérêts pouvant rapporter gros

angel dust ['eɪndʒəldʌst] *n* PCP *f*, phéncyclidine □ *f*

ankle-biter ['æŋkəlbaɪtə(r)] *n* gosse *mf*

anorak ['ænəræk] *n Br Péj (person)* ringard *m*

Ce terme désigne un type de jeune homme généralement solitaire dont les activités vont à l'encontre de ce qui est considéré comme "cool". Un "anorak" ne s'intéresse pas à la mode (d'où le terme "anorak", symbole de l'absence de goût en matière vestimentaire) ni à l'actualité musicale ou sportive, et ne fréquente aucun endroit branché.

A-OK [eɪəʊ'keɪ] *Am* **1** *adj* super, génial; **everything's A-OK** tout baigne dans l'huile

2 *adv* **to go A-OK** se passer vachement bien

ape [eɪp] *adj* **to go ape (over)** *(lose one's temper)* piquer une crise, péter les plombs (à cause de); *(enthuse)* s'emballer (pour)

apeshit ! ['eɪpʃɪt] *adj* **to go apeshit (over)** *(lose one's temper)* piquer une crise, péter les plombs (à cause de); *(enthuse)* s'emballer (pour)

apple ['æpəl] *n* **(a) the (Big) Apple** New York ▫ **(b)** *Br* **apples and pears** *(rhyming slang* **stairs)** escaliers ▫ *mpl*

-arama [ə'rɑːmə] *suffixe Hum* **you should have seen how much we ate – it was pigarama!** t'aurais vu tout ce qu'on a mangé – une vraie orgie!; **try that new bar – it's babearama!** essaye ce nouveau bar – il y a toujours plein de canons

Ce suffixe dénote l'abondance de ce qui le précède. On peut l'ajouter à presque n'importe quel nom, verbe ou adjectif pour introduire la notion de foisonnement.

armpit ['ɑːmpɪt] *n* **the armpit of the universe** *(place)* un coin paumé, un trou

arse ! [ɑːs] *Br* **1** *n* **(a)** *(buttocks)* cul *m*; **a kick up the arse** un coup de pied au cul; **to make an arse of sth** complètement foirer qch; **to get one's arse in(to) gear** se remuer le cul; **to work one's arse off** bosser comme un nègre;

to talk out of one's arse dire des conneries; **to be out on one's arse** *(get fired)* se faire virer; **to go arse over tit** *or* **tip** ramasser une gamelle; **my arse!** mon cul!; **to kiss** *or* **lick sb's arse** faire du lèche-cul à qn; **kiss my arse!** va te faire foutre!; **get your arse over here!** ramène ta fraise!, amène-toi!; **move** *or* **shift your arse!** pousse ton cul!; **stick** *or* **shove it up your arse!** tu peux te le mettre au cul!; **a nice piece of arse** une nénette bandante; **he's been sitting on his arse all day** il a rien foutu de la journée; **he doesn't know his arse from his elbow** il est complètement nul; **she thinks the sun shines out of his arse** elle le prend pour un dieu; **it's my arse that's on the line** ça risque de me retomber sur la gueule

(b) *(person)* crétin(e) *m,f*; **to make an arse of oneself** se ridiculiser ▫

2 *vt* **why don't you come with us? – I can't be arsed** tu viens avec nous? – non, j'ai trop la flemme; **he can't be arsed doing it himself** il a pas envie de se faire chier à le faire lui-même

▶ *voir aussi* **pain**

arse about !, **arse around** ! *vi Br (act foolishly)* faire le con, déconner; *(waste time)* glander, glandouiller

arse up ! *vt sép Br* **to arse sth up** foirer qch

arse-bandit ! ['ɑːsbændɪt] *n Br Injurieux* pédale *f*, tapette *f*

arsehole ! ['ɑːshəʊl] *n Br* **(a)** *(anus)* trou *m* du cul; **the arsehole of nowhere** *or* **of the universe** *(place)* un coin paumé, un trou **(b)** *(person)* trou *m* du cul; **to make an arsehole of oneself** se ridiculiser ▫

arseholed ! ['ɑːshəʊld] *adj Br (drunk)* bourré comme un coing, complètement pété

arse-kisser ! ['ɑːskɪsə(r)] *n Br* lèche-cul *mf*

arse-kissing[!] [ˈɑːskɪsɪŋ] *Br* **1** *n* lèche *f*
2 *adj* **he's nothing but an arse-kissing bastard!** c'est qu'un lèche-cul!

arse-licker[!] [ˈɑːslɪkə(r)] = **arse-kisser**

arse-licking[!] [ˈɑːslɪkɪŋ] = **arse-kissing**

arty-farty [ˈɑːtɪˈfɑːtɪ], *Am* **artsy-fartsy** [ˈɑːtsɪˈfɑːtsɪ] *adj* (*person*) qui se donne un genre artiste□; (*film, activities*) qui se veut artistique□

as if [æzˈɪf] *exclam* **am I a nag? – as if!** est-ce que je suis une emmerdeuse? – mais non! (*dit ironiquement*); **I'm going on a diet tomorrow – as if!** je commence un régime demain – c'est ça! (*dit ironiquement*)

ass[!] [æs] *n Am* cul *m*; **a kick in the ass** un coup de pied au cul; **to get one's ass in gear** se remuer le cul; **to work one's ass off** bosser comme un nègre; **to be on sb's ass** être sur le dos de qn; **to do sth ass backwards** faire qch à l'envers□; **to get one's ass in a sling** avoir des emmerdes; **to go ass over teakettle** ramasser une gamelle; **my (aching) ass!** mon cul!; **I don't want to put my ass on the line** je veux pas que ça me retombe sur la gueule; **to be out on one's ass** (*get fired*) se faire virer; **to haul** *or* **tear ass** se grouiller; **to kiss sb's ass** faire du lèche-cul à qn; **kiss my ass!** va te faire foutre!; **get your ass over here!** ramène ta fraise!, amène-toi!; **move your ass!** pousse ton cul!; **stick** *or* **shove it up your ass!** tu peux te le mettre au cul!; **a nice piece of ass** une nénette bandante; **he's been sitting on his ass all day** il n'a rien foutu de la journée; **he doesn't know his ass from his elbow** *or* **from a hole in the ground** il est complètement nul; **it's my ass that's on the line** ça risque de me retomber sur la gueule; **to kick sb's ass** (*defeat*) ratatiner qn; **to kick ass** assurer un max; **to break** *or* **bust one's ass** se casser le cul; **to be up to one's ass in work** crouler sous le travail; **up your ass!** va te faire mettre!; **you can**

bet your ass I will! un peu que je vais le faire!; **your ass is grass!** tu vas voir ce que tu vas prendre!; **they oughta fire his sorry ass!** ils devraient le virer!
▶ *voir aussi* **bite, pain, rat**

ass-bandit[!] [ˈæsbændɪt] *n Am Injurieux* pédale *f*, tapette *f*

asshole[!] [ˈæshəʊl] *n Am* (**a**) (*anus*) trou *m* du cul; **the asshole of the universe** *or* **world** (*place*) un coin paumé, un trou (**b**) (*person*) trou *m* du cul

ass-kisser[!] [ˈæskɪsə(r)] *n Am* lèche-cul *mf*

ass-kissing[!] [ˈæskɪsɪŋ] *Am* **1** *n* lèche *f*
2 *adj* **he's nothing but an ass-kissing bastard!** c'est qu'un lèche-cul!

ass-licker[!] [ˈæslɪkə(r)] = **ass-kisser**

ass-licking[!] [ˈæslɪkɪŋ] = **ass-kissing**

ass-wipe[!] [ˈæswaɪp] *n Am* (*person*) trou *m* du cul

at [æt] *prép* **that club is where it's at** c'est la boîte *in*, **that's not where I'm at** c'est pas mon truc

attitude [ˈætɪtjuːd] *n* (*self-assurance, assertiveness*) assurance□ *f*; **to have attitude** avoir du caractère; **a car with attitude** une voiture qui a du caractère

Auntie [ˈɑːntɪ] *n Br* **Auntie (Beeb)** la BBC

> "Auntie" se traduit littéralement "tatie"; c'est le surnom affectueux donné à la BBC par les Britanniques, qui met en relief l'attitude quelque peu paternaliste de l'institution vis-à-vis du public, et un style qui manque parfois d'audace.

away [əˈweɪ] **1** *adj Br* **well away** (*drunk*) bourré, beurré, pété
2 *adv* **to be away with the fairies** (*senile*) être complètement gaga; (*eccentric*) être farfelu; (*daydreaming*) être dans les nuages

awesome [ˈɔːsəm] *adj Am* super, génial

axe, *Am* **ax** [æks] *n* (*guitar*) gratte *f*, râpe *f*

B

babe [beɪb] n (**a**) *(attractive woman)* canon m (**b**) *(term of address)* chéri(e) m,f (**c**) Am *(attractive man)* beau mec m
▶ voir aussi **magnet**

backside [bæk'saɪd] n derrière m

bad [bæd] adj (**a**) *(not good)* **I'm having a bad hair day** *(my hair's a mess)* je n'arrive pas à me coiffer aujourd'hui [□]; *(I'm having a bad day)* aujourd'hui c'est un jour sans; **he's bad news** c'est quelqu'un de pas fréquentable [□] (**b**) *(excellent)* super, génial; **this music's so bad** cette musique est vraiment super

badass [!] ['bædæs] Am **1** n *(person)* dur(e) m,f (à cuire)

2 adj (**a**) *(intimidating, tough)* **to be badass** être un(e) dur(e) à cuire (**b**) *(excellent)* super, génial; **her new sneakers are so badass** ils sont super, ses nouveaux tennis

bad-mouth ['bædmaʊθ] vt Am débiner

bag [bæg] n (**a**) Péj *(woman)* **old bag** vieille bique f
(**b**) *(quantity of drugs)* dose f *(en sachet ou dans un papier plié)*
(**c**) *(interest)* dada m; **he has a new bag** il a un nouveau dada; **it's not my bag** c'est pas mon truc
(**d**) **it's in the bag** c'est dans la poche
▶ voir aussi **bum**

ball [!!] [bɔːl] Am **1** vt *(have sex with)* *(of man)* baiser, tringler, troncher; *(of woman)* baiser avec, s'envoyer
2 vi *(have sex)* baiser

ball up [!] [bɔːl] Am = **balls up**

ball-breaker [!] ['bɔːlbreɪkə(r)], **ball-buster** [!] ['bɔːlbʌstə(r)] n Am (**a**) *(woman)* femme f de tête [□] (**b**) *(problem,*

situation) casse-tête m

ballistic [bə'lɪstɪk] adj **to go ballistic** piquer une crise, péter une durite

balls [!] [bɔːlz] npl (**a**) *(testicles)* couilles fpl; **to have blue balls** avoir les couilles pleines et douloureuses (**b**) *(nonsense)* conneries fpl (**c**) *(courage)* cran m; **to have the balls to do sth** avoir assez de cran pour faire qch

balls up [!] vt sép Br **to balls sth up** *(interview, exam)* foirer qch, se planter à qch; *(plan, arrangement)* faire foirer qch; **you've ballsed everything up** tu as tout fait foirer

balls-up [!] ['bɔːlzʌp] n Br merdier m; **to make a balls-up of sth** *(interview, exam)* foirer qch, se planter à qch; *(plan, arrangement)* faire foirer qch

ballsy ['bɔːlzɪ] adj qui en a

ball-up [!] ['bɔːlʌp] Am = **balls-up**

baloney [bə'ləʊnɪ] **1** n *(nonsense)* foutaises fpl
2 exclam foutaises!

baltic ['bɔːltɪk] adj Br *(weather)* **it's baltic** il fait un froid de canard

bananas [bə'nɑːnəz] adj *(mad)* dingue, cinglé, timbré; **to go bananas** devenir dingue ou cinglé ou timbré

bang [bæŋ] **1** n (**a**) *(sexual intercourse)* **to have a bang** [!!] baiser
(**b**) Am **to get a bang out of sb/sth** s'éclater avec qn/en faisant qch
2 adv Br (**a**) *(exactly)* **bang on time** pile à l'heure; **bang up-to-date** hypermoderne; **bang in the middle** en plein milieu
(**b**) **bang on** *(guess, answer, calculation)* qui tombe pile; *(arrive, start)* pile à

l'heure

(c) **bang goes that idea** c'est râpé;
bang goes my holiday c'est foutu
pour mes vacances

3 !! vt (have sex with) (of man) baiser,
tringler, troncher; (of woman) baiser
avec, s'envoyer

4 !! vi (have sex) baiser

bang on vi Br (talk at length) rabâcher;
**he's forever banging on about the
Spice Girls** il n'arrête pas de nous
rebattre les oreilles avec les Spice Girls

bang up vt sép Br (imprison) boucler,
coffrer

banger ['bæŋə(r)] n (**a**) (car) tas m de
ferraille, vieille bagnole f (**b**) Br (sausage) saucisse □ f; **bangers and mash**
des saucisses et de la purée

banging ['bæŋɪŋ] adj Br (club, party)
hyper animé

barf [bɑːf] vi dégueuler, gerber

barfly ['bɑːflaɪ] n Am pilier m de bistrot

barhop ['bɑːhɒp] vi Am faire la tournée
des bars □

barking ['bɑːkɪŋ] adj Br **barking (mad)**
cinglé, toqué, taré

barmy ['bɑːmɪ] adj Br barjo

bash [bæʃ] **1** n (**a**) (party) fiesta f (**b**) Br
(attempt) **to have a bash (at sth/at
doing sth)** essayer (qch/de faire qch) □;
I'll give it a bash je vais essayer un coup
2 vt (hit) cogner; (dent) cabosser

basket case ['bɑːskɪtkeɪs] n cinglé(e)
m,f, barjo mf

bastard ! ['bɑːstəd] n (**a**) (person) salaud (salope) m,f; **poor bastard!** le
pauvre!; **lucky bastard!** le veinard!;
you sad bastard! pauvre mec ou type,
va!; **some bastard traffic warden
gave me a parking ticket** une salope
de contractuelle m'a collé un papillon
(**b**) (thing) truc m chiant; **a bastard of
a job** un travail à la con; **this oven is a
bastard to clean** ce four est vraiment
chiant à nettoyer; **I can't get the bas-**

tard thing to start j'arrive pas à faire
démarrer cette saloperie

bat [bæt] n (**a**) Péj (woman) **old bat** vieille
bique f (**b**) Am (drinking spree) **to be on
a bat** sortir prendre une cuite
▸ voir aussi **hell**

battleaxe, Am **battleax** ['bætəlæks]
n (woman) dragon m, virago f

batty ['bætɪ] adj fêlé, timbré

bawl out [bɔːl] vt sép **to bawl sb out**
enguirlander qn, passer un savon à qn

beak [biːk] n (nose) quart de brie m

beam [biːm] vt Hum **beam me up,
Scotty!** que quelqu'un me sorte de là!

Il s'agit de l'expression utilisée par les
membres d'équipage du vaisseau
"Starship Enterprise" dans la série
télévisée américaine culte Star Trek
pour demander au technicien de
l'équipe (nommé Scotty) de les
ramener à bord du vaisseau grâce à un
rayon spécial. Aujourd'hui, on utilise
cette expression lorsque l'on se trouve
dans une situation très désagréable,
dont on voudrait bien être sorti
comme par miracle.

bear [beə(r)] n Hum **does a bear shit in
the woods?** ! à ton avis?
▸ voir aussi **Pope**

beast [biːst] n Am (ugly woman) boudin
m, cageot m

beat [biːt] vt (**a**) **to beat it**, Am **to beat
feet** (go away) se tirer, se barrer (**b**) **to
beat one's meat** !! (masturbate) se
branler
▸ voir aussi **rap**

beat off !! vi (masturbate) se branler

beat-'em-up ['biːtəmʌp] n = film ou
jeu vidéo comportant de nombreuses
bagarres

beauty ['bjuːtɪ] **1** n (beautiful thing)
splendeur f; **his new hi-fi's a beauty**
sa nouvelle chaîne est géniale; **that
black eye is a real beauty!** quel beau
coquard!

2 *exclam Br* **(you) beauty!** super!

beaver [!!] ['biːvə(r)] *n (woman's genitals)* chatte *f*, cramouille *f*, chagatte *f*

bed [bed] *vt (have sex with)* coucher avec

beef [biːf] **1** *n (complaint)* **what's your beef?** c'est quoi, ton problème?; **my beef is with him** c'est avec lui que j'ai un problème
2 *vi (complain)* râler (**about** à propos de)

beefcake ['biːfkeɪk] *n (attractive men)* beaux mecs *mpl* musclés; *Br* **he's a real beefcake** il est vraiment bien foutu

beemer ['biːmə(r)] *n (BMW)* BM *f*

beezer ['biːzə(r)] *n Am (nose)* tarin *m*, blaire *m*

bell [bel] *n Br (phone call)* **to give sb a bell** passer un coup de fil à qn, bigophoner qn

bellyache ['belɪeɪk] *vi* râler (**about** à propos de)

bellyful ['belɪfʊl] *n* **to have had a bellyful of sb/sth** en avoir ras le bol de qn/qch

belt [belt] **1** *n (blow)* gnon *m*, un pain *m*; **to give sb a belt in the face** flanquer un gnon *ou* un pain dans la tronche à qn
2 *vt (hit) (person)* flanquer un gnon *ou* un pain à; *(ball)* flanquer un grand coup dans
3 *vi (move quickly)* **to belt along** aller à fond la caisse *ou* à toute blinde; **to belt down the stairs** descendre les escaliers à fond la caisse *ou* à toute blinde

belt up *vi Br (be quiet)* la fermer, la boucler; **belt up!** la ferme!, ta gueule!

bend [bend] *n* **to be round the bend** être dingue *ou* cinglé; **to go round the bend** devenir dingue *ou* cinglé; **to drive sb round the bend** rendre qn dingue *ou* cinglé
▸ *voir aussi* **ear, elbow**

bender ['bendə(r)] *n* **(a)** *(drinking session)* beuverie *f*; **to go on a bender** aller se cuiter **(b)** *Injurieux (homosexual)*

pédale *f*, tantouze *f*

Dans la catégorie (b), ce terme perd son caractère injurieux quand il est utilisé par des homosexuels.

bent [bent] *adj* **(a)** *Br Injurieux (homosexual)* pédé; **as bent as a nine bob note** *or* **as a three pound note** pédé comme un phoque **(b)** *Br (corrupt, dishonest)* pourri, ripou **(c)** *Am* **bent out of shape** *(angry, upset)* dans tous ses états **(d)** *Am* **get bent!** [!] va te faire voir!

Dans la catégorie (a), ce terme perd son caractère injurieux quand il est utilisé par des homosexuels.

berk [bɜːk] *n Br* andouille *f*, débile *mf*

bet [bet] *vi* **you bet!** y a intérêt!, un peu!; **he says he's sorry – I bet!** il dit qu'il regrette – c'est ça! *ou* mon œil, oui!

bevvied ['bevɪd] *adj Br* bourré, beurré; **to get bevvied** se cuiter, prendre une cuite

bevvy ['bevɪ] *n Br* **(a)** *(alcohol)* alcool *m*, bibine *f* **(b)** *(alcoholic drink)* **to have a bevvy** boire un coup **(c)** *(drinking session)* beuverie *f*; **to go on the bevvy** aller se cuiter, aller prendre une cuite

bi [baɪ] *adj (abrév* **bisexual)** bi

Bible-basher ['baɪbəlbæʃə(r)], **Bible-thumper** ['baɪbəlθʌmpə(r)] *n* grenouille *f* de bénitier

biddy ['bɪdɪ] *n* **old biddy** vieille bique *f*

biff [bɪf] *vt (person)* foutre un pain *ou* un gnon à; *(object)* foutre un grand coup dans

big [bɪg] *adj* **(a)** **to be into sb/sth big time** *or* **in a big way** être dingue de qn/qch; **he's been doing smack big time** *or* **in a big way** depuis quelque temps il arrête pas de prendre de l'héro; **did you have fun? – big time!** vous vous êtes bien amusés? – oui, vachement bien! **(b)** **to make a big deal out of sth** faire tout un fromage de qch; **it's no big deal** c'est pas grave; *Ironique* **big deal!**

la belle affaire!

(**c**) *Br* **big girl's blouse** *(wimp)* femme-lette *f*

(**d**) **to have big hair** = avoir une coiffure bouffante tenue par une grande quantité de laque

(**e**) *Am* **big house** *(prison)* taule *f*, placard *m*; **he's gone to the big house** on l'a mis à l'ombre

▶ *voir aussi* **cheese, E, enchilada, mama, shot, smoke, wheel**

biggie, biggy ['bɪgɪ] *n* **it's going to be a biggie** *or* **biggy!** *(new film, CD)* ça va faire un carton!; *(storm)* ça va faire mal!; *Am* **no biggie!** pas de problèmes!

bike [baɪk] *n* (**a**) *Br* **on your bike!** *(go away)* casse-toi!, tire-toi!; *(don't talk nonsense)* n'importe quoi!; *(I don't believe you)* c'est ça! (**b**) **she's the town bike** [!] *(promiscuous)* il n'y a que le train qui ne lui soit pas passé dessus

Bill [bɪl] *n Br* **the (Old) Bill** les flics *mpl*

bimbo ['bɪmbəʊ] *n (woman)* jolie nana pas très futée

bin [bɪn] *n (psychiatric hospital)* maison *f* de fous

bint [bɪnt] *n Br* greluche *f*; **you stupid bint!** espèce d'andouille!

bird [bɜːd] *n* (**a**) *Br (woman)* nana *f*, gonzesse *f* (**b**) *Am (man)* mec *m* (**c**) *Am* **to give sb the bird** *(make fun of)* se foutre de la gueule de qn; *(gesture at)* faire un doigt d'honneur à qn; **to flip sb the bird** *(gesture at)* faire un doigt d'honneur à qn

birdbrain ['bɜːdbreɪn] *n* cervelle *f* d'oiseau

bishop ['bɪʃəp] *n* **to bang** *or Br* **bash the bishop** [!!] *(masturbate)* se branler, se taper sur la colonne

▶ *voir aussi* **actress**

bit [bɪt] *n* (**a**) *Br* **a bit on the side** *(man)* amant □ *m*; *(woman)* maîtresse □ *f*; **she's a bit of all right!** elle est gironde!

(**b**) *Am (term of imprisonment)* peine *f* de prison □; **he did a bit in Fort Worth**

il a fait de la taule à Fort Worth

▶ *voir aussi* **stuff**

bitch [bɪtʃ] **1** *n* (**a**) *(woman)* salope *f*; *Br* **the poor bitch** la pauvre; **the lucky bitch** la veinarde

(**b**) *(thing)* truc *m* chiant; **life's a bitch!** chienne de vie!; **I've had a bitch of a day** j'ai passé une sale journée; **her place is a bitch to find without a map** sa maison est vraiment chiante à trouver sans carte

2 *vi* (**a**) *Br (say nasty things)* déblatérer (**about** contre)

(**b**) *(complain)* râler (**about** à propos de)

bitch up *vt sép* **to bitch sth up** saloper qch

bitchin ['bɪtʃɪn] *adj Am* super, génial

bitchy ['bɪtʃɪ] *adj (person)* salaud, dégueulasse; *(remark)* dégueulasse; **that was a bitchy thing to do** c'est vraiment salaud *ou* dégueulasse d'avoir fait ça

bite [baɪt] *Am* **1** *vt* **bite me!, bite my ass!** [!] va te faire voir!

2 *vi (be bad)* craindre; **this really bites!** ça craint vraiment!

biz [bɪz] *n Br (abrév* **business**) **it's the biz!** c'est impec'!

blab [blæb] **1** *vt (tell)* raconter □

2 *vi* (**a**) *(tell secret)* vendre la mèche (**b**) *(chatter)* bavarder, jacasser

blabbermouth ['blæbəmaʊθ] *n* **he's a blabbermouth** il ne sait pas tenir sa langue

black man's wheels [blækmænz-'wiːlz] *npl Br (BMW)* BM *f*

blade [bleɪd] *n (knife)* lame *f*, surin *m*

blag [blæg] *Br* **1** *n (robbery)* braquage *m*

2 *vt* (**a**) *(steal)* piquer (**b**) *(con)* **to blag oneself sth** obtenir qch au culot; **to blag one's way in** resquiller

blah [blɑː] **1** *n* (**a**) *(meaningless remarks, nonsense)* blabla *m*, baratin *m* (**b**) **blah, blah, blah** *(to avoid repetition)* etc etc;

he went on for half an hour about how we all had to work harder, **blah, blah, blah** il nous a rabâché pendant une demi-heure qu'il fallait qu'on fasse tous plus d'efforts, etc etc **2** *adj (dull)* sans intérêt [□]

blank [blæŋk] *n* **to shoot** or **fire blanks** *(of man)* être stérile [□]

blast [blɑ:st] **1** *n Am (good time)* **it was a blast** c'était l'éclate; **we had a blast** on s'est éclatés
2 *exclam Br* **blast (it)!** crotte!, zut!

blasted ['blɑ:stɪd] **1** *adj* **(a)** *(drunk)* bourré, beurré; *(on drugs)* défoncé **(b)** *(for emphasis)* **the blasted car** cette saleté de voiture; **the blasted child** ce sale môme; **it's a blasted nuisance** c'est sacrément embêtant
2 *adv (for emphasis)* **don't go so blasted fast!** ne va pas si vite, bon sang!

blazes ['bleɪzɪz] *npl* **(a)** **to run/work like blazes** courir/travailler comme un(e) fou (folle) **(b)** **what/who/why the blazes...?** que/qui/pourquoi diable...? **(c)** **go** or *Br* **get to blazes!** va au diable!

bleeder ['bli:də(r)] *n Br (person)* salaud (salope) *m,f*; **the poor bleeder** le pauvre; **you lucky bleeder!** sacré veinard!

bleeding ['bli:dɪŋ] *Br* **1** *adj (for emphasis)* **you bleeding idiot!** espèce de con!; **what a bleeding nuisance!** quelle saloperie!
2 *adv (for emphasis)* foutrement; **you're bleeding (well) coming with me!** tu viens avec moi, un point c'est tout!; **that was bleeding stupid!** c'est vraiment con, ce que tu as fait/dit!

blimey ['blaɪmɪ] *exclam Br* zut alors!, la vache!

blinder ['blaɪndə(r)] *n Br* **(a)** *(drinking session)* beuverie *f*; **to go on a blinder** aller se cuiter, aller prendre une cuite **(b)** *(excellent performance)* sacrée prestation *f*; **to play a blinder** faire un match/une partie d'enfer

blinding ['blaɪndɪŋ] *adj Br (excellent)* super, génial

blink [blɪŋk] *n* **to be on the blink** *(of TV, machine)* déconner

blinking ['blɪŋkɪŋ] *Br* **1** *adj (for emphasis)* sacré; **the blinking thing won't work!** pas moyen de faire marcher cette saloperie!

Black American slang

Il existe de nombreux termes d'argot Noir américain, qui, bien que désormais largement utilisés en Amérique du Nord et en Grande-Bretagne, retiennent néanmoins leur identité afro-américaine. Ces termes portent la mention *Noir Am* dans ce dictionnaire.

C'est dans le monde des musiciens, et particulièrement le monde des jazzmen des années trente, que tout un pan de l'argot Noir américain trouve ses origines. Le jargon des musiciens de jazz a par la suite été progressivement adopté par la jeunesse américaine. Depuis le début des années 80, c'est le rap qui est une source importante de termes d'argot. L'orthographe de ces termes est souvent modifiée de façon à en transcrire fidèlement la prononciation (par ex "ho", "nigga", "gangsta"). Le rap, en tant que forme d'expression d'une communauté défavorisée qui connaît un taux de criminalité très élevé, est une musique souvent violente, qui véhicule volontiers des clichés emprunts de misogynie. Le rap continue d'exercer une très grande influence sur la façon dont s'expriment les jeunes.

2 *adv (for emphasis)* sacrément; **you're so blinking stubborn!** ce que tu peux être têtu!

blitzed [blɪtst] *adj (drunk)* bourré, beurré; *(on drugs)* défoncé

bloke [bləʊk] *n Br* type *m*, mec *m*

blokeish [ˈbləʊkɪʃ] *adj Br* = typique d'un style de vie caractérisé par de fréquentes sorties entre copains, généralement copieusement arrosées, et un goût prononcé pour le sport et les activités de groupe

bloody ☒ [ˈblʌdɪ] *Br* **1** *adj (for emphasis)* **you bloody idiot!** espèce de con!; **bloody hell!** putain!; **where's my bloody pen?** où est ce putain de stylo? **2** *adv (for emphasis)* foutrement; **it's bloody hot!** il fait foutrement chaud!, il fait une chaleur à crever!; **it was bloody brilliant!** putain, c'était génial!; *Ironique* **that's just bloody marvellous!** il manquait plus que ça!; **I wish he'd bloody stop it!** quand est-ce qu'il va s'arrêter, merde!

blooming [ˈbluːmɪŋ] *Br* **1** *adj (for emphasis)* **I've lost my blooming keys** j'ai perdu ces saletés de clefs **2** *adv (for emphasis)* sacrément; **he's blooming useless!** il est vraiment nul!

blotto [ˈblɒtəʊ] *adj* complètement paf *ou* pété, bourré comme un coing

blow [bləʊ] **1** *n Br (cannabis)* shit *m*; *Am (cocaine)* coke *f*, neige *f*; *(heroin)* héro *f*, blanche *f*
2 *vt* **(a) to blow a gasket** *or* **a fuse** *(of person)* péter une durite, péter les plombs; **to blow one's top** *or* **one's stack** péter une durite, péter les plombs; **it blew my mind!** *(of film, experience)* ça m'a complètement emballé!
(b) *(reveal)* **to blow the gaff** vendre la mèche
(c) to blow the whistle on sb balancer qn; **to blow the whistle on sth** dénoncer qch ▫

(d) *(waste) (chance)* gâcher; **we should have won but we blew it** on aurait dû gagner mais on a tout fait foirer; **that's blown it!** ça a tout fait foirer!
(e) *(money)* claquer; **he blows all his salary on holidays/CDs** il claque tout son salaire en voyages/CD; **they blew £2,000 on an engagement ring** ils ont claqué 2.000 livres dans une bague de fiançailles
(f) ☒☒ *(fellate)* tailler une pipe à
(g) *Am* **to blow chunks** *(vomit)* gerber, dégobiller

blow away *vt sép* **(a)** *Am* **to blow sb away** *(shoot dead)* flinquer qn, descendre qn; *(defeat)* flanquer une raclée à qn **(b) to blow sb away** *(impress, bowl over)* complètement emballer qn; **the Grand Canyon just blew me away** le Grand Canyon m'a coupé le souffle

blower [ˈbləʊə(r)] *n Br (telephone)* bigophone *m*

blow-job ☒☒ [ˈbləʊdʒɒb] *n* pipe *f*; **to give sb a blow-job** tailler une pipe à qn

blub [blʌb], **blubber** [ˈblʌbə(r)] *vi* chialer comme un veau

blue-arsed fly ☒ [ˈbluːɑːstˈflaɪ] *n Br* **to run about** *or* **around like a blue-arsed fly** courir dans tous les sens

blues [bluːz] *npl Am* **to sing the blues** *(complain)* geindre ▫, pleurnicher

boat [bəʊt] *n Br* **boat (race)** *(rhyming slang* **face***)* tronche *f*, trombine *f*

Bob [bɒb] *npr Br* **...and Bob's your uncle!** ...et le tour est joué!

bod [bɒd] *n (abrév* **body***)* **(a)** *Br (person)* individu ▫ *m*; **he's a strange bod** c'est un drôle de numéro *ou* de zèbre **(b)** *(physique)* corps ▫ *m*; **she's got a great bod** elle est super bien roulée *ou* foutue

bodacious [bəʊˈdeɪʃəs] *adj Am* incroyable

bog ☒ [bɒg] *n Br (toilet)* chiottes *fpl*; **bog roll** papier cul *m*, PQ *m*

bog off ☐ *vi Br* se barrer, se casser; **bog off!** *(go away)* barre-toi!, casse-toi!; *(expressing contempt, disagreement)* va te faire voir!

bogart [ˈbəʊgɑːt] *vt* **to bogart a joint** squatter un joint, bogarter

bogey [ˈbəʊgɪ] *n Br (nasal mucus)* crotte *f* de nez

bog-standard [ˈbɒgstændəd] *adj Br* tout ce qu'il y a d'ordinaire

bogus [ˈbəʊgəs] *adj Am (unpleasant)* chiant; *(unfashionable)* ringard

bohunk [ˈbəʊhʌŋk] *n Am* **(a)** *Injurieux (Eastern European immigrant)* = terme désignant un Américain originaire d'un pays d'Europe de l'Est ou ses descendants **(b)** *(country bumpkin)* bouseux(euse) *m,f*

boiler [ˈbɔɪlə(r)] *n Péj* **(old) boiler** vieille peau *f*

bollock ☐ [ˈbɒlək] *Br* **1** *adv* **bollock naked** à poil, le cul à l'air
2 *vt* **to bollock sb** engueuler qn, passer un savon à qn

bollocking ☐ [ˈbɒləkɪŋ] *n Br* engueulade *f*, savon *m*; **to give sb a bollocking** engueuler qn, passer un savon à qn; **to get a bollocking** se faire engueuler, se faire passer un savon

bollocks ☐ [ˈbɒləks] *Br* **1** *npl* **(a)** *(testicles)* couilles *fpl* **(b)** *(nonsense)* conneries *fpl*; **the film was a load of bollocks** c'était de la merde, ce film **(c) bollocks to him!** qu'il aille se faire foutre!
2 *exclam* des conneries, tout ça!
▸ *voir aussi* **dog**

bollocks up ☐ *vt sép Br* **to bollocks sth up** *(interview, exam)* foirer qch, se planter à qch; *(plan, arrangement)* faire foirer qch

bolshie, bolshy [ˈbɒlʃɪ] *adj Br* râleur

bomb [bɒm] **1** *n* **(a)** *Br* **to go like a bomb** *(of fast car)* être un vrai bolide; *(of party)* se passer super bien; **he/the car was going like a bomb** il/la voiture

roulait à fond la caisse
(b) *Br (large sum of money)* **to cost a bomb** coûter bonbon *ou* la peau des fesses; **to make a bomb** se faire un fric fou
(c) *Am (failure)* bide *m*
2 *vt Am (fail) (test)* se planter complètement à
3 *vi* **(a)** *(fail) (of film)* faire un four *ou* un bide; *Am (of student)* se planter complètement
(b) to bomb along aller à fond la caisse *ou* à toute blinde

bomb out 1 *vt sép Br* **to bomb sb out** poser un lapin à qn
2 *vi (fail)* se faire sortir; **to bomb out of sth** se faire éjecter de qch

bombed [bɒmd] *adj (drunk)* bourré, beurré; *(on drugs)* défoncé

bomber [ˈbɒmə(r)] *n (cannabis cigarette)* cône *m*

bonce [bɒns] *n Br* caboche *f*, ciboulot *m*

bone ☐☐ [bəʊn] *Am* **1** *vt* baiser, troncher, tringler
2 *vi* baiser, s'envoyer en l'air

bone up on *vt insép Am* **to bone up on sth** potasser qch

bonehead [ˈbəʊnhed] *Am* **1** *n* débile *mf*, crétin(e) *m,f*
2 *adj* débile

boner [ˈbəʊnə(r)] *n* **(a)** *(erection)* **to have a boner** ☐☐ bander, avoir la trique **(b)** *Am (mistake)* bourde *f*, boulette *f*

bong [bɒŋ] *n* pipe *f* à eau □, bang *m*

bonk [bɒŋk] *Br* **1** *n* **to have a bonk** faire une partie de jambes en l'air
2 *vt* s'envoyer en l'air avec
3 *vi* faire une partie de jambes en l'air

bonkers [ˈbɒŋkəz] *adj* cinglé, fêlé, dingue, tapé

bonzo [ˈbɒnzəʊ] *adj Am* cinglé, fêlé, dingue, tapé

boob [buːb] **1** *n* **(a)** *(breast)* nichon *m*; **to have a boob job** se faire refaire les nichons; **boob tube** *(garment)* bustier *m* extensible □

  (b) *Br (mistake)* boulette *f*, bourde *f*; **to make a boob** faire une boulette

  (c) *Am (person)* abruti(e) *m,f*, andouille *f*, courge *f*; **boob tube** *(television)* téloche *f*

  2 *vi Br (make mistake)* faire une bourde *ou* une boulette

boo-boo ['buːbuː] *n Am* boulette *f*, bourde *f*; **to make a boo-boo** faire une boulette *ou* une bourde

booger ['buːgə(r)] *n Am* **(a)** *(nasal mucus)* crotte *f* de nez **(b)** *(person)* garnement □ *m* **(c)** *(thing)* bidule *m*, machin *m*, truc *m*

boogie ['buːgɪ] **1** *n (dance)* **to have a boogie** danser □, guincher

  2 *vi* **(a)** *(dance)* danser □, guincher

  (b) *Am (leave)* mettre les bouts, se casser, s'arracher; **let's boogie on out of here** on met les bouts, on se casse

book [bʊk] *Am* **1** *vt* **to book it** *(leave)* mettre les bouts, se casser, s'arracher; **let's book it!** on se casse!, on s'arrache!

  2 *vi* **(a)** *(leave)* mettre les bouts, se casser, s'arracher **(b)** *(move quickly)* foncer

boondocks ['buːndɒks] *npl Am* **the boondocks** la cambrousse; **in the boondocks** en pleine cambrousse

boost [buːst] *Am* **1** *vt* **(a)** *(steal)* piquer, faucher **(b)** *(break into)* cambrioler □

  2 *vi (steal)* voler □

boot [buːt] **1** *n* **(a)** *(kick)* **to give sth a boot** donner un coup de latte dans qch; *Br* **he was trying to get up when they put the boot in** il essayait de se relever quand ils se sont mis à lui donner des coups de latte; *Br* **he'd already apologized, you didn't have to put the boot in like that** il s'était excusé, tu n'avais pas besoin d'insister à ce point □

  (b) to give sb the boot *(fire)* virer qn; **to get the boot** *(get fired)* se faire virer

  (c) *Br Péj (ugly woman)* **(old) boot**

boudin *m*, cageot *m*

  2 *vt (kick)* donner un coup de latte/des coups de latte à

boot out *vt sép* **to boot sb out** foutre qn à la porte, vider qn

booty ['buːtɪ] *n Noir Am* **(a)** *(buttocks)* cul *m*, derche *m* **(b)** *(sexual intercourse)* **to get some booty** s'envoyer en l'air

booze [buːz] **1** *n* alcool □ *m*, bibine *f*; **to be on the booze** picoler

  2 *vi* picoler

boozehound ['buːzhaʊnd] *n Am* ivrogne *mf*, poivrot(e) *m,f*

boozer ['buːzə(r)] *n* **(a)** *Br (pub)* pub □ *m*, troquet *m* **(b)** *(person)* ivrogne *mf*, poivrot(e) *m,f*

booze-up ['buːzʌp] *n* beuverie *f*; **to have a booze-up** prendre une cuite

boozy ['buːzɪ] *adj (person)* qui aime picoler; *(occasion)* où l'on picole beaucoup

bop[1] [bɒp] *Br* **1** *n (dance)* **to have a bop** danser □, guincher

  2 *vi (dance)* danser □, guincher

bop[2] **1** *n (punch)* coup *m* de poing □, ramponneau *m*; **she gave him a bop on the head** elle lui a donné un coup de poing dans la tête

  2 *vt (hit)* frapper □; **she bopped him on the head** elle lui a donné un coup de poing dans la tête

boss [bɒs] *adj (excellent)* super; **you're looking boss!** tu es superbe!

bottle ['bɒtəl] *n* **(a)** *Br (courage)* courage □ *m*, cran *m* **(b)** *(alcohol)* **the bottle** l'alcool □ *m*; **to be on the bottle** picoler; **to hit the bottle** se mettre à picoler

bottle out *vi Br* se dégonfler; **he bottled out of the fight** il s'est dégonflé au dernier moment et a refusé de se battre; **he bottled out of telling her the truth** finalement il a eu la trouille de lui dire la vérité

bouncer ['baʊnsə(r)] *n (doorman)* videur *m*

box [bɒks] *n* (**a**) *Br* **to be out of one's box** *(drunk)* être complètement pété, être plein comme une barrique (**b**) **the box** *(television)* la télé, la téloche (**c**) !! *(vagina)* chatte *f*, con *m*

boyf [bɔɪf] *n Br* abrév **boyfriend**) **my/ her boyf** mon/son mec

boy racer [bɔɪ'reɪsə(r)] *n Br* jeune conducteur *m* imprudent □

> Le "boy racer" est un jeune homme qui vient d'obtenir son permis de conduire et dont l'activité principale consiste à faire des tours en voiture avec ses copains, sans destination précise, pied au plancher, toutes vitres baissées tout en écoutant de la musique à plein volume.

boy toy ['bɔɪtɔɪ] *n Am Hum* jeune amant □ *m (d'une femme plus âgée)*

bozo ['bəʊzəʊ] *n Am* crétin(e) *m,f*, andouille *f*, cruche *f*

bracelets ['breɪslɪts] *npl (handcuffs)* menottes □ *fpl*, bracelets *mpl*

brain [breɪn] **1** *n* (**a**) **to have brains** en avoir dans le ciboulot; *Br* **to have sth on the brain** faire une fixette sur qch (**b**) *(person)* tête *f*; **he's a real brain** c'est une vraie tête
2 *vt (hit)* donner un coup sur la cafetière à

brass [brɑːs] *n Br* (**a**) *(money)* blé *m*, flouze *m*
(**b**) **brass (neck)** *(cheek, nerve)* culot *m*, toupet *m*; **to have a brass neck** être culotté; **to have the brass (neck) to do sth** avoir le culot de faire qch
(**c**) **it's brass monkeys** *or* **brass monkey weather** *(very cold)* il fait un froid de canard
(**d**) *(prostitute)* pute *f*

brass off *vt sép Br* **to brass sb off** gonfler qn; **to be brassed off (with)** en avoir marre (de)

bread [bred] *n* (**a**) *(money)* blé *m*, oseille *f* (**b**) *Br* **it's the best thing since sliced bread** c'est ce qu'on a fait de mieux depuis l'invention du fil à couper le beurre

break [breɪk] *n* **give me a break!** *(don't talk nonsense)* dis pas n'importe quoi!; *(stop nagging)* fiche-moi la paix!

breeze [briːz] *n* **it was a breeze** *(simple)* c'était du gâteau
▸ *voir aussi* **shoot**

brew [bruː] *n Am (beer)* mousse *f*

brewer's droop ['bruːəz'druːp] *n Br Hum* = impuissance temporaire due à l'alcool; **he had brewer's droop** il bandait mou parce qu'il avait trop picolé

brewski ['bruːskɪ] *n Am* mousse *f*

brill [brɪl] *adj Br (abrév* **brilliant)** super, génial

bring off !! [brɪŋ] *vt sép (masturbate)* **to bring sb off** branler qn; **to bring oneself off** se branler

Brit [brɪt] **1** *n (abrév* **Britisher)** Angliche *mf*
2 *adj (abrév* **British)** angliche

bro [brəʊ] *n (abrév* **brother)** (**a**) *(family member)* frangin *m*, frérot *m* (**b**) *Am (male friend)* pote *m*; **yo, bro!** salut mon pote!

broad [brɔːd] *n Am (woman)* gonzesse *f*, nana *f*

broke [brəʊk] *adj (having no money)* fauché, raide; **to go for broke** jouer le tout pour le tout

brolly ['brɒlɪ] *n Br* pébroc *m*, pépin *m*

brother ['brʌðə(r)] *n Noir Am (black male)* Noir *m* américain □; **a brother got capped last night** un des nôtres s'est fait buter hier soir
▸ *voir aussi* **soul**

browned-off ['braʊnd'ɒf] *adj Br* **to be browned-off (with)** en avoir marre (de); **to be browned-off with doing sth** en avoir marre de faire qch

brown-nose ! ['braʊnnəʊz] **1** *n* lèche-cul *mf*
2 *vi* faire de la lèche

Brum [brʌm] *npr Br* (*abrév* **Birmingham**) = surnom donné à la ville de Birmingham

Brummie ['brʌmɪ] *n Br* = natif de la ville de Birmingham

bubbly ['bʌblɪ] *n* (*champagne*) champ' *m*

buck [bʌk] *n Am* (*dollar*) dollar □ *m*; **got any bucks?** t'as du fric?

buddy ['bʌdɪ] *n* (**a**) (*friend*) pote *m* (**b**) (*term of address*) **thanks, buddy** (*to friend*) merci, vieux; (*to stranger*) merci, chef; **hey, buddy!** hé, toi!

buddy up *vi Am* **to buddy up to sb** faire de la lèche à qn

buddy-buddy ['bʌdɪbʌdɪ] *adj Am Péj* copain-copain; **they're very buddy-buddy** ils sont très copain-copain

buff [bʌf] *n* **in the buff** à poil

bug [bʌg] *vt* (*annoy, nag*) enquiquiner, emmerder (**about** à cause de)

bug off *vi Am* (*leave*) se casser, s'arracher; **bug off!** casse-toi!

bug out *vi Am* (**a**) (*leave*) se casser, s'arracher (**b**) (*go mad*) déjanter

bugger [!] ['bʌgə(r)] *Br* **1** *n* (**a**) (*person*) salaud *m*; **the poor bugger** le pauvre; **the silly bugger** cet espèce d'imbécile; **to play silly buggers** faire le con (**b**) (*thing*) truc *m* chiant; **a bugger of a job** un travail à la con; **her house is a bugger to find** sa maison est vachement dure à trouver (**c**) **bugger all** (*nothing*) que dalle; **bugger all money/thanks** pas un sou/un merci; **that was bugger all help** ça n'a servi à rien (**d**) **I don't give a bugger!** je m'en fous pas mal!

2 *exclam* **bugger (it)!** merde!

3 *vt* (**a**) (*exhaust*) mettre sur les genoux, crever (**b**) (*ruin, break*) bousiller (**c**) (*for emphasis*) **bugger me!** putain!; **bugger the expense, let's buy it!** et puis merde, tant pis si c'est cher, achetons-le!

bugger about [!], **bugger around** [!] *Br* **1** *vt sép* **to bugger sb about** (*treat badly*) se foutre de la gueule de qn; (*waste time of*) faire perdre son temps à qn □

2 *vi* (*waste time*) glander, glandouiller

bugger off [!] *vi Br* se barrer, se casser, s'arracher; **bugger off!** (*go away*) barre-toi!, casse-toi!; (*expressing contempt, disagreement*) va te faire foutre!

bugger up [!] *vt sép* **to bugger sth up** (*ruin*) foutre qch en l'air; (*break*) bousiller qch

buggered [!] ['bʌgəd] *adj Br* (**a**) (*exhausted*) crevé, naze (**b**) (*broken*) foutu, naze (**c**) (*amazed*) **well, I'm buggered!** ben merde alors! (**d**) (*in trouble*) foutu; **if we don't get the money soon, we're buggered** si on a pas l'argent rapidement, on est foutus (**e**) (*for emphasis*) **I'll be buggered if I'm going to apologize!** plutôt crever que de m'excuser!; **I'm buggered if I know!** j'en sais foutre rien!

buggery [!] ['bʌgərɪ] *n Br* **like buggery!** ouais, mon cul!; **to run like buggery** courir comme un(e) dératé(e); **is he a good cook? – is he buggery!** il fait bien la cuisine? – tu veux rire!

bull [bʊl] **1** *n* (*nonsense*) conneries *fpl*; **he's talking bull** il raconte des conneries, il dit n'importe quoi

2 *exclam* n'importe quoi!

▶ *voir aussi* **shoot**

bulldyke ['bʊldaɪk] *n Injurieux* gouine *f* (*d'apparence masculine*)

bullshit [!] ['bʊlʃɪt] **1** *n* conneries *fpl*

2 *exclam* des conneries, tout ça!

3 *vt* **to bullshit sb** raconter des conneries à qn; **she bullshitted her way into the job** elle a eu le boulot au culot

4 *vi* raconter des conneries

bum [bʌm] **1** *n* (**a**) (*buttocks*) fesses *fpl*,

derrière m; **bum bag** banane f (sac); **bum fluff** (beard) barbe f très peu fournie □
(b) Am (tramp) **(stew) bum** clodo mf
(c) (enthusiast) **to be a beach/ski bum** passer son temps à la plage/sur les pistes □
(d) **to give sb the bum's rush** (dismiss) envoyer paître qn; (from work) virer qn; **to give sth the bum's rush** (idea, suggestion) rejeter qch □; **my idea got the bum's rush** mon idée est passée à la trappe
2 adj (worthless) merdique; **to get a bum deal** se faire avoir; **a bum rap** (false charge) une fausse accusation □
3 vt (scrounge) **to bum sth (from** or **off sb)** taxer qch (à qn); **to bum a lift** or **a ride** se faire emmener en voiture □; **can I bum a lift** or **a ride to the station?** est-ce que tu peux me déposer à la gare?

bum about, bum around 1 vt insép (spend time in) **to bum about Australia/the country** parcourir l'Australie/le pays sac au dos □; **to bum about the house** rester chez soi à glander
2 vi (hang around) glander

bum-freezer ['bʌmfriːzə(r)] n Br Hum (jacket) veste f ultra-courte □; (skirt) jupe f ultra-courte □, jupe ras la touffe

bummed [bʌmd] adj **to be bummed** l'avoir mauvaise

bummer ['bʌmə(r)] n (situation) **what a bummer!** la poisse!, c'est chiant!; **it was a real bummer being stuck at home all day** c'était vraiment la poisse ou chiant de devoir rester enfermé toute la journée

bump off [bʌmp] vt sép **to bump sb off** (murder) supprimer ou zigouiller ou buter qn

bun [bʌn] n (a) **to have a bun in the oven** (be pregnant) être en cloque
(b) Am **buns** (buttocks) fesses fpl,

miches fpl

bundle ['bʌndəl] n (a) (large sum of money) **to cost a bundle** coûter bonbon ou la peau des fesses; **to make a bundle** se faire un fric fou (b) Br **to go a bundle on sb** en pincer drôlement pour qn; **to go a bundle on sth** être fan de qch

bung [bʌŋ] Br **1** n (bribe) pot-de-vin □ m
2 vt (put) flanquer; (throw) balancer

bunk [bʌŋk] n Br **to do a bunk** (from home) fuguer, faire une fugue; (from prison) se faire la belle

bunk off vt insép & vi Br sécher

bunny ['bʌnɪ] n Am **ski** or **snow bunny** jeune minette f qui fait du ski
▸ voir aussi **jungle**

burbs [bɜːbz] npl Am (abrév **suburbs**) banlieue □ f; **they live in the burbs** ils habitent en banlieue

burn [bɜːn] vt Am (a) (swindle) arnaquer
(b) (anger) foutre en rogne

burn up vt sép Am (anger) foutre en rogne

bush [bʊʃ] n (a) [!] (woman's pubic hair) barbu m (b) (marijuana) herbe f

bushed [bʊʃt] adj crevé, lessivé, naze

business ['bɪznɪs] n **like nobody's business** (sing, tell jokes) vachement bien; (work) comme une bête; Br **it's the business** c'est impec'
▸ voir aussi **monkey**

bust [bʌst] **1** n (police raid) descente f; **drug bust** descente des stups
2 adj (a) (broken) foutu (b) (having no money) fauché; **to go bust** (of person, business) boire un bouillon
3 vt (a) (arrest) agrafer (**for** pour)
(b) (raid) faire une descente dans
(c) Am (demote) dégrader □; **he got busted to sergeant** il est repassé sergent

buster ['bʌstə(r)] n Am (term of address) mec m; **who are you looking at, buster?** tu veux ma photo, Ducon?

bust-up ['bʌstʌp] n (**a**) *(quarrel)* engueulade f; **to have a bust-up** s'engueuler (**b**) *(of relationship)* rupture □ f

butch [bʊtʃ] **1** n *(masculine lesbian)* lesbienne f à l'allure masculine □ **2** adj *(woman)* hommasse; *(man)* macho

butcher's ['bʊtʃəz] n Br *(rhyming slang* **butcher's hook = look)** **to have a butcher's (at sb/sth)** mater (qn/qch)

butt [bʌt] n *(buttocks)* fesses fpl; **move your butt!** bouge-toi!

butt out vi s'occuper de ses fesses; **butt out!** occupe-toi de tes fesses!; **just butt out of my life!** laisse-moi vivre!

butthead ['bʌthed] n Am crétin(e) m,f,

andouille f, cruche f

buttinski [bʌ'tɪnskɪ] n Am fouille-merde mf

button ['bʌtən] vt **to button it** *(be quiet)* la fermer; **button it!** ferme-la!

butty ['bʌtɪ] n Br sandwich □ m, casse-dalle m; **chip butty** sandwich aux frites

buzz [bʌz] n (**a**) *(phone call)* **to give sb a buzz** passer un coup de fil à qn, bigophoner qn (**b**) *(thrill)* **to give sb a buzz** exciter qn □; **to get a buzz out of doing sth** prendre son pied à faire qch

buzz off vi dégager, mettre les bouts, se tirer; **buzz off!** dégage!, tire-toi!

C

cabbage ['kæbɪdʒ] n (**a**) Br (brain-damaged person) légume m; (dull person) larve f (**b**) Am (money) fric m, blé m, oseille f

cack [kæk] Br **1** n (**a**) (excrement) caca m (**b**) (nonsense) conneries fpl; **don't talk cack!** arrête de raconter n'importe quoi! (**c**) (worthless things) camelote f; **the film was a load of cack** le film était nul

2 adj (bad) nul; **her music is cack** sa musique est nulle

3 vt **he was cacking himself** (scared) il faisait dans son froc

cack-handed [kæk'hændɪd] adj Br maladroit□, manche

cahoots [kə'huːts] n **to be in cahoots (with sb)** être de mèche (avec qn)

cakehole ['keɪkhəʊl] n Br bouche□ f, clapet m; **shut your cakehole!** ferme-la!, ferme ton clapet!

calaboose ['kæləbuːs] n Am taule f, placard m; **in the calaboose** en taule, au placard, à l'ombre

can¹ [kæn] **1** n (**a**) Am (toilet) chiottes fpl (**b**) Am (prison) taule f, placard m; **in the can** en taule, au placard, à l'ombre (**c**) Am (buttocks) fesses fpl; **to kick sb in the can** botter les fesses à qn (**d**) Br **to carry the can** (take the blame) porter le chapeau

2 vt Am (**a**) (dismiss) virer, saquer (**b**) **to can it** (shut up) la fermer, la boucler; **can it!** ferme-la!, boucle-la!

can² modal aux v **no can do!** impossible!; Am **can do!** pas de problème!

cancer stick ['kænsəstɪk] n clope f

canned [kænd] adj (drunk) beurré, bourré, pété

cap [kæp] Am **1** n (bullet) bastos f
2 vt (shoot) descendre

carpet ['kɑːpɪt] **1** n **to be on the carpet** (in trouble) être dans le caca; **to put sb on the carpet** (reprimand) enguirlander qn, passer un savon à qn

2 vt Br (reprimand) enguirlander, passer un savon à

carve up [kɑːv] vt sép **to carve sb up** (attack with knife) donner des coups de couteau au visage à qn□; (in car) faire une queue de poisson à qn

case [keɪs] **1** n **he's always on my case** je l'ai tout le temps sur le dos; **get off my case!** lâche-moi les baskets!, oublie-moi!

2 vt **to case the joint** repérer les lieux (avant un cambriolage)

cash in [kæʃ] Am **1** vt sép **to cash in one's chips** (die) calancher, clamser, passer l'arme à gauche

2 vi (die) calancher, clamser, passer l'arme à gauche

casual ['kæʒʊəl] n Br jeune supporter m de foot

> Ce terme désigne un certain type de supporter de football. Le "casual" est un jeune homme, généralement issu d'un milieu modeste, qui dépense beaucoup d'argent en vêtements mais ne fait pas preuve d'un goût très sûr (ainsi les chaussures de sport et survêtements de marque côtoieront-ils les polos en laine vierge de coupe classique). Le "casual" se déplace le plus souvent en bande, consomme de la bière en grande quantité et est

souvent l'auteur de violences lors des matchs.

cat [kæt] n (**a**) Am (man) mec m ; (woman) nana f, gonzesse f (**b**) **to look like something the cat dragged in** ne ressembler à rien
▶ voir aussi **fat**

cathouse ['kæthaʊs] n bordel m, claque m

cattle market ['kætəlmɑːkɪt] n Br Péj (nightclub) = boîte réputée pour être un lieu de drague

cha [tʃɑː] n Br (tea) thé ᵈ m

champers ['ʃæmpəz] n Br (abrév **champagne**) champ' m

chance [tʃɑːns] **1** n **no chance!** des clous!
2 vt **to chance one's arm** (take a risk) risquer le coup ; (push one's luck) exagérer ᵈ, pousser

chancer ['tʃɑːnsə(r)] n Br opportuniste ᵈ mf

char [tʃɑː(r)] = **cha**

charge [tʃɑːdʒ] n Am (thrill) **to get a charge out of sth/doing sth** s'éclater ou prendre son pied avec qch/en faisant qch

charlie ['tʃɑːlɪ] n (**a**) (cocaine) coke f, neige f (**b**) Br (person) andouille f, crétin(e) m,f ; **to look/feel a right charlie** avoir l'air/se sentir con

chase [tʃeɪs] vt **to chase the dragon** chasser le dragon

chassis ['ʃæsɪ] n (woman's body) châssis m ; Hum **she's got a classy chassis** elle est super bien foutue ou balancée ou carrossée

chat up [tʃæt] vt sép Br **to chat sb up** baratiner qn, draguer qn

chat-up line ['tʃætʌplaɪn] n Br = formule d'entrée en matière pour commencer à draguer quelqu'un

cheapskate ['tʃiːpskeɪt] n radin(e) m,f

check out [tʃek] **1** vt sép (look at) to

check sb/sth out mater qn/qch ; **there's a new pub we could check out** il y a un nouveau pub qu'on pourrait essayer ; **check it/her out!** mate-moi ça!
2 vi Am (die) passer l'arme à gauche

cheers [tʃɪəz] exclam (**a**) Br (thank you) merci! ᵈ (**b**) Br (goodbye) salut!, ciao! (**c**) (as toast) santé!, à la tienne/vôtre!

cheese [tʃiːz] n (**a**) Br **hard cheese!** pas de pot ou veine! (**b**) **big cheese** (important person) huile f (**c**) **to cut the cheese** (fart) larguer une caisse

cheese off vt sép **to cheese sb off** gonfler qn ; **to be cheesed off (with)** en avoir marre (de)

cheesecake ['tʃiːzkeɪk] n (attractive women) belles nanas fpl ; Br **she's a real cheesecake** elle est vraiment bien foutue ou balancée ou carrossée

cheesy ['tʃiːzɪ] adj (**a**) (tasteless) ringard (**b**) **cheesy grin** large sourire ᵈ m

cheggers ['tʃegəz] adj Br en cloque

cherry ['tʃerɪ] **1** n (**a**) (virginity) berlingot m ; **to lose one's cherry** perdre son berlingot (**b**) (virgin) puceau (pucelle) m,f (**c**) Am (newcomer) bleu m
2 adj Am (in perfect condition) en parfait état ᵈ, impec'

chew [tʃuː] vt **to chew the fat** or **the rag** tailler une bavette

chew out vt sép Am **to chew sb out** souffler dans les bronches à qn, passer un savon à qn ; **to get chewed out** se faire souffler dans les bronches, se faire passer un savon

chick [tʃɪk] n (woman) nana f, gonzesse f
▶ voir aussi **magnet**

chicken ['tʃɪkɪn] **1** n (coward) dégonflé(e) m,f
2 adj (cowardly) dégonflé
▶ voir aussi **spring**

chicken out vi se dégonfler ; **he chickened out of the fight** il s'est dégonflé au dernier moment et a refusé de se battre; **he chickened out of telling her the truth** finalement il a eu la trouille de lui dire la vérité

chickenfeed ['tʃɪkɪnfiːd] *n (small amount of money)* cacahuètes *fpl*

chickenshit ! ['tʃɪkɪnʃɪt] *adj Am* dégonflé

chill (out) [tʃɪl] *vi* se détendre □; **I wish he'd chill out a bit** ça serait bien qu'il soit un peu plus cool; **he likes chilling out at home** il aime bien être chez lui, peinard; **chill (out)!** relax!, calmos!

chillin ['tʃɪlɪn] *adj Am* super, génial, cool

Chink [tʃɪŋk] *n Injurieux* Chinetoc *mf*, Chinetoque *mf*

Chinky ['tʃɪŋkɪ] *n Injurieux* (**a**) *(person)* Chinetoc *mf*, Chinetoque *mf* (**b**) *Br (meal)* repas *m* chinois □; *(restaurant)* (resto *m*) chinois *m*; **to go for a Chinky** manger chinois

> Lorsqu'il est question de nourriture, de cuisine, de restaurants, le terme "chinky" perd sa connotation raciste. Il est toutefois déconseillé de l'utiliser.

chinless wonder ['tʃɪnləs'wʌndə(r)] *n Br* = individu de bonne famille dépourvu de volonté et d'intelligence

> Ce terme signifie littéralement "merveille au menton fuyant", ce trait physique étant censé être le signe d'un caractère faible et d'un patrimoine génétique peu enviable.

chintzy ['tʃɪntsɪ] *adj Am* (**a**) *(cheap, of poor quality)* toc et tape-à-l'œil (**b**) *(miserly)* radin

chinwag ['tʃɪnwæg] *n Br* converse *f*; **to have a chinwag (with sb)** tailler une bavette (avec qn)

chip in [tʃɪp] **1** *vt sép (contribute)* donner □; **everyone chipped in a fiver** tout le monde a donné cinq livres **2** *vi (contribute money)* participer □, donner □; **they all chipped in to buy her a present** ils se sont cotisés pour lui

offrir un cadeau □

chippy ['tʃɪpɪ] *n Br* = boutique qui vend du poisson frit et des frites

chisel ['tʃɪzəl] *vt (cheat)* arnaquer; **to chisel sb out of sth** arnaquer qn de qch

chocka ['tʃɒkə], **chock-a-block** [tʃɒkə'blɒk] *adj Br* plein à craquer

chop [tʃɒp] *n* **to get the chop** *(of person)* se faire virer; *(of plan)* passer à la trappe

chopper ['tʃɒpə(r)] *n* (**a**) *(helicopter)* hélico *m* (**b**) *Br (penis)* pine *f*, queue *f*

chow [tʃaʊ] *n (food)* bouffe *f*

chow down *vi Am* attaquer

chowderhead ['tʃaʊdəhed] *n Am* crétin(e) *m,f*, imbécile *mf*

Christ [kraɪst] *exclam* **Christ (Almighty)!** nom de Dieu!; **for Christ's sake!** bon sang!

chronic ['krɒnɪk] *adj Br (very bad)* nul

chuck [tʃʌk] **1** *n Br* **to give sb the chuck** plaquer qn **2** *vt* (**a**) *(throw)* balancer (**b**) *(boyfriend, girlfriend)* plaquer

chuck down *vt sép Br* **it's chucking it down** *(raining)* il tombe des cordes

chuck in *vt sép Br* **to chuck sth in** *(job, studies)* plaquer qch; *(habit)* se débarrasser de qch □

chuck out *vt sép* **to chuck sb out** flanquer qn à la porte; **to chuck sth out** balancer qch

chuck up *vi Br (vomit)* dégobiller, gerber, dégueuler

chucker-out [tʃʌkə'raʊt] *n Br (doorman)* videur *m*

chucking-out time ['tʃʌkɪŋ'aʊtaɪm] *n Br (in pub)* heure *f* de la fermeture □

chuffed [tʃʌft] *adj Br* content □; **I was chuffed to bits** j'étais vachement content

chug [tʃʌg] **1** *n Br* **to have a chug** ! *(masturbate)* se branler **2** *vt (drink quickly)* descendre

3 ⚠ vi Br (masturbate) se branler

chug down vt sép **to chug sth down** descendre qch

chump [tʃʌmp] n (**a**) Br **to be off one's chump** être cinglé ou timbré; **to go off one's chump** perdre la boule, disjoncter (**b**) Am **chump change** (small amount of money) cacahuètes fpl

chunder ['tʃʌndə(r)] vi Br dégobiller, gerber, dégueuler

cig [sɪg] n Am (abrév **cigarette**) clope f, tige f

cigar [sɪ'gɑː(r)] n **close, but no cigar!** c'est presque ça, mais pas tout à fait!

> Il s'agit d'une expression humoristique utilisée lorsqu'une personne à qui l'on a posé une devinette donne une réponse inexacte mais très proche de la réponse juste, le cigare étant la récompense fictive à laquelle cette personne aurait eu droit si elle avait deviné juste. Cette expression a été popularisée par les animateurs de jeux télévisés.

ciggy ['sɪgɪ] n (abrév **cigarette**) clope f, tige f

cissy ['sɪsɪ] Br = **sissy**

city ['sɪtɪ] n Am **you should see the people at the gym – it's fat city!** si tu voyais les gens qui vont au club de gym – c'est tous des gros lards!; **try the park, it's dope city!** va voir au parc, c'est pas les dealers qui manquent!

> ▶ voir aussi **fat**

> Ce mot dénote l'abondance de ce qui le précède. On peut l'ajouter à presque n'importe quel nom, verbe ou adjectif pour introduire la notion de foisonnement.

clap [klæp] n **the clap** la chaude-pisse; **to have (a dose of) the clap** avoir la chaude-pisse

clapped-out [klæpt'aʊt] adj Br (person) crevé, lessivé, naze; (car, TV) fichu

clappers ['klæpəz] npl Br **to do sth like**

the clappers faire qch comme un dingue

class [klɑːs] adj (excellent) classe; **a class car/hi-fi** une voiture/chaîne classe

classic ['klæsɪk] **1** n **it was a classic!** ça payait!

   2 adj **it was classic!** ça payait!

clean [kliːn] adj **to be clean** (not carrying drugs) ne pas avoir de drogue sur soi ▫; (not carrying weapons) ne pas être armé ▫; (no longer addicted to drugs) avoir décroché

> ▶ voir aussi **nose**

clean out vt sép **to clean sb out** (leave penniless) nettoyer qn

clean up vi (make large profit) gagner gros

clear off [klɪə(r)] vi Br dégager, se tirer; **clear off!** dégage!, tire-toi!

clear out vi dégager, se tirer; **clear out!** dégage!, tire-toi!

clever clogs ['klevəklɒgz], **clever dick** ['klevədɪk] n Br gros (grosse) malin(igne) m,f; **OK, clever clogs** or **dick, what do we do now?** alors, gros malin, qu'est-ce qu'on fait maintenant?

clink [klɪŋk] n (prison) taule f, placard m; **in the clink** en taule, à l'ombre, en cabane

clip [klɪp] **1** n (**a**) Br (blow) **to give sb a clip round the ear** flanquer une calotte à qn (**b**) **clip joint** = bar ou boîte de nuit où l'on se fait escroquer

   2 vt Br **to clip sb round the ear** flanquer une calotte à qn

clit ⚠⚠ [klɪt] n (abrév **clitoris**) clito m

clobber[1] ['klɒbə(r)] n Br (clothes) frusques fpl; (belongings) barda m

clobber[2] vt (**a**) (hit) (once) flanquer un pain ou gnon à; (repeatedly) flanquer une raclée à (**b**) (defeat) flanquer une raclée à (**c**) (penalize) écraser ▫, accabler ▫

clock [klɒk] vt (**a**) (hit) flanquer un pain ou un gnon à (**b**) (notice) repérer

clogs [klɒgz] *npl Br* **to pop one's clogs** passer l'arme à gauche, calancher
▶ *voir aussi* **clever clogs**

closet ['klɒzɪt] **1** *n* **to come out of the closet** *(of homosexual)* faire son come-out
2 *adj* **closet communist/alcoholic** communiste *mf*/alcoolique *mf* honteux(euse); **closet queen** homo *m* honteux

clot [klɒt] *n Br (person)* nouille *f*, courge *f*, andouille *f*

cloud-cuckoo-land ['klaʊd'kʊkuːlænd] *n Br* **to be living in cloud-cuckoo-land** ne pas avoir les pieds sur terre

clout [klaʊt] **1** *n* **(a)** *(influence)* influence *f* □, **to have a lot of clout** avoir le bras long **(b)** *(blow)* calotte *f*; **to give sb a clout** flanquer une calotte à qn; **to give sth a clout** flanquer un coup dans qch
2 *vt (hit) (person)* flanquer une calotte à; *(thing)* flanquer un coup dans

club [klʌb] *n* **(a)** *Br* **to be in the (pudding) club** *(pregnant)* être en cloque **(b)** **join the club!** t'es pas le (la) seul(e)!

clueless ['kluːlɪs] *adj* nul

C-note ['siːnəʊt] *n Am* billet *m* de cent dollars □

cobblers [!] ['kɒbləz] *Br* **1** *npl* **(a)** *(testicles)* balloches *fpl*, boules *fpl* **(b)** *(nonsense)* foutaises *fpl*
2 *exclam* n'importe quoi!, des foutaises, tout ça!

cock [kɒk] *n* **(a)** [!!] *(penis)* queue *f*, bite *f* **(b)** *Br (term of address)* mon pote; **alright, me old cock!** salut, mon pote!

cock up *vt sép Br* **to cock sth up** *(interview, exam)* foirer qch, se planter à qch; *(plan, arrangement)* faire foirer qch

cocksucker [!!] ['kɒksʌkə(r)] *n* enculé *m*

cocktease [!!] ['kɒktiːz], **cockteaser** [!!] ['kɒktiːzə(r)] *n* allumeuse *f*

cock-up ['kɒkʌp] *n Br* foirade *f*; **to make a cock-up of sth** *(interview, exam)* foirer qch, se planter à qch; *(plan, arrangement)* faire foirer qch

coco ['kəʊkəʊ] *n Br* **I should coco!** tu l'as dit!

cod [kɒd] *n Br (nonsense)* foutaises *fpl*

codger ['kɒdʒə(r)] *n* **old codger** vieux croulant *m*

codswallop ['kɒdzwɒləp] *n Br* foutaises *fpl*; **it's a load of codswallop** tout ça, c'est des foutaises

coffin ['kɒfɪn] *n* **(a)** *Br Péj* **coffin dodger** *(old person)* croulant(e) *m,f* **(b)** **coffin nail** *(cigarette)* clope *f*, tige *f*

coke [kəʊk] *n (abrév* **cocaine)** coke *f*

coked up [kəʊkt'ʌp] *adj* défoncé à la coke

cokehead ['kəʊkhed] *n* **to be a cokehead** consommer beaucoup de cocaïne □

coldcock ['kəʊldkɒk] *vt Am* assommer □, estourbir

cold turkey [kəʊld'tɜːkɪ] *n* **to be cold turkey** être en manque; **to go cold turkey** décrocher d'un seul coup

comatose ['kəʊmətəʊs] *adj (drunk)* ivre mort □

come [kʌm] **1** [!] *n (semen)* foutre *m*
2 *vi* **(a)** [!] *(reach orgasm)* jouir **(b)** *Br* **to come it** bluffer; **don't come it with me!** arrête ton cinéma!

come off 1 *vt insép* **come off it!** arrête ton char!
2 [!] *vi (reach orgasm)* jouir

come on *vi* **(a)** **to come on to sb** faire du rentre-dedans à qn **(b)** *Br (start menstruating)* avoir ses ragnagnas; **I came on this morning** les Anglais ont débarqué ce matin

come out *vi (reveal homosexuality)* faire son comeout

come up *vi Br* **(a)** [!] *(ejaculate)* décharger **(b)** *(after taking drugs)* décoller

come-on ['kʌmɒn] *n* **to give sb the come-on** faire du rentre-dedans à qn

commie ['kɒmɪ] *n* (*abrév* **communist**) coco *mf*

con¹ [kɒn] **1** *n* (*abrév* **confidence trick**) (*swindle*) arnaque *f*; **con man** arnaqueur *m*

   2 *vt* **to con sth out of sb** arnaquer qn de qch; **to con sb into doing sth** persuader qn de faire qch par la ruse
   ▶ *voir aussi* **merchant**

con² *n* (*abrév* **convict**) taulard(e) *m, f*

conk [kɒŋk] *n Br* (*nose*) tarin *m*, blaire *m*

conk out *vi* (**a**) (*break down*) tomber en rade (**b**) (*fall asleep*) s'endormir □, piquer du nez

connection [kə'nekʃən] *n Am* (*drug dealer*) dealer *m*

cook [kʊk] **1** *vt* **to cook a shot** préparer un shoot d'héroïne

   2 *vi* **what's cooking?** (*what's happening?*) quoi de neuf?; **now we're cooking with gas!** maintenant tout marche comme sur des roulettes!

cook up 1 *vt sép* **to cook up a shot** préparer un shoot d'héroïne

   2 *vi* (*heat heroin*) préparer un shoot d'héroïne

cookie ['kʊkɪ] *n* (**a**) (*person*) **a tough cookie** un(e) dur(e) *m,f* à cuire; **a smart cookie** une tête (**b**) **that's the way the cookie crumbles** c'est la vie (**c**) **to toss** *or Am* **shoot one's cookies** (*vomit*) gerber, dégueuler

cool [kuːl] **1** *adj* (**a**) (*fashionable, sophisticated*) branché; **Glasgow's a really cool city** Glasgow est une ville hyper-branchée; **he still thinks it's cool to smoke** il pense encore que ça fait bien de fumer

   (**b**) (*excellent*) cool, super; **we had a really cool weekend** on a passé un super week-end; **that's a cool jacket** elle est cool *ou* super, cette veste

   (**c**) (*allowed, acceptable*) **is it cool to skin up in here?** on peut se rouler un joint ici?; **it's not cool to wear jeans in that restaurant** on ne peut pas entrer dans ce restaurant si on porte un jean □

   (**d**) (*accepting, not upset*) **are you cool with that?** ça te va?; **they're not cool about me smoking at home** ils n'aiment pas que je fume à la maison □; **I thought she'd be angry, but she was really cool about it** je pensais qu'elle se fâcherait, mais en fait elle a été très cool

   2 *exclam* cool!, super!

   3 *vt* **to cool it** se calmer □; **cool it!** du calme!, calmos!
   ▶ *voir aussi* **lose**

cooler ['kuːlə(r)] *n* (*prison*) taule *f*, cabane *f*; **in the cooler** en taule, en cabane, à l'ombre

coon [kuːn] *n Injurieux* (*black person*) nègre (négresse) *m,f*

cop [kɒp] **1** *n* (**a**) (*police officer*) flic *m*; **cop shop** (*police station*) poste *m*

   (**b**) *Br Hum* (*arrest*) **it's a fair cop!** je suis fait, y a rien à dire!

   (**c**) *Br* **it's not much cop** (*not very good*) ce n'est pas terrible, ça ne casse pas trois pattes à un canard

   2 *vt* (**a**) (*catch*) **to cop sb** pincer qn; **to get copped doing sth** se faire pincer en train de faire qch; **to cop hold of sth** choper qch; **cop (a load of) this!** (*listen*) écoute-moi ça!; (*look*) mate-moi ça!

   (**b**) *Br* **to cop it** (*be punished*) prendre un savon; (*die*) clamser, calancher

   (**c**) **to cop some** *Br* **zeds** *or Am* **zees** roupiller

cop out *vi* (*avoid responsibility*) se défiler; (*choose easy solution*) choisir la solution de facilité □; **to cop out of doing sth** ne pas avoir le cran de faire qch

cop-out ['kɒpaʊt] *n* solution *f* de facilité □

copper ['kɒpə(r)] *n* (*police officer*) flic *m*

cottage ['kɒtɪdʒ] *n Br* (*public toilet*)

tasse f, toilettes publiques ᵒfpl (utilisées comme lieu de rencontre par certains homosexuels)

cottaging ['kɒtɪdʒɪŋ] n Br = drague homosexuelle dans les toilettes publiques

couch potato ['kaʊtʃpə'teɪtəʊ] n flemmard(e) m,f qui passe sa vie devant la télé

cough up [kɒf] **1** vt sép (money) cracher, allonger
2 vi cracher ou allonger le fric

cow [kaʊ] n Br Péj (woman) vache f, chameau m; **poor cow!** la pauvre!; **lucky cow!** la veinarde!; **you silly cow!** espèce de cloche!
▸ voir aussi **holy**

cowabunga [kaʊə'bʌŋgə] exclam Am = cri de joie ou de victoire

Il s'agit d'un terme du monde des surfers, rendu célèbre par le personnage de dessin animé Bart Simpson.

cowboy ['kaʊbɔɪ] n Br Péj (workman) mauvais artisan ᵒm, fumiste m

crab [kræb] n (pubic louse) morpion m; **to have crabs** avoir des morpions

crack [kræk] **1** n (**a**) **crack (cocaine)** crack m
(**b**) ⚠⚠ (woman's genitals) chatte f, con m, cramouille f
(**c**) ⚠⚠ (anus) troufignon m, trou m du cul
(**d**) (attempt) **to have a crack at sth, to give sth a crack** essayer qch ᵒ
2 vi **to get cracking** (make a start) se mettre au boulot; (speed up) se grouiller, se magner

crack up **1** vt sép **to crack sb up** (cause to laugh hysterically) faire éclater qn de rire
2 vi (**a**) Br (get angry) péter les plombs (**b**) (have nervous breakdown) craquer (nerveusement) (**c**) (laugh hysterically) éclater de rire

cracked [krækt] adj (mad) cinglé, toqué

cracker ['krækə(r)] n (**a**) Br (excellent thing) **to be a cracker** être génial; **it was a cracker of a goal** c'était un but magnifique; **she's a cracker** (gorgeous) elle est hyper canon (**b**) Am (poor white person) = pauvre originaire du sud des États-Unis

crackerjack ['krækədʒæk] Am **1** n **to be a crackerjack** (person) être un crack ou un as; (thing) être génial
2 adj (excellent) génial, du tonnerre

crackers ['krækəz] adj Br (mad) cinglé, toqué

crackhead ['krækhed] n accro mf au crack

crackhouse ['krækhaʊs] n = lieu où l'on achète, vend et consomme du crack

cracking ['krækɪŋ] adj Br (excellent) super, génial

crackpot ['krækpɒt] **1** n (person) allumé(e) m,f
2 adj (scheme, idea) loufoque

cradle-snatcher ['kreɪdəlsnætʃə(r)] n **he's a cradle-snatcher** il les prend au berceau

crank [kræŋk] n (**a**) (eccentric) allumé(e) m,f (**b**) Am (grumpy person) râleur(euse) m,f

crank up **1** vt sép **to crank sth up** (music, volume) monter qch
2 vi (inject drugs) se piquer

cranky ['kræŋkɪ] adj (**a**) Br (eccentric) excentrique ᵒ, loufoque (**b**) Am (grumpy) grognon, grincheux

crap ⚠ [kræp] **1** n (**a**) (excrement) merde f; **to have** or **take a crap** chier, couler un bronze
(**b**) (nonsense) conneries fpl; **he's full of crap** il raconte n'importe quoi; **you're talking crap!** tu racontes n'importe quoi!; **cut the crap!** arrête tes conneries!, arrête de dire n'importe quoi!; **don't believe all that crap!** il faut pas écouter toutes ces conneries!; **that's crap, I never said that!** c'est des conneries, j'ai jamais dit ça!; **what he's**

saying **is a load of crap** il raconte n'importe quoi

(**c**) *(worthless things)* **the film/book was a load of crap** il était nul, ce film/ bouquin

(**d**) *(useless things)* bazar *m*; **clear all your crap off the bed** enlève ton bazar du lit

(**e**) *(disgusting substance)* merde *f*, saloperie *f*; **he eats nothing but crap** il bouffe que de la merde

(**f**) *(unfair treatment)* **I'm not taking that crap from you!** si tu crois que je vais supporter tes conneries, tu te gourres!; **I don't need this crap!** je me passerais bien de ce genre de conneries!

(**g**) **to feel like crap** *(ill)* se sentir vraiment patraque

2 *adj (worthless)* merdique; *(nasty)* dégueulasse; **to feel crap** *(ill)* se sentir vraiment mal fichu; *(guilty)* se sentir coupable □; **her work is crap** elle fait de la merde; **he's a crap teacher** il est complètement nul comme prof

3 *vt* **to crap oneself** *(defecate, be scared)* faire dans son froc

4 *vi (defecate)* chier, couler un bronze

crap out ⚠ *vi* se dégonfler; **he crapped out of the fight** il s'est dégonflé au dernier moment et a refusé de se battre; **he crapped out of telling her the truth** finalement il a eu la trouille de lui dire la vérité

crapper ⚠ ['kræpə(r)] *n (toilet)* chiottes *fpl*, gogues *mpl*

crappy ⚠ ['kræpɪ] *adj (worthless)* merdique; **to feel crappy** *(ill)* se sentir vraiment mal fichu; *(guilty)* se sentir coupable □; **he's a crappy teacher** il est complètement nul comme prof

crash [kræʃ] **1** *vt (party)* s'inviter à, taper l'incruste à

2 *vi (spend night, sleep)* pieuter; *(fall asleep)* s'endormir □; **can I crash at your place?** est-ce que je peux pieuter chez toi?

crash out *vi (spend night, sleep)* pieuter; *(fall asleep)* s'endormir □; **he was crashed out on the sofa** il roupillait dans le canapé

crate [kreɪt] *n (old car)* vieille bagnole *f*; *(old plane)* vieux coucou *m*

cream [kriːm] **1** *vt* (**a**) *(defeat)* battre à plates coutures; *Am (beat up)* tabasser (**b**) **to cream one's jeans** ⚠⚠ *(of man)* décharger dans son froc; *(of woman)* mouiller sa culotte

2 ⚠⚠ *vi* (**a**) *(become sexually aroused) (of woman)* mouiller (**b**) *(ejaculate)* décharger

crease up [kriːs] *Br* **1** *vt sép* **to crease sb up** *(cause to laugh hysterically)* faire se tordre qn de rire

2 *vi (laugh hysterically)* se tordre de rire

cred [kred] *n Br (abrév* **credibility***)* **to have (street) cred** être branché *ou* dans le coup; **he wants to get some (street) cred** il veut faire branché *ou* dans le coup

creep [kriːp] *n* (**a**) *(unpleasant man)* type *m* répugnant; *Br (obsequious person)* lèche-bottes *mf* (**b**) **to give sb the creeps** *(scare)* donner la chair de poule à qn; *(repulse)* débecter qn

creepy ['kriːpɪ] *adj* **it's creepy** *(scary)* ça me donne la chair de poule; *(repulsive)* ça me débecte

creepy-crawly ['kriːpɪ'krɔːlɪ] *n* bébête *f*

cretin ['kretɪn] *n (idiot)* crétin(e) *m,f*

crikey ['kraɪkɪ] *exclam* bigre!

croak [krəʊk] *vi (die)* calancher, passer l'arme à gauche

crock [krɒk] *n Am* **to be a crock** *or* **a crock of shit** ⚠ *(nonsense)* être des foutaises *ou* des conneries; **don't believe that crock he told you!** ne crois pas ce qu'il t'a dit, c'est des foutaises!

crone [krəʊn] *n* **old crone** vieille toupie *f*

cropper ['krɒpə(r)] *n* **to come a cropper** *(fall)* prendre une gamelle; *(fail)* se planter

crown jewels [!] [ˈkraʊnˈdʒʊəlz] *npl Hum (man's genitals)* bijoux *mpl* de famille

crucial [ˈkruːʃəl] *adj Br (excellent)* super, génial; **the DJ at the club last night was well crucial** le DJ de la boîte, hier soir, était vraiment super

crucify [ˈkruːsɪfaɪ] *vt (defeat, criticize)* démolir

crud [krʌd] *n* (a) *(dirt)* crasse *f* (b) *(nonsense)* conneries *fpl*; **he was talking some crud about the dangers of drugs** il était en train de raconter des conneries sur les dangers de la drogue (c) *(person)* ordure *f*, saloperie *f*

cruddy [ˈkrʌdɪ] *adj* (a) *(dirty)* cradingue, dégueulasse (b) *(worthless)* merdique

cruise [kruːz] **1** *vt (person)* draguer; *(place)* aller draguer dans
2 *vi* (a) *(look for sexual partner)* draguer (b) *Am (leave)* mettre les bouts, se casser, s'arracher; **ready to cruise?** on y va? (c) *Hum* **you're cruising for a bruising!** toi, tu cherches les emmerdes!

crumb [krʌm] *n Péj (person)* minable *mf*

crumbly [ˈkrʌmblɪ] *n Br (old person)* croulant(e) *m,f*

crummy [ˈkrʌmɪ] *adj* minable

crumpet [ˈkrʌmpɪt] *n Br (women)* nanas *fpl*, gonzesses *fpl*; **a nice bit of crumpet** une belle nana; **the thinking man's/woman's crumpet** une belle nana /une beau mec intelligent(e)

crust [krʌst] *n Br* **to earn a** *or* **one's crust** gagner sa croûte

crustie, crusty [ˈkrʌstɪ] *n Br* jeune hippie *mf* crado

Le type "crusty" est apparu au début des années 90 avec l'émergence du mouvement alternatif des "New Age travellers" (communautés néo-hippies parcourant la Grande-Bretagne dans des caravanes et des autobus aménagés, dont les membres sont de tous les combats pour la défense de l'environnement). Le "crusty" est généralement sans emploi et sans domicile fixes, d'une hygiène pas toujours irréprochable, et il se déplace souvent avec un chien tenu au bout d'une ficelle.

cry out [kraɪ] *vi* **for crying out loud!** c'est pas possible!

cuckoo [ˈkʊkuː] *adj (mad)* cinglé, toqué

cuff [kʌf] **1** *n* (a) *(blow)* beigne *f*, torgnole *f*
2 *vt* flanquer une beigne à; **to cuff sb round the ear** donner une claque sur l'oreille à qn

cuffs [kʌfs] *npl (abrév* **handcuffs***)* menottes □ *fpl*, bracelets *mpl*

cum [!!] [kʌm] *n* foutre *m*, jute *m*

cunt [!!] [kʌnt] *n* (a) *(woman's genitals)* chatte *f*, con *m* (b) *(man)* enculé *m*; *(woman)* sale pute *f*; **he's a stupid cunt!** c'est qu'un enculé!

Il s'agit du terme le plus grossier de la langue anglaise, loin devant "fuck". Même les gens qui ont l'habitude de jurer évitent généralement de l'utiliser, y compris entre amis, car son utilisation ne manquerait pas de choquer. Il est préférable de le bannir complètement de son vocabulaire.

cupcake [ˈkʌpkeɪk] *n* (a) *(eccentric person)* allumé(e) *m,f* (b) *Am Injurieux (homosexual)* pédale *f*, tantouze *f*

curse [kɜːs] *n* **to have the curse** avoir ses ragnagnas

cushti [ˈkʊʃtɪ] *adj Br* super, génial

cut out [kʌt] **1** *vt sép* **cut it out!** ça suffit!
2 *vi Am (leave)* mettre les bouts, calter

D

daffy ['dæfɪ] *adj* loufoque, loufedingue

Dago ['deɪgəʊ] *Injurieux* **1** *n* métèque *mf* (*personne d'origine espagnole, italienne, portugaise ou latino-américaine*)
2 *adj* métèque

daisy ['deɪzɪ] *n* **to be pushing up the daisies** manger les pissenlits par la racine

damage ['dæmɪdʒ] *n* **what's the damage?** (*how much does it cost?*) ça fait combien?

dame [deɪm] *n Am* gonzesse *f*

dammit ['dæmɪt] **1** *n Br* **as near as dammit** dans ces eaux-là
2 *exclam* merde!

damn [dæm] **1** *n* (**a**) **I don't give a damn** j'en ai rien à cirer, je m'en balance (**b**) *Br* **damn all** (*nothing*) que dalle; **damn all money/thanks** pas un sou/un merci; **they had damn all to do with it** ils n'y étaient pour rien
2 *adj* sacré, foutu; **he's a damn nuisance!** c'est un sacré emmerdeur!; **it's one damn thing after another!** ça n'arrête pas!
3 *adv* vachement; **a damn good idea** une super bonne idée; **you're damn right** t'as parfaitement raison; **he's so damn slow** il est hyper lent; **she knows damn well what I'm talking about** elle sait parfaitement de quoi je parle □
4 *exclam* **damn (it)!** merde!
5 *vt* **damn you!** va te faire voir!; **he lied to me, damn him!** il m'a menti, le salaud!; **damn the expense/the consequences!** tant pis pour les frais/les conséquences!; **well, I'll be damned!** eh ben ça alors!; **I'm** *or* **I'll be damned if I'm going to apologize** plutôt crever que de m'excuser
► *voir aussi* **sight**

damnation [dæm'neɪʃən] *exclam* zut!

damned [dæmd] *adj & adv* = **damn**

damnedest ['dæmdəst] **1** *n* **to do one's damnedest (to do sth)** faire tout son possible (pour faire qch)
2 *adj Am* **it was the damnedest thing!** c'était carrément incroyable!

dandy ['dændɪ] *adj* super; **everything's just (fine and) dandy!** tout baigne!

darky ['dɑːkɪ] *n Injurieux* bronzé(e) *m,f*

darn [dɑːn] **1** *adj* sacré, foutu; **the darn car won't start** cette saloperie de voiture ne veut pas démarrer; **you're a darn fool** t'es un vrai con
2 *adv* vachement; **we were darn lucky** on a eu une sacrée veine; **you know darn well what I mean!** tu comprends parfaitement ce que je veux dire! □; **it's too darn hot** il fait vraiment trop chaud □
3 *exclam* **darn (it)!** zut!
4 *vt* **he's late, darn him!** il est en retard, il fait vraiment chier!; **well, I'll be darned!** eh ben ça alors!
► *voir aussi* **sight**

darned [dɑːnd] *adj & adv* = **darn**

dash [dæʃ] *exclam* **dash (it)!** zut!, mince!

daylights ['deɪlaɪts] *npl* **to beat the living daylights out of sb** flanquer une dérouillée *ou* une raclée à qn; **you scared the living daylights out of me!** tu m'as foutu une de ces trouilles!

dead [ded] **1** *adj* (**a**) (*not alive*) **to be dead from the neck up** ne rien avoir dans le citron; **to be dead to the world** en écraser; **I wouldn't be seen dead there/ in that dress** je préférerais mourir que d'y aller/que de porter cette robe

(b) *(absolute)* **to be a dead ringer for sb** être le portrait tout craché de qn; **he's a dead loss** c'est un bon à rien; **it was a dead loss** ça n'a servi à rien [□]

2 *adv Br (very)* vachement; **it's dead easy/good** c'est vachement facile/bon; **you were dead lucky** tu as eu une sacrée veine; **I'm dead bored** je m'ennuie à mort

▸ *voir aussi* **knock, meat**

deadbeat ['dedbi:t] *n Am (lazy person)* glandeur(euse) *m,f; (tramp)* clodo *mf; (parasite)* pique-assiette *mf*

death [deθ] *n* **to look like death warmed up** avoir l'air d'un(e) déterré(e); **to feel like death warmed up** se sentir patraque

▸ *voir aussi* **sick**

deck [dek] **1** *n* **(a) to hit the deck** *(get out of bed)* sortir de son pieu, se dépagnoter; *(fall)* se foutre la gueule par terre; *(lie down)* se jeter à terre **(b)** *Hum* **he's not playing with a full deck** c'est pas une lumière, il n'a pas inventé l'eau chaude

2 *vt* **to deck sb** foutre qn par terre

deep-six ['di:p'sıks] *vt Am* **(a)** *(throw away)* balancer, foutre en l'air **(b)** *(rule out)* mettre au placard

def [def] *adj* super, génial

deffo ['defəu] *adv Br (abrév* **definitely)** absolument [□]; **are you coming tonight? – deffo!** tu viens ce soir? – je veux!

dekko ['dekəu] *n Br* **to have** *or* **take a dekko at sb/sth** mater qn/qch

demo ['deməu] *n (abrév* **demonstration)** manif *f*

dense [dens] *adj (stupid)* débile

devil ['devəl] *n* **(a)** *(person)* **the lucky devil!** le veinard!; *Br* **poor devil!** le pauvre!; *Br* **go on, be a devil!** allez, laisse-toi tenter! **(b)** *(for emphasis)* **what/who/why the devil...?** que/qui/pourquoi diable...?; **how the devil**

should I know? comment veux-tu que je sache?; **we had a devil of a job getting here on time** on a eu un mal de chien à arriver à l'heure

dexy ['deksı] *n (abrév* **dexampheta-mine)** amphé *f*, amphet *f*

diabolical [daıə'bɒlıkəl] *adj Br (very bad)* nul

dick [dık] *n* **(a)** ![] *(penis)* bite *f*, queue *f* **(b)** ![] *(man)* trou *m* du cul, trouduc *m* **(c)** *Am (detective)* privé *m*

▸ *voir aussi* **clever clogs, features**

dickhead ![] ['dıkhed] *n* trou *m* du cul

dicky-bird ['dıkıbз:d] *n Br (rhyming slang* **word)** mot [□] *m;* **not a dicky-bird!** motus et bouche cousue!

diddly ['dıdəlı] *n Am* **that's not worth diddly** ça ne vaut pas un clou

diddlyshit ![] [dıdəlı'ʃıt] *n Am* **I don't give a diddlyshit** je m'en balance, je m'en fous complètement

diesel (dyke) ['di:zəl(daık)] *n Injurieux* gouine *f (à l'allure masculine)*

dig [dıg] **1** *vt* **(a)** *(like)* aimer [□], apprécier [□]; **I really dig that kind of music** ça me branche vraiment, ce genre de musique **(b)** *(look at)* mater; **dig that guy over there** mate un peu le mec, là-bas **(c)** *(understand)* piger

2 *vi (understand)* piger; **you dig?** tu piges?

dig in *vi (start eating)* attaquer *(un repas)*

dike [daık] *Am =* **dyke**

dildo ![] ['dıldəu] *n Péj (person)* trou *m* du cul, trouduc *m*

dimwit ['dımwıt] *n* andouille *f*, courge *f*

dip [dıp] *n Am (idiot)* andouille *f*, courge *f*, cruche *f*

▸ *voir aussi* **wick**

dippy ['dıpı] *adj* loufoque, loufedingue

dipshit ![] ['dıpʃıt] *n Am* taré(e) *m,f*, crétin(e) *m,f*

dipso ['dıpsəu] *n (abrév* **dipsomaniac)** alcolo *mf*, poivrot(e) *m,f*

dipstick ['dɪpstɪk] n (idiot) andouille f, cruche f

dirt [dɜːt] n (**a**) **to dish the dirt (about)** tout raconter (sur); **come on, dish the dirt!** allez, dis-moi tout! (**b**) Am **to do sb dirt** faire une crasse à qn

dirtbox [!!] ['dɜːtbɒks] n Br trou m du cul, boîte f à pâté

dirty ['dɜːtɪ] **1** n Br **to do the dirty on sb** faire une crasse à qn
   2 adj **dirty old man** vieux cochon m; **dirty weekend** week-end m coquin; Br Hum **dirty stop-out** débauché(e) m,f qui découche

dis [dɪs] = **diss**

disaster area [dɪ'zɑːstəreərɪə] n **to be a walking disaster area** être une catastrophe ambulante

disco biscuit ['dɪskəʊ'bɪskɪt] n Br cachet m d'ecstasy, bonbec m

dishwater ['dɪʃwɔːtə(r)] n **this coffee's like dishwater!** c'est vraiment de l'eau de vaisselle, ce café!

dishy ['dɪʃɪ] adj mignon

diss [dɪs] vt Am débiner

ditch [dɪtʃ] vt (boyfriend, girlfriend) plaquer, larguer; (thing) balancer, foutre en l'air; (plan, idea) laisser tomber

div [dɪv] n Br andouille f, cruche f

dive [daɪv] n (place) bouge □ m

divvy ['dɪvɪ] n Br (idiot) andouille f, courge f

DL [diː'el] n Noir Am = **down-low**

do [duː] **1** vt (**a**) (take) **to do drugs** se droguer □; **let's do lunch** il faudrait qu'on déjeune ensemble un de ces jours (**b**) Br (prosecute) poursuivre □; **to get done for speeding** se faire pincer pour excès de vitesse (**c**) Br (rob) **to do a jeweller's/bank** braquer une bijouterie/une banque (**d**) (cheat) arnaquer; **to do sb out of sth** arnaquer qn de qch; **I've been done!** j'ai été refait! (**e**) (visit) **to do Paris/the sights** faire

Paris/les monuments (**f**) Br (beat up) tabasser; **I'll do you!** je vais te casser la gueule! (**g**) (kill) zigouiller, buter (**h**) (have sex with) (of man) baiser, tringler, troncher; (of woman) baiser avec, s'envoyer
   2 n (party) fête f, boum f

do in vt sép Br (**a**) (exhaust) vanner, pomper, crever; **to feel done in** être crevé ou naze ou sur les rotules (**b**) (kill) **to do sb in** buter ou zigouiller qn
   ▶ voir aussi **head**

do over vt sép Br (**a**) (beat up) **to do sb over** tabasser qn (**b**) (rob) **to do sb over** dépouiller qn; **to do sth over** dévaliser qch □

do with vt insép (tolerate) **I can't be doing with people like that** je peux pas blairer les gens comme ça; **he couldn't be doing with living in London** il pouvait pas supporter de vivre à Londres

doddle ['dɒdəl] n Br **it's a doddle** c'est hyper fastoche

dodgy ['dɒdʒɪ] adj Br (**a**) (unsafe, untrustworthy) louche; **he's OK, but all his friends are well dodgy** lui, ça va, mais ses amis craignent vraiment; **the house is nice, but it's in a really dodgy area** la maison est bien mais elle est dans un quartier vraiment craignos; **investing money in a scheme like that is just too dodgy** c'est vraiment trop risqué d'investir dans ce genre de truc; **they were involved in a couple of dodgy business deals** ils ont été impliqués dans des transactions plutôt louches
   (**b**) (not working properly, unstable) merdique; **don't sit on that chair, it's a bit dodgy** ne t'assieds pas sur cette chaise, elle est un peu branlante □; **the ceiling looks a bit dodgy** le plafond n'a pas l'air en très bon état □; **my stomach's been a bit dodgy for the last couple of days** ça fait deux jours que j'ai l'estomac un peu dérangé □; **we can't go camping**

while the weather's so dodgy on ne peut pas aller camper alors que le temps risque de se gâter à tout moment ▫

dog [dɒg] *n* **(a)** *(ugly woman)* cageot *m*, boudin *m*
(**b**) **dog's breakfast** *or* **dinner** *(mess)* merdier *m*; **to make a dog's breakfast** *or* **dinner of sth** complètement foirer qch; *Br* **to be dressed up like a dog's dinner** être attifé de façon ridicule
(**c**) *Br* **to be the dog's bollocks** [!] *(excellent)* être génial
(**d**) *Hum* **I'm going to see a man about a dog** *(going to the toilet)* je vais aux toilettes ▫; *(going somewhere unspecified)* j'ai un truc à faire
(**e**) *Br* **to give sb dog's abuse** traiter qn de tous les noms
(**f**) *Am (useless thing)* merde *f*
(**g**) *Am (foot)* arpion *m*, pinglot *m*
▶ *voir aussi* **hair, sausage**

dog-end [ˈdɒgend] *n Br* mégot *m*, clope *m*

doggone [ˈdɒgɒn] *Am* **1** *adj* sacré, foutu; **I've lost the doggone car keys** j'ai perdu ces saletés de clés de bagnole
2 *adv* vachement; **it's so doggone hot!** il fait une chaleur à crever!
3 *exclam* **doggone (it)!** zut!

doggy-fashion [ˈdɒgɪfæʃən] *adv (have sex)* en levrette

doll [dɒl] *n* **(a)** *(attractive woman)* canon *m* **(b)** *(term of address)* poupée *f* **(c)** *Am (kind person)* trésor *m*, chou *m*

doll up *vt sép* **to doll oneself up, to get dolled up** se faire belle ▫

dong [!] [dɒŋ] *n* bite *f*, queue *f*

doobie [ˈduːbɪ] *n* joint *m*, pétard *m*

doodah [ˈduːdɑː], *Am* **doodad** [ˈduːdæd] *n* truc *m*, machin *m*

doofus [ˈduːfəs] *n Am* andouille *f*, cruche *f*, courge *f*

doo-lally [duːˈlælɪ] *adj Br* zinzin, timbré

doorstep [ˈdɔːstep] *n Br (slice of bread)* grosse tranche *f* de pain ▫

dope [dəʊp] **1** *n* **(a)** *(cannabis)* shit *m*

(**b**) *(person)* crétin(e) *m,f*, abruti(e) *m,f*
2 *adj Am (excellent)* génial, super

dopehead [ˈdəʊphed] *n* **to be a dopehead** fumer beaucoup de cannabis ▫

dopey [ˈdəʊpɪ] *adj* empoté, cruche

do-re-mi [dəʊreɪˈmiː] *n Am (money)* fric *m*, blé *m*, oseille *f*, artiche *f*

dork [dɔːk] *n* ringard *m*, bouffon *m*

dorky [ˈdɔːkɪ] *adj* ringard, nul

dose [dəʊs] *n* **(a)** *(venereal disease)* chtouille *f*; **to catch a dose** attraper la chtouille **(b)** *Br* **to get through sth like a dose of salts** faire qch en deux coups de cuillère à pot

dosh [dɒʃ] *n Br* blé *m*, oseille *f*

doss [dɒs] *Br* **1** *n* **(a)** *(bed)* plumard *m* **(b)** *(sleep)* **to have a doss** piquer un roupillon **(c)** **it was a doss** *(easy)* c'était fastoche
2 *vi (sleep)* roupiller

doss about, doss around *vi Br* traîner

doss down *vi Br* pieuter

dosser [ˈdɒsə(r)] *n Br* **(a)** *(tramp)* clodo *mf* **(b)** *(hostel)* asile *m* de nuit ▫

doss-house [ˈdɒshaʊs] *n Br* asile *m* de nuit ▫

dotty [ˈdɒtɪ] *adj* maboule, loufedingue; **to be dotty about sb/sth** être dingue de qn/qch

douche-bag [ˈduːʃbæg] *n Am (person)* ordure *f*

dough [dəʊ] *n (money)* blé *m*, oseille *f*

down [daʊn] *vt (eat, drink)* s'enfiler; **he downed his pint and left** il a descendu sa pinte puis il est parti

down-and-out [ˈdaʊnənaʊt] **1** *n* clodo *mf*
2 *adj* à la rue ▫

downer [ˈdaʊnə(r)] *n* **(a)** *(drug)* barbiturique ▫ *m*, downer *m* **(b)** *(depressing experience)* **to be on a downer** avoir le bourdon; **it was a real downer** c'était vraiment déprimant ▫; **the film's a**

complete downer c'est un film qui file le bourdon

down-low [daʊn'ləʊ] *n Noir Am* **on the down-low** (*confidential*) confidentiel [□]; **I'm telling you this on the down-low** je te dis ça, mais c'est entre nous

drag [dræg] *n* (**a**) (*bore*) truc *m* chiant, galère *f*; **he's such a drag** c'est vraiment un emmerdeur; **the party was a real drag** la soirée était vraiment chiante; **what a drag!** quelle galère!
  (**b**) (*on cigarette, joint*) bouffée *f*, taffe *f*; **she took** *or* **had a drag on her cigarette** elle tira sur sa cigarette
  (**c**) *Am* (*influence*) influence [□] *f*; **to have drag** avoir le bras long
  ▸ *voir aussi* **main**

drat [dræt] *exclam* **drat (it)!** zut!, mince!

dratted ['drætɪd] *adj* sacré, foutu; **where's that dratted brother of mine?** mais où est passé mon frangin?

draw [drɔː] *n Br* (*cannabis*) shit *m*

dream [driːm] **1** *n* **in your dreams!** tu peux toujours rêver!
  2 *vi* **dream on!** tu peux toujours rêver!

drip [drɪp] *n* (*person*) mollusque *m*

drop [drɒp] **1** *vt* **drop it!** (*I don't want to talk about it*) tu me lâches?; (*I don't want to hear about it*) change de disque!
  2 *vi* **drop dead!** ta gueule!
  ▸ *voir aussi* **log**

drop-dead gorgeous [drɒpded-'gɔːdʒəs] *adj* hyper canon

dross [drɒs] *n* (*worthless things*) **it's (a load of) dross** ça ne vaut pas un clou

druggie, druggy ['drʌgɪ] *n* camé(e) *m,f*

dry up [draɪ] *vi* **dry up!** (*be quiet*) la ferme!

ducats ['dʌkəts] *npl Am* fric *m*, blé *m*, oseille *f*

dude [djuːd, duːd] *n Am* (**a**) (*man*) mec *m* (**b**) (*term of address*) mec *m*, vieux *m*; **hey, dude!** (*as greeting*) salut vieux!; (*to attract attention*) excusez-moi! [□]

duff [dʌf] **1** *n* (**a**) *Br* **up the duff** (*preg-*

nant) en cloque; **to get sb up the duff** mettre qn en cloque (**b**) *Am* (*buttocks*) cul *m*, derche *m*; **get up off your duff!** bouge ton cul!
  2 *adj* (*bad, useless*) merdique

duff up *vt sép Br* **to duff sb up** tabasser qn

duffer ['dʌfə(r)] *n* (*incompetent person*) branleur(euse) *m,f*; **old duffer** vieux schnock *m*

dumb [dʌm] *adj Am* (*stupid*) bête [□], débile

dumbass [!] ['dʌmæs] *Am* **1** *n* taré(e) *m,f*, débile *mf*, abruti(e) *m,f*
  2 *adj* débile

dumbbell ['dʌmbel] *n* (*person*) cloche *f*, cruche *f*

dumbfuck [!!] ['dʌmfʌk] *n* connard (connasse) *m,f*

dump [dʌmp] **1** *n* (**a**) *Péj* (*house, room*) taudis [□] *m*; (*town*) trou *m*, bled *m*; (*pub*) bouge [□] *m* (**b**) **to** *Br* **have** *or Am* **take a dump** [!] (*defecate*) chier, couler un bronze
  2 *vt* (*boyfriend, girlfriend*) plaquer, larguer

dumpling ['dʌmplɪŋ] *n* (*fat man*) gros patapouf *m*; (*fat woman*) grosse dondon *f*

dunno [dʌ'nəʊ] *contraction* (*abrév* **I don't know**) j'sais pas!

dustbins ['dʌstbɪnz] *npl Br* (*rhyming slang* **dustbin lids** = **kids**) gosses *mpl*, mômes *mpl*

Dutch [dʌtʃ] **1** *adj* **Dutch courage** = courage puisé dans la bouteille; **I need some Dutch courage before I phone him** il faut que je boive quelque chose avant de l'appeler
  2 *adv* **to go Dutch** payer chacun sa part [□]

dweeb [dwiːb] *n Am* crétin(e) *m,f*, abruti(e) *m,f*

dyke [daɪk] *n Injurieux* (*lesbian*) gouine *f*, gousse *f*

E

E [i:] *n* (**a**) (*abrév* **ecstasy**) ecsta *f* (**b**) *Br*
(*abrév* **elbow**) **to give sb the big E**
plaquer qn, larguer qn

ear [ɪə(r)] *n* (**a**) **to be up to one's ears in
work** avoir un boulot dingue *ou* pas
possible; **to be up in one's ears in
debt** être couvert de dettes (**b**) **to
throw sb out on his ear** vider qn
(**c**) **to bend sb's ear** pomper l'air à qn
▸ *voir aussi* **pig, thick**

earbashing ['ɪəbæʃɪŋ] *n Br* **to give sb
an earbashing** passer un savon à qn,
souffler dans les bronches à qn; **to get
an earbashing** se faire passer un savon,
se faire souffler dans les bronches

earful ['ɪəfʊl] *n* **to give sb an earful**
passer un savon à qn, souffler dans les
bronches à qn; **to get an earful** se faire
passer un savon, se faire souffler dans
les bronches; **get an earful of this!**
écoute un peu ça!

early doors ['ɜːlɪ'dɔːz] *adv Br* tôt □;
we'll have to get there early doors il
faut qu'on se pointe de bonne heure

earner ['ɜːnə(r)] *n Br* **a nice little earner** une affaire juteuse

earth [ɜːθ] *n* (**a**) *Hum* **did the earth
move for you?** *(when having sex)* alors,
c'était comment pour toi?; **the earth
moved!** c'était divin!
(**b**) *Hum* **earth to Jane, earth to Jane,
can you hear me?** allô, Jane, est-ce que
tu me reçois?
(**c**) *(for emphasis)* **what/who/why on
earth...?** que/qui/pourquoi diable...?;
how on earth should I know? comment veux-tu que je le sache?; **to look
like nothing on earth** ne ressembler à
rien; **to feel like nothing on earth**

n'être vraiment pas dans son assiette
▸ *voir aussi* **scum**

Dans la catégorie (b), il s'agit d'une
phrase humoristique dont le style
rappelle un dialogue de film de
science-fiction. On l'utilise pour attirer
l'attention d'un interlocuteur distrait.

earwig ['ɪəwɪɡ] *Br* **1** *vt* écouter de façon
indiscrète □
2 *vi* écouter aux portes □

easy ['i:zɪ] **1** *adj* (**a**) *Br (promiscuous)*
facile (**b**) **to be on easy street** avoir la
belle vie
2 *adv* **to take it** *or* **things easy** ne pas
s'en faire; **take it easy!** du calme!,
calmos!
▸ *voir aussi* **lay**

eat [i:t] *vt* (**a**) *(worry)* **what's eating
you?** qu'est-ce qui te tracasse? (**b**) *Am*
eat it *or* **me** *or* **shit!** [!] va te faire voir!
(**c**) [!!] *(perform cunnilingus on)* brouter
le cresson à, sucer (**d**) *Am* **to eat sb's
lunch** battre qn à plates coutures

eat out *vt sép* (**a**) [!!] *(perform
cunnilingus on)* brouter le cresson à,
sucer (**b**) **eat your heart out, Claudia
Schiffer!** ça va faire des jalouses, n'est-
ce pas, Claudia Schiffer?

eats [i:ts] *npl* bouffe *f*

ecofreak ['i:kəʊfri:k] *n* écolo *mf* radi-
cal(e)

ecstasy ['ekstəsɪ] *n (drug)* ecstasy *f*

eff [ef] *vi Br* **to eff and blind** [!] jurer
comme un charretier

eff off [!] *vi* se barrer; **eff off!** va te
faire!

effing [!] ['efɪŋ] **1** *n Br* **stop that effing
and blinding!** arrête de jurer comme

un charretier!

2 *adj* fichu, foutu; **the effing telly's on the blink** cette saloperie de télé déconne!

3 *adv* sacrément, vachement; **don't be so effing lazy!** remue-toi, espèce de feignasse!

egg [eg] *n* **a good egg** *(man)* un chic type; *(woman)* une brave femme; **a bad egg** *(man)* un sale type; *(woman)* une sale bonne femme

eggbeater ['egbiːtə(r)] *n* *Am* (helicopter) hélico *m*

egghead ['eghed] *n* *Hum ou Péj* intello *mf*

eightball ['eɪtbɔːl] *n* *Am* **to be behind the eightball** être dans la mouise

Il s'agit à l'origine d'un terme de billard; la boule numéro huit est celle qui doit être jouée en dernier et il est donc très délicat de se retrouver dans une position où l'on risque de toucher cette boule avant la fin de la partie.

eighty-six ['eɪtɪ'sɪks] *Am* **1** *adj* **to be eighty-six on sth** *(in restaurant, bar)* manquer de qch ⁰; **tell the customer we're eighty-six on the chicken** dis au client qu'il n'y a plus de poulet

2 *vt* **(a)** *(eject)* vider **(b)** *(kill)* buter, refroidir

elbow ['elbəʊ] *n* **(a)** *Br* **to give sb the elbow** *(employee)* virer qn; *(boyfriend, girlfriend)* plaquer qn, larguer qn; **to get the elbow** *(of employee)* se faire virer; *(of boyfriend, girlfriend)* se faire plaquer *ou* larguer **(b)** *Hum* **to bend one's elbow** *(drink)* lever le coude
▶ *voir aussi* **arse, ass**

El Cheapo [el'tʃiːpəʊ] *Hum* **1** *n* article *m* bas de gamme ⁰

2 *adj* bas de gamme ⁰; **an El Cheapo restaurant** un resto bon marché

elevator ['elɪveɪtə(r)] *n* *Hum* **the elevator doesn't go up to the top floor** c'est pas une lumière

eliminate [ɪ'lɪmɪneɪt] *vt* *(kill)* liquider

enchilada [entʃɪ'lɑːdə] *n* **big enchilada** *(person)* huile *f*; **the whole enchilada** *(everything)* tout le tremblement

end [end] *n* **(a)** *Br* **to get one's end away** tremper son biscuit **(b)** **to go off (at) the deep end** péter les plombs, péter une durite

equalizer ['iːkwəlaɪzə(r)] *n* *Am* (handgun) flingue *m*, feu *m*

Essex ['esɪks] *npr* *Br* *Péj* **Essex Girl** minette *f* de l'Essex; **Essex Man** ≃ beauf *m*

Il s'agit de stéréotypes sociaux apparus au cours des années 80. L'"Essex Girl" (originaire de l'Essex, comté situé à l'est de Londres) est censée être une jeune femme d'origine modeste aux mœurs légères, vulgaire, bruyante, et peu intelligente. L'"Essex Man" est lui aussi vulgaire et bruyant; de plus, il est réactionnaire et inculte.

eyeball ['aɪbɔːl] *vt* mater

eyeful ['aɪfʊl] *n* **to get an eyeful (of sb/sth)** mater (qn/qch); **get an eyeful of that!** mate un peu ça!; **she's quite an eyeful!** elle est vachement bien foutue!

eye-popping ['aɪpɒpɪŋ] *adj* *Am* sensationnel

Eyetie ['aɪtaɪ] *Injurieux* **1** *n* Rital(e) *m,f*, macaroni *mf*

2 *adj* rital

F

FA [ef'eɪ] n Br (abrév **Fanny Adams** or **fuck all**) **sweet FA** que dalle

fab [fæb] adj Br (abrév **fabulous**) génial, super

face [feɪs] n (**a**) Br **to be off one's face** (drunk) être pété ou bourré; (on drugs) être défoncé (**b**) **in your face** (unsubtle) percutant □
▸ voir aussi **feed, shut, waste**

faceache ['feɪseɪk] n Br **to be a face-ache** (ugly) être une mocheté; (miserable) toujours faire la gueule

fade [feɪd] vi Am (leave) s'esbigner, calter

fadge [!!] [fædʒ] n Br (woman's genitals) chatte f, cramouille f

faff about, faff around [fæf] vi Br (**a**) (waste time) glander (**b**) (potter) s'occuper □, bricoler

fag [fæg] n (**a**) Br (cigarette) clope f; **fag end** mégot □ m, clope m (**b**) Am Injurieux (homosexual) pédale f, tapette f, tantouze f; **fag hag** fille f à pédés

> Dans la catégorie (b), ce terme perd son caractère injurieux quand il est utilisé par des homosexuels.

fagged (out) [fægd('aʊt)] adj Br lessivé, crevé, naze

faggot ['fægət] n Am Injurieux (homosexual) pédale f, tapette f, tantouze f

> Quand il est utilisé par des homosexuels, ce terme perd son caractère injurieux.

faggy ['fægɪ] adj Am Injurieux qui fait tapette

> Quand il est utilisé par des homosexuels, ce terme perd son caractère injurieux.

fairy ['feərɪ] n Injurieux (homosexual) tante f, pédé m
▸ voir aussi **away**

fall out [fɔːl] vi Noir Am (fall asleep) s'endormir □

fall guy ['fɔːlgaɪ] n (dupe) pigeon m; (scapegoat) bouc m émissaire □

family jewels [!] ['fæməlɪ'dʒuːəlz] npl Hum (man's genitals) bijoux mpl de famille

fancy ['fænsɪ] **1** adj (**a**) Br **fancy man** amant □ m; **fancy woman** maîtresse □ f (**b**) Am **Fancy Dan** (dandy) dandy m; (show-off) frimeur m
2 vt Br (**a**) (be attracted to) **to fancy sb** en pincer pour qn (**b**) (have high opinion of) **to fancy oneself** se gober (**c**) (want) **do you fancy a drink/going to the cinema?** ça te dirait d'aller boire un coup/d'aller au cinéma?

fancy-dan ['fænsɪ'dæn] adj Am frimeur

fanny ['fænɪ] n (**a**) [!] Br (woman's genitals) chatte f, foufoune f (**b**) Am (buttocks) derrière m; **fanny pack** banane f (sac)
▸ voir aussi **magnet**

fanny about [!], **fanny around** [!] vi Br perdre son temps à des bricoles, glander

far-out [fɑː'raʊt] **1** adj (**a**) (strange) zarbi; (avant-garde) d'avant-garde □ (**b**) (excellent) génial, géant
2 exclam super!, génial!

fart [fɑːt] **1** n pet m, prout m; **a boring old fart** (person) un(e) vieux (vieille) con (conne)
2 vi péter
▸ voir aussi **pissed**

fart about, fart around vi perdre son temps à des bricoles, glander

fartsack ['fɑːtsæk] n Am (bed) pieu m, plumard m; (sleeping bag) sac m à viande

fashion victim ['fæʃənvɪktɪm] n Péj esclave mf de la mode

fast [fɑːst] adj **to pull a fast one on sb** rouler qn

fat [fæt] adj (**a**) **fat cat** richard(e) m,f; Am **to be in fat city** avoir la belle vie (**b**) Ironique (for emphasis) **a fat lot of good that'll do me!** ça me fera une belle jambe!; **you're a fat lot of help!** merci! tu m'aides vachement!; **fat chance!** on peut toujours rêver! (**c**) Noir Am (excellent) super, génial ▸ voir aussi **chew**

fathead ['fæthed] n andouille f, courge f

fatso ['fætsəʊ], **fatty** ['fætɪ] n (man) gros lard m; (woman) grosse dondon f

faze [feɪz] vt déconcerter □

features ['fiːtʃəs] npl Br **monkey features** Duconnoque; **dick features** ⚠ Ducon

Fed [fed] n Am (**a**) **the Feds** (abrév **Federal Government**) = toute agence dépendant du gouvernement fédéral, aux États-Unis (**b**) **the Fed** (abrév **Federal Reserve Board**) = agence gouvernementale américaine dont le rôle est de réguler le système bancaire (**c**) (abrév **Federal Agent**) agent m du gouvernement fédéral □

federal case ['fedərəl'keɪs] adj Am **to make a federal case out of sth** faire toute une histoire de qch

feeb [fiːb] n Am crétin(e) m,f, débile mf

feed [fiːd] **1** n (large meal) gueuleton m **2** vt **to feed one's face** s'en mettre plein la lampe, se goinfrer

feedbag ['fiːdbæg] n Am **to put on the (old) feedbag** bouffer

feel up [fiːl] vt sép **to feel sb up** peloter qn

fem [fem] n lesbienne f féminine □

fence [fens] **1** n (person) receleur □ m, fourgueur m **2** vi faire du recel □

fender-bender ['fendəbendə(r)] n Am accrochage □ m

fess up [fes] vi Am (confess) se mettre à table

-fest [fest] suffixe **drinkfest** beuverie f; Br **shagfest** séance f de baise intense

> Le suffixe "-fest" dénote l'excès. On l'ajoute à des termes désignant une activité.

fifth wheel ['fɪfθ'wiːl] n Am **to feel like a fifth wheel** tenir la chandelle

figure ['fɪɡə(r)] vi Am **go figure!** va comprendre!

filth [fɪlθ] n Br Péj **the filth** (the police) les flics mpl, les poulets mpl

fin [fɪn] n Am (five-dollar note) billet m de cinq dollars □

finagle [fɪ'neɪɡəl] vt Am obtenir en magouillant

finger ['fɪŋɡə(r)] **1** n **to pull one's finger out** s'enlever les doigts du cul; **to give sb the finger,** Br **to give sb the fingers** faire un doigt d'honneur à qn; **to put the finger on sb** (denounce) balancer qn; (blame) accuser qn □ **2** vt (**a**) ⚠ (woman) mettre le doigt dans la chatte de, masturber □ (**b**) (denounce) balancer; (blame) accuser □

> En Grande-Bretagne, on utilise l'expression "to give sb the fingers" au pluriel car ce geste se fait à l'aide de l'index et du majeur.

finger-fuck ⚠⚠ ['fɪŋɡəfʌk] vt (woman) mettre le doigt dans la chatte de

fink [fɪŋk] Am **1** n (**a**) (informer) mouchard m (**b**) (unpleasant person) blaireau m, enflure f (**c**) (strikebreaker) jaune m **2** vi moucharder; **to fink on sb** balancer qn

firewater ['faɪəwɔːtə(r)] *n* tord-boyaux *m*

fish [fɪʃ] *n* (**a**) *(person)* **cold fish** pisse-froid *mf*; **queer fish** drôle d'oiseau *m* (**b**) **to drink like a fish** boire comme un trou

fist-fuck ‼️ ['fɪstfʌk] *vt* insérer le poing dans l'anus de◻, pratiquer le fist-fucking sur

fit [fɪt] **1** *n* **to have** *or* **throw a fit** piquer une crise, péter les plombs; *Br* **to be in fits** se tenir les côtes, hurler de rire; *Br* **to have sb in fits** faire hurler qn de rire
2 *adj Br (attractive)* bien foutu

fit up *vt sép* **to fit sb up** monter un coup contre qn; **they fitted him up** il a été victime d'un coup monté

five [faɪv] *n* (**a**) **to take five** faire un break de cinq minutes (**b**) **gimme five!** tape-moi dans la main!
▶ *voir aussi* **high-five**

> Dans la catégorie (b), il s'agit d'une façon de signifier à quelqu'un que l'on veut lui taper dans la main pour le saluer, le féliciter, ou en signe de victoire.

fiver ['faɪvə(r)] *n Br (sum)* cinq livres◻ *fpl*; *(note)* billet *m* de cinq livres◻

five-spot ['faɪvspɒt] *n Am* billet *m* de cinq dollars◻

fix [fɪks] **1** *n* (**a**) *(of drugs)* fix *m*; **I need my daily fix of chocolate** il me faut ma dose quotidienne de chocolat (**b**) **to be a fix** *(of election, contest)* être truqué
2 *vt* (**a**) *(rig)* truquer (**b**) *(bribe)* graisser la patte à (**c**) *(get even with)* régler ses comptes avec; **I'll fix him!** il va me le payer!

fixer ['fɪksə(r)] *n (person)* combinard(e) *m,f*, magouilleur(euse) *m,f*

flake [fleɪk] *n (person)* allumé(e) *m,f*

flake out *vi* s'écrouler de fatigue

flaky ['fleɪkɪ] *adj* loufoque, loufedingue

flamer ['fleɪmə(r)] *n Am* enflure *f*

flaming ['fleɪmɪŋ] *Br* **1** *adj (for emphasis)* **you flaming idiot!** espèce de crétin!; **he's a flaming pest** c'est un sacré emmerdeur; **flaming hell!** merde alors!
2 *adv (for emphasis)* vachement, super; **it was flaming expensive** c'était vachement cher; **you're flaming well staying here!** tu ne bouges pas d'ici, enfonce-toi bien ça dans la tête!

flap [flæp] **1** *n* **to be in a flap** être dans tous ses états; **to get in a flap** se mettre dans tous ses états, faire un caca nerveux
2 *vi* s'exciter, paniquer; **stop flapping!** du calme!, calmos!
▶ *voir aussi* **jaw**

flash [flæʃ] **1** *adj Br (car, clothes, jewellery)* tape-à-l'œil; *(person)* frimeur; **Flash Harry** frimeur *m*
2 *vt Am (expose oneself to)* s'exhiber devant◻
3 *vi (expose oneself)* s'exhiber◻; *Br* **to flash at sb** s'exhiber devant qn

flash on *vt insép Am* **to flash on sth** se remémorer qch◻; **I flashed on what had happened** tout d'un coup j'ai revu tout ce qui s'était passé◻

flashback ['flæʃbæk] *n (hallucination)* flashback *m*, retour *m* d'acide

flasher ['flæʃə(r)] *n (man)* exhibitionniste◻ *m*

flatfoot ['flætfʊt] *n Am (police officer)* flic *m*, poulet *m*

fleabag ['fliːbæg] *n* (**a**) *Br (person)* pouilleux (euse) *m,f*; *(animal)* sac *m* à puces (**b**) *Am (hotel)* hôtel *m* borgne

fleapit ['fliːpɪt] *n Br (cinema)* = vieux cinéma de quartier mal tenu

fleece [fliːs] *vt (overcharge)* écorcher; *(cheat)* arnaquer, plumer

flesh [fleʃ] *n* **to press the flesh** = serrer des mains au cours d'un bain de foule

fling [flɪŋ] **1** *n* (**a**) *(sexual relationship)* aventure◻ *f*, passade◻ *f*; **to have a fling (with sb)** avoir une aventure (avec qn) **(b)** (period of enjoyment) bon temps □ m; **to have a final fling** s'éclater une dernière fois

flip [flɪp] **1** vt **to flip one's lid** or Am **wig** (get angry) piquer une crise, péter les plombs; (go mad) devenir cinglé, perdre la boule; (get excited) devenir dingue

    2 vi (get angry) piquer une crise, péter les plombs; (go mad) devenir cinglé, perdre la boule; (get excited) devenir dingue

    ▸ voir aussi **bird**

flip out vi (get angry) piquer une crise, péter les plombs; (go mad) devenir cinglé, perdre la boule; (get excited) devenir dingue

flipping ['flɪpɪŋ] Br **1** adj (for emphasis) foutu, fichu; **get that flipping dog out of here!** fous-moi cette saleté de clébard dehors!; **flipping heck!** mince alors!

    2 adv (for emphasis) sacrément; **he's so flipping annoying!** ce qu'il peut être embêtant!; **don't flipping well talk to me like that!** t'as intérêt à me parler sur un autre ton!

float about, float around [fləʊt] vi Br traîner

flog [flɒɡ] vt Br (sell) fourguer

floor [flɔː(r)] **1** n **to wipe the floor with sb** (defeat) battre qn à plates coutures

    2 vt **(a)** (knock down) foutre par terre **(b)** (shock) secouer; (baffle) dérouter □

floosie, floozie, floozy ['fluːzɪ] n pétasse f, roulure f

flop [flɒp] **1** n **(a)** (failure) bide m **(b)** Am (hotel) hôtel m borgne; (hostel) asile m de nuit □

    2 vi **(a)** (fail) faire un bide **(b)** Am (sleep) pioncer, roupiller

flophouse ['flɒphaʊs] n Am (hotel) hôtel m borgne; (hostel) asile m de nuit □

fluff [flʌf] n Br **a bit of fluff**, Am **a fluff** une gonzesse, une nana

    ▸ voir aussi **bum**

flunk [flʌŋk] Am **1** vt (exam) rater □, foirer; (student) ne pas accorder d'unité de valeur à □

    2 vi (in exam) échouer □, se planter

flunk out vi Am se faire virer (à cause de ses mauvais résultats)

flush [flʌʃ] adj (rich) **to be flush** avoir des ronds; **I'm feeling flush so I'll pay** j'ai des ronds, donc c'est moi qui paie

fly [flaɪ] **1** adj Noir Am (excellent) génial, super, géant; (stylish, attractive) chouette

    2 vt **to fly the coop** (escape) se faire la belle

    3 vi **to send sb/sth flying** envoyer qn/qch valser; **to fly off the handle** sortir de ses gonds, piquer une crise

    ▸ see also **kite**

fly-by-night ['flaɪbənaɪt] **1** n (person) fumiste mf, artiste m; (company) entreprise f pas sérieuse

    2 adj pas sérieux

fogey ['fəʊɡɪ] n **old fogey** (man) vieux schnock m; (woman) vieille bique f; Hum **young fogey** jeune con (conne) m,f (vieux avant l'âge)

foggy ['fɒɡɪ] adj **I haven't the foggiest (idea)!** aucune idée!

fool about, fool around [fuːl] vi **(a)** (act foolishly) faire l'idiot; **to fool about with sth** jouer avec qch **(b)** (waste time) glander, glandouiller **(c)** (have affairs) fricoter (**with** avec) **(d)** (of couple) se bécoter

foot [fʊt] n **my foot!** mon œil!

footer ['fʊtə(r)], **footie** ['fʊtɪ] n Br (abrév **football**) foot m

footsie ['fʊtsɪ] n **to play footsie with sb** faire du pied à qn

fork out [fɔːk] **1** vt sép allonger

    2 vi casquer (**for** pour)

foul up [faʊl] **1** vt **to foul sth up** foirer qch, merder qch

    2 vi foirer, merder

foul-up ['faʊlʌp] n ratage □ m, foirade f

four-eyes [ˈfɔːraɪz] n Péj (term of address) binoclard(e) m,f

fox [fɒks] n Am (woman) canon m

foxy [ˈfɒksɪ] adj (sexually attractive) sexy

fraidy cat [ˈfreɪdɪkæt] n Am poule f mouillée

frat [fræt] n Am (abrév **fraternity**) club m d'étudiants□; **frat rat** membre m d'un club d'étudiants□

Les "fraternities" sont des organisations d'étudiants dont chacune possède ses locaux ("fraternity house") et dont la principale raison d'être est de fournir instantanément à ses membres un cercle d'amis et de connaissances. Les étudiants désireux de faire partie d'une "fraternity" doivent être parrainés par des membres et doivent se soumettre à de nombreuses épreuves souvent aussi stupides qu'humiliantes. Le nom de chaque "fraternity" est composé de trois lettres de l'alphabet grec.

frazzled [ˈfræzəld] adj (exhausted) naze, flagada; (bothered) à cran

freak [friːk] 1 n (a) (odd person) monstre m (b) (fan) **a computer/tennis freak** un fana d'informatique/de tennis
   2 vt (shock, scare) faire flipper
   3 vi (panic, become scared) flipper, paniquer; (become angry) piquer une crise, péter les plombs
   ▸ voir aussi **Jesus**

freak out 1 vt sép **to freak sb out** (shock, scare) faire flipper qn
   2 vi (a) (panic, become scared) flipper, paniquer; (become angry) piquer une crise, péter les plombs (b) (abandon restraint) s'éclater; **look at him freaking out on the dancefloor!** regarde-le s'éclater sur la piste de danse!

freaking [ˈfriːkɪŋ] Am 1 adj (for emphasis) sacré, foutu; **where are those freaking kids?** mais où sont passés ces foutus gamins?

   2 adv (for emphasis) vachement; **it's freaking cold out there** ça pince vachement dehors; **I don't freaking know!** j'en sais foutre rien!

freak-out [ˈfriːkaʊt] n trip m

freaky [ˈfriːkɪ] adj (strange) bizarre□, zarbi

freebase [ˈfriːbeɪs] vi = chauffer de la cocaïne et en inhaler la fumée

freeload [ˈfriːləʊd] vi vivre au crochet des autres

freeloader [ˈfriːləʊdə(r)] n parasite□ m

French [frentʃ] 1 n Hum **pardon** or **excuse my French!** (after swearing) passez-moi l'expression!
   2 adj **French kiss** baiser m avec la langue□, pelle f, patin m; **to give sb a French kiss** rouler une pelle ou un patin à qn; Br **French letter** capote f anglaise

L'image stéréotypée que se font les Britanniques et les Américains des Français est celle d'un peuple très porté sur le sexe, aux moeurs exotiques. Ces clichés sont à l'origine de nombreuses expressions argotiques. Il est amusant de noter que les "French letters" des Anglais sont les "capotes anglaises" des Français.

French-kiss [frentʃˈkɪs] 1 vt rouler une pelle ou un patin à
   2 vi se rouler une pelle ou un patin

fresh [freʃ] adj Am (a) (cheeky) culotté; **don't get fresh with me, young man!** ne soyez pas insolent, jeune homme! (b) (sexually bold) déluré□; **to get fresh with sb** faire des avances à qn□ (c) (excellent) super, génial

fresher [ˈfreʃə(r)] n Br étudiant(e) m,f de première année□

fried [fraɪd] adj (a) Am (drunk) bourré, beurré, pété, poivré; (on drugs) raide, parti, défoncé (b) Hum **fried eggs** (breasts) œufs mpl sur le plat

frig [!] [frɪg] 1 exclam **frig (it)!** merde!
   2 vt (a) (have sex with) (of man) baiser,

tringler, troncher; *(of woman)* baiser avec, s'envoyer (**b**) *(masturbate)* branler **3** *vi (masturbate)* s'astiquer le bouton, se branler

frig about⚠, **frig around**⚠ *vi (act foolishly)* faire le con, déconner; *(waste time)* glander, glandouiller

frigging⚠ ['frɪgɪn] **1** *adj (for emphasis)* fichu, foutu; **what a frigging waste of time!** tu parles d'une perte de temps!; **shut your frigging mouth!** ferme-la!, ferme ta gueule!
2 *adv (for emphasis)* **don't frigging lie to me!** ne me mens pas, bordel!; **I'm frigging freezing!** je me les gèle!

frighteners ['fraɪtnəz] *npl Br* **to put the frighteners on sb** menacer qn □

Frisco ['frɪskəʊ] *npr Am* = surnom donné à la ville de San Francisco

fritz [frɪts] *n Am* **to be on the fritz** *(of TV, machine)* déconner, débloquer

Frog [frɒg], **Froggy** ['frɒgɪ] *Injurieux* **1** *n* Français(e) *m,f*, fransquillon(onne) *m,f*
2 *adj* français □; **they've got some Frog footballer playing for them** il y a un joueur français dans leur équipe; **I hate Frog food** j'ai horreur de la cuisine française

C'est la réputation de mangeurs de cuisses de grenouilles des Français qui leur valut ce surnom. Selon le ton et le contexte, ce terme peut être soit injurieux, soit humoristique.

front [frʌnt] **1** *vt Am* (**a**) *(pay in advance)* avancer □; **the cashier can front you the money** le caissier peut vous faire une avance *ou* vous avancer l'argent (**b**) *(give, lend money to)* filer; **can you front me five bucks?** tu pourrais pas me filer cinq dollars?
2 *vi Noir Am* (**a**) *(show off)* frimer (**b**) *(tell lies)* baratiner, raconter des craques

frosh [frɒʃ] *n Am* étudiant(e) *m,f* de première année □

fruit [fruːt] *n Am Injurieux (homosexual)* pédé *m*, tapette *f*

fruitcake ['fruːtkeɪk] *n (person)* dingo *mf*, allumé(e) *m,f*
▶ *voir aussi* **nutty**

fry [fraɪ] *Am* **1** *vt (convict)* faire passer à la chaise électrique □
2 *vi (of convict)* passer à la chaise électrique □

fuck‼ [fʌk] **1** *n* (**a**) *(sexual intercourse)* baise *f*; **to have a fuck** baiser, s'envoyer en l'air (**b**) *(person)* **to be a good fuck** bien baiser, être un bon coup; **you stupid fuck!** espèce d'enculé! (**c**) *(for emphasis)* **who the fuck left the window open?** quel est le con qui a laissé la fenêtre ouverte?; **why the fuck didn't you tell me?** pourquoi est-ce que tu m'as pas prévenu, bordel!; **what the fuck are you doing?** mais qu'est-ce que tu fous, bordel!; **I can't really afford it, but what the fuck!** c'est un peu cher pour moi, mais je m'en fous!; **it costs a fuck of a lot of money** ça coûte la peau du cul; **it's been a fuck of a long day!** putain, la journée a été longue!; **shut the fuck up!** ferme ta gueule!; *Br* **get to fuck!** va te faire enculer!; **get the fuck out of here!** fous-moi le camp!, dégage! (**d**) *(expressing surprise, disbelief)* **for fuck's sake!** merde!, putain!; *Br* **fuck knows where he is!** j'ai pas la moindre idée d'où il peut être! (**e**) *(in comparisons)* **as stupid as fuck** con comme la lune; **as boring as fuck** chiant comme la pluie; **he ran like fuck** il a pris ses jambes à son cou (**f**) **not to give a (flying) fuck (about)** se foutre complètement (de); **who gives a fuck!** tout le monde s'en fout! (**g**) **can I borrow the car? – like fuck you can** *or Br* **can you fuck!** est-ce que je peux prendre la voiture? – alors là tu peux te brosser!; **are you going to apologize? – like fuck I am** *or Br* **am I**

fuck! est-ce que tu vas t'excuser? – des clous!

(**h**) **fuck all** que dalle; *Br* **fuck all money/time** pas un flèche/une minute; **she's done fuck all today** elle a rien foutu de la journée; **she knows fuck all about it** elle y connaît que dalle

2 *exclam* **fuck (it)!** bordel de merde!

3 *vt* (**a**) *(have sex with) (of man)* baiser, tringler, troncher; *(of woman)* baiser avec; **he fucked her brains out** il l'a baisée comme il faut

(**b**) *(for emphasis)* **fuck him!** qu'il aille se faire enculer!; **fuck me!** merde alors!; **fuck you!** va te faire enculer!; *Br* **go and fuck yourself,** *Am* **go fuck yourself!** va te faire enculer!

4 *vi* (**a**) *(have sex)* baiser

(**b**) **to fuck with sb** jouer au con avec qn; **don't fuck with me!** joue pas au con avec moi!

▸ *voir aussi* **holy, rabbit**

fuck about ⚠️, **fuck around** ⚠️
1 *vt sép* **to fuck sb about** *(treat badly)* se foutre de la gueule de qn; *(waste time of)* faire perdre son temps à qn □

2 *vi* (**a**) *(be promiscuous)* baiser à droite à gauche (**b**) *(act foolishly)* déconner, faire le con; *(waste time)* glander, glandouiller; **to fuck about with sth** tripoter qch

fuck off ⚠️ **1** *vt sép* **to fuck sb off** faire chier qn; **to be fucked off (with)** en avoir plein le cul (de)

2 *vi* (**a**) *(leave)* se casser, calter; **fuck off!** *(go away)* casse-toi!; *(expressing contempt, disagreement)* va te faire foutre! (**b**) *Am (waste time, be idle)* glander

fuck over ⚠️ *vt sép* **to fuck sb over** baiser qn, arnaquer qn

fuck up ⚠️ **1** *vt sép* (**a**) *(person)* rendre cinglé; *(plan, situation)* faire foirer; **she's totally fucked up** *(psychologically)* elle est complètement à côté de ses pompes; **you've fucked every-**

thing up tu as tout fait foirer *ou* merder (**b**) *Am* **fucked up** *(drunk)* bourré, beurré, pété, poivré; *(on drugs)* raide, parti, défoncé

2 *vi* merder, foirer

fuckable ⚠️ ['fʌkəbəl] *adj* baisable

fucked ⚠️ [fʌkt] *adj* (**a**) *(exhausted)* naze, crevé, lessivé (**b**) *(broken, not working properly)* foutu; **my leg's fucked** j'ai la jambe qui déconne (**c**) *(in trouble)* foutu; **if they don't win this game, they're fucked** si ils gagnent pas ce match, ils sont foutus (**d**) *(for emphasis)* **I'm fucked if I'm going to apologize!** plutôt crever que de m'excuser!; **I'm fucked if I know!** j'en sais foutre rien!

fucker ⚠️ ['fʌkə(r)] *n* (**a**) *(man)* enculé *m*, enfoiré *m*; *(woman)* connasse *f*; **some fucker's stolen my bike** il y a un enculé qui m'a piqué mon vélo; **you lazy fucker!** espèce de grosse feignasse!; **you stupid fucker!** pauvre con! (**b**) *(thing)* saloperie *f*; **I can't get the fucker to start** j'arrive pas à faire démarrer cette saloperie

fuckfest ⚠️ ['fʌkfest] *n* séance *f* de baise intense

fuckhead ⚠️ ['fʌkhed] *n* connard (connasse) *m,f*

fucking ⚠️ ['fʌkɪŋ] **1** *adj* **fucking hell!** merde alors!, putain!; **where the fucking hell have you been?** où est-ce que t'étais passé, bordel?; **she's here all the fucking time!** elle est toujours fourrée ici!; **where are my fucking cigarettes?** où sont mes putains de cigarettes?; **he's a fucking bastard!** c'est un véritable enculé!; **you fucking idiot!** espèce de crétin!; *Am* **fucking A!** *(absolutely)* absolument!, tu parles!; *(great)* super!, génial!

2 *adv* **it's fucking freezing!** on se les gèle!; **I'm fucking well going home!** merde! moi je rentre chez moi!; **the film was fucking crap!** c'était de la merde ce film!; **we had a fucking amazing weekend!** on a passé un week-end vraiment génial!; **fucking stop it!** arrête, bordel de merde!; **I don't fucking know!** j'en sais foutre rien!

fuck-me !! ['fʌkmi:] adj **fuck-me dress** robe f affriolante; **fuck-me shoes** chaussures fpl de pute

fuck-off !! ['fʌkɒf] **1** n Am (person) glandeur(euse) m,f
  2 adj Br (for emphasis) mastoc; **they've got a huge fuck-off house in the country** ils ont une baraque énorme à la campagne

fuckpad !! ['fʌkpæd] n Br baisodrome m

fuck-up !! ['fʌkʌp] n **(a)** (bungle) ratage m, foirade f; **to make a fuck-up of sth** foirer qch **(b)** Am (bungler) manche m; (misfit) paumé(e) m,f

fuckwit !! ['fʌkwɪt] n connard (connasse) m,f

fudge-packer !! ['fʌdʒpækə(r)] n Injurieux tantouze f, pédale f, tapette f

fugly !! ['fʌglɪ] adj (abrév **fucking ugly**) hyper moche; **she's really fugly** c'est un vrai boudin ou cageot

funky ['fʌŋkɪ] adj **(a)** (fashionable, excellent) cool **(b)** Am (smelly) qui pue, qui schlingue

funny farm ['fʌnɪfɑ:m] n maison f de fous

furpie !! ['fɜ:'paɪ] n (woman's genitals) tarte f aux poils

fuzz [fʌz] n **the fuzz** (the police) les flics mpl, les poulets mpl

G

gab [gæb] **1** *n* **to have the gift of the gab** avoir du bagout
2 *vi* jacter, jacasser

gabfest ['gæbfest] *n Am* converse *f*

gaff [gæf] *n* (**a**) *Br* (*home*) baraque *f*; **he's staying at my gaff for the weekend** il crèche chez moi ce week-end (**b**) *Am* **to stand the gaff** encaisser
▶ *voir aussi* **blow**

gaffer ['gæfə(r)] *n* (*boss*) patron⌐ *m*, taulier *m*

gag [gæg] **1** *vt Am Hum* **gag me (with a spoon)!** ça me fout la nausée!
2 *vi Br* **to be gagging for it** [!] avoir envie de se faire tirer

gaga ['gɑːgɑː] *adj* (**a**) (*deranged*) toqué, timbré; *Br* (*senile*) gaga (**b**) (*besotted*) **to be gaga about** *or* **over sb** être dingue de qn

gal [gæl] *n Am* nana *f*, gonzesse *f*

game [geɪm] *n Br* **to be on the game** se prostituer⌐, michetonner
▶ *voir aussi* **mug, skin**

gander ['gændə(r)] *n* **to have a gander (at sb/sth)** jeter un œil (à qn/qch), mater (qn/qch)

ganga ['gændʒə] *n* herbe *f*

gang-bang ['gæŋbæŋ] **1** *n* = coïts entre une femme et plusieurs hommes à la suite; (*rape*) viol *m* collectif⌐
2 *vt* **to gang-bang sb** baiser qn à tour de rôle; (*rape*) commettre un viol collectif sur qn⌐

ganja ['gændʒə] = **ganga**

gannet ['gænət] *n Br* (*person*) morfal(e) *m,f*

garbage ['gɑːbɪdʒ] **1** *n* (**a**) (*nonsense*) âneries *fpl*; **don't talk garbage!** ne dis

pas n'importe quoi!; **that's garbage, you never said anything of the sort!** tu racontes n'importe quoi, t'as jamais dit ça!
(**b**) (*worthless things*) **their new album is a load of garbage** leur dernier album est vraiment nul; **I've been eating too much garbage lately** je mange trop de cochonneries en ce moment
(**c**) (*useless things*) bazar *m*; **chuck out all that garbage of yours** fous-moi tout ton bazar en l'air, balance-moi tout ton bazar

gas [gæs] **1** *n* (**a**) (*amusing thing, situation*) **what a gas!** quelle rigolade!; **the film was a real gas!** c'était un film vachement marrant!; *Br* **to have a gas** se marrer, s'en payer une tranche (**b**) (*amusing person*) **he's a real gas!** c'est un vrai boute-en-train! (**c**) *Am* **to be out of gas** (*exhausted*) être crevé *ou* naze
2 *vi* (*chat*) jacter, jacasser
▶ *voir aussi* **cook**

gasbag ['gæsbæg] *n* (*chatterbox*) moulin *m* à paroles; (*boaster*) fanfaron(onne) *m,f*

gas-guzzler ['gæsgʌzlə(r)] *n* voiture *f* qui bouffe beaucoup d'essence

gash [!!] [gæʃ] *n* (*woman's genitals*) craquette *f*, fente *f*, cramouille *f*

gasp [gɑːsp] *vi* **to be gasping for a cigarette/a drink** mourir d'envie de fumer une cigarette/de boire un verre

gasper ['gɑːspə(r)] *n Br* clope *f*

gassed [gæst] *adj* (*drunk*) bourré, pété

gasser ['gæsə(r)] *n Am* **to have a gasser** se marrer, s'en payer une tranche; **what a gasser!** quelle rigolade!; **the**

film was a real gasser! c'était un film vachement marrant!

gay-basher ['geɪbæʃə(r)] *n* = individu qui attaque des homosexuels

gay-bashing ['geɪbæʃɪŋ] *n* = violences contre des homosexuels

gay plague ['geɪpleɪg] *n* sida $^\square$ *m*

> L'expression signifie littéralement "peste gay". Elle est aujourd'hui politiquement incorrecte, mais désignait le sida dans les années 80, à une époque où l'on pensait que cette maladie n'affectait que les homosexuels.

GBH [dʒiːbiːˈeɪtʃ] *n Br* (*abrév* **grievous bodily harm**) **to give sb GBH of the earholes** raser qn

GD [dʒiːˈdiː] *adj Am* (*abrév* **goddamn(ed)**) foutu, sacré; **he's a GD fool** c'est un sacré con

gear [gɪə(r)] *n* (**a**) (*equipment*) matos *m*; (*belongings*) barda *m* (**b**) (*clothes*) fringues *fpl* (**c**) *Br* (*drugs*) dope *f* (**d**) *Am* **to get it in gear** se magner
▸ *see also* **arse, ass**

gee [dʒiː] *exclam Am* **gee (whiz)!** ça alors!

geek [giːk] *n Am* (**a**) (*strange person*) zarbi(e) *m,f*, allumé(e) *m,f* (**b**) (*misfit*) ringard(e) *m,f*

geezer ['giːzə(r)] *n* (**a**) *Br* (*man*) mec *m*, type *m* (**b**) *Am* (*old person*) vioque *mf*

gelt [gelt] *n Am* fric *m*, flouze *m*, pognon *m*

gender-bender ['dʒendəbendə(r)] *n* travesti $^\square$ *m*, travelo *m*

Geordie ['dʒɔːdɪ] *n Br* = natif de Newcastle-upon-Tyne ou de ses environs

get [get] **1** *n Br* (*man*) salopard *m*; (*woman*) salope *f*
2 *vt* (**a**) (*annoy*) énerver $^\square$, prendre la tête à; **it really gets me the way he's late for everything** il me gonfle à toujours être en retard
(**b**) (*understand*) comprendre $^\square$, piger; **I**

get it! j'ai pigé!
(**c**) **to get it** (*be reprimanded*) se faire passer un savon; (*be beaten up*) prendre une raclée
(**d**) **to get it together** se remuer le cul; (*in one's life*) se prendre en main $^\square$
(**e**) **get you!** (*listen to*) écoute-toi!; (*look at*) regarde-toi!
3 *exclam* (*go away*) casse-toi!, dégage!

get away *exclam* (*expressing disbelief*) tu déconnes!
▸ *voir aussi* **end**

get by *vi* (*manage*) y arriver $^\square$, se démerder

get down 1 *vt sép* **to get sb down** foutre le bourdon à qn
2 *vi* (**a**) (*abandon restraint*) s'éclater; (*dance with abandon*) s'éclater en dansant (**b**) *Am* (*get to work, begin*) s'y mettre, attaquer (**c**) *Am* (*have sex*) s'envoyer en l'air

get off *vi* (**a**) (*reach orgasm*) jouir $^\square$ (**b**) **to tell sb where to get off** envoyer balader qn

get off on *vt insép* **to get off on sth** prendre son pied avec qch; **to get off on doing sth** prendre son pied à faire qch

get off with *vt insép Br* **to get off with sb** faire une touche avec qn

get on *vt sép* (**a**) **to get it on (with)** (*have sex*) s'envoyer en l'air (avec); *Am* (*fight*) se friter (avec) (**b**) *Am* **to get it on** (*get started, get busy*) s'y mettre

get to *vt insép* **to get to sb** déprimer qn $^\square$, foutre le bourdon à qn; **don't let it get to you** il faut pas que ça te sape le moral

get up ⚠ *vt sép* **to get it up** bander; **he couldn't get it up** il a pas réussi à bander
▸ *voir aussi* **nose**

get up to *vt insép* se livrer à $^\square$; **what have you been getting up to?** qu'est-ce que tu deviens?

get-go ['getgəʊ] n Noir Am **from the get-go** (from the beginning) dès le début □; **he's a crook from the get-go** (completely) c'est un escroc total, c'est un véritable escroc

get-together ['gettəgeðə(r)] n réunion f entre amis □

get-up ['getʌp] n accoûtrement m

ghetto blaster ['getəʊblɑːstə(r)] n gros radio-cassette m portable □, ghetto blaster m

gig [gɪg] n (**a**) (concert) concert □ m, gig m (**b**) (job) boulot m

gimme ['gɪmɪ] contraction (abrév **give me**) donne-moi □; Am **the gimmes** la cupidité □
▶ voir aussi **five**

ginormous [dʒaɪ'nɔːməs, Am dʒɪ'nɔː-məs] adj énorme □, mastoc

girlfriend ['gɜːlfrend] n Am (term of address) = terme utilisé par les Américaines pour s'adresser les unes aux autres; **yo, girlfriend!** salut frangine!

À l'origine, ce terme n'était utilisé que par les Noires américaines. Aujourd'hui, son usage s'est généralisé.

girlie ['gɜːlɪ] n fille □ f, nana f; **girlie mag** revue f porno; Br **to have a girlie chat** bavarder entre filles □

gism ['dʒɪzəm] = **jism (a)**

git [gɪt] n (man) salopard m; (woman) salope f

give [gɪv] vi Am **what gives?** quoi de neuf?
▶ voir aussi **one**

give over Br **1** vt insép **give over shouting!** arrête de gueuler comme ça! **2** vi arrêter □

gizmo ['gɪzməʊ] n truc m, bidule m

glitterati [glɪtə'rɑːtɪ] npl **the glitterati** le beau monde

glitz [glɪts] n clinquant m, tape-à-l'œil m

glitzy ['glɪtsɪ] adj tape-à-l'œil

glom [glɒm] vt Am (seize) arracher □

glom onto vt insép Am (**a**) (seize) arracher □ (**b**) (catch sight of) apercevoir □

G-man ['dʒiːmæn] n Am agent m du FBI

gnarly ['nɑːlɪ] adj Am (excellent, awful) mortel

gnat [næt] n Br **gnat's piss** !! (drink) eau f de vaisselle, pipi m de chat

go [gəʊ] vt (**a**) (say) dire; **so she goes "you're lying!" and I go "no, I'm not!"** alors elle me fait "tu mens!" et je lui fais "non, je mens pas!" (**b**) **I could really go a beer/ciggy/pizza** je me taperais bien une bière/une clope/une pizza
▶ voir aussi **way**

go down vi (**a**) (go to prison) aller en taule; **he went down for ten years** il en a pris pour dix ans
(**b**) Br (be received) **to go down like a ton of bricks** or **a lead balloon** faire un bide total, se casser la gueule
(**c**) Am (fall) **to go down like a ton of bricks** se casser la gueule
(**d**) (happen) se passer □, avoir lieu □; **what's going down?** quoi de neuf?

go down on !! vt insép **to go down on sb** (fellate) sucer qn, tailler une pipe à qn; (perform cunnilingus on) sucer qn, brouter le cresson à qn

go for vt insép **go for it!** vas-y!

go over vi Am (be received) **to go over like a ton of bricks** or **a lead balloon** faire un bide total, se casser la gueule

go under vi (of company) se casser la gueule

go with vt insép (**a**) (be romantically involved with) sortir avec □ (**b**) **to go with the flow** suivre le mouvement □

goat [gəʊt] n (**a**) Br **to act the goat** (act foolishly) faire l'imbécile, déconner (**b**) **to get sb's goat** (annoy) irriter qn □, prendre la tête à qn (**c**) Péj **old goat** (lecherous man) vieux m cochon; Am (old man) vieux schnock m; (old woman) vieille toupie f

gob [gɒb] *Br* **1** *n (mouth)* gueule *f*; **shut your gob!** ferme ta gueule!

   2 *vi (spit)* mollarder (**at/on** vers/sur)

gobble !! ['gɒbəl] *vt (fellate)* sucer, tailler une pipe à

gobbledygook ['gɒbəldɪguːk] *n* (**a**) *(jargon)* charabia *m* (**b**) *(nonsense)* conneries *fpl*

gobby ['gɒbɪ] *adj Br* **to be gobby** être une grande gueule

gobshite ! ['gɒbʃaɪt] *n Br (man)* trouduc *m*; *(woman)* connasse *f*

gobsmacked ['gɒbsmækt] *adj Br* estomaqué

God [gɒd] *n* (**my**) **God!** mon Dieu!; **for God's sake!** bon Dieu!; **God knows** va savoir; **what in God's name are you doing?** mais qu'est-ce que tu es en train de faire?; **he thinks he's God's gift (to women)** il s'imagine que toutes les femmes sont folles de lui; **the God squad** les culs bénis

godawful ['gɒdɔːfʊl] *adj* dégueulasse, nul

goddammit ! [gɒd'dæmɪt] *exclam* bordel!

goddamn ! ['gɒd'dæm], **goddamned** ! ['gɒd'dæmd] **1** *adj* foutu, fichu; **he's a goddamn** *or* **goddamned fool!** c'est un pauvre con!

   2 *adv* vachement; **that was goddamn** *or* **goddamned stupid!** c'est vraiment pas malin!

   3 *exclam* **goddamn (it)!** bordel!

goer ['gəʊə(r)] *n Br (woman)* **she's a bit of a goer** elle couche à droite à gauche

gofer ['gəʊfə(r)] *n* larbin *m*

Le terme "gofer" est une altération des termes "go for" qui signifie "aller chercher", ce qui résume le genre de tâches confiées aux employés subalternes.

goldbrick ['gəʊldbrɪk] *Am* **1** *n (malingerer)* tire-au-flanc *m*

   2 *vi (malinger)* tirer au flanc

gold-digger ['gəʊld'dɪgə(r)] *n Péj (woman)* croqueuse *f* de diamants

golden showers !! ['gəʊldən'ʃaʊəz] *npl* = pratique sexuelle qui consiste à uriner sur son ou sa partenaire

golly ['gɒlɪ] *exclam* bon Dieu!

gone [gɒn] *adj* (**a**) **to be gone on sb** être dingue de qn (**b**) **to be well gone** *(drunk)* être beurré *ou* bourré *ou* pété

goner ['gɒnə(r)] *n* **to be a goner** être foutu

gong [gɒŋ] *n (medal)* médaille □ *f*, breloque *f*

gonna ['gɒnə] *contraction (abrév* **going to**) **I'm gonna kill him!** je vais le buter!

Cette contraction n'est utilisée que pour exprimer le futur proche.

gonzo ['gɒnzəʊ] *adj Am* dingue, dément

goober ['guːbə(r)] *n Am* crétin(e) *m,f*, andouille *f*, tache *f*

goods [gʊdz] *npl Am* **to have the goods on sb** avoir la preuve de la culpabilité de qn □

goof [guːf] *Am* **1** *n* (**a**) *(person)* crétin(e) *m,f*, andouille *f*, tache *f* (**b**) *(mistake)* boulette *f*, bourde *f*

   2 *vi* (**a**) *(make mistake)* faire une boulette *ou* une bourde (**b**) *(joke)* rigoler; **to goof with sb** *(tease)* faire enrager qn (**c**) *(stare)* **to goof at sb/sth** regarder qn/qch bêtement □

goof about, goof around *vi Am* (**a**) *(act foolishly)* faire le con, déconner (**b**) *(waste time)* glander, glandouiller

goof off *Am* **1** *vt insép* **to goof off school** sécher l'école; **to goof off work** ne pas aller bosser

   2 *vi* glander, glandouiller

goof up *Am* **1** *vt insép* **to goof sth up** foirer qch, merder qch

   2 *vi* foirer, merder

goofball ['guːfbɔːl] *n Am* (**a**) *(person)* crétin(e) *m,f*, andouille *f*, tache *f* (**b**) *(barbiturate)* mélange *m* de barbituriques et d'amphétamines □

goofy ['gu:fɪ] *adj* (**a**) *(stupid)* débile, abruti (**b**) *Br* **to have goofy teeth** avoir les dents qui courent après le bifteck

gook [gu:k] *n Am Injurieux* bridé(e) *m,f*

goolies ⚠ ['gu:lɪz] *npl Br* couilles *fpl*, valseuses *fpl*

goon [gu:n] *n* (**a**) *(idiot)* andouille *f*, cruche *f*, courge *f* (**b**) *(hired thug)* gorille *m*

goose [gu:s] *vt* **to goose sb** mettre la main au cul à qn

gooseberry ['gʊzbərɪ] *n Br* **to play gooseberry** tenir la chandelle

gorblimey [gɔ:'blaɪmɪ] *exclam Br* nom de Dieu!, merde alors!

Gordon Bennett ['gɔ:dən'benɪt] *exclam Br* nom d'une pipe!

> Il s'agit d'un euphémisme du mot "God" utilisé comme juron. Gordon Bennett était un journaliste américain du 19ème siècle haut en couleurs.

gorilla [gə'rɪlə] *n Péj (man)* grosse brute *f*

gosh [gɒʃ] *exclam* la vache!

gotcha ['gɒtʃə] *exclam (abrév* **I got you)** *(I understand)* je comprends, d'accord; *(when catching hold of someone)* pris!; *(when catching someone doing something)* je t'y prends!; *(when one has an advantage over someone)* je te tiens!

gotta ['gɒtə] *contraction* (**a**) *(abrév* **got to)** **I('ve) gotta go** (il) faut que j'y aille; **it's gotta be done** il faut que ce soit fait □ (**b**) *(abrév* **got a)** **he's gotta new girlfriend** il a une nouvelle copine

grand [grænd] *n (thousand pounds)* mille livres □ *fpl; (thousand dollars)* mille dollars □ *mpl*

grass [grɑ:s] **1** *n* (**a**) *(marijuana)* herbe *f* (**b**) *Br (informer)* mouchard *m*, balance *f* **2** *vi Br (inform)* moucharder; **to grass on sb** balancer qn, moucharder qn

grass up *vt sép Br* **to grass sb up** balancer qn, moucharder qn

gravy ['greɪvɪ] *n Am (easy money)* argent *m* facile □; **to get on the gravy train** profiter d'un filon

greased lightning [gri:st'laɪtnɪŋ] *n* **like greased lightning** à tout berzingue, à fond la caisse

greaser ['gri:sə(r)] *n* (**a**) *(biker)* motard *m* (**b**) *Am Injurieux (Latin American)* métèque *mf* (d'origine latino-américaine)

greasy spoon [gri:sɪ'spu:n] *n (café)* boui-boui *m*

greedy-guts ['gri:dɪgʌts] *n* morfal(e) *m,f*

green [gri:n] *n Am (money)* fric *m*, flouze *m*, blé *m*

greenback ['gri:nbæk] *n Am* fafiot *m*

greenhorn ['gri:nhɔ:n] *n* bleu *m*

green-welly [gri:n'welɪ] *adj Br Hum* **the green-welly brigade** la grande bourgeoisie rurale

> Le terme "green welly" signifie littéralement "botte de caoutchouc verte". Par métonymie, il désigne les aristocrates et les grands bourgeois vivant à la campagne, que l'on voit souvent chaussés de bottes de caoutchouc vertes et vêtus de vestes de chasse.

greeny ['gri:nɪ] *n Br* (**a**) *(phlegm)* mollard *m* (**b**) *(nasal mucus)* morve *f*

grief [gri:f] *n (trouble, inconvenience)* embêtements *mpl*; **to give sb grief** embêter qn; **I'm getting a lot of grief from my parents** mes parents n'arrêtent pas de m'embêter *ou* de me prendre la tête

grifter ['grɪftə(r)] *n Am* escroc □ *m*, arnaqueur *m*

grill [grɪl] *vt (interrogate)* cuisiner

grip [grɪp] *n* **to get a grip** se ressaisir □; **get a grip!** ressaisis-toi!, assure!

grody ['grəʊdɪ] *adj Am* dégueulasse; **grody to the max** franchement dégueulasse

groovy ['gruːvɪ] **1** *adj* bath, super
2 *exclam* super!, cool!

gross [grəʊs] *adj (disgusting)* dégueulasse

gross out *vt sép* **to gross sb out** répugner qn ❑, dégoûter qn ❑, débecter qn

gross-out ['grəʊsaʊt] *n Am* = chose ou situation répugnante; **what a gross-out!** c'est vraiment dégueulasse!

grot [grɒt] *n Br* crasse ❑ *f*

grotty ['grɒtɪ] *adj* dégueulasse, dégueu

groupie ['gruːpɪ] *n* groupie *f*

grub [grʌb] *n (food)* bouffe *f*; **grub's up!** à la soupe!

grungy ['grʌndʒɪ] *adj Am (dirty)* dégueulasse, dégueu

grunt [grʌnt] *n Am (soldier)* bidasse *m*

guff [gʌf] *n (nonsense)* âneries *fpl*; **don't talk guff!** ne dis pas d'âneries!; **the film was a load of guff** le film était vraiment débile

guinea ['gɪnɪ] *n Am Injurieux (Italian)* Rital(e) *m,f*, macaroni *mf*

gutless ['gʌtlɪs] *adj* **to be gutless** ne rien avoir dans le bide; **a gutless performance** une prestation sans intérêt ❑

gutrot ['gʌtrɒt] *n* (**a**) *(drink)* tord-boyaux *m* (**b**) *(stomach upset)* mal *m* de bide

guts [gʌts] *npl* (**a**) *(insides)* **to hate sb's guts** ne pas pouvoir blairer qn; **to work one's guts out** travailler comme un nègre (**b**) *(courage)* cran *m*; **to have guts** en avoir dans le bide, avoir du cran; **to have the guts to do sth** avoir le cran de faire qch
▸ *voir aussi* **spew, spill**

gutsy ['gʌtsɪ] *adj* (**a**) *(courageous)* **to be gutsy** en avoir dans le bide, avoir du cran (**b**) *(greedy)* morfal

gutted ['gʌtɪd] *adj Br (disappointed)* dégoûté, hyper déçu

guttered ['gʌtəd] *adj Br (drunk)* bourré, pété, beurré, poivré

guv [gʌv], **guvnor** ['gʌvnə(r)] *n Br* (*abrév* **governor**) (**a**) *(boss)* **the guv** *or* **guvnor** le patron, le chef (**b**) *(term of address)* chef *m*, patron *m*

guy [gaɪ] *n* (**a**) *(man)* mec *m*, type *m* (**b**) *(person)* **hi, guys!** salut!; **what are you guys doing tonight?** qu'est-ce vous faites ce soir?
▸ *voir aussi* **tough**

gyp [dʒɪp] **1** *n* (**a**) *Br (pain)* **to give sb gyp** faire déguster qn (**b**) *Am (swindler)* escroc ❑ *m*, arnaqueur *m*
2 *vt Am (swindle)* arnaquer

H

H [eɪtʃ] n (abrév **heroin**) blanche f, héro f

habit ['hæbɪt] n (drug addiction) accoutumance □ f; **to have a drug habit** être toxico; **to have a coke/smack habit** être accro à la coke/à l'héro; **to kick the habit** décrocher

hack [hæk] **1** n (**a**) Péj (writer) pisse-copie mf (**b**) Am (taxi) taxi □ m, tacot m; (taxi driver) chauffeur m de taxi □

2 vt (cope with) **he can't hack the pace** il n'arrive pas à tenir le rythme; **he can't hack it** il s'en sort pas

hack off vt sép **to hack sb off** prendre la tête à qn; **to be hacked off (with)** en avoir marre (de)

hackette [hæ'ket] n Br Péj pisse-copie f

hag [hæg] n (ugly woman) **(old) hag** vieille peau f

▶ voir aussi **fag**

hair [heə(r)] n **to get in sb's hair** taper sur les nerfs à qn; **to let one's hair down** se laisser aller; **keep your hair on!** du calme!, calmos!; Hum **this'll put hairs on your chest!** tiens, bois/mange ça, c'est bon pour la santé!; **I need a hair of the dog (that bit me)** j'ai besoin d'un verre pour soigner ma gueule de bois

hairpie [‼] [heə'paɪ] n (woman's genitals) tarte f aux poils

half [hɑːf] **1** n (**a**) **a party/day/hangover and a half** une sacrée nouba/journée/gueule de bois (**b**) **my other** or **better half** ma moitié

2 adv Br (for emphasis) **you don't half talk rubbish** tu racontes vraiment n'importe quoi; **it's not half bad** c'est pas mal du tout; **he hasn't half changed** il a vachement changé; **not half!** et comment!

half-arsed [‼] [hɑːf'ɑːst], Am **half-assed** [‼] [hɑːf'æst] adj foireux

half-cut [hɑːf'kʌt] adj Br (drunk) bourré, pété, fait

half-inch [hɑːf'ɪntʃ] vt Br (rhyming slang **pinch**) piquer, faucher, chouraver; **he got his wallet half-inched** il s'est fait piquer son portefeuille

halfwit ['hɑːfwɪt] n abruti(e) m,f, débile mf

halfwitted [hɑːf'wɪtɪd] adj abruti, débile

ham-fisted [hæm'fɪstɪd] adj maladroit □, manche

hammer ['hæmə(r)] **1** n Am **to let the hammer down** appuyer sur le champignon, mettre les gaz

2 vt (**a**) (beat up) tabasser (**b**) (defeat) écraser, battre à plates coutures (**c**) (criticize) éreinter, démolir

hammered ['hæməd] adj (drunk) bourré, beurré, pété, fait

hammering ['hæmərɪŋ] n (**a**) (beating) **to give sb a hammering** tabasser qn; **to get a hammering** se faire tabasser (**b**) (defeat) branlée f, pâtée f; **to give sb a hammering** battre qn à plates coutures, foutre la pâtée à qn; **to get a hammering** être battu à plates coutures (**c**) (criticism) **to give sb/sth a hammering** éreinter ou démolir qn/qch; **to get a hammering** se faire éreinter ou démolir

hand-job [‼] ['hændʤɒb] n **to give sb a hand-job** branler qn

hand shandy ⚠️ [ˈhændˈʃændɪ] *n Br Hum* **to have a hand shandy** se branler, faire cinq contre un; **to give sb a hand shandy** branler qn

handsome [ˈhændsəm] *exclam Br* super!, génial!

hang [hæŋ] **1** *vt Am* **to hang a left/a right** tourner à gauche/à droite □ **2** *vi* (**a**) *Am (spend time)* traîner; **he's hanging with his friends** il traîne avec ses copains (**b**) **how's it hanging?** *(how are you?)* comment ça va? (**c**) *Am* **to hang loose** rester cool; **hang loose!** détends-toi!, cool!; **to hang tough** s'accrocher

hang about, hang around *vi* (**a**) *(spend time)* traîner; **who does she hang about or around with?** avec qui est-ce qu'elle sort? (**b**) *(wait)* poireauter; **to keep sb hanging about or around** faire poireauter qn; **hang about, that's not what I meant!** attends voir, c'est pas ce que je voulais dire!

hang in *vi* **to hang in there** tenir bon, tenir le coup; **hang in there!** tiens bon!

hang on *vt sép Am* **to hang one on** *(get drunk)* prendre une cuite

hang out *vi* (**a**) *(spend time)* traîner; **he hangs out at the local bar** c'est un habitué du café du coin; **who's that guy she hangs out with?** c'est qui ce mec avec qui elle sort? (**b**) **to let it all hang out** être relax

hang up *vt sép* (**a**) **to be hung up on sb/sth** *(obsessed)* être obsédé par qn/qch □ (**b**) *Am* **to hang it up** *(stop)* laisser tomber

hang-out [ˈhæŋaʊt] *n* **that bar's my favourite hang-out** c'est le bar où je vais d'habitude □; **it's a real student hang-out** c'est un endroit très fréquenté par les étudiants □

hang-up [ˈhæŋʌp] *n* complexe □ *m*

hanky-panky [ˈhæŋkɪˈpæŋkɪ] *n (sexual activity)* galipettes *fpl*; *(underhand behaviour)* coups *mpl* fourrés

happening [ˈhæpənɪŋ] *adj* branché, dans le coup

happy [ˈhæpɪ] *adj Hum* **he's not a happy camper** *or Br* **chappy** *or* **bunny** il est pas jouasse

happy-clappy [hæpɪˈklæpɪ] *n Br Hum Péj* chrétien(enne) *m,f* évangélique □

hard-ass ⚠️ [ˈhɑːdæs] *n Am (person)* dur(e) *m,f* à cuire

hard-on ⚠️ [ˈhɑːdɒn] *n* **to have a hard-on** bander; **to get a hard-on** se mettre à bander

hash [hæʃ] *n* (**a**) *(abrév* **hashish)** hasch *m* (**b**) *(mess)* **to make a hash of sth** saloper qch

hassle [ˈhæsəl] **1** *n (trouble, inconvenience)* embêtements *mpl*; **to give sb hassle** harceler qn; **it's too much hassle** c'est trop de tintouin, c'est trop galère; **moving house is such a hassle** c'est vraiment galère de déménager **2** *vt* **to hassle sb** harceler qn □; **to hassle sb into doing sth** harceler qn jusqu'à ce qu'il fasse qch □

hatchet [ˈhætʃɪt] *n* (**a**) **hatchet job** très mauvaise critique □ *f*; **to do a hatchet job on sb/sth** éreinter *ou* démolir qn/qch (**b**) **hatchet man** *(hired killer)* tueur *m* à gages □; *(in industry, politics)* = personne dont le rôle est de restructurer une entreprise ou une organisation, le plus souvent à l'aide de mesures impopulaires

hatstand [ˈhætstænd] *adj Br (mad)* toqué, timbré, cinglé

have [hæv] *vt* (**a**) **to have had it** *(be ruined, in trouble)* être foutu; *Am (be exhausted)* être crevé *ou* naze *ou* lessivé; **to have had it up to here (with)** en avoir marre (de), avoir eu sa dose (de); **to let sb have it** *(physically)* casser la gueule à qn; *(verbally)* souffler dans les bronches à qn; **he had it coming** il l'a

48

cherché
  (**b**) *(cheat)* **to be had** se faire avoir
  (**c**)⚠ *(have sex with) (of man)* baiser, s'envoyer; *(of woman)* baiser avec, s'envoyer avec

have away *vt sép Br* **to have it away (with sb)**⚠ s'envoyer en l'air (avec qn)

have in *vt sép* **to have it in for sb** avoir qn dans le nez

have off *vt sép Br* **to have it off (with sb)**⚠ s'envoyer en l'air (avec qn)

have on *vt sép* **to have sb on** faire marcher qn

hay [heɪ] *n* **to hit the hay** *(go to bed)* se pieuter, se bâcher

hayseed ['heɪsiːd] *n Am* bouseux(euse) *m,f*, péquenaud(e) *m,f*

head [hed] *n* (**a**) **to get one's head together** se mettre en train□; **to laugh one's head off** être mort de rire; **to shout one's head off** gueuler comme un sourd; *Br* **to do sb's head in** prendre la tête à qn; *Br* **go and boil your head!** va te faire cuire un œuf!
  (**b**) *Br* **to be off one's head** *(mad)* être cinglé *ou* toqué; **to be out of one's head** *(mad)* être cinglé *ou* toqué; *(drunk)* être bourré *ou* beurré *ou* pété; *(on drugs)* être défoncé *ou* parti
  (**c**) **to give sb head**⚠⚠ sucer qn
  ▸ *voir aussi* **hole, honcho, knock, lose, rush, upside**

-head [hed] *suffixe* **she's a bit of a whiskyhead** elle a un faible pour le whisky; **he's a real jazzhead** c'est un vrai fana de jazz

> Le suffixe "-head" dénote l'enthousiasme de quelqu'un pour une activité ou une substance.

headbanger ['hedbæŋə(r)] *n* (**a**) *(heavy metal fan)* hardeux(euse) *m,f* (**b**) *Br (mad person)* cinglé(e) *m,f*, toqué(e) *m,f*

headcase ['hedkeɪs] *n* cinglé(e) *m,f*, toqué(e) *m,f*

headshrinker ['hedʃrɪŋkə(r)] *n Am* psy *mf*

heap [hiːp] *n (car)* poubelle *f*

heaps [hiːps] *Br* **1** *npl (a lot)* **I've got heaps to do** j'ai un tas de trucs à faire; **heaps of time/money** vachement de temps/d'argent
  2 *adv* **I like him heaps** je l'aime vachement

heart-throb ['hɑːtθrɒb] *n* idole *f*

heave [hiːv] **1** *n* **to give sb the heave** *(employee)* virer qn, sacquer qn; *(boyfriend, girlfriend)* plaquer qn, larguer qn; **to get the heave** *(of employee)* se faire virer *ou* sacquer; *(of boyfriend, girlfriend)* se faire plaquer *ou* larguer
  2 *vi (retch)* avoir un haut-le-cœur□; *(vomit)* gerber, dégueuler, dégobiller

heave-ho [hiːv'həʊ] *n* **to give sb the (old) heave-ho** *(employee)* virer qn, sacquer qn; *(boyfriend, girlfriend)* plaquer qn, larguer qn; **to get the (old) heave-ho** *(of employee)* se faire virer *ou* sacquer; *(of boyfriend, girlfriend)* se faire plaquer *ou* larguer

heaving ['hiːvɪŋ] *adj Br (extremely busy)* hyper animé

heavy ['hevɪ] **1** *n (man)* balaise *m*, grosse brute *f*
  2 *adj* (**a**) *(frightening, troublesome)* craignos; **to get heavy with sb** devenir agressif avec qn□; **things started to get a bit heavy** ça a commencé à craindre (**b**) *(profound, affecting)* profond□; **to get heavy with sb** prendre la tête à qn

hebe [hiːb] *n Am Injurieux* youpin(e) *m,f*; youtre *mf*

heck [hek] **1** *n* **who the heck said you could borrow my car?** bon sang! qui t'as dit que tu pouvais prendre ma voiture?; **why the heck didn't you tell me?** pourquoi est-ce que tu m'as pas prévenu, nom de nom!; **what the heck are you doing?** mais qu'est-ce que tu fous, nom de nom!; **there were a heck**

of a lot of people there il y avait un maximum de monde; **he misses her a heck of a lot** elle lui manque vachement; **I can't afford it, but what the heck!** c'est un peu cher pour moi mais je m'en fous!; **to do sth just for the heck of it** faire qch juste pour le plaisir
2 *exclam* mince alors!

heebie-jeebies ['hi:bɪ'dʒi:bɪz] *npl* **to have the heebie-jeebies** avoir la trouille *ou* les chocottes; **to give sb the heebie-jeebies** *(scare)* foutre la trouille à qn; *(repulse)* débecter qn

heel [hi:l] *n (person)* chameau *m*

heifer ['hefə(r)] *n* **(a)** *Péj (fat woman)* grosse dondon *f* **(b)** *Am (attractive woman)* canon *m*

Heinz [haɪnz] *n Hum (dog)* bâtard□ *m*

C'est parce que la marque Heinz se vantait jadis d'offrir une gamme de 57 variétés de produits différents que l'on gratifie parfois un chien bâtard de cette appellation. Le sous-entendu est que l'animal est issu d'un nombre comparable de variétés canines.

heist [haɪst] **1** *n Am (robbery)* cambriolage□ *m*; *(hold-up)* braquage *m*, casse *m*
2 *vt (money)* rafler; *(bank)* braquer

hell [hel] **1** *n* **(a) the boyfriend/flatmate/neighbours from hell** un petit ami/un colocataire/des voisins de cauchemar; **to give sb hell** engueuler qn; **to knock hell out of sb** tabasser qn; **all hell broke loose** ça a chié; **this weather plays hell with my joints** ce temps est mauvais pour mes articulations□; **there'll be hell to pay** on va avoir des embêtements; **hell for leather** à fond la caisse, à tout berzingue; **like a bat out of hell** comme une furie; **go to hell!** va te faire voir!
(b) *(for emphasis)* **what the hell** *or* **in hell's name are you doing?** mais qu'est-ce que tu fous, nom de Dieu!; **who the hell are you talking about?** mais tu parles de qui, nom de Dieu!;

why the hell did you say that? pourquoi t'as dit ça, nom de Dieu!; **how the hell should I know?** mais comment veux-tu que je le sache?; **what the hell, you only live once!** et puis merde, on ne vit qu'une fois!; **are you going? – like** *or* **the hell I am!, am I hell!** est-ce que tu y vas? – tu rigoles!; **get the hell out of here!** fous-moi le camp!; **I did it just for the hell of it** je l'ai fait rien que pour le plaisir; **to hell with it!** et puis merde!; **I wish to hell I knew** c'est ce que j'aimerais bien savoir; **it was hell on wheels** c'était l'enfer; **hell's bells** *or Br* **teeth!** nom de Dieu!
(c) he's in a hell of a bad mood il est d'humeur massacrante; **he had a hell of a job carrying the wardrobe** il en a chié pour porter l'armoire; **to have a hell of a time** *(very good)* s'éclater; *(very bad)* passer un très mauvais moment; **he likes her a hell of a lot** il est dingue d'elle; **it could have been a hell of a lot worse** ça aurait pu être bien pire; *Br* **it's a hell of a cold outside** il fait un froid de canard dehors
(d) *(in comparisons)* **to work/run like hell** travailler/courir comme un dingue; **as jealous as hell** hyper jaloux; **as mad as hell** fou à lier; **I'm as sure as hell not going** il est pas question que j'y aille
2 *exclam* bon Dieu!

hellacious [hel'eɪʃəs] *adj Am* **(a)** *(bad, unpleasant)* infernal **(b)** *(excellent)* super, génial

hellhole ['helhəʊl] *n* trou *m* à rats

hellish ['helɪʃ] *adj (very bad)* infernal; **the weather was hellish** il a fait un temps dégueulasse; **I feel hellish** je me sens vraiment pas dans mon assiette

hellishly ['helɪʃlɪ] *adv* vachement

helluva ['heləvə] *contraction (abrév* **hell of a)** **they're making a helluva noise** ils font un boucan pas possible; **he's a helluva nice guy** c'est un type formidable; **I miss him a helluva lot** il me manque vachement; **it costs a helluva**

lot of money ça coûte vachement cher, ça coûte bonbon; **we had a helluva time getting there** on en a chié pour arriver là-bas

herb [hɜːb] n (marijuana) herbe f

her indoors [hɜːrɪnˈdɔːz] n Br Hum la patronne

hick [hɪk] n Am bouseux(euse) m,f, péquenaud(e) m,f

hickey [ˈhɪkɪ] n Am suçon m

hide [haɪd] n **to tan sb's hide** tanner le cuir à qn

high [haɪ] adj **(a)** (on drugs) défoncé, parti, raide; **to get high** se défoncer; **as high as a kite** (on drugs) complètement parti, raide; Br (very excited) surexcité □ **(b)** Br **he's for the high jump** (in trouble) son compte est bon
▸ voir aussi **hog**

high-five [ˈhaɪˈfaɪv] n = tape amicale donnée dans la paume de quelqu'un, bras levé, pour le saluer, le féliciter, ou en signe de victoire

hightail [ˈhaɪteɪl] vt **to hightail it** décamper, mettre les bouts en vitesse; **he hightailed it home** il est rentré chez lui à fond de train

hike [haɪk] n Am **take a hike!** va te faire voir!

himbo [ˈhɪmbəʊ] n Hum beau mec pas très futé

> Il s'agit d'un jeu de mots sur le terme "bimbo" et le pronom "him". Le mot "bimbo" désigne une belle fille pas très intelligente.

hip [hɪp] **1** adj (fashionable) cool, branché
2 vt Am **to hip sb to sth** mettre qn au courant de qch □; **let me hip you to the latest** je vais te mettre au parfum

hipped [hɪpt] adj Am **to be hipped on sb/sth** être dingue de qn/qch

history [ˈhɪstərɪ] n **he's history!** (in trouble) il est fini!; (no longer in my life) avec lui, c'est terminé

hit [hɪt] **1** n **(a)** (of hard drugs) fix m; (of joint) taffe f; (effect of drugs) effet □ m (procuré par une drogue); **you get a good hit off that grass** cette herbe fait rapidement de l'effet
(b) (murder) meurtre m sur commande □
2 vt **(a) to hit the road** (leave) mettre les bouts, se barrer, s'arracher
(b) to hit the roof or Am **the ceiling** (lose one's temper) piquer une crise, péter les plombs
(c) (go to) **to hit the shops** aller faire du shopping; Br **to hit the town** aller faire la fête en ville; Br **to hit the pub** aller au pub
(d) (murder) buter, zigouiller, refroidir
(e) to hit sb for sth (borrow) emprunter qch à qn □; (scrounge from) taper qch à qn
(f) Am **to hit the bricks** (be released from prison) sortir de taule
(g) Am **that hit the spot** (was satisfying, refreshing) ça fait du bien par où que ça passe
▸ voir aussi **deck, hay, rack, sack**

hit on vt insép Am **to hit on sb** draguer qn, faire du plat à qn

hit up vt sép **to hit it up** se piquer, se shooter

hitch [hɪtʃ] vt **to get hitched** (married) se maquer, se passer la corde au cou

hitman [ˈhɪtmæn] n tueur m à gages □, tueur professionnel □

hiya [ˈhaɪjə] exclam salut!

ho [həʊ] n Noir Am (abrév **whore**) pouffiasse f, grognasse f

> Il s'agit de la transcription phonétique du mot "whore", tel que le prononcent certains Noirs américains. C'est un terme sexiste très employé par les chanteurs de rap et qui désigne une fille ou une femme.

hog [hɒg] **1** n **(a)** Am (person) goinfre m, porc m **(b)** Am (motorbike) grosse bécane f, gros cube m **(c)** Noir Am (luxury *car)* **voiture** *f* **de luxe**□ *(généralement une Cadillac ou une Lincoln Continental)* **(d)** *Am* **to live high on the hog** se la couler douce; **to be in hog heaven** être au septième ciel

hogwash ['hɒgwɒʃ] *n* foutaises *fpl*; **that's a lot of hogwash!** tout ça c'est des foutaises!

hokey ['hǝʊkɪ] *adj Am (nonsensical)* absurde□; *(sentimental)* à la guimauve

hokum ['hǝʊkǝm] *n Am (nonsense)* foutaises *fpl*; *(sentimentality)* guimauve *f*

hole [hǝʊl] *n* **(a)** *(house, room)* taudis □ *m*; *(town)* trou *m*, bled *m*; *(pub)* bouge□ *m* **(b)** *(difficult situation)* **to be in a hole** être dans la mouise; **to get sb out of a hole** sortir qn de la mouise **(c) hole in the wall** *(restaurant)* petit restaurant□ *m*; *(shop)* petite boutique□ *f*; *(cash dispenser)* distributeur *m* automatique de billets□; *Am (apartment)* appartement *m* minuscule□ **(d) I need that like I need a hole in the head!** j'ai vraiment pas besoin de ça! **(e)** ‼ *(vagina)* chagatte *f*, chatte *f*; *Br* **to get one's hole** baiser

hole up *vi (hide)* se planquer

-holic ['hɒlɪk] *suffixe Hum* **chocoholic** accro *mf* au chocolat; **workaholic** bourreau *m* de travail; **shopaholic** maniaque *mf* du shopping; *Am* **foodaholic** goinfre *mf*

holy ['hǝʊlɪ] *adj Am* **(a) holy cow** *or* **smoke** *or* **mackerel!** ça alors!; **holy shit** ❗ *or* **fuck!** ‼ putain de merde! **(b) holy Joe** cul *m* béni

homeboy ['hǝʊmbɔɪ] *n Noir Am* **(a)** *(man from one's home town)* compatriote *m* **(b)** *(friend)* pote *m* **(c)** *(fellow gang member)* = membre de la même bande

homegirl ['hǝʊmgɜːl] *n Noir Am* **(a)** *(woman from one's home town)* compatriote *f* **(b)** *(friend)* copine *f* **(c)** *(fellow*

gang member) = membre de la même bande

homegrown ['hǝʊmgrǝʊn] *n* = cannabis cultivé chez soi ou dans son jardin

homey ['hǝʊmɪ] = **homeboy, homegirl**

homo ['hǝʊmǝʊ] *n Injurieux (abrév* **homosexual)** homo *m*, pédale *f*

hon [hʌn] *n Am (abrév* **honey)** *(term of address)* chéri(e) *m,f*

honcho ['hɒntʃǝʊ] *n Am* chef *m*; **head honcho** grand chef *m*

honey ['hʌnɪ] *n* **(a)** *(term of address)* chéri(e) *m,f* **(b)** *(person, thing)* **he's a honey** *(good-looking)* il est vachement mignon; *(nice)* il est vachement gentil; **a honey of a car/dress** une voiture/robe très chouette

honk [hɒŋk] *vi Br* **(a)** *(smell bad)* schlinguer, fouetter **(b)** *(vomit)* gerber, dégueuler

honker ['hɒŋkǝ(r)] *n Am* **(a)** *(nose)* blaire *m*, tarin *m*, pif *m* **(b)** *(breast)* nichon *m* **(c)** *(device)* bécane *f*

honkie, honky ['hɒŋkɪ] *n Noir Am Injurieux* sale Blanc (Blanche) *m,f*

hooch [huːtʃ] *n Am* alcool *m* de contrebande□

hood [hʊd] *n* **(a)** *(abrév* **hoodlum)** *(delinquent)* voyou *m*, loubard *m*; *Am (gangster)* truand *m*, gangster□ *m* **(b)** *Noir Am (abrév* **neighborhood)** quartier□ *m*

hoodlum ['huːdlǝm] *n (delinquent)* voyou *m*, loubard *m*; *Am (gangster)* truand *m*, gangster□ *m*

hooey ['huːɪ] *n* foutaises *fpl*

hoof [huːf] *vt* **to hoof it** aller à pinces

hoo-ha ['huːhɑː] *n (fuss)* raffut *m*, barouf *m*

hook [hʊk] **1** *n Br* **to sling one's hook** mettre les bouts, foutre le camp, se casser; **sling your hook!** fous le camp!, casse-toi! **2** *vt Am* **to hook school** faire l'école buissonnière

3 *vi Am (work as prostitute)* faire le trottoir

hooked [hʊkt] *adj* **to be hooked (on)** être accro (à)

hooker ['hʊkə(r)] *n* **(a)** *(prostitute)* pute *f* **(b)** *Am (of drink)* **a hooker of gin/ bourbon** un bon coup de gin/de bourbon

hookey, hooky ['hʊkɪ] *n Am* **to play hookey** faire l'école buissonnière

hoops [huːps] *npl Am (basketball)* basket *m*; **to shoot hoops** jouer au basket

Hooray Henry ['hʊreɪ'henrɪ] *n Br* fils *m* à papa *(exubérant et bruyant)*

Il s'agit d'un homme issu de la grande bourgeoisie, généralement jeune, qui parle très fort et aime se faire remarquer lorsqu'il s'amuse.

hoosegow ['huːsgaʊ] *n Am* taule *f*; **in the hoosegow** en taule, en cabane

hoot [huːt] *n* **(a)** **I don't give a hoot** *or* **two hoots (about)** j'en ai rien à fiche (de) **(b)** *(amusing person, situation)* **to be a hoot** être marrant *ou* crevant

hooter ['huːtə(r)] *n* **(a)** *(nose)* pif *m*, blaire *m*, tarin *m* **(b)** *Am (breast)* nichon *m*

hop [hɒp] *vt* **to hop it** mettre les bouts, foutre le camp, se casser; **hop it!** casse-toi!, fous le camp!

hophead ['hɒphed] *n Am* toxico *mf*

horn [hɔːn] *n* **(a)** ⚠ *Br (erection)* érection ᵈ *f*; **to have the horn** avoir la trique *ou* le gourdin; **to give sb the horn** *(arouse)* exciter qn **(b)** *Am (telephone)* bigophone *m*; **to get on the horn to sb** passer un coup de fil *ou* de bigophone à qn

horny ['hɔːnɪ] *adj* **(a)** *(sexually aroused)* excité **(b)** *Br (sexually attractive)* sexy

horror ['hɒrə(r)] *n* **(a)** *(person, thing)* horreur *f*; **that kid's a little horror** ce gosse est un petit monstre **(b)** *Br* **to**

have the horrors faire dans son froc; **to give sb the horrors** donner le frisson à qn

horse [hɔːs] *n (heroin)* blanche *f*, héro *f* ▸ *voir aussi* **hung**

horseshit ⚠ ['hɔːsʃɪt] *n Am (nonsense)* conneries *fpl*

hot [hɒt] *adj* **(a)** *(sexually aroused)* excité; *(sexually attractive)* chaud, sexy; **to be hot to trot** *(of man)* être en rut; *(of woman)* être en chaleur **(b)** *(excellent)* génial, super **(c)** *(stolen)* volé ᵈ **(d)** *Am* **the hot seat** *(electric chair)* la chaise électrique ᵈ

hot-knife ['hɒtnaɪf] *vi* se droguer au hasch *(en coinçant un morceau de haschich entre deux lames de couteau préalablement chauffées)*

hotrod ['hɒtrɒd] *n* bagnole *f* trafiquée

hots [hɒts] *npl* **to have the hots for sb** craquer pour qn

hotshot ['hɒtʃɒt] **1** *n (expert)* crack *m*; *Br (important person)* huile *f*; *Am Péj (self-important person)* gros bonnet *m*
2 *adj* **a hotshot lawyer** un super avocat; **a hotshot pool player** un as du billard

house ape [haʊs'eɪp] *n Am Hum (child)* môme *mf*, chiard *m*

how's-your-father [haʊzjə'fɑːðə(r)] *n Br Hum (sexual intercourse)* **a bit of how's-your-father** une partie de jambes en l'air

hubba-hubba ['hʌbə'hʌbə] *exclam Am* la super gonzesse!

hubby ['hʌbɪ] *n* mari ᵈ *m*

huff [hʌf] **1** *n* **to be in a** *or* **the huff** faire la tête, bouder ᵈ; **to take the huff, to go in a huff** se mettre à bouder ᵈ
2 *vt Am (glue, solvents)* sniffer

huffy ['hʌfɪ] *adj* **to be huffy** *(in a bad mood)* faire la tête, bouder ᵈ; *(by nature)* être susceptible ᵈ, être chatouilleux

hum [hʌm] *Br* **1** *n (bad smell)* puanteur ᵈ *f*; **there's a bit of a hum in here!** ça coince *ou* ça fouette ici!

2 *vi (smell bad)* coincer, fouetter

humdinger [hʌm'dɪŋə(r)] *n* **to be a humdinger** être génial; **a humdinger of a football match** un match de foot magnifique; **she's a humdinger!** elle est hyper canon!

humongous [hju:'mʌŋgəs] *adj* énorme◻, mastoc

hump [hʌmp] **1** *n* **(a)** *Br* **to have the hump** être de mauvais poil; **to get** *or* **take the hump** se mettre à faire la gueule; **to give sb the hump** mettre qn de mauvais poil

(b) *Am (person)* crétin(e) *m,f*, andouille *f*

2 *vt* **(a)** ❗ *(have sex with) (of man)* baiser, se taper; *(of woman)* baiser avec, se taper

(b) *(carry)* trimballer

3 ❗ *vi (have sex)* baiser, s'envoyer en l'air

hung [hʌŋ] *adj* **to be hung like a horse** *or* **a whale** *or Br* **a donkey** *or Am* **a mule** ❗ être monté comme un âne *ou* un taureau *ou* un bourricot

hunk [hʌŋk] *n (man)* beau mec *m*

hunky ['hʌŋkɪ] *adj* bien foutu

hunky-dory [hʌŋkɪ'dɔ:rɪ] *adj* au poil; **everything's hunky-dory** tout baigne

hurl [hɜ:l] *vi (vomit)* dégobiller, gerber

hurting ['hɜ:tɪŋ] *adj Am* **(a)** *(in need)* **to be hurting for sth** avoir méchamment besoin de qch **(b)** *(in trouble)* dans la mouise

hush money ['hʌʃmʌnɪ] *n* = argent versé à quelqu'un pour acheter son silence

hustle ['hʌsəl] *Am* **1** *n (swindle)* arnaque *f*

2 *vt* **(a)** *(swindle)* arnaquer; **to hustle sb out of sth** soutirer qch à qn; **to hustle some pool** jouer au billard pour de l'argent◻ **(b)** *(sell)* fourguer **(c)** *(obtain dishonestly)* soutirer; *(steal)* piquer, faucher

3 *vi (work as prostitute)* faire le tapin

hustler ['hʌslə(r)] *n Am* **(a)** *(energetic person)* battant(e) *m,f* **(b)** *(swindler)* magouilleur(euse) *m,f* **(c)** *(prostitute)* pute *f*

hype¹ [haɪp] **1** *n* **(a)** *(abrév* **hypodermic)** shooteuse *f*, pompe *f* **(b)** *(drug addict)* toxico *mf*, camé(e) *m,f*

2 *adj Noir Am (excellent)* super, génial, grand

hype² *n (publicity)* battage *m*, matraquage *m*

hype up *vt sép* **to hype sth up** faire du battage autour de qch

hyper ['haɪpə(r)] *adj (excited)* surexcité◻

hypo ['haɪpəʊ] *n (abrév* **hypodermic)** shooteuse *f*, pompe *f*

I

ice [aɪs] **1** n (**a**) (diamonds) diams mpl (**b**) (drug) ice f
2 vt (kill) buter, refroidir, zigouiller

icky ['ɪkɪ] adj (repulsive) dégueulasse; (sticky) poisseux; (sentimental) mièvre □, à la guimauve

idea [aɪ'dɪə] n **what's the big idea?** à quoi tu joues?

idiot box ['ɪdɪətbɒks] n Am (television) téloche f

iffy ['ɪfɪ] adj (**a**) (doubtful, unreliable) **our holidays are looking very iffy** nos

Insults

Son but principal étant de choquer, l'insulte est sans doute la forme la plus pure et la plus immédiate d'utilisation de la langue familière. On trouvera ci-dessous certains des mécanismes de formation les plus répandus en anglais. La forme d'insulte la plus simple est un substantif utilisé comme exclamation (cf colonne "nom") et parfois précédé de "you". Cette combinaison peut à son tour être renforcée par un adjectif. Le tableau ci-dessous illustre ce procédé à l'aide de quelques mots très communs. Il faut remarquer que, bien que les combinaisons soient en principe multiples, certaines sont plus fixes que d'autres.

	ADJECTIF	NOM
	stupid □	idiot □
	Br bleeding	Br pillock
	goddamn	bitch
(you)	Br bloody !	prat
	Br sodding !	bastard !
	Am dumbass !	Br arsehole, Am asshole !!
	fucking !!	Br wanker !!
	Am motherfucking !!	Am motherfucker !!
		cunt !!

Pour un effet tout aussi percutant, on pourra utiliser un impératif, tel que "get lost", "push off", Br "bugger off" !, "piss off" ! ou "fuck off" !!.

L'expression "go (and)..." est également très productive lorsqu'elle précède un infinitif, comme dans:

> go (and) boil your head!
> go (and) jump in the lake!
> go (and) play in the traffic!
> go (and) fuck yourself! !!

Enfin, et notamment lorsque le locuteur veut être sarcastique, l'expression "Why don't you..." revient souvent dans la formation d'insultes; elle peut servir à introduire n'importe laquelle des tournures impératives ci-dessus.

vacances risquent de tomber à l'eau; **the brakes are a bit iffy** les freins déconnent un peu; *Br* **my stomach's been a bit iffy lately** je me sens un peu barbouillé ces temps-ci

(b) *(suspicious)* louche, chelou; **it all sounded rather iffy** tout ça m'avait l'air plutôt louche; **her new man sounds really iffy** son nouveau copain a l'air vraiment louche

illin' ['ɪlɪn] *adj Noir Am* **(a)** *(unpleasant)* merdique **(b)** *(mad)* cinglé, toqué, timbré

in [ɪn] **1** *adj (fashionable)* in, branché; **it's the in place** c'est l'endroit le plus branché; **it's the in thing/colour** c'est le truc/la couleur à la mode; **the in crowd** les gens branchés

2 *adv* **(a) to be in on a secret/a plan** être au courant d'un secret/d'un projet □; **I wasn't in on it** j'étais pas dans la confidence; **I want in** *(include me)* ça me branche **(b) you're going to be in for it!** tu vas voir ce que tu vas prendre!

inhale [ɪnˈheɪl] *vt Am* **to inhale sth** *(eat quickly)* engouffrer qch; *(drink quickly)* descendre qch

inside 1 *adj* ['ɪnsaɪd] **it was an inside job** c'est quelqu'un de l'intérieur qui a fait le coup

2 *adv* [ɪnˈsaɪd] *(in prison)* en taule, à l'ombre, au frais; **to put sb inside** mettre qn en taule *ou* à l'ombre

into ['ɪntʊ] *prép (keen on)* **to be into sb** en pincer pour qn; **to be into sth** être branché qch; **to be into doing sth** s'éclater à faire qch; **he's into drugs** il se drogue □; **I'm not into that sort of thing** c'est pas mon truc

Irish ['aɪrɪʃ] *adj Br (contradictory, illogical)* loufoque

"Irish" signifie littéralement "irlandais". En Grande-Bretagne les Irlandais sont la cible de nombreuses plaisanteries où ils apparaissent généralement comme des gens peu intelligents et manquant de bon sens. Bien que ce terme ne témoigne pas nécessairement d'une attitude xénophobe de la part de celui qui l'utilise, il est préférable de ne pas l'employer.

iron ['aɪən] *n Br Injurieux (rhyming slang* **iron hoof = poof)** pédale *f*, tantouze *f*, tapette *f*
▶ *voir aussi* **pump**

it [ɪt] *pron* **she thinks she's IT** elle se prend pas pour de la merde; **it girl** jeune mondaine □ *f*

item ['aɪtəm] *n* **they're an item** *(of couple)* ils sont maqués

J

J [dʒeɪ] *n* (*abrév* **joint**) (*cannabis cigarette*) joint *m*

Jack [dʒæk] *npr Am Péj* (*term of address*) Duchnoque

jack [dʒæk] *n* (**a**) **every man jack (of them)** absolument tout le monde (**b**) **jack shit** ⚠ que dalle

jack around *Am* **1** *vt sép* **to jack sb around** (*treat badly*) se ficher de qn; (*waste time of*) faire perdre son temps à qn ▫
2 *vi* (*waste time*) glander, glandouiller

jack in *vt sép Br* **to jack sth in** laisser tomber qch, plaquer qch; **to jack it all in** tout plaquer

jack off ⚠ **1** *vt sép* **to jack sb off** branler qn
2 *vi* se branler, se paluener

jack up **1** *vt sép* (**a**) *Br* (*drugs*) s'injecter ▫, se piquer à (**b**) (*prices, profits*) gonfler
2 *vi Br* se piquer, se shooter

jacksie, jacksy ['dʒæksɪ] *n Br* (*buttocks*) fesses *fpl*, popotin *m*; (*anus*) troufignon *m*, trou *m* de balle

Jack-the-lad [dʒækðə'læd] *n Br* = jeune homme exubérant et insolent d'origine modeste

Jag [dʒæg] *n* (*abrév* **Jaguar**) Jaguar ▫ *f*

jailbait ['dʒeɪlbeɪt] *n* fille *f* mineure ▫, poids *m* mort

jake [dʒeɪk] *n Br* joint *m*, pétard *m*

jalopy [dʒə'lɒpɪ] *n* vieille bagnole *f*, guimbarde *f*

jam [dʒæm] **1** *n* **jam (session)** bœuf *m*, jam-session *f*; **to have a jam (session)** faire un bœuf *ou* une jam-session
2 *vi* faire un bœuf *ou* une jam-session

jammy ['dʒæmɪ] *adj Br* (*lucky*) veinard; **you jammy bugger!** ⚠ sacré veinard!

JAP [dʒæp] *n Am Péj* (*abrév* **Jewish American Princess**) = jeune Américaine juive issue de la grande bourgeoisie

Jap [dʒæp] *Injurieux* (*abrév* **Japanese**) **1** *n* Jap *mf*
2 *adj* jap

jar [dʒɑː(r)] *n Br* (*drink*) pot *m*, godet *m*; **let's go out for a couple of jars** allons boire un pot

java ['dʒɑːvə] *n Am* (*coffee*) kawa *m*

jaw [dʒɔː] **1** *n Am* **to flap one's jaw** gueuler
2 *vi* tailler une bavette

jazz [dʒæz] *n* **...and all that jazz** ...et tout le tremblement

jeepers (creepers) ['dʒiːpəz('kriː-pəz)] *exclam* bon Dieu!, bon sang!

Jeez [dʒiːz] *exclam* bon Dieu!, bon sang!

jelly ['dʒelɪ] *n Br* (*drug*) gélule *f* de Temazepam ▫

jerk [dʒɜːk] *n* (*person*) abruti(e) *mf*, crétin(e) *m,f*

jerk off ⚠ **1** *vt sép* **to jerk sb off** branler qn
2 *vi* se branler, se paluener

jerk-off ⚠ ['dʒɜːkɒf] *n Am* (*person*) connard (connasse) *m,f*

jerky ['dʒɜːkɪ] *adj Am* (*stupid*) débile, abruti

Jesus ['dʒiːzəs] **1** *n* **Jesus freak** chrétien(enne) *m,f* hippie
2 *exclam* **Jesus (Christ)!** nom de Dieu!; *Br* **Jesus wept!** bon sang!

jiff [dʒɪf], **jiffy** ['dʒɪfɪ] *n* seconde □ *f*, instant □ *m*; **in a jiff** dans une seconde

jiggered ['dʒɪgəd] *adj Br (exhausted)* naze, crevé, lessivé

jimjams ['dʒɪmdʒæmz] *npl* **(a) to have the jimjams** être sur les nerfs **(b)** *Br (pyjamas)* pyjama □ *m*

Jimmy ['dʒɪmɪ] *npr Br (rhyming slang* **Jimmy Riddle = piddle**) **to have a Jimmy** pisser; **to go for a Jimmy** aller pisser

jism ['dʒɪzəm] *n* **(a)** ⚠️⚠️ *(semen)* foutre *m* **(b)** *Am (energy)* ressort □ *m*

jive [dʒaɪv] *Noir Am* **1** *n (nonsense)* foutaises *fpl*; *(insincerity)* craques *fpl* **2** *adj (unpleasant)* à la noix

jive-ass ⚠️ ['dʒaɪvæs] *adj Noir Am* à la noix

job [dʒɒb] *n* **(a)** *(thing)* truc *m*; **her new car is one of those sporty jobs** sa nouvelle voiture est un de ces modèles style ''sport''; **their latest hi-fi is a lovely job** leur nouvelle chaîne stéréo est super
(b) *(crime)* coup *m*; **to do** *or* **pull a job** faire un coup; **he did** *or* **pulled that bank job** c'est lui qui a braqué la banque
(c) *Br* **to be on the job** ⚠️ *(having sex)* être en train de baiser
(d) *Br (excrement)* caca *m*
(e) *Am* **to do a job on sth** *(ruin, damage)* bousiller qch
▶ *voir aussi* **boob, hatchet, nose, snow**

Jock [dʒɒk] *npr Injurieux (Scotsman)* Écossais □ *m*

> ''Jock'' est un diminutif un peu désuet de ''John'' qui est parfois utilisé en Écosse. Bien que ce terme ne témoigne pas nécessairement d'une attitude xénophobe de la part de celui qui l'utilise, il est préférable de ne pas l'employer.

jock [dʒɒk] *n Am* **(a)** *(athlete)* sportif(ive) *m,f (pas très brillant intellectuellement)* **(b)** *(abrév* **disc jockey**) disc-jockey *mf*

Joe [dʒəʊ] *npr* **(a)** *Am (man)* mec *m*, type *m*; **a good Joe** *(man)* un chic type; *(woman)* une brave femme **(b)** *Br* **Joe Public, Joe Bloggs, Joe Soap,** *Am* **Joe Blow, Joe Schmo, Joe Six-Pack** Monsieur Tout-le-Monde
▶ *voir aussi* **holy**

john [dʒɒn] *n Am* **(a)** *(toilet)* chiottes *fpl* **(b)** *(prostitute's client)* micheton *m*

johnny ['dʒɒnɪ] *n Br (condom)* **(rubber)** johnny capote *f*

johnson ['dʒɒnsən] *n Am* quéquette *f*

joint [dʒɔɪnt] *n* **(a)** *(cannabis cigarette)* joint *m* **(b)** *(place)* turne *f* **(c)** *Am (prison)* taule *f*, placard *m*; **in the joint** en taule, à l'ombre **(d)** ⚠️ *Am (penis)* pine *f*, bite *f*
▶ *voir aussi* **case, clip**

jollies ['dʒɒlɪz] *npl Am* **to get one's jollies (doing sth)** prendre son pied (en faisant qch), s'éclater (en faisant qch)

journo ['dʒɜːnəʊ] *n Br (abrév* **journalist**) journaleux(euse) *m,f*

joypop ['dʒɔɪpɒp] *vi* = prendre de la drogue sans devenir dépendant

jug [dʒʌg] *n* **(a)** *(prison)* taule *f*, cabane *f*; **in (the) jug** en taule, à l'ombre **(b) jugs** ⚠️ *(breasts)* nichons *mpl*, lolos *mpl*

juice [dʒuːs] *n* **(a)** *(petrol)* essence □ *f*; *(electricity)* jus *m*; *Br (gas)* gaz □ *m* **(b)** *Noir Am (popularity, recognition)* succès □; **to have a lot of juice** faire un tabac
▶ *voir aussi* **jungle**

juiced [dʒuːst] *adj Am (drunk)* pété, bourré, beurré

juicer ['dʒuːsə(r)] *n Am* alcolo *mf*, poivrot(e) *m,f*

jump [dʒʌmp] *vt* **(a)** *(attack)* **to jump sb** sauter sur le paletot à qn; **to get jumped** se faire agresser □ **(b) to jump**

sb's bones sauter sur qn
▸ *voir aussi* **high, throat**

jumping ['dʒʌmpɪŋ] *adj (party, night-club)* hyper animé

jungle ['dʒʌŋgəl] *n* (**a**) *Injurieux* **jungle bunny** nègre (négresse) *m,f* (**b**) **jungle juice** tord-boyaux *m (le plus souvent produit artisanalement)*

junk [dʒʌŋk] **1** *n* (**a**) *(worthless things)* **his new book is a pile of junk** son nouveau bouquin ne vaut pas un clou; **she eats nothing but junk** elle mange que des saloperies
(**b**) *(useless things)* bazar *m*; **move all that junk of yours off the bed** enlève ton bazar du lit
(**c**) *(drug)* drogue *f* dure □ *(le plus souvent héroïne)*
2 *vt* (**a**) *(throw away)* balancer, foutre en l'air
(**b**) *(criticize)* débiner, éreinter

junkie ['dʒʌŋkɪ] *n* junkie *mf*; **a chocolate/soap opera junkie** un accro du chocolat/des feuilletons télé

K

Kaffir ['kæfə(r)] *n Br Injurieux* nègre (négresse) *m,f* d'Afrique du Sud

karsey, karzey, kazi ['kɑːzɪ] *n Br* chiottes *fpl*, gogues *mpl*

kazoo [kə'zuː] *n Am (buttocks)* derrière *m*, arrière-train *m*; **to have problems/debts up the kazoo** *(in excess)* avoir des problèmes/des dettes jusqu'au cou

kecks [keks] *npl Br* fute *m*, falzar *m*

keel over [kiːl] *vi* **(a)** *(faint)* tourner de l'œil **(b)** *(die)* calancher, passer l'arme à gauche

keister ['kiːstə(r)] *n Am (buttocks)* fesses *fpl*, derrière *m*, derche *m*

keks [keks] = **kecks**

Kevin ['kevɪn] *npr Br Péj* jeune beauf *m*

> Il s'agit d'un stéréotype social comparable à celui de l'**Essex Man** (voir cette entrée). Le "Kevin" est jeune, d'origine modeste, peu cultivé, parfois violent, et ne fait pas toujours preuve d'un goût très sûr. Kevin est un prénom très courant dans les milieux populaires et, de ce fait, est considéré comme vulgaire par beaucoup de gens.

kick [kɪk] **1** *n (thrill)* **to get a kick out of sth/doing sth** prendre son pied avec qch/en faisant qch; **to do sth for kicks** faire qch histoire de rigoler
2 *vt* **to kick the bucket** *(die)* calancher, passer l'arme à gauche
3 *vi Am (die)* calancher, passer l'arme à gauche
▶ *voir aussi* **ass, shit**

kick about, kick around 1 *vt insép (spend time in)* **to kick about the world/Africa** rouler sa bosse *ou* traîner ses guêtres autour du monde/en Afrique; *Br* **is my purse kicking about the kitchen somewhere?** est-ce que mon porte-monnaie traîne quelque part dans la cuisine?
2 *vi (hang around)* traîner (**with** avec); *Br* **have you seen my lighter kicking about?** t'as pas vu mon briquet (traîner) quelque part?

kick off *vi* **(a)** *Am (die)* calancher, passer l'arme à gauche **(b)** *Br (get violent)* **it's going to kick off** ça va bastonner

kickback ['kɪkbæk] *n (bribe)* pot-de-vin *m*

kicker ['kɪkə(r)] *n Am* **(a)** *(hidden drawback)* os *m*, hic *m* **(b)** *(worst part of situation)* **the work's tough and the kicker is the pay's lousy** le travail est dur, et en plus de ça, c'est payé avec un lance-pierres

kicking ['kɪkɪŋ] **1** *n Br* **to give sb a kicking** tabasser qn à coups de latte; **to get a kicking** se faire tabasser à coups de latte
2 *adj (party, nightclub)* hyper animé

kicky ['kɪkɪ] *adj Am (excellent)* super, génial, géant

kid [kɪd] *n (child)* gosse *mf*; *(young adult)* jeune □ *mf*, gamin(e) *m,f*; *Br* **our kid** *(brother)* le petit frère; *(sister)* la petite sœur

kike [kaɪk] *n Am Injurieux* youpin(e) *m,f*, youtre *mf*

kill [kɪl] **1** *vt Br* **to kill oneself (laughing)** être mort de rire; *Ironique* **you kill me!** toi alors!
2 *vi* **I'd kill for a beer** je me damnerais pour une bière

killer ['kɪlə(r)] n (**a**) (difficult thing) **those steps were a killer!** ces marches m'ont lessivé!; **the English exam was a killer** l'examen d'anglais était vraiment coton (**b**) (excellent thing) **their new album's a killer** leur dernier album est vraiment génial ou mortel; **this one's a killer** (joke) elle est bien bonne, celle-là

killing ['kɪlɪŋ] adj Br (**a**) (very amusing) marrant, crevant, mortel (**b**) (exhausting) crevant, tuant

kinda ['kaɪndə] contraction (abrév **kind of**) **this is my kinda party!** c'est le genre de soirée que j'aime!; **that kinda thing** ce genre de truc; **you look kinda tired** t'as l'air un peu fatigué; **I kinda expected this** je m'y attendais un peu; **do you like it? – kinda** tu trouves ça comment? – pas mal

kinky ['kɪŋkɪ] adj (person) (sexually) qui a des goûts spéciaux; (eccentric) loufoque; (clothing, sex) très spécial

kip [kɪp] Br 1 n **to have a kip, to get some kip** piquer un roupillon, pioncer; **to get an hour's kip** piquer un roupillon d'une heure; **I didn't get much kip last night** j'ai pas beaucoup roupillé la nuit dernière
2 vi roupiller, pioncer

kip down vi Br pieuter

kiss [kɪs] vt **to kiss sth goodbye, to kiss goodbye to sth** faire une croix sur qch; **you can kiss your money/promotion goodbye!** tu peux faire une croix sur ou dire adieu à ton argent/ta promotion!
▸ voir aussi **arse, ass, French**

kiss off vt sép Am (**a**) **to kiss sb off** (dismiss) envoyer balader ou promener qn; (kill) buter ou zigouiller qn (**b**) **to kiss sth off** (give up hope of) faire une croix sur qch; **you can kiss off your promotion!** tu peux faire une croix sur ou dire adieu à ta promotion!

kisser ['kɪsə(r)] n (mouth) bec m, museau m

kiss-off ['kɪsɒf] n Am **to give sb the kiss-off** envoyer balader ou promener qn

kit [kɪt] n Br (clothes) **to get one's kit off** se désaper, se mettre à poil; **get your kit off!** à poil!

kite [kaɪt] n **go fly a kite!** va voir ailleurs si j'y suis!
▸ voir aussi **high**

kittens ['kɪtənz] npl **to have kittens** (become agitated) faire un caca nerveux

Kiwi ['kiːwiː] n (person) Néo-Zélandais(e)◻ m,f, kiwi mf

klutz [klʌts] n Am (stupid person) abruti(e) m,f, tache f; (clumsy person) manche m

knacker ['nækə(r)] Br 1 n **knackers**⚠ (testicles) couilles fpl, balloches fpl
2 vt (**a**) (exhaust) crever, lessiver (**b**) (break, wear out) bousiller

knackered ['nækəd] adj Br (**a**) (exhausted) crevé, lessivé, naze (**b**) (broken, worn out) bousillé

knees-up ['niːzʌp] n Br (party) sauterie f

knee-trembler ['niːtremblə(r)] n Br **to have a knee-trembler** baiser debout

knickers ['nɪkəz] Br 1 npl **to get one's knickers in a twist** (become agitated) s'affoler, s'exciter; (become angry) piquer une crise, se mettre en pétard; **to get into sb's knickers** s'envoyer qn
2 exclam n'importe quoi!

knob [nɒb] 1 n (**a**) ⚠ (penis) bite f, queue f (**b**) ⚠ Br (man) trou m du cul (**c**) Br **the same to you with knobs on!** toi-même!
2 ⚠ vt Br (have sex with) baiser, tringler, troncher

knock [nɒk] vt (**a**) (criticize) éreinter, débiner; **don't knock it till you've tried it!** n'en dis pas de mal avant d'avoir essayé◻
(**b**) Br (have sex with) (of man) baiser,

tringler, troncher; (of woman) baiser
avec, s'envoyer
  (c) Br **to knock sth on the head** (put a
stop to) faire cesser qch □; **knock it on
the head, will you!** c'est pas bientôt
fini?
  (d) Am **to knock sb for a loop** (amaze)
scier qn, en boucher un coin à qn
  (e) to knock sb dead (impress) en
mettre plein la vue à qn; **Oasis knocked
them dead last night** hier soir, Oasis a
fait un tabac

knock about, knock around
  1 vt insép (spend time in) **to knock
about the world/Africa** rouler sa
bosse ou traîner ses guêtres autour du
monde/en Afrique; Br **are my keys
knocking about the kitchen somewhere?** est-ce que mes clés traînent
quelque part dans la cuisine?
  2 vi (hang around) traîner (**with** avec);
Br **are my fags knocking about?**
est-ce que mes clopes sont dans le
coin?

knock back vt sép **(a)** (drink)
descendre
  (b) Br (cost) coûter à □; **it knocked
me back a few hundred pounds** ça
m'a coûté quelques centaines de livres;
**that must have knocked you back
a bit!** ça a dû te coûter un paquet de
fric!
  (c) Br (reject) **to knock sb back** rejeter
qn □; **to knock sth back** (offer,
invitation) refuser qch □; **she knocked
him back** il s'est pris une veste

knock off **1** vt sép **(a)** (stop) **knock it
off!** arrête!
  (b) (steal) piquer, faucher; **to knock
off a bank/jeweller's** (rob) braquer
une banque/une bijouterie
  (c) (murder) buter, refroidir, zigouiller
  (d) (have sex with) (of man) baiser,

tringler, troncher; (of woman) baiser
avec, s'envoyer
  2 vi (stop working) dételer

knock out vt sép Am **to knock oneself
out** (indulge oneself) se faire plaisir;
**there's plenty food left, knock
yourself out!** il reste plein de
nourriture, sers-toi autant que tu
veux! □

knock over vt sép Am (rob) braquer

knock up vt sép **to knock sb up** (make
pregnant) engrosser qn

knockback ['nɒkbæk] n Br (rejection)
veste f; **to get a knockback** prendre
une veste

knockers ⚠ ['nɒkəz] npl (breasts) nichons mpl, roberts mpl

knocking shop ['nɒkɪŋʃɒp] n Br bordel m, boxon m, claque m

knockout ['nɒkaʊt] **1** n (excellent
thing) merveille □ f, **she's a knockout**
(gorgeous) elle est vachement sexy
  2 adj super

knockover ['nɒkəʊvə(r)] n Am (robbery) casse m

knot [nɒt] **1** n **to tie the knot** (get
married) se maquer, se passer la corde
au cou
  2 vt Br **get knotted!** (go away) casse-
toi!, va te faire voir ailleurs!; (expressing
contempt, disagreement) la ferme!

kook [kuːk] n Am zigoto m, zigomar m

kooky ['kuːkɪ] adj Am loufoque, loufedingue

kosher ['kəʊʃə(r)] adj (legitimate, honest) réglo, régulier

Kraut [kraʊt] Injurieux **1** n Boche mf
  2 adj boche

kvetch [kvetʃ] vi Am râler, geindre

L

lad [læd] *n Br* (**a**) *(young man)* garçonᵈ *m*, petit gars *m*; **he's a bit of a lad** c'est un sacré fêtard; **he's one of the lads** on se marre bien avec lui (**b**) **the lads** *(friends)* les copains; **he's gone out for a couple of drinks with the lads** il est sorti boire un coup avec les copains
▸ *voir aussi* **new**

laddish ['lædɪʃ] *adj Br* = typique d'un style de vie caractérisé par de fréquentes sorties entre copains, généralement copieusement arrosées, un comportement arrogant et macho et un goût prononcé pour le sport et les activités de groupe

la-di-da [lɑːdɪ'dɑː] **1** *adj (person, attitude)* prétentieuxᵈ, snobinard; *(voice)* affectéᵈ
2 *adv* d'une façon prétentieuseᵈ

lager lout ['lɑːgəlaʊt] *n Br* = jeune voyou buveur de bière

lah-di-dah [lɑːdɪ'dɑː] = **la-di-da**

laid-back [leɪd'bæk] *adj* décontractéᵈ, relax

La-la land ['lɑːlɑːlænd] *n Am Péj* = surnom donné à la ville de Los Angeles

lame [leɪm] *Am* **1** *n (stupid person)* andouille *f*, cruche *f*, courge *f*
2 *adj (stupid)* cloche, nouille

lamebrain ['leɪmbreɪn] *n Am* andouille *f*, cruche *f*, courge *f*

land [lænd] *vt* (**a**) *Br* **to get landed with sb/sth** se retrouver avec qn/qch sur les bras; **I got landed with doing the dishes** c'est moi qui me suis tapé *ou* coltiné la vaisselle (**b**) *(hit)* **to land sb a punch** coller une châtaigne *ou* un ramponneau à qn; **he landed me one on the chin** il m'a envoyé un marron dans le menton

lardarse ! ['lɑːdɑːs], *Am* **lardass** ! ['lɑːdæs] *n (man)* gros *m* plein de soupe; *(woman)* grosse vache *f*

large [lɑːdʒ] *adv* (**a**) *Br (to a large extent)* **Arsenal got thrashed large** Arsenal s'est fait ratatiner *ou* s'est fait battre à plates coutures; **we got pissed large last night** ! on s'est pris une cuite maison hier soir (**b**) *Noir Am* **to live large** mener la belle vieᵈ

lark [lɑːk] *n Br* (**a**) *(joke)* rigolade *f*; **to do sth for a lark** faire qch histoire de rigoler (**b**) *(activity)* **I'm fed up with this dieting lark** j'en ai marre de ce régime que je suis en train de faire; **I can't be doing with that fancy dress lark** je n'aime pas du tout cette histoire de bal masqué

lark about, lark around *vi Br* faire l'idiot

later ['leɪtə(r)], *Br* **laters** ['leɪtəz] *exclam* salut!, à la prochaine!

laugh [lɑːf] **1** *n* **to have a laugh** se marrer; **to do sth for a laugh** faire qch histoire de rigoler; **he's always good for a laugh** c'est un marrant; **you're having a laugh, aren't you?** tu déconnes?
2 *vi* (**a**) **don't make me laugh!** ne me fais pas rigoler!, laisse-moi rire!
(**b**) *Br* **if we win this match, we'll be laughing** si on gagne ce match, on n'a plus de souci à se faire; **if your offer's accepted, you'll be laughing** si ils acceptent ta proposition, ce sera super pour toi

laughing gear [ˈlɑːfɪŋɡɪə(r)] *n Br* bouche [□] *f*, clapet *m*

lav [læv] *n Br* (*abrév* **lavatory**) vécés *mpl*

law [lɔː] *n* **the law** les flics *mpl*; **I'll get the law on you!** j'appelle les flics!

lay [leɪ] **1** *n* **to be a good lay** être un bon coup; **to be an easy lay** avoir la cuisse légère
2 *vt* (**a**) (*have sex with*) **to lay sb** s'envoyer qn; **to get laid** s'envoyer en l'air (**b**) *Am* **to lay one** (*fart*) péter, larguer une caisse

lay off *vt insép* (**a**) **to lay off sb** (*stop annoying, nagging*) ficher la paix à qn; **just lay off me!** fiche-moi la paix!, fais-moi des vacances! (**b**) (*abstain from*) **to lay off the chocolate** ne plus manger de chocolat [□]; **to lay off the cigarettes** s'arrêter de fumer [□]; **you'd better lay off the booze for a while** tu devrais t'arrêter de boire pendant quelque temps [□]

lazybones [ˈleɪzɪbəʊnz] *n* flemmard(e) *m,f*

lead [led] *n* **to fill** *or* **pump sb full of lead** plomber qn; *Am Hum* **to get lead poisoning** (*get shot dead*) se faire buter

leak [liːk] *n* **to take** *or* **have a leak** (*urinate*) pisser un coup

leatherboy [ˈleðəbɔɪ] *n* cuir *m*, pédé *m* cuir

leatherneck [ˈleðənek] *n Am* marine [□] *m* (*américain*), ≃ marsouin *m*

leave out [liːv] *vt sép Br* **leave it out!** arrête!

lech [letʃ] **1** *n* obsédé *m*
2 *vi* regarder/agir avec concupiscence [□]; **to lech after sb** baver devant qn (*de concupiscence*)

leery [ˈlɪərɪ] *adj* **to be leery of sb/sth** se méfier de qn/qch [□]

left field [left'fiːld] *n* **to be way out in left field** être complètement loufoque; **it came out of left field** (*comment,*

question) c'est tombé comme un cheveu sur la soupe

left-footer [left'fʊtə(r)] *n Br Péj* catholique [□] *mf*, catho *mf*

leftie, lefty [ˈleftɪ] *n* gaucho *mf*

leg [leg] **1** *n* (**a**) *Br* **to get one's leg over** s'envoyer en l'air (**b**) **to shake a leg** (*get moving*) se magner, se grouiller; **shake a leg!** magne-toi!, grouille-toi!
2 *vt* **to leg it** (*run, run away*) cavaler

legit [ləˈdʒɪt] *adj* (*abrév* **legitimate**) réglo, régulier

legless [ˈleglɪs] *adj Br* (*drunk*) pété, bourré, beurré

lemon [ˈlemən] *n* (**a**) *Br* (*person*) abruti(e) *m,f*; **I felt a total lemon** je me suis senti tout con (**b**) *Am* (*useless thing*) **it's a lemon** c'est de la camelote

length [leŋθ] *n Br* **to slip sb a length** [!] glisser un bout à qn, tringler qn

lesbo [ˈlezbəʊ] *n Injurieux* (*abrév* **lesbian**) gouine *f*

> Ce terme perd son caractère injurieux lorsqu'il est utilisé par des lesbiennes.

let off [let] *vi Br* (*fart*) larguer, lâcher

lettuce [ˈletɪs] *n Am* (*money*) blé *m*, oseille *f*, artiche *m*

level [ˈlevəl] *n* **on the level** réglo, régulier

lez [lez], **lezzy** [ˈlezɪ] *n Injurieux* (*abrév* **lesbian**) gouine *f*

> Ce terme perd son caractère injurieux lorsqu'il est utilisé par des lesbiennes.

lick [lɪk] *vt* (*defeat*) battre à plates coutures, mettre la pâtée à, ratatiner; **to get licked** être battu à plates coutures ▸ *voir aussi* **arse**

lick out [!!] *vt sép Br* **to lick sb out** brouter le cresson à qn

life [laɪf] *n* **get a life!** t'as rien de mieux à faire de ton temps?; *Br* **my life!** c'est pas vrai!

lifer [ˈlaɪfə(r)] *n* prisonnier *m* condamné à perpète

lift [lɪft] *vt* (**a**) *(steal)* piquer, faucher (**b**) *Br (arrest)* agrafer, alpaguer; **he got lifted for stealing cars** il s'est fait agrafer *ou* alpaguer pour vol de voitures

light [laɪt] *n Hum* **the lights are on but there's nobody home** c'est pas une lumière

lighten up ['laɪtən] *vi* se détendre □

like [laɪk] *adv* (**a**) **there were like three thousand people there** il devait y avoir environ trois mille personnes □; **I was busy, like, that's why I didn't call you** j'étais occupé, c'est pour ça que je t'ai pas appelé, tu comprends?; **he just came up behind me, like** il s'est approché de moi par derrière □
(**b**) *(in reported speech)* **I was like "no way"** alors je lui ai fait "pas question"; **so he was like "in your dreams, pal!"** alors il a dit "c'est ça, compte là-dessus mon vieux!"

> "Like" est très souvent utilisé pour combler les temps morts lorsque l'on parle, ou après une expression peu claire ou inhabituelle.

limey ['laɪmɪ] *Am* **1** *n* Angliche *mf*, Rosbif *mf*
2 *adj* angliche

limp-wristed [lɪmp'rɪstɪd] *adj* efféminé □, chochotte

line [laɪn] *n (of powdered drugs)* ligne *f*
▶ *voir aussi* **main**

lip [lɪp] *n (cheek)* toupet *m*; **don't give me any of your lip!** ne sois pas insolent! □

lippy ['lɪpɪ] **1** *n Br (abrév* **lipstick**) rouge *m* à lèvres □
2 *adj (cheeky)* insolent □

lipstick lesbian ['lɪpstɪk'lezbɪən] *n* lesbienne *f* glamoureuse □

liquidate ['lɪkwɪdeɪt] *vt (kill)* liquider, refroidir

load [ləʊd] *n* (**a**) **a load of** un tas de; **it's a load of rubbish** c'est un tas de conneries; **get a load of this!** *(look)* mate-

moi ça!; *(listen)* écoute un peu ça!
(**b**) **loads of** des tas de; **loads of money/time** vachement d'argent/de temps (**c**) *Am* **to have a load on** être complètement bourré *ou* beurré *ou* pété
▶ *voir aussi* **shoot**

loaded ['ləʊdɪd] *adj* (**a**) *(wealthy)* plein aux as (**b**) *(drunk)* bourré, beurré, pété; *(on drugs)* défoncé, raide

loaf [ləʊf] *n Br (rhyming slang* **loaf of bread** = **head**) citron *m*, cigare *m*; **use your loaf!** réfléchis une minute!

loan shark ['ləʊnʃɑːk] *n* usurier(ère) □ *m,f*

lob [lɒb] *vt (throw)* balancer

local ['ləʊkəl] *n Br (pub)* pub *m* du coin *(où l'on a ses habitudes)*

loco ['ləʊkəʊ] *adj Am* timbré, toqué, cinglé

locoweed ['ləʊkəʊwiːd] *n (marijuana)* herbe *f*

log [lɒg] *n Br* **to drop a log** [!] *(defecate)* couler un bronze

lolly ['lɒlɪ] *n Br (money)* oseille *f*, artiche *m*, fric *m*, pognon *m*

loo [luː] *n Br* vécés *mpl*

looker ['lʊkə(r)] *n* **she's a real looker** elle est vraiment canon; **she's not much of a looker** c'est pas une beauté

loon [luːn] *n* cinglé(e) *m,f*, dingue *mf*, toqué(e) *m,f*

loony ['luːnɪ] **1** *n* cinglé(e) *m,f*, dingue *mf*, toqué(e) *m,f*; **loony bin** maison *f* de fous
2 *adj* timbré, dingue, cinglé

loony-tune ['luːnɪtjuːn] *n Am* cinglé(e) *m,f*, dingue *mf*, toqué(e) *m,f*

loony-tunes ['luːnɪtjuːnz] *adj Am* cinglé, toqué, timbré

loop [luːp] *n Am* **to be out of the loop** ne pas être dans le coup; **to cut sb out of the loop** mettre qn aux oubliettes
▶ *voir aussi* **knock**

loopy ['luːpɪ] *adj* cinglé, chtarbé, dingue

loose [lu:s] *adj (promiscuous)* facile; **to be loose** être une fille facile
▸ *voir aussi* **hang, screw**

loot [lu:t] *n (money)* fric *m*, pèse *m*, flouze *m*; *(goods)* marchandise ⁰ *f*; *(presents)* cadeaux ⁰ *mpl*

lorry ['lɒrɪ] *n Br Hum* **it fell off the back of a lorry** c'est de la marchandise volée ⁰

lose [lu:z] *vt* **(a)** **to lose one's cool** se démonter; **to lose one's head** piquer une crise, voir rouge, se mettre en pétard; **to lose it** *(go mad)* perdre la boule; *(lose one's temper)* piquer une crise, péter les plombs; *Br* **to lose the plot** perdre la boule; *Br* **to lose the place** devenir gaga **(b)** **get lost!** *(go away)* casse-toi!, tire-toi!; *(expressing contempt, disagreement)* n'importe quoi!
▸ *voir aussi* **lunch, marbles, rag, shirt**

loser ['lu:zə(r)] *n (man)* raté *m*, loser *m*; *(woman)* ratée *f*

louse [laʊs] *n (person)* peau *f* de vache

louse up *vt sép Am* **to louse sth up** foirer qch

lousy ['laʊzɪ] *adj* **(a)** *(very bad)* merdique; **to feel lousy** *(ill)* se sentir vraiment mal fichu; *(guilty)* se sentir coupable ⁰, avoir les boules *ou* les glandes; **we had a lousy time** on s'est vraiment fait suer; **he's in a lousy mood** il est d'humeur dégueulasse **(b)** **to be lousy with sth** être bourré de qch; **the streets were lousy with cops** les rues étaient pleines de flics; **to be lousy with money** être bourré de fric, être plein aux as

love [lʌv] *n* **(a)** *Br (term of address) (to one's spouse, partner, child)* chéri(e) *m,f*; *(to male stranger)* Monsieur *m*; *(to female stranger)* Madame *f* **(b)** **love handles** poignées *fpl* d'amour

loved up [lʌvd'ʌp] *adj Br* tout gentil *(sous l'effet de l'ecstasy)*

lover boy ['lʌvəbɔɪ] *n Ironique* **she's gone out with lover boy** elle est sortie avec son Jules; **when's lover boy coming round to see you?** quand est-ce qu'il vient te voir ton Jules?

lovey-dovey [lʌvɪ'dʌvɪ] *adj (behaviour)* sentimental ⁰; **to be all lovey-dovey** *(of two lovers)* être comme des tourtereaux

luck into [lʌk] *vt insép Am* **to luck into sth** dégoter qch

luck out, luck up *vi Am* décrocher le gros lot

luck up on *vt insép Am* **to luck up on sth** dégoter qch

lug¹ [lʌg] *n Am (man)* abruti *m*, crétin *m*

lug², **lughole** ['lʌghəʊl] *n Br (ear)* esgourde *f*, portugaise *f*

lulu ['lu:lu:] *n Am* **to be a lulu** être génial

lumber ['lʌmbə(r)] *vt Br* **to get lumbered with sb/sth** se taper *ou* se coltiner qn/qch; **I got lumbered with doing the dishes** je me suis coltiné *ou* farci la vaisselle

lunch [lʌntʃ] *n* **to be out to lunch** *(mad)* travailler du chapeau, être cinglé; **to lose** *or Am* **shoot one's lunch** *(vomit)* gerber, dégobiller; **liquid lunch** = alcool qui tient lieu de déjeuner

lunchbox ['lʌntʃbɒks] *n Br (man's genitals)* service *m* trois pièces, bijoux *mpl* de famille

lunkhead ['lʌŋkhed] *n Am* cruche *f*, andouille *f*, courge *f*

lush [lʌʃ] *n* alcolo *mf*, poivrot(e) *m,f*

lushed [lʌʃt] *adj Am* pété, bourré, beurré

luvved up [lʌvd'ʌp] = **loved up**

luvvie, luvvy ['lʌvɪ] *n Br Péj (man)* acteur ⁰ *m*; *(woman)* actrice ⁰ *f*

Le mot "luvvie" signifie littéralement "chéri" ou "chérie" et est censé être un terme communément utilisé par les acteurs pour s'adresser les uns aux autres.

M

Mac [mæk] *npr Am (term of address)* chef *m*

mack [mæk] *n* (**a**) *Am (pimp)* maquereau *m*, mac *m* (**b**) *Noir Am (expert seducer)* tombeur *m*

mack on *vt insép Noir Am* **to mack on sb** draguer qn

mad [mæd] *adj* (**a**) **to be mad about sb/sth** être dingue de qn/qch; *Br* **to be mad for it** *(raring to go)* être prêt à s'éclater (**b**) **to run/work like mad** courir/travailler comme un dingue

madam ['mædəm] *n* (**a**) *(of brothel)* mère *f* maquerelle (**b**) *Br (arrogant girl)* **she's a little madam** c'est une petite pimbêche (**c**) *Br (term of address)* madame *f*; **that's enough of your cheek, madam!** ça suffit comme ça petite insolente!

madhouse ['mædhaʊs] *n (psychiatric hospital, busy place)* maison *f* de fous; **it's like a madhouse in here** c'est une vraie maison de fous ici

mag [mæg] *n (abrév* **magazine**) revue □ *f*, magazine □ *m*
▶ *voir aussi* **girlie, skin**

magic ['mædʒɪk] *adj* (**a**) *Br (excellent)* super, génial (**b**) **magic mushrooms** champignons *mpl* hallucinogènes □, champignons *mpl*

magnet ['mægnɪt] *n* **his new car's a babe** *or* **chick** *or* **fanny** ! **magnet** sa nouvelle voiture est super pour emballer les gonzesses

main [meɪn] *adj* (**a**) *Am* **main man** *(friend)* pote *m*; **yo, my main man, how ya doin'?** salut mon pote, comment ça va?; *Br* **when it comes to scoring goals, Robbie Fowler's the main man** pour ce qui est de marquer des buts, Robbie Fowler est champion (**b**) **main squeeze** *(boyfriend)* mec *m*, Jules *m*; *(girlfriend)* nana *f*, gonzesse *f* (**c**) **main line** *(vein)* veine *f* apparente □ *(choisie pour s'injecter de la drogue)* (**d**) *Am* **main drag** rue *f* principale □

mainline ['meɪnlaɪn] **1** *vt (drugs)* se faire un shoot de; *(habitually)* se shooter à
2 *vi* se shooter, se piquer

mainliner ['meɪnlaɪnə(r)] *n* junkie *mf*, shooté(e) *m,f*

make [meɪk] **1** *n* **to be on the make** *(financially)* chercher à s'en mettre plein les poches; *(sexually)* draguer
2 *vt Am* **to make sb, to make it with sb** coucher avec qn
3 *vi Am* **to make like sb** *(pass oneself off as)* essayer de passer pour qn □; **he's always making like a tough guy** il essaie toujours de jouer les durs; **make like you don't know anything** fais comme si tu savais pas

make out *vi Am (sexually)* se peloter; **to make out with sb** peloter qn

mama, mamma ['mæmə] *n Am* (**a**) *(woman)* bonne femme *f* (**b**) **big mama** *(large object)* mastodonte *m*

man [mæn] **1** *n* (**a**) *Br (husband, boyfriend)* mec *m*; **she's got a new man** elle a un nouveau mec (**b**) *(term of address)* **hey, man!** *(as greeting)* salut vieux!; **how are you doing, man?** comment ça va, vieux?; **come on, man!** allez! (**c**) *Noir Am* **the Man** *(white people)* les

Blancs *mpl*; *(the police)* les flics *mpl*; *(drug dealer)* dealer *m*

2 *exclam* la vache!; **man, am I tired!** la vache, je suis crevé!

▸ *voir aussi* **con, dog, hatchet, main, new, old, play**

Manc [mæŋk] *n Br (abrév* **Mancunian)** = natif de la ville de Manchester

maneater ['mæni:tə(r)] *n (woman)* mangeuse *f* d'hommes

manky ['mæŋkı] *adj Br* cradingue, crado

map [mæp] *n Am (face)* tronche *f*, trombine *f*

marbles ['mɑ:bəlz] *npl* **to lose one's marbles** perdre la boule; **to have all one's marbles** ne pas être gâteux du tout

mare[1] [meə(r)] *n Br Péj (woman)* grognasse *f*; **you silly mare!** espèce d'andouille!

mare[2] *n Br (abrév* **nightmare)** cauchemar □ *m*; **it was a total mare!** c'était un vrai cauchemar!; **her new boyfriend's a complete mare** c'est une vraie tache son nouveau copain; **we had a bit of a mare finding somewhere to park** on a eu vachement de mal pour trouver une place où se garer

mate [meıt] *n Br* **(a)** *(friend)* pote *m* **(b)** *(term of address)* **thanks, mate** *(to friend)* merci vieux; *(to stranger)* merci chef; **watch where you're going, mate!** hé, regarde devant toi!

matey ['meıtı] *Br* **1** *n (term of address)* **how's it going, matey?** comment ça va vieux?; **just watch it, matey!** fais gaffe!

2 *adj (friendly)* **to be matey with sb** être pote avec qn; **they're very matey all of a sudden** ils sont très potes tout d'un coup

max [mæks] *(abrév* **maximum) 1** *n Am* **to the max** *(totally)* un max; **did you have a good time? – to the max!** tu

t'es bien amusé? – vachement bien!, un max!

2 *adv (at the most)* maxi; **it'll take three days max** ça prendra trois jours maxi

3 *vt Am* **to max an exam** obtenir le maximum de points à un examen □

▸ *voir aussi* **grody**

max out *Am* **1** *vt sép* **to max out one's credit card** dépenser le maximum autorisé avec sa carte de crédit □

2 *vi* **to max out on chocolate** se goinfrer de chocolat; **to max out on booze** picoler un max

maxed [mækst] *adj Am (extremely drunk)* bourré comme un coing, pété à mort

maxed out [mækst'aʊt] *adj Am* **(a) to be maxed out on one's credit card** avoir dépensé le maximum autorisé avec sa carte de crédit □ **(b) to be maxed out on chocolate/sci-fi movies** avoir fait une overdose de chocolat/de films de science-fiction

mean [mi:n] *adj (excellent)* super, génial; **she's a mean chess player** elle joue super bien aux échecs, elle touche (sa bille) aux échecs; **he makes a mean curry** il fait super bien le curry

meat [mi:t] *n* **(a) you're dead meat!** t'es mort!

(b) !! *(penis)* bite *f*, queue *f*

(c) meat rack lieu *m* de drague *(en particulier chez les homosexuels)*

(d) *Am* **meat wagon** *(ambulance)* ambulance □ *f*

(e) *Br Péj* **meat market** *(nightclub)* = boîte réputée pour être un lieu de drague

▸ *voir aussi* **beat**

meatball ['mi:tbɔ:l], **meathead** ['mi:thed] *n Am (person)* crétin(e) *m,f*, truffe *f*, andouille *f*

meatheaded ['mi:thedıd] *adj Am* débile

medallion man [mɪˈdæljənmæn] n Br macho m à chaîne en or

> Le "medallion man" est généralement un homme entre deux âges traversant une crise d'identité. Il porte une chemise ouverte sur un torse velu et des bijoux clinquants (dont le fameux médaillon). Il fréquente les boîtes de nuit en compagnie de gens nettement moins âgés que lui, et tente de séduire les jeunes femmes.

mega [ˈmegə] **1** adj (excellent) génial, super, géant; (enormous) énorme
2 adv (very) hyper, méga

mega- [ˈmegə] préfixe hyper; **mega-rich** hyper riche; **mega-famous** hyper célèbre; **mega-angry** hyper en colère

megabucks [ˈmegəbʌks] n un fric fou, une fortune

megastar [ˈmegəstɑː(r)] n superstar f

megilla [məˈgɪlə] n Am **the whole megilla** tout le tremblement; **I don't need the whole megilla, just give me the main points** t'as pas besoin de tout me raconter en détail ou par le menu, dis-moi le principal

mellow [ˈmeləʊ] **1** n Noir Am (friend) pote m
2 adj **(a)** Noir Am (attractive) sexy, craquant **(b)** Noir Am (fine, acceptable) cool; **see you at six? – yeah, that's mellow** on se voit à six heures? – ouais, ça marche! **(c)** (relaxed, unexcited) cool, décontract, relaxe; **stay mellow!** calmos!, du calme! **(d)** (on drugs) **to be mellow** être parti, planer

mellow out vi (relax) se calmer

melons [ˈmelənz] npl (breasts) nichons mpl, roberts mpl

mensch [menʃ] n Am (man) chic type m; (woman) brave femme f

mental [ˈmentəl] adj (mad) dingue, cinglé; **to go mental** (go mad) devenir dingue ou cinglé, perdre la boule; (lose one's temper) péter les plombs, péter une durite, piquer une crise; Br **it was a mental party!** c'était une fête vraiment démente ou dingue!; Br **you should have seen the way they were shouting at each other, it was mental!** t'aurais vu comme ils se criaient dessus, c'était dingue!

Merc [mɜːk] n (abrév **Mercedes**) Mercedes □ f

merchant [ˈmɜːtʃənt] n **speed merchant** Br (fast driver) chauffard m; Am (athlete) = coureur à pied très rapide; Br **gossip merchant** commère f; Br **rip-off** or **con merchant** arnaqueur(euse) m,f

> Ce terme peut s'ajouter à de nombreux noms pour désigner quelqu'un qui s'adonne à une activité.

merry [ˈmerɪ] adj Br (slightly drunk) éméché

meshuga [məˈʃuːgə] adj Am dingue, taré, cinglé

mess [mes] vi **(a)** Br **no messing!** sans blagues! **(b)** **to mess with sb** embêter qn; **don't mess with him!** le cherche pas!, te frotte pas à lui!

mess about, mess around vi **(a)** (act foolishly) faire l'imbécile **(b)** (waste time) glander, glandouiller **(c)** (potter) bricoler **(d)** **to mess about with sb** (sexually) coucher avec qn

metalhead [ˈmetəlhed] n fan mf de heavy metal □, hardeux(euse) m,f

Mex [meks] Am Injurieux (abrév **Mexican**) **1** n Mexicain(e) □ m,f
2 adj mexicain □

Mick [mɪk] npr Injurieux (Irishman) Irlandais □ m

> "Mick" est le diminutif de "Michael", l'un des prénoms les plus courants en Irlande. Bien que ce terme ne témoigne pas nécessairement d'une attitude xénophobe de la part de celui qui

l'utilisé, il est préférable de ne pas
l'employer.

mick [mɪk], **mickey** ['mɪkɪ] *n Br* **to
take the mick out of sb/sth** se ficher
de qn/qch; **are you taking the mick?**
tu te fiches de moi?

Mickey (Finn) ['mɪkɪ('fɪn)] *n* = boisson alcoolisée dans laquelle on a versé
un sédatif

Mickey Mouse ['mɪkɪ'maʊs] *adj Péj* à
la gomme, à la noix

middle finger salute ['mɪdəlfɪŋgə-
sə'luːt] *n Br* doigt *m* d'honneur; **to give
sb the middle finger salute** faire un
doigt d'honneur à qn

mighty ['maɪtɪ] *adv Am* vachement, hyper

Mike [maɪk] *npr* **for the love of Mike!**
c'est quelque chose!, c'est pas vrai!

miles [maɪlz] *adv Br (very much)* vachement; **I feel miles better** je me sens
vachement mieux; **it's miles more interesting** c'est vachement plus intéres-
sant; **you're miles too slow** t'es
vachement trop lent, t'es mille fois trop
lent

million ['mɪljən] *adj* **to look (like)
a million dollars** en jeter; **to feel (like)
a million dollars** être au septième
ciel

mind [maɪnd] *n* **to be out of one's
mind** être cinglé *ou* dingue *ou* fêlé; **to
be bored out of one's mind** mourir
d'ennui; **to be out of one's mind with
worry** être malade d'inquiétude
► *voir aussi* **blow, pissed**

mind-blowing ['maɪndbləʊɪŋ] *adj*
époustouflant

minder ['maɪndə(r)] *n Br (bodyguard)*
garde *m* du corps ⁰, gorille *m*

minge [mɪndʒ] *n Br* chatte *f*

mingy ['mɪndʒɪ] *adj Br (person)* radin;
(sum, portion, amount) ridicule ⁰, minable

missis, missus ['mɪsɪz] *n Br (wife)*
bourgeoise *f*; **the missis** la patronne,
ma bourgeoise

mitt [mɪt] *n (hand)* pogne *f*, patte *f*; **get
your mitts off me!** bas les pattes!

mix up [mɪks] *vt sép Am* **to mix it up**
(fight) se castagner, se bastonner

mo [məʊ] *n Br (abrév* **moment)** instant ⁰
m, seconde ⁰ *f*; **half a mo!, wait a mo!**
une seconde!

Mob [mɒb] *n* **the Mob** la mafia ⁰

mobster ['mɒbstə(r)] *n* gangster ⁰ *m*
(particulièrement de la mafia)

mofo [!] ['məʊfəʊ] *n Noir Am (abrév*
motherfucker) enfoiré *m*

mog [mɒg], **moggy** ['mɒgɪ] *n Br* greffier *m*

mondo ['mɒndəʊ] *adv Am* vachement

money ['mʌnɪ] *n* **(a) to be in the
money** avoir du fric **(b)** *Noir Am (term
of address)* chef *m*; **what's up, money?**
ça va, chef?

moneybags ['mʌnɪbægz] *n (person)*
richard(e) *m,f*, rupin(e) *m,f*; **lend us a
fiver, moneybags!** passe-moi cinq
livres, toi qui es plein aux as!

money-grubber ['mʌnɪgrʌbə(r)] *n*
rapace *m*, requin *m*

mong [mɒŋ] *n Br (abrév* **mongol)** mon-
gol(e) *m,f*, gol *m*

Bien que ce terme soit très injurieux et
politiquement incorrect lorsqu'il
s'applique à un trisomique, il est
relativement anodin lorsqu'il désigne
simplement un imbécile.

moniker ['mɒnɪkə(r)] *n* blase *m*

monkey ['mʌŋkɪ] *n* **(a)** *Br (£500)* cinq
cents livres ⁰ *fpl*
(b) *Br* **I don't give a monkey's** je m'en
fiche pas mal, j'en ai rien à battre
(c) monkey business magouilles *fpl*
(d) *Am* **to have a monkey on one's
back** être accro
(e) monkey suit *(formal suit)* costard

m chic; *Am (uniform)* uniforme ⁻ *m*
▶ *voir aussi* **brass, features**

monkey about, monkey around *vi* faire l'imbécile

Montezuma's Revenge ['mɒntɪ-'zuːmərə'vendʒ] *n Hum* la turista

monty ['mɒntɪ] *n Br* **the full monty** le grand jeu, la totale

moo [muː] *n Br Péj (woman)* vieille bique *f*, vieille toupie *f*; **you silly moo!** espèce d'andouille!; **shut up, you old moo!** la ferme, espèce de vieille toupie!

mooch [muːtʃ] **1** *vt* taper, taxer; **to mooch sth off sb** taper *ou* taxer qch à qn
2 *vi* taxer

mooch about, mooch around
1 *vt* **to mooch about the house** traîner dans la maison
2 *vi* glander, glandouiller

moody ['muːdɪ] *adj Br (goods)* volé ⁻; *(passport, document)* faux ⁻

moola, moolah ['muːlə] *n Am* flouze *m*, fric *m*, pognon *m*

moon [muːn] *vi (expose one's buttocks)* montrer ses fesses

moonshine ['muːnʃaɪn] *n Am* **(a)** *(nonsense)* foutaises *fpl* **(b)** *(illegal alcohol)* alcool *m* de contrebande ⁻

morning glory ['mɔːnɪŋ'glɔːrɪ] *n Br* érection *f* au réveil ⁻

moron ['mɔːrɒn] *n* crétin(e) *m,f*, imbécile *mf*

moronic [mə'rɒnɪk] *adj* débile

mother ['mʌðə(r)] *n* **(a)** *(large person, thing)* mastodonte *m*; **I've got a mother of a hangover** j'ai une vache de gueule de bois; **her boyfriend's a big mother** son copain est un balaise **(b)** ⚠ *(abrév* **motherfucker)** *(person)* enfoiré *m*; *(thing)* saloperie *f*; **some mother's stolen my drink** il y a un enfoiré qui m'a pris mon verre; **the mother's broken down again** cette saloperie est encore tombée en panne

motherfucker ⚠⚠ ['mʌðəfʌkə(r)] *n* **(a)** *(person)* enculé *m*; **he's a stupid motherfucker** c'est un pauvre con **(b)** *(thing)* saloperie *f*; **the motherfucker won't start** cette saloperie ne veut pas démarrer; **I've a motherfucker of a hangover** j'ai une gueule de bois d'enfer

motherfucking ⚠⚠ ['mʌðəfʌkɪŋ] *adj* foutu; **where's that motherfucking bastard?** où est passé cet enculé?; **open up or I'll kick the motherfucking door in!** ouvre ou j'enfonce cette putain de porte!

mothering ⚠ ['mʌðərɪŋ] *adj Am* foutu; **where's that mothering bitch?** où est passée cette conne?

motor ['məʊtə(r)] *Br* **1** *n (car)* bagnole *f*
2 *vi* **to be motoring** *(going fast)* foncer

motormouth ['məʊtəmaʊθ] *n* moulin *m* à paroles

mouth [maʊθ] *n* **to be all mouth** n'avoir que (de) la gueule; *Br* **he's all mouth and no trousers** il a que (de) la gueule; **to shoot one's mouth off** parler à tort et à travers; **me and my big mouth!** j'ai encore perdu une occasion de me taire!
▶ *voir aussi* **shut**

mouth off [maʊð] *vi (brag)* se vanter ⁻, crâner; *(talk impudently)* la ramener; *(talk indiscreetly)* parler à tort et à travers

mouthful ['maʊθfʊl] *n* **(a)** *(word)* mot *m* imprononçable ⁻; *(name)* nom *m* à coucher dehors **(b)** *Br* **to give sb a mouthful** traiter qn de tous les noms **(c)** *Am* **you said a mouthful!** tu l'as dit, bouffi!

move [muːv] *n* **(a)** **to get a move on** se magner; **get a move on!** magne-toi! **(b)** **to make a move** *(leave)* y aller ⁻, bouger; **to make a move on sb** faire des avances à qn ⁻

muck [mʌk] *n Br (worthless things)* **his book's a load of muck** son livre ne vaut pas un clou; **he eats nothing but muck** il mange que des saloperies

mucker ['mʌkə(r)] *n Br* (**a**) *(friend)* pote *m* (**b**) *(term of address)* vieux *m*; **alright, me old mucker!** salut vieux!, salut mon pote!

muff ⚠️ [mʌf] *n (woman's genitals)* chatte *f*, con *m*, cramouille *f*

muff-diving ⚠️ ['mʌfdaɪvɪŋ] *n* descente *f* au barbu; **to go muff-diving** faire une descente au barbu

mug [mʌg] *n* (**a**) *(face)* tronche *f*, trombine *f*; **mug shot** = photo d'identité prise par la police ou en prison (**b**) *(gullible person)* poire *f*; **it's a mug's game** le jeu n'en vaut pas la chandelle; **the lottery's a mug's game** le loto, c'est un attrape-couillons

muggins ['mʌgɪnz] *n Br* mézigue; **muggins (here) paid the bill as usual** comme d'habitude c'est mézigue qui a payé l'addition

mule [mju:l] *n (drug smuggler)* mule *f* ► *voir aussi* **hung**

munch out [mʌntʃ] *vi Am* se goinfrer, s'empiffrer

munchies ['mʌntʃɪz] *npl* (**a**) *(hunger)* fringale *f*, **to have the munchies** avoir la dalle (**b**) *(food)* amuse-gueule *mpl*

muppet ['mʌpɪt] *n Br (person)* andouille *f*

murder ['mɜ:də(r)] **1** *n (difficult task, experience)* **it was murder** c'était l'enfer; **the traffic was murder** il y avait une circulation dingue; **it's murder trying to park in the town centre** c'est l'enfer pour trouver à se garer dans le centre-ville; **standing all day is murder on your feet** ça fait vachement mal aux pieds de rester debout toute la journée

2 *vt* (**a**) *(song, language)* massacrer (**b**) *Br* **I could murder a fag/beer** je me taperais bien une clope/une bière (**c**) *(defeat)* ratatiner, écrabouiller, foutre la pâtée à

mush [mʊʃ] *n Br (term of address)* **oi, mush!** hé, Duchenoque!

muso ['mju:zəʊ] *Br (abrév* **musician)** musico *m*

mutha ['mʌðə] *Noir Am =* **mother**

muthafucka ['mʌðəfʌkə] *Noir Am =* **motherfucker**

mutt [mʌt] *n* clébard *m*, clebs *m*

N

nab [næb] vt (**a**) (catch, arrest) pincer, alpaguer (**b**) (steal) piquer, faucher

naff [næf] adj Br (clothes, place, person) ringard; (comment, behaviour) débile; **naff all** que dalle; **I've got naff all money** j'ai que dalle comme argent

naff off vi Br s'arracher, se casser; **naff off!** (go away) casse-toi!; (expressing contempt, disagreement) va te faire voir!

naffing ['næfɪŋ] Br 1 adj (for emphasis) foutu, sacré; **shut your naffing mouth!** ferme-la!, ferme ton clapet!; **naffing hell!** putain!

2 adv (for emphasis) vachement; **you're so naffing stupid!** t'es vraiment débile!; **you're naffing well coming with me!** tu viens avec moi, un point c'est tout!

Nam [næm] npr (abrév **Vietnam**) le Vietnam

Le terme "Nam" n'est utilisé que dans le contexte de la guerre du Vietnam.

nancy (boy) ['nænsɪ(bɔɪ)] n (effeminate man) chochotte f; (homosexual man) homo m

narc [nɑːk] n Am (abrév **narcotics agent**) agent m de la Brigade des stups

nark [nɑːk] 1 n (**a**) (informer) mouchard(e) m,f (**b**) Br (grumbler) râleur(euse) m,f

2 vt Br (annoy) foutre en rogne ou en boule

3 vi (inform) **to nark on sb** balancer qn

narked [nɑːkt] adj Br en rogne

narky ['nɑːkɪ] adj Br ronchon

nasty ['nɑːstɪ] adj Am (excellent) super, génial; **she makes a nasty pizza** elle fait super bien la pizza

natch [nætʃ] exclam (abrév **naturally**) bien sûr!

natter ['nætə(r)] Br 1 n converse f; **to have a natter** tailler une bavette

2 vi papoter

neat [niːt] Am 1 adj (excellent) super, génial

2 exclam super!, génial!

neck [nek] 1 n (**a**) Br (cheek) culot m; **she's got some neck!** elle a un sacré culot! (**b**) Br **to get it in the neck** se faire remonter les bretelles

2 vi (of couple) se peloter

▶ voir aussi **brass, dead, pain**

needful ['niːdful] n Br (what is necessary) **to do the needful** faire le nécessaire ▫; **have you got the needful?** (money) t'as du fric?

needle ['niːdəl] 1 n **to get the needle** se foutre en boule ou en rogne; **to give sb the needle** foutre qn en boule ou en rogne

2 vt (irritate) foutre en boule ou en rogne

3 vi (inject drugs) se shooter, se piquer

nelly ['nelɪ] n Br **not on your nelly!** des clous!

nerd [nɜːd] n ringard m

Le "nerd" est une personne, généralement jeune, qui par son désintérêt pour les activités prisées par les gens de son âge, son absence de goût en matière vestimentaire et son incapacité à communiquer de façon satisfaisante avec autrui, se rend

impopulaire auprès des autres. Le
"nerd" est souvent un passionné
d'informatique.

nerdy ['nɜːdɪ] *adj* ringard

never-never ['nevə'nevə(r)] *n Br* **to
buy sth on the never-never** acheter
qch à crédit □

new [njuː] *adj Br* **new lad** jeune homme
m moderne □; **new man** homme *m*
moderne □

Les concepts de "new lad" et de "new
man" sont apparus à la fin des années
80. Le "new lad" est un jeune homme
dont les centres d'intérêt ne diffèrent
en rien de ceux de n'importe quel
autre jeune homme (à savoir les
sorties, les rencontres, le sport...)
mais dont l'attitude témoigne d'une
certaine sophistication absente chez le
"lad" moyen. Le "new lad" sait boire
avec modération et n'est pas sexiste.
Le "new man", lui, ne craint pas de
laisser s'exprimer sa sensibilité. Il est
constamment à l'écoute des besoins
de sa compagne et participe
équitablement à l'éducation des
enfants et aux tâches ménagères.

newbie ['njuːbɪ] *n Am* bleu(e) *m,f (personne nouvellement recrutée)*

newsie ['njuːzɪ] *n Am* **(a)** *(newspaper
vendor)* vendeur(euse) *m,f* de journaux □
(b) *(journalist)* journaleux(euse) *m,f*

next [nekst] *adv Am* **to get next to sb**
(ingratiate oneself with) faire de la lèche
à qn; *(become emotionally involved with)*
se lier avec qn □; *(have sex with)* coucher
avec qn

nibs [nɪbz] *n Br* **his/her nibs** son altesse,
cézigue

nice [naɪs] *adj Br* **nice one!** bravo!
▸ *voir aussi* **earner**

nick [nɪk] *Br* **1** *n* **(a)** *(police station)* poste
m; *(prison)* bloc *m* **(b)** *(condition)* condition □ *f*, état □ *m*; **in good/bad nick** en
bon/mauvais état

2 *vt* **(a)** *(arrest)* agrafer, alpaguer; **he
got nicked for stealing a car** il s'est
fait arrêter pour vol de voiture □
(b) *(steal)* piquer, faucher

nickel ['nɪkəl] *n Am* **(a)** *(five cents)* **it's
not worth a plugged nickel** ça vaut
pas un clou **(b)** *(five dollars)* cinq dollars □ *mpl*; **to buy a nickel of weed**
acheter pour cinq dollars d'herbe

nicker ['nɪkə(r)] *n Br (pounds sterling)*
livres *fpl* sterling □

niff [nɪf] *Br* **1** *n* puanteur □ *f*
2 *vi* refouler, schlinguer, fouetter

niffy ['nɪfɪ] *adj Br* qui fouette *ou* refoule

nifty ['nɪftɪ] *adj* astucieux □

nigga ['nɪɡə] *n Noir Am Injurieux* nègre
(négresse) *m,f*

Lorsqu'il est utilisé par des Noirs
américains, le terme "nigga" perd son
caractère injurieux et acquiert une
connotation positive.

nigger ['nɪɡə(r)] *n Injurieux* nègre (négresse) *m,f*

Lorsqu'il est utilisé par des Noirs
américains, le terme "nigger" perd son
caractère injurieux et acquiert une
connotation positive.

Nip [nɪp] *n Injurieux Jap mf*

nipper ['nɪpə(r)] *n Br* môme *m*, gosse *m*

nippy ['nɪpɪ] *adj* **(a)** *(weather)* **it's nippy**
ça pince, il fait frisquet **(b)** *Br (car)*
maniable □

nit [nɪt], **nitwit** ['nɪtwɪt] *n Br* andouille
f, courge *f*

nob [nɒb] *n Br (rich person)* rupin(e) *m,f*,
richard(e) *m,f*

noddle ['nɒdəl] *n Br (head)* caboche *f*,
cafetière *f*, ciboulot *m*; **use your noddle!** fais marcher ton ciboulot *ou* tes
méninges!

noggin ['nɒɡɪn] *n* caboche *f*, cafetière *f*,
ciboulot *m*

noise [nɔɪz] *n Br* **shut your noise!** la
ferme!, boucle-la!

no-no ['nəʊnəʊ] *n* **it's a no-no** ça ne se fait pas □; **asking him for more money is a definite no-no** il est hors de question de lui demander plus d'argent

noodle ['nuːdəl] *n* (*head*) caboche *f*, cafetière *f*, ciboulot *m*

nookie, nooky ['nʊkɪ] *n* partie *f* de jambes en l'air; **to have a bit of nookie** *or* **nooky** faire une partie de jambes en l'air

nope [nəʊp] *adv* non □, nan

north and south ['nɔːθən'saʊθ] *n Br* (*rhyming slang* **mouth**) bouche □ *f*, clapet *m*

nose [nəʊz] *n* **to have a nose job** se faire refaire le nez □; *Br* **to get up sb's nose** taper sur les nerfs à qn; **to keep one's nose clean** se tenir à carreau; **nose candy** (*cocaine*) coco *f*, neige *f*

nose-rag ['nəʊzræg] *n* tire-jus *m*

nosey parker [nəʊzɪ'pɑːkə(r)] *n Br* fouine *f*

nosh [nɒʃ] **1** *n* bouffe *f*
2 *vi* bouffer

nosh-up ['nɒʃʌp] *n Br* gueuleton *m*

not [nɒt] *adv* **it was a great party... not!** c'était pas vraiment génial comme soirée!; **he's really gorgeous...not!** c'est pas exactement un Apollon!

Cette structure a été rendue célèbre par le film comique américain *Wayne's World*, l'histoire de deux adolescents prolongés. Ce film est à l'origine d'expressions désormais couramment utilisées par de nombreux jeunes, aussi bien en Grande-Bretagne qu'aux États-Unis.

nothing doing ['nʌθɪŋ'duːɪŋ] *exclam* pas question!

nowt [naʊt] *pron Br* (*nothing*) rien □, que dalle

nudge nudge wink wink ['nʌdʒ-'nʌdʒ'wɪŋk'wɪŋk] *exclam Br* vous voyez ce que je veux dire!

Cette expression fut popularisée par l'émission de télévision *Monty Python's Flying Circus* au cours des années 70. On l'emploie pour indiquer à son interlocuteur que ce que l'on dit comporte des sous-entendus, souvent de nature grivoise.

nuke [njuːk] *vt* (**a**) (*attack with nuclear weapons*) atomiser □ (**b**) (*cook in microwave*) faire cuire au four à micro-ondes □ (**c**) (*defeat*) ratatiner, battre à plates coutures

number ['nʌmbə(r)] *n* (**a**) (*cannabis cigarette*) joint *m* (**b**) **to do a number one/two** (*urinate/defecate*) faire la petite/grosse commission (**c**) **I've got your number!** j'ai repéré ton manège! (**d**) *Am* **to do a number on sth** (*spoil, ruin*) bousiller qch

numbskull ['nʌmskʌl] *n* crétin(e) *m,f*, andouille *f*, cruche *f*

numero uno ['nuːmərəʊ'uːnəʊ] *n & adj Am* numéro un; **don't forget who's numero uno round here** n'oublie pas qui commande *ou* qui est le patron ici; **he's the numero uno coke dealer** c'est le principal dealer de coke

nurd [nɜːd] *Am* = **nerd**

nut [nʌt] *n* (**a**) (*head*) caboche *f*, cafetière *f*, ciboulot *m*; **to be off one's nut** (*mad*) être dingue *ou* cinglé; **to go off one's nut** (*go mad*) perdre la boule, devenir cinglé; (*get angry*) péter les plombs, péter une durite, piquer une crise; *Br* **to do one's nut** (*get angry*) péter les plombs, péter une durite, piquer une crise
(**b**) (*person*) cinglé(e) *m,f*, dingue *mf*; **a football/computer nut** un fana de football/d'informatique
(**c**) **he can't drive/sing for nuts** il conduit/chante comme un pied
(**d**) **nuts**[!] (*testicles*) boules *fpl*, couilles *fpl*
▶ *voir aussi* **sweet**

nutcase ['nʌtkeɪs] *n* cinglé(e) *m,f*, dingue *mf*

nuthouse ['nʌthaʊs] *n* maison *f* de fous

nuts [nʌts] **1** *adj* (*mad*) dingue, cinglé, timbré; **to go nuts** (*go mad*) devenir cinglé, perdre la boule; (*get angry*) péter les plombs, péter une durite; **to drive sb nuts** rendre qn chèvre; **to be nuts about sb/sth** être dingue de qn/qch **2** *exclam* mince!, zut!; **nuts to that!** plutôt crever!

nutso ['nʌtsəʊ] *Am adj* dingue, cinglé, timbré; **to go nutso** (*go mad*) devenir cinglé, perdre la boule; (*get angry*) péter les plombs, péter une durite; **to drive sb nutso** rendre qn chèvre; **to be nutso about sb/sth** être dingue de qn/qch

nutter ['nʌtə(r)] *n Br* cinglé(e) *m,f*, dingue *m,f*

nutty ['nʌtɪ] *adj* (*mad*) dingue, cinglé, timbré; *Hum* **as nutty as a fruitcake** complètement ravagé

nympho ['nɪmfəʊ] *n* (*abrév* **nymphomaniac**) nympho *f*

O

-o [əʊ] *suffixe* **sicko** malade *mf*, tordu(e) *m,f*; **thicko** nouille *f*, andouille *f*; **pinko** gaucho *mf*

> Le suffixe "-o" s'utilise pour construire un nom à partir d'un adjectif. Il s'agit d'un procédé générateur en anglais.

oar [ɔː(r)] *n* Br **to stick one's oar in** ramener sa fraise

oats [əʊts] *npl* **(a) to sow one's (wild) oats** jeter sa gourme; Br **to get one's oats** tirer un coup **(b)** Am **to feel one's oats** *(feel full of energy)* être en pleine forme; *(be self-important)* faire l'important

OD [əʊ'diː] *(abrév* **overdose)** **1** *n* overdose *f*
2 *vi* faire une overdose **(on** de); **I've OD'd on pizzas/soap operas lately** j'ai tellement mangé de pizza/regardé de feuilletons télé ces derniers temps que j'en suis dégoûté

oddball ['ɒdbɔːl] **1** *n* allumé(e) *m,f*, farfelu(e) *m,f*
2 *adj* loufoque, farfelu

odds [ɒdz] *npl* Br *(difference)* **it makes no odds** ça change rien; **it makes no odds what I say** ce que je dis ne sert à rien □; **what's the odds?** qu'est-ce que ça peut faire?

ofay [əʊ'feɪ] *n* Am Injurieux sale Blanc (Blanche) *m,f*

off [ɒf] **1** *adj* Br *(unacceptable)* **that was a bit off** c'est un peu fort de café
2 *vt* Am *(kill)* buter, refroidir, zigouiller

offie ['ɒfɪ] *n* Br *(abrév* **off-licence)** magasin *m* de vins et spiritueux □

off-the-wall ['ɒfðə'wɔːl] *adj* bizarroïde

oi [ɔɪ] *exclam* hé!

oik [ɔɪk] *n* Br plouc *mf*

oiled [ɔɪld] *adj* **(well) oiled** *(drunk)* bourré, beurré, pété

okay-dokay, okey-dokey ['əʊkɪ-'dəʊkɪ] *exclam* OK, d'accord, dac

old [əʊld] *adj* **old lady** *(wife)* bourgeoise *f*; *(mother)* vieille *f*; Br **old dear** *(elderly woman)* grand-mère *f*; *(mother)* vieille *f*; Br **old lag** truand *m*; **old man** *(husband)* Jules *m*; *(father)* vieux *m*; **old woman** *(wife)* bourgeoise *f*; *(mother)* vieille *f*; *(timid, fussy man)* chochotte *f*

oldie ['əʊldɪ] *n (person)* vieux (vieille) *m,f*; **(golden) oldie** *(song)* vieux succès □ *m*; *(film)* classique *m* du cinéma populaire □

on [ɒn] **1** *adj* **(a)** Br **it's not on!** *(unacceptable)* ça va pas du tout!
(b) fancy a pint? – you're on! tu bois une bière? – je veux!; **if you wash the dishes, I'll dry them – you're on!** si tu fais la vaisselle, je l'essuie – ça marche!
(c) Br **to be on** *(menstruating)* avoir ses ragnagnas
2 *adv* Br **to be** *or* **go on about sth** jacter de qch sans arrêt; **what's she (going) on about now?** qu'est-ce qu'elle raconte maintenant?
3 *prép* **what's he on?** il se sent bien?

one [wʌn] *n* **(a) to give sb one**[!] *(have sex with)* en glisser une paire à qn
(b) to have had one too many avoir bu un coup de trop
(c) *(blow)* **to belt/thump sb one** en coller une à qn
(d) Br *(person)* **you are a one!** toi alors!; **he's a right one, him!** lui alors,

il est impayable!

(e) Br **to go into one** (lose one's temper) péter les plombs, péter une durite ▸ voir aussi **lay, nice**

one-night stand [wʌnnaɪt'stænd] n aventure f sans lendemain

oodles ['uːdəlz] npl **oodles of** un max de, des masses de; **to have oodles of money** avoir un max de fric, être plein aux as; **to have oodles of time** avoir vachement de temps

oomph [ʊmf] n (a) (sex appeal) sex-appeal □ m; **she's got plenty of oomph** elle est vachement sexy (b) (vigour) punch m, pêche f, **their new album lacks the oomph of the last one** leur nouvel album n'a pas la pêche du précédent

oreo (cookie) ['ɔːrɪəʊ('kʊkɪ)] n Am Péj (person) = personne de couleur qui adopte les valeurs des Blancs

Un "Oreo® cookie" est un type de biscuit au chocolat fourré à la crème: noir à l'extérieur mais blanc à l'intérieur.

orgasmic [ɔː'gæzmɪk] adj (food, smell, taste) jouissif

OTT [əʊtiː'tiː] adj Br (abrév **over the top**) **the house is nice, but the decor's a bit OTT** la maison est bien, mais la décoration est un peu lourdingue; **it's a bit OTT to call him a fascist** c'est un peu exagéré de le traiter de fasciste; **he went completely OTT when he** heard what she'd said il a pété les plombs quand il a appris ce qu'elle avait dit

out [aʊt] **1** adj (a) (not in fashion) démodé □ (b) (openly homosexual) ouvertement homosexuel □ **2** adv (a) **to be out of it** (drunk, on drugs) être raide; **I felt a bit out of it** (excluded) je me sentais un peu de trop (b) **out of order** (unacceptable) inacceptable □; **that was a bit out of order!** c'est un peu fort de café!; **you were out of order to call her a slut** t'aurais pas dû la traiter de salope (c) **I'm out of here** je me casse; **let's get out of here** allez, on se casse **3** vt (homosexual) dévoiler l'homosexualité de □

outta ['aʊtə] contraction (abrév **out of**) **let's get outta here!** allez, on se casse!; **you must be outta your mind!** mais t'es complètement dingue!; Am **outta sight** (excellent) dingue, dément

owt [aʊt] pron Br (anything) quelque chose □; **he never said owt** il n'a jamais rien dit □; **is there owt the matter?** il y a quelque chose qui va pas?

Oz [ɒz] npr (abrév **Australia**) Australie □ f

Ozzie ['ɒzɪ] n (abrév **Australian**) Australien(enne) □ m,f

P

pack [pæk] **1** vt **to pack a gun** être armé □, être chargé
  2 vi **to send sb packing** envoyer qn balader
  ▶ voir aussi **fanny**

pack in vt sép **to pack sb/sth in** plaquer ou laisser tomber qn/qch; **pack it in!** ça suffit!

pack up vi Br **(a)** (stop work) dételer **(b)** (break down) tomber en panne □; **the telly packed up just as Gazza was about to score** la télé m'a/nous a lâché(s) juste au moment où Gazza allait marquer

packet ['pækɪt] n Br **(a)** (large amount of money) **to cost a packet** coûter bonbon; **to earn a packet** gagner des mille et des cents **(b)** (man's genitals) service m trois pièces

pad [pæd] n (home) casbah f; **you can crash at my pad** tu peux pieuter chez moi

Paddy ['pædɪ] npr Injurieux (Irishman) Irlandais □ m

> "Paddy" est le diminutif de "Patrick", l'un des prénoms les plus courants en Irlande. Bien que ce terme ne témoigne pas nécessairement d'une attitude xénophobe de la part de celui qui l'utilise, il est préférable de ne pas l'employer.

paddy ['pædɪ] n **(a)** Br **to be in a paddy** (angry) être en rogne **(b)** Am **paddy wagon** (police van) panier m à salade

pain [peɪn] n **to be a pain (in the neck)** être casse-pieds; Am **to give sb a pain (in the neck)** taper sur le système à qn; **to be a pain in the** Br **arse** or Am **ass** ⚠️ être casse-couilles ou chiant; **it's a real pain in the** Br **arse** or Am **ass having to get up so early** ⚠️ ça fait vraiment chier de devoir se lever si tôt

Paki ['pækɪ] n Br Injurieux (abrév **Pakistani**) (person) Pakistanais(e) □ m,f; **Paki shop, Paki's** = épicerie de quartier tenue par un Pakistanais

> Lorsqu'il est question d'une épicerie de quartier tenue par un Pakistanais, le terme "Paki" perd sa connotation raciste. Il est toutefois déconseillé de l'utiliser.

Paki-basher ['pækɪbæʃə(r)] n Br = individu qui attaque des immigrés pakistanais

Paki-bashing ['pækɪbæʃɪŋ] n Br = violences à l'encontre d'immigrés pakistanais

pal [pæl] n **(a)** (friend) pote m **(b)** (term of address) **thanks, pal** (to friend) merci, vieux; (to stranger) merci, chef; **watch where you're going, pal** hé, regarde où tu vas!

pal around vi **to pal around with sb** être pote avec qn; **they palled around for a while at high school** il y a un moment où ils étaient potes au lycée

palaver [pə'lɑːvə(r)] n Br (fuss) **what a palaver!** quelle histoire!; **it was a real palaver getting a work permit** ça a été la croix et la bannière pour obtenir un permis de travail; **we had the usual palaver about who was going to pay** ça a été le cirque habituel pour décider qui allait payer

pally ['pælɪ] adj Br **to be pally with sb** être pote avec qn; **they're very pally**

all of a sudden ils sont très potes tout d'un coup

palooka [pə'lu:kə] n Am (**a**) (clumsy man) manche m; (stupid man) andouille f, crétin m (**b**) (inept fighter) mauvais boxeur □ m

palsy-walsy ['pælzɪ'wælzɪ] adj **to be palsy-walsy with sb** être comme cul et chemise avec qn, être à tu et à toi avec qn; **they're very palsy-walsy all of a sudden** ils sont très potes ou copain-copain tout d'un coup

pan [pæn] **1** n Br **to go down the pan** être foutu en l'air; **that's our holidays down the pan** on peut faire une croix sur nos vacances
  2 vt (criticize) éreinter

panic button ['pænɪkbʌtən] n Am **to hit the panic button** paniquer, flipper

pansy ['pænzɪ] n (effeminate man) chochotte f; (homosexual man) tante f

pants [pænts] npl (**a**) **to beat the pants off sb** battre qn à plates coutures; **to scare the pants off sb** foutre une trouille pas possible à qn; **to bore the pants off sb** ennuyer qn à mourir; **he charmed the pants off my parents** il a conquis mes parents
  (**b**) **to be caught with one's pants down** être pris sur le fait en train de faire une bêtise
▸ voir aussi **pee**

papers ['peɪpəz] npl Am **go peddle your papers!** va voir ailleurs si j'y suis!

paralytic [pærə'lɪtɪk] adj Br (very drunk) pété à mort, bourré comme un coing, rond comme une queue de pelle

park [pɑːk] vt **to park oneself beside sb/on sth/etc** se poser ou poser ses fesses à côté de qn/sur qch/etc; **park your** Br **bum** or Am **butt over here beside me!** pose-toi ici, à côté de moi!
▸ voir aussi **walk**

parky ['pɑːkɪ] adj Br frisquet; **it's parky today** il fait frisquet aujourd'hui

party ['pɑːtɪ] **1** n **party animal** fêtard(e) m,f
  2 vi faire la fête

party-pooper ['pɑːtɪpuːpə(r)] n rabat-joie mf

pass [pɑːs] n **to make a pass at sb** faire du plat à qn

past [pɑːst] prép Br **to be past it** (of person) avoir passé l'âge; (of thing) avoir fait son temps

paste [peɪst] vt (beat up) tabasser; (defeat) battre à plates coutures; **to get pasted** (beaten up) se faire tabasser; (defeated) être battu à plates coutures

pasting ['peɪstɪŋ] n **to give sb a pasting** (beat up) tabasser qn; (defeat) battre qn à plates coutures; **to** Br **get** or Am **take a pasting** (be beaten up) se faire tabasser; (be defeated) être battu à plates coutures

patch [pætʃ] n Br (of prostitute, salesperson, police officer) secteur m

patsy ['pætsɪ] n Am pigeon m

paw [pɔː] **1** n (hand) pogne m, patte f; Br **paws off!**, Am **keep your (big) paws off!** bas les pattes!
  2 vt (touch sexually) peloter

payoff ['peɪɒf] n (bribe) pot-de-vin m

pdq [pi:di:'kju:] adv (abrév **pretty damn quick**) illico presto

peach [pi:tʃ] n **she's a peach** elle est canon; **a peach of a goal/dress** un but/une robe magnifique

peachy (keen) ['pi:tʃɪ(ki:n)] adj Am super, génial, grand

peanuts ['pi:nʌts] npl (small amount of money) cacahuètes fpl

pear-shaped ['peəʃeɪpt] adj Br **to go pear-shaped** partir en eau de boudin

pecker ['pekə(r)] n (**a**) [!] Am (penis) bite f, queue f (**b**) Br **to keep one's pecker up** ne pas se laisser abattre □

peckerwood ['pekəwuːd] n Noir Am **to be a peckerwood** être génial ou super

pecs [peks] *npl* (*abrév* **pectoral muscles**) pectoraux□ *mpl*; **he's got a great set of pecs** il a des super pectoraux

pee ⚠ [piː] **1** *n* pipi *m*; **to have a pee** faire pipi; **to go for a pee** aller faire pipi **2** *vt* **to pee oneself** *or Br* **one's pants** faire pipi dans sa culotte; **to pee oneself (laughing)** rire à en faire dans sa culotte **3** *vi* faire pipi; **it's peeing down** (*raining*) il pleut comme vache qui pisse

pee off ⚠ *vt sép* (*annoy*) **to pee sb off** faire chier qn; **to be peed off** être fumasse *ou* furibard; **to be peed off at sb/about sth** être en pétard contre qn/à cause de qch; **to be peed off with sb/sth** (*have had enough of*) en avoir ras le bol de qn/qch

peg out [peg] *vi* (*die*) passer l'arme à gauche, calancher

pen [pen] *n* (**a**) *Am* (*abrév* **penitentiary**) taule *f*; **in the pen** en taule, en cabane (**b**) *Br* (*abrév* **penalty**) péno *m*

pen-and-ink [penən'ɪŋk] *vi Br* (*rhyming slang* **stink**) schlinguer, fouetter

penguin suit ['pengwɪnsuːt] *n Br* costard *m* chic

penny ['penɪ] *n Br* **to spend a penny** (*urinate*) faire la petite commission

perp [pɜːp] *n Am* (*abrév* **perpetrator**) criminel(elle)□ *m,f*

perv [pɜːv] *n* (*abrév* **pervert**) pervers(e)□ *m,f*, détraqué(e) *m,f*

pervy ['pɜːvɪ] *adj Br* pervers

pet [pet] *n Br* (*term of address*) chéri(e) *m,f*

Pete [piːt] *npr* **for Pete's sake!** bon sang!

peter ['piːtə(r)] *n Am* (*penis*) quéquette *f*, zizi *m*

pew [pjuː] *n Br* **take** *or* **have a pew!** (*sit down*) pose-toi quelque part!

phat [fæt] *adj Noir Am* super, génial

pick up [pɪk] *vt sép* **to pick sb up** (*sexual partner*) lever qn; (*criminal*) agrafer qn, coffrer qn

pickled ['pɪkəld] *adj* (*drunk*) bourré, pété, beurré

picnic ['pɪknɪk] *n* **it was no picnic!** c'était pas de la tarte!
▸ *voir aussi* **sandwich**

picture ['pɪktʃə(r)] *n* (*film*) film□ *m*; *Br* **the pictures** (*the cinema*) le cinoche, le ciné

piddle ['pɪdəl] **1** *n* pipi *m*; **to have a piddle** faire pipi; **to go for a piddle** aller faire pipi **2** *vi* faire pipi

piddling ['pɪdəlɪŋ] *adj* (*details, amount*) insignifiant□

piece [piːs] *n* (**a**) **a piece of cake**, *Br* **a piece of piss** ⚠ un jeu d'enfant (**b**) *Am* (*gun*) flingue *m*

pie-eyed [paɪ'aɪd] *adj* rond, bourré

pig [pɪg] **1** *n* (**a**) (*greedy person*) goinfre *mf*; **to make a pig of oneself** se goinfrer
(**b**) (*ugly person*) mocheté *f*; (*unpleasant person*) chameau *m*
(**c**) *Br* (*thing*) truc *m* chiant; **cleaning the oven is a pig of a job** c'est vraiment chiant de nettoyer le four; **the desk was a pig to move** le bureau était vachement chiant à déménager
(**d**) (*police officer*) flic *m*, poulet *m*; **the pigs** les flics *mpl*, les poulets *mpl*
(**e**) *Br* **to make a pig's ear of sth** foirer qch; **he made a pig's ear of laying the carpet** il a posé la moquette comme un vrai sagouin
2 *vt Br* **to pig oneself (on)** se goinfrer (de)

pig out *vi* se goinfrer (**on** de)

pigeon ['pɪdʒɪn] *n Am* (*person*) pigeon *m*, poire *f*
▸ *voir aussi* **stool**

pig-thick ['pɪg'θɪk] *adj Br* con comme un balai

pig-ugly ['pɪg'ʌglɪ] *adj Br* moche comme un pou

pillock ['pɪlək] *n Br* andouille *f*, courge *f*

pillow-biter ['pɪləʊbaɪtə(r)] *n Injurieux* pédé *m*, tantouze *f*

pill-popper ['pɪlpɒpə(r)] *n* accro *mf* aux tranquillisants

pinch [pɪntʃ] *vt Am (arrest)* alpaguer, agrafer, serrer

pinhead ['pɪnhed] *n* crétin(e) *m,f*, andouille *f*, courge *f*

pinko ['pɪŋkəʊ] **1** *n* gaucho *mf*
2 *adj* gaucho

pins [pɪnz] *npl (legs)* cannes *fpl*, gambettes *fpl*; **she's got a great pair of pins** elle a des super gambettes

piss [!] [pɪs] **1** *n* **(a)** *(urine)* pisse *f*; **to have** *or Am* **take a piss** pisser; **to go for a piss** aller pisser; *Br* **piss flaps** [!!] grandes lèvres □ *fpl*, escalopes *fpl*
(b) *Br* **to take the piss out of sb/sth** se foutre de qn/qch; **are you taking the piss?** tu te fous de moi?
(c) *Br* **to be on the piss** se péter, se bourrer la gueule, prendre une cuite; **to go on the piss** aller se bourrer la gueule, aller prendre une cuite
(d) *Br (worthless things)* **the film/book was piss** le film/le bouquin ne valait pas un clou; **their beer is piss** leur bière, c'est du pipi de chat
2 *vt* **to piss oneself** se pisser dessus; **to piss oneself (laughing)** rire à en pisser dans sa culotte
3 *vi* **(a)** *(urinate)* pisser; **it's pissing down, it's pissing with rain** il pleut comme vache qui pisse
(b) **to piss all over sb** *(defeat)* battre qn à plates coutures
(c) *Am* **to piss and moan** geindre, pleurnicher
4 *adv* **piss poor** merdique; *Br* **piss easy** fastoche
▸ *voir aussi* **gnat, piece, pot, streak**

piss about [!], **piss around** [!] **1** *vt Br* **to piss sb about** *(cause problems for)* se foutre de la gueule de qn; *(waste time of)* faire perdre son temps à qn □
2 *vi (waste time)* glander, glandouiller

piss away [!] *vt sép* **to piss sth away** *(winnings, inheritance)* gaspiller qch □

piss off [!] **1** *vt sép (annoy)* **to piss sb off** faire chier qn; **to be pissed off** être fumasse; **to be pissed off at sb/about sth** être en pétard contre qn/à cause de qch; **to be pissed off with sb/sth** *(have had enough of)* en avoir ras le bol de qn/qch
2 *vi (go away)* se casser, se tirer; **piss off!** *(go away)* fous le camp!, tire-toi!, dégage!; *(expressing contempt, disagreement)* va te faire foutre!

piss-artist [!] ['pɪsɑːtɪst] *n Br* poivrot(e) *m,f*, alcolo *mf*

pissed [!] [pɪst] *adj* **(a)** *Br (drunk)* pété, bourré; **to get pissed** se péter la gueule; **as pissed as a fart** *or* **a newt, pissed out of one's head** *or* **mind** bourré comme un coing, plein comme une barrique, rond comme une queue de pelle
(b) *Am (annoyed)* **to be pissed** être fumasse; **to be pissed at sb/about sth** être en pétard contre qn/à cause de qch; **to be pissed with sb/sth** *(have had enough of)* en avoir ras le bol de qn/qch

pissed-up [!] ['pɪst'ʌp] *adj Br (drunk)* bourré, pété, beurré

pisser [!] ['pɪsə(r)] *n* **(a)** *(annoying situation)* **what a pisser!** quelle merde!; **it was a real pisser that the weather wasn't better** c'était vraiment chiant qu'il fasse pas plus beau **(b)** *Am (remarkable situation)* **what a pisser!** c'est génial *ou* super! **(c)** *Am (annoying person)* emmerdeur(euse) *m,f*; *(remarkable person)* **to be a pisser** être un mec/une nana génial(e)

pisshead [!] ['pɪshed] *n* **(a)** *Br (drunkard)* poivrot(e) *m,f*, alcolo *mf* **(b)** *Am (unpleasant person)* connard (connasse) *m,f*

pisshole [!] ['pɪʃhəʊl] *n* **his eyes are like pissholes in the snow** il a des petits yeux

piss-take [!] ['pɪsteɪk] *n Br* satire□ *f*; **this is a piss-take, isn't it?** non mais tu te fous de ma gueule ou quoi?

piss-up [!] ['pɪsʌp] *n Br* beuverie *f*; **to have a piss-up** prendre une cuite, se bourrer la gueule; **to go on a piss-up** aller prendre une cuite *ou* se bourrer la gueule; *Hum* **he couldn't organize a piss-up in a brewery** c'est un incompétent de première

pit [pɪt] *n* **(a)** *(untidy place)* foutoir *m* **(b)** *Br (bed)* plumard *m*, pieu *m* **(c) to be the pits** être complètement nul

pixilated ['pɪksɪleɪtəd] *adj Br* bourré, pété, beurré

pizza ['pi:tsə] *n Hum* **to have a face like a pizza** être une vraie calculette

pizza-face ['pi:tsəfeɪs] *n Hum* calculette *f*

PJs ['pi:dʒeɪz] *npl (abrév* **pyjamas)** pyjama□ *m*

plant [plɑ:nt] *n (person)* taupe *f*; *(thing)* = objet caché dans le but d'incriminer quelqu'un

plastered ['plɑ:stəd] *adj (drunk)* bourré, pété, beurré

plastic ['plæstɪk] *n (credit cards)* cartes *fpl* de crédit□; **to put sth on the plastic** payer qch avec une carte de crédit; **do they take plastic?** est-ce qu'ils acceptent *ou* prennent les cartes de crédit?; **can I pay with plastic?** vous prenez les cartes de crédit?

plates [pleɪts] *npl Br (rhyming slang* **plates of meat = feet)** arpions *mpl*, panards *mpl*

play [pleɪ] **1** *vt Br* **play the white man!** sois sympa!
2 *vi* **(a) to play hard to get** se faire désirer□ **(b) to play with oneself** *(masturbate)* se caresser, se toucher
▸ *voir aussi* **deck, hell**

pleb [pleb] *n Br Péj (abrév* **plebeian)** prolo *mf*

plebby ['plebɪ] *adj Br Péj (abrév* **plebeian)** prolo

plod [plɒd] *n Br (police officer)* flic *m*; **the plod** les flics, les poulets, la flicaille

plonk [plɒŋk] **1** *n Br (wine)* piquette *f*
2 *vt (put, place)* flanquer, coller, foutre; **just plonk your stuff on the table** t'as qu'à foutre tes affaires sur la table; **plonk yourself down over there** pose-toi là-bas

plonker ['plɒŋkə(r)] *n Br* **(a)** *(person)* andouille *f*, courge *f*, truffe *f* **(b)** *(penis)* quéquette *f*, zizi *m*

plowed [plaʊd] *adj Am (drunk)* pété, bourré, beurré

plug [plʌg] **1** *n* **to pull the plug on sth** *(stop financing)* arrêter de financer qch□
2 *vt Am (shoot)* flinguer

plug-ugly ['plʌg'ʌglɪ] *adj* moche comme un pou

pocket billiards ['pɒkɪt'bɪljədz], *Am* **pocket pool** ['pɒkɪt'pu:l] *n Hum* **to play** *Br* **pocket billiards** *or Am* **pocket pool** se caresser les boules à travers sa poche de pantalon

poison ['pɔɪzən] *n* **name your poison!**, *Br* **what's your poison?** qu'est-ce que tu bois?

poke [pəʊk] **1** *n* **(a)** [!] *(sexual intercourse)* **to have a poke** tirer un coup **(b)** *Hum* **it's better than a poke in the eye with a sharp stick** c'est mieux que rien□
2 [!] *vt (have sex with)* tringler, troncher

pokey ['pəʊkɪ] *n Am (prison)* taule *f*, cabane *f*; **in the pokey** en taule, en cabane, à l'ombre

polack ['pəʊlæk] *n Injurieux* Polack *mf*

pole [pəʊl] *n* **(a)** *Br* **to be up the pole** *(mad)* être dingue *ou* cinglé; **to be up the pole with worry** être fou *ou* malade d'inquiétude□; **to drive sb up the**

pole rendre qn chèvre (**b**)|!| *(penis)* queue *f*, bite *f*

polluted [pə'lu:tɪd] *adj Am (drunk)* pété, beurré, bourré, rond

ponce [pɒns] *n Br* (**a**) *(effeminate man)* chochotte *f* (**b**) *(pimp)* maquereau *m*

ponce about, ponce around *vi Br* (**a**) *(of effeminate man)* faire chochotte (**b**) *(waste time)* glander, glandouiller

poncy ['pɒnsɪ] *adj Br* qui fait chochotte

pond [pɒnd] *n* **the pond** *(the Atlantic)* l'Océan *m* Atlantique□; **across the pond** outre-Atlantique□

pong [pɒŋ] *Br* **1** *n* puanteur□ *f*
2 *vi* schlinguer, fouetter

pony ['pəʊnɪ] *n Br (£25)* vingt-cinq livres□ *fpl*

poo [pu:] **1** *n* (**a**) *(excrement)* caca *m*; **to do** *or Br* **have a poo** faire caca (**b**) *Br (worthless things)* **it's a load of poo** ça vaut pas un clou; **he's talking a load of poo** il raconte n'importe quoi
2 *vi* faire caca

pooch [pu:tʃ] *n (dog)* clébard *m*, clebs *m*
▸ *voir aussi* **screw**

poof [pu:f], **poofter** ['pu:ftə(r)] *n Br Injurieux* pédé *f*, pédale *f*, tantouze *f*, tapette *f*

poofy ['pu:fɪ] *adj Br Injurieux* qui fait tapette

Pool [pu:l] *npr (abrév* **Liverpool**) **the Pool** = surnom donné à la ville de Liverpool

poop [pu:p] *Am* **1** *n* caca *m*; **to take a poop** faire caca
2 *vi* faire caca

pooped [pu:pt] *adj Am* crevé, nase, lessivé

pop[1] [pɒp] **1** *n (fizzy drink)* soda□ *m*
2 *vt* (**a**) **to pop the question** proposer le mariage□ (**b**) **to pop pills** prendre des pilules□
▸ *voir aussi* **clogs**

pop[2] *n Am (father)* papa *m*

pop off *vi (die)* calancher, passer l'arme à gauche

Pope [pəʊp] *n Hum* **is the Pope Catholic?** à ton avis?

> Il s'agit d'une expression utilisée lorsque quelqu'un vient de poser une question que l'on juge superflue tant il paraît évident que la réponse ne peut être qu'affirmative.

popper ['pɒpə(r)] *n (drug)* popper *m*, nitrate *m* d'amyle□

pops [pɒps] = **pop**[2]

pork|!| [pɔ:k] **1** *n Hum* **pork (sword)** *(penis)* queue *f*, bite *f*
2 *vt (have sex with)* tringler, troncher

porker ['pɔ:kə(r)] *n (man)* gros lard *m*; *(woman)* grosse vache *f*

porky ['pɔ:kɪ] **1** *n Br* **porky (pie)** *(rhyming slang* **lie**) mensonge□ *m*, craque *f*
2 *adj (fat)* gros□, mastard

posse ['pɒsɪ] *n* (**a**) *(group of friends)* bande *f*; **he's out with the posse** il est sorti avec ses potes *ou* avec sa bande (**b**) *Noir Am (entourage)* clique *f* (**c**) *Noir Am (criminal gang)* gang *m*

pot [pɒt] *n* (**a**) *(marijuana)* herbe *f*, beu *f* (**b**) **to go to pot** *(deteriorate)* aller à vau-l'eau (**c**) **he hasn't got a pot to piss in** |!| il est complètement fauché
▸ *voir aussi* **shit**

pothead ['pɒthed] *n* **to be a pothead** fumer beaucoup de cannabis□

potted ['pɒtɪd] *adj Am (drunk)* pété, fait, bourré, rond

potty ['pɒtɪ] *adj Br* dingue, cinglé, timbré; **to be potty about sb/sth** être dingue de qn/qch

pox [pɒks] *n Br* **the pox** *(syphilis)* la vérole□

poxy ['pɒksɪ] *adj Br (worthless)* minable; **he only gave me a poxy five pounds for it** il me l'a acheté cinq malheureuses livres

prang [præŋ] Br 1 n accrochage ᵒ m; **to have a prang** avoir un accrochage 2 vt (vehicle) bigorner

prat [præt] n crétin(e) m,f, courge f, andouille f, cruche f

prat about, prat around vi Br (act foolishly) faire l'idiot; (waste time) glander, glandouiller

preggers ['pregəz] adj en cloque

preppy ['prepi] Am 1 n ≃ BCBG mf 2 adj ≃ BCBG

pressie, prezzie ['prezi] n Br (abrév **present**) cadeau ᵒ m

priceless ['praɪslɪs] adj (amusing) impayable, crevant

prick ⚠⚠ [prɪk] n (a) (penis) bite f, queue f, pine f; **to feel like a spare prick (at a wedding)** tenir la chandelle (b) (man) tête f de nœud, connard m, blaireau m

pricktease ⚠⚠ ['prɪktiːz], **prickteaser** ⚠⚠ ['prɪktiːzə(r)] n allumeuse f

private parts ['praɪvɪt'pɑːts], **privates** ['praɪvɪts] npl parties fpl génitales ᵒ

pro [prəʊ] n (a) (abrév **prostitute**) pute f (b) (abrév **professional**) pro mf

prob [prɒb] n (abrév **problem**) problème ᵒ m, blème m; Br **no probs!** pas de problèmes!

Prod [prɒd] n Br (abrév **Protestant**) protestant(e) ᵒ m,f

profile ['prəʊfaɪl] vi Noir Am (show off) frimer, crâner

pronto ['prɒntəʊ] adv illico (presto), pronto

psycho ['saɪkəʊ] n (abrév **psychopath**) psychopathe ᵒ mf, cinglé(e) m,f

pub-crawl ['pʌbkrɔːl] n Br tournée f des bars ᵒ; **to go on a pub-crawl** faire la tournée des bars

pubes [pjuːbz] npl (abrév **pubic hairs**) poils mpl pubiens ᵒ

puff [pʌf] n Br (marijuana) herbe f, beu f; (cannabis) shit m, hasch m

puke [pjuːk] 1 n dégueulis m 2 vi dégueuler, gerber

pukka ['pʌkə] adj Br (a) (excellent) génial, super (b) (genuine) réglo, régulier ᵒ

pull [pʊl] 1 n (a) **to be on the pull** chercher à lever une nana/un mec (b) (influence) piston m; **to have a lot of pull** avoir le bras long 2 vt (sexual partner) lever, emballer 3 vi (find sexual partner) faire une touche ▶ voir aussi **fast, plug**

pull off ⚠⚠ vt sép **to pull sb off** branler qn; **to pull oneself off** se branler

pulling power ['pʊlɪŋpaʊə(r)] n Br pouvoir m de séduction ᵒ; **he thinks his new sports car will do wonders for his pulling power** il croit que sa nouvelle voiture de sport l'aidera à lever les nanas

pump [pʌmp] vt **to pump iron** faire de la gonflette ▶ voir aussi **lead**

pumped [pʌmpt] adj Am (excited) surexcité; (enthusiastic) emballé

punch out [pʌntʃ] vt sép Br **to punch sb's lights out**, Am **to punch sb out** amocher qn, arranger le portrait à qn

punk [pʌŋk] n Am (worthless person) ordure f

punter ['pʌntə(r)] n Br (a) (gambler) parieur(euse) ᵒ m,f (b) (consumer, customer) client(e) ᵒ m,f (c) (prostitute's client) micheton m

push [pʊʃ] 1 n Br **to give sb the push** (employee) virer qn; (boyfriend, girlfriend) plaquer qn; **to get the push** (of employee) se faire virer; (of boyfriend, girlfriend) se faire plaquer 2 vt (a) (drugs) dealer (b) **to be pushing forty/fifty** friser la quarantaine/cinquantaine (c) **it'll be pushing it to finish by five** ça va faire un peu juste pour finir à cinq heures; **that's pushing it a bit** c'est un peu exagéré; **don't push your luck!**

fais gaffe à toi!

▸ *voir aussi* **daisy**

push off *vi Br* mettre les bouts, se casser, se tirer; **push off!** tire-toi!, casse-toi!

pusher ['pʊʃə(r)] *n (drug dealer)* dealer *m*

pushover ['pʊʃəʊvə(r)] *n* **(a)** *(person)* poire *f*, pigeon *m* **(b)** *(thing)* jeu *m* d'enfant; **the German exam was a pushover** l'examen d'allemand était hyper fastoche

puss [pʊs] *n* **(a)** *(cat)* minou *m*, minet *m* **(b)** *(face)* binette *f*, frimousse *f*

pussy ['pʊsɪ] *n* **(a)** *(cat)* minou *m*, minet *m*

(b) [!!] *(woman's genitals)* chatte *f*, chagatte *f*, cramouille *f*

(c) [!!] *(women)* nanas *fpl*, cuisse *f*; *(sex)* baise *f*; **they're out looking for pussy** ils cherchent des meufs; **he hasn't had any pussy for weeks** ça fait des semaines qu'il a pas baisé *ou* qu'il a pas tiré un coup

(d) [!] *(weak, cowardly man)* lavette *f*

pussy-whipped [!] ['pʊsɪwɪpt] *adj* dominé par sa femme□; **he's totally pussy-whipped** c'est sa femme qui porte la culotte

put [pʊt] *vt Br* **put it there!**, *Am* **put 'er there!** *(shake hands)* serrons-nous la pince!

put about *vt sép Br* **(a) to put a rumour about** répandre une rumeur□; **to put it about that...** répandre la rumeur comme quoi... **(b) to put it** *or* **oneself about** *(be promiscuous)* coucher à droite à gauche

put away *vt sép* **(a) to put sb away** *(in prison)* mettre qn à l'ombre; *(in psychiatric hospital)* interner qn□, enfermer qn chez les fous **(b) to put sth away** *(food, drink)* s'envoyer qch; **he can really put it away!** *(food)* il a un sacré appétit!; *(drink)* qu'est-ce qu'il descend!

put on *vt sép* **(a) to put sb on** *(tease)* faire marcher qn **(b) to put it on** *(pretend)* faire du cinéma *ou* du chiqué

put out *vi Am (of woman)* accepter de coucher *(for* avec); **did she put out?** est-ce qu'elle a bien voulu coucher?; **she'd put out for anybody** elle coucherait avec le premier venu

put over *vt sép* **to put one over on sb** gruger qn

putrid ['pju:trɪd] *adj (worthless)* pourri

putz [pʌts] *n Am* andouille *f*, truffe *f*

putz around *vi Am* **(a)** *(act foolishly)* faire l'idiot, faire l'imbécile **(b)** *(waste time)* glander, glandouiller

Q

q.t. [kju:'ti:] *n* **on the q.t.** en douce, en loucedé

quack [kwæk] *n Br Péj (doctor)* toubib *m*

queen [kwi:n] *n* **(a)** *(effeminate homosexual)* folle *f* **(b)** *Injurieux (any homosexual man)* pédé *m*, tantouze *f*, tapette *f*

> Ce terme perd son caractère injurieux lorsqu'il est utilisé par des homosexuels. Par ailleurs, lorsqu'il désigne un individu efféminé (sens (a)), il n'est jamais véritablement injurieux. Il convient toutefois de l'utiliser avec circonspection.

queer [kwɪə(r)] **1** *n Injurieux (homosexual)* pédé *m*, pédale *f*, tantouze *f*
2 *adj* **(a)** *Injurieux (homosexual)* pédé, homo **(b)** *Br* **to be in queer street** être dans la mouise *ou* dans la panade
▸ *voir aussi* **act, fish**

> Ce terme perd son caractère injurieux quand il est utilisé par des homosexuels.

queer-basher ['kwɪəbæʃə(r)] *n* = individu qui se livre à des violences à l'encontre d'homosexuels

queer-bashing ['kwɪəbæʃɪŋ] *n* = violences à l'encontre d'homosexuels

quickie ['kwɪkɪ] **1** *n* **to have a quickie** *(drink)* boire un coup en vitesse; *(sex)* tirer un coup vite fait
2 *adj* **quickie divorce** divorce *m* express

quid [kwɪd] *n Br (pound sterling)* livre *f* sterling □; **to be quids in** être à l'aise, avoir du fric

quim !! [kwɪm] *n* chatte *f*, chagatte *f*, con *m*

R

rabbit ['ræbɪt] *n* (**a**) *Péj* **rabbit food** *(salad)* verdure *f*; *Br* **rabbit hutch** *(accommodation)* cage *f* à lapins (**b**) **to fuck like rabbits** ⚠️⚠️ baiser comme des lapins

rabbit on *vi Br* bavasser (**about** à propos de); **what's he rabbiting on about?** qu'est-ce qu'il bave?

rack [ræk] *n Am* **to hit the rack** *(go to bed)* se pieuter, se bâcher

rack back *vt sép Am* **to rack sb back** passer un savon à qn, remonter les bretelles à qn

racket ['rækɪt] *n* (**a**) *(noise)* boucan *m*, barouf *m*; **to make a racket** faire du boucan *ou* du barouf (**b**) *(criminal activity)* activité *f* criminelle◻; **protection racket** racket *m*; **drugs racket** trafic *m* de drogue

rad [ræd] *adj (abrév* **radical)** super, génial, géant

radical ['rædɪkəl] *adj* super, génial, géant

rag [ræg] *n* (**a**) *(newspaper)* torchon *m* (**b**) *Br* **to lose one's** *or* **the rag** piquer une crise, péter les plombs (**c**) **to be on the rag** ⚠️ avoir ses ragnagnas (**d**) **to feel like a wet rag** *or Am* **a dish rag** se sentir ramollo (**e**) *Am* **rags** *(clothes)* fringues *fpl*
▶ *voir aussi* **chew**

raghead ['ræghed] *n Am Injurieux* raton *m*, bicot *m*

ragtop ['rægtɒp] *n Am* décapotable◻ *f*

rake in [reɪk] *vt sép* **to rake sth in** *(money)* ramasser qch à la pelle; **he must be raking it in!** il doit s'en mettre plein les poches!

rake-off ['reɪkɒf] *n* commission *f* illicite◻, ristourne *f*

ralph [rælf] *vi* gerber, dégueuler

randy ['rændɪ] *adj* excité *(sexuellement)*

rank [ræŋk] *adj Br (worthless)* merdique

rank on *vt insep Am* **to rank on sb** agonir qn d'injures, traiter qn de tous les noms

rap [ræp] *n* (**a**) *(blame)* **to take the rap (for sth)** écoper (pour qch); *Am* **to beat the rap** échapper à la condamnation◻, être acquitté◻; *Am* **rap sheet** casier *m* judiciaire◻ (**b**) *Am (speech)* **don't give me that rap!** raconte pas n'importe quoi!; **he was laying down some rap about the new model** il était en train de faire un baratin sur le nouveau modèle
2 *vt Am (criticize)* éreinter, descendre
3 *vi Noir Am (talk)* causer; **what's he rapping about now?** qu'est-ce qu'il raconte maintenant?
▶ *voir aussi* **bum**

rat [ræt] *n* (**a**) *(person)* salaud *m*, salopard *m*, ordure *f* (**b**) *Am* **I don't give a rat's ass** ⚠️ je m'en fous pas mal, je m'en balance
▶ *voir aussi* **frat**

rat on *vt insép* **to rat on sb** balancer qn, moucharder qn

rat out *vt sép Am* **to rat sb out** balancer qn, moucharder qn

rat-arsed ⚠️ ['rætɑːst] *adj Br* bourré comme un coing, pété à mort, plein comme une barrique

ratbag ['rætbæg] *n Br* salaud *m*, salopard *m*, ordure *f*

ratfink ['rætfɪŋk] n Am salaud m, salopard m, ordure f

ratty ['rætɪ] adj râleur, rouspéteur

raunchy ['rɔ:ntʃɪ] adj sexy

raver ['reɪvə(r)] n Br (**a**) (socially active person) noceur(euse) m,f (**b**) (person who attends raves) raver mf

rave-up ['reɪvʌp] n Br boum f

razz [ræz] vt Am (jeer at) chambrer

razzle ['ræzəl] n Br **to go on the razzle** faire la bringue ou la nouba

readies ['redɪz] npl Br liquide m

real [rɪəl] **1** adj **is he for real?** il est sérieux?; **get real!** arrête de rêver!, redescends sur terre!
  2 adv Am (very) vachement; **you were real lucky** t'as eu une sacré veine; **it's real hot** il fait vachement chaud; **we had a real good time** on s'est vachement bien amusés

ream out [ri:m] vt sép Am **to ream sb out** (scold) passer un savon à qn, remonter les bretelles à qn

rear end [rɪər'end] n (buttocks) arrière-train m

redneck ['rednek] n Am plouc mf, bouseux(euse) m,f (du Sud des États-Unis); **a redneck politician/cop** un homme politique/flic tout ce qu'il y a de plus réactionnaire

reefer ['ri:fə(r)] n (cannabis cigarette) joint m, stick m

ref [ref] n (abrév **referee**) arbitre □ m

rent boy ['rentbɔɪ] n Br jeune prostitué m homosexuel □

rents [rents] npl Am (abrév **parents**) vieux mpl, renps mpl

repo ['ri:pəʊ] **1** n (abrév **repossession**) **repo man** huissier □ m (chargé par une société de saisir des biens non payés)
  2 vt (abrév **repossess**) saisir □

result [rɪ'zʌlt] n Br **to get a result** (in sport) gagner □, l'emporter □; **he had a result last night, he pulled some gorgeous bird** il a fait fort hier soir, il a levé une super nana; **a 20% pay rise? what a result!** 20% d'augmentation? tu as fait fort!

retard ['ri:tɑ:d] n crétin(e) m,f, débile mf mental(e)

Richard ⚠ ['rɪtʃəd] npr Br (rhyming slang **Richard the Third** = **turd**) étron m

ride [raɪd] **1** n (**a**) ⚠⚠ (sexual partner) **to be a good ride** être un bon coup (**b**) Noir Am (car) bagnole f, caisse f, tire f
  2 ⚠⚠ vt (have sex with) (of man) baiser, tringler, troncher, sauter; (of woman) baiser avec, s'envoyer

rig [rɪg] n (large truck) gros-cul m

right [raɪt] **1** adj (**a**) **too right!** tu l'as dit, bouffi! (**b**) Am **a right guy** un chic type
  2 adv (**a**) Br (for emphasis) vachement, drôlement; **I was right angry** j'étais vachement en colère; **it's a right cold day** ça pince drôlement aujourd'hui, il fait drôlement frisquet aujourd'hui

---

Rhyming slang

Il s'agit d'un procédé argotique complexe consistant à remplacer un mot par une expression dont le dernier terme rime avec le mot en question; bien souvent n'est prononcé que le premier terme de l'expression, à savoir celui qui ne rime pas avec le mot remplacé. Exemple: kids = dustbin lids = dustbins; head = loaf of bread = loaf. À l'origine ce type d'argot était pratiqué par les Cockneys (les habitants de l'est de Londres) mais certains termes sont maintenant passés dans le langage courant et sont connus de la plupart des Britanniques (c'est le cas de la grande majorité des termes figurant dans ce dictionnaire).

(b) **right on!** bravo!
▶ voir aussi **yeah**

righteous ['raɪtʃəs] adj Noir Am (a) (genuine) authentique▯ (b) (excellent) génial, super, géant

right-on ['raɪt'ɒn] adj (socially aware) politiquement correct

Riley ['raɪlɪ] npr **to lead the life of Riley** se la couler douce, avoir la belle vie

ringpiece‼ ['rɪŋpiːs] n rondelle f, troufignon m

rinky-dink ['rɪŋkɪdɪŋk] adj Am (goods) merdique; (business, businessman) minable

riot ['raɪət] n (a) (amusing person, thing) **he's a complete riot** il est vraiment tordant, il est impayable; **the party was a riot** la soirée était vraiment démente (b) **to read sb the riot act** souffler dans les bronches à qn, passer un savon à qn

rip [rɪp] vi Br **to let rip** (behave unrestrainedly) se déchaîner; (fart) larguer une caisse; **to let rip at sb** se mettre en pétard contre qn

rip off vt sép **to rip sb off** (cheat, swindle) arnaquer qn; **to rip sth off** (steal) piquer qch, faucher qch

rip-off ['rɪpɒf] n arnaque f; **what a rip-off!** quelle arnaque!
▶ voir aussi **merchant**

ripped [rɪpt] adj (drunk) bourré, beurré, pété; (on drugs) raide, défoncé; Br **ripped to the tits**! (drunk) bourré comme un coing, plein comme une barrique, rond comme une queue de pelle; (on drugs) complètement raide ou défoncé

rise [raɪz] n **to take** or **get a rise out of sb** faire enrager qn

ritzy ['rɪtsɪ] adj tape-à-l'œil, clinquant

river ['rɪvə(r)] n Am **to send sb up the river** (to prison) mettre qn à l'ombre ou en taule ou en cabane

roach [rəʊtʃ] n (a) (of cannabis cigarette) mégot▯ m (d'une cigarette de marijuana) (b) (abrév **cockroach**) cafard▯ m

roadhog ['rəʊdhɒg] n (man) chauffard m, écraseur m; (woman) écraseuse f

roasting ['rəʊstɪŋ] n **to give sb a roasting** souffler dans les bronches à qn, passer un savon à qn; **to get a roasting** se faire souffler dans les bronches, prendre ou se faire passer un savon

robbery ['rɒbərɪ] n **it's** Br **daylight** or Am **highway robbery** c'est de l'arnaque

rock [rɒk] 1 n (a) (diamond) diam m (b) (crack cocaine) crack m; Br (cocaine) coco f, neige f (c) **rocks**! (testicles) couilles fpl, boules fpl; **to get one's rocks off** (have sex) baiser, s'envoyer en l'air; (have orgasm) jouir, prendre son pied, (enjoy oneself) s'éclater, prendre son pied; **to get one's rocks off doing sth** s'éclater ou prendre son pied en faisant qch (d) **on the rocks** (drink) aux glaçons▯; (relationship, marriage, business) en train de battre de l'aile (e) Am **to have rocks in one's head** être bête comme ses pieds
2 vi **the party was really rocking** il y avait une ambiance d'enfer à la soirée

rocker ['rɒkə(r)] n **to be off one's rocker** (mad) être cinglé, avoir une araignée dans le plafond; **to go off one's rocker** (go mad) perdre la boule, devenir dingue ou cinglé; (lose one's temper) péter les plombs, péter une durite, piquer une crise

rocket ['rɒkɪt] n Br (telling-off) engueulade f; **to give sb a rocket** remonter les bretelles à qn, passer un savon à qn, engueuler qn; **to get a rocket** se faire remonter les bretelles, prendre ou se faire passer un savon, se faire engueuler

rockhouse ['rɒkhaʊs] n Am = lieu où l'on achète, vend et consomme du crack

rocky ['rɒkɪ] n Br (abrév **Moroccan**) (cannabis) marocain m

rod [!] [rɒd] n (penis) pine f, bite f, tige f

roger [!] ['rɒdʒə(r)] vt Br baiser, sauter, sabrer

roid [rɔɪd] n Am (abrév **steroid**) roids stéroïdes □ mpl; **roid rage** = état d'agressivité extrême causé par l'absorption de stéroïdes

L'expression "roid rage" est un jeu de mots sur l'expression "road rage", qui désigne l'état d'agressivité irrationnel de certains automobilistes.

roll [rəʊl] **1** n **to have a roll in the hay** faire une partie de jambes en l'air
2 vt (**a**) **to roll one's own** se rouler ses cigarettes □ (**b**) Am (rob) faire les poches à (une personne ivre ou endormie)
3 vi **to be rolling in it** (very rich) être plein aux as

Roller ['rəʊlə(r)] n Br (abrév **Rolls Royce**) Rolls Royce f

rollick ['rɒlɪk] vt Br engueuler, remonter les bretelles à

rollicking ['rɒlɪkɪŋ] n Br **to give sb a rollicking** engueuler qn, remonter les bretelles à qn; **to get a rollicking** se faire engueuler, se faire remonter les bretelles

Rolls [rəʊlz] = **Roller**

roll-up ['rəʊlʌp], **roll-your-own** ['rəʊljɔːr'əʊn] n Br cigarette f roulée à la main □

rook [rʊk] vt Am (cheat) arnaquer

roomie ['ruːmɪ] n Am (abrév **roommate**) colocataire mf, coloc mf

rot [rɒt] n Br (nonsense) foutaises fpl; **don't talk rot!** arrête de raconter n'importe quoi!

rotgut ['rɒtgʌt] n tord-boyaux m, gnôle f

rotten ['rɒtən] adj (**a**) (worthless) nul, pourri, merdique; **he's a rotten cook** il est vraiment complètement nul comme cuisinier; **the weather was really rotten** le temps était vraiment pourri; **we had a rotten time** on a passé un moment dégueulasse
(**b**) (unkind) vache, dégueulasse; **to be rotten to sb** être vache ou dégueulasse avec qn; **that was a rotten thing to say/do** c'est vraiment salaud ou vache ou dégueulasse d'avoir dit/fait ça
(**c**) **to feel rotten** (ill) se sentir patraque; (guilty) se sentir coupable □
▸ voir aussi **something**

rotter ['rɒtə(r)] n Br pourriture f, ordure f

rough [rʌf] **1** n **she likes a bit of rough** (person) elle aime s'envoyer un prolo de temps en temps; (sexual activity) elle aime qu'on la malmène un peu pendant l'amour
2 adj (**a**) Br (ill) **to feel/look rough** ne pas être/ne pas avoir l'air dans son assiette
(**b**) **rough trade** (male prostitute) = jeune prostitué homosexuel à tendances violentes; (working-class male homosexual) homosexuel m prolo

rough up vt sép **to rough sb up** tabasser qn

royal ['rɔɪəl] adj (for emphasis) sombre, de première; **her whining gives me a royal pain** elle me fait vraiment chier avec ses jérémiades; **he's a royal idiot** c'est un sombre crétin ou un crétin de première

royally ['rɔɪəlɪ] adv (for emphasis) dans les grandes largeurs; **they messed up royally** ils se sont plantés dans les grandes largeurs, ils se sont plantés, et pas qu'un peu

rozzer ['rɒzə(r)] n Br flic m, poulet m

rub out [rʌb] vt sép Am **to rub sb out** zigouiller ou buter ou refroidir qn

rubber ['rʌbə(r)] n (**a**) (condom) capote f (anglaise) (**b**) **rubber** Br **cheque** or Am **check** chèque m en bois

rubberneck ['rʌbənek] Péj **1** n (**a**) (at scene of accident) curieux(euse) m,f (qui s'attarde sur le lieu d'un accident) (**b**) (tourist) touriste⁓ mf (qui assiste à des visites guidées)
 2 vi (**a**) (at scene of accident) = faire le curieux sur le lieu d'un accident (**b**) (of tourist) faire le touriste⁓ (en assistant à des visites guidées)

rubbish ['rʌbɪʃ] Br **1** n (nonsense) foutaises fpl; **don't talk rubbish!** arrête de raconter n'importe quoi!; **his book's a load of rubbish** son livre ne vaut pas un clou, son livre est vraiment nul
 2 exclam n'importe quoi!
 3 adj (worthless) nul, pourri; **that was a rubbish film/meal** le film/repas était nul
 4 vt (criticize) éreinter

rube [ru:b] n Am plouc mf, péquenaud(e) m,f

rub-out ['rʌbaʊt] n Am assassinat⁓ m

ruby ['ru:bɪ] n Br (rhyming slang **Ruby Murray** = curry) curry⁓ m

ruck [rʌk] n Br (fight) baston m ou f; **there was a bit of a ruck after the match** il y a eu du grabuge ou du baston après le match

ruddy ['rʌdɪ] Br **1** adj (for emphasis) sacré; **you ruddy idiot!** espèce d'andouille!; **he's a ruddy liar!** c'est un sacré menteur!
 2 adv (for emphasis) sacrément, vachement, drôlement; **you look ruddy ridiculous** t'as l'air vraiment ridicule

rug [rʌg] n (hairpiece) moumoute f

rug-rat ['rʌgræt] n (child) môme mf, chiard m

rumble ['rʌmbəl] **1** n (fight) baston m ou f
 2 vt Br (see through) (scheme, plot) découvrir⁓, flairer; (person) démasquer⁓, voir venir
 3 vi (fight) se friter, se castagner

rum-dum ['rʌmdʌm] n Am (**a**) (idiot) abruti(e) m,f, crétin(e) m,f (**b**) (drunken tramp) **he's a rum-dum** c'est un clodo et un poivrot

rump [rʌmp] n (buttocks) croupe f

rumpy-pumpy ['rʌmpɪ'pʌmpɪ] n Br Hum zig-zig m, crac-crac m; **to have a bit of rumpy-pumpy** faire une partie de jambes en l'air, faire zig-zig ou craccrac

runner ['rʌnə(r)] n Br **to do a runner** (run away) décaniller, se débiner, mettre les bouts; (leave without paying) partir sans payer⁓

running jump ['rʌnɪŋ'dʒʌmp] n Br **take a running jump!**, Am **take a running jump at the moon!** va voir ailleurs si j'y suis!

runs [rʌnz] npl (diarrhoea) **the runs** la courante

rush [rʌʃ] n (after taking drugs) flash m; **I got a real rush from that coffee** ce café m'a donné un coup de fouet; **to get a head rush** avoir la tête qui tourne
 ▶ voir aussi **bum**

rustbucket ['rʌstbʌkɪt] n (car) poubelle f, tas m de ferraille

S

sack [sæk] 1 *n* (**a**) *(dismissal)* **to get the sack** se faire virer *ou* sacquer; **to give sb the sack** virer qn, sacquer qn (**b**) *(bed)* pieu *m*, plumard *m*; **to hit the sack** se pieuter, se pagnoter; **to be good/no good in the sack** être/ne pas être une affaire au pieu (**c**) *Am* **sad sack** *(person)* raté(e) *m,f*
2 *vt (dismiss)* virer, sacquer

sack out *vi Am* se pieuter, se bâcher, se pager

sad [sæd] *adj Péj (pitiful)* pitoyable ⁻; **he's still living with his parents, how sad can you get?** il habite toujours chez ses parents, il est grave *ou* il craint!; **what a sad bastard!** ⚠ quel branleur!; **he's got really sad taste in music** il écoute de la musique vraiment craignos
► *voir aussi* **sack**

salami [sə'lɑːmɪ] *n Hum* **to play hide the salami** *(have sex)* s'envoyer en l'air

sambo ['sæmbəʊ] *n Br Injurieux (black man)* nègre *m*, bamboula *m*; *(black woman)* négresse *f*

sandwich ['sændwɪtʃ] *n* (**a**) *Br Hum* **to be one sandwich short of a picnic** ne pas être net (**b**) **knuckle sandwich** coup *m* de poing dans la gueule, bourre-pif *m*; **to give sb a knuckle sandwich** mettre son poing dans la gueule à qn (**c**) *Br Hum* **to give sb a tongue sandwich** rouler une pelle *ou* un patin à qn

sap [sæp] *n (person)* poire *f*

sarky ['sɑːkɪ] *adj Br (abrév* **sarcastic)** sarcastique ⁻

sarnie ['sɑːnɪ] *n Br (abrév* **sandwich)** casse-dalle *m*

Saturday night special ['sætədɪnaɪt'speʃəl] *n Am (gun)* flingue *m*, feu *m (bon marché et de qualité médiocre, que l'on peut se procurer facilement)*

sauce [sɔːs] *n* (**a**) *Br (cheek)* insolence ⁻ *f*; **that's enough of your sauce!** arrête de faire l'insolent! (**b**) *(alcohol)* alcool ⁻ *m*, bibine *f*; **to hit the sauce** se mettre à picoler; **to be on the sauce** s'être mis à picoler; **to be off the sauce** être au régime sec

sauced [sɔːst] *adj (drunk)* beurré, bourré, pété

sausage ['sɒsɪdʒ] *n Br* (**a**) *not a sausage (nothing)* que dalle; **you silly sausage!** espèce de nouille! (**b**) **sausage dog** saucisse *f* à pattes (**c**) *Hum (penis)* chipolata *f*

savvy ['sævɪ] *n* jugeote *f*

sawbuck ['sɔːbʌk] *n Am* billet *m* de dix dollars ⁻

sawed-off [sɔːd'ɒf] *adj Am Hum (person)* petit ⁻

scab [skæb] 1 *n (strikebreaker)* jaune *m (non-gréviste)*
2 *vi Am (work as a strikebreaker)* briser une grève ⁻

scabby ['skæbɪ] *adj Br* (**a**) *(worthless)* merdique; **you can keep your scabby car!** tu peux te la garder, ta caisse de merde! (**b**) *(shabby)* merdique, craignos; *(dirty)* cradingue, crado, dégueu

scads [skædz] *npl Am* **scads (of)** un paquet (de), des tas (de), une tapée (de)

scag [skæg] *n* (**a**) *(heroin)* héro *f*, blanche *f* (**b**) *Am (ugly woman)* boudin *m*, cageot *m*

scam [skæm] 1 *n* arnaque *f*

2 *vt* arnaquer

scank [skæŋk] = **skank**

scanky ['skæŋkɪ] = **skanky**

scants [skænts] *npl Br* (men's) calcif *m*; (women's) petite culotte *f*

scaredy cat ['skeədɪkæt] *n* poule *f* mouillée

scarf [skɑːf] *vt Am* (eat) bouffer, boulotter

scarper ['skɑːpə(r)] *vi Br* (go away) se casser, se barrer, trisser, se tirer

scat [skæt] *vi* (go away) se casser, se barrer, se tirer, trisser; **scat!** casse-toi!, dégage!

scene [siːn] *n* **it's not my scene** c'est pas mon truc

schiz [skɪts] *Am* = **schizo**

schizo ['skɪtsəʊ] (abrév **schizophrenic**)
1 *n* cinglé(e) *m,f*, dingue *mf*
2 *adj* cinglé, timbré, toqué

schlemiel [ʃləˈmiːl] *n Am* minable *mf*

schlep [ʃlep] **1** *n* (a) (person) lourdaud(e) *m,f* (b) (journey) trotte *f*; **it's a bit of a schlep to the supermarket** ça fait une trotte jusqu'au supermarché
2 *vt* (carry) trimballer
3 *vi* (walk) crapahuter; **to schlep home** rentrer chez soi à pinces; **I had to schlep to the grocery store** il a fallu que je crapahute jusqu'à l'épicerie

schlep around 1 *vt insép* **to schlep around the town** crapahuter en ville
2 *vi Am* crapahuter

schlock [ʃlɒk] *Am* **1** *n* (worthless things) saloperies *fpl*, daube *f*
2 *adj* (worthless) qui ne vaut pas un clou, nul; **schlock jewelry** bijoux *mpl* en toc

schlong [!] [ʃlɒŋ] *n Am* queue *f*, bite *f*, pine *f*

schmaltz [ʃmɔːlts] *n* guimauve *f*

schmaltzy ['ʃmɔːltsɪ] *adj* à la guimauve

schmo [ʃməʊ] *n Am* (unlucky person) guignard(e) *m,f*; (stupid person) nul (nulle) *m,f*
▶ *voir aussi* **Joe**

schmooze [ʃmuːz] *vi Am* bavarder, jaspiner, jacasser

schmuck [ʃmʌk] *n Am* andouille *f*, courge *f*

schnook [ʃnʊk] *n Am* poire *f*, pigeon *m*

schnozz [ʃnɒz], **schnozzle** ['ʃnɒzəl] *n* blaire *m*, tarin *m*

schtuk [ʃtʊk] *n Br* **to be in schtuk** être dans le pétrin, être dans la panade

schtum [ʃtʊm] *adj Br* **to keep schtum** ne pas piper mot

schwing [ʃwɪŋ] *exclam* putain, la supernana!

> Il s'agit d'une onomatopée censée reproduire le son que produirait une érection. Ce terme a été popularisé par le film américain *Wayne's World*.

sci-fi ['saɪfaɪ] (abrév **science-fiction**) **1** *n* SF *f*
2 *adj* de SF

scoff [skɒf] **1** *n Br* (food) boutте *f*, graille *f*
2 *vt* (eat) bouffer, boulotter

scooby ['skuːbɪ] *n Br* (rhyming slang **Scooby Doo** = **clue**) **he hasn't got a scooby** (is incompetent) il est vraiment nul; (doesn't suspect) il se doute de rien; (doesn't know) il en a pas la moindre idée

> Ce terme vient du dessin animé américain *Scooby Doo*.

scoot [skuːt] *vi* se sauver, filer; **scoot!** du vent!, file!

scoot away, scoot off *vi* se sauver, filer

scope [skəʊp] *vt Am* (a) (look at) mater, reluquer; **he's at the beach scoping the babes** il est à la plage en train de mater les nanas (b) (see) voir □; **did you scope that ring he was wearing?** t'as vu un peu la bague qu'il avait au doigt?

scope out *vt sép* = **scope**

scorcher ['skɔːtʃə(r)] *n* journée *f* de forte chaleur □; **today's been a scorcher** il en a fait un plat aujourd'hui

score [skɔ:(r)] **1** n **to know the score** savoir à quoi s'en tenir ▫; **what's the score?** qu'est-ce qui se passe?
  2 vt (drugs) acheter ▫
  3 vi **(a)** (buy drugs) acheter de la drogue ▫ **(b)** (find sexual partner) faire une touche; **to score with sb** emballer qn

Scouse [skaʊs] Br **1** n (person) = natif de la ville de Liverpool; (dialect) = dialecte de la ville de Liverpool
  2 adj de Liverpool

Scouser ['skaʊsə(r)] n Br = natif de la ville de Liverpool

scram [skræm] vi se casser, se barrer, trisser, se tirer; **scram!** du vent!, file!

scran [skræn] n Br bouffe f, graille f

scrap [skræp] **1** n (fight) baston m ou f; **to get into a scrap** se bagarrer; **to get into a scrap with sb** se friter ou se castagner avec qn
  2 vi (fight) se friter, se castagner

scratch [skrætʃ] n Am (money) fric m, pognon m, flouze m, oseille f

scream [skri:m] n **he's a scream** il est impayable; **it was a scream** c'était tordant, c'était à se tordre de rire; **the book/film's a scream** le livre/le film est tordant

screw [skru:] **1** n **(a)** [!] (sexual intercourse) baise f; **to have a screw** baiser, tirer un coup, s'envoyer en l'air; **to be a good screw** (of person) être un bon coup
  (b) to have a screw loose (be mad) avoir une case de vide
  (c) Br (prison officer) maton(onne) m,f
  (d) Br (salary) salaire ▫ m; **to be on a good screw** avoir un super bon salaire
  2 vt **(a)** [!] (have sex with) (of man) baiser, troncher, tringler, limer; (of woman) baiser avec, s'envoyer
  (b) [!] (for emphasis) **screw you!** va te faire foutre!; **screw him!** qu'il aille se faire foutre!; **go and screw yourself!** va te faire foutre!
  (c) (cheat) arnaquer

  (d) Am **to screw the pooch** (blunder) faire une gaffe ou une boulette
  3 [!] vi (have sex) baiser, s'envoyer en l'air

screw around 1 vt sép **to screw sb around** (treat badly) se foutre de la gueule de qn; (waste time of) faire perdre son temps à qn ▫
  2 vi **(a)** (act foolishly) faire l'andouille; (waste time) glander, glandouiller **(b)** [!] (be promiscuous) coucher à droite à gauche

screw over vt sép **to screw sb over** arnaquer qn, refaire qn

screw up 1 vt sép (person) rendre cinglé; (plan, situation) faire foirer, foutre en l'air; **she's totally screwed up** elle est complètement à côté de ses pompes; **you've screwed everything up** tu as tout foutu en l'air
  2 vi foirer, merder

screwball ['skru:bɔ:l] **1** n allumé(e) m,f, barge mf
  2 adj allumé, barge

screwed [skru:d] adj (in trouble) **to be screwed** être foutu

screw-loose ['skru:lu:s] adj Am loufoque, loufedingue

screw-up ['skru:ʌp] n Am (bungler) manche m; (misfit) paumé(e) m,f

screwy ['skru:ɪ] adj Am dingue, cinglé, toqué

scrote [!] [skrəʊt] n Br (abrév **scrotum**) (person) gland m, taré m

scrubber ['skrʌbə(r)] n Br (woman) roulure f, salope f

scrummy ['skrʌmɪ] adj Br délicieux ▫, super bon

scum [skʌm] n **(a)** (people) ordures fpl; **he's scum** c'est une ordure; **he's the scum of the earth** c'est le dernier des derniers; **she treats him like scum** elle le traite comme de la merde **(b)** [!] Am (semen) foutre m

scumbag ['skʌmbæg] n **(a)** (person) ordure f, raclure f (**b**) ! Am (condom) capote f (anglaise)

scumbucket ['skʌmbʌkɪt] n Am (person) ordure f, raclure f

scuzzy ['skʌzɪ] adj Am dégueulasse, cradingue

search [sɜːtʃ] vt **search me!** (I don't know) j'en ai pas la moindre idée!

sec [sek] n (abrév **second**) seconde □ f, instant □ m; **half a sec!** une seconde!; **wait a sec!** attends une seconde!

seeing-to ['siːɪŋtuː] n Br **to give sb a good seeing-to** (beat up) tabasser qn; (have sex with) faire passer qn à la casserole

see ya ['siːjə] exclam salut!, à pluss!

serious ['sɪərɪəs] adj (for emphasis) **she makes serious money** elle gagne un fric fou; **we did some serious drinking last night** on a picolé hier soir, et on n'a pas fait semblant; **that is one serious computer** c'est pas de la gnognotte, cet ordinateur

seriously ['sɪərɪəslɪ] adv (for emphasis) sérieusement, vachement; **she's getting seriously fat** elle devient énorme; **he was seriously drunk** il était sérieusement éméché; **her boyfriend is seriously gorgeous** son petit ami est super beau

sesh [seʃ] n Br (abrév **session**) **to have a drinking sesh** se pinter; **we had a bit of a sesh last night** on s'en est donné hier soir

set back [set] vt sép (cost) coûter à □; **it set me back twenty quid** ça m'a coûté vingt livres; **that must have set you back a bit** ça a dû te coûter bonbon

set up vt sép (trap, trick) piéger □; **they were set up** ils ont été victimes d'un coup monté

set-to ['settuː] n Br baston m ou f

set-up ['setʌp] n (trap, trick) machination □ f, coup m monté

severe [sɪ'vɪə(r)] adj Br (for emphasis)

sacré, vache (de); **he is a severe pain** c'est un sacré emmerdeur

severely [sɪ'vɪəlɪ] adv Br (for emphasis) sérieusement, vachement; **we were severely drunk last night** on était sérieusement déchirés hier soir; **you are severely annoying me!** tu me cours sérieusement sur le haricot!

sewermouth ['suːməʊθ] n Am **to be a sewermouth** jurer comme un charretier

sex [seks] n **sex god** apollon m; **sex goddess** vénus f; **sex kitten** nana f sexy, joli petit colis m

sexpot ['sekspɒt] n (man) homme m hyper sexy; (woman) bombe f sexuelle

sex-starved ['seks'stɑːvd] adj frustré

shack up [ʃæk] vi **to shack up with sb** se mettre à la colle avec qn; **to be shacked up (with sb)** être à la colle (avec qn); **they shacked up together** ils se sont mis à la colle

shades [ʃeɪdz] npl (sunglasses) lunettes fpl noires □

shaft ! [ʃɑːft] **1** n (**a**) (penis) chibre m, queue f (**b**) Am **to get the shaft** (get cheated) se faire baiser ou arnaquer
2 vt (**a**) Br (have sex with) baiser, tringler, troncher (**b**) (cheat) baiser, arnaquer; **to get shafted** se faire baiser ou arnaquer

shag ! [ʃæg] Br **1** n (**a**) (sexual intercourse) baise f; **to have a shag** baiser, tirer un coup, s'envoyer en l'air; **to be a good shag** (of person) être un bon coup (**b**) (boring task) plaie f; **it's a real shag having to get up so early every morning** c'est vraiment chiant ou la plaie de devoir se lever si tôt tous les matins
2 vt (have sex with) (of man) baiser, troncher, tringler, limer; (of woman) baiser avec, s'envoyer
3 vi (have sex) baiser, s'envoyer en l'air

shaggable ! ['ʃægəbəl] adj Br baisable

shagged (out) ! [ʃægd('aʊt)] adj Br (tired) naze, lessivé

shake [ʃeɪk] n (**a**) **in two shakes (of a lamb's tail)** en moins de deux, en deux temps trois mouvements, en deux coups de cuiller à pot (**b**) **it's no great shakes** ça casse pas des briques, ça casse pas trois pattes à un canard ▸ voir aussi **leg, stick**

shake down vt sép Am (**a**) (blackmail) **to shake sb down** faire chanter qn ▯ (**b**) (search) **to shake sb down** fouiller qn ▯, palper qn; **to shake sth down** fouiller qch ▯

shakedown ['ʃeɪkdaʊn] n Am (**a**) (blackmail) chantage ▯ m (**b**) (search) fouille ▯ f

shamus ['ʃeɪməs] n Am (private detective) privé m

shank [ʃæŋk] Am 1 n (knife) surin m, lame f
2 vt (stab) planter

Sharon and Tracy ['ʃærənən'treɪsɪ] npr Br = type de jeune femme d'origine modeste aux mœurs légères, vulgaire, bruyante, et peu intelligente

"Sharon" et "Tracy" sont des prénoms très courants dans les milieux populaires et, de ce fait, sont considérés comme vulgaires par beaucoup de gens. On utilise cette expression de la façon suivante: "the club was full of Sharon and Tracys", "she's a bit of a Sharon and Tracy (type)".

sharp [ʃɑːp] adj (stylish) chicos, classe ▸ voir aussi **poke**

sharpish ['ʃɑːpɪʃ] adv Br illico presto, vite fait; **you'd better do it sharpish** t'as intérêt à le faire illico presto, t'as intérêt à faire fissa

shattered ['ʃætəd] adj Br (exhausted) naze, lessivé, crevé, claqué

shebang [ʃə'bæŋ] n **the whole shebang** et tout le tremblement, et tout le bataclan

shekels ['ʃekəlz] npl (money) fric m, flouze m, pognon m

shell out [ʃel] 1 vt sép raquer
2 vi raquer, casquer (**for** pour)

shellac [ʃə'læk] vt Am (defeat) battre à plates coutures, écrabouiller, filer une raclée ou une déculottée à; **to get shellacked** être battu à plates coutures, se faire écrabouiller, prendre une raclée ou une déculottée

shellacking [ʃə'lækɪŋ] n Am (**a**) (beating) **to give sb a shellacking** tabasser qn, passer qn à tabac; **to take a shellacking** se faire tabasser, se faire passer à tabac, prendre une raclée (**b**) (defeat) raclée f, déculottée f; **to give sb a shellacking** battre qn à plates coutures, écrabouiller qn, filer une raclée ou une déculottée à qn; **to take a shellacking** être battu à plates coutures, se faire écrabouiller, prendre une raclée ou une déculottée

shemozzle [ʃə'mɒzəl] n Am merdier m

sherman [!] ['ʃɜːmən] n Br (rhyming slang **Sherman tank** = **wank**) branlette f; **to have a sherman** se branler, se faire une branlette, faire cinq contre un

shift [ʃɪft] 1 vt (**a**) (sell) fourguer (**b**) (eat, drink) s'envoyer; **hurry up and shift that pint!** dépêche-toi d'écluser ta pinte! (**c**) **shift yourself!** (move) pousse tes fesses!; (hurry up) magne-toi!, remue-toi!
2 vi (move quickly) foncer

shifty ['ʃɪftɪ] adj (person) louche; (look) fuyant ▯

shindig ['ʃɪndɪg] n (**a**) (party) fête ▯ f, fiesta f; **to have a shindig** faire la fiesta (**b**) (commotion) raffut m, ramdam m; **to kick up a shindig** faire du raffut

shine [ʃaɪn] 1 n Am Injurieux (black man) nègre m, bamboula m; (black woman) négresse f
2 vi **stick it where the sun don't shine!** [!] tu peux te le mettre où je pense!
▸ voir aussi **arse**

shiner ['ʃaɪnə(r)] n (black eye) œil m au

beurre noir, coquard m

shirt [ʃɜːt] n **keep your shirt on!** t'énerve pas!, du calme!; *Br* **to put one's shirt on sth** miser jusqu'à son dernier centime sur qch □; **to lose one's shirt** tout perdre □; **to take the shirt off sb's back** faire cracher jusqu'à son dernier centime à qn; **stuffed shirt** *(person)* collet m monté

shirt-lifter ['ʃɜːtlɪftə(r)] n *Br Injurieux* pédé m, tantouze f, tapette f

shit ⚠ [ʃɪt] **1** n **(a)** *(excrement)* merde f; **to** *Br* **have** *or Am* **take a shit** chier, couler un bronze; **to have the shits** avoir la chiasse; **to be in the shit** être dans la merde; **to drop sb in the shit** foutre qn dans la merde; **I don't give a shit** j'en ai rien à battre *ou* à secouer; **who gives a shit?** qu'est-ce que ça peut foutre?; **to treat sb like shit** traiter qn comme de la merde; **to beat the shit out of sb** défoncer la gueule à qn; **to scare the shit out of sb** foutre une trouille pas possible à qn; **to get one's shit together** se ressaisir □; **to be up shit creek (without a paddle)** être dans une merde noire; **when the shit hits the fan** quand ça pètera; **he thinks his shit doesn't stink** il se prend pas pour de la merde; **eat (and die)!** va te faire foutre!; **tough shit!** tant pis!; **shit happens** ce sont des choses qui arrivent □

(b) *(nonsense)* conneries fpl; **he's full of shit** il dit que des conneries, il sait pas ce qu'il dit; **to talk shit** raconter des conneries; **that's shit!** c'est des conneries!; **don't believe that shit** n'écoute pas ces conneries; **no shit?** sans déconner?, sans dec?; **no shit!** sans déconner!, sans dec!

(c) *(worthless things)* **to be a load of shit,** *Am* **to be the shits** être de la merde

(d) *(useless things)* bordel m, foutoir m; **clear all that shit off your desk** vire-moi ce bordel de ton bureau

(e) *(disgusting substance)* merde f, saloperie f; **I can't eat this shit** je peux pas bouffer cette merde

(f) *(person)* ordure f, bâton m merdeux; **he's been a real shit to her** il s'est vraiment conduit en salaud avec elle

(g) *(unfair treatment)* **to give sb shit** faire chier qn; **the press have been giving him a lot of shit lately** la presse l'a traîné dans la merde ces derniers temps; **don't take his shit!** le laisse pas te traiter comme de la merde!; **I don't need this shit!** j'ai pas envie de m'emmerder avec ce genre de conneries!

(h) *(anything)* **he doesn't do shit** il en rame pas une, il en fout pas une rame; **I can't see shit** j'y vois goutte

(i) to feel/look like shit *(ill)* se sentir/avoir l'air patraque

(j) *(cannabis)* shit m, chichon m; *(heroin)* héro f, blanche f

2 adj *(worthless)* merdique; **to feel shit** *(ill)* se sentir patraque; *(guilty)* se sentir coupable □, avoir les boules *ou* les glandes; **I had a really shit time** j'ai passé un moment dégueulasse; **he's a shit driver** il conduit comme un pied

3 adv **to be shit out of luck** ne pas avoir de bol *ou* de pot

4 exclam merde!

5 vt **(a) to shit oneself** *(defecate, be scared)* chier dans son froc; *(react with anger)* piquer une crise; *(react with surprise)* ne pas en revenir; **to shit a brick** *or* **bricks** chier dans son froc

(b) *Am* **to shit sb** *(lie to)* raconter des craques à qn; *(deceive)* se foutre de la gueule de qn

6 vi **(a)** *(defecate)* chier; **shit or get off the pot!** alors, tu te décides? □

(b) to shit on sb *(treat badly)* traiter qn comme de la merde; *Br* **to shit on sb from a great height** *(treat badly)* traiter qn comme de la merde; *(defeat)* battre qn à plates coutures, écrabouiller qn, foutre une déculottée à qn; *Am* **shit**

on that! et puis merde!

(c) *Am (react with anger)* piquer une crise; *(react with surprise)* ne pas en revenir; **your parents will shit when they see what you've done!** tes parents vont piquer une crise quand ils se rendront compte de ce que t'as fait

▶ *voir aussi* **bear, crock, eat, holy, jack**

shit-ass [!] ['ʃɪtæs] *n Am (person)* salaud (salope) *m,f*

shit-can [!] ['ʃɪtkæn] *vt Am (discard)* balancer, foutre en l'air; *(disregard, abandon)* laisser tomber

shite [!] [ʃaɪt] *Br* **1** *n* (a) *(excrement)* merde *f* (b) *(nonsense)* conneries *fpl*; **he's full of shite** il raconte que des conneries, il sait pas ce qu'il dit; **to talk shite** raconter des conneries, déconner; **that's shite!** c'est des conneries!; **don't believe that shite!** n'écoute pas ces conneries!

2 *adj (bad)* merdique; **to feel shite** *(ill)* se sentir patraque; *(guilty)* se sentir coupable □, avoir les boules *ou* les glandes; **I had a really shite time** j'ai passé un moment dégueulasse; **he's a shite singer** il chante comme un pied

3 *exclam* merde!

shit-faced [!] ['ʃɪtfeɪst] *adj (drunk)* bourré, pété, beurré; *(on drugs)* défoncé, raide

shit-for-brains [!] ['ʃɪtfəbreɪnz] *n* tache *f*, gogol *mf*

shithead [!] ['ʃɪthed] *n* enfoiré(e) *m,f*

shit-heel [!] ['ʃɪthi:l] *n Am (person)* pécore *mf*, bouseux(euse) *m,f*

shithole [!] ['ʃɪthəʊl] *n (dirty place)* porcherie *f*, taudis *m*; **this town's a complete shithole** *(boring, ugly)* cette ville est un vrai trou

shit-hot [!] [ʃɪt'hɒt] *adj* super, génial

shithouse [!] ['ʃɪthaʊs] *n* chiottes *fpl*, gogues *mpl*; **to be built like a brick shithouse** être une armoire à glace

shit-kicker [!] ['ʃɪtkɪkə(r)] *n Am (farmhand)* garçon *m* de ferme □; *(rustic)*

pedzouille *mf*, pécore *mf*

shitless [!] ['ʃɪtlɪs] *adj* **to be bored shitless** se faire chier à mort; **to be scared shitless** être mort de trouille

shitload [!] ['ʃɪtləʊd] *n* **a (whole) shitload (of)** une chiée de, une tapée de

shit-scared [!] [ʃɪt'skeəd] *adj* **to be shit-scared** être mort de trouille

shit-stirrer [!] ['ʃɪtstɜ:rə(r)] *n* fouteur (euse) *m,f* de merde

shitter [!] ['ʃɪtə(r)] *n (toilet)* chiottes *fpl*, gogues *mpl*

shitty [!] ['ʃɪti] *adj (worthless)* merdique; *(nasty)* dégueulasse; **that was a shitty thing to do/say** c'est salaud *ou* dégueulasse d'avoir fait/dit ça; **to feel shitty** *(ill)* se sentir patraque; *(guilty)* se sentir coupable □, avoir les boules *ou* les glandes

shiv [ʃɪv] *Am* **1** *n (knife)* surin *m*, lame *f*
2 *vt (stab)* planter

shock jock [ˈʃɒkdʒɒk] *n Am* = animateur ou animatrice de radio au ton irrévérencieux et provocateur

shoot [ʃu:t] **1** *exclam Am* zut!, mince!

2 *vt* (a) *Am* **to shoot the breeze** *or* **the bull** *(chat)* papoter (b) **to shoot one's load** *or* **wad** [!!] *(ejaculate)* décharger, balancer la purée; *Am* **to shoot one's wad** *or* **the works** *(do all one can)* se donner à fond

3 *vi (speak)* **shoot!** vas-y, je t'écoute!

▶ *voir aussi* **blank, cookie, hoops, lunch, mouth**

shoot through *vi Br (leave)* se tirer, mettre les bouts

shoot up 1 *vt sép (drugs)* se faire un shoot de; *(habitually)* se shooter *ou* se piquer à

2 *vi (inject drugs)* se piquer, se shooter

shoot-'em-up ['ʃu:təmʌp] *n* = film ou jeu vidéo comportant de nombreux échanges de coups de feu

shooter ['ʃu:tə(r)] *n (gun)* flingue *m*, feu *m*
▶ *voir aussi* **square, straight**

shooting-gallery ['ʃuːtɪŋgæləri] n Am (for buying drugs) = lieu où l'on achète, vend et consomme de la drogue

shooting-iron ['ʃuːtɪŋaɪən] n Am (gun) flingue m, feu m

shooting-match ['ʃuːtɪŋmætʃ] n **the whole shooting-match** tout le bataclan, tout le tremblement

shop [ʃɒp] vt Br (inform on) dénoncer □, balancer

short [ʃɔːt] adj **to have sb by the short hairs** or Br **by the short and curlies** avoir qn à sa merci □

shortarse [!] ['ʃɔːtɑːs] n Br rase-bitume mf, bas-du-cul mf

shorts [ʃɔːts] npl **(a) to have the shorts** (have little money) être fauché, être raide **(b)** Am **eat my shorts!** tu me gonfles!

shorty ['ʃɔːti] n rase-bitume mf, bas-ducul mf, **hey, shorty!** hé, rase bitume!

shot [ʃɒt] **1** n **(a) to do sth like a shot** (speedily) faire qch à tout berzingue; (with no hesitation) faire qch sans hésiter □ **(b) big shot** gros bonnet m, huile f **(c)** Noir Am **the whole shot** tout le tremblement
    2 adj **(a)** Br **to get shot of sb/sth** se débarrasser de qn/qch □; **I can't wait to be shot of this house** j'ai hâte de me débarrasser de cette maison **(b)** Am (wasted, ruined) fichu, foutu; **that's another day shot!** encore une journée de foutue (en l'air)!
    ▸ voir aussi **cook, cook up, mug**

shotgun wedding ['ʃɒtgʌn'wedɪŋ] n mariage m forcé □ (lorsque la future mariée est enceinte)

shout [ʃaʊt] n Br (round of drinks) tournée □ f; **it's my shout** c'est ma tournée; **whose shout is it?** c'est la tournée de qui?

shove off [ʃʌv] vi décaniller, se barrer, se tirer; **shove off!** dégage!, fous le camp!

show [ʃəʊ] vi (arrive) se pointer

showboat ['ʃəʊbəʊt] Am **1** n (show-off) crâneur(euse) m,f, frimeur(euse) m,f
    2 vi (show off) crâner, frimer

shower ['ʃaʊə(r)] n Br Péj (people) **what a shower!** quel bande de nuls!; **you lazy shower!** bande de flemmards!

shredded ['ʃredɪd] adj Am (drunk) bourré, pété, beurré, fait

shrink [ʃrɪŋk] n (psychiatrist) psy mf

shrooms [ʃruːmz] npl (abrév **mushrooms**) champignons hallucinogènes □ mpl, champignons mpl

shtuk [ʃtʊk] = **schtuk**

shtum [ʃtʊm] = **schtum**

shuck [ʃʌk] Noir Am **1** n (trick) arnaque f
    2 vt (trick) arnaquer
    3 vi **to shuck (and jive)** (act foolishly) faire l'andouille; (speak misleadingly, bluff) baratiner

shucks [ʃʌks] exclam mince!, punaise!

shufty ['ʃʊfti] n Br **to have a shufty at sth** jeter un coup d'œil à qch; **have a quick shufty at this!** regarde un peu ça!

shut [ʃʌt] vt **shut your mouth** or **face, shut it!** ferme ton clapet!, la ferme!
    ▸ voir aussi **noise, trap**

shut up 1 vt sép **to shut sb up** clouer le bec à qn; **that shut him up!** ça lui a cloué le bec!
    2 vi fermer son clapet, la fermer, la boucler; **shut up!** la ferme!, ferme ton clapet!, boucle-la!

shut-eye ['ʃʌtaɪ] n **to get some shuteye** piquer un roupillon, roupiller

shyster ['ʃaɪstə(r)] n Am (businessman, politician) homme m d'affaires/politicien m véreux; (lawyer) avocat m marron

sick [sɪk] adj **(a) to be sick (and tired) of sb/sth** en avoir marre ou ras le bol de qn/qch; **to be sick to death** or **sick of the sight of sb/sth** en avoir sa claque

de qn/qch **(b)** Br **(as) sick as a parrot** (disappointed) déçu □, dégoûté
▶ voir aussi **teeth**

sickbag ['sɪkbæg] n Br **pass the sickbag!** ça me fout la nausée!

sickie ['sɪkɪ] n Br **to take a sickie** se faire porter pâle (lorsqu'on est bien portant)

sicko ['sɪkəʊ] n malade mf, tordu(e) m,f

sight [saɪt] n **(a)** **she can't stand** or Br **stick the sight of him** elle ne peut pas le voir en peinture **(b)** (mess) **to be** or Br **look a sight** être dans un bel état; Br **what a sight!** quel tableau! **(c)** (for emphasis) **a damn** or **darn sight better/easier** vachement mieux/plus facile; **a damn** or **darn sight more/less** vachement plus/moins
▶ voir aussi **outta, sick**

signify ['sɪɡnɪfaɪ] vi Noir Am = se livrer à des joutes verbales entre amis; **they were signifying back and forth** ils se chambraient, ils s'envoyaient des vannes

Le "signifying" est une sorte de joute verbale improvisée au cours de laquelle des amis se lancent des remarques sarcastiques et grotesques.

simoleon [sɪ'məʊlɪən] n Am (dollar) dollar □ m

simp [sɪmp] n Am (abrév **simpleton**) andouille f, crétin(e) m,f

sing [sɪŋ] vi (confess, inform) cracher ou lâcher le morceau
▶ voir aussi **blues**

singer ['sɪŋə(r)] n Br (informer) indic mf

sis [sɪs] n (abrév **sister**) frangine f

sissy ['sɪsɪ] n femmelette f

sister ['sɪstə(r)] n **(a)** Noir Am (fellow black woman) Noire f américaine □; **you don't treat your sisters like that!** c'est pas des façons de traiter d'autres Noires! **(b)** (fellow feminist) camarade f féministe □
▶ voir aussi **soul**

six-pack ['sɪkspæk] n **(a)** Hum (stomach muscles) abdos mpl; **he's got a great six-pack** il a des supers abdos **(b)** Br Hum **to be one can short of a six-pack** ne pas être net
▶ voir aussi **sandwich**

sixty-nine [sɪkstɪ'naɪn] n (sexual position) soixante-neuf m

skag [skæɡ] n = **scag**

skank [skæŋk] n Am cageot m, boudin m

skanky ['skæŋkɪ] adj Am hyper moche

skate [skeɪt] n **to get one's skates on** (hurry up) se magner, se grouiller; **get your skates on!** magne-toi!, grouille-toi!

skedaddle [skɪ'dædəl] vi décamper, se tailler, décaniller

skeezer ['skiːzə(r)] n Noir Am **(a)** (ugly woman) cageot m, boudin m **(b)** (promiscuous woman) pouffiasse f, traînée f

skid [skɪd] n **(a)** **to be on the skids** (of company, marriage) battre de l'aile; Am **to hit the skids** (of company, sales, prices) dégringoler **(b)** Am **skid row** bas-fonds □ mpl; **to be on skid row** être dans la dèche **(c)** Br **skid lid** casque □ m (de moto) **(d)** **skid marks** ! traces fpl de pneus (traces d'excrément sur le slip)

skin [skɪn] **1** n **(a)** (abrév **skinhead**) skinhead mf, skin mf **(b)** Br (cigarette paper) papier m à cigarette □ **(c)** Am **gimme some skin!** tape-moi dans la main! **(d)** **skin flick** film m de cul; **skin mag** magazine m de cul **(e)** Am **skin game** (swindle) arnaque f
2 vt **(a)** (swindle) arnaquer **(b)** Am **skin me!** tape-moi dans la main!

Dans les catégories 1 (c) et 2(b), il s'agit d'une façon de signifier à quelqu'un que l'on veut lui taper dans la main pour le saluer, le féliciter, ou en signe de victoire.

skin up vi Br rouler un joint

skinflint ['skɪnflɪnt] n radin(e) m,f

skinful ['skɪnfʊl] n **to have had a skin-ful** tenir une bonne cuite

skinny ['skɪnɪ] n Am (inside information) renseignements ᵍ mpl; **what's the skinny on the situation?** résume-moi la situation ᵍ

skinny-dipping ['skɪnɪdɪpɪŋ] n **to go skinny-dipping** se baigner à poil

skin-pop ['skɪnpɒp] **1** vt (drugs) se piquer ou se shooter à
2 vi (inject drugs) se piquer, se shoo-ter

skint [skɪnt] adj Br fauché, raide

skirt [skɜːt] n (women) nanas fpl, gon-zesses fpl; **they've gone out looking for skirt** ils sont allés draguer; Br **a bit of skirt** une nana, une gonzesse

skive [skaɪv] Br **1** n (easy job) planque f; **she's taking PE because it's such a skive** elle a choisi éducation physique parce que c'est pépère
2 vi tirer au flanc, tirer au cul

skive off Br **1** vt insép **to skive off school** sécher les cours, **to skive off work** ne pas aller bosser
2 vi tirer au flanc, tirer au cul

skiver ['skaɪvə(r)] n Br tire-au-flanc mf, tire-au-cul mf

skivvies ['skɪvɪz] npl Am calbute m, calcif m

skull [skʌl] n **to be out of one's skull** (drunk) être plein comme une barrique, être rond comme une queue de pelle
▸ voir aussi **thick**

skunk [skʌŋk] n Péj (person) salaud (salope) m,f

slacker ['slækə(r)] n bon (bonne) m,f à rien, raté(e) m,f

Il s'agit d'un stéréotype social apparu aux États-Unis, au début des années 90. Ce terme désigne une personne jeune (entre vingt et trente ans), qui a fait des études, mais que le monde du travail et la notion de carrière rebutent, et qui se contente le plus souvent de travaux subalternes qui ne comportent aucune responsabilité.

slag [slæg] Br **1** n (a) (promiscuous wo-man) pouffiasse f, traînée f (b) Péj (per-son) enfoiré(e) m,f; **some slag's stolen my fags** il y a un enfoiré qui m'a piqué mes clopes
2 vt (a) (criticize) débiner, éreinter, descendre en flammes (b) (make fun of) se foutre de

slag off vt sép Br (a) (criticize) débiner, éreinter, descendre en flammes (b) (make fun of) se foutre de

slam [slæm] vt (a) (criticize) éreinter, descendre en flammes; **to get slammed** se faire éreinter, se faire des-cendre en flammes (b) [!] Am (have sex with) (of man) baiser, s'envoyer; (of wo-man) baiser avec, s'envoyer (c) (drink quickly) descendre, écluser; **let's go slam some beers** allons écluser quel-ques blères

slammer ['slæmə(r)] n taule f, cabane f; **in the slammer** en taule, en cabane, à l'ombre

slanging match ['slæŋɪŋmætʃ] n Br prise f de bec, engueulade f; **to have a slanging match (with sb)** avoir une prise de bec (avec qn), s'engueuler (avec qn)

slant [slɑːnt] n Injurieux (Oriental) bridé(e) m,f

slap [slæp] n Br (make-up) maquillage ᵍ m

slaphead ['slæphed] n Br chauve ᵍ m; **he's a slaphead** il n'a pas un poil sur le caillou, il a une casquette en peau de fesse

slapper ['slæpə(r)] n Br (a) (promiscuous woman) pouffiasse f, traînée f, salope f (b) Péj (any woman) gonzesse f, gro-gnasse f

slash [slæʃ] n Br **to have a slash** pisser; **to go for a slash** aller pisser un coup

slasher film ['slæʃəfɪlm] n = film d'horreur particulièrement sanglant

slate [sleɪt] *Br* **1** *n* **to have a slate loose** avoir une case de vide, avoir une araignée au plafond
2 *vt (criticize)* éreinter, débiner, descendre en flammes

slaughter ['slɔːtə(r)] *vt (defeat)* écrabouiller, battre à plates coutures, mettre une raclée *ou* une déculottée à

slaughtered ['slɔːtəd] *adj Br (drunk)* bourré, beurré, pété

slay [sleɪ] *vt (amuse)* faire mourir de rire; *Ironique* **you slay me!** tu es impayable!

sleazebag ['sliːzbæg], **sleazeball** ['sliːzbɔːl] *n* **(a)** *(despicable person)* ordure *f*, raclure *f* **(b)** *(repulsive man)* gros dégueulasse *m*

sleep around [sliːp] *vi* coucher à droite à gauche

slick up [slɪk] *vi Am (dress smartly)* se mettre sur son trente-et-un, se faire beau

slimebag ['slaɪmbæg], **slimeball** ['slaɪmbɔːl] *n* **(a)** *(despicable person)* ordure *f*, raclure *f* **(b)** *(repulsive man)* gros dégueulasse *m*

slit !! [slɪt] *n (vagina)* craque *f*, cramouille *f*

Sloane (Ranger) [sləʊn('reɪndʒə(r))] *n Br* ≃ jeune femme *f* BCBG

Une "Sloane Ranger" est une jeune femme à la mode, fille de grands bourgeois ou d'aristocrates. À l'origine, ce terme ne désignait que les jeunes femmes dont la famille habitait Sloane Square (quartier chic du sud-ouest de Londres); aujourd'hui, sa sphère géographique s'est étendue au reste de Londres et à ses environs. "Sloane Ranger" est un jeu de mots sur "Lone Ranger", qui est le nom du héros d'une série télévisée américaine des années 50 qui avait pour cadre le FarWest.

Sloaney ['sləʊnɪ] *adj Br* ≃ BCBG
slog [slɒg] **1** *n* **(a)** *(task)* tâche *f* duraille,

corvée *f*
2 *vi (work hard)* trimer; **to slog away (at sth)** travailler comme un dingue (à qch)

sloshed [slɒʃt] *adj* bourré, pété, beurré

slug [slʌg] **1** *n* **(a)** *(of drink)* goulée *f*, lampée *f*; **to take** *or* **have a slug of sth** boire une lampée de qch **(b)** *(bullet)* pruneau *m*, bastos *f*
2 *vt (hit)* cogner; **to slug it out** se bastonner, se friter, se castagner

slugfest ['slʌgfest] *n Am* baston *m ou f*, castagne *f*

slut [slʌt] *n* **(a)** *(promiscuous woman)* pouffiasse *f*, traînée *f* **(b)** *(prostitute)* pute *f*

smack [smæk] *n (heroin)* héro *f*, blanche *f*

smacker ['smækə(r)] *n* **(a)** *(kiss)* gros bisou *m* **(b)** *(pound sterling)* livre *f* sterling ▫; *(dollar)* dollar ▫ *m*; **fifty smackers** cinquante livres/dollars

smalls [smɔːlz] *npl Br* sous-vêtements ▫ *mpl*

smart [smɑːt] **1** *n Am* **smarts** *(intelligence)* intelligence ▫ *f*; **to have smarts** en avoir dans le ciboulot; **he's pretty low on smarts** c'est pas une lumière
2 *adj* **smart alec** petit(e) malin(igne) *m,f*, je-sais-tout *mf*
▶ *voir aussi* **cookie**

smartarse ! ['smɑːtɑːs], *Am* **smartass** ! ['smɑːtæs] *n* petit(e) malin(igne) *m,f*

smashed [smæʃt] *adj (drunk)* bourré, pété, beurré; *(on drugs)* raide, défoncé

smasher ['smæʃə(r)] *n Br* **to be a smasher** être génial; **she's a smasher** *(gorgeous)* elle est hyper canon

smashing ['smæʃɪŋ] *adj Br* super, génial, géant

smeggy ! ['smegɪ] *adj Br (disgusting)* dégueulasse, cradingue

smoke [sməʊk] *n* **(a)** *(cigarette)* clope *f*; *(cannabis cigarette)* joint *m*; *(cannabis)*

chichon *m*, shit *m*, teuch *m* **(b)** *Br* **the (Big) Smoke** *(London)* = surnom donné à la ville de Londres
▸ *voir aussi* **holy**

smooch [smu:tʃ] *vi* se bécoter

smoothie, smoothy ['smu:ðɪ] *n* individu *m* mielleux

snaffle ['snæfəl] *vt Br* piquer, faire main basse sur; **who's snaffled my pen?** qui est-ce qui m'a piqué mon stylo?

snail mail ['sneɪlmeɪl] *n Hum* = terme humoristique désignant les services postaux par opposition aux messageries électroniques

snakebite ['sneɪkbaɪt] *n Br (drink)* = boisson comprenant une mesure de bière et une mesure de cidre

snap [snæp] *exclam Br* **I'm on holiday next week – snap!** je suis en vacances la semaine prochaine – moi aussi! □

> "Snap" est un jeu de cartes dans lequel deux joueurs retournent leurs cartes une par une et simultanément, jusqu'au moment où deux cartes de la même valeur sont retournées; le premier à dire "snap" remporte alors les cartes accumulées. On utilise cette expression lorsque l'on remarque deux choses identiques.

snatch [!!] [snætʃ] *n (woman's genitals)* craque *f*, cramouille *f*, chatte *f*

snazzy ['snæzɪ] *adj* chicos, classe

sneak [sni:k] **1** *n* **(a)** *Br (tell-tale)* cafard(e) *m,f*, cafteur(euse) *m,f* **(b)** *Am* **sneaks** *(abrév* **sneakers)** baskets *fpl*
2 *vi (tell tales)* cafter, cafarder; **to sneak on sb** cafter qn, cafarder qn

snit [snɪt] *n Am* **to be in a snit** être fumasse *ou* furibard

snitch [snɪtʃ] **1** *n* **(a)** *(tell-tale)* cafard(e) *m,f*, cafteur(euse) *m,f* **(b)** *Br (nose)* blaire *m*, tarin *m*, pif *m*
2 *vi (tell tales)* cafter, cafarder; **to snitch on sb** cafter qn, cafarder qn

snockered ['snɒkəd] *adj Am (drunk)* bourré, pété, fait, beurré

snog [snɒg] *Br* **1** *n* **to have a snog** se bécoter, se rouler des pelles *ou* des patins
2 *vt* bécoter, rouler des pelles *ou* des patins à
3 *vi* se bécoter, se rouler des pelles *ou* des patins

snooker ['snu:kə(r)] *vt* **(a)** *Br (thwart)* mettre dans l'embarras □; **if that doesn't work, we're snookered!** si ça marche pas, on est foutu! **(b)** *Am (swindle, trick)* arnaquer; **don't get snookered into anything!** te laisse pas arnaquer!

snoot [snu:t] *n (nose)* blaire *m*, tarin *m*, pif *m*

snort [snɔ:t] **1** *n (of drug)* **to have a snort** se faire une ligne
2 *vt (drug)* sniffer

snot [snɒt] *n (mucus)* morve *f*

snotrag ['snɒtræg] *n* tire-jus *m*, tire-moelle *m*

snotty ['snɒtɪ] *adj* **(a)** *(nose, handkerchief)* morveux, plein de morve **(b)** *(haughty)* bêcheur, prétentiard; *(insolent)* insolent □

snout [snaʊt] *n Br* **(a)** *(cigarette)* clope *f*; *(tobacco)* tabac □ *m*, foin *m* **(b)** *(informer)* indic *mf*

snow [snəʊ] **1** *n* **(a)** *(cocaine)* coco *f*, neige *f*; *(heroin crystals)* cristaux *mpl* d'héroïne □ **(b)** *Am* **snow job** baratin *m*; **to give sb a snow job** baratiner qn, rouler qn dans la farine
2 *vt Am* **to snow sb** *(charm, persuade)* baratiner qn, rouler qn dans la farine; **to snow sb into doing sth** baratiner qn pour qu'il fasse qch
▸ *voir aussi* **bunny, pisshole**

snuff [snʌf] **1** *n* **snuff movie** = film pornographique au cours duquel un participant est réellement assassiné
2 *vt* **(a)** *Br* **to snuff it** *(die)* calancher, passer l'arme à gauche **(b)** *Am (murder)* buter, refroidir, zigouiller

soak [səʊk] **1** *n* **old soak** vieux (vieille) poivrot(e) *m,f*

2 *vt Am* **to soak sb** *(charge heavily)* écorcher qn; *(tax heavily)* accabler qn d'impôts ⃞

sob ⚠, **SOB** ⚠ [esəʊˈbiː] *n Am (abrév* **son-of-a-bitch)** salaud *m*, fils *m* de pute

sock [sɒk] **1** *n* **(a)** *(blow)* beigne *f*, chataîgne *f*; **she gave him a sock in the face** elle lui a filé une beigne

(b) to put a sock in it la fermer, la mettre en veilleuse, la boucler; **put a sock in it!** la ferme!, ferme ton clapet!, mets-la en veilleuse!

2 *vt* **(a)** *(hit)* filer une beigne *ou* une chataîgne à; **she socked him in the face** elle lui a filé une beigne

(b) to sock it to sb montrer à qn ce que l'on sait faire; **sock it to them!** vas-y, montre-leur ce que tu sais faire!, vas-y, donne le maximum!

sod ⚠ [sɒd] *Br* **1** *n* **(a)** *(person)* con (conne) *m,f*; **the poor sod** le pauvre, le pauvre bougre; **you're a lazy sod** t'es vraiment un flemmard

(b) *(thing)* saloperie *f*; **it's a sod of a job** c'est un boulot vraiment chiant

(c) **sod all** que dalle; **sod all money** pas un flèche, pas un rond; **there's sod all to eat** il y a que dalle à bouffer

2 *vt* **sod it!** merde!; **sod him!** qu'il aille se faire voir!; **sod the expense, let's just go!** tant pis si ça coûte cher, allons-y!

sod off ⚠ *vi Br* foutre le camp, décamper, décaniller; **sod off!** fous le camp!, dégage!

sodding ⚠ [ˈsɒdɪŋ] *Br* **1** *adj (for emphasis)* sacré, foutu; **get that sodding dog out of here!** fous-moi cette saleté de clébard dehors!; **he's a sodding nuisance!** c'est un sacré emmerdeur!; **sodding hell!** merde alors!

2 *adv (for emphasis)* vachement; **you can sodding well do it yourself!** démerde-toi tout seul pour le faire!; **don't be so sodding lazy!** ce que tu peux être flemmard!

Sod's law [ˈsɒdzˈlɔː] *n Br* la loi de l'emmerdement maximum

softie, softy [ˈsɒftɪ] *n (gentle person)* bonne pâte *f*; *(coward)* poule *f* mouillée

solid [ˈsɒlɪd] *Noir Am* **1** *adj (excellent)* génial, super, géant

2 *adv (absolutely)* absolument ⃞; **I solid gotta do it!** il faut absolument que je le fasse!

some [sʌm] *adj* **(a)** *(for emphasis)* **that was some party/meal!** c'était une sacrée fête!/un sacré gueuleton!; **she's some cook!** c'est une sacrée cuisinière!

(b) *Ironique* **some friend he is!** tu parles d'un copain!; *Br* **some hope!** on peut toujours rêver!

something [ˈsʌmθɪŋ] **1** *pron* **that meal was something else!** c'était quelque chose, ce repas!; **he really is something else!** il est pas possible!

2 *adv Br* **something rotten** *or* **awful** *(lots)* vachement; **he fancies her something rotten** *or* **awful** il est dingue d'elle

son-of-a-bitch ⚠⚠ [sʌnəvəˈbɪtʃ] *Am* **1** *n* **(a)** *(man)* salaud *m*, fils *m* de pute; **you old son-of-a-bitch, how ya doin'?** comment ça va, enfoiré? **(b)** *(object)* saloperie *f*; **this son-of-a-bitch is too heavy to carry** cette saloperie est trop lourde à porter

2 *exclam* putain!

son-of-a-bitching ⚠⚠ [sʌnəvəˈbɪtʃɪŋ] *adj Am (for emphasis)* foutu, putain de; **where'd that son-of-a-bitching letter go?** où est passée cette putain de lettre?

son-of-a-gun [sʌnəvəˈgʌn] *Am* **1** *n* salaud *m*; **hi, you old son-of-a-gun!** salut, vieux bandit!

2 *exclam* putain!

soph [sɒf] *n Am (abrév* **sophomore)** étudiant(e) *m,f* de deuxième année ⃞

sorehead [ˈsɔːhed] *n Am (person)* ronchon(onne) *m,f*, grincheux(euse) *m,f*

sorry-ass [!] [ˈsɔːrɪˈæs], **sorry-assed** [!] [ˈsɔːrɪæst] *adj Am (inferior, contemptible)* à la con; **that sorry-ass bastard stole my woman!** cet enfoiré m'a piqué ma gonzesse!

sorted [ˈsɔːtɪd] *Br* **1** *adj* **to be sorted** *(psychologically)* être équilibré □, être bien dans ses baskets; *(have everything one needs)* être paré; **she's the most sorted person I know** c'est la personne la plus équilibrée que je connaisse □; **if I get that pay rise, I'll be sorted** si j'obtiens cette augmentation j'aurai plus à m'en faire; **to be sorted for sth** disposer de qch □; **are you sorted for E's/whizz?** t'as ce qu'il te faut comme ecsta/speed?
2 *exclam* super!, génial!

soul [soul] *n Noir Am* **soul brother** Noir *m* américain □; **soul sister** Noire *f* américaine □

Il s'agit d'expressions utilisées par les Noirs américains pour se désigner eux-mêmes et s'adresser les uns aux autres. Ces expressions sont souvent abrégées en "brother" et "sister".

sound [saʊnd] *Br* **1** *adj* super, génial, géant
2 *exclam* super!, génial!, cool!

sounds [saʊndz] *npl (music)* zizique *f*, zicmu *f*

soup [suːp] *n* **to be in the soup** être dans le pétrin *ou* dans la panade

soup-strainer [ˈsuːpstreɪnə(r)] *n Am Hum (large moustache)* grosses bacchantes *fpl*

sourpuss [ˈsaʊəpʊs] *n (ill-tempered person)* grincheux(euse) *m,f*

souse [saʊs] *n Am (person)* alcolo *m,f*, poivrot(e) *m,f*

soused [saʊst] *adj Am (drunk)* bourré, pété, fait, beurré

sozzled [ˈsɒzəld] *adj Br* bourré, beurré, pété, fait

SP [esˈpiː] *n Br (abrév **starting price**)* to

give sb the SP (on) mettre qn au parfum (à propos de *ou* concernant)

Il s'agit au départ d'une expression de turfistes. Le "starting price" est la cote d'un cheval juste avant le départ.

space [speɪs] *n* **(a)** *Hum* **space cadet,** *Am* **space case** allumé(e) *m,f*; **he's a bit of a space cadet** *or Am* **space case** il est toujours en train de planer **(b)** *Br* **space cakes** gateaux *mpl* au cannabis □, space cakes *mpl*

spaced out [speɪstˈaʊt], **spacey** [ˈspeɪsɪ] *adj* **to be** *or* **feel spaced out** *or* **spacey** *(dazed)* être dans le coaltar; *(after taking drugs)* être raide, planer

spade [speɪd] *n Injurieux (black man)* nègre *m*, bamboula *m*; *(black woman)* négresse *f*

spag bol [ˈspægˈbɒl] *n Br (abrév **spaghetti bolognese**)* spaghettis *mpl* (à la) bolognaise

spare [speə(r)] *adj* **(a)** *(mad) Br* **to go spare** péter les plombs, péter une durite; **to drive sb spare** rendre qn chèvre, faire tourner qn en bourrique **(b)** *Hum Br* **spare tyre,** *Am* **spare tire** *(roll of fat)* poignée *f* d'amour, pneu *m* de secours
▸ *voir aussi* **prick**

sparkler [ˈspɑːklə(r)] *n (diamond)* diam *m*

spastic [ˈspæstɪk] *n Injurieux* gol *mf*, gogol *mf*

Ce terme signifie littéralement "handicapé moteur". Il s'agit d'une injure extrêmement politiquement incorrecte qu'il est préférable de bannir complètement de son vocabulaire.

spaz [spæz] *n Injurieux* gol *mf*, gogol *mf*

Il s'agit d'une abréviation du mot "spastic" utilisé comme injure. Bien que cette injure ne soit pas aussi choquante que le mot dont elle est dérivée, il est préférable de l'utiliser avec beaucoup de circonspection.

spaz out vi faire le con

spazzy ['spæzi] = **spaz**

speccy ['spekɪ] Br **1** n binoclard(e) m,f **2** adj binoclard

specs [speks] npl (abrév **spectacles**) carreaux mpl, hublots mpl

speed [spi:d] **1** n (**a**) (amphetamines) amphets fpl, speed m (**b**) **to be up to speed on sth** être au courant de qch □ **2** vi **to be speeding** (have taken amphetamines) être sous amphets, speeder ▶ voir aussi **merchant**

speedball ['spi:dbɔ:l] n speedball m (mélange d'héroïne et de cocaïne)

speedfreak ['spi:dfri:k] n **to be a speedfreak** consommer beaucoup d'amphets

spew [spju:] Br **1** vt dégueuler, gerber; **to spew one's guts up** rendre tripes et boyaux **2** vi dégueuler, gerber

spic, spick [spɪk] n Am Injurieux métèque mf (d'origine latino-américaine)

spike [spaɪk] n (hypodermic needle) shooteuse f, pompe f

spill [spɪl] **1** vt **to spill the beans, to spill one's guts** vendre la mèche; (under interrogation) cracher ou lâcher le morceau **2** vi vendre la mèche; (under interrogation) cracher ou lâcher le morceau; **come on, spill!** allez, accouche!

spins [spɪnz] npl **to have the spins** avoir le tournis (généralement après avoir trop bu)

spit [spɪt] n (**a**) Br **to be the (very) spit of sb** être le portrait craché de qn (**b**) Br **it's a bit of a spit and sawdust pub** c'est un pub sans prétentions □ (**c**) Hum **to swap spit** se rouler des pelles ou des patins

spit out vt sép **spit it out!** accouche!

splatter movie ['splætəmu:vɪ] n =

film violent et sanglant

spliced [splaɪst] adj **to get spliced** (marry) se marier □, se maquer

spliff [splɪf] n splif m, joint m

split [splɪt] **1** vt **to split one's sides (laughing)** se tenir les côtes (de rire) **2** vi (**a**) Am (leave) se casser, se barrer, s'arracher; **come on, let's split** allez, on se casse (**b**) Br (inform) **to split on sb** balancer qn

spondulicks [spɒn'du:lɪks] npl fric m, pognon m, flouze m

sponge [spʌndʒ] **1** vt **to sponge sth (off sb)** taper qch (à qn) **2** vi jouer au parasite; **to sponge off sb** vivre aux crochets de qn

sponger ['spʌndʒə(r)] n pique-assiette mf

spook [spu:k] **1** n Am (**a**) (spy) barbouze f (**b**) Injurieux (black man) nègre m, bamboula m; (black woman) négresse f **2** vt (startle) faire sursauter, foutre la trouille à; (frighten, disturb) donner la chair de poule à

spot-on ['spɒtɒn] Br **1** adj (accurate) **his guess was spot-on** il a mis en plein dans le mille; **his remark was spot-on** sa remarque était vachement bien vue **2** exclam (excellent) super!, génial!

spout [spaʊt] n Br **to be up the spout** (pregnant) être en cloque; (ruined) être foutu; **that's our holidays up the spout** on peut faire une croix sur nos vacances

spread [spred] vt Br **to spread it** or **oneself about a bit** (be promiscuous) avoir la cuisse légère, coucher à droite à gauche

spring [sprɪŋ] **1** n **she's no spring chicken** (no longer young) elle a pas mal d'heures de vol, elle est plus de la première jeunesse **2** vt (prisoner) faire évader □

sprog [sprɒg] n Br (child) môme mf, gosse mf

spud [spʌd] n (potato) patate f

spunk [!!] [spʌŋk] *n (semen)* foutre *m*

squaddie ['skwɒdɪ] *n Br* bidasse *m*

square [skweə(r)] **1** *n* **(a)** *(unfashionable person)* ringard(e) *m,f* **(b)** *Am* **square shooter** *(candid person)* personne *f* franche □

2 *adj (unfashionable)* ringard

square up *vi Am (of criminal)* raccrocher, se ranger des voitures; *(of drug addict)* décrocher

squawk [skwɔːk] *Am* **1** *n (complaint)* plainte □ *f*; **what's your squawk?** c'est quoi ton problème?

2 *vi (complain)* râler

squeal [skwiːl] *vi (inform)* moucharder; **to squeal on sb** balancer *ou* moucharder qn

squealer ['skwiːlə(r)] *n (informer)* indic *mf*

squeeze [skwiːz] *n* **(a)** **(main) squeeze** *(boyfriend)* mec *m*, Jules *m*; *(girlfriend)* nana *f*, gonzesse *f* **(b)** **to put the squeeze on sb** faire pression sur qn □

squiffy ['skwɪfɪ] *adj Br* éméché

squillion ['skwɪljən] *n Br Hum* **squillions (of)** une foultitude (de), une ribambelle (de)

squirrelly ['skwɪrəlɪ] *adj Am (eccentric)* loufedingue

squirt [skwɜːt] *n (person)* avorton *m*, demi-portion *f*

squits [skwɪts] *npl Br* **the squits** la courante

stache [stæʃ] *n Am (abrév* **mustache***)* bacchantes *fpl*, moustagache *f*

stacked [stækt] *Am* = **well-stacked**

staggered ['stægəd] *adj (amazed)* estomaqué

stallion ['stæljən] *n* **(a)** *(man)* étalon *m* **(b)** *Noir Am (woman)* canon *m*, bombe *f*

stand up [stænd] *vt sép* **to stand sb up** poser un lapin à qn

starkers ['stɑːkəz] *adj Br* à poil

stash [stæʃ] **1** *n* **(a)** *(hidden supply)* provision □ *f*; *(hiding place)* planque *f*

(b) *(supply of drugs)* réserve *f* de drogue □; **the police found his stash under the floorboards** la police a trouvé sa réserve de drogue cachée sous le plancher

2 *vt (hide)* planquer

static ['stætɪk] *n Am* **(a)** *(insolence)* insolence □ *f*; **I'm not taking that static from you!** arrête de faire l'insolent! **(b)** *(hassle, interference)* embêtements *mpl*; **you can expect plenty of static from mom** tu vas avoir Maman sur le dos

steal [stiːl] *n* **to be a steal** *(very cheap)* être donné

steam up [stiːm] *vt sep Am* **to steam sb up** *(infuriate)* mettre qn en pétard *ou* en boule; **to be steamed up** être en pétard *ou* en boule

steaming ['stiːmɪŋ] *adj* **(a)** *Br (drunk)* rond comme une queue de pelle, plein comme une barrique, pété à mort **(b)** *Am (angry)* en pétard, en boule

steamy ['stiːmɪ] *adj (erotic)* chaud, sexy

stems [stemz] *npl Am (legs)* quilles *fpl*, gambettes *fpl*, cannes *fpl*

stew [stjuː] **1** *n Am (abrév* **stewardess***)* hôtesse *f* de l'air □

2 *vi Br* **to be stewing** *(of person)* crever de chaleur; **it's stewing in here** il fait une chaleur à crever ici

▶ *voir aussi* **bum**

stewed [stjuːd] *adj* **stewed (to the gills)** rond comme une queue de pelle, plein comme une barrique, pété à mort

stick [stɪk] **1** *n* **(a)** *Br* **up the stick** *(pregnant)* en cloque **(b)** **the sticks** *(place)* la cambrousse; **to live in the sticks** habiter en pleine cambrousse **(c)** *Br* **to give sb stick (for sth)** *(tease)* faire enrager qn, chambrer qn (à cause de qch); **they're giving him stick for buying platform shoes** ils le font enrager parce qu'il a acheté des platform shoes

(d) Am *(cannabis cigarette)* stick *m*
(e) Br Hum **he's won more awards than you can shake a stick at** on lui a décerné une flopée de prix; **there was more talent than you can shake a stick at** ça grouillait de beaux mecs/de belles nanas
2 vt (a) *(place, put)* flanquer, coller
(b) Br *(tolerate) (person)* encadrer, blairer, piffer, encaisser; *(thing)* encaisser; **I can't stick him** je peux pas le blairer; **how have you stuck it for so long?** comment t'as fait pour supporter ça aussi longtemps?
(c) **you can stick your job!** ton boulot, tu peux te le mettre où je pense!; **he can stick his money!** son fric, il peut se le mettre *ou* coller où je pense!; **stick it!** va te faire voir!
▶ *voir aussi* **arse, ass, oar, poke, shine, sight**

sticky fingers ['stɪkɪ'fɪŋgəz] *npl* **to have sticky fingers** *(steal things)* avoir tendance à piquer tout ce qui traîne

stiff [stɪf] **1** *n* (a) *(corpse)* macchabée *m* (b) Br *(failure)* bide *m* (c) Am *(tramp)* clodo *mf* (d) Am *(stupid person)* nul (nulle) *m,f*
2 *adj* Am *(drunk)* bourré, rond, fait, beurré

stiffy [!] ['stɪfɪ] *n* Br **to have a stiffy** bander, avoir la trique *ou* le gourdin; **to get a stiffy** se mettre à bander

sting [stɪŋ] **1** *n* (a) *(swindle)* arnaque *f* (b) Am *(police operation)* coup *m* monté *(dans le cadre d'une opération de police)*
2 *vt (swindle)* arnaquer, refaire; **to get stung** se faire arnaquer, se faire refaire; **they stung him for a hundred quid** ils l'ont arnaqué *ou* refait de cent livres

stink [stɪŋk] **1** *n (fuss)* foin *m*, pataquès *m*; **to raise** *or* **make** *or* Br **kick up a stink (about sth)** faire toute une histoire (de qch)
2 *vi (be bad)* être nul, craindre; **don't bother going to the concert, it stinks!** ne vas pas au concert, c'est

nul!; **what do you think of my plan? – it stinks!** qu'est-ce que tu penses de mon projet? – il est nul!
▶ *voir aussi* **shit**

stinker ['stɪŋkə(r)] *n* (a) *(person)* ordure *f* (b) *(difficult thing)* **to be a stinker** être vachement dur, être coton; **the German exam was a real stinker** l'examen d'allemand était vraiment coton (c) *(worthless thing)* **to be a stinker** être nul, être merdique; **his new film's a total stinker** son nouveau film est complètement nul (d) **to have a stinker of a cold** avoir un sacré rhume *ou* un rhume carabiné

stinking ['stɪŋkɪŋ] **1** *adj* (a) *(worthless)* merdique, nul (b) **to have a stinking cold** avoir un sacré rhume *ou* un rhume carabiné
2 *adv* **to be stinking rich** être plein aux as, être bourré de fric

stinko ['stɪŋkəʊ] *adj* Am *(drunk)* pété, bourré, fait

stir [stɜː(r)] **1** *n (prison)* taule *f*, placard *m*, cabane *f*; **in stir** en taule, en cabane, à l'ombre; **stir crazy** cinglé *(à force d'être en prison)*
2 *vt* Br **to stir it** semer la zizanie

stitch [stɪtʃ] *n* (a) Am *(amusing person, thing)* **to be a stitch** être tordant *ou* crevant (b) **to be in stitches** *(laugh)* se tenir les côtes (de rire), être plié de rire; **to have sb in stitches** faire rire qn aux larmes

stitch up *vt sép* Br **to stitch sb up** *(frame)* piéger qn □, monter un coup contre qn; **he was stitched up** il a été victime d'un coup monté

stogie ['stəʊgɪ] *n* Am *(cigar)* cigare □ *m*

stoked [stəʊkt] *adj* Am *(excited, enthusiastic)* emballé

stomach ['stʌmək] *vt (tolerate) (person)* blairer, piffer, piffrer, encaisser; *(thing)* encaisser; **I like him but I can't stomach his brother** lui, je l'aime bien, mais je peux pas blairer son frère; **I can't**

stomach the way he looks at me il a une façon de me regarder qui me débecte
▶ *voir aussi* **throat**

stomp [stɒmp] *vt Am (defeat)* flanquer une peignée *ou* une déculottée *ou* une tannée à

stone [stəʊn], **stone-cold** ['stəʊn-'kəʊld] *adj Noir Am (absolute, real)* véritable [□], total; **she is a stone babe!** c'est une supernana!; **this is turning into a stone drag!** ça devient vraiment galère!

stoned [stəʊnd] *adj (on drugs)* raide, défoncé; **to get stoned** se défoncer

stoner ['stəʊnə(r)] *n* adepte *mf* de la fumette

stony (broke) ['stəʊnɪ('brəʊk)] *adj* fauché (comme les blés), raide, à sec

stooge [stuːdʒ] *n* (**a**) *(dupe)* pigeon *m*, poire *f* (**b**) *(idiot)* andouille *f*, crétin(e) *m,f*

stool [stuːl], **stoolie** ['stuːlɪ], **stool pigeon** ['stuːlpɪdʒɪn] *n* indic *mf*

straight [streɪt] **1** *n* (**a**) *(heterosexual)* hétéro *mf*
(**b**) *Am (conventional person)* personne *f* conventionnelle *ou* sérieuse [□]; **don't be such a straight!** sois pas si sérieux!
2 *adj* (**a**) *(heterosexual)* hétéro
(**b**) *(not on drugs)* **to be straight** ne pas avoir pris de drogue [□]
(**c**) *(conventional)* conventionnel [□], sérieux [□]
(**d**) *Am* **a straight arrow** *(man)* un brave type; *(woman)* une brave femme; **a straight shooter** *(person)* une personne franche [□]
(**e**) *Am (true)* vrai [□]
(**f**) *Am* **to get straight** = prendre une dose d'héroïne (ou d'une drogue comparable) de façon à éviter l'effet de manque
3 *adv* (**a**) **to go straight** *(of criminal)* se ranger des voitures
(**b**) *Br* **straight up?** sans déconner?,

sans dec?; **straight up!** sans déconner!, je t'assure!, sans dec!

straight-edge [streɪt'edʒ] *adj Am* sérieux [□], rangé [□]

strapped [stræpt] *adj* (**a**) **to be strapped (for cash)** être fauché, ne pas avoir un rond (**b**) *Am (armed)* armé [□], chargé

streak [striːk] *n Br* **he's a long streak of piss** [!] *(tall and thin)* c'est une grande perche; *(insipid in character)* c'est une lavette

street [striːt] *n* (**a**) **to be on the street** *or* **streets** *(of homeless person)* être à la rue; *(of prostitute)* faire le trottoir *ou* le tapin; **to walk the streets** *(of prostitute)* faire le trottoir *ou* le tapin (**b**) *Br* **this job should be right up your street** ce boulot devrait être dans tes cordes; **there'll be loads of drink and drugs, it should be right up your street** il y aura beaucoup d'alcool et de drogue, c'est tout à fait ton truc
▶ *voir aussi* **cred, easy, queer**

streetwalker ['striːtwɔːkə(r)] *n* prostituée [□] *f*, **to be a streetwalker** faire le trottoir

streetwise ['striːtwaɪz] *adj* qui sait se débrouiller tout seul, déluré

strength [streŋθ] *n* **give me strength!** pitié!

stretch [stretʃ] *n (term of imprisonment)* peine *f* de prison [□]; **to do a stretch** faire de la taule; **he was given a five-year stretch** il a écopé de cinq ans

strewth [struːθ] *exclam Br (abrév* **God's truth)** mince alors!

strides [straɪdz] *npl Br (trousers)* bénard *m*, bène *m*, futal *m*, fute *m*

stringbean ['strɪŋbiːn] *n Am (person)* grande perche *f*, asperge *f*

stroke [strəʊk] *vt Am (flatter)* passer de la pommade à

strop [strɒp] *n Br* **to be in a strop** être mal luné, être de mauvais poil

stroppy ['strɒpɪ] *adj Br* mal luné, de mauvais poil

stuck [stʌk] *adj Br* **to get stuck into sb** *(physically, verbally)* rentrer dans le lard à qn; **to get stuck into sth** *(book, work, meal)* attaquer qch; **get stuck in!** attaque!

stud [stʌd] *n (man)* étalon *m*; *Am* **stud muffin** super beau mec *m*

stuff [stʌf] **1** *n* **(a)** *Br* **she's a lovely bit of stuff** elle est vraiment bien balancée, elle est canon; **he was there with his bit of stuff** il était là avec sa gonzesse
  (b) go on, do your stuff! allez, à toi de jouer!; **to know one's stuff** s'y connaître, connaître son affaire; **that's the stuff!** parfait!
  (c) *(drugs)* came *f*
  2 *vt* **(a) to stuff oneself** *or* **one's face** se goinfrer, s'empiffrer, s'en mettre plein la lampe, s'en mettre jusque-là
  (b) get stuffed!, stuff you! va te faire cuire un œuf!; **stuff this, I'm going home!** rien à foutre de ce truc, moi je rentre chez moi!; **I've had enough, he can stuff his job!** j'en ai marre, son boulot il peut se le mettre où je pense!
  (c) *(defeat)* écrabouiller, foutre une déculottée à, battre à plates coutures
  (d) ‼ *(have sex with)* baiser, troncher, tringler

stumblebum ['stʌmbəlbʌm] *n Am*
  (a) *(drunken vagrant)* clodo *mf* alcolo
  (b) *(clumsy, incompetent person)* manche *m*

stumm [ʃtʊm] = **schtum**

stump up [stʌmp] *Br* **1** *vt sép* cracher, casquer
  2 *vi* casquer, raquer **(for** pour); **come on, stump up!** allez, raque!

stunner ['stʌnə(r)] *n Br (woman)* canon *m*, bombe *f*

stupe [stjuːp] *n Am* andouille *f*, truffe *f*, crétin(e) *m,f*

style [staɪl] *vi Noir Am (show off)* frimer, flamber; *(do well)* bien se démerder

sub [sʌb] *Br* **1** *n (abrév* **subsistence allowance)** *(small loan)* prêt □ *m*; **to give sb a sub** dépanner qn; **to get a sub** se faire dépanner
  2 *vt (lend)* **to sub sb sth** dépanner qn de qch; **can you sub me a fiver?** tu peux me dépanner de cinq livres?

suck [sʌk] **1** *vt Am* **to suck face** se rouler des pelles *ou* des patins *ou* des galoches
  2 *vi (be bad)* craindre, être nul *ou* merdique; **this bar/film sucks** ce bar/film est vraiment nul; **this sucks, let's do something else** c'est nul, si on faisait autre chose?; **I've got to work all weekend – that sucks!** il faut que je travaille tout le week-end – ça craint!

suck off ‼ *vt sép* **to suck sb off** sucer qn, tailler une pipe à qn, faire un pompier à qn

suck up *vi* **to suck up to sb** faire de la lèche à qn, cirer les pompes à qn

sucker ['sʌkə(r)] **1** *n* **(a)** *(gullible person)* poire *f*, pigeon *m*; **he's a sucker for blondes/chocolate ice-cream** il adore les blondes/la glace au chocolat **(b)** *Am (despicable man)* blaireau *m* **(c)** *Am (object)* truc *m*, machin *m*, bitoniau *m*; **what's this sucker for?** à quoi ça sert, ce truc?
  2 *vt (trick, swindle)* arnaquer

sugar ['ʃʊgə(r)] **1** *n* **(a)** *(term of address)* chéri(e) *m,f* **(b)** **sugar daddy** = homme âgé qui entretient une jeune maîtresse
  2 *exclam* miel!, punaise!

suit [suːt] *n Péj (person)* employé(e) *m,f* de bureau □ *(en costume ou tailleur)*
  ▶ *voir aussi* **monkey, penguin**

sunshine ['sʌnʃaɪn] *n Br (term of address)* chéri(e) *m,f*; **watch it, sunshine!** fais gaffe, mon coco!

supergrass ['suːpəgrɑːs] *n Br* indic *mf* de choc

sure [ʃɔː(r)] **1** *adj* **sure thing!** et comment!
  2 *exclam* **(a)** *Am (you're welcome)* de rien! □, il n'y a pas de quoi! □ **(b) (for)**

sure! *(of course)* bien sûr!

suss [sʌs] *vt Br (work out)* découvrir ᵈ; *(realize)* se rendre compte de ᵈ; **I soon sussed what he was up to** j'ai vite compris son petit manège; **I haven't sussed where the good pubs are yet** j'ai pas encore repéré les bons pubs

suss out *vt sép Br* **to suss sth out** *(work out)* découvrir ᵈ; *(realize)* se rendre compte de ᵈ; **I couldn't suss out how the modem worked** j'ai pas pigé comment le modem fonctionnait; **I can't quite suss her out** c'est quelqu'un que j'ai du mal à cerner; **I haven't sussed out his motives yet** j'ai toujours pas pigé ses motivations, **we have to suss out the best places to go at night** il faut qu'on repère les endroits où sortir le soir

sussed [sʌst] *adj* **(a)** *(astute)* rusé, malin **(b) I haven't got her sussed yet** je l'ai pas encore vraiment cernée; **I haven't got this computer sussed yet** j'ai pas encore pigé comment fonctionne cet ordinateur

swacked [swækt] *adj Am (drunk)* bourré, fait, beurré

swanky ['swæŋkɪ] *adj* **(a)** *(chic, posh)* classe, chicos **(b)** *(boastful)* frimeur

sweat [swet] *n* **no sweat!** pas de problèmes!

sweet [swiːt] **1** *adj (excellent)* génial, super
2 *exclam Br* **sweet (as a nut)!** cool!, génial!
▶ *voir aussi* **FA**

sweetie(-pie) ['swiːtɪ(paɪ)] *n (term of address)* mon (ma) chéri(e) *m,f*

swift [swɪft] *adj Am (clever)* malin; **that was a real swift move** c'était bien joué; **she's not real swift** c'est pas une lumière, elle est pas très maligne

swine [swaɪn] *n Br (person)* salaud *m*; **he's a lazy swine!** c'est une grosse feignasse!

swing [swɪŋ] *vi* **(a)** *(be hanged)* être pendu; **he should swing for that!** il mériterait douze balles dans la peau! **(b)** *(exchange sexual partners)* faire de l'échangisme ᵈ **(c) to swing both ways** *(be bisexual)* marcher à voile et à vapeur **(d) to swing for sb** *(hit out at)* essayer d'en coller une à qn

swinger ['swɪŋə(r)] *n* **(a)** *(sociable person)* fêtard(e) *m,f* **(b)** *(who exchanges sexual partners)* échangiste ᵈ *mf*

swipe [swaɪp] *vt (steal)* piquer, chouraver, barboter; **who's swiped my pen?** qui m'a piqué *ou* chouravé *ou* barboté mon stylo?

swish [swɪʃ] **1** *n Am Injurieux (effeminate homosexual)* folle *f*
2 *adj Br (chic)* classe, chicos

swishy ['swɪʃɪ] *adj Am Injurieux (effeminate)* chochotte

switch-hitter ['swɪtʃhɪtə(r)] *n Injurieux (homosexual)* pédé *m*, tante *f*, tapette *f*

swizz [swɪz] *n Br* arnaque *f*

swot [swɒt] *Br* **1** *n Péj* bûcheur(euse) *m,f*
2 *vi* bûcher

swot up on *vt insép Br* bûcher

syrup ['sɪrəp] *n Br (rhyming slang* **syrup of figs = wig)** moumoute *f*

T

ta [tɑː] *exclam Br* merci! □

tab [tæb] *n* (**a**) *(of LSD)* buvard *m* (**b**) *Br (cigarette)* clope *f*, tige *f*, sèche *f*

table ['teɪbəl] *n* **to drink sb under the table** = tenir encore debout quand tout le monde a roulé sous la table

tackle ['tækəl] *n Br Hum* **(wedding) tackle** *(man's genitals)* service *m* trois pièces, bijoux *mpl* de famille

tad [tæd] *n* **a tad** un tantinet; **it's a tad expensive** c'est un peu chérot; **it's a tad long** c'est un peu longuet; **it's a tad worrying** c'est un tantinet inquiétant; **I think you're exaggerating a tad** je crois que t'exagères un tantinet; **you were being a tad naive if you believed him** si tu l'as cru, t'as été un tantinet naïf

tadger ['tædʒə(r)] *n Br (penis)* chipolata *f*

Taffy ['tæfɪ] *n Br Péj (Welshman)* Gallois □ *m*

> "Taffy" est censé être la transcription phonétique du prénom "David" tel que le prononcent les Gallois, et désigne une personne originaire du pays de Galles. Bien que ce terme ne témoigne pas nécessairement d'une attitude xénophobe de la part de celui qui l'utilise, il est préférable de ne pas l'employer.

tail [teɪl] **1** *n* (**a**) *(buttocks)* derrière *m*; **to work one's tail off** bosser comme un malade (**b**) *(person following a criminal)* filocheur *m*; **to put a tail on sb** faire filer le train à qn, faire filocher qn (**c**) [!] *Am (woman)* **she's a great piece of tail** c'est une nana super bandante; **he's looking for some tail** il cherche une

femme à se mettre sur le bout

2 *vt (follow)* filocher, filer le train à
▶ *voir aussi* **shake**

tailgate ['teɪlgeɪt] *vt Am* **to tailgate sb** coller au cul à qn

take [teɪk] *n* **to be on the take** toucher des pots-de-vin, palper

take off *vi (leave hurriedly)* se barrer, se tirer

take out *vt sép* **to take sb out** *(kill)* buter qn, zigouiller qn, refroidir qn

tale [teɪl] *n* **to tell tales** *(inform)* cafter; **she's been telling tales to the teacher again** elle est encore allée cafter à la maîtresse

talent ['tælənt] *n Br (attractive men)* beaux mecs *mpl*; *(attractive women)* belles nanas *fpl*; **he's out chatting up the local talent** il est en train de draguer les minettes du coin; **it's an OK bar, but there's not much talent** c'est pas mal comme bar, mais question mecs/nanas, ça casse pas des briques

talk [tɔːk] *vi* **talk about lucky!** tu parles d'un coup de bol!; **talk about a waste of time!** tu parles d'une perte de temps; **now you're talking!** à la bonne heure!, voilà, c'est beaucoup mieux!; **you can talk!, look who's talking!** tu peux parler!

tank [tæŋk] *n* **to be built like a tank** être une armoire à glace

tanked [tæŋkt] *adj Am (drunk)* bourré, beurré, pété; **to get tanked** prendre une cuite

tanked up [tæŋkt'ʌp] *adj Br (drunk)* bourré, beurré, pété; **to get tanked up** prendre une cuite

tap [tæp] *vt Br* **to tap sb for sth** taper qch à qn; **he tapped me for a loan but I refused** il a voulu me taper du fric, mais j'ai refusé

ta-ra [tə'rɑ:] *exclam Br* salut!, ciao!

tart [tɑːt] *n Br* (**a**) *(prostitute)* pute *f* (**b**) *Péj (promiscuous woman)* salope *f*, traînée *f*, Marie-couche-toi-là *f*, pétasse *f*

tart up *vt sép Br* **to tart oneself up** se pomponner; **to tart sth up** décorer qch [□] *(le plus souvent avec mauvais goût)*

tarty ['tɑːtɪ] *adj Br* qui fait pute

tasty ['teɪstɪ] *adj (attractive)* bien foutu, bien balancé

tea leaf ['tiːliːf] *n Br (rhyming slang* **thief)** voleur(euse) [□] *m,f*

technicolour, *Am* **technicolor** ['teknɪkʌlə(r)] *adj Hum* **to have a** *Br* **technicolour** *or Am* **technicolor yawn** *(vomit)* gerber, dégobiller

teenybopper ['tiːnɪbɒpə(r)] *n* petite minette *f (qui suit la mode)*

teeth [tiːθ] *npl Br* **to be fed up** *or* **sick to the back teeth of sb/sth** en avoir plus que marre de qn/qch
▶ *voir aussi* **hell**

tell-tale ['telteɪl] *n Br* cafteur(euse) *m,f*

tenner ['tenə(r)] *n Br (ten-pound note)* billet *m* de dix livres [□]; *Am (ten-dollar note)* billet *m* de dix dollars [□]; *Br (sum)* dix livres [□] *fpl*

ten-spot ['tenspɒt] *n Am* billet *m* de dix dollars [□]

there [ðeə(r)] *adv* **been there, done that (got the T-shirt)** non merci, j'ai déjà donné

thick [θɪk] *adj* (**a**) *(stupid)* bête [□], débile; *Br* **to be as thick as two short planks** être bête comme ses pieds *ou* bête à manger du foin; **will you get that into your thick skull!** tu vas te mettre ça dans la tête, oui ou non?
(**b**) *Br (unreasonable)* **that's a bit thick!** c'est un peu fort!; **it's a bit thick expecting us to take them to the**

airport! ils exagèrent de compter sur nous pour les conduire à l'aéroport!
(**c**) *Br* **to give sb a thick ear** flanquer une taloche à qn

thickie ['θɪkɪ], **thicko** ['θɪkəʊ] *n Br* nouille *f*, andouille *f*

thing [θɪŋ] *n* (**a**) **to have a thing about sb/sth** *(like)* avoir un faible pour qn/qch; *(dislike)* avoir horreur de qn/qch; **he's got a real thing about tidiness/ punctuality** il est très à cheval sur la propreté/la ponctualité (**b**) *(penis)* chose *f*
▶ *voir aussi* **sure**

thingumabob ['θɪŋəmɪbɒb], **thingumajig** ['θɪŋəmɪdʒɪg], **thingummy** ['θɪŋəmɪ], **thingy** ['θɪŋɪ] *n (person)* Bidule *mf*, Machin(e) *m,f*; *(thing)* truc *m*, machin *m*

third degree ['θɜːdɪ'griː] *n* **to give sb the third degree** cuisiner qn

thrash [θræʃ] **1** *n Br (party)* fiesta *f*
2 *vt* (**a**) *(beat up)* tabasser, casser la gueule à (**b**) *(defeat)* foutre la pâtée *ou* une raclée *ou* une déculottée à, écrabouiller, battre à plates coutures (**c**) *Br (car)* conduire comme un dingue

thrashing ['θræʃɪŋ] *n* (**a**) *(beating)* **to give sb a thrashing** tabasser qn, casser la gueule à qn, foutre une raclée à qn; **to get a thrashing** prendre une raclée, se faire tabasser
(**b**) *(defeat)* déculottée *f*, dégelée *f*, raclée *f*; **to give sb a thrashing** foutre la pâtée *ou* une raclée *ou* une déculottée à qn, écrabouiller qn, battre qn à plates coutures; **to get a thrashing** prendre une raclée *ou* une déculottée, se faire battre à plates coutures

threads [θredz] *npl (clothes)* fringues *fpl*

throat [θrəʊt] *n* (**a**) *Hum* **my stomach thinks my throat's cut** je crève la dalle (**b**) **to be at each other's throats** *(arguing)* se disputer, se chamailler; **to jump down sb's throat** *(shout at)* rentrer dans qn, gueuler sur qn

throw up [θrəʊ] vi (vomit) dégobiller

thunderthighs ['θʌndəθaɪz] n Hum = femme aux grosses cuisses

tick [tɪk] n Br (a) (moment) seconde⁰ f, instant⁰ m; **hang on a tick** or **two ticks** attends une seconde; **I'll just be a tick** or **two ticks** j'en ai pour une seconde ou deux secondes (b) (credit) **to buy sth on tick** acheter qch à crédit⁰

tick off vt sép (a) Br (scold) passer un savon à (b) Am (annoy) prendre la tête à; **to be ticked off (with)** en avoir marre (de)

ticker ['tɪkə(r)] n (heart) palpitant m

ticket ['tɪkɪt] n **that's (just) the ticket!** c'est exactement ce qu'il me/te/etc faut!

tiddly ['tɪdlɪ] adj Br (a) (drunk) éméché (b) (small) minus

tie on [taɪ] vt sép Am **to tie one on** (get drunk) prendre une cuite, se cuiter

tight [taɪt] adj (a) (miserly) pingre, radin (b) (drunk) pompette

tight-arsed[!] ['taɪtɑːst], Am **tight-assed**[!] ['taɪtæst] adj (uptight) coincé

tight-fisted [taɪt'fɪstɪd] adj pingre, radin

tightwad ['taɪtwɒd] n radin(e) m,f

time [taɪm] n (a) **to do time** (in prison) faire de la taule (b) Am **to make time with sb** (chat up) draguer qn; (have sex with) s'envoyer en l'air avec qn

tinkle ['tɪŋkəl] 1 n (a) Br (phone call) **to give sb a tinkle** passer un coup de fil à qn (b) (act of urinating) Br **to have** or **do a tinkle** faire pipi; **to go for a tinkle** aller faire pipi
2 vi (urinate) faire pipi

tip [tɪp] n Br (untidy place) taudis m
▶ voir aussi **arse**

tipsy ['tɪpsɪ] adj éméché

tit[!] [tɪt] n (a) (breast) nichon m, robert m; Br **to get on sb's tits** courir sur le haricot à qn, taper sur les nerfs à qn (b) Br (person) con (conne) m,f; **I felt a right tit** je me suis senti tout con
▶ voir aussi **arse, ripped**

titty[!] ['tɪtɪ] n (a) (breast) nichon m, robert m (b) **tough titty!** dur! dur!

toast [təʊst] n **to be toast** (in trouble) être foutu; (exhausted) être naze ou crevé ou lessivé ou claqué; **if Mum finds out, you're toast** si Maman s'en rend compte, t'es mort ou foutu!; **I can't drink any more or I'll be toast tomorrow** il faut que j'arrête de boire, sinon demain je serai dans le coaltar

tod [tɒd] n Br (rhyming slang **Tod Sloan** = **own**) **on one's tod** tout seul⁰

to-die-for [tə'daɪfɔː(r)] adj craquant

toff [tɒf] n Br rupin(e) m,f

toffee ['tɒfɪ] n Br **he can't sing/act for toffee!** il chante/joue comme un pied!

toffee-nosed ['tɒfɪnəʊzd] adj Br bêcheur, snob

together [tə'geðə(r)] adj (well-adjusted) équilibré⁰, bien dans ses baskets

togs [tɒgz] npl Br fringues fpl, sapes fpl

toilet ['tɔɪlɪt] n **to go down the toilet** (of plan, career, work) être foutu en l'air; **that's our holidays down the toilet!** on peut faire une croix sur nos vacances!

toke [təʊk] 1 n (of joint) taffe f; **to take a toke** prendre une taffe
2 vi **to toke on a joint** prendre une taffe d'un joint

tomcat around ['tɒmkæt] vi Am courir les filles

Tom, Dick and Harry ['tɒm'dɪkən'hærɪ] npr **every** or Br **any Tom, Dick and Harry** le premier venu, n'importe qui

tonsil hockey ['tɒnsɪl'hɒkɪ] n Hum **to play tonsil hockey** se rouler des pelles ou des patins

tool[!] [tuːl] n (a) (penis) engin m (b) (man) con m, connard m

toot [tuːt] 1 n (a) (of cocaine) prise f de cocaïne⁰ (b) Am (drinking spree) cuite f;

to go out on a toot sortir prendre une cuite

2 vt (cocaine) sniffer

3 vi (sniff cocaine) sniffer de la coke

toots [tu:ts] n (term of address) chéri(e) m,f

top [tɒp] **1** n (**a**) **to pay top dollar (for sth)** payer le prix fort (pour qch) (**b**) Br to **pay/earn top whack** payer/gagner un max; **we can offer you £50 top whack** on vous propose 50 livres mais pas plus ou et c'est notre dernier prix (**c**) **top banana** huile f, gros bonnet m

2 vt Br (kill) buter, zigouiller, refroidir; **to top oneself** se suicider ▢, se foutre en l'air

▶ voir aussi **blow, totty, up**

tops [tɒps] adv (at the most) maxi; **it'll cost a fiver tops** ça coûtera cinq livres maxi ou à tout casser

torqued [tɔːkt] adj Am (**a**) (angry) furibard, furax, fumasse (**b**) (drunk) bourré, fait, beurré

tosh [tɒʃ] Br **1** n foutaises fpl; **that's a load of tosh!** c'est des foutaises!

2 exclam n'importe quoi!

toss [tɒs] n Br **I don't give a toss!** je m'en fiche pas mal!; **who gives a toss?** qu'est-ce que ça peut foutre?

▶ see also **cookie**

toss off [!] Br **1** vt sép **to toss sb off** branler qn; **to toss oneself off** se branler, se palucher, se pogner

2 vi se branler, se palucher, se pogner

tosser ['tɒsə(r)], **tosspot** ['tɒspɒt] n Br tache f, branque m

total ['təʊtəl] vt Am (vehicle) fusiller, bousiller

totally ['təʊtəlɪ] adv Am (very much) vachement; **I don't smoke but my parents totally smoke** moi je fume pas, mais mes parents ils fument vachement ou ils fument comme des malades

totty ['tɒtɪ] n Br (attractive women) belles nanas fpl, belles gonzesses fpl; **he's at the beach checking out the totty** il est en train de mater les nanas sur la plage; **check out the top totty!** vise un peu les canons!

touch [tʌtʃ] **1** n **to be a soft touch** être un pigeon ou une poire

2 vt **to touch sb for sth** taper qch à qn

touch up vt sép Br **to touch sb up** peloter qn; **to touch oneself up** se toucher

touched [tʌtʃt] adj (mad) timbré, toqué, cinglé

tough [tʌf] **1** adj **a tough guy** un dur

2 exclam tant pis!

▶ voir aussi **cookie, hang, shit, titty**

towelhead ['taʊəlhed] n Injurieux raton m, bicot m

toyboy ['tɔɪbɔɪ] n = jeune amant d'une femme plus âgée

tracks [træks] npl (**a**) **to make tracks** (leave) mettre les bouts, se casser (**b**) (on arm) traces fpl de piquouses

tradesman's entrance [!] ['treɪdzmənz'entrəns] n Br Hum (anus) entrée f de service

traffic ['træfɪk] n **go play in the traffic!** va voir ailleurs si j'y suis!

trainspotter ['treɪnspɒtə(r)] n Br Péj ringard(e) m,f

À l'origine, le terme "trainspotter" désigne un passionné des chemins de fer dont le passe-temps consiste à noter les numéros des locomotives qu'il aperçoit. Au sens large, ce terme désigne une personne généralement solitaire et ennuyeuse, qui ne sait pas s'habiller (il porte le plus souvent un anorak). Un "trainspotter" ne s'intéresse pas à l'actualité musicale ou sportive, et ne fréquente aucun endroit branché.

tramlines ['træmlaɪnz] npl Br (on arm) traces fpl de piquouses

tramp [træmp] n Péj (promiscuous woman) Marie-couche-toi-là f, pétasse f, traînée f

trank [træŋk], **trankie** ['træŋkɪ] n (abrév **tranquillizer**) tranquillisant □ m

trannie, tranny ['trænɪ] n Br (abrév **transvestite**) travelo m

trap [træp] n (mouth) clapet m; **shut your trap!** ferme ton clapet, ferme-la!; **to keep one's trap shut** la fermer, la boucler

trash [træʃ] 1 n (a) (nonsense) foutaises fpl; **his new film's a load of trash** son dernier film ne vaut pas un clou (b) (people) ordures fpl; **he's just trash** c'est un moins que rien; **white trash** petits Blancs mpl pauvres (c) Noir Am **to talk trash** (converse, gossip) tailler une bavette
2 vt (a) (vandalize) foutre en l'air, bousiller (b) (criticize) éreinter, démolir

trashed [træʃt] adj (drunk) rond, fait, bourré; (on drugs) défoncé, raide

tree [triː] n **to be out of one's tree** (mad) être cinglé ou givré; (drunk) être rond ou rétamé ou bourré; (on drugs) être défoncé ou raide

trendy ['trendɪ] 1 n branché(e) m,f
2 adj branché

trick [trɪk] n (a) **how's tricks?** comment ça va? (b) **to do the trick** faire l'affaire (c) (prostitute's client) micheton m; **to turn a trick** faire une passe; **she's been turning tricks for years** ça fait des années qu'elle fait la pute

trim [trɪm] n (women) nanas fpl, gonzesses fpl; **that's his new bit of trim** c'est sa nouvelle nana ou gonzesse

trip [trɪp] 1 n (a) (after taking drugs) trip m; **to have a good/bad trip** avoir un bon/mauvais trip (b) (quantity of LSD) dose f de LSD □, trip m (c) (experience) **to be on a guilt trip** culpabiliser; **to be on a power trip** être en plein trip mégalo; **to be on an ego trip** se faire mousser
2 vi (after taking drugs) triper

trip out vi (after taking drugs) triper

tripe [traɪp] n (nonsense) foutaises fpl, conneries fpl; **don't talk tripe!** dis pas n'importe quoi!, raconte pas de conneries!; **what a load of tripe!** n'importe quoi!; **the film is absolute tripe!** il vaut pas un clou, ce film!

trolley ['trɒlɪ] n (a) **to be off one's trolley** avoir un grain, être cinglé (b) Br Hum Péj **trolley dolly** (air hostess) hôtesse f de l'air □

trots [trɒts] npl **the trots** (diarrhoea) la courante

trouble ['trʌbəl] n (a) **man/woman trouble** peines fpl de cœur (b) Br **trouble and strife** (rhyming slang **wife**) femme □ f, bourgeoise f

trounce [traʊns] vt battre à plates coutures, écrabouiller, mettre la pâtée à; **to get trounced** être battu à plates coutures, prendre une déculottée

trout [traʊt] n Péj (woman) **(old) trout** vieille bique f

try on [traɪ] vt sép Br **to try it on with sb** (attempt to deceive) essayer d'embobiner qn; (attempt to seduce) faire des avances à qn □; (test someone's tolerance) essayer de faire le coup à qn

tube [tjuːb] n (a) **to go down the tubes** (of plans) tomber à l'eau; **that's £500 down the tubes** ça fait 500 livres de foutues en l'air (b) **the tube** (television) la téloche (c) **to have one's tubes tied** (be sterilized) se faire ligaturer les trompes □
▶ voir aussi **boob**

tubular ['tjuːbjʊlə(r)] adj Am (excellent) génial, super, géant

turd [!] [tɜːd] n (a) (excrement) merde f (b) (person) ordure f

turd-burglar [!] ['tɜːdbɜːglə(r)] n Br Injurieux pédale f, tantouze f, lope f

turf [tɜːf] n (a) (territory) territoire m (b) Am (field of expertise, authority) domaine □ m, truc m, rayon m; **that's not my turf** c'est pas mon rayon

turf out vt sép Br **to turf sb out** vider qn, foutre qn dehors

turkey ['tɜ:kɪ] n Am **(a)** (unsuccessful film, book) bide m **(b)** (person) crétin(e) m,f, andouille f, courge f **(c) to talk turkey** passer aux choses sérieuses □
▶ voir aussi **cold turkey**

turn off [tɜ:n] vt sép **to turn sb off** (repulse) débecter qn

turn on 1 vt sép (excite) **to turn sb on** exciter qn; **to be turned on** être excité **2** vi (take drugs) se camer

turn over vt sép Br (rob, burgle) **to turn sth over** (house) cambrioler qch □; (bank, shop) cambrioler qch □, braquer qch

turn-off ['tɜ:nɒf] n (sexually) **it's a turn-off** ça coupe l'envie

turn-on ['tɜ:nɒn] n (sexually) **it's a real turn-on for him** il trouve ça super excitant

TV [ti:'vi:] n (abrév **transvestite**) travelo m

twat [twæt] n **(a)**|!| (woman's genitals) chatte f, chagatte f **(b)** (person) tache f, taré(e) m,f

tweaked [twi:kt] adj Am (drunk) bourré, fait, beurré; (on drugs) raide, défoncé

twenty-four seven ['twentɪfɔ:'sevən] adv (constantly) sans arrêt □

Cette expression (à laquelle on ajoute parfois "365") signifie littéralement 24 heures par jour, 7 jours par semaine (et 365 jours par an).

twerp [twɜ:p] n courge f, nouille f

twinky ['twɪŋkɪ] n Am (homosexual) homo m

twist [twɪst] n Br **to be round the twist** être dingue, avoir un grain; **to go round the twist** devenir dingue ou cinglé, perdre la boule; **to drive sb round the twist** rendre qn chèvre
▶ voir aussi **knickers**

twister ['twɪstə(r)] n **(a)** Br (crook) arnaqueur(euse) m,f **(b)** Am (tornado) tornade □ f

twit [twɪt] n Br courge f, nouille f

two-time [tu:'taɪm] vt **to two-time sb** tromper qn □, faire porter des cornes à qn

two-timer [tu:'taɪmə(r)] n personne f infidèle □

tyke [taɪk] n **(a)** Br (coarse person) lourdaud(e) m,f **(b)** (child) morveux(euse) m,f, môme mf

U

uh-huh [ˈʌhʌ, ʌˈhʌ] *exclam* ouais!

umpteen [ˈʌmptiːn] *adj* des tas de; **I've told you umpteen times** je te l'ai déjà dit trente-six fois

umpteenth [ˈʌmptiːnθ] *adj* énième; **for the umpteenth time** pour la énième fois

uncool [ʌnˈkuːl] *adj* **(a)** *(unfashionable, unsophisticated)* ringard; **it's a really uncool place** c'est nul comme endroit; **what an uncool thing to do!** c'est vraiment nul de faire un truc pareil! **(b)** *(not allowed, not accepted)* mal vu □; **I think it's a bit uncool to smoke in here** je pense pas que ce soit permis de fumer ici □ **(c)** *(upset)* **she was a bit uncool about me moving in with them** elle tenait pas trop à ce que je m'installe chez eux

undies [ˈʌndɪz] *npl* (abrév **underwear**) sous-vêtements *mpl* féminins □

unhip [ʌnˈhɪp] *adj* ringard

uni [ˈjuːnɪ] *n* **(a)** *Br* (abrév **university**) fac *f*; **he's doing law at uni** il fait une fac de droit **(b)** *Am* (abrév **uniform**) uniforme □ *m*

unreal [ʌnˈrɪəl] *adj* **(a)** *(unbelievable)* pas possible, pas croyable, dingue **(b)** *(excellent)* dément, super, génial

up [ʌp] **1** *n* *(drug)* amphet *f*, amphé *f*

2 *adj* **(a) what's up?** *(what's happening)* qu'est-ce qui se passe?; *(what's wrong)* qu'est-ce qui va pas?; *Am (as greeting)* salut!; **what's up with him?** qu'est-ce qui lui arrive?; **there's something up with the TV** la télé débloque **(b)** *Br* **we're going clubbing tonight, are you up for it?** on va en boîte ce soir,

ça te branche?; **was she up for it?** *(willing to have sex)* alors, elle a bien voulu coucher?

3 *adv Br* **he doesn't have very much up top** c'est pas une lumière, il a pas inventé l'eau chaude *ou* le fil à couper le beurre; **she's got plenty up top** elle en a dans le ciboulot

4 *prép* **up yours!** [!!] va te faire foutre!

upchuck [ˈʌptʃʌk] *vi Hum* dégobiller

upper [ˈʌpə(r)] *n* **(a)** *(drug)* amphet *f*, amphé *f*; **he's on uppers** il est sous amphets *ou* amphés **(b)** *Br* **to be on one's uppers** être dans la dèche

upside [ˈʌpsaɪd] *prép Noir Am* **to go upside sb's head** filer un coup sur le ciboulot *ou* la cafetière à qn

upstairs [ʌpˈsteəz] *adv* **(a) he hasn't got much upstairs** c'est pas une lumière, il a pas inventé l'eau chaude *ou* le fil à couper le beurre **(b) to kick sb upstairs** *(promote)* se débarrasser de qn en lui donnant de l'avancement □

uptight [ʌpˈtaɪt] *adj Noir Am* *(excellent)* super, génial, géant

us [ʌs] *pron Br (me)* **give us a kiss** embrasse-moi □; **give us a look** fais voir □; **he bought us a drink** il m'a payé un verre □

use [juːz] *vi* *(take drugs)* se camer

user [ˈjuːzə(r)] *n* drogué(e) □ *m,f*; **heroin user** héroïnomane □ *mf*; **cocaine user** cocaïnomane □ *mf*

usual [ˈjuːʒəl] *n* *(drink, food)* **the usual, sir?** comme d'habitude, monsieur?; **I'll just have my usual** je prends comme d'habitude

V

vag¹ [!!] [væʤ] *n* (*abrév* **vagina**) chatte *f*, cramouille *f*

vag² [væg] *n Am* (*abrév* **vagrant**) clodo *mf*

vamoose [vəˈmuːs] *vi* se tirer, se casser; **vamoose!** tire-toi!, casse-toi!

vamp [væmp] *vi Noir Am* (*leave*) se casser, se tirer, s'arracher

veep [viːp] *n Am* (*abrév* **vice-president**) vice-président □ *m*

veg [veʤ] *npl Br* (*abrév* **vegetables**) légumes □ *mpl*, verdure *f*

veg out *vi* traîner, glandouiller

veggie [ˈveʤɪ] (*abrév* **vegetarian**) **1** *n* végétarien(enne) □ *m,f*
2 *adj* végétarien □

velvet [ˈvelvɪt] *n Am* (*profit*) bénef *m*; (*easy money*) argent *m* facile □

verbal [ˈvɜːbəl] **1** *n Br* (*insults*) insultes □ *fpl*; **to give sb some verbal** traiter qn de tous les noms
2 *adj Hum* **to have verbal** *Br* **diar-** rhoea *or Am* **diarrhea** être atteint de diarrhée verbale

vibes [vaɪbz] *npl* (*abrév* **vibrations**) **to get good/bad vibes about sb/sth** bien/mal sentir qn/qch; **he gives me good/bad vibes** il y a quelque chose chez lui que j'aime/que j'aime pas; **this place gives me strange vibes** cet endroit me donne de drôles de sensations

-ville [vɪl] *suffixe* **boresville** hyper chiant; **sleazeville** hyper corrompu

> Le suffixe "-ville" sert à former des noms et des adjectifs. Il indique que le terme qui le précède caractérise ce dont on parle.

vines [vaɪnz] *npl Noir Am* (*clothes*) fringues *fpl*, sapes *fpl*

vino [ˈviːnəʊ] *n* pinard *m*, picrate *m*

vom [vɒm] (*abrév* **vomit**) **1** *n* dégueulis *m*
2 *vi* dégueuler, gerber

Valley speak

"Valley speak" ou "Valspeak" est le jargon utilisé par les riches adolescentes de la Vallée de San Fernando, près de Los Angeles. C'est Frank Zappa et sa fille Moon Unit qui ont popularisé ce jargon au début des années 80, notamment avec la sortie du disque *Valley Girl* en 1982.

Bien que l'engouement pour le "Valley speak" ait été de courte durée, quelques expressions ont survécu et figurent dans ce dictionnaire. Le "Valley speak" a beaucoup emprunté à l'argot des surfeurs. Le sarcasme et l'exagération en sont les caractéristiques principales, ainsi qu'une bonne dose d'ironie qui transparaît dans des expressions telles que "for sure" et "as if". Bien qu'encore adolescente, la "valley girl" jette sur le monde un regard désabusé. Elle constitua le thème de livres, de chansons et de films, le plus célèbre étant *Clueless*, sorti en 1995.

wack [wæk] *adj Noir Am* (**a**) *(worthless)* nul (**b**) *(mad)* cinglé, toqué, timbré (**c**) *(stupid)* débile

wacko ['wækəʊ] **1** *n* cinglé(e) *m,f,* dingue *mf*
2 *adj* cinglé, dingue, timbré, toqué

wacky ['wækɪ] *adj* loufoque; *Hum* **wacky baccy** *(marijuana)* herbe *f*

wagon ['wægən] *n* **to be on the wagon** être au régime sec; **to be off** *or* **have fallen off the wagon** s'être remis à picoler
▶ *voir aussi* **meat, paddy**

walk [wɔːk] **1** *n* **take a walk!** va voir ailleurs si j'y suis!, dégage!; **it was a walk in the park** *(very easy)* c'était un jeu d'enfant
2 *vt* **to walk it** gagner les doigts dans le nez
▶ *voir aussi* **street**

wall [wɔːl] *n* (**a**) **off the wall** *(eccentric)* loufoque, zarbi (**b**) **to be up the wall** *(mad)* être cinglé *ou* givré, avoir un grain; **to drive sb up the wall** rendre qn chèvre
▶ *voir aussi* **hole**

wallop ['wɒləp] **1** *n* **to give sb a wallop** foutre une beigne *ou* un gnon à qn; **to give sth a wallop** foutre un coup dans qch
2 *vt* (**a**) *(hit)* *(person)* foutre une beigne *ou* un gnon à; *(object)* foutre un coup dans (**b**) *(defeat)* foutre la pâtée *ou* une raclée *ou* une déculottée à, écrabouiller, battre à plates coutures

wally ['wɒlɪ] *n Br* andouille *f,* nouille *f*

wank [wæŋk] *Br* **1** *n* branlette *f;* **to have a wank** se branler, se pogner, se paluches
2 *vi* se branler, se pogner, se paluches

wank off *Br* **1** *vt sép* **to wank sb off** se branler qn; **to wank oneself off** se branler, se pogner, se palucher
2 *vi* se branler, se pogner, se palucher

wanker ['wæŋkə(r)] *n Br (idiot)* connard *m*

wannabe ['wɒnəbiː] *n* (**a**) *(who wants money, success)* arriviste *mf* (**b**) *(who wants to be like someone famous)* = personne qui cherche à être comme son idole; **the place was full of Spice Girl wannabes** c'était plein de filles habillées en Spice Girls

warpaint ['wɔːpeɪnt] *n Hum (make-up)* maquillage *m;* **to put the warpaint on** se maquiller

washed-up [wɒʃt'ʌp] *adj* **to be (all) washed-up** *(of person)* être fini; *(of plan)* être tombé à l'eau

washout ['wɒʃaʊt] *n (failure)* fiasco *m,* bide *m*

waste [weɪst] *vt (attack)* casser la gueule à, démonter le portrait à; *(kill)* buter, refroidir, zigouiller; *Br* **to waste sb's face** casser *ou* défoncer la gueule à qn, faire une tête au carré à qn

wasted ['weɪstɪd] *adj (drunk)* pété, bourré, fait; *(on drugs)* défoncé, raide

waster ['weɪstə(r)] *n Br* glandeur(euse) *m,f,* glandouilleur(euse) *m,f*

watering hole ['wɔːtərɪŋhəʊl] *n Hum (bar)* troquet *m,* rade *m*

water sports ['wɔːtəspɔːts] *npl* = pratique sexuelle qui consiste à uriner sur son ou sa partenaire

way [weɪ] **1** *n* (**a**) **no way!** pas question!; **no way am I going!** il est pas question que j'y aille!; **no way, José!** pas question! (**b**) **to go all the way** *or* **the**

whole way with sb coucher avec qn;
they went all the way or **the whole
way** ils ont couché ensemble **(c)** Am
way to go! super!
  2 exclam Am si! (en réponse à "no way!")
3 adv (very) vachement; **he is way
crazy** il est vachement atteint
▸ voir aussi **swing**

L'usage figurant dans la catégorie 2 a
été popularisé par le film comique
américain Wayne's World.

way-out [wer'aʊt] adj (eccentric) loufoque

wazoo [wə'zu:] n Am (buttocks) fesses □
fpl, miches fpl

wedge [wedʒ] n Br (money) fric m, flouze
m, pognon m, oseille f

wee [wi:] Br **1** n pipi m; **to have a wee**
faire pipi
  2 vi faire pipi

weed [wi:d] n **(a)** Br (person) femmelette
f, mauviette f, lavette f **(b)** (marijuana)
herbe f **(c)** Am (cigarette) clope f, sèche
f, tige f; (cannabis cigarette) joint m
(d) the weed (tobacco) tabac □ m; **I've
given up the weed** j'ai arrêté de fumer □

weedy ['wi:dɪ] adj Br (physically) racho;
(in character) faible □, mou

weenie ['wi:nɪ] n Am **(a)** (frankfurter)
saucisse f de Francfort □ **(b)** (idiot) andouille f, truffe f, courge f **(c)** (student)
bûcheur(euse) m,f **(d)** Hum (penis) chipolata f; **to play hide the weenie**
(have sex) s'envoyer en l'air

"Weenie" est le diminutif de "wiener"
(qui signifie "viennois" en allemand), qui
est le nom donné aux saucisses de
Francfort aux États-Unis.

weird out [wɪəd] vt sép Am **to weird
sb out** faire flipper qn

weirded out ['wɪədɪdaʊt] adj Am
(strange) loufoque, zarbi; (mad) cinglé,
dingue, timbré

weirdo ['wɪədəʊ] n (man) hurluberlu □
m; drôle de zèbre m; (woman) hurluberlu □ m

well [wel] adv Br (very) vachement; **he
looks well dodgy** il a l'air vachement
louche; **the club was well cool** la boîte
était vachement cool

well-hung [!] ['wel'hʌŋ] adj (man) bien
monté

well-stacked ['wel'stækt] adj (woman)
qui a de gros nichons; **she's well-
stacked** il y a du monde au balcon

welly ['welɪ] n Br **to give it some welly**
mettre le paquet

wet [wet] **1** n Br (feeble person) mauviette f, lavette f
  2 adj **(a)** Br (feeble) faible □, mou
(b) wet blanket rabat-joie mf **(c)** Am
to be all wet (mistaken) se gourer
▸ voir aussi **rag**

wetback ['wetbæk] n Am Injurieux =
travailleur clandestin mexicain

"Wetback" signifie littéralement "dos
mouillé". Cette appellation vient du fait
que de nombreux Mexicains traversent le
Rio Grande à la nage pour aller travailler
clandestinement aux États-Unis.

whack [wæk] **1** n (attempt) essai □ m,
tentative □ f; **to give sth a whack, to
take a whack at sth** essayer qch
  2 vt (kill) buter, zigouiller, refroidir
▸ voir aussi **top**

whack off [!] vi se branler, se pogner,
se palucher, faire cinq contre un

whacked [wækt] adj crevé, naze, lessivé, claqué

whacky ['wækɪ] = **wacky**

whang [!] [wæŋ] n Am (penis) bite f, zob
m, queue f

whatever ['wɒtevə(r)] exclam laisse
tomber!

what-for ['wɒt'fɔ:(r)] n **to give sb
what-for** (physically) foutre une raclée
à qn; (verbally) passer un savon à qn,
remonter les bretelles à qn; **to get
what-for** (physically) prendre une raclée; (verbally) se faire passer un savon,
se faire remonter les bretelles

what's-her-face ['wɒtsɜːfeɪs], **what's-her-name** ['wɒtsɜːneɪm] n Machine f

what's-his-face ['wɒtsɪzfeɪs], **what's-his-name** ['wɒtsɪzneɪm] n Machin m

whatsit ['wɒtsɪt], **whatsitsname** ['wɒtsɪtsneɪm] n machin m, truc m, bidule m

wheel [wiːl] **1** n (**a**) **(big) wheel** (person) huile f, gros bonnet m (**b**) **(set of) wheels** (car) bagnole f, caisse f, tire f
2 vi **to wheel and deal** magouiller
▶ voir aussi **fifth wheel**, **hell**

wheeler-dealer ['wiːlə'diːlə(r)] n magouilleur(euse) m,f

whipped [wɪpt] adj Am = **pussy-whipped**

whistle ['wɪsəl] n Br (rhyming slang **whistle and flute** = suit) costard m
▶ voir aussi **blow**

white [waɪt] adj (**a**) **white stuff** (morphine) morphine⁰ f, lili-pioncette f; (heroin) blanche f, héro f; (cocaine) coco f, neige f, coke f (**b**) **white lightning** tord-boyaux m (distillé illégalement)

whitebread ['waɪtbred] adj Am Péj (dull, conventional) conventionnel et ennuyeux⁰

Whitey ['waɪtɪ] n Noir Am Blanc (Blanche) m,f

whizz [wɪz] **1** n (**a**) (expert) as m; **a computer whizz** un as de l'informatique; **he's a whizz at chess** c'est un crack aux échecs; **whizz kid** jeune prodige m (**b**) Br (amphetamines) amphés fpl, amphets fpl (**c**) Am **to take a whizz** (urinate) faire pipi
2 vi Am (urinate) faire pipi

whizzbang ['wɪzbæŋ] adj Am (excellent) super, génial, géant

whopper ['wɒpə(r)] n (**a**) (huge object) mastodonte m (**b**) (lie) craque f

whore [hɔː(r)] n (**a**) (prostitute) pute f (**b**) (promiscuous woman) salope f, pétasse f, traînée f

whorehouse ['hɔːhaʊs] n bordel m, claque m

wick [wɪk] n (**a**) Br **to get on sb's wick** taper sur les nerfs à qn, courir sur le haricot à qn (**b**) **to dip one's wick** [!] tremper son biscuit

wicked ['wɪkɪd] **1** adj (excellent) super, génial, géant
2 exclam super!, génial!

widget ['wɪdʒɪt] n (**a**) (thing, object) bidule m, machin m (**b**) (gadget) gadget⁰ m

wig out [wɪg] vi Am (get angry) piquer une crise, péter les plombs; (go mad) devenir cinglé, perdre la boule; (get excited) devenir dingue

wigged (out) [wɪgd('aʊt)] adj Am (crazy) cinglé, tapé, timbré

wigger ['wɪgə(r)] n Am Péj = Blanc qui cherche à copier le mode de vie des Noirs

"Wigger" est la contraction de "white" et de "nigger".

wiggy ['wɪgɪ] adj Am (mad) cinglé, tapé, timbré; (eccentric) loufoque, allumé

wild [waɪld] adj (**a**) (angry) en pétard, fumasse, furibard, furax; **to go wild** se mettre en pétard (**b**) (enthusiastic) **to be wild about sb/sth** être dingue de qn/qch; **I wasn't exactly wild about it** ça ne m'a pas vraiment emballé (**c**) (excellent) super, génial, géant (**d**) **to do the wild thing** (have sex) s'envoyer en l'air

willies ['wɪlɪz] npl Br **to give sb the willies** donner la chair de poule à qn

willy ['wɪlɪ] n quéquette f, zizi m

wimp [wɪmp] n mauviette f, femmelette f, lavette f

wimp out vi se dégonfler; **he wimped out of the fight** il s'est dégonflé au dernier moment et a refusé de se battre; **he wimped out of telling her the truth** finalement il a eu la trouille de lui dire la vérité

wind up [waɪnd] vt sép Br **to wind sb up** (tease) faire enrager qn, taquiner qn; (fool) mettre qn en boîte; (irritate) foutre qn en rogne

windbag ['wɪndbæg] n moulin m à paroles

window ['wɪndəʊ] n **to go out (of) the**

window (of plans) tomber à l'eau; **that's my chances of promotion out the window** je peux faire une croix sur mon avancement

wind-up ['waɪndʌp] n Br mise f en boîte; **this has to be a wind-up!** dis-moi que c'est une plaisanterie!

wingding ['wɪŋdɪŋ] n Am (celebration) bringue f, bombe f, fiesta f

winkle ['wɪŋkəl] n Br (penis) quéquette f, zizi m

wino ['waɪnəʊ] n poivrot(e) m,f, alcolo mf

wipe out [waɪp] vt sép **to wipe sb out** (exhaust) lessiver qn; (kill) buter ou refroidir ou zigouiller qn

wiped (out) [waɪpt('aʊt)] adj (exhausted) crevé, naze, lessivé, claqué

wired ['waɪəd] adj (highly strung) sur les nerfs, à cran; (after taking drugs) défoncé (après avoir pris de la cocaïne ou des amphétamines)

wise up [waɪz] vi **to wise up to sb** voir qn sous son vrai jour ◻; **to wise up to sth** se rendre compte de qch ◻; **wise up!** réveille-toi!, ouvre les yeux!

wiseass ⚠ ['waɪzæs] n Am je-sais-tout mf

wiseguy ['waɪzgaɪ] n Am (a) (know-all) je-sais-tout mf (b) (criminal) truand m

with it ['wɪθɪt] adj (a) (fashionable) dans le coup, dans le vent (b) (awake) bien réveillé ◻; **to get with it** se réveiller ◻

wizz [wɪz] = **whizz**

wobbler ['wɒblə(r)], **wobbly** ['wɒblɪ] n Br **to throw a wobbler** piquer une crise, péter les plombs, péter une durite

wog [wɒg] n Injurieux (black man) nègre m, bamboula m; (black woman) négresse f

wolf [wʊlf] n (womanizer) coureur m

wombat ['wɒmbæt] n Am (man) hurluberlu ◻ m, drôle de zèbre m; (woman) hurluberlu ◻ m

wonga ['wɒŋgə] n Br fric m, flouze m, pognon m

wonk [wɒŋk] n Am (a) (student) bû-

cheur(euse) m,f (b) (intellectual, expert) intello mf (qui ne s'intéresse qu'à sa discipline)

wood [wʊd] n Am (a) **to put the wood to sb** (beat up) tabasser qn; (defeat) écrabouiller qn, battre qn à plates coutures, mettre une raclée ou une déculottée à qn (b) **to put the wood to sb** ⚠ (have sex with) tringler ou troncher qn

wooden overcoat ['wʊdən'əʊvəkəʊt] n Hum (coffin) costume m de sapin

woodie ⚠ ['wʊdɪ] n Am (erection) érection ◻ f, bandaison f; **to have a woodie** avoir la trique ou le gourdin, bander

woof [wʊf] vi Noir Am (boast, bluff) frimer, flamber

wop [wɒp] n Injurieux **1** n Rital(e) m,f **2** adj rital

word [wɜːd] exclam Noir Am **word (up)!** (I agree) parfaitement!; (it's true) sans dec!

working girl ['wɜːkɪŋgɜːl] n Am (prostitute) prostituée ◻ f, putain f

work over [wɜːk] vt sép **to work sb over** (beat up) tabasser qn, filer une raclée à qn, dérouiller qn

works [wɜːks] npl (a) **the works** (everything) la totale, tout le toutim (b) (drug paraphernalia) matos m de drogué ▶ voir aussi **shoot**

worm [wɜːm] n (person) larve f

wotcha ['wɒtʃə], **wotcher** ['wɒtʃə(r)] exclam Br bonjour! ◻, salut!

wow [waʊ] exclam oh là là!, la vache!

wrap up [ræp] vi Br (be quiet) la fermer, la boucler; **wrap up!** la ferme!, boucle-la!, écrase!

wrecked [rekt] adj (drunk) bourré, pété, beurré, fait; (on drugs) défoncé, raide; (exhausted) crevé, naze, lessivé, claqué

wrinkly ['rɪŋklɪ] n Br (old person) croulant(e) m,f

wuss [wʊs] n mauviette f, lavette f

wussy ['wʊsɪ] **1** n mauviette f, lavette f **2** adj mou, mollasson

X, Y, Z

X [eks] *n (abrév* **ecstasy)** X *f,* ecsta *f*

X-rated ['eks'reɪtɪd] *adj (lewd, erotic)* osé, salé; *(violent)* violent [□], saignant

> "X-rated" signifie littéralement "classé X". Cette appellation n'est plus utilisée par les commissions de censure américaine et britannique mais l'expression perdure.

yack [jæk] = **yak**

yah [jɑː] *n Br Péj* **(OK) yah** ≃ bourge *mf*

> "Yah" est la transcription phonétique du mot "yes" tel qu'il est prononcé par certains éléments de la grande bourgeoisie et de l'aristocratie anglaises. Par extension, le mot "yah" désigne une personne d'un milieu très aisé, arrogante et imbue d'elle-même, qui adopte une attitude méprisante avec ceux qu'elle considère comme ses inférieurs.

yak [jæk] **1** *n (conversation)* converse *f*; **to have a yak** papoter

2 *vi* **(a)** *(chat)* papoter **(b)** *Am (vomit)* gerber, dégueuler

Yank [jæŋk] **1** *n* Amerloque *mf,* Ricain(e) *m,f*

2 *adj* ricain

> Lorsqu'il est utilisé par les Américains eux-mêmes, ce terme n'a aucune connotation péjorative. Lorsqu'il est utilisé par une personne d'une autre nationalité, il peut être soit injurieux, soit humoristique, selon le ton et le contexte.

Yankee ['jæŋkɪ] **1** *n* **(a)** *Br Injurieux (American)* Amerloque *mf,* Ricain(e) *m,f*

(b) *Am (person from Northern USA)* = natif du Nord des États-Unis

2 *adj* **(a)** *Br Injurieux (American)* ricain **(b)** *Am (from Northern USA)* du Nord des États-Unis [□]

> Dans la catégorie l (a), ce terme peut être soit injurieux, soit humoristique, selon le ton et le contexte.

yap [jæp] **1** *n* **(a)** *(mouth)* clapet *m,* gueule *f*; **shut your yap!** ferme ton clapet!, la ferme!, écrase! **(b)** *Am (idiot)* andouille *f,* truffe *f; (country bumpkin)* pécore *mf,* péquenaude(e) *m,f*

2 *vi* jacasser, bavasser

yawn [jɔːn] *n (boring person, event)* **to be a yawn** être rasoir

▸ *voir aussi* **technicolour**

yay [jeɪ] *n Am (cocaine)* coco *f,* neige *f*

yeah [jeə] *exclam* ouais!; *Ironique* **yeah, right!, yeah sure!** oui, c'est ça!

yellow ['jeləʊ] *adj (cowardly)* trouillard; **to have a yellow streak** être un peu trouillard sur les bords

yellow-belly ['jeləʊbelɪ] *n (coward)* poule *f* mouillée

yep [jep] *exclam* ouais!

Yid [jɪd] *n Injurieux* youpin(e) *m,f,* youde *mf*

ying-yang ⚠ ['jɪŋjæŋ] *n Am* **(a)** *(anus)* troufignon *m,* fion *m,* rondelle *f* **(b)** *(penis)* bite *f,* biroute *f,* pine *f*

yo [jəʊ] *exclam Noir Am* salut!

yob [jɒb], **yobbo** ['jɒbəʊ] *n Br* loubard *m*

yonks [jɒŋks] *npl Br* une éternité; **I haven't seen him for yonks** ça fait un bail *ou* une paye que je l'ai pas vu

yup [jʌp] *exclam* = **yep**

yuppie, yuppy [ˈjʌpɪ] *n* (*abrév* **young upwardly-mobile professional**) yuppie *mf*; **yuppie flu** syndrome *m* de fatigue chronique □

za [tsɑ:] *n* *Am Hum* (*abrév* **pizza**) pizza □ *f*

zap [zæp] **1** *vt* (*kill*) buter, refroidir, zigouiller
2 *vi* (*change TV channels*) zapper

zapper [ˈzæpə(r)] *n* (*TV remote control*) télécommande □ *f*, zappette *f*

zebra [ˈzi:brə] *n* *Am* (*American football referee*) arbitre □ *m*

> C'est à cause de leur chemise à bandes noires et blanches que l'on donne ce surnom aux arbitres.

zeds [zedz], *Am* **zees** [zi:z] *npl* **to catch some** *Br* **zeds** *or* *Am* **zees** piquer un roupillon
► *voir aussi* **cop**

> C'est la bande dessinée qui est à l'origine de cette expression: "zzzz" est l'onomatopée la plus fréquemment utilisée pour évoquer le sommeil.

zero [ˈzi:rəʊ] **1** *n* (*person*) nul (nulle) *m,f*
2 *adj* aucun □; **he's got zero charm** il a aucun charme; **they've got zero chance of winning** ils ont pas la moindre chance de gagner

zilch [zɪltʃ] *n* (*nothing*) que dalle

zillion [ˈzɪljən] *n Hum* **a zillion** *or* **zillions (of)** des millions et des millions (de)

zing [zɪŋ] *vt Am* (*tease*) vanner, chambrer

zinger [ˈzɪŋə(r)] *n Am* (*pointed remark*) vanne *f*

zip [zɪp] **1** *n Am* (*nothing*) que dalle; (*zero*) zéro *m*; **the score was four-zip** le score était de quatre à zéro
2 *vt* **to zip it** (*be quiet*) la fermer, la boucler; **zip it!** la ferme!, ferme ton clapet!, écrase!

zit [zɪt] *n* (*pimple*) bouton □ *m*

zone [zəʊn] *n Am* **to be in a zone** (*dazed*) être dans le coaltar; (*after taking drugs*) être raide, planer

zoned (out) [zəʊnd(ˈaʊt)] *adj Am* **to be zoned out** (*dazed*) être dans le coaltar; (*after taking drugs*) être raide, planer

zonked (out) [zɒŋkt(ˈaʊt)] *adj* (*exhausted*) crevé, naze, lessivé, claqué; (*drunk*) bourré, rond, pété, fait; (*on drugs*) défoncé, raide

zoom [zu:m] *vt Am* (**a**) (*fool, deceive*) se foutre de, duper □ (**b**) (*flirt with*) faire du rentre-dedans à

zooted [ˈzu:tɪd] *adj Am* (*drunk*) bourré, pété, fait (**b**) (*on drugs*) raide, défoncé

zowie [ˈzaʊɪ] *exclam Am* oh là là!, la vache!

Français-Anglais
French-English

A

abattis [abati] *nmpl* **t'as intérêt à numéroter tes abattis** start saying your prayers!

abeilles [abɛj] *nfpl* **avoir les abeilles** to be hacked off *or* cheesed off

abîmer [abime] *vt* **abîmer qn** to beat sb up, to give sb a hammering *or* a pasting; **se faire abîmer** to get beaten up, to *Br* get *or Am* take a hammering *or* a pasting ▸ *see also* **portrait**

abonné, -e [abɔne] *adj* **être abonné à qch** to be prone to sth □; **décidément, je suis abonné!** this is happening to me all the time!

abouler [abule] **1** *vt* (*apporter*) to bring □; (*passer*) to pass □; **allez, aboule le fric!** come on, cough up!
2 s'abouler *vpr* to turn up, to show up, to roll up; **alors, tu t'aboules?** you coming, then?
▸ *see also* **viande**

accoucher [akuʃe] *vi* **accouche!** spit it out!, out with it!

accro [akro] **1** *adj* **être accro à qch** (*drogué*) to be hooked on sth; (*fanatique*) to be really into sth, to be mad about sth
2 *nmf* (**a**) (*drogué*) addict, junkie; **être accro à qch** to be hooked on sth (**b**) (*fanatique*) addict, nut, fanatic; **un accro du jazz** a jazzhead; **un accro du yoga** a yoga nut

accrocher [akrɔʃe] **s'accrocher** *vpr* (**a**) (*persévérer*) to stick at it, to hang in there; **accroche-toi Jeannot!** the best of luck *or Br* British! (**b**) **tu peux te l'accrocher!** you can forget it!; **s'il continue comme ça, sa médaille, il**

peut se l'accrocher if he carries on like that he can kiss goodbye to his chances of winning a medal

acide [asid] *nm (LSD)* acid

activer [aktive] *vi* to get a move on, to move it, to get one's skates on, *Am* to get it in gear; **allez, active!** come on, get a move on!

ado [ado] *nmf* (*abbr* **adolescent, -e**) teenager □

à donf [adɔ̃f] *adv* (*verlan* **à fond**) (*vite*) *Br* like the clappers, *Am* like sixty; (*très fort*) at full blast

affaire [afɛr] *nf* **être/ne pas être une affaire (au pieu)** to be good/no good in the sack
▸ *see also* **faire, juteux**

affirmatif [afirmatif] *exclam* you bet!, sure thing!

agité, -e [aʒite] *nm,f Hum* **agité du bocal** *Br* nutter, headcase, *Am* wacko, screwball

agrafer [agrafe] *vt* (**a**) (*retenir*) to corner (**b**) (*arrêter*) *Br* to nick, *Am* to bust

aidé, -e [ɛde] *adj* **il est pas aidé** (*bête*) he's not too bright; (*laid*) he's no oil painting

aile [ɛl] *nf* **avoir un coup dans l'aile** to have had one too many; **battre de l'aile** to be in a bad way, to be struggling

-aille [aj] *suffix* **boustifaille** food □, chow, grub; **duraille** tough; **la flicaille** the cops, the pigs, *Br* the filth; **marmaille** kids, brats

This suffix is found at the end of many French slang nouns and adjectives and indicates that the word is rather pejorative.

air [ɛr] nm **de l'air!** get lost!, get out of here!; **ficher** ou **foutre**[!] **qch en l'air** (mettre sens dessus dessous) to turn sth upside down; (jeter aux ordures) to chuck sth (out), to bin sth, Am to trash sth; **se foutre en l'air** (se suicider) to kill oneself □, Br to top oneself; (avoir un accident de la route) to have a crash □; **avoir l'air con et la vue basse**[!] to look like a real jerk

▸ see also **envoyer, jambe, pomper**

airbags [ɛrbag] nmpl tits, jugs, knockers, Am hooters

aise [ɛz] nf **à l'aise** (facilement) easily □, no problem, Br no probs; **ça coûte 500 balles à l'aise** it's easily worth 500 francs, it's worth 500 francs no problem or Br no probs; **et lui il se tournait les pouces, à l'aise, Blaise!** and there HE was, twiddling his thumbs without a care in the world!

alcolo, alcoolo [alkɔlo] nmf (abbr **alcoolique**) alky, lush, boozer, Am juicer

aligner [aliɲe] **1** vt (a) **les aligner** to pay up, to cough up (b) **il s'est fait aligner par un flic en moto** a motorcycle cop slapped a fine on him

2 s'aligner vpr to go without; **tu peux t'aligner pour que je te prête du fric, maintenant!** you can get lost if you think I'm going to lend you any money now!

aller [ale] vi (a) **tu peux y aller, c'est ce qui se fait de mieux!** you can take it from me, it's the best of stuff! (b) **où tu vas?** are you mad?, have you got a screw loose?, Br are you off your head?

aller-retour [aleratur], **aller et retour** [aleertur] nm slap on the face □ (first with the palm and then with the back of the hand)

allô [alo] exclam (à quelqu'un qui n'écoute pas) **allô?** hello? (to attract sb's attention)

allocs [alɔk] nfpl (abbr **allocations**) Br child benefit □, Am dependents' allowances □

allonger [alɔ̃ʒe] vt (a) (donner) **allonger une baffe à qn** to give sb a slap □, to slap sb □; **allonger un coup de poing à qn** to punch sb □ (b) **les allonger, allonger le fric** to pay up, to cough up

allouf [aluf] nf match □ (for lighting fire, cigarette)

allumé, -e [alyme] nm,f crackpot, crank

allumer [alyme] vt (a) (battre) to beat up, Br to do over; **se faire allumer** to get beaten up or Br done over (b) (tuer) to kill □, to waste, Br to do in (c) (exciter) to turn on, to make horny

allumeuse [alymøz] nf pricktease(r)

allure [alyr] nf Hum **à toute allure!** see you later!

This expression, which literally means "at full speed", is a pun on the phrase "à tout à l'heure".

alpaguer [alpage] vt to collar, to nab; **se faire alpaguer** to get collared or nabbed

amazone [amazon] nf = prostitute who works from a car

amener [amne] **s'amener** vpr (venir) to come □; (arriver) to turn up, to show up, to roll up

▸ see also **viande**

Amerloque [amɛrlɔk] nmf Yank, Yankee

amocher [amɔʃe] vt (personne, objet) to smash up

amortisseurs [amɔrtisœr] nmpl tits, jugs, knockers, Am hooters

amphés [ãfe], **amphets** [ãfɛt] nfpl (abbr **amphétamines**) speed, Br whizz

amphi [ãfi] nm (abbr **amphithéâtre**) lecture room or hall □

anar [anar] nmf (abbr **anarchiste**) anarchist □

andouille [ãduj] *nf* dope, *Br* divvy, *Am* dork

Anglais [ãglɛ] *nmpl* **les Anglais ont débarqué** I've/she's got my/her period ◻, I'm/she's on the rag

angliche [ãgliʃ] **1** *adj* British ◻, Brit **2** *nm (langue)* English ◻ **3** *nmf* **Angliche** *(personne)* Brit

angoisse [ãgwas] *nf* **c'est l'angoisse!, bonjour l'angoisse!** what a pain *or* drag *or* bummer!

angoisser [ãgwase] *vi* to be all uptight *or* worked up

antisèche [ãtisɛʃ] *nf Br* crib sheet, *Am* trot

apéro [apero] *nm (abbr* **apéritif)** aperitif ◻

à pluss [aplys] *exclam* see you later!, ciao!, *Br* laters!

appart' [apart] *nm (abbr* **appartement)** pad, *Br* flat ◻, *Am* apartment ◻

appuyer [apɥije] **s'appuyer** *vpr* **s'appuyer qn** to get stuck *or Br* lumbered *or* landed with sb; **s'appuyer le menage/la vaisselle** to get stuck *or Br* lumbered *or* landed with the housework/the dishes

▸ *see also* **champignon**

aprème [aprɛm] *nm or nf (abbr* **après-midi)** **cet** *ou* **cette aprème** this afternoon ◻

Arbi [arbi] *nm Offensive =* racist term used to refer to a North African Arab

archi- [arʃi] *prefix* extremely ◻, seriously, *Br* dead, well, *Am* real; **les magasins sont archibondés le samedi après-midi** the shops are *Br* chock-a-block *or Am* jammed on Saturday afternoons; **c'est faux, archifaux!** it's so ◻ *or Br* dead wrong!; **c'est un air archiconnu** it's a *Br* dead *or Am* real well-known tune

-ard [ar] *suffix* **connard** ⚠ stupid bastard, prick, *Br* arsehole, *Am* asshole; **faiblard** weakish, on the weak side;

flemmard lazy so-and-so; **salopard** ⚠ bastard

This suffix is found at the end of many French slang nouns and adjectives and indicates that the word is rather pejorative.

ardoise [ardwaz] *nf (pour inscrire des dettes)* slate, tab; **laisser une ardoise** to disappear without paying one's debts ◻

aristo [aristo] *nmf (abbr* **aristocrate)** aristo, *Br* toff, nob

arme [arm] *nf* **passer l'arme à gauche** to croak, to kick the bucket, *Br* to snuff it, *Am* to check out

armoire [armwar] *nf* **c'est une armoire à glace** he's built like a tank

arnaque [arnak] *nf* **c'est (de) l'arnaque!** what a rip-off!, it's *Br* daylight *or Am* highway robbery!

arnaquer [arnake] *vt* **arnaquer qn** to rip sb off; **se faire arnaquer** to get ripped off

arnaqueur, -euse [arnakœr, -øz] *nm,f Br* rip-off merchant, *Am* hustler

arpion [arpjɔ̃] *nm* foot ◻, *Br* plate, *Am* dog

arquer [arke] *vi* to walk ◻

arracher [araʃe] **1** *vt* **(a)** **ça t'arracherait la gueule de dire merci/de t'excuser?** it wouldn't kill you to say thanks/to apologize!

(b) **ça arrache (la gueule)** it blows the top of your head off **2 s'arracher** *vpr* to hit the road, to make tracks; **il faut que je m'arrache** I must be off, I've got to make tracks

arranger [arãʒe] *vt* **arranger qn** *(battre)* to beat sb up, to clobber sb, *Br* to kick sb's head in

arroser [aroze] **1** *vt* **(a)** *(fêter)* **arroser qch** to celebrate sth with a few drinks ◻; **il faut arroser ça** that calls for a celebration *or* a drink **(b)** *(mitrailler)* to spray with bullets

2 s'arroser vpr **ça s'arrose** that calls for a celebration or a drink

arsouille [arsuj] nm hood, hooligan, Br yob

Arthur [artyr] npr **se faire appeler Arthur** to get one's head bitten off, to get bawled out or Am chewed out

artiche [artiʃ] nm dough, bread, Br dosh, Am bucks

as [ɑs] nm (**a**) (expert) whizz; **un as du volant** an ace driver
  (**b**) **passer à l'as** to go out of the window, to go down the tubes or Br pan
  (**c**) **être fichu** ou **foutu** ou **fagoté comme l'as de pique** Br to be dressed like a scarecrow or a tramp, Am to look like a bum
  (**d**) **être plein aux as** to be loaded, Br to be rolling in it, Am to be rolling in dough

asperge [aspɛrʒ] nf (personne) bean-pole

aspi [aspi] nm (abbr **aspirant**) = soldier with the rank of lieutenant engaged in military service

assaisonner [asezɔne] vt (réprimander) **assaisonner qn** to give sb a roasting, to bawl sb out, Am to chew sb out; **se faire assaisonner** to get a roasting, to get bawled out, Am to get chewed out

asseoir [aswar] **s'asseoir** vpr **s'asseoir sur qch** (ne pas en tenir compte) not to give a damn or a hoot about sth

assis, -e [asi, -iz] adj **en rester assis** to be speechless or Br gobsmacked

assurer [asyre] vi (**a**) (être compétent) **il assure vachement en anglais** he's brilliant at English; **elle assure à la batterie** she's a brilliant drummer (**b**) (garder son sang-froid) to stay in control, to keep one's head; **vas-y, assure!** go for it!

astap [astap] adj inv (abbr **à se taper le cul par terre**) hysterical, side-splitting;

c'était astap it was a scream or a hoot

Athénien [atenjɛ̃] nm **c'est là que les Athéniens s'atteignirent** it was at that point that things started to go wrong□

atout [atu] nm (coup) clout, thump; **prendre un atout** to get clouted or thumped

attaque [atak] **d'attaque** adj **être d'attaque** to be on top form; **se sentir d'attaque pour faire qch** to feel up to doing sth

attaquer [atake] **1** vt (entamer) to tackle, Br to get stuck into
  2 vi (commencer à manger) Br to get stuck in, Am to chow down

atteint, -e [atɛ̃, -ɛ̃t] adj **être atteint** (ne pas être sain d'esprit) to be touched, to have a screw or Br slate loose

attrape-couillon [atrapkujɔ̃] nm scam, swindle, con, Am hustle

auge [oʒ] nf (assiette) plate□

autre [otr] pron **qu'est-ce qu'il a, l'autre?** what's up with him or Br your man there?; **oh l'autre eh! Il sait pas faire du vélo!** he can't even ride a bike!; **à d'autres!** come off it!, gimme a break!, yeah right!, Br do me a favour!

avaler [avale] vt (**a**) **avaler son bulletin de naissance** to croak, to kick the bucket, Am to cash in one's chips (**b**) **avaler la fumée** ‼ (au cours d'une fellation) to swallow

avoine [avwan], **avoinée** [avwane] nf thrashing, hammering; **prendre une avoine** to Br get or Am take a thrashing or a hammering; **filer une avoine à qn** to give sb a thrashing or a hammering

avoir [avwar] vt (**a**) **se faire avoir** to be had or conned or done (**b**) **en avoir** to have guts or balls

azimut [azimyt] **tous azimuts** adv all over the place or Br shop

azimuté, -e [azimyte] adj crackers, Br barking, Am wacko

B

baba [baba] **1** adj *(stupéfait)* flabbergasted, Br gobsmacked; **j'en suis resté baba** I was flabbergasted or Br gobsmacked

2 nmf *(hippie)* **baba (cool)** hippy

3 nm **l'avoir dans le baba** to be had or conned

"Baba" in sense 2 is a term used to refer to a second-generation hippy who has adopted the image and lifestyle of the original hippy generation of the 60s and 70s.

babtou [babtu] nmf *(verlan* **toubab**) Frenchman, f Frenchwoman □

baby [bɛbi] nm = half-measure of whisky

bac [bak] nm *(abbr* **baccalauréat**) = secondary school examinations qualifying for entry to university, Br ≃ A-levels □, Am ≃ high school diploma □

bacchantes [bakɑ̃t] nfpl moustache □, tash

bâcher [baʃe] **se bâcher** vpr to hit the sack or the hay or Am the rack

bachot [baʃo] nm = secondary school examinations qualifying for entry to university, Br ≃ A-levels □, Am ≃ high school diploma □; **boîte à bachot** crammer

bachotage [baʃɔtaʒ] nm cramming, Br swotting

bachoter [baʃɔte] vi to cram, Br to swot

bachoteur, -euse [baʃɔtœr, -øz] nm,f = student cramming for an exam

bâdrage [bɑdraʒ] nm Can nuisance, pain (in the neck)

bâdrant, -e [bɑdrɑ̃, -ɑ̃t] adj Can **être bâdrant** to be a nuisance or a pain (in the neck)

bâdrer [bɑdre] vt Can **bâdrer qn** to bug sb, Br to do sb's head in, Am to give sb a pain (in the neck)

baffe [baf] nf clout, cuff

baffer [bafe] vt to clout, to cuff

bafouille [bafuj] nf letter □

bâfrer [bɑfre] vi to stuff oneself or one's face, to pig out

bâfreur, -euse [bɑfrœr, -øz] nm,f pig, Br greedy-guts, gannet, Am hog

bagne [baɲ] nm **c'est le bagne ici** it's like a sweatshop here

bagnole [baɲɔl] nf car □, wheels, Br motor

bagou [bagu] nm gift of the gab; **avoir du bagou** to have the gift of the gab

bagouse [baguz] nf **(a)** ring □ *(for finger)* **(b)** **être de la bagouse !!** to be Br a poof or a shirt-lifter or Am a fag

baguenauder [bagnode] **1** vi to saunter or wander around □

2 se baguenauder vpr to saunter or wander around □

bahut [bay] nm **(a)** *(camion)* lorry □, truck **(b)** *(taxi)* taxi □, cab **(c)** *(lycée)* high school □

baigner [beɲe] vi **(a)** **tout baigne (dans l'huile)** everything's hunky-dory or Am A-OK **(b)** **avoir les dents du fond qui baignent** to have stuffed oneself or one's face, to have pigged out

baigneur ! [beɲœr] nm **(a)** *(sexe de la femme)* pussy, snatch, Br fanny **(b)** *(postérieur)* Br arse, Am ass, fanny

bail [baj] nm **ça fait un bail** it's been ages or Br yonks

baille [baj] nf water □; **tomber à la baille** to fall in

bain [bɛ̃] nm **être/se mettre dans le bain** to be in/get into the swing of things

baisable ‼ [bɛzabl] adj fuckable, Br shaggable

baise ‼ [bɛz] nf (amour physique) fucking, screwing, Br shagging

baise-en-ville [bɛzɑ̃vil] nm inv overnight bag □

baiser ‼ [beze] **1** vt (**a**) (faire l'amour avec) to fuck, to screw, to lay, Br to shag (**b**) (duper) to shaft, to screw; **se faire baiser** to get shafted or screwed (**c**) (surprendre) to nab; **se faire baiser** to get nabbed
  2 vi to fuck, to screw, Br to shag; **il baise bien** he's a great fuck or lay or screw or Br shag
  ▶ see also **couille, lapin**

baiseur, -euse ‼ [bɛzœr, -øz] nm,f **c'est une sacrée baiseuse** she's a great fuck or lay or screw or Br shag

baisodrome ‼ [bɛzɔdrom] nm fuck-pad

bakchich [bakʃiʃ] nm Br backhander, bung, Am payoff

balader [balade] vi **envoyer balader qn** to tell sb where to go, Br to send sb packing; **envoyer balader qch** (lancer) to send sth flying; (abandonner) to quit sth, Br to chuck or pack sth in

baladeuse [baladøz] adj **avoir les mains baladeuses** to have wandering hands

balai [balɛ] nm (an) year □; **il a cinquante balais** he's fifty □

> This word is used only when referring to people's ages.

balaise [balɛz] **1** adj (**a**) (fort) (physiquement) hefty, burly; (intellectuellement) brainy; **être balaise en qch** to be brilliant at sth (**b**) (difficile) tough, tricky
  2 nm big guy

balance [balɑ̃s] nf (dénonciateur) squealer, Br grass, Am rat

balancé, -e [balɑ̃se] adj **être bien balancé** to have a great bod

balancer [balɑ̃se] **1** vt (**a**) (dénoncer) to squeal on, Br to grass on, Am to rat on (**b**) (lancer) to chuck (**c**) (mettre aux ordures) to chuck (out), to bin, Am to trash
  2 vi (médire) to dish the dirt, Br to bitch
  3 s'en balancer ‼ vpr not to give a shit or Br a toss or Am a rat's ass
  ▶ see also **purée, sauce**

balcon [balkɔ̃] nm **il y a du monde au balcon** she's well-stacked, she's a big girl, Br you don't get many of those to the pound

baliser [balize] vi to be scared stiff or witless

balle [bal] nf (franc) franc □; **t'as pas cent balles?** got any change?
  ▶ see also **peau, trou**

balloches ‼ [balɔʃ] nfpl balls, nuts, Br bollocks

ballon [balɔ̃] nm (alcootest) **faire souffler qn dans le ballon** to get sb to blow into the bag

ballot [balo] nm (idiot) Br divvy, wally, Am goof, geek

baloche [balɔʃ] nm local dance □

baltringue [baltrɛ̃g] nmf wimp, chicken, Br big girl's blouse

bambou [bɑ̃bu] nm **avoir le coup de bambou** (avoir un accès de folie) to crack up, to go nuts, Br to go off one's head; (être épuisé) to be wiped or Br shattered or Am pooped; **attraper un coup de bambou** (avoir une insolation) to get sunstroke □; **c'est le coup de bambou** (c'est très cher) it costs an arm and a leg or Br a bomb or a packet

bamboula [bɑ̃bula] **1** nf (fête) wild party; **faire la bamboula** to party, Br to go on the razzle
  2 nm Offensive (homme de race noire)

nigger, Br wog, Am coon

banane [banan] nf **(a)** (coiffure) quiff **(b)** (insulte) **banane!** you moron or Br plonker or Am geek! **(c)** **avoir la banane**‼ to have a hard-on or Br a stiffy

bandaison‼ [bɑ̃dɛzɔ̃] nf hard-on, boner, Br stiffy

bandant, -e‼ [bɑ̃dɑ̃, -ɑ̃t] adj **(a)** (désirable sexuellement) **elle est bandante** she's really horny, she really turns me on **(b)** (enthousiasmant) thrilling □

bander‼ [bɑ̃de] vi to have a hard-on; **il bande pour elle** he's got the hots for her, she really turns him on, Br he thinks she's really horny; **faire bander qn** (exciter sexuellement) to turn sb on, to make sb horny, Br to give sb the horn; **ce genre de musique, ça me fait pas vraiment bander** I can't really get into this sort of music

bang [bɑ̃g] nm (pipe à eau) bong

banquer [bɑ̃ke] vi to cough up, to hand over the cash

baquer [bake] **se baquer** vpr to go for a dip

baraka [baraka] nf **avoir la baraka** to be lucky □ or Br jammy

baraque [barak] nf (maison) place, pad; **casser la baraque** (remporter un vif succès) to bring the house down;

casser la baraque à qn (faire échouer ses projets) to mess things up for sb

baraqué, -e [barake] adj hefty, burly

baratin [baratɛ̃] nm (d'un vendeur) sales talk or pitch; (pour séduire) sweet talk, Br patter; **c'est du baratin** it's a load of bull or tripe or Br waffle

baratiner [baratine] vt **baratiner qn** (essayer de convaincre) to shoot sb a line, to try to talk sb round; (pour séduire) Br to chat sb up, Am to hit on sb; **baratiner qn pour qu'il fasse qch** to try to talk sb into doing sth □

baratineur, -euse [baratinœr, -øz] nm,f smooth talker

barbant, -e [barbɑ̃, -ɑ̃t] adj deadly dull; **c'est barbant, mais il faut le faire** it's a drag, but it's got to be done

barbaque [barbak] nf meat □

barbe [barb] nf **c'est la barbe** it's a drag; **la barbe!** give it a rest!

barber [barbe] **1** vt **barber qn** to bore sb stiff or to tears **2 se barber** vpr to be bored stiff or to tears

barboter [barbote] vt (voler) to pinch, Br to nick; **barboter qch à qn** to pinch or Br nick sth from sb; **se faire barboter qch** to get sth pinched or Br nicked

barbouze [barbuz] nf **(a)** (barbe) beard □ **(b)** (espion) spy □, plant

barbu[!] [barby] nm (poils pubiens de la

l'Argot des banlieues

Around twenty years ago a new form of slang, quite unlike traditional "argot", began to emerge in the impoverished suburban areas of large cities, especially Paris. This new slang reflects the cultural and ethnic diversity of these neighbourhoods, with expressions originating from Arabic (eg "chouf"), African languages (eg "toubab" and its verlan form "babtou") and Romany (eg "bouillaver", "raclo"), whilst the popularity of rap music has led to an influx of English expressions (eg "dope", "shit", "splif").

Verlan (see entry) is omnipresent and words are often abbreviated. It is a form of slang essentially created and used by young people as a linguistic expression of their social, economic and geographical marginalization.

femme) bush

barda [barda] *nm* stuff, gear

barder [barde] *v imp* **ça va barder!** there's going to be trouble!

barge [barʒ], **barjo, barjot** [barʒo] **1** *adj* nuts, bananas, *Br* off one's head, *Am* wacko
2 *nmf* headcase, nutcase *Br* nutter, *Am* wacko

baron [barɔ̃] *nm (compère)* plant

barouf [baruf], **baroufle** [barufl] *nm* racket, din

barre [bar] *nf* (a) **avoir un coup de barre** to be bushed *or* wiped *or* *Br* shattered *or* *Am* beat (b) **c'est le coup de barre** it costs an arm and a leg *or* a bundle *or* *Br* a packet
▶ *see also* **couille**

barré, -e [bare] *adj* **être bien barré** to be looking good; **être mal barré** to be heading for trouble

barreau, -x [baro] *nm* **barreau de chaise** *(cigare)* fat cigar □

barrer [bare] **se barrer** *vpr (partir)* to hit the road, to get going, to make tracks; *(se sauver)* to beat it, *Br* to clear off, *Am* to book it; **barre-toi!** get out of here!, beat it!, *Am* take a hike!

barrette [barɛt] *nf (de haschich)* = thin strip

basket [baskɛt] *nf* (a) **être bien dans ses baskets** to be very together *or* *Br* sorted (in one's head) *or* *Am* very together (b) **lâche-moi les baskets!** get off my back!, don't hassle me!

bassiner [basine] *vt* **bassiner qn** to bug sb, *Br* to do sb's head in, to get up sb's nose, *Am* to give sb a pain

bassinet [basinɛ] *nm* **cracher au bassinet** to cough up, to hand over the cash

basta [basta] *exclam* that'll do!

Bastoche [bastɔʃ] *nf* **la Bastoche** = the Bastille area of Paris

baston [bastɔ̃] *nm or nf* scuffle, *Br* punch-up, *Am* fist fight

bastonner [bastɔne] **1** *v imp* **ça a bastonné** there was a scuffle *or* *Br* a punch-up *or* *Am* a fist fight
2 **se bastonner** *vpr* to have a scuffle *or* *Br* a punch-up *or* *Am* a fist fight

bastos [bastos] *nf* bullet □, slug

bastringue [bastrɛ̃g] *nm* (a) *(vacarme)* racket, din (b) *(désordre)* shambles (c) **et tout le bastringue** blah blah blah

bataclan [bataklɑ̃] *nm* **et tout le bataclan** blah blah blah

bataillon [batajɔ̃] *nm* **inconnu au bataillon** never heard of him

bâtard ‼ [batar] *nm* bastard

bateau [bato] *adj inv (banal)* hackneyed □, trite □

bâton [batɔ̃] *nm (dix mille francs)* ten thousand francs □

battant [batɑ̃] *nm (cœur)* ticker

battre [batr] **1** *vt* **j'en ai rien à battre** ! I don't give a shit *or* *Br* a toss *or* *Am* a rat's ass
2 **se battre** *vpr* **je m'en bats l'œil** I don't give a damn *or* a hoot *or* *Br* a stuff; **je m'en bats les couilles** ‼ I don't give a (flying) fuck
▶ *see also* **aile**

bavard [bavar] *nm (avocat)* lawyer □, brief

bavarde [bavard] *nf (langue)* tongue □; **tenir sa bavarde** to hold one's tongue, to keep one's mouth shut

bavasser [bavase] *vi* to yak, *Br* to natter

baver [bave] **1** *vt* (a) *(dire)* **qu'est-ce que tu baves?** what are you rambling *or* jabbering *or* *Br* wittering on about? (b) **en baver** to have a hard *or* tough time of it; **en faire baver à qn** to give sb a hard time
2 *vi (bavarder)* to chat, to yak, *Br* to natter; **baver sur qn** to dish the dirt about sb, *Br* to bitch about sb, *Am* to bad-mouth sb

bavette [bavɛt] *nf* **tailler une bavette (avec qn)** to have a chat *or* *Br* a natter

(with sb)

baveux, -euse [bavø, -øz] **1** *nm,f Can (enfant effronté)* brat

2 *nm* (**a**) *(savon)* soap □ (**b**) *(journal)* paper □ (**c**) *(baiser)* sloppy kiss

bazarder [bazarde] *vt* (**a**) *(jeter)* to chuck (out), to bin, *Am* to trash (**b**) *(dénoncer)* to squeal on, *Br* to grass on, *Am* to rat on

BCBG [besebeʒe] *(abbr* **bon chic bon genre) 1** *nmf Br* ≃ Sloane (Ranger), *Am* ≃ preppy

2 *adj inv Br* ≃ Sloany, *Am* ≃ preppy

This term refers to someone whose classic, elegant style of dress suggests a wealthy, conservative social background.

BD [bede] *nf (abbr* **bande dessinée)** comic strip □, cartoon □

beauf [bof] *(abbr* **beau-frère) 1** *adj (caractéristique du Français moyen)* = stereotypically narrow-minded and middle class

2 *nm* (**a**) *(beau-frère)* brother-in-law □ (**b**) *(Français moyen)* = stereotypical narrow-minded, middle-class man

The term "beauf" – short for "beau-frère" – comes from a character in a comic strip created in the 1960s by the French cartoonist Cabu. A "beauf" is the average middle-class Frenchman with a racist, reactionary and jingoistic outlook on life.

beaujolpif [boʒɔlpif] *nm* Beaujolais □

bec [bɛk] *nm (bouche)* mouth □, *Br* gob, cakehole; **clouer le bec à qn** to shut sb up; **puer du bec** to have rotten breath ▸ *see also* **claquer**

bécane [bekan] *nf* (**a**) *(bicyclette, moto)* bike (**b**) *(machine)* machine □, *Am* honker

because [bikoz] *prep* because of □

bècebège [bɛsbɛʒ] = **BCBG**

bêcheur, -euse [bɛʃœr, -øz] **1** *adj* stuck-up, snooty

2 *nm,f* stuck-up *or* snooty person

bécot [beko] *nm* kiss □

bécoter [bekɔte] **1** *vt Br* to snog, *Am* to neck

2 **se bécoter** *vpr Br* to snog, *Am* to neck, to suck face

becter [bɛkte] *vt & vi* to eat □

bédave [bedav], **bédaver** [bedave] *vi* to smoke □

bédé [bede] *nf* = **BD**

bédo [bedo] *nm* joint, doobie, spliff, number

bégueule [begœl] *adj* fussy □

beigne [bɛɲ] *nf* clout, cuff; **flanquer une beigne à qn** to clout *or* cuff sb

belette [bəlɛt] *nf* chick, *Br* bird

belle [bɛl] *nf* **se faire la belle** *(faire une fugue)* to run away □, *Br* to do a bunk; *(s'évader)* to break out □

belle-doche [bɛldɔʃ] *nf* mother-in-law □

bénard [benar], **bène** [bɛn] *nm Br* trousers □, keks, *Am* pants □

bénef [benɛf] *nm (abbr* **bénéfice)** profit □; **c'est tout bénef** it's all profit

béni-oui-oui [beniwiwi] *nm inv* yes-man

berceau [bɛrso] *nm* **les prendre au berceau** to be a cradle-snatcher

Bérézina [berezina] *npr* **c'est la Bérézina** it's a disaster □

This expression refers to the Berezina river in Belarus which Napoleon's Grande Armée crossed during its hectic retreat from Russia in 1812. Many soldiers lost their lives during the disorganized crossing.

berge [bɛrʒ] *nf (an)* year □; **elle a cinquante berges** she's fifty □

This term is used only when referring to people's ages.

berlingot [!] [bɛrlɛ̃go] *nm* (**a**) *(clitoris)* clit (**b**) *(virginité)* **avoir son berlingot**

to be a virgin $^\square$; **perdre son berlingot** to lose one's virginity $^\square$ or cherry

berlue [bɛrly] *nf* **avoir la berlue** to be seeing things

berzingue [bɛrzɛ̃g] **à tout berzingue** *adv* at top speed, *Br* like the clappers, *Am* like sixty

bésef [bezɛf] *adv* **pas bésef** not a lot $^\square$, not much $^\square$

besogner [!] [bəzɔɲe] *vt* to hump, to screw, *Br* to shaft

bête [bɛt] *nf* (**a**) (*expert*) **être une bête (en)** to be brilliant (at) (**b**) **comme une bête** like crazy (**c**) **faire la bête à deux dos** to make the beast with two backs

béton [betɔ̃] *vi* (*verlan* **tomber**) **laisse béton!** forget it!, drop it!

beu [bø] *nf* grass, weed, herb

beur [bœr], **beurette** [bœrɛt] *nm,f* (*verlan* **arabe**) = person born and living in France of North African immigrant parents

beurré, -e [bœre] *adj* (*ivre*) wasted, plastered, loaded, *Br* pissed, legless; **beurré comme un petit Lu** *Br* (as) pissed as a newt, *Am* stewed to the gills

bézef [bezɛf] = **bésef**

bi [bi] *adj inv* (*abbr* **bisexuel, -elle**) bi

biberonner [bibrɔne] *vi* to be a boozer or an alky or a lush; **qu'est-ce qu'il biberonne!** he can really put it away, he's a terrible boozer or alky or lush!

bibi [bibi] **1** *pron* (*moi*) yours truly; **et qui c'est qu'a payé l'addition? c'est bibi!** and who paid the bill? yours truly or *Br* muggins here!
2 *nm* (*chapeau*) (woman's) hat $^\square$

bibiche [bibiʃ] *nf* sweetheart, honey, sugar

bibine [bibin] *nf* (*alcool*) gutrot, rotgut, *Am* alky; (*bière*) dishwater

bibli [bibli] *nf* (*abbr* **bibliothèque**) library $^\square$

biche [biʃ] *nf* **ma biche** darling, sweetheart

bicher [biʃe] *vi* (**a**) (*bien se passer*) **ça biche?** how's it going?, how are things? (**b**) (*être satisfait*) to be tickled pink; **ça me fait bicher** that makes me happy $^\square$

biclo [biklo], **biclou** [biklu] *nm* bike

bicoque [bikɔk] *nf* (*maison*) place, pad

bicot [biko] *nm Offensive* = racist term used to refer to a North African Arab

bicrave [bikrav], **bicraver** [bikrave] *vt* to sell $^\square$, *Br* to flog; (*drogue*) to deal

bidasse [bidas] *nm Br* squaddie, *Am* grunt

bide [bid] *nm* (**a**) (*ventre*) belly, gut; **il n'a rien dans le bide** (*il n'a pas de courage*) he's got no guts or balls (**b**) (*échec*) flop, washout, *Am* bomb; **faire un bide** to be a flop or a washout, *Am* to bomb

bidoche [bidɔʃ] *nf* meat $^\square$

bidochon [bidɔʃɔ̃] *nmf* = stereotypical working-class, reactionary person

This word is an allusion to *Les Bidochon*, a comic strip by the cartoonist Binet, about an ordinary French couple who embody the stereotypical behaviour and values of the working class.

bidon [bidɔ̃] **1** *adj inv* phoney
2 *nm* (**a**) (*ventre*) belly, gut (**b**) **c'est du bidon** it's a load of baloney or garbage or *Br* rubbish; **c'est pas du bidon** it's gospel, it's the honest truth; **c'est pas du bidon, il a vraiment mal** he's not putting it on, he's in real pain

bidonnant, -e [bidɔnɑ̃, -ɑ̃t] *adj* sidesplitting, hysterical; **c'était bidonnant!** it was a scream or a hoot!

bidonner [bidɔne] **se bidonner** *vpr* to kill oneself (laughing), to crack up, to laugh one's head off

bidouillage [bidujaʒ] *nm* **c'est du bidouillage** it's just been thrown together

bidouiller [biduje] *vt (bricoler)* to tinker with; *(trafiquer)* to fiddle

bidule [bidyl] **1** *nm (chose)* thingy, whatsit
  2 *npr* **Bidule** *(personne)* thingy, whatshis-name, *f* whats-her-name

biffe [bif] *nf* **la biffe** the infantry □

biffeton [biftɔ̃] = **bifton**

biffin [bifɛ̃] *nm* **(a)** *(soldat)* infantryman □ **(b)** *(personne ridicule)* buffoon, clown

bifteck [biftɛk] *nm* **défendre son bifteck** to look after number one; **gagner son bifteck** to earn one's crust *or* one's bread and butter

bifton [biftɔ̃] *nm (billet de banque)* note □, *Am* greenback; *(de transport, de spectacle)* ticket □

bigler [bigle] **1** *vt (observer)* to eyeball, to check out, *Br* to clock
  2 *vi (loucher)* to have a squint □

bigleux, -euse [biglø, -øz] *adj* **(a)** *(qui louche)* cross-eyed **(b)** *(qui voit mal)* short-sighted □

bigophone [bigɔfɔn] *nm Br* blower, *Am* horn

bigophoner [bigɔfɔne] *vi* to make a phone call □; **bigophoner à qn** to give sb a buzz *or Br* a bell

bigorner [bigɔrne] **1** *vt* to smash up, *Br* to prang; **bigorner sa bagnole contre un arbre** to smash one's car into a tree
  2 se bigorner *vpr* to have a scrap *or Br* a punch-up *or Am* a fist fight

bijoux [biʒu] *nmpl Hum* **les bijoux de famille** *(sexe de l'homme)* the crown jewels

bilan [bilɑ̃] *nm* **déposer le bilan** *(mourir)* to croak, to kick the bucket, *Br* to snuff it, *Am* to check out; *(déféquer)* to *Br* have *or Am* take a crap *or* a dump

billard [bijar] *nm* **passer sur le billard** to go under the knife

bille [bij] *nf* **(a)** *(visage)* face □, mug; **une bille de clown** a funny face □ **(b) reprendre** *ou* **retirer ses billes** to pull

out □ *(from a deal)* **(c) toucher sa bille (en/à)** to know a thing or two (about)

binette [binɛt] *nf (visage)* face □, mug

biniou [binju] *nm (téléphone) Br* blower, *Am* horn; **filer un coup de biniou** to make a phone call □; **filer un coup de biniou à qn** to give sb a buzz *or Br* a bell

binoclard, -e [binɔklar, -ard] *nm,f* four-eyes, *Br* speccy

binz [bins] *nm* **(a)** *(chose compliquée)* **quel binz pour trouver sa maison!** it was a real performance or hassle *or Br* carry-on finding his house! **(b)** *(désordre)* shambles

bio [bjo] *nf (abbr* **biographie)** biog; **une bio d'Elvis** an Elvis biog

bique [bik] **1** *nm Offensive* = racist term used to refer to a North African Arab
  2 *nf* **une vieille bique** an old bag

biroute [!] [birut] *nf* dick, knob, *Am* schlong

biscoteaux [biskɔto] *nmpl* biceps □

biscuit [biskɥi] *nm* **tremper son biscuit** [!!] to dip one's wick

bistouquette [bistukɛt] *nf* willy, *Am* peter

bite [!!] [bit] *nf* dick, cock, prick, knob; **rentrer la bite sous le bras** to go home without getting laid *or Br* without getting one's oats

biter [!] [bite] *vt* **j'y bite rien** I don't understand a *Br* bloody *or Am* goddamn thing

bitoniau [bitɔnjo] *nm* thingy, whatsit, *Br* doodah, *Am* doodad

bitos [bitos] *nm* hat □

biture [bityr] *nf* **il tenait une de ces bitures!** he was completely plastered *or* wasted *or Br* legless *or* pissed!; **prendre une biture** to get plastered *or* wasted *or Br* legless *or* pissed

biturer [bityre] **se biturer** *vpr* to get plastered *or* wasted *or Br* legless *or* pissed

bizut [bizy] *nm* = first-year student in a

"grande école"

bizutage [bizytaʒ] *nm Br* ragging, *Am* hazing *(in "grandes écoles")*

bizuter [bizyte] *vt Br* to rag, *Am* to haze *(in "grandes écoles")*

blabla [blabla] *nm inv* baloney, *Br* waffle

blablater [blablate] *vi* to waffle on, *Br* to witter on

black [blak] **1** *nmf (personne de race noire)* Black

2 *nm* **travailler au black** *(clandestinement)* = to work without declaring one's earnings; *(en plus de son travail habituel)* to moonlight

blague [blag] *nf* **(a) sans blague!** *(je t'assure)* no kidding!, it's true!; **sans blague?** *(est-ce vrai?)* no kidding?, yeah? **(b) blagues à tabac** saggy boobs

blair, blaire [blɛr] *nm Br* conk, hooter, *Am* schnozzle, honker

blaireau, -x [blɛro] *nm (individu)* jerk, *Br* prat

blairer [blɛre] *vt* **je peux pas le blairer** I can't stand *or* stomach *or Br* stick him

blanche [blɑ̃ʃ] *nf (héroïne)* smack, scag, skag

Blanche-Neige [blɑ̃ʃnɛʒ] *nm inv Offensive* nigger, *Br* wog, *Am* coon

blase, blaze [blaz] *nm* name ᵈ, handle, moniker

blé [ble] *nm (argent)* dough, *Br* dosh, *Am* bucks

blèche [blɛʃ] *adj* hideous, *Br* pig-ugly

bled [blɛd] *nm (localité)* place ᵈ; *Pej* hole, dump, dive

blème [blɛm] *nm (abbr* **problème)** problem, *Br* prob

bleu [blø] *nm* **(a)** *(novice)* rookie, *Am* cherry **(b) un petit bleu** a telegram ᵈ **(c)** *(policier)* cop, *Br* plod, *Am* flatfoot

bleue [blø] *nf* **la grande bleue** the sea ᵈ; *(la Méditerranée)* the Med

bleubite [bløbit] *nm* rookie, *Am* cherry

bleusaille [bløzaj] *nf* **la bleusaille** the

new recruits ᵈ, the rookies

blinde [blɛ̃d] **à toute blinde** *adv* at full speed, like lightning, *Br* like the clappers

blindé, -e [blɛ̃de] *adj (ivre)* blitzed, plastered, wasted, loaded

blinder [blɛ̃de] **1** *vi* to bomb along
2 se blinder *vpr (s'enivrer)* to get blitzed *or* plastered *or* wasted *or* loaded

blobote [bloblot] *nf* **avoir la blobote** to have the shakes

bloc [blok] *nm (prison)* slammer, clink, *Br* nick, *Am* pen

blonde [blɔ̃d] *nf Can* girlfriend ᵈ, (main) squeeze, *Br* bird

bloquer [bloke] *vi* **bloquer sur qn** to have the hots for sb, *Br* to fancy sb

blouser [bluze] *vt* **blouser qn** to put one over on sb, to take sb for a ride; **se faire blouser** to get taken for a ride

bobard [bobar] *nm* fib, *Br* porky, whopper; **raconter des bobards** to tell fibs *or Br* porkies *or* whoppers

bobinard [!] [bobinar] *nm* whorehouse, *Br* knocking shop

bobine [bobin] *nf (visage)* face ᵈ, mug

bobonne [bobon] *nf* the old lady, *Br* the missus, her indoors

boche [boʃ] *Offensive* **1** *adj* Kraut
2 *nmf* **Boche** *(personne)* Kraut

Depending on the context and the tone of voice used, this term may be either offensive or affectionately humorous. It is nonetheless inadvisable to use it unless one is quite sure of the reaction it will receive.

bœuf [bœf] **1** *adj* **faire un effet bœuf** to cause a stir, to make a splash
2 *nm* **(a) faire un bœuf** to have a jam session, to jam **(b) on n'est pas des bœufs** you can't treat us like slaves

bof [bof] *exclam* **c'était bien? – bof** was it good? – not particularly

Normally accompanied by an expression of utter indifference, this term is used in numerous situations to express a disdainful lack of enthusiasm.

bogarter [bɔgaʀte] *vi* to bogart a joint

boîte [bwat] *nf* (**a**) *(société)* firm ᵠ, company ᵠ (**b**) **boîte (de nuit)** club, nightclub ᵠ; **sortir en boîte** to go clubbing (**c**) **boîte à ouvrage** [!!] box, twat, *Br* fanny; **boîte à pâté** [!!] *Br* dirtbox, arsehole, *Am* asshole
▸ *see also* **bachot**

boit-sans-soif [bwasɑ̃swaf] *nmf inv* alky, lush, boozer, *Am* juicer

bol [bɔl] *nm (chance)* luck ᵠ; **un coup de bol** a stroke of luck ᵠ; **manque de bol, il était déjà parti** as bad luck would have it, he'd already left ᵠ
▸ *see also* **ras**

bombarder [bɔ̃baʀde] **1** *vt* **on l'a bombardé ministre** he's been made a minister out of the blue
2 *vi (fumer beaucoup)* to smoke like a chimney

bombe [bɔ̃b] *nf* (**a**) *(fête)* **faire la bombe** to party
(**b**) *(jolie fille)* babe, knockout, *Br* cracker
(**c**) **à toute bombe** at top speed, *Br* like the clappers, *Am* like sixty; **aller à toute bombe** to bomb along, to belt along

bomber [bɔ̃be] *vi* to bomb along, to belt along

bon app' [bɔnap] *exclam (abbr* **bon appétit***)* enjoy your meal!, *Am* enjoy!

bonbec [bɔ̃bɛk] *nm (cachet d'ecstasy)* E, *Br* disco biscuit

bonbon [bɔ̃bɔ̃] **1** [!] *nm* (**a**) *(clitoris)* clit (**b**) **bonbons** *(testicules)* balls, *Br* bollocks; **casser les bonbons à qn** to piss sb off, *Br* to get on sb's tits, *Am* to break sb's balls
2 *adv* **coûter bonbon** to cost an arm and a leg *or* a bundle *or Br* a bomb

bonhomme [bɔnɔm] *nm (mari)* old man
▸ *see also* **nom**

bonjour [bɔ̃ʒuʀ] *exclam* **bonjour l'ambiance/l'odeur!** what an atmosphere/a smell!; **bonjour les dégâts!** what a mess!

bonnard [bɔnaʀ] *adj* **c'est bonnard!** cool!

bonne [bɔn] **1** *adj (belle)* gorgeous, stunning, *Br* fit; **elle est bonne, la sœur de Frédo** Frédo's sister is a real babe *or Br* cracker
2 *nf* **avoir qn à la bonne** to like sb ᵠ
▸ *see also* **pâte, poire**

bonnet [bɔnɛ] *nm* (**a**) **un gros bonnet (de)** a big shot *or* big cheese (in) (**b**) **te casse pas le bonnet** don't worry about it ᵘ, don't let it bother you ᵘ

bonniche [bɔniʃ] *nf* servant ᵠ, *Br* skivvy

bord [bɔʀ] *nm* **sur les bords** a bit ᵠ, a tad; **il est un peu menteur sur les bords** he's a bit of a liar

bordel [!!] [bɔʀdɛl] **1** *nm* (**a**) *(maison close)* brothel ᵘ, whorehouse, *Br* knocking shop
(**b**) *(désordre)* shambles, mess; **foutre le bordel (dans)** *(mettre en désordre)* to make a fucking mess (of); **il fout le bordel en classe** he creates fucking havoc in the classroom
2 *exclam* fuck!; **bordel de merde!** fucking hell!; **mais qu'est-ce qu'il fout, bordel!** what the fuck is he doing?

bordélique [bɔʀdelik] *adj* **être bordélique** *(endroit, situation)* to be a mess *or* a shambles; *(personne)* to be messy

borne [bɔʀn] *nf (kilomètre)* kilometre ᵠ

bosse [bɔs] *nf* **rouler sa bosse** to knock about; **il a roulé sa bosse un peu partout** he's been around a bit

bosser [bɔse] *vi* to work ᵠ; **bosser comme un nègre** to slog one's guts out

bosseur, -euse [bɔsœʀ, -øz] **1** *adj* hard-working ᵠ
2 *nm,f* hard worker ᵠ

botte [bɔt] *nf* **en avoir plein les bottes**

to be *Br* knackered *or Am* pooped; **lécher les bottes à qn** to lick sb's boots; **chier dans les bottes à qn**[‼] to piss sb off, *Br* to get on sb's tits, *Am* to break sb's balls; **il lui a proposé la botte**[!] he asked her straight out to sleep with him

botter [bɔte] *vt* (**a**) *(plaire à)* **ça me botte** I like it □, I dig it; **ça te botterait d'y aller?** do you want to go?□, *Br* do you fancy going? (**b**) *(donner des coups de pied à)* **botter le cul à qn**[!] to give sb *Br* a boot up the arse *or Am* a kick in the ass; **botter les fesses** *ou* **le train à qn** to give sb a kick in the pants

boucan [bukã] *nm* racket, din

boucane [bukan] *nf Can* smoke□

bouché, -e [buʃe] *adj* **être bouché (à l'émeri)** *Br* to be thick (as two short planks), *Am* to have rocks in one's head

boucher [buʃe] *vt* **en boucher un coin à qn** to leave sb flabbergasted *or Br* gobsmacked

boucler [bukle] *vt* (**a**) *(fermer)* to shut□, to close□; **boucler la lourde** to shut *or* close the door□ (**b**) *(emprisonner)* to lock up, to put away (**c**) **la boucler** *(se taire)* to shut up, to button it, *Br* to belt up; **tu vas la boucler?** shut up *or* button it *or Br* belt up, will you?

boudin [budɛ̃] *nm* (**a**) *(femme laide)* dog, *Br* boot, *Am* beast (**b**) **faire du boudin** to be in a *or* the huff

▸ *see also* **eau, rond**

bouffarde [bufard] *nf* pipe□

bouffe [buf] *nf* (**a**) *(aliments)* food□, eats, chow, grub (**b**) *(repas)* meal□; **faire la bouffe** to do the cooking□; **se faire une bouffe** to have a meal together□

bouffer [bufe] **1** *vt (manger)* to eat□; **bouffer de l'essence** to be a gas-guzzler; **bouffer du kilomètre** to clock up a lot of miles; **bouffer du curé/du coco** to be a priest-/commie-hater

2 *vi* to eat□

3 se bouffer *vpr* **se bouffer le nez** to have a shouting match, *Br* to have a go at each other

▸ *see also* **chancre, vache**

bouffi [bufi] *nm* **tu l'as dit, bouffi!** you said it!, *Am* you said a mouthful!

bouffon [bufɔ̃] *nm (personne ridicule)* buffoon, clown

bougeotte [buʒɔt] *nf* **avoir la bougeotte** to be fidgety; *(avoir envie de voyager)* to have itchy feet

bouger [buʒe] *vi (sortir)* to make a move, to move on; **on bouge?** shall we make a move?

bougnoul, bougnoule [buɲul] *nm Offensive* = racist term used to refer to a North African Arab

boui-boui [bwibwi] *nm* greasy spoon

bouillave [bujav], **bouillaver** [bujave] *vt* to screw, to hump, *Br* to shag

bouille [buj] *nf (visage)* face□, mug; **avoir une bonne bouille** to look nice□

bouillie [buji] *nf* **de la bouillie pour les chats** *(texte)* a load of garbage *or Br* rubbish

bouillon [bujɔ̃] *nm (eau)* water□; **tomber dans le bouillon** to fall in; **boire le bouillon** *(avaler de l'eau)* to get a mouthful of water□; *(faire faillite)* to go bust

boule [bul] *nf* (**a**) *(tête)* **perdre la boule** to crack up, to lose one's marbles, to go round the bend, *Br* to lose the plot; **donner un coup de boule à qn** to headbutt sb; **prendre un coup de boule** to get headbutted; **avoir la boule à zéro** to have a skinhead (haircut)

(**b**) *(angoisse)* **avoir les boules** to be upset□; **ça me fout les boules** it makes me upset; **les boules!** how awful!

(**c**) **se mettre en boule** to hit the roof *or Am* ceiling, to blow one's top *or Am* stack, to fly off the handle

(**d**) **boules**[!] *(testicules)* balls, nuts

bouler [bule] *vi* **envoyer bouler qn** to tell sb where to go, *Br* to send sb packing

boulette [bulɛt] *nf* (*erreur*) *Br* boob, *Am* boo-boo; **faire une boulette** to make a *Br* boob or *Am* boo-boo

Boul' Mich' [bulmiʃ] *npr* **le Boul' Mich'** = the Boulevard Saint-Michel in Paris

boulonner [bulɔne] *vi* to work □

boulot [bulo] *nm* work □; (*tâche, emploi*) job □; **se mettre au boulot** to get to work □, to get down to it

boulotter [bulɔte] *vi* to eat □

boum [bum] **1** *nf* party □ (*for young people*)
  2 **être en plein boum** to be up to one's neck, to be rushed off one's feet

boumer [bume] *vi* **ça boume?** how are things?, how's it going?

bouquin [bukɛ̃] *nm* book □

bouquiner [bukine] *vi* to read □

bourdon [burdɔ̃] *nm* **avoir le bourdon** (*être déprimé*) to feel down, to be on a downer

bourge [burʒ] *Pej* (*abbr* **bourgeois, -e**)
  1 *adj* middle-class □
  2 *nmf* middle-class person □

bourgeoise [burʒwaz] *nf* (*épouse*) old lady

bourlinguer [burlɛ̃ge] *vi* to knock about

bourrage [buraʒ] *nm* **bourrage de crâne** *ou* **de mou** brainwashing □, eyewash

bourre [bur] **1** *nm* cop
  2 *nf* **être à la bourre** to be running late □; **coup de bourre** busy time □; **entre midi et deux heures c'est le coup de bourre** the busiest time is between twelve and two

bourré, -e [bure] *adj* wasted, plastered, *Br* legless, pissed
  ▸ *see also* **coing**

bourre-pif [burpif] *nm inv* punch on the nose □

bourrer [bure] **1** ⚠⚠ *vt* (*posséder sexuellement*) to hump, *Br* to poke, to shaft
  2 *vi* (*aller très vite*) to belt along, to bomb along
  3 **se bourrer** *vpr* **se bourrer la gueule** ⚠ to get shit-faced or *Br* rat-arsed or pissed
  ▸ *see also* **mou**

bourrichon [buriʃɔ̃] *nm* **monter le bourrichon à qn** to put ideas in sb's head; **se monter le bourrichon** to get carried away

bourrin [burɛ̃] *nm* (**a**) (*cheval*) horse □ (**b**) (*policier*) cop, pig (**c**) (*femme laide*) dog, *Br* boot, *Am* beast

bourrique [burik] *nf* (**a**) (*personne têtue*) pig-headed person (**b**) **être soûl comme une bourrique** *Br* to be (as) pissed as a newt or a fart, *Am* to be stewed to the gills (**c**) **faire tourner qn en bourrique** to drive sb round the bend

bouseux, -euse [buzø, -øz] *nm,f Pej* yokel, peasant, *Am* hick, hayseed

bousiller [buzije] *vt* to wreck, to bust, *Br* to knacker

boussole [busɔl] *nf* **perdre la boussole** to crack up, to lose one's marbles, to go round the bend or *Br* the twist

boustifaille [bustifaj] *nf* food □, chow, grub

bout [bu] *nm* (**a**) ⚠⚠ (*sexe de l'homme*) dick, prick, cock; **se mettre une femme sur le bout** to get laid, *Br* to get one's end away (**b**) **tenir le bon bout** to be on the right track
  ▸ *see also* **mettre**

boutanche [butɑ̃ʃ] *nf* bottle □

bouteille [butɛj] *nf* (*âge*) **avoir de la bouteille** to have been around a long time; **prendre de la bouteille** to be getting on a bit

boutique [butik] *nf* (**a**) **parler boutique** to talk shop (**b**) (*sexe de l'homme*) dick, *Br* tadger, *Am* schlong

bouton !⃞ [butɔ̃] *nm (clitoris)* clit

boxon !!⃞ [bɔksɔ̃] *nm* **(a)** *(maison close)* brothel ᐤ, whorehouse, *Br* knocking shop **(b)** *(désordre)* mess, shambles; **foutre le boxon (dans)** *(mettre en désordre)* to make a fucking mess (of); **il fout le boxon en classe** he creates fucking havoc in the classroom

bracelets [braslɛ] *nmpl (menottes)* cuffs, bracelets

braire [brɛr] *vi* **ça me fait braire** it hacks me off, *Br* it gets up my nose *or* does my head in, *Am* it gives me a pain

branché, -e [brɑ̃ʃe] *adj (bar, discothèque, personne)* hip, trendy; **être branché cinéma/jazz** to be into movies/jazz

brancher [brɑ̃ʃe] *vt* **(a)** *(plaire à)* **ça me branche** I'm really into it; **ça me brancherait de venir avec vous** I'd be into coming with you
(b) *(pour séduire)* *Br* to chat up, *Am* to hit on
(c) *(mettre en contact)* **brancher qn avec qn** to introduce sb to sb ᐤ
(d) *(faire parler)* **brancher qn sur un sujet** to get sb started *or* to start sb off on a subject

branlée !⃞ [brɑ̃le] *nf (défaite, correction)* thrashing, pasting; **prendre une branlée** to get thrashed, to *Br* get *or* *Am* take a pasting

branler !!⃞ [brɑ̃le] **1** *vt* to jerk off, *Br* to toss off, to wank off; **j'en ai rien à branler** I don't give a (flying) fuck *or* a shit; **mais qu'est-ce qu'il branle?** what the fuck is he doing?, what the fuck is he up to?
2 se branler *vpr* to jerk off, *Br* to toss oneself off, to wank, to have a wank; **s'en branler** not to give a (flying) fuck *or* a shit

branlette !!⃞ [brɑ̃lɛt] *nf* hand-job, *Br* wank; **se faire une branlette** to jerk off, *Br* to toss oneself off, to wank, to

have a wank; **faire une branlette à qn** to give sb a hand-job, to jerk sb off, *Br* to toss sb off, to wank sb off

branleur, -euse !⃞ [brɑ̃lœr, -øz] *nm,f* loser, *Br* waster, *Am* slacker

branque [brɑ̃k] **1** *adj (fou)* bonkers, nuts, *Br* off one's head, barking (mad)
2 *nmf (imbécile)* dope, jerk, *Br* prat, feeb; *(fou)* *Br* nutter, headcase, *Am* wacko, screwball

braque [brak] *adj* crazy, off one's rocker, *Br* mental

braquemart !⃞ [brakmar] *nm* dick, prick, *Br* knob

braquer [brake] *vt* **(a)** *(voler)* **braquer une banque/une bijouterie** to hold up a bank/a jeweller's; **braquer qch à qn** to pinch *or* *Br* nick sth from sb **(b)** *(rendre hostile)* **braquer qn** *Br* to get sb's back up, *Am* to tick sb off

braqueur [brakœr] *nm* armed robber ᐤ

bras [bra] *nm* **un gros bras** a big guy; **jouer les gros bras** to act the tough guy
▶ *see also* **bite, pine, yeux**

brêle [brɛl] *nf* **(a)** *(cyclomoteur)* (motor) scooter ᐤ, moped ᐤ **(b)** *(personne)* cretin, jerk, *Br* tosspot, *Am* fathead

Brésilienne [breziljɛn] *nf (prostitué)* = Brazilian transsexual *or* transvestite male prostitute

bretelles [brətɛl] *nfpl* **remonter les bretelles à qn** to bawl sb out, *Br* to give sb an earful, *Am* to chew sb out; **se faire remonter les bretelles** to get bawled out, *Br* to get an earful, *Am* to get chewed out
▶ *see also* **piano**

bricheton [briʃtɔ̃] *nm* bread ᐤ

bricole [brikɔl] *nf (chose insignifiante)* little thing ᐤ; **il va lui arriver des bricoles** he's heading for trouble

bricoler [brikɔle] **(a)** *vi (faire des petits boulots)* to do odd jobs, to do this and that **(b)** *(se livrer à de menus travaux)* to mess around, to potter around

bridé, -e [bride] *nm,f Offensive* slant, *Am* gook

brignolet [briɲɔlɛ] *nm* bread □

bringue [brɛ̃g] *nf* **(a)** *(fête)* **faire la bringue** to party, *Br* to go on the razzle **(b) une grande bringue** a beanpole

brioche [brijɔʃ] *nf* **avoir de la brioche** to have a paunch *or* a pot-belly; **prendre de la brioche** be getting a paunch *or* a pot-belly

brique [brik] *nf (dix mille francs)* ten thousand francs □
▸ see also **casser**

briser [brize] *vt* **il/ça me les brise** he/it really bugs me *or* hacks me off *or Br* gets up my nose *or* does my head in

Bronx [brɔks] *npr* **mettre le Bronx dans qch** to turn sth upside down, to make a mess of sth

bronze [brɔ̃z] *nm* **couler un bronze** [!!] to *Br* have *or Am* take a dump *or* a crap, *Br* to drop a log

bronzé, -e [brɔ̃ze] *nm,f Offensive* nigger, *Br* darky, *Am* coon

brosse [brɔs] *nf* **prendre une brosse** to get wrecked *or* smashed *or Br* slaughtered *or* pissed

brosser [brɔse] **se brosser** *vpr* to do without; **tu peux te brosser pour que je te prête ma caisse, maintenant!** if you think I'm going to lend you my car now, you can forget it!

broue [bru] *nf Can* lather □; **faire de la broue** to show off

brouille-ménage [brujmenaʒ] *nm inv* red wine □, *Br* plonk

brouter [brute] *vt* **les brouter à qn** [!] to piss sb off, *Br* to get on sb's tits, *Am* to break sb's balls; **brouter la tige à qn** [!!] to go down on sb, to suck sb off, to give sb head; **brouter le cresson à qn** [!!] to go down on sb, *Br* to lick sb out

brouteuse [!!] [brutøz] *nf* dyke

brûlé, -e [bryle] *adj* **être brûlé** *(être compromis)* to be finished

bûche [byʃ] *nf* **ramasser une bûche** *(tomber)* to go flying

bûcher [byʃe] **1** *vt Br* to swot up on, *Am* to bone up on
2 *vi Br* to swot, *Am* to bone up

bûcheur, -euse [byʃœr, -øz] **1** *adj* hard-working □
2 *nm,f* hard worker □

buffet [byfɛ] *nm (ventre)* belly

bulle [byl] *nf* **(a)** *(à un devoir)* zero □, *Am* goose egg; **prendre une bulle** to get a zero □ *or Am* a goose egg **(b) coincer la bulle** to get some shut-eye *or* some *Br* zeds *or Am* zees
▸ see also **chier**

buller [byle] *vi* to laze about

burettes [!] [byrɛt] *nfpl (testicules)* balls, nuts, *Br* bollocks; **se vider les burettes** [!!] to shoot one's load; **casser les burettes à qn** to piss sb off, *Br* to get on sb's tits, *Am* to break sb's balls

burlingue [byrlɛ̃g] *nm* office □

burnes [!!] [byrn] *nfpl* balls, nuts, *Br* bollocks; **se vider les burnes** to shoot one's load; **casser les burnes à qn** to piss sb off, *Br* to get on sb's tits, *Am* to break sb's balls

buter [byte] *vt* to kill □, *Br* to do in, *Am* to eighty-six; **se faire buter** to get killed □, *Br* to get done in, *Am* to get eighty-sixed

buvable [byvabl] *adj* **pas buvable** *(très antipathique)* unbearable □; **c'est un mec pas buvable** he's a complete pain (in the neck)

buvard [byvar] *nm (dose de LSD)* tab, trip

Byzance [bizɑ̃s] *npr* **c'est Byzance** it's the last word in luxury; **c'est pas Byzance** it's not exactly luxurious

C

cabane [kaban] *nf (prison)* slammer, clink, *Br* nick, *Am* joint; **en cabane** in the slammer *or* clink *or Br* nick *or Am* joint

cabanon [kabanɔ̃] *nm* **il est bon pour le cabanon** he should be locked up *or* put away

câblé, -e [kɑble] *adj (à la page)* hip, trendy

cabochard, -e [kabɔʃar, -ard] *adj* pig-headed

caboche [kabɔʃ] *nf* head □, nut

cabot [kabo] *nm (chien)* mutt

caca [kaka] *nm* poo, poop; **il nous fait un caca nerveux, l'autre!** he's having kittens!, he's having a fit!
  ▶ see also **nez**

cadavre [kadavr] *nm (bouteille vide)* empty, *Br* dead man

cadeau, -x [kado] *nm* **ce mec, c'est pas un cadeau!** that guy's a total pain (in the neck)!

cador [kadɔr] *nm* **(a)** *(chien)* mutt **(b)** *(personne influente)* big shot, big cheese, bigwig; *(d'une bande)* leader □

cafard [kafar] *nm* **(a)** *(tristesse)* **avoir le cafard** *ou* **un coup de cafard** to feel down *or* low; **ça m'a foutu le cafard** it got me down **(b)** *(délateur)* sneak, tell-tale, *Am* snitch

cafarder [kafarde] **1** *vt* **cafarder qn** to sneak on sb, to tell tales on sb, *Am* to snitch on sb
  2 *vi* **(a)** *(être triste)* to feel down *or* low **(b)** *(rapporter)* to sneak, to tell tales, *Am* to snitch

cafardeur, -euse [kafardœr, -øz] *nm,f* sneak, tell-tale, *Am* snitch

cafardeux, -euse [kafardø, -øz] *adj (personne)* down, low

cafèt' [kafɛt] *nf (abbr* **cafétéria)** cafeteria □

cafeter [kafte] = **cafter**

cafeteur, -euse [kaftœr, -øz] = **cafteur**

cafetière [kaftjɛr] *nf (tête)* head □, nut

cafouiller [kafuje] *vi* **(a)** *(mal fonctionner)* to be a shambles *or* a muddle; *(machine)* to play up, to be on the blink *or Am* on the fritz **(b)** *(s'embrouiller)* to get in a muddle, to tie oneself in knots

cafouillis [kafuji] *nm* shambles, muddle

cafter [kafte] *vi* to sneak, to tell tales, *Am* to snitch

cafteur, -euse [kaftœr, -øz] *nm,f* sneak, tell-tale, *Am* snitch

cage [kaʒ] *nf* **(a)** **cage à lapins** *(logement)* rabbit hutch **(b)** *(buts)* goal □ *(posts, nets)*

cageot [kaʒo] *nm (femme laide)* dog, *Br* boot, *Am* beast, skank

cagnard [kaɲar] *nm (soleil)* blazing sunshine □; **quel cagnard!** what a scorcher!, *Br* it's roasting!

caïd [kaid] *nm (gros bonnet)* big shot, big cheese, bigwig; *(d'une bande)* leader □; **jouer les caïds** to act tough, *Br* to act the hard man

caillasse [kajas] *nf (argent)* dough, bread, *Br* dosh, *Am* bucks, gelt

caille [kaj] *nf* **ma caille** honey, sweetheart

cailler [kaje] **1** *v imp* **ça caille** it's freezing *or Br* baltic, *Br* it's brass monkeys

2 se cailler vpr to be freezing; **se les cailler** ! to be freezing one's Br **arse** or Am **ass off**

caillera [kajra] nf (verlan **racaille**) scum

caillou, -x [kaju] nm (a) (tête) head ▫, nut; **il a plus un poil sur le caillou** he's as bald as a coot; **elle en a dans le caillou** she's a smart cookie (b) (pierre précieuse) rock, sparkler

cainf [kɛ̃f], **cainfri** [kɛ̃fri] nmf (verlan **Africain**) African ▫

caisse [kɛs] nf (a) (voiture) car ▫, wheels, Br motor (b) **passer à la caisse** (être payé) to collect (c) (pet) **lâcher** ou **larguer une caisse** ! to fart, Br to let off, Am to lay one

cake [kɛk] nm (imbécile) dope, jerk, moron, Br plonker, Am goober

calancher [kalɑ̃ʃe] vi to croak, Br to snuff it, Am to check out

calbar [kalbar], **calbute** [kalbyt] nm Br scants, Am shorts, skivvies

calcaire [kalkɛr] nm **avoir** ou **faire un coup de calcaire** to have a fit, to go off (at) the deep end

calcif [kalsif] = **calbar**

calculer [kalkyle] vt (regarder) to check out, to eye (up)

calebar [kalbar], **calecif** [kalsif] = **calbar**

calendos [kalɑ̃dos] nm camembert ▫

caleter [kalte] = **calter**

calibre [kalibr] nm (pistolet) shooter, Am piece, equalizer

calmos [kalmos] exclam chill (out)!, take it easy!

calots [kalo] nmpl (yeux) eyes ▫

calotte [kalɔt] nf **la calotte** (le clergé) the clergy ▫

calter [kalte] vi to beat it, Br to clear off, Am to split

calva [kalva] nm (abbr **calvados**) calvados ▫

Camarde [kamard] nf **la Camarde** death ▫

cambrouse [kɑ̃bruz], **cambrousse** [kɑ̃brus] nf **la cambrousse** the sticks, Am the boondocks; **en pleine cambrousse** in the sticks, in the middle of nowhere, Br in the back of beyond

cambuse [kɑ̃byz] nf dump, hole, hovel

came [kam] nf drugs ▫, stuff, Br gear

camé, -e [kame] **1** adj **être camé** to be on something; **il était complètement camé** he was totally loaded or wrecked or wasted
2 nm,f druggie, junkie, Br drughead, Am dope fiend

camelote [kamlɔt] nf (a) (marchandise) stuff, Br gear (b) (objets de mauvaise qualité) trash, junk, garbage, Br rubbish

camer [kame] **se camer** vpr to do drugs; **se camer à l'héroïne/à la cocaïne** to be on heroin/cocaine; **il s'est jamais camé à l'héroïne** he's never done heroin

camp [kɑ̃] nm **ficher le camp** to clear off, to beat it, Am to split; **foutre le camp** ! to go to hell, Br to piss off, to bugger off; **fiche(-moi) le camp!** get lost!, beat it!, Br sling your hook!, Am take a walk!; **fous(-moi) le camp!** ! go to hell!, get the hell out of here!, Br piss off!, bugger off!

canard [kanar] nm (journal) rag
▶ see also **casser**

canarder [kanarde] vt to snipe at ▫, to take pot shots at

canasson [kanasɔ̃] nm horse ▫

cané, -e [kane] adj (épuisé) Br knackered, shattered, Am beat

caner¹ [kane] vi (renoncer) to throw in the towel, to chuck it in

caner², canner [kane] vi (a) (mourir) to croak, Br to snuff it, Am to cash in (one's chips) (b) (s'enfuir) to beat it, Br to leg it, Am to bug out

cannes [kan] nfpl (jambes) legs ▫, pins

canon [kanɔ̃] **1** adj gorgeous, stunning, Br fit

  2 nm (belle femme) babe, knockout, Br smasher

cantoche [kãtɔʃ] nf canteen □

caoua [kawa] = **kawa**

cap [kap] adj (abbr **capable**) **t'es pas cap de…!** I bet you can't…!

capo [kapo] nm (abbr **caporal**) Br ≃ lance corporal □, Am ≃ private first class □

capote [kapɔt] nf **capote (anglaise)** condom □, French letter, Br durex ®, Am rubber

capter [kapte] vt (comprendre) to get; **répète, j'ai pas capté** say that again, I didn't get it

carabiné, -e [karabine] adj (café, cocktail) powerful □; (rhume) stinking; (fièvre) raging □; **tenir une cuite carabinée** to be off one's face or totally plastered or Br completely legless

carafe [karaf] **en carafe** adv **rester en carafe** to be left stranded or high and dry; **tomber en carafe** (en panne) to break down □

carafon [karafɔ̃] nm (tête) head □, nut; **il a vraiment rien dans le carafon** he's got nothing between his ears, Br he's as thick as two short planks, Am he's got rocks in his head

carapater [karapate] **se carapater** vpr to scram, to make oneself scarce

carat [kara] nm **dernier carat** (dernière limite) at the very latest □, tops

carburer [karbyre] vi **il carbure au whisky/au café** whisky/coffee keeps him going

carne [karn] nf bad-quality meat □; **vieille carne** old bag, old witch

carotter [karɔte] vt **carotter qch à qn** (dérober) to pinch or Br nick sth from sb; (escroquer) to swindle or Br do sb out of sth

carpette [karpɛt] nf (lâche) doormat

carreaux [karo] nmpl (lunettes) specs

carrer [kare] vt **tu peux te le carrer dans le cul** ou **dans l'oignon!** ⚠️ you can shove or stick it up your Br arse or Am ass!

carton [kartɔ̃] nm (a) **faire un carton** (tirer sur quelqu'un) to take pot shots at somebody; (avoir du succès) to be a hit (b) **(se) prendre un carton** (essuyer une défaite) to get thrashed or Br trounced; (avoir une mauvaise note) to get a bad mark □ (c) **taper le carton** (jouer aux cartes) to have a game of cards □

cartonner [kartone] vi (a) (avoir une bonne note) to pass with flying colours (b) (musique) to be mind-blowing

casbah [kasba] nf (maison) place, pad, Br gaff

case [kaz] nf **il lui manque une case** he's got a screw loose, he's off his rocker, he's not all there; **retour à la case départ!** back to square one!

cash [kaʃ] adv **payer cash** to pay cash □

casquer [kaske] vt & vi to fork out, to cough up

casquette [kaskɛt] nf (a) **avoir la casquette de plomb** to have a hangover □, to be hungover □ (b) (contrôleur dans les transports en commun) ticket inspector □

  ▸ see also **ras**

casse [kas] **1** nm break-in □, Am heist; **faire un casse chez un bijoutier** to Br do over or Am boost a jeweller's

  2 nf trouble; **va y avoir de la casse** there's going to be trouble

cassé, -e [kase] adj (drogué) stoned, wrecked, flying; (ivre) smashed, plastered, Br legless

casse-bonbons ⚠️ [kasbɔ̃bɔ̃] **1** adj inv **être casse-bonbons** to be a pain (in the neck)

  2 nmf inv pain (in the neck)

casse-couilles ⚠️ [kaskuj] **1** adj inv **être casse-couilles** to be a pain in the

Br arse *or Am* ass

  2 *nmf inv* pain in the *Br* arse *or Am* ass

casse-cul [!!] [kasky] **1** *adj inv* **être casse-cul** to be a pain in the *Br* arse *or Am* ass

  2 *nmf inv* pain in the *Br* arse *or Am* ass

casse-dalle [kasdal] *nm inv* sandwich ▢, *Br* butty, sarny

casse-graine [kasgrɛn] *nm inv* snack ▢

casse-gueule [kasgœl] *adj inv* (*sport, acrobaties*) death-defying; (*entreprise*) risky ▢, *Br* dodgy

casse-pieds [kaspje] **1** *adj inv* **être casse-pieds** to be a pain (in the neck)

  2 *nmf inv* pain (in the neck)

casse-pipe [kaspip] *nm inv* **envoyer qn/aller au casse-pipe** (*à la guerre*) to send sb/go to the front

casser [kase] **1** *vt* (**a**) **casser la figure** *ou* **la gueule** [!] **à qn** to smash sb's face in, to waste sb's face; **casser la gueule à une bouteille** to down a bottle in one (**b**) (*critiquer*) to tear *or* rip to bits (**c**) (*agresser*) **casser du pédé** [!] to go queer-bashing *or* gay-bashing; **casser du flic** [!] to beat up some cops (**d**) **les casser à qn** [!] (*l'importuner*) *Br* to get on sb's tits, *Am* to break sb's balls (**e**) **ça casse pas des briques, ça casse pas trois pattes à un canard, ça casse rien** it's nothing to write home about (**f**) **à tout casser** (*au maximum*) max, tops; **ça doit coûter cent francs à tout casser** it must cost a hundred francs max *or* tops; **faire une fiesta à tout casser** to have a hell of a party

  2 **se casser** *vpr* (**a**) (*partir*) to clear off, *Am* to split; **bon, faut que je me casse** I'd better be off, I've got to make tracks; **casse-toi!** get lost!, get the hell out of here!

  (**b**) **se casser la figure** *ou* **la gueule** [!] (*tomber*) to fall flat on one's face; (*échouer*) to be a flop

  (**c**) (*s'inquiéter*) **te casse pas!** take it easy!, chill (out)!

(**d**) **se casser (à faire qch)** to go out of one's way (to do sth); **se casser le cul (à faire qch)** [!] to bust a gut *or Am* one's ass (doing sth)

  ▸ *see also* **baraque, bonbon, bonnet, burettes, burnes, couille, croûte, graine, margoulette, morceau, nénette, pipe, rondelle, tronc**

casserole [kasrɔl] *nf Hum* **passer à la casserole** (*subir un rapport sexuel*) *Br* to get a good seeing-to, *Am* to get a balling; (*être assassiné*) to get bumped off

castagne [kastaɲ] *nf* (*coup*) clout, wallop; **va y avoir de la castagne** there's going to be a *Br* punch-up *or Am* fist fight

castagner [kastaɲe] **1** *vt* to clout, to wallop

  2 **se castagner** *vpr* to have a *Br* punch-up *or Am* fist fight

cata [kata] *nf* (*abbr* **catastrophe**) **c'est la cata** it's a disaster

catho [kato] *adj & nmf* (*abbr* **catholique**) Catholic ▢

causant, -e [kozɑ̃, -ɑ̃t] *adj* **il n'est pas très causant** he's not very chatty, he doesn't have much to say for himself

causer [koze] *vi* to chat

cavale [kaval] *nf* **être en cavale** to be on the run

cavaler [kavale] **1** *vi* (**a**) (*courir, se dépêcher*) to run around ▢, to charge around (**b**) (*rechercher les aventures*) to chase after women/men

  2 *vt* **tu commences à me cavaler!** you're starting to *Br* get on my wick *or* up my nose *or Am* tick me off!

cavaleur, -euse [kavalœr, -øz] **1** *adj* (*homme*) womanizing; (*femme*) man-eating

  2 *nm,f* (*homme*) womanizer, skirt-chaser; (*femme*) man-eater

cave [kav] *nm* (*imbécile*) sucker, *Br* mug, *Am* patsy

céfran [sefrã] (verlan **français**) **1** adj French □

2 nmf Frenchman, f Frenchwoman □

ceinture [sɛ̃tyr] nf **faire ceinture** (être privé de nourriture, être forcé à l'abstinence) to go without; **ce soir, mon vieux, ceinture!** you'll have to go without tonight!

cendar [sɑ̃dar] nm ashtray □

ceusses [søs] pron Hum **les ceusses qui...** them who...

cézigue [sezig] pron his lordship, Br his nibs

chagatte [!!] [ʃagat] nf pussy, snatch, Br fanny

chambard [ʃɑ̃bar] nm **(a)** (remue-ménage) upheaval □ **(b)** (vacarme) racket, din; **faire du chambard** to make a racket or a din

chambardement [ʃɑ̃bardəmɑ̃] nm upheaval □

chambarder [ʃɑ̃barde] vt **tout chambarder** (mettre en désordre, bouleverser) to turn everything upside-down

chambrer [ʃɑ̃bre] vt (taquiner) **chambrer qn** to make fun of sb □, Br to wind sb up, to take the mickey out of sb, Am to goof with sb

chameau, -x [ʃamo] **1** adj **être chameau** (homme) to be a Br swine or Am stinker; (femme) to be a witch or Br a cow

2 nm (homme) Br swine, Am stinker; (femme) witch, Br cow

champ' [ʃɑ̃p] nm (abbr **champagne**) bubbly, Br champers

champignon [ʃɑ̃piɲɔ̃] nm **appuyer sur le champignon** (accélérer) Br to put one's foot down, Am to step on the gas, to let the hammer down

champion, -onne [ʃɑ̃pjɔ̃, -ɔn] adj great, Br fab, Am aces

Champs [ʃɑ̃] npr **les Champs** the Champs-Elysées □

chancre [ʃɑ̃kr] nm **bouffer comme un chancre** to stuff oneself or one's face, to pig out, Br to make a pig of oneself

chandelle [ʃɑ̃dɛl] nf **(a)** (morve) drip of snot **(b) tenir la chandelle** (être de trop) Br to play gooseberry, Am to be the fifth wheel

▸ see also **trente-six**

chanson [ʃɑ̃sɔ̃] nf **c'est toujours la même chanson** it's always the same old story; **ça va, je connais la chanson!** I've heard it all before!

chapeau [ʃapo] nm **1** nm **travailler du chapeau** to have a screw loose, to be off one's rocker, to be not all there

2 exclam good for you/him/etc!

char [ʃar] nm **arrête ton char (Ben Hur)!** come off it!, yeah right!

charas [ʃaras] nm cannabis resin □

charbon [ʃarbɔ̃] nm **aller au charbon** (à son travail) to go to work □

charcler [ʃarkle] vt to kill □, to waste, Br to do in, Am to eighty-six; **ça va charcler!** there's going to be trouble!

charclo [ʃarklo] nmf (verlan **clochard**) tramp, Br dosser, Am hobo, bum

charcuter [ʃarkyte] vt (sujet: chirurgien) to butcher, to hack up

chargé, -e [ʃarʒe] adj (ivre, drogué) loaded, wrecked, wasted

charlot [ʃarlo] nm (personne qui manque de sérieux) clown

charogne [!] [ʃarɔɲ] nf (homme méprisable) bastard; (femme méprisable) bitch

charre [ʃar] = **char**

charrette [ʃarɛt] **1** nf (voiture) car □, wheels, Br motor

2 adj inv (en retard) **être charrette** to be working against the clock

charrier [ʃarje] **1** vt (se moquer de) **charrier qn** to make fun of sb □, Br to take the mickey out of sb, to wind sb up, Am to goof with sb; **il s'est fait charrier** he got made fun of □, Br he got the mickey taken out of him

2 vi **charrier (dans les bégonias)** (exagérer) to go too far; **faut pas charrier!** come off it!, gimme a break!

châsses [ʃas] nmpl (yeux) eyes □

châssis [ʃasi] nm (silhouette) chassis, bod; **mate un peu le châssis!** check out the chassis or bod on that!

chat [ʃa] nm **il n'y avait pas un chat** there wasn't a soul
▶ see also **pipi**

châtaigne [ʃatɛɲ] nf (**a**) (coup) clout, thump; **mettre une châtaigne à qn** to clout or thump sb (**b**) (bagarre) **il va y avoir de la châtaigne** there's going to be a Br punch-up or Am fist fight (**c**) (décharge électrique) **(se) prendre une châtaigne** to get a shock

châtaigner [ʃatɛɲe] **1** vt to clout, to thump; **se faire châtaigner** to get clouted or thumped
2 se châtaigner vpr to trade punches

Château [ʃato] nm **le Château** the Élysée Palace □ (official residence of the French President)

Château-Lapompe [ʃatolapɔ̃p] nm Hum **du Château-Lapompe** water □

This humorous expression, imitating a typical name for French wine, is used to mean water when served or ordered instead of wine with a meal.

chatte ⚠️⚠️ [ʃat] nf (sexe de la femme) pussy, snatch, Br fanny; **avoir de la chatte** to be fucking lucky or Br jammy

chaud, -e [ʃo, ʃod] **1** adj (sexuellement) hot; **être (un) chaud lapin** to be permanently horny; **être chaud de la pince** ⚠️ to be a horny bastard
2 nm **on a eu chaud (aux fesses)!** we had a narrow escape!
▶ see also **eau**

chaude-pisse ⚠️ [ʃodpis] nf **la chaude-pisse** the clap

chauffer [ʃofe] v imp **ça va chauffer** there's going to be trouble

chaussure [ʃosyr] nf **avoir mis ses**

chaussures à bascule (être ivre) to be staggering all over the place

chébran [ʃebrɑ̃] adj (verlan **branché**) hip, trendy

chef [ʃɛf] nm (**a**) (terme d'adresse) pal, Br mate, Am buddy (**b**) **se débrouiller comme un chef** to do really well □

chefaillon [ʃefajɔ̃] nm little Hitler

chelou [ʃəlu] adj (verlan **louche**) shady, seedy, Br dodgy

chèque [ʃɛk] nm **chèque en bois** rubber Br cheque or Am check

chercher [ʃɛrʃe] vt (provoquer) to pick a fight with; **tu me cherches, là?** do you want a fight?; **si tu me cherches, tu vas me trouver!** if you're looking for trouble, you've come to the right place, if you're looking for a fight, you'll get one!
▶ see also **crosses, pou**

chérot [ʃero] adj inv pricey

chetron [ʃətrɔ̃] nf (verlan **tronche**) face □, mug

cheval, -aux [ʃəval, -o] nm **c'est pas le mauvais cheval** he's a nice enough guy

cheveu, -x [ʃəvø] nm **se faire des cheveux (blancs)** to worry oneself sick, to give oneself grey hairs

cheville [ʃəvij] nf **avoir les chevilles qui enflent** to get big-headed, to get too big for one's Br boots or Am britches

chèvre [ʃɛvr] nf **rendre qn chèvre** to drive sb nuts or crazy or round the bend; **devenir chèvre** to go nuts or crazy or round the bend

chiadé, -e [ʃjade] adj elaborate □

chiader [ʃjade] vt to take care over □

chialer [ʃjale] vi (**a**) (pleurer) to blubber, to snivel (**b**) (se plaindre) to whinge

chiant, -e ⚠️ [ʃjɑ̃, -ɑ̃t] adj (**a**) (monotone) Br bloody or Am goddamn boring; **chiant comme la pluie** as boring as hell, Br piss-boring (**b**) (agaçant) **être chiant** Br to be a bloody nuisance, to be a pain in the Br arse or Am ass

chiard [!] [ʃjar] nm brat

chiasse [!!] [ʃjas] nf (a) (diarrhée) **la chiasse** the runs, the shits, the trots; **foutre la chiasse à qn** (lui faire peur) to scare sb shitless (b) (ennui) **quelle chiasse!** what a fucking pain (in the Br arse or Am ass)!

chiatique [!!] [ʃjatik] adj **être chiatique** to be a pain in the Br arse or Am ass

chibre [!] [ʃibr] nm dick, Br tadger, Am schlong

chicha [ʃiʃa] nm (verlan **haschich**) hash, dope, Br blow

chichon [ʃiʃɔ̃] nm hash, dope, Br blow

chicos [ʃikos] adj classy, smart

chié, -e [!] [ʃje] adj (a) (formidable) shit-hot, Am awesome (b) (qui exagère) **il est chié, lui!** he's got a Br bloody or Am goddamn nerve!

chiée [!] [ʃje] nf **(toute) une chiée de** a (whole) shitload of

chien, chienne [ʃjɛ̃, ʃjɛn] 1 nm,f **avoir un mal de chien à faire qch** to have a hell of a job doing sth; **c'est pas fait pour les chiens** it's there for a reason; **les paillassons c'est pas fait pour les chiens!** the doormat's not there as an ornament!; **chienne de vie!** what a life!

 2 adj (méchant) **être chien avec qn** to be rotten to sb
▸ see also **nom**

chienlit [ʃjɑ̃li] nf (désordre) shambles, muddle; **c'est la chienlit** it's a complete shambles or muddle

chier [!!] [ʃje] 1 vi (a) (déféquer) to shit, to Br have or Am take a shit or a crap or a dump

 (b) **chier dans la colle** to be out of order, Br to take the piss; **chier dans son froc** (avoir peur) to shit oneself, to be shit-scared; **à chier** (très mauvais) fucking awful; **y a pas à chier** there are no two fucking ways about it; **en chier (pour faire qch)** to have a hell of a time

(doing sth); **ça va chier (des bulles)!** the shit's going to hit the fan!, all hell's going to break loose!; **va chier!** fuck off!; **faire chier qn** (mettre en colère) Br to piss sb off, to get on sb's tits, Am to break sb's balls; (ennuyer) to bore sb shitless; **se faire chier** (s'ennuyer) to be bored shitless; **se faire chier à faire qch** (se donner du mal) to bust a gut or Am one's ass doing sth; **envoyer chier qn** to tell sb where to get off, Br to tell sb to piss off

 2 vt **tu vas pas nous chier une pendule!** don't make such a fuss or Br a bloody song and dance about it!
▸ see also **botte, nul, rat, tortiller**

chierie [!] [ʃiri] nf **quelle chierie!** Br what a bloody pain!, what a pain in the Br arse or Am ass!

chieur, -euse [!] [ʃjœr, -øz] nm,f pain in the Br arse or Am ass

chinetoc, chinetoque [ʃintɔk] nmf Offensive Chink, Chinky

chinois [ʃinwa] nm **se polir le chinois** [!] to beat one's meat, to bang or Br bash the bishop

chiotte [!] [ʃjɔt] nf (a) (voiture) car □, wheels, Br motor; (moto) bike, Am hog; (cyclomoteur) (motor) scooter □, moped □ (b) (ennui) **quelle chiotte!** what a pain in the Br arse or Am ass! (c) **chiottes** (W-C) Br bog, Am john; **il a un goût de chiottes** he's got shit taste; **aux chiottes, l'arbitre!** Br ≃ the referee's a wanker!, Am ≃ kill the umpire!

chiper [ʃipe] vt **chiper qch à qn** to pinch or Br nick sth from sb

chipolata [!] [ʃipolata] nf (pénis) sausage, Br pork sword, Am salami

chique [ʃik] nf **avoir la chique** (mal aux dents) to have a swollen cheek □ (because of toothache); **ça m'a coupé la chique** (surpris) I was speechless or Br gobsmacked; **mou comme une chique** spineless, Br wet
▸ see also **jus**

chiqué [ʃike] nm **c'est du chiqué** it's all put on or pretend

chlass, chlasse, chlâsse [ʃlas] = **schlass²**

chleu, chleuh [ʃlø] nm Offensive Kraut

> Depending on the context and the tone of voice used, this term may be either offensive or affectionately humorous. It is nonetheless inadvisable to use it unless one is quite sure of the reaction it will receive.

chlinguer [ʃlɛ̃ge] vi to stink, Br to pong, to hum

chnoc, chnoque [ʃnɔk] = **schnock**

chnouf, chnouffe [ʃnuf] nf (héroïne) junk, horse; (cocaïne) snow, charlie, coke

chochotte [ʃoʃot] nf (personne maniérée) wimp, wuss; **fais pas ta chochotte** stop mincing or Br poncing about!

chocolat [ʃokola] adj inv **on est chocolat!** (on a été dupés) we've been done!; (dans une situation sans issue) we've been left high and dry or stranded!
▶ see also **turbine**

chocottes [ʃokɔt] nfpl **avoir les chocottes** to be scared witless or stiff, to have the wind up; **foutre les chocottes à qn** to scare sb witless or stiff, to put the wind up sb

choir [ʃwar] vi **laisser choir qn** to let sb down □; **tout laisser choir** to pack it all in, Br to jack it all in, Am to chuck everything

chôm'du, chômedu [ʃomdy] nm (chômage) **être au chôm'du** to be out of work □; **pointer au chôm'du** to be Br on the dole or Am on welfare □

choper [ʃope] vt (a) (saisir) to grab □ (b) (surprendre) to catch □, to nab; **se faire choper** to get caught □ or nabbed (c) (maladie, coup de soleil) to catch □

chopine [ʃopin] nf **boire une chopine** to have a drink □

chose [ʃoz] nf **être porté sur la chose** to have a one-track mind, Br to have sex on the brain

chou, choute [ʃu, ʃut] **1** adj inv (mignon) cute
2 nm,f (a) **rentrer dans le chou à qn** to give sb an earful or Br a mouthful (b) **mon (petit) chou, ma (petite) choute** darling, sweetie (c) **c'est bête comme chou** it's as easy as pie

chouette [ʃwɛt] **1** adj great, fantastic, fabulous; Ironic **ah t'as l'air chouette, avec cet anneau dans le nez!** you look something else with your nose pierced!
2 exclam **chouette (alors)!** great!, fantastic!, fabulous!
3 nm **refiler du chouette** [!!] to take it up the Br arse or Am ass
4 nf **une vieille chouette** (femme) an old bag or witch

chouf [ʃuf] exclam look!

chouïa [ʃuja] nm **un chouïa (de)** a smidgen (of), a touch (of)

choullle [ʃuj] nf party □, bash

chouiller [ʃuje] vi to party

chouraver [ʃurave], **chourer** [ʃure] vt to pinch, Br to nick; **chouraver ou chourer qch à qn** to pinch or Br nick sth from sb

chrono [krɔno] adv **faire du 140 km/h chrono** to be clocked at 140 kmh

chtar [ʃtar] nm (a) (cachot) slammer, clink, Br nick, Am pen (b) (coup) clout, wallop (c) (policier) cop

chtarbé, -e [ʃtarbe] adj crazy, nuts, off one's rocker

chtouille [!] [ʃtuj] nf **la chtouille** the clap

cibiche [sibiʃ] nf gasper, cig

ciboulot [sibulo] nm **en avoir dans le ciboulot** to have brains, to have a lot between one's ears; **se creuser le ciboulot** to rack or Am cudgel one's brains; **travailler du ciboulot** to to be off one's rocker or Br trolley, Br to have lost the plot

cigare [sigar] *nm* (**a**) *(tête)* head □, nut (**b**) **avoir le cigare au bord des lèvres**‼ to be dying for a shit

cinglé, -e [sɛ̃gle] **1** *adj* crazy, off one's rocker *or Br* head

2 *nm,f* nutcase, *Br* nutter, headcase, *Am* screwball, flamer

cinoche [sinɔʃ] *nm* **aller au cinoche** to go to the *Br* pictures *or Am* movies □; **faire du cinoche** to cause a scene, to make a fuss

cinoque [sinɔk] *adj* crazy, loopy, off one's rocker

cinq [sɛ̃k] *adj inv* **en cinq sec** in no time at all, in two shakes; *Hum* **faire cinq contre un**❗ *(se masturber)* to beat one's meat, *Br* to have a hand shandy

cintré, -e [sɛ̃tre] *adj* cracked, *Br* barmy, *Am* screwy, wacko

cirage [siraʒ] *nm* **être dans le cirage** *(soûl)* to be out of it *or Br* off one's face; *(étourdi)* to be feeling out of it *or* woozy

cirer [sire] *vt* (**a**) **cirer les pompes à qn** to lick sb's boots (**b**) **j'en ai rien à cirer**❗ I don't give a shit *or Br* a toss *or Am* a rat's ass

citron [sitrɔ̃] *nm (tête)* head □, nut; **se presser** *ou* **se creuser le citron** to rack *or Am* cudgel one's brains

citrouille [sitruj] *nf (tête)* head □, nut

clacos [klakos] *nm* camembert □

clair [klɛr] *exclam* I get the message!, I hear you!

clamser [klamse] *vi* to croak, to kick the bucket, *Br* to snuff it, *Am* to check out

clandos [klɑ̃dos] *nm* illegal immigrant □

claouis❗ [klawi] *nmpl* balls, nuts, *Br* bollocks

clapet [klapɛ] *nm* **ferme ton clapet!** shut your trap!, put a lid on it!, *Br* belt up!

claque [klak] **1** *nf* **en avoir sa claque (de)** to have had it up to here (with), to have had a bellyful (of)

2 *nm (maison close)* whorehouse, *Br* knocking shop

▶ see also **clique, tête**

claqué, -e [klake] *adj (épuisé)* bushed, *Br* knackered, shattered, *Am* beat

claquer [klake] **1** *vt (dépenser)* to blow

2 *vi* (**a**) *(mourir)* to croak, to kick the bucket, *Br* to snuff it, *Am* to cash in (one's chips) (**b**) **claquer du bec** to be starving *or* ravenous

classe [klas] **1** *adj (élégant)* classy; *(formidable)* class

2 *adv* **s'habiller classe** to be a classy dresser

3 *nf* **la classe!** classy!

classieux, -euse [klasjø, -øz] *adj* classy

clean [klin] **1** *adj* clean-cut □

2 *adv* **s'habiller clean** to dress in a clean-cut way □

clébard [klebar], **clebs** [klɛps] *nm* mutt

clim [klim] *nf (abbr* **climatisation)** air conditioning □

clique [klik] *nf* (**a**) *(bande)* gang, crowd (**b**) **prendre ses cliques et ses claques** to pack one's bags and go

cloche [klɔʃ] **1** *nf* (**a**) *(imbécile)* jerk, *Br* prat, pillock, *Am* geek (**b**) **être de la cloche** to be a tramp *or Am* hobo (**c**) **se taper la cloche** to feed one's face, *Br* to have a slap-up meal

2 *adj* daft, thick, *Am* dumb

▶ see also **sonner**

clocher [klɔʃe] *vi* **il y a quelque chose qui cloche** there's something wrong somewhere; **qu'est-ce qui cloche?** what's up?

clodo [klɔdo] *nmf* tramp, *Am* hobo

clope [klɔp] *nf* smoke, *Br* fag, ciggy

cloper [klɔpe] *vi* to smoke □

clopinettes [klɔpinɛt] *nfpl* **des clopinettes** *(presque rien)* peanuts

cloque [klɔk] *nf* **être en cloque** *Br* to be up the duff *or* spout, to be in the club,

Am to be knocked up

clou [klu] *nm* **(a)** **ça ne vaut pas un clou** it's not worth a *Br* penny *or Am* red cent **(b)** **des clous!** no way!, no chance! **(c)** *(bicyclette)* bike

coaltar [koltar] *nm* **être dans le coaltar** *(étourdi)* to be in a daze, to be feeling out of it *or* spaced out

cocard [kokar] *nm* black eye □, shiner

cochonceté [koʃõste] *nf* **(a)** *(action obscène)* repulsive act □; **allez faire vos cochoncetés ailleurs!** go and do that sort of thing somewhere else! **(b)** *(remarque obscène)* obscenity □; **dire des cochoncetés** to talk dirty

cochonner [koʃone] *vt* *(salir)* to dirty □, to make a mess of □

coco [koko] **1** *nm* **(a)** *(personne)* **un drôle de** *ou* **un sacré coco** a weirdo, an oddball; **toi mon coco, je t'ai à l'œil!** just watch it, *Br* pal *or* mate *or Am* buddy! **(b)** *(estomac)* **bien se remplir le coco** to stuff oneself *or* one's face, to feed one's face
   2 *nmf* *(abbr* **communiste***)* commie
   3 *nf* *(cocaïne)* coke, snow
   ▶ see also **noix**

cocoter [kokote] *vi* to stink, *Br* to pong, to hum

cocotte [kokot] *nf* **ma cocotte** darling, honey

cocotter [kokote] = **cocoter**

cocu, -e [koky] **1** *adj* **je suis cocu** my wife's cheating on me; **un mari cocu** a man whose wife is cheating on him; **faire qn cocu** to cheat on sb
   2 *nm* deceived husband □; **avoir une chance** *ou* **veine de cocu** to have the luck of the devil

cocufier [kokyfje] *vt* to cheat on

coffrer [kofre] *vt* to put inside *or* away *or* behind bars; **se faire coffrer** to get put inside *or* away *or* behind bars

cogne [koɲ] *nm* cop, *Br* bobby, *Am* flatfoot

cogner [koɲe] **1** *vt* to knock about, to beat (up)
   2 *vi* **(a)** *(puer)* to stink (to high heaven), *Br* to pong, to hum **(b)** **ça cogne** *(le soleil chauffe)* it's scorching *or Br* roasting
   3 **se cogner** *vpr* **(a)** **se cogner qn/qch** *(corvée)* to get stuck *or Br* lumbered *or* landed with sb/sth **(b)** **se cogner qn** [!!] *(posséder)* to screw sb, *Br* to have it off with sb, *Am* to ball sb

coincer [kwɛ̃se] **1** *vt* *(attraper)* to nab, to collar; **se faire coincer** to get nabbed *or* collared
   2 *vi* *(puer)* to stink, *Br* to pong, to hum
   ▶ see also **bulle**

coinços [kwɛ̃sos] *adj* full of hang-ups, screwed-up

coing [kwɛ̃] *nm* **bourré comme un coing** trashed, wasted, plastered, *Br* off one's face, legless

coke [kok] *nf* *(cocaïne)* coke

colbac [kolbak] *nm* **attraper qn par le colbac** to grab sb by the scruff of the neck

colis [koli] *nm* *(fille)* chick, *Br* bird; **un joli petit colis** a knockout, a babe, *Br* a cracker, a bit of all right

colle [kol] *nf* **être à la colle** to be shacked up together
   ▶ see also **chier**

coller [kole] **1** *vt* **(a)** *(placer)* to stick, to dump; **il a collé tous les cartons dans un coin** he stuck *or* dumped all the cardboard boxes in a corner **(b)** *(administrer)* **coller qch à qn** *(claque, baiser, rhume)* to give sb sth □; *(amende)* to slap sth on sb; **il m'a collé les gosses pour le week-end** he dumped the kids on me for the weekend **(c)** *(suivre)* **coller qn** to stick to sb like glue, to follow sb around
   2 *vi* **(a)** **ça colle!** OK!, cool!; **ça ne colle pas très bien entre eux** they don't really see eye to eye **(b)** **il arrête pas de me coller au cul** [!]

he keeps following me around like a lost dog; *(en voiture)* Br he keeps driving up my arse, Am he keeps tailgating me

3 s'y coller *vpr* **c'est encore moi qui m'y colle!** I'm stuck or Br lumbered with it again!; **c'est toi qui t'y colles** it's your turn

▸ *see also* **pain**

collimateur [kɔlimatœr] *nm* **avoir qn dans le collimateur** to keep one's eye on sb, to keep tabs on sb

colo [kɔlo] *nf (abbr* **colonie de vacances)** Br (children's) holiday camp □, Am summer camp □

colon [kɔlɔ̃] *nm* **(a)** *(abbr* **colonel)** colonel □ **(b) ben mon colon!** goodness me!, Br blimey!, Am gee (whiz)!

colonne [kɔlɔn] *nf* **se taper (sur) la colonne, s'astiquer la colonne** [!!] to jerk off, to beat off, to beat one's meat

coltiner [kɔltine] **se coltiner** *vpr* **se coltiner qn/qch** to get stuck or Br lumbered or landed with sb/sth

comac [kɔmak] *adj* ginormous, humongous, massive

comme d'hab [kɔmdab] *adv (abbr* **comme d'habitude)** as per usual

commission [kɔmisjɔ̃] *nf* **faire la petite/grosse commission** to do a number one/number two

compagnie [kɔ̃paɲi] *nf* **salut, la compagnie!** hi, guys or folks!; **ces mecs, c'est racaille et compagnie** these guys are a bunch of scumbags

compète [kɔ̃pɛt] *nf (abbr* **compétition)** competition □ *(in sport)*; **faire de la compète** to enter competitions

compil' [kɔ̃pil] *nf (abbr* **compilation)** compilation □

comprenette [kɔ̃prənɛt] *nf* **avoir la comprenette un peu dure** to be a bit slow on the uptake

compte [kɔ̃t] *nm* **avoir son compte** *(être condamné)* to have had it, to be done for; *(être ivre)* to have had enough

(to drink) □; **ça va, j'ai eu mon compte** *(j'en ai assez)* that's enough, I've had it; **régler son compte à qn** *(punir sévèrement)* to give sb what for, to give sb what's coming to him/her; *(tuer)* to bump sb off, Br to do sb in, Am to eighty-six sb; **son compte est bon** he's had it, Br he's for it

con, conne [!] [kɔ̃, kɔn] **1** *adj* **(a)** *(stupide)* Br bloody or Am goddamn stupid; **être con comme la lune** ou **comme un balai** Br to be thick (as two short planks), to be as daft as a brush, Am to have rocks in one's head

(b) *(regrettable)* **c'est con, je ne vais pas pouvoir me libérer** it's a bummer, but I'm not going to be able to get away **(c) à la con** *(médiocre)* crappy, lousy, Br poxy

2 *nm,f* **(a)** *(imbécile)* Br arsehole, twat, Am asshole; **faire le con** *(faire le clown)* Br to arse around, to piss about, Am to screw around; **faire le con, jouer au con** *(faire semblant de ne pas comprendre)* to act dumb; **fais pas le con, ça va s'arranger** don't do anything stupid, it'll sort itself out; **se retrouver comme un con** to be left feeling a complete Br arsehole or Am asshole; **si les cons volaient, tu serais chef d'escadrille** if being an Br arsehole or Am asshole was an Olympic event, you'd be a gold medallist

(b) *(homme déplaisant)* bastard; *(femme déplaisante)* bitch

3 [!!] *nm (sexe de la femme)* cunt

▸ *see also* **air, gueule, piège, tête**

conard, -asse [kɔnar, -as] = **connard**

condé [kɔ̃de] *nm (policier)* cop

conduite [kɔ̃dɥit] *nf* **s'acheter une conduite** to turn over a new leaf, to mend one's ways; *(criminel)* to go straight

confiote [kɔ̃fjɔt] *nf (confiture)* jam □

congélo [kɔ̃ʒelo] *nm (abbr* **congélateur)** freezer □

connard, -asse⚠ [kɔnar, -as] nm,f
(**a**) (homme stupide) stupid bastard,
prick, Br arsehole, Am asshole; (femme
stupide) stupid bitch, Br arsehole, Am
asshole (**b**) (homme déplaisant) bastard;
(femme déplaisante) bitch

connement⚠ [kɔnmɑ̃] adv stupidly □;
**il s'est fait connement piquer sa
caisse** the stupid idiot got his car
pinched; **et connement j'ai accepté**
and like the idiot that I am, I said yes

connerie⚠ [kɔnri] nf (**a**) (acte stupide)
faire une connerie to do a Br bloody or
Am goddamn stupid thing; **j'ai peur
qu'il fasse une connerie** (un acte in-
considéré) I'm scared he's going to do
something Br bloody or Am goddamn
stupid
(**b**) (remarque stupide) **dire** ou **raconter
des conneries** to talk crap or bullshit
(**c**) (caractère stupide) stupidity □; **il est
d'une connerie!** he's so Br bloody or
Am goddamn stupid!

conso [kɔ̃so] nf (abbr **consommation**)
drink □ (in bar, club)

constipé, -e [kɔ̃stipe] adj (gêné) uptight; (sourire) strained □

contrat [kɔ̃tra] nm (d'un tueur) contract

contredanse [kɔ̃trədɑ̃s] nf (document)
(parking) ticket □; (amende) parking
fine □

contrefiche [kɔ̃trəfiʃ], **contreficher** [kɔ̃trəfiʃe] **se contrefiche** ou
contreficher de vpr not to give a damn
or a hoot or Br a stuff about

contrefoutre [kɔ̃trəfutr] **se contrefoutre de** vpr not to give a damn or a
hoot or Br a stuff about

cool [kul] adj inv (**a**) (détendu) laid-back,
cool; **cool, mon vieux!** chill (out)!, take
it easy! (**b**) (bien, beau) cool

coolos [kulos] adj (**a**) (détendu) laid-
back, cool (**b**) (bien) cool

coopé [kɔpe] nf (abbr **coopération**)
(aide aux PVD) aid to developing countries □; (service militaire) = voluntary

work overseas carried out as an alter-
native to national service

coquard [kɔkar] = **cocard**

corbeau, -x [kɔrbo] nm (personne)
Goth

corde [kɔrd] nf (**a**) **se passer la corde
au cou** to get spliced or hitched (**b**) **être
dans les cordes de qn** to be (right) up
sb's street (**c**) **il pleut** ou **tombe des
cordes** it's raining cats and dogs, Br it's
bucketing down, it's chucking it down

cornes [kɔrn] nfpl **faire porter des
cornes à qn** (tromper) to cheat on sb

cornet [kɔrnɛ] nm (estomac) **qu'est-ce
qu'on s'est mis dans le cornet!** we
totally stuffed ourselves or our faces!,
we really pigged out

corniaud [kɔrnjo] nm moron, Br twit,
Am fathead

cornichon [kɔrniʃɔ̃] nm (niais) Br plonker, pillock, Am lamebrain, meathead

corrida [kɔrida] nf (agitation) hassle, Br
carry-on; **quelle corrida hier soir,
pour rentrer chez moi!** what a hassle
or Br carry-on I had getting home last
night!

cossard, -e [kɔsar, -ard] **1** adj lazy □
2 nm,f lazybones

cossin [kɔsɛ̃] nm Can thingy, whatsit

costard [kɔstar] nm suit □ (clothing)
▸ see also **tailler**

costaud, -e [kɔsto, -od] **1** adj (**a**) (personne) big □, hefty; (objet) sturdy □
(**b**) (café, alcool) strong □
2 nm big guy

cote [kɔt] nf **avoir la cote (avec qn)** to
be popular (with sb) □

côte [kot] nf (**a**) **avoir les côtes en long**
to be bone idle (**b**) **se tenir les côtes** to
be in stitches, to kill oneself (laughing),
to split one's sides

coton [kɔtɔ̃] **1** adj inv tough, tricky
2 nm **filer un mauvais coton** to be in a
bad way

couche [kuʃ] nf **en tenir une couche** to

have nothing between one's ears, *Br* to be as thick as two short planks, *Am* to have rocks in one's head

coucheries [kuʃri] *nfpl* sleeping around, casual sex □

coucou [kuku] *nm (avion)* **un vieux coucou** an old crate

couenne [kwan] *nf* skin □
▸ see also **sucer**

couillave [kujav], **couillaver** [kujave] *vt* to do, to con

couille‼ [kuj] *nf* **(a)** *(testicule)* ball, nut, *Br* bollock; **avoir des couilles (au cul)** to have (a lot of) balls; **baiser à couilles rabattues** to fuck like rabbits; **casser les couilles à qn** *Br* to get on sb's tits, *Am* to break sb's balls; **se faire des couilles en or** to make a bundle *or Br* a packet; **partir en couille** to go down the tubes *or Br* pan; **c'est de la couille (en barre)** it's a load of balls *or Br* bollocks; **mes couilles!** my *Br* arse *or Am* ass!; **couille molle** wimp, *Br* big girl's blouse

(b) *(erreur) Br* cock-up, balls-up, *Am* ball-up

(c) *(ennui)* problem □; **il m'arrive une couille** I'm in deep shit
▸ see also **battre**

couillon, -onne! [kujɔ̃, -ɔn] **1** *adj Br* bloody *or Am* goddamn stupid

2 *nm,f Br* arsehole, twat, tosser, *Am* asshole, dumbass; **faire le couillon** *Br* to arse about, to piss about, *Am* to screw around

couillonnade! [kujɔnad] *nf* **(a)** *(discours stupide)* **dire des couillonnades** to talk crap *or* bull *or Br* bollocks **(b)** *(acte stupide)* **faire des couillonnades** *Br* to cock *or* balls things up, *Am* to ball things up

couillonner! [kujɔne] *vt* to screw, to rip off; **se faire couillonner** to get screwed *or* ripped off

coulant, -e [kulã, -ãt] **1** *adj (arrangeant)* easy-going

2 *nm (fromage)* = very ripe cheese, particularly camembert

couler [kule] **1** *vt* **(a)** *(discréditer)* **couler qn** to bring sb down, to ruin sb **(b)** **se la couler douce** to take things easy

2 *vi (entreprise)* to go under
▸ see also **bronze**

couleur [kulœr] *nf* **annoncer la couleur** *(déclarer ses intentions)* to lay one's cards on the table; *(au restaurant, au café)* = to say what one is having; **allez, annonce la couleur!** what's it to be, then?
▸ see also **voir**

coup [ku] *nm* **(a)** *(boisson)* drink □; **boire un coup** to have a drink □; **un coup de rouge** a glass of red wine □

(b) *(acte criminel)* job, operation; **il m'a fait le coup de la panne** he tried to pull the old "the car won't start" routine on me; **coup fourré** dirty trick

(c) **un bon coup**! *(partenaire sexuel)* a good lay *or* screw *or Br* shag

(d) **avoir le coup (pour faire qch)** to have the knack (of doing sth); **être dans le coup** *(être au courant)* to know what's going on; *(être dans la confidence)* to be in on it; **mettre qn dans le coup** to fill sb in, to put sb in the picture; **en mettre un coup** to pull out all the stops; **coup dur** setback □; **en deux coups les gros** in a jiffy, in next to no time
▸ see also **tirer**

coupe-choux [kupʃu] *nm inv (rasoir)* cut-throat razor □

couper [kupe] **1** *vt* **ça te la coupe, hein?** you weren't expecting that one, were you!, that shut you up, didn't it!

2 *vi* **couper à qch** *(éviter)* to get out of sth
▸ see also **chique, sifflet**

courailler [kuraje] *vi Can* to chase after women

courailleur [kurajœr] *nm Can* womanizer, skirt-chaser

courante [kurɑ̃t] *nf* **la courante** the runs, the trots

coureur, -euse [kurœr, -øz] **1** *adj* *(homme)* womanizing; *(femme)* man-eating

2 *nm,f* *(homme volage)* womanizer, skirt-chaser; *(femme volage)* man-eater

courge [kurʒ] *nf Br* pillock, plonker, *Am* meathead, bonehead

courir [kurir] **1** *vi* **tu peux toujours courir!** not a chance!, no way!; **tu peux toujours courir pour que je te prête ma caisse!** no way am I lending you my car!; **laisse courir!** forget it!, drop it!

2 *vt* **tu commences à me courir!** you're starting to bug me *or Br* do my head in *or Am* give me a pain!

▶ see also **galipote, haricot**

court-jus [kurʒy] *nm* short-circuit □

cousu [kuzy] *adj* **c'est du cousu main** *(facile)* it's in the bag, *Br* it's a dead cert; *(très bien fait)* it's a work of art

▶ see also **motus**

couvrante [kuvrɑ̃t] *nf* blanket □, cover □

crac-crac [krakrak] *nm* **faire crac-crac** to have a bit of nooky *or Br* rumpy-pumpy

cracher [kraʃe] **1** *vi* **(a)** *(payer)* to fork out, to cough up **(b) cracher dans la soupe** to bite the hand that feeds; **il crache pas dessus** he never turns up his nose at it, he never says no to it

2 *vt* *(argent)* to fork out, to cough up

▶ see also **bassinet, gueule, morceau**

crachoir [kraʃwar] *nm* **tenir le crachoir** to go *or* ramble on and on; **tenir le crachoir à qn** to listen to sb go *or* ramble on and on

crack [krak] *nm* **(a)** *(drogue)* crack **(b)** *(personne douée)* whizz

cracra [krakra], **crade** [krad], **cradingue** [kradɛ̃g], **crado** [krado] *adj* filthy □

craignos [krɛɲos] *adj* **(a)** *(louche)* shady, *Br* dodgy **(b)** *(laid)* hideous **(c)** *(mauvais)* crap, lousy, the pits

craindre [krɛ̃dr] *vi* **(a)** *(être louche)* to be shady *or Br* dodgy

(b) *(être laid)* to be hideous

(c) *(être mauvais)* to be crap, to be the pits, to suck, *Am* to bite

(d) ça craint! it's crap!, it sucks!

cramé, -e [krame] *adj* *(ivre)* blitzed, wasted, *Br* off one's face, *Am* stewed (to the gills)

cramer [krame] **1** *vt* **(a)** *(brûler)* to burn □ **(b)** *(repérer)* to spot □, to clock, *Br* to rumble

2 *vi* *(brûler)* to burn □

cramouille [!!] [kramuj] *nf* pussy, snatch, twat, *Br* fanny

crampe [krɑ̃p] *nf* **tirer sa crampe** [!] *(s'enfuir)* to beat it, *Br* to piss off, to bugger off, *Am* to book it; *(coïter)* to screw, *Br* to have a bonk, to have it off, *Am* to bang

crampon [krɑ̃pɔ̃] *nm* *(personne importune)* leech

cran [krɑ̃] *nm* **(a)** *(couteau)* **cran (d'arrêt)** *Br* flick knife □, *Am* switchblade □ **(b) être à cran** to be about to crack up, to have reached boiling point

crâner [krɑne] *vi* to swagger, to show off

crâneur, -euse [krɑnœr, -øz] **1** *adj* swaggering; **être crâneur** to be a show-off *or* a poser

2 *nm,f* show-off, poser

crapahuter [krapayte] *vi* *(marcher)* to schlep *or* traipse about

crapoter [krapɔte] *vi* = to smoke without inhaling

crapoteux, -euse [krapɔtø, -øz] *adj* filthy □

craquant, -e [krakɑ̃, -ɑ̃t] *adj* *(personne)* gorgeous, stunning, *Br* fit

craque [krak] *nf* **(a)** *(mensonge)* lie □, fib, *Br* porky (pie) **(b)** *Vulg (sexe de la femme)* crack, gash

craquer [krake] *vi* (**a**) *(nerveusement)* to crack up (**b**) *(succomber)* to crack, to give in; **finalement j'ai craqué** in the end I couldn't resist it; **craquer pour qn/qch** to fall for sb/sth; **il me fait vraiment craquer** I've got the hots for him, *Br* I really fancy him

craquette [!] [krakɛt] *nf* pussy, twat, gash, *Br* minge

crasher [kraʃe] **se crasher** *vpr (avion, automobiliste, motard)* to crash □

craspec [kraspɛk] *adj* filthy □

crasse [kras] *nf* **faire une crasse à qn** to play a dirty trick on sb, *Br* to do the dirty on sb, *Am* to do sb dirt

cravacher [kravaʃe] *vi* to work like mad

cravate [kravat] *nf* **c'est de la cravate** it's a load of baloney *or* bull
▶ see also **jeter**

crécher [kreʃe] *vi* to live □

crémerie [krɛmri] *nf* **changer de crémerie** to go somewhere else □, to move on □

crétin, -e [kretɛ̃, -in] **1** *nm,f* cretin
2 *adj* cretinous

creuser [krøze] **se creuser** *vpr (réfléchir)* to rack *or Am* cudgel one's brains
▶ see also **ciboulot, citron**

crevant, -e [krəvɑ̃, -ɑ̃t] *adj* (**a**) *(épuisant)* exhausting □, *Br* killing, knackering (**b**) *(hilarant)* hysterical, side-splitting

crevard, -e [krəvar, -ard] *nm,f (glouton)* pig, *Br* gannet, *Am* hog

crève [krɛv] *nf* **la crève** a stinking cold

crevé, -e [krəve] *adj* (**a**) *(épuisé) Br* knackered, shattered, *Am* beat (**b**) *(mort)* dead □

crever [krəve] **1** *vt* (**a**) *(épuiser)* to wear out □, *Br* to knacker
(**b**) *(tuer)* to kill □, to waste, *Br* to do in
(**c**) **crever la dalle** to be starving *or* ravenous

2 *vi (mourir)* to kick the bucket, to croak, *Br* to snuff it, *Am* to check out; **crever de faim/de chaleur** *(avoir faim/chaud)* to be starving/boiling; **à crever de rire** hysterical; **c'était à crever de rire** it was hysterical *or* a scream; **je peux crever la gueule ouverte, t'en as rien à faire!** I could die tomorrow for all you care!; **qu'il crève!** he can go to hell!

3 **se crever** *vpr* (**a**) *(s'épuiser)* to wear oneself out, *Br* to get knackered
(**b**) *(se donner du mal)* **se crever (à faire qch)** to go out of one's way (to do sth); **se crever le cul (à faire qch)** [!] to bust a gut *or Am* one's ass (doing sth)

Crim', Crime [krim] *nf (abbr* **Brigade Criminelle) la Crim'** the crime squad □

crincrin [krɛ̃krɛ̃] *nm* racket, din *(especially loud music)*

crise [kriz] *nf* **la crise (de rire)!** what a scream *or* hoot!

criser [krize] *vi* to lose it, to go ape, *Br* to go off one's head

croco [krɔko] *nm (abbr* **crocodile)** crocodile (skin) □; **un sac en croco** a crocodile handbag □

crocs [kro] *nmpl* (**a**) *(dents)* teeth □, *Br* gnashers, *Am* choppers (**b**) **avoir les crocs** *(avoir faim)* to be hungry □

croire [krwar] **1** *vt* **j'te crois!** *(je suis d'accord)* absolutely!, *Br* too right!; *Ironic* yeah right!, *Br* I believe you (thousands wouldn't)!
2 **se croire** *vpr* **s'y croire** to think a lot of oneself, *Br* to fancy oneself

croquenots [krɔkno] *nmpl* shoes □, clodhoppers

croqueuse [krɔkøz] *nf* **croqueuse de diamants** gold-digger

croquignolet, -ette [krɔkiɲɔlɛ, -ɛt] *adj Ironic* cutesy

crosses [krɔs] *nfpl* **chercher des crosses à qn** to try to pick a fight with sb

crouille [kʁuj] *nm Offensive* = racist term used to refer to a North African Arab

croulant,-e [kʁulɑ̃,-ɑ̃t] *nm,f* old codger, *Br* wrinkly, *Am* geezer

croupion [kʁupjɔ̃] *nm* behind, rear (end), rump

croûte [kʁut] *nf* (**a**) *(tableau)* bad painting □, daub (**b**) **casser la** *ou* **une croûte** to have a snack □ *or* a bite to eat (**c**) **gagner sa croûte** to earn a *or* one's crust

croûter [kʁute] *vi (manger)* to eat □, to chow

croûton [kʁutɔ̃] *nm* **vieux croûton** old fossil, *Br* crumbly, *Am* geezer

cruche [kʁyʃ] **1** *nf (imbécile) Br* plonker, pillock, *Am* goof, geek **2** *adj* dense

cube [kyb] *nm* **un gros/petit cube** a big/small bike

cucul [kyky] *adj inv (personne, air)* cutesy, *Br* twee; *(film, livre)* corny

cueillir [kœjiʁ] *vt (arrêter)* to pick up, *Br* to lift

cuiller, cuillère [kɥijɛʁ] *nf* **elle n'y va pas avec le dos de la cuiller** she doesn't go in for half measures, she doesn't do things by halves; **être à ramasser à la petite cuiller** to be completely *Br* shattered *or Am* beat; **en deux** *ou* **trois coups de cuiller à pot** in next to no time, in two shakes (of a lamb's tail)

cuir [kɥiʁ] *nm* (**a**) *(peau)* skin □; **tanner le cuir à qn** to tan sb's hide (**b**) *(blouson)* leather jacket □ (**c**) *(homosexuel)* leather-boy

cuisiner [kɥizine] *vt (interroger)* to grill

cuisse [kɥis] *nf* **avoir la cuisse légère** to sleep around, to be an easy lay; **il y a de la cuisse!** there's plenty of babes *or Br* talent *or* totty!

cuistot [kɥisto] *nm* cook □

cuit, -e [kɥi, -it] *adj* (**a**) **être cuit** *(être pris)* to have had it, to be done for; *(être ivre)* to be wasted *or* plastered *or* smashed; **c'est cuit** I've/we've/*etc* had it (**b**) **c'est du tout cuit** it's in the bag, *Br* it's a dead cert, *Am* it's a lock (**c**) **les carottes sont cuites** the game's up

cuite [kɥit] *nf* **il tient une sacrée cuite** he's totally wrecked *or* wasted *or Br* legless *or* pissed; **prendre une cuite** to get wrecked *or* wasted *or Br* legless *or* pissed; **tu te souviens de ta première cuite?** do you remember the first time you got wrecked *or* wasted *or Br* legless *or* pissed?

cuiter [kɥite] **se cuiter** *vpr* to get wrecked *or* wasted *or Br* legless *or* pissed

cul [ky] *nm* (**a**) [!!] *(postérieur) Br* arse, *Am* ass; **en avoir plein le cul (de)** *(en avoir assez)* to be pissed off *or Am* pissed (with); **en avoir plein le cul** *(être fatigué)* to be *Br* shagged *or Am* beat; **l'avoir dans le cul** [!!] to have been shafted *or* screwed; **tu peux te le mettre au cul!** [!!] shove it up your *Br* arse *or Am* ass!; **lécher le cul à qn** [!!] *Br* to lick *or* kiss sb's arse, *Am* to kiss sb's ass; **avoir qn au cul** to have sb on one's tail; **en rester sur le cul** to be flabbergasted *or Br* gobsmacked; **avoir le cul bordé de nouilles** to be a lucky bastard; **et mon cul, c'est du poulet?** *Br* you're taking the piss, aren't you!, *Am* gimme a break!; **parle à mon cul, ma tête est malade** [!!] *(personne ne m'écoute)* I might as well talk to the fucking wall; *(laisse-moi tranquille)* fuck off!; **mon cul!** [!!] no fucking way!, my *Br* arse *or Am* ass!; **être comme cul et chemise** to be as thick as thieves; **avoir le cul entre deux chaises** to be in an awkward position; **il y a des coups de pied au cul qui se perdent** a kick in the *Br* arse *or Am* ass is too good for some people; *Can* **n'avoir rien que le cul et les dents** to be at rock bottom (**b**) [!] *(sexe)* screwing, *Br* shagging; **un**

film de cul a porn movie, *Am* a skin flick; **un magazine de cul** a porn or skin or girlie mag; **il s'intéresse qu'au cul** all he thinks about is sex □, *Br* he's got sex on the brain

(**c**) *(chance)* **avoir du cul**⚠ to be a lucky bastard

(**d**) *Pej* **cul béni**⚠ Bible-basher, Bible-thumper, *Am* holy Joe

(**e**) *(camion)* **un gros cul** *Br* a juggernaut, *Am* a semi, an eighteen-wheeler

(**f**) **faire cul sec** to down one's drink in one; **cul sec!** down in one!

▶ see *also* **carrer, casser, coller, couille, crever, doigt, feu, geler, lécher, magner, papier, peau, péter, ras, taper, tête, tirer, tortiller, trou**

culbute [kylbyt] *nf* **faire la culbute** *(faire faillite)* to go bust or under

culbuter⚠ [kylbyte] *vt (posséder sexuellement)* to screw, to shaft, *Br* to shag

culot [kylo] *nm* cheek, nerve; **avoir du culot** to have a lot of nerve, *Br* to have a brass neck; **y aller au culot** to brazen or

bluff it out

culotte [kylɔt] *nf* **poser culotte** to *Br* have or *Am* take a dump or a crap
▶ see *also* **pisser**

culotté, -e [kylɔte] *adj* **être culotté** to have a lot of nerve, *Br* to have a brass neck

cul-terreux [kytɛrø] *nm Pej* yokel, peasant, *Am* hick, hayseed

cureton [kyrtɔ̃] *nm Pej* priest □

curie [kyri] *nm (billet de cinq cents francs)* five-hundred franc note □

A "curie" is so called because a picture of Pierre and Marie Curie features on the banknote.

cuti [kyti] *nf* **virer sa cuti** to change one's whole lifestyle □; *(changer d'opinion)* to switch allegiances □; *(devenir homosexuel)* to become gay □

cuver [kyve] **1** *vt* **cuver son vin/sa bière** to sleep it off
2 *vi* to sleep it off

D

dab, dabe [dab] *nm* old man *(father)*

dac [dak] *exclam* OK!

dalle [dal] *nf* **avoir la dalle** to be hungry □; **avoir la dalle en pente** to be fond of the bottle, to like a drink; **se rincer la dalle** to have a drink □
▸ *see also* **crever, que dalle**

damer [dame] *vt* **damer le pion à qn** to go one better than sb, to outdo sb □; **se faire damer le pion** to be outdone □

dard [!!] [dar] *nm* dick, prick, cock, *Am* joint
▸ *see also* **pomper**

dare-dare [dardar] *adv* at the double, double quick

daron [darɔ̃] *nm* old man *(father)*

dass [das] *nm (verlan* **sida***)* AIDS □

daube [dob] *nf* **de la daube** (a load of) garbage *or Br* rubbish

dauber [dobe] *vi* to stink, *Br* to pong, to hum

dauffer [!!] [dofe] *vt* **dauffer qn** to bugger sb, to fuck sb up the *Br* arse *or Am* ass

deal [dil] *nm* (drug) deal; **il a fait de la taule pour deal d'héro** he did time for dealing smack

dealer¹ [dilœr] *nm* (drug) dealer

dealer² [dile] *vt & vi* to deal *(drugs)*

deb [dɛb] *adj (abbr* **débile***)* daft, *Am* dumb

déballer [debale] *vt (avouer)* to pour out, to spill, to come clean about

débander [!!] [debɑ̃de] *vi* to lose one's hard-on

débarquer [debarke] *vi* **tu débarques?** where have you been?, what

planet have you been on?
▸ *see also* **Anglais**

débarrasser [debarase] *vt* **débarrasser le plancher** to hit the road, to be off, to make tracks, *Am* to book it; **tu vas me faire le plaisir de me débarrasser le plancher!** would you kindly get lost!

débouler [debule] *vi* to burst in; **les flics ont déboulé dans le café** the cops burst into the café

dèbe [dɛb] *adj (abbr* **débile***)* daft, *Am* dumb

débecter [debɛkte] *vt* **débecter qn** to turn sb's stomach, to make sb feel sick

débile [debil] *adj* daft, *Am* dumb

débine [debin] *nf* **être dans la débine** to be totally broke *or Br* skint *or* strapped

débiner [debine] **1** *vt Br* to bitch about, to slag off, *Am* to bad-mouth
2 se débiner *vpr* to take off, to make oneself scarce, *Br* to scarper, *Am* to bug out

débiter [debite] *vt (dire)* to come out with, to trot out

débloquer [deblɔke] *vi* **(a)** *(ne plus avoir toute sa tête)* to be off one's rocker, to be not all there, *Br* to be away with the fairies **(b)** *(dire n'importe quoi)* to talk crap *or* bull **(c)** *(ne pas fonctionner correctement)* to be on the blink, *Am* to be on the fritz

débourrer [!!] [debure] *vi* to *Br* have *or Am* take a dump *or* a crap

déboussolé, -e [debusɔle] *adj* lost □, disorientated □

débrancher [debrɑ̃ʃe] *vt Hum* **débran-**

chez-le! shut him up, will you!

débris [debri] *nm* **un vieux débris** an old codger, an old fogey, *Am* a geezer

dec [dɛk] (*abbr* **déconner**) **sans dec** *adv* **sans dec!** (*je t'assure*) no kidding!, *Br* straight up!; **sans dec?** (*est-ce vrai?*) no kidding?, yeah?, *Br* straight up?

décalcifier [dekalsifje] **se décalcifier** *vpr Hum* to take one's *Br* trousers or *Am* pants off▢, *Br* to get one's keks off

> This verb derives its humour from the pun on the word "calcif" – slang for "caleçon" – and the literal translation of the verb "to become decalcified".

décamper [dekɑ̃pe] *vi* to clear off, to make oneself scarce, to take off

décaniller [dekanije] *vi* to clear off, to make oneself scarce, to take off

décarcasser [dekarkase] **se décarcasser** *vpr* to sweat blood, to bust a gut (**pour** over); **se décarcasser pour faire qch** to sweat blood or bust a gut to do sth

décharger [!!] [deʃarʒe] *vi* (*éjaculer*) to shoot one's load

dèche [dɛʃ] *nf* poverty▢; **être dans la dèche** to be broke or *Br* skint or strapped; **en ce moment c'est la dèche chez nous** we're broke or *Br* skint or strapped at the moment

déchiqueté, -e [deʃikte] *adj* (*ivre*) plastered, trashed, *Br* off one's face, *Am* stiff; (*drogué*) wrecked, ripped, loaded

déchiré, -e [deʃire] *adj* (*ivre*) wasted, trashed, *Br* pissed, *Am* fried; (*drogué*) stoned

déchiros [deʃiros] *nm* weirdo, *Am* wacko

décoiffant, -e [dekwafɑ̃, -ɑ̃t] *adj* mind-blowing

décoiffer [dekwafe] *vi* **ça décoiffe** it's mind-blowing, it takes your breath away

décoller [dekɔle] *vi* (**a**) (*partir*) to be off, to get going, to make a move; **il ne décolle plus de chez nous** we can't get rid of him, he's never away from our place (**b**) (*maigrir*) to lose weight▢

déconner [dekɔne] *vi* (**a**) (*dire n'importe quoi*) to talk crap or bull or *Br* bollocks; **sans déconner!** (*je t'assure*) no kidding!, *Br* straight up!; **sans déconner?** (*est-ce vrai?*) no kidding?, yeah?, *Br* straight up?
(**b**) (*faire le clown*) to fool around
(**c**) (*ne pas fonctionner correctement*) to play up, to be on the blink, *Am* to be on the fritz
(**d**) (*ne plus avoir toute sa tête*) to be off one's rocker, to be not all there, *Br* to be away with the fairies
(**e**) (*ne pas être raisonnable*) **allez, déconne pas, viens avec nous!** come on, don't be like that, come with us! ▢

déconneur, -euse [dekɔnœr, -øz]
1 *adj* **être déconneur** to be a clown or a troublemaker
2 *nm,f* clown, troublemaker

décor [dekɔr] *nm* **la voiture est allée dans le décor** (*hors de la route*) the car left the road▢; **envoyer qn dans le décor** (*le faire tomber*) to send sb flying

décrocher [dekrɔʃe] **1** *vt* (*obtenir*) to land
2 *vi* (*drogué*) to kick the habit

décuiter [dekɥite] *vi* to sober up▢

déculottée [dekylɔte] *nf* hammering, trouncing; **prendre une déculottée** to get hammered or trounced

défait, -e [defɛ, -ɛt] *adj* (*ivre*) wasted, *Br* slaughtered, *Am* tanked; (*drogué*) wrecked, ripped, loaded

défendre [defɑ̃dr] **se défendre** *vpr* (*avoir un niveau honorable*) to get by, to hold one's own
▸ see also **bifteck**

défonce [defɔ̃s] *nf* **la défonce** getting stoned; **à part la défonce, rien ne l'intéresse** the only thing he's interested in is getting stoned

défoncé, -e [defɔ̃se] adj stoned, wrecked, shit-faced

défoncer [defɔ̃se] **1** vt **défoncer la gueule à qn** to smash sb's face in, Br to punch sb's lights out, Am to punch sb out

2 se défoncer vpr (**a**) (se droguer) to get stoned or wrecked or shit-faced (**b**) (faire des efforts) to sweat blood, to work flat out
▸ see also **rondelle**

défriser [defrize] vt **et alors, ça te défrise?** have you got a problem with that?

défroquer [defrɔke] **se défroquer** vpr to take one's Br trousers or Am pants off [□], Br to get one's keks off

dég [deg] adj inv (abbr **dégueulasse**) disgusting [□], gross

dégager [degaʒe] vi (**a**) (sentir mauvais) to stink, Br to pong, to hum (**b**) (produire un effet puissant) (musique) to be mind-blowing, to kick ass; (plat, épice) to blow the top of one's head off, to pack a punch (**c**) (partir) to clear off, to get moving; **allez, dégage!** get out of here!, get lost!, beat it!, Am take a hike!

dégaine [degɛn] nf strange appearance [□]; **il a vraiment une dégaine pas possible!** he looks like nothing on earth or like something from another planet!

dégelée [deʒle] nf thrashing, hiding; **foutre une dégelée à qn** to give sb a thrashing or a hiding; **prendre une dégelée** to get a thrashing or a hiding

déglingué, -e [deglɛ̃ge] adj (**a**) (cassé) falling apart, bust, Br knackered (**b**) (ivre) wrecked, Br off one's face, Am fried

dégobiller [degɔbije] vi to puke, to chunder, to barf

dégoiser [degwaze] **1** vt to come out with, to trot out

2 vi **dégoiser sur qn** Br to bitch about sb, to slag sb off, Am to bad-mouth sb

dégommer [degɔme] vt (**a**) (tuer) to blow away, to gun down (**b**) (tirer sur) to shoot at [□] (**c**) (évincer) to kick out, to boot out

dégonflard, -e [degɔ̃flar, -ard], **dégonflé, -e** [degɔ̃fle] nm,f chicken (person)

dégonfler [degɔ̃fle] **se dégonfler** vpr to chicken out, Br to bottle out, to lose one's bottle

dégoter, dégotter [degɔte] vt to unearth, to stumble upon

dégoûté, -e [degute] adj (découragé) bummed (out), Br gutted; **putain, je suis trop dégoûté!** what a bummer!, Br I'm gutted or as sick as a parrot!

dégringoler [degrɛ̃gɔle] vi (**a**) (personne) to tumble (**b**) (entreprise) to collapse; (prix, cours) to slump (**c**) (pleuvoir) **ça dégringole** it's raining cats and dogs, Br it's bucketing down, it's chucking it down

dégrouiller [degruje] **se dégrouiller** vpr to get a move on, to shake a leg, Am to get it in gear

dégueu [degø] adj inv (abbr **dégueulasse**) (sale) disgusting [□], gross; (mauvais) crappy, lousy, Br poxy; **pas dégueu** (bon) pretty good

dégueulasse [degœlas] **1** adj (**a**) (sale) disgusting [□], gross; (mauvais) crappy, lousy, Br poxy; **pas dégueulasse** (bon) pretty good (**b**) (moralement) rotten

2 nm,f (**a**) (sale) filthy Br pig or Am hog (**b**) (moralement) Br swine, Am stinker

dégueulasser [degœlase] vt to dirty, to mess up

dégueuler ⚠ [degœle] vi to throw up, to puke, to barf, to hurl
▸ see also **tripes**

dégueulis ⚠ [degøli] nm puke, vom, barf

déguster [degyste] vi (souffrir) to have a hellish time of it, to have a hell of a time, Am to stand the gaff

déj [dεʒ] nm (abbr **déjeuner**) **petit déj** breakfast □

déjanter [deʒɑ̃te] vi to flip one's lid, to lose it, Br to lose the plot

delacroix [dəlakrwa] nm one-hundred franc note □

> A "delacroix" is so called because a picture of the painter Eugène Delacroix features on the banknote.

délire [delir] nm (moment amusant) **le délire!** it was wicked or Br mental or Am awesome!; **on s'est tapés un super délire!** we had a wicked or Br mental or Am awesome time!, Am we had a blast!

délirer [delire] vi (s'amuser) to have a wicked or Br mental or Am awesome time, Am to have a blast

déménager [demenaʒe] vi (**a**) (être fou) to be off one's rocker or trolley, to have lost it, Br to have lost the plot (**b**) (produire un effet puissant) (musique) to be mind-blowing, to kick ass; (plat, épice) to blow the top of one's head off, to pack a punch

dément, -e [demɑ̃, -ɑ̃t] adj (excellent) brilliant, wicked, Br fab, Am awesome

démerdard, -e [demεrdar, -ard] **1** adj resourceful □; **il est vachement démerdard** he can wangle or Am finagle anything
2 nm,f **être un démerdard** to know a trick or two

démerde [demεrd] nf **dans ce pays, tout marche à la démerde** you have to use your wits to get anything done in this country

démerder [demεrde] **se démerder** vpr (**a**) (se débrouiller) to manage □, to get by □; **t'en fais pas, je me démerderai tout seul** don't worry, I'll manage on my own; **tu ne voulais pas que je t'aide, maintenant démerde-toi!** you didn't want me to help you, so you can manage on your own now!; **je sais pas comment il se démerde, il casse tout**

ce qu'il touche I don't know how he does it, he breaks everything he gets his hands on
(**b**) (dans une discipline) to manage □, to get by □
(**c**) (se dépêcher) to get a move on, Am to get it in gear

demi-portion [dəmiporsjɔ̃] nf weed, squirt

dentelle [dɑ̃tεl] nf **ne pas faire dans la dentelle** to be really unsubtle □ or in your face

dep [dεp] nm Offensive (verlan **pédé**) queer, Br poof, Am fag

dépatouiller [depatuje] **se dépatouiller** vpr to manage □, to get by □; **se dépatouiller de qch** to get (oneself) out of sth

déplumé, -e [deplyme] adj bald □

déplumer [deplyme] **se déplumer** vpr to go bald □

dépoiler [depwale] **se dépoiler** vpr to strip off

dépoter [depɔte] vi (aller très vite) to go like a bomb

dépouiller [depuje] vt (**a**) (voler) **dépouiller qn** to rob sb, Br to do sb over; **se faire dépouiller** to get robbed, Br to get done over (**b**) (scandaliser) **ça me dépouille!** it's an outrage or a scandal!

dépuceler [depysle] vt to deflower □

dérailler [deraje] vi (tenir des propos insensés) to talk drivel, to ramble

derche [!] [dεrʃ] nm butt, Br bum, Am fanny; **se magner le derche** to move one's butt or Br bum; **un faux derche** a two-faced Br swine or Am stinker

dérouillée [deruje] nf (correction, défaite) thrashing, hammering; **flanquer une dérouillée à qn** to thrash or hammer sb; **prendre une dérouillée** to get thrashed or hammered

dérouiller [deruje] **1** vt (battre) **dérouiller qn** to thrash sb, to hammer sb
2 vi (se faire battre) to get thrashed or

hammered; *(souffrir)* to go through hell, to have a hellish time of it, *Am* to stand the gaff

derrière [dɛʀjɛʀ] *nm* behind, backside; **c'était à se taper le derrière par terre** it was hysterical, it was a scream *or* a hoot

désaper [desape] **se désaper** *vpr* to strip off

descendre [desɑ̃dʀ] *vt* **(a)** *(tuer)* to blow away, to blast **(b)** *(boire)* to put away, to knock back, *Am* to inhale; **qu'est-ce qu'il descend!** he can really put it away *or* knock it back! **(c)** *(critiquer)* **descendre qn en flammes** to give sb a roasting, to crucify sb

descente [desɑ̃t] *nf* **il a une bonne** *ou* **sacrée descente** he can really put it away *or* knock it back

dessin [desɛ̃] *nm* **tu veux que je te fasse un dessin?** do you want me to draw you a map?, do I have to spell it out for you?

dessouder [desude] *vt* to kill □, to waste, *Br* to do in

destroy [dɛstʀɔj] *adj (musique)* = loud, fast and aggressive; *(personne)* self-destructive □; *(jean)* ripped □; *(voiture)* beat up, wrecked, *Br* knackered

dételer [detle] *vi (arrêter de travailler)* to knock off; **sans dételer** non-stop

détente [detɑ̃t] *nf* **être long** *ou* **dur à la détente** to be a bit slow on the uptake

déterré, -e [deteʀe] *nm,f* **avoir une mine de déterré** to look like death warmed up

deuche [dœʃ], **deudeuche** [dœdœʃ] *nf* Citroën 2CV □

deuil [dœj] *nm Hum* **il a les ongles en deuil** you could grow potatoes under his nails

deux [dø] *pron* **en moins de deux** in less than no time, in two shakes; **cette bagnole de mes deux** [!] that *Br* bloody *or Am* goddamn car; **les ordina-**

teurs et moi, ça fait deux I don't know the first thing about computers; **lui et moi, ça fait deux** him and I are two different people; **il est radin comme pas deux** he's as stingy as they come; **il est menteur comme pas deux** he's an out-and-out liar

deux-pattes [døpat] *nf* Citroën 2CV □

deuzio [døzjo] *adv* secondly □

devanture [dəvɑ̃tyʀ] *nf* **se faire refaire la devanture** *(un lifting)* to have a face-lift □; *(se faire battre)* to get one's face wasted *or* one's features re-arranged

déveine [devɛn] *nf* rotten luck; **être dans la déveine** to have a run of bad luck □

diam [djam] *nm (abbr* **diamant)** sparkler, rock

dico [diko] *nm (abbr* **dictionnaire)** dictionary □

dingo [dɛ̃go] **1** *adj* crazy, bonkers, *Br* barking (mad), *Am* bonzo
  2 *nmf* maniac, nutcase

dingue [dɛ̃g] **1** *adj* **(a)** *('fou)* crazy, crackers, off one's rocker *or Br* head **(b)** *(frappant)* unreal, incredible, crazy; **c'est dingue ce qu'il fait chaud!** it's unreal *or* incredible how hot it is!; **en ce moment j'ai un boulot dingue!** the amount of work I have at the moment is unreal *or* crazy!
  2 *nmf* headcase, nutcase, *Br* nutter; **il va finir chez les dingues** he's going to end up in the nuthouse *or* the loony bin

dinguer [dɛ̃ge] *vi* **envoyer dinguer qch** *(jeter brutalement)* to send sth flying; **envoyer dinguer qn** *(le faire tomber)* to send sb flying; *(l'éconduire)* to tell sb where to go, *Br* to send sb packing

dire [diʀ] *vt* **je te dis pas!** I can't describe it!, you wouldn't believe it!; **il s'est foutu dans une colère, je te dis pas!** he went absolutely ballistic, you wouldn't have believed it!

directo [dirɛkto] *adv* (*abbr* **directement**) right away, *Br* straight

dirlo [dirlo] *nm Br* headmaster□, head, *Am* principal□

discrétos [diskrɛtos] *adv* on the quiet, on the q.t.

discutailler [diskytaje] *vi* to quibble

disjoncter [disʒɔ̃kte] *vi* (*devenir fou*) to crack up, to go round the bend, to lose it, *Br* to lose the plot

disque [disk] *nm* **change de disque!** (*change de sujet*) change the record!

dissert, disserte [disɛrt] *nf* (*abbr* **dissertation**) essay□

djig [dʒig] *nf* chick, *Br* bird

doc [dɔk] *nf* (*abbr* **documentation**) info

doigt [dwa] *nm* (a) **faire qch les doigts dans le nez** to do sth standing on one's head *or* with one's eyes closed
  (b) **s'enlever les doigts du cul** !! to pull one's finger out
  (c) **faire un doigt d'honneur à qn** to give sb the finger, *Am* to flip sb the bird
  (d) **se mettre** *ou* **se fourrer le doigt dans l'œil (jusqu'au coude)** to be barking up the wrong tree
  (e) **avoir les doigts de pied en éventail** (*paresser*) to laze around; (*avoir un orgasme*) to come, to get off

dondon [dɔ̃dɔ̃] *nf* **grosse dondon** fat lump, fatty

donner [dɔne] **1** *vt* (a) (*dénoncer*) to squeal on, *Br* to grass on, to shop, *Am* to rat on (b) **j'ai déjà donné** been there, done that (got the T-shirt)
  2 *vi* **ça donne** it's something else!, it's wicked *or Br* mental!
  3 se donner *vpr* (a) **s'en donner** to have the time of one's life (b) **se la donner** to show off, to pose

donneur [dɔnœr] *nm Br* grass, *Am* fink

donneuse [dɔnøz] *nf Br* grass, *Am* fink

"Donneuse" is not used as the feminine form of "donneur" – both terms always

refer to a man. The use of the feminine form in this way makes the term sound even more pejorative. See also the entry **salope**.

donzelle [dɔ̃zɛl] *nf* little madam

dope [dɔp] *nf* dope, stuff, *Br* gear

dort-en-chiant [dɔrɑ̃ʃjɑ̃] *nm Br* slowcoach, *Am* slowpoke

dos [do] *nm* **l'avoir dans le dos** to get done *or* conned; **en avoir plein le dos** (*être épuisé*) to be *Br* knackered *or* shattered *or Am* beat *or* pooped; (*être excédé*) to be hacked off *or* cheesed off; **avoir qn sur le dos** to have sb on one's back; **je l'ai tout le temps sur le dos** she's always on *or* never off my back; **il a bon dos, le métro!** blame it on the *Br* underground *or Am* subway, why don't you!; **faire un enfant dans le dos à qn** to stab sb in the back
  ▸ see *also* **bête, cuiller**

dose [doz] *nf* (a) **en avoir sa dose** to have had one's fill, to have had it up to here (b) **en tenir une dose** to have nothing between one's ears, *Br* to be as thick as two short planks, *Am* to have rocks in one's head

doser [doze] *vi* **ça dose!** wicked!, *Br* fab, *Am* awesome!

douce [dus] **en douce** *adv* **faire qch en douce** to do sth on the quiet *or* on the q.t.
  ▸ see *also* **couler**

douiller [duje] **1** *vt* (*payer*) to fork out for
  2 *vi* (*être cher*) to cost a bundle *or* an arm and a leg *or Br* a bomb

douilles [duj] *nmpl* (*cheveux*) hair□, mop

douleur [dulœr] *nf* **si je le chope, il va comprendre sa douleur** if I catch him, he'll get what's coming to him *or* his worst nightmares will come true

douloureuse [dulurøz] *nf* (*addition*) *Br* bill□, *Am* check□

drague [drag] *nf Br* chatting up, *Am* hitting on; **ce mec-là, c'est un pro de la drague** he's a bit of a pro at *Br* chatting up *or Am* hitting on women, that guy; **c'est un lieu de drague idéal** it's an ideal place for *Br* chatting people up *or Am* hitting on people

draguer [drage] **1** *vt* to come on to, *Br* to chat up, *Am* to hit on
  2 *vi* to be *Br* on the pull *or Am* on the make

dragueur, -euse [dragœr, -øz] **1** *adj* **il est très dragueur** he's always *Br* chatting up *or Am* hitting on women; **il n'a jamais été très dragueur** he's never been one for *Br* chatting up *or Am* hitting on women
  2 *nm,f* **c'est un dragueur** he's always *Br* chatting up *or Am* hitting on women

drepou [drɔpu] *nf* (*verlan* **poudre**) (*hé-roïne*) smack, scag, skag; (*cocaïne*) coke, snow, charlie

Duchnoque [dyʃnɔk] *nm* his nibs; (*terme d'adresse*) *Br* pal, matey, *Am* bud, buddy

Ducon ⚠ [dykɔ̃], **Ducon-la-joie** ⚠ [dykɔ̃laʒwa] *nm* shit-for-brains, *Br* dick features

dur, -e [dyr] **1** *nm* (*train*) train □
  2 *nm,f* **un dur à cuire, une dure à cuire** a hard nut
  3 *exclam* **dur dur!** bummer!, what a drag!
  ▶ see *also* **coup, détente, feuille**

Duralille [dyralij] *adj* tough

durite [dyrit] *nf* **péter une durite** (*se mettre en colère*) to go ape *or* ballistic, to hit the *Br* roof *or Am* ceiling

E

eau, -x [o] *nf* (**a**) **finir** *ou* **partir en eau de boudin** *(mal se terminer)* to end in tears; *(échouer)* to go down the tubes (**b**) **il n'a pas inventé l'eau chaude** *ou* **tiède** he's not exactly bright, he's no Einstein, *Br* he'll never set the Thames on fire (**c**) **dans ces eaux-là** thereabouts ▫, more or less ▫
► *see also* **pomme**

échauffer [eʃofe] *vt* **échauffer les oreilles à qn** to bug sb, *Br* to do sb's head in, to get up sb's nose, *Am* to give sb a pain (in the neck)

éclate [eklat] *nf* **c'est l'éclate** it's a laugh *or* a hoot; **c'est pas l'éclate** it's not exactly a barrel of laughs

éclater [eklate] **1** *vt* **éclater qn, éclater la gueule à qn** to smash sb's face in, to waste sb's face
2 s'éclater *vpr* to have a fantastic time, *Am* to have a blast

écluser [eklyze] *vt* to knock back, to down, to sink

écolo [ekolo] (*abbr* **écologiste**) *adj & nmf* green

éconocroques [ekɔnɔkrɔk] *nfpl* savings ▫

écoper [ekɔpe] *vi* **écoper d'une amende/de cinq ans de prison** to get *or* cop a fine/five years in prison

écorcher [ekɔrʃe] *vt* (*faire trop payer*) to fleece, *Am* to soak

écrase-merde [ekrazmɛrd] *nmpl* shoes ▫, clodhoppers

écraser [ekraze] **1** *vt* **en écraser** to sleep like a log
2 *vi* **écrase!** shut up!, *Br* belt up!
3 s'écraser *vpr* to shut up, *Br* to belt up

écroulé, -e [ekrule] *adj* **être écroulé (de rire)** to be doubled up (with laughter), to be killing oneself (laughing), to be in stitches

ecsta [ɛksta] *nf* (*abbr* **ecstasy**) E

écumoire [ekymwar] *nf* **transformer qn en écumoire** to pump sb full of lead

effeuilleuse [efœjøz] *nf* stripper

emballer [ɑ̃bale] **1** *vt* (**a**) (*enthousiasmer*) **ça ne m'a pas emballé** I wasn't wild about it *or Br* mad keen on it, it didn't do much for me; **ça l'a vraiment emballé** he was really taken with it (**b**) (*séduire*) *Br* to pull, to get off with, *Am* to pick up
2 s'emballer *vpr* to get carried away

emberlificoter [ɑ̃bɛrlifikɔte] **1** *vt* to hoodwink; **se laisser emberlificoter** to let oneself be hoodwinked
2 s'emberlificoter *vpr* to tie oneself in knots; **s'emberlificoter dans ses explications** to get tangled up *or* tied up in one's explanations

embobiner [ɑ̃bɔbine] *vt* **embobiner qn** to take sb in, to con sb

embouché, -e [ɑ̃buʃe] *adj* **être mal embouché** to be in a foul mood

embrayer [ɑ̃brɛje] *vi* to spit it out, to get to the point; **embrayer sur qch** to launch into the subject of sth

embringuer [ɑ̃brɛ̃ge] **1** *vt* **embringuer qn dans qch** to get sb mixed up in sth
2 s'embringuer *vpr* **s'embringuer dans qch** to get mixed up in sth

embrouille [ɑ̃bruj] *nf* (**a**) (*situation confuse*) muddle; **il s'est foutu dans une embrouille** he got himself in a

169

embrouiller ▸ enculage
complete muddle **(b)** *(problème)* **tenez-vous tranquilles, je veux pas d'embrouilles!** keep quiet, I don't want any trouble or hassle!; **je vois venir les embrouilles** I can see trouble ahead

embrouiller [ɑ̃bruje] *vt (duper)* to muddle; **ni vu ni connu je t'embrouille** no one is/was/etc any the wiser

éméché, -e [emeʃe] *adj* tipsy, merry

emmanché [ɑ̃mɑ̃ʃe] *nm* jerk, *Br* pillock, *Am* dork

emmerdant, -e ! [ɑ̃mɛrdɑ̃, -ɑ̃t] *adj* **être emmerdant** to be a pain in the *Br* arse or *Am* ass, to be damn or *Br* bloody annoying

emmerde ! [ɑ̃mɛrd] *nm or nf* trouble ▫, hassle; **avoir des emmerdes** to have a hell of a lot of problems; **en ce moment, j'ai que des emmerdes** at the moment, it's just one damn or *Br* bloody thing or hassle after another; **j'ai encore eu un emmerde avec la bagnole** I've had more damn or *Br* bloody trouble with the car

emmerdé, -e ! [ɑ̃mɛrde] *adj* **avoir l'air/être emmerdé** to look/be in a bit of a mess

emmerdement ! [ɑ̃mɛrd(ə)mɑ̃] = **emmerde**

emmerder ! [ɑ̃mɛrde] **1** *vt* **(a)** *(contrarier)* **emmerder qn** to bug sb to death, to get up sb's nose, *Br* to piss sb off; **ça m'emmerde de devoir aller à cette réunion** it's a damn or *Br* bloody nuisance having to go to this meeting **(b)** *(ennuyer)* **emmerder qn** to bore sb stiff or rigid **(c)** *(mépriser)* **le directeur, je l'emmerde!** the manager can go to hell or *Br* bugger or sod off!

2 s'emmerder *vpr* **(a)** *(s'ennuyer)* to be bored stiff or rigid; **s'emmerder à cent sous de l'heure** to be bored shitless **(b)** *(se donner du mal)* **s'emmerder à faire qch** to go to the bother or trouble of doing sth

(c) tu t'emmerdes pas! *(tu ne te refuses rien)* you're not doing too badly for yourself!; *(tu as du culot)* you've got a *Br* bloody or *Am* goddamn nerve!
▸ see also **rat**

emmerdeur, -euse ! [ɑ̃mɛrdœr, -øz] *nm,f* pain in the *Br* arse or *Am* ass, damn or *Br* bloody nuisance

empaffé !! [ɑ̃pafe] *nm* dickhead, prick, *Br* wanker

empapaouté ! [ɑ̃papaute] *nm* arsehole, *Am* asshole

empapaouter ! [ɑ̃papaute] *vt* to bugger, to take up the *Br* arse or *Am* ass; **va te faire empapaouter!** go to hell!, *Br* bugger off!, sod off!

emperlousé, -e [ɑ̃pɛrluze] *adj* dripping with pearls

empiffrer [ɑ̃pifre] **s'empiffrer** *vpr* to stuff oneself or one's face, to pig out

empiler ! [ɑ̃pile] *vt* to screw, to fleece; **se faire empiler** to get screwed or fleeced

emplafonner [ɑ̃plafɔne] *vt* to crash or smash into ▫

emplâtre [ɑ̃plɑtr] *nm Br* waster, *Am* klutz

empoté, -e [ɑ̃pote] *nm,f* clumsy or *Br* cack-handed idiot, *Am* klutz

en [ɑ̃] *pron* **en être** *(être homosexuel)* to be one of THEM

encadrer [ɑ̃kadre] *vt* **(a)** *(rentrer dans)* to smash or crash into ▫ **(b)** **je ne peux pas l'encadrer** I can't stand (the sight of) him, *Br* I can't stick him

encaisser [ɑ̃kɛse] **1** *vt* *(tolérer)* to stand, *Br* to stick

2 *vi* *(supporter les coups)* **il sait encaisser** he can take a lot of punishment; **qu'est-ce qu'il a encaissé!** what a hammering or pasting he took!

encaldosser !! [ɑ̃kaldɔse] *vt* to bugger, to fuck up the *Br* arse or *Am* ass

enculage !! [ɑ̃kylaʒ] *nm* **(a)** *(sodomisation)* buggery **(b)** **de l'enculage de**

mouches hair-splitting, nit-picking

enculé [!!] [ãkyle] *nm* prick, *Br* arsehole, wanker, *Am* asshole
▶ see *also* **mère**

enculer [!!] [ãkyle] *vt* (**a**) *(sodomiser)* to bugger, to fuck up the *Br* arse *or Am* ass; **va te faire enculer!** fuck off!, go and fuck yourself! (**b**) *(duper)* to screw, to shaft (**c**) **enculer les mouches** to split hairs, to nit-pick

enculeur, -euse [ãkylœr, -øz] *nm,f* **enculeur de mouches** hair-splitter, nit-picker

enfarinée [ãfarine] *adj* **arriver la gueule enfarinée** to turn up like an idiot *or* quite unsuspecting

enfer [ãfɛr] *nm* (**a**) **c'est l'enfer** it's hell (on earth) (**b**) **d'enfer** *(excellent)* great, wicked, *Br* fab, *Am* awesome
▶ see *also* **look**

enfiler [ãfile] **1** [!!] *vt* to fuck, to screw, *Br* to shag
2 s'enfiler *vpr* (**a**) *(nourriture)* to scoff; *(boisson)* to guzzle, to down, to sink (**b**) [!!] *(coïter)* to fuck, to screw, *Br* to shag

enflé [!] [ãfle] *nm* prick, *Br* arsehole, tosser, *Am* asshole

enflure [!] [ãflyr] *nf* prick, *Br* arsehole, tosser, *Am* asshole

enfoiré, -e [!!] [ãfware] *nm,f (homme)* bastard, fucker; *(femme)* bitch

engin [!] [ãʒɛ̃] *nm (pénis)* prick, tool

engrosser [!] [ãgrose] *vt* **engrosser qn** to knock sb up, *Br* to get sb up the duff

engueulade [ãgœlad] *nf* bawling out, roasting, earful; **se prendre une engueulade** to get bawled out, to get a roasting *or* an earful

engueuler [ãgœle] **1** *vt* **engueuler qn** to bawl sb out, to give sb hell *or* a roasting; **se faire engueuler** to get bawled out, to get a roasting
2 s'engueuler *vpr* to be at each other's throats, *Br* to have a slanging match;

ses parents n'arrêtent pas de s'engueuler his parents are always at each other's throats
▶ see *also* **poisson**

enguirlander [ãgirlãde] *vt* **enguirlander qn** to read sb the riot act; **se faire enguirlander** to get read the riot act

enquiquinant, -e [ãkikinã, -ãt] *adj* (**a**) *(ennuyeux)* deadly dull (**b**) *(contrariant)* **être enquiquinant** to be a pain

enquiquiner [ãkikine] *vt* (**a**) *(ennuyer)* to bore stiff *or* rigid (**b**) *(contrarier)* **enquiquiner qn** to bug sb, *Br* to get up sb's nose, *Am* to give sb a pain

enquiquineur, -euse [ãkikinœr, -øz] *nm,f* pain (in the neck), pest, nuisance

entourloupe [ãturlup], *nf* dirty trick

entourlouper [ãturlupe] *vt* **entourlouper qn** to play a dirty trick on sb, *Br* to do the dirty on sb, *Am* to do sb dirt

entourloupette [ãturlupɛt] = **entourloupe**

entraver [ãtrave] *vt* to understand □, to get; **j'entrave que dalle** I don't understand a damn *or Br* bloody thing

entuber [!] [ãtybe] *vt (flouer)* to rip off, to swindle; **se faire entuber** to get ripped off *or* swindled

envapé, -e [ãvape] *adj* out of it, ripped, *Br* off one's face

envoyer [ãvwaje] **s'envoyer** *vpr* (**a**) *(absorber) (nourriture)* to scoff; *(boisson)* to guzzle, to down, to sink; *(livre)* to devour (**b**) [!] *(avoir des relations sexuelles avec) Br* to bonk, to have it off with, *Am* to ball; **s'envoyer en l'air (avec qn)** *Br* to bonk (sb), to have it off (with sb), *Am* to ball (sb)
▶ see *also* **balader, bouler, chier, décor, dinguer, paître, péter, pisser, promener, rose, valdinguer, valser, vanne**

épais [epɛ] *adv* **il y en a pas épais** there isn't much/aren't many

épate [epat] *nf* **c'est de l'épate** it's just showing off, it's all an act; **faire de l'épate** to show off

épingler [epēgle] *vt* (*arrêter*) to nab, *Br* to lift, *Am* to nail; **se faire épingler** to get nabbed *or Br* lifted *or Am* nailed

éponge [epɔ̃ʒ] *nf* **(a)** (*ivrogne*) lush, alky, boozer, *Am* juicer **(b) éponges** lungs □; **avoir les éponges mitées** = to have a disease of the lungs such as tuberculosis or silicosis

éreinter [erēte] *vt* (*critiquer sévèrement*) to pull to pieces, to slam, *Br* to slag off

esbigner [esbiɲe] **s'esbigner** *vpr* to clear off, to take off, *Am* to book it

esbroufe, esbrouffe [esbruf] *nf* showing off; **faire de l'esbroufe** to show off; **décrocher un boulot à l'esbroufe** to bluff one's way into a job; **il a eu l'oral à l'esbroufe** he bluffed his way through the oral

esgourde [esgurd] *nf* ear □, *Br* lug, lughole

esgourder [esgurde] *vt* (*entendre*) to hear □; (*écouter*) to listen □

espèce [espɛs] *nf* **espèce de con!** [!] you *Br* arsehole! *or Am* asshole!; **espèce de menteur!** you filthy liar!; **c'est une espèce d'empoté!** he's a *Br* cack-handed idiot *or Am* klutz!; **il s'est marié avec une espèce de pouffiasse!** [!] he married some old tart *or Br* slapper

espingouin [espēgwē] *Offensive* **1** *adj* Dago
2 *nm* **Espingouin** Dago

> Depending on the context and the tone of voice used, this term may be either offensive or affectionately humorous. It is nonetheless inadvisable to use it unless one is quite sure of the reaction it will receive.

esquinter [eskēte] *vt* **(a)** (*endommager*) to wreck, to bust, *Br* to knacker **(b)** (*blesser*) to smash up; **se faire**

esquinter to get smashed up

estomaquer [estomake] *vt* to stagger, to flabbergast; **il a été estomaqué** he was staggered *or* flabbergasted *or Br* gobsmacked

estourbir [esturbir] *vt* **(a)** (*assommer*) to knock out **(b)** (*tuer*) to kill □, *Br* to do in

étendre [etɑ̃dr] *vt* **(a)** (*faire tomber*) to floor, to deck **(b)** (*tuer*) to kill □, *Br* to do in **(c) se faire étendre (à un examen)** (*échouer*) to fail □ *or Am* flunk (an exam)

Étienne [etjɛn] *npr* **à la tienne, Étienne!** cheers!

étonner [etone] *vt Ironic* **tu m'étonnes!** you're telling ME!, you DO surprise me!

étriper [etripe] **s'étriper** *vpr* to knock lumps out of each other, to make mincemeat of each other

étron [etrɔ̃] *nm* turd

exam [egzam] *nm* (*abbr* **examen**) exam

exciter [eksite] **s'exciter** *vpr* (*s'énerver*) to get worked up *or* excited; **t'excite pas, je vais te le rendre ton fric!** calm down *or* don't get worked up, I'll give you your money back!

exo [egzo] *nm* (*abbr* **exercice**) exercise □

expliquer [eksplike] *vt* **je t'explique pas** I can't describe it, you wouldn't believe it; **on s'est pris un de ces savons, je t'explique pas...** you wouldn't have believed the telling-off we got

exploser [eksploze] **1** *vt* **(a)** (*battre*) **exploser qn** to kick sb's head in, to smash sb's face in **(b) être explosé (de rire)** to be killing oneself (laughing), to be cracking up, to be in stitches
2 *vi* **ils ont explosé sur la scène rock il y a vingt ans** they burst onto the rock scene twenty years ago

expo [ekspo] *nf* (*abbr* **exposition**) exhibition □

extra [ekstra] *adj inv* great, terrific, *Br* fab, *Am* awesome

F

fac [fak] *nf* (*abbr* **faculté**) *Br* uni, *Am* school □

façade [fasad] *nf* **se ravaler la façade** to put one's face on, to put on one's warpaint; **se faire ravaler la façade** to have a face-lift □

face [fas] *nf* **face de rat** ratbag, *Am* ratfink

facho [faʃo] *adj & nmf* fascist □

facile [fasil] *adv* easily □, no problem, *Br* no probs

fada [fada] **1** *adj* crazy, crackers, off one's rocker, *Am* wacko
2 *nmf* nutcase, nutter, *Am* wacko

fadé, -e [fade] *adj* **être fadé** to take the *Br* biscuit *or Am* cake; **habituellement, ses films cassent pas des briques, mais le dernier est particulièrement fadé** his films usually aren't much to write home about, but his last one really takes the *Br* biscuit *or Am* cake

faf¹ [faf] *adj & nmf* (*fasciste*) fascist □

faf², faffe [faf], **fafiot** [fafjo] *nm* (**a**) (*billet de banque*) *Br* banknote □, *Am* greenback (**b**) **fafs, faffes, fafiots** (*papiers d'identité*) ID

fagoté, -e [fagɔte] *adj* **être mal/bizarrement fagoté** to be badly-/strangely-dressed
▶ *see also* **as**

faire [fɛr] **1** *vt* (**a**) **on ne me la fait pas, à moi!** you can't fool me!, there's no flies on me! (**b**) **faire son affaire à qn** to bump sb off, *Br* to do sb in
2 se faire *vpr* (**a**) **se faire qn** ⚠ (*avoir des rapports sexuels avec*) to screw *or Br* shag sb; (*battre*) to beat the shit out of sb

(**b**) (*supporter*) **celui-là, il faut se le faire!** he's a total pain (in the neck)!
(**c**) **va te faire!** get out of here!, *Br* sling your hook!, eff off!, *Am* bug off!
(**d**) **on se fait un film/un resto chinois?** do you fancy going to see a film/ going for a Chinese?

fait, -e [fɛ, fɛt] *adj* (*ivre*) blitzed, wasted, gassed

falloir [falwar] *v imp* **il l'a remis à sa place, comme il faut** he put him well and truly in his place; **ils leur ont mis la pâtée, comme il faut** they absolutely pasted *or* thrashed them

falzar [falzar] *nm Br* trousers □, keks, *Am* pants □

famille [famij] *nf* **des familles** nice little; **un petit gueuleton des familles** a nice little meal
▶ *see also* **bijou**

fana [fana] (*abbr* **fanatique**) **1** *adj* **être fana de football** to be into football, to be a football fan *or* nut
2 *nmf* fan, nut, freak; **un fana de football** a football fan *or* nut

farcir [farsir] **se farcir** *vpr* (**a**) (*consommer*) to scoff, to guzzle (**b**) (*supporter*) to have to put up with; **celui-là, il faut se le farcir!** he's a total pain! (**c**) (*faire*) **se farcir qch** to get stuck *or Br* lumbered *or* landed with sth (**d**) ⚠⚠ (*posséder sexuellement*) to screw, *Br* to have it off with, *Am* to ball

fard [far] *nm* **piquer un fard** to go red

farine [farin] *nf* (*héroïne*) smack, scag, skag, H; (*cocaïne*) charlie, snow

fastoche [fastɔʃ] *adj* dead *or Am* real easy; **c'était hyper fastoche** it was dead easy, it was a walk in the park or Br a doddle

fauche [foʃ] nf thieving □, pinching, Br nicking; **à chaque fois, il y a de la fauche** things get pinched or Br nicked every time

fauché, -e [foʃe] adj broke, Br skint, strapped (for cash)

faucher [foʃe] vt (voler) to pinch, Br to nick

Faucheuse [foʃøz] nf **la Faucheuse** (la mort) the Grim Reaper

fauteuil [fotœj] nm **arriver dans un fauteuil** to win hands down, Br to walk it

faux [fo] adv **avoir tout faux** (se tromper) to have it all wrong
▶ see also **derche, jeton**

faux-cul [foky], **faux-derche** [fodɛrʃ] nm two-faced Br swine or Am stinker

fayot [fajo] nm (a) (personne) crawler, Br creep (b) (haricot) bean □

fayoter [fajɔte] vi to crawl, Br to creep

féca [feka] nm (verlan café) coffee □, Am java

feeling [filiŋ] nm **faire qch au feeling** to do sth by intuition □

feignasse [fɛɲas] nf lazy so-and-so

feignasser [fɛɲase] vi to lounge or laze around

feinter [fɛ̃te] vt (duper) to take in, to con

fêlé, -e [fele] adj (fou) crackers, nuts, Br barking, Am wacko

femmelette [famlɛt] nf wimp, drip, sissy, Br big girl's blouse

fendant, -e [fɑ̃dɑ̃, -ɑ̃t] adj hysterical, side-splitting

fendante [fɑ̃dɑ̃t] nf **quelle fendante!, la fendante!** what a scream or a hoot!

fendard, -e [fɑ̃dar, -ard] **1** adj (amusant) hysterical, side-splitting; **c'est fendard** it's hysterical or side-splitting
2 nm (pantalon) Br trousers □, keks, Am pants □

fendre [fɑ̃dr] **se fendre** vpr (a) (rire) **se fendre (la gueule** ou **la poire** ou **la pêche** ou **la pipe)** to kill oneself (laughing), to crack up, to split one's sides
(b) **se fendre de qch** to come up with sth; **je me suis fendu de deux cents balles** I coughed up two hundred francs; **il s'est pas fendu** he wasn't exactly generous, it didn't cost him much; **il s'est même pas fendu d'un sourire** he didn't even crack a smile

fente [!!] [fɑ̃t] nf (sexe de la femme) crack, gash

fer [fɛr] nm **se retrouver les quatre fers en l'air** to fall flat on one's back

fermer [fɛrme] vt **ferme ta gueule!, la ferme!, ferme-la!** shut your face or mouth!, shut it!, Br belt up!
▶ see also **clapet**

ferraille [fɛraj] nf (petite monnaie) small change □, Br coppers

fesse [fɛs] nf (a) (sexe) sex □, Br bonking; **il s'intéresse qu'à la fesse** he's got a one-track mind, Br he's got sex on the brain; **film de fesse** porn movie, Am skin flick; **magazine de fesse** porn or skin or girlie mag (b) **s'occuper de ses fesses** to mind one's own business
▶ see also **chaud, feu, peau**

fête [fɛt] nf **faire sa fête à qn** to give sb a hammering, Br to do sb over; **ça va être ma/ta/etc fête** I'm/you're/etc in for it

feu, -x [fø] nm (a) (pistolet) shooter, Am piece (b) **avoir le feu au cul** [!] ou **aux fesses** (être pressé) to be in a hell of a rush; (aimer les plaisirs charnels) to be horny as hell or Br gagging for it
▶ see also **péter, plancher**[1]

feuille [fœj] nf (a) **être dur de la feuille** to be hard of hearing □ (b) (billet de banque) note □, Am greenback

feuj [fœʒ] (verlan juif) **1** adj Jewish □
2 nmf Jew □

fiasse [fjas] nf (a) (prostituée) whore, hooker (b) (femme aux mœurs légères) slut, tart, tramp, *Br* scrubber **(c)** *(femme désagréable)* bitch, *Br* cow

ficelé, -e [fisle] *adj* **(a)** *(habillé)* **être mal ficelé** *Br* to be dressed like a scarecrow *or* a tramp, *Am* to look like a bum **(b)** *(structuré) (histoire, scénario)* **bien/ bizarrement ficelé** well-/strangely-structured □

fiche [fiʃ], **ficher** [fiʃe] **1** *vt (faire)* to do □; **mais qu'est-ce qu'il fiche?** what on earth is he doing?

2 se fiche, se ficher *vpr* **se fiche** *or* **se ficher de qn/qch** not to give a damn about sb/sth; **je m'en fiche pas mal!** I don't give a damn, I couldn't care less!; **tu te fiches de moi?** are you making a fool of me?

fichu, -e [fiʃy] *adj* **(a)** *(hors d'usage)* **être fichu** to have had it, to be done for, *Br* to be knackered

(b) *(condamné à une mort certaine)* **être fichu** to be done for, to have had it

(c) *(dépréciatif) Br* blasted, *Am* darn(ed); **il a un fichu caractère** he's so *Br* blasted *or* *Am* darn(ed) difficult

(d) *(fait)* **être bien/mal fichu** to have/ not to have a great bod; **elle est bien fichue, votre cuisine** your kitchen's really well designed □; **un roman bien fichu** a well-structured novel □

(e) mal fichu *(malade)* under the weather, *Br* off-colour, *Am* off-color

(f) *(capable)* **être fichu de faire qch** to be quite capable of doing sth □; **il est pas fichu de le faire** he can't do it □

▸ see also **as**

fiesta [fjɛsta] *nf* wild party □; **faire la fiesta** to party

fifty-fifty [fiftififti] *adv* fifty-fifty

filer [file] **1** *vt (donner)* to give □; **file-moi une clope** give me a *Br* fag *or* *Am* cig; **filer une baffe à qn** to smack *or* clout sb

2 *vi (partir)* to get going *or* moving; **il faut que je file** I must be off, I have to get going; **allez, file, tu vas être en**

retard! go on, off you go, you're going to be late!

filoche [filɔʃ] *nf* shadowing, tailing

filocher [filɔʃe] **1** *vt (suivre)* to shadow, to tail

2 *vi (se dépêcher)* to get a move on, to move it, to get one's skates on, *Am* to get it in gear

fiole [fjɔl] *nf* **(a)** *(visage)* face □, mug **(b)** *(tête)* head □, nut

fion ⚠ [fjɔ̃] *nm* **(a)** *(postérieur) Br* arse, *Am* ass; **se casser le fion (pour faire qch)** to bust a gut *or* *Am* one's ass (doing sth) **(b)** *(anus) Br* arsehole, *Am* asshole **(c)** *(chance)* luck □; **avoir du fion** to be lucky □; **ne pas avoir de fion** to be unlucky □

fiotte ⚠⚠ [fjɔt] *nf Offensive* queer, *Br* poof, *Am* fag

fissa [fisa] *adv* **faire fissa** to get a move on, to get one's skates on, *Am* to get it in gear

fix, fixe [fiks] *nm* fix *(of drug)*

fixette [fiksɛt] *nf* **faire une fixette sur qn/qch** to be obsessed with sb/sth □, *Br* to have sb/sth on the brain

flag [flag] **en flag** *adv (abbr en flagrant délit)* **être pris en flag** to get caught red-handed *or* with one's pants down

flagada [flagada] *adj inv* washed-out

flamber [flɑ̃be] **1** *vt (dépenser)* to blow **2** *vi* **(a)** *(jouer avec passion)* to be a heavy gambler □ **(b)** *(se donner des airs)* to show off

flambeur, -euse [flɑ̃bœr, -øz] *nm,f* **(a)** *(joueur)* heavy gambler □ **(b)** *(personne qui se donne des airs)* show-off

flan [flɑ̃] *nm* **(a) en rester comme deux ronds de flan** to be flabbergasted *or* *Br* gobsmacked **(b) c'est du flan** it's a load of nonsense *or* *Br* rubbish

flancher [flɑ̃ʃe] *vi (abandonner)* to chuck it in, to throw in the towel; **son cœur a flanché** his heart gave out; **j'ai la mémoire qui flanche** my memory's going

flanquer [flãke] **1** vt **flanquer une claque/un coup à qn** to smack/punch sb; **flanquer qch par terre** (en le faisant exprès) to chuck or fling sth on the floor; (accidentellement) to knock sth onto the floor □; **flanquer qn à la porte** to kick sb out; **flanquer la trouille à qn** to put the wind up sb, to scare sb stiff or witless

2 se flanquer vpr **se flanquer (la gueule) par terre** to fall flat on one's face

flapi, -e [flapi] adj dead beat, bushed, Br knackered

flash [flaʃ] nm rush (after taking drugs)

flasher [flaʃe] vi **(a)** (après absorption de drogue) to get a rush **(b) flasher sur qn/qch** to fall for sb/sth

flèche [flɛʃ] nm **j'ai pas un flèche** I'm totally broke or Br skint or strapped

flémingite [flemɛ̃ʒit] nf Hum laziness □, lazyitis; **être atteint de flémingite aiguë** to suffer from acute laziness or lazyitis

flemmard, -e [flɛmar, -ard] **1** adj lazy □

2 nm,f lazy so-and-so

flemmarder [flɛmarde] vi to laze or lounge about

flemme [flɛm] nf laziness □; **j'ai la flemme** I can't be bothered doing anything, I don't feel like doing anything; **j'ai la flemme de le faire maintenant** I can't be bothered doing it just now

flic [flik] nm cop, Br plod, Am flatfoot

flicage [flikaʒ] nm police surveillance □

flicaille [flikaj] nf **la flicaille** the cops, the pigs, Br the filth

flingue [flɛ̃g] nm shooter, Am piece

flinguer [flɛ̃ge] **1** vt **(a)** (tuer) to blow away **(b)** (abîmer) to wreck, to bust, Br to knacker

2 se flinguer vpr to blow one's brains out

flip [flip] nm **(a)** (déprime) **être en plein flip** to be on a real downer; **c'est le flip!** what a downer! **(b)** (après l'absorption de drogue) depression □, downer (as the after-effect of taking cocaine or amphetamines)

flippant, -e [flipã, -ãt] adj (déprimant) depressing □; **être flippant** to be a downer

flipper [flipe] vi **(a)** (être angoissé) to feel down, to be on a downer; **faire flipper qn** to get sb down **(b)** (avoir peur) to be scared □ **(c)** (après absorption de drogue) to feel down (as the after-effect of taking cocaine or amphetamines)

▸ see also **mère**

fliqué, -e [flike] adj crawling or heaving with cops

fliquer [flike] vt Pej **(a)** (population, employés) to keep under surveillance □; **il flique complètement sa femme** he watches his wife like a hawk **(b)** (quartier) to police □

flopée, floppée [flope] nf **une flopée (de)** a whole bunch (of), loads (of), tons (of)

flotte [flɔt] nf (eau) water □; **prendre la flotte** to get soaked (in the rain)

flotter [flɔte] vi (pleuvoir) to rain □

flouse, flouze [fluz] nm cash, dough, Br dosh, Am bucks

flûte [flyt] nf (mensonges) lies □, Br porkies

flûter [flyte] vi (dire des mensonges) to tell lies □ or Br porkies

flûteur, -euse [flytœr, -øz] nm,f liar □

foies [fwa] nmpl **avoir les foies** to be scared stiff or to death or out of one's wits

foin [fwɛ̃] nm **faire du foin** (du tapage) to make a racket; (du scandale) to make waves, to cause a stink

foire [fwar] nf **(a)** (désordre) chaos □, Br bedlam; **c'est la foire, là-dedans!** it's a

madhouse or Br it's bedlam in there!
(b) faire la foire to have a wild time; **il
ne pense qu'à faire la foire** all he
thinks about is having a good time

foirer [fware] **1** vi (échouer) to be a Br
cock-up or balls-up or Am ball-up
  2 vt (rater) to make a Br cock-up or
balls-up or Am ball-up of

foireux, -euse [fwarø, -øz] adj hopeless, useless

foldingue [fɔldɛ̃g] adj crazy, loopy, Br
mental, Am wacko

folichon, -onne [fɔliʃɔ̃, -ɔn] adj **pas
folichon** not much fun; **ça n'a rien de
folichon** it's no fun

folklo [fɔlklo] adj inv (abbr **folklorique**)
bizarre, weird and wonderful; (per-
sonne) eccentric ▫, loopy, off-the-wall,
Am kooky

folle [fɔl] nf (homosexuel) queen

fondu, -e [fɔ̃dy] adj (fou) round the
bend, out to lunch, off one's rocker or
trolley

fonsdé, -e [fɔ̃sde] adj (verlan **défoncé**)
stoned, wrecked

foot [fut] nm (abbr **football**) soccer ▫, Br
football ▫, footie

fort [fɔr] **1** adj **c'est fort** that's quite
something; **c'est un peu fort (de café)**
that's a bit much or rich
  2 adv **(a) y aller un peu fort** to go a bit
over the top or Br OTT; **tu y es allé un
peu fort avec le poivre** you overdid it a
bit with the pepper **(b) faire fort** to do
really well ▫, to excel oneself ▫
  ▸ see also **gueule**

fortiche [fɔrtiʃ] adj clever ▫, smart ▫

fossile [fɔsil] nm (individu rétrograde)
fossil

fouetter [fwɛte] vi (sentir mauvais) to
stink, Br to pong

foufoune [!] [fufun] nf pussy, Br fanny,
snatch

fouille [fuj] nf (poche) pocket ▫

fouille-merde [!] [fujmɛrd] nmf inv

shit-stirrer, Am buttinski

fouiller [fuje] **se fouiller** [!] vpr **tu
peux toujours te fouiller!** you haven't
a hope in hell!

fouiner [fwine] vi to nose or ferret
about (**dans** in)

fouler [fule] **se fouler** vpr **se fouler (la
rate)** to strain or overexert oneself ▫;
t'aurais pu te fouler un peu plus! you
could have made a bit more of an
effort!; **tu t'es vraiment pas foulé (la
rate)!** you didn't exactly strain or overexert yourself!

foultitude [fultityd] nf **une foultitude
(de)** masses (of), loads (of), tons (of)

four [fur] nm (échec) flop, Br washout,
Am bomb, turkey; **faire un four** to be a
flop or Br a washout, Am to bomb

fourbi [furbi] nm **(a)** (désordre) shambles, mess **(b)** (affaires) stuff, Br gear

fourguer [furge] vt **(a)** (vendre) to flog;
(placer) to unload, to palm off; **fourguer qch à qn** (vendre) to flog sth to sb;
(placer) to unload sth on sb, to palm sth
off on sb **(b)** (dénoncer) to squeal on, Br
to grass on, to shop, Am to rat on

fourmi [furmi] nf (petit revendeur de
drogue) (small-time) dealer

fourrer [fure] vt **(a)** (mettre) to stick, to
shove **(b)** [!!] (posséder sexuellement) to
shaft, to poke, to ride
  ▸ see also **doigt**

foutaise [futɛz] nf **de la foutaise, des
foutaises** crap, bull; **raconter des foutaises** to talk crap or bull

fouteur, -euse [futœr, -øz] nm,f **fouteur de merde** [!] shit-stirrer, Am buttinski

foutoir [futwar] nm shambles; **quel
foutoir dans sa chambre!** her room's
a complete pigsty or tip!

foutre [futr] **1** vt **(a)** [!] (faire) to do ▫; **ne
rien foutre, ne pas en foutre une** to
do damn all or Br bugger or sod all; **j'en
ai rien à foutre!** I don't give a shit!;

qu'est-ce qu'il fout? what the hell is he doing?; **qu'est-ce que tu veux que ça me foute?** what the hell do I care?, what the hell does it matter to me?; **qu'est-ce que j'ai bien pu foutre de mes clés?** what the hell can I have done with my keys?

(b) [!] (mettre) to stick, to dump, Br to bung; **il sait pas où il a foutu les clés** he doesn't know what the hell he's done with the keys; **il peut pas bouffer sans en foutre partout** he can't eat without getting his food everywhere; **foutre qch par terre** (en le faisant exprès) to stick or dump or Br bung sth on the floor, (accidentellement) to knock sth onto the floor □; **foutre qn à la porte** to chuck or kick sb out; **foutre son poing dans la gueule à qn** to give sb a punch in the face; **foutre la paix à qn** to get off sb's back; **ça la fout mal** it doesn't look too good; **foutre qn dedans** to mislead sb □; **j't'en foutrais, moi, de l'esprit d'équipe!** team spirit, I'll give you Br bloody or Am goddamn team spirit!; **qui est-ce qui m'a foutu un empoté pareil?** how the hell did I end up with such a total Br arsehole or Am asshole?

(c) **va te faire foutre**[!!] fuck off!; **qu'il aille se faire foutre!**[!!] he can fuck right off!

2 vi **foutre sur la gueule à qn**[!] to waste sb's face, to smash sb's face in

3 se foutre[!] vpr (a) (se mettre) **se foutre à faire qch** to start doing sth □; **il s'est foutu de l'encre partout** he covered himself in ink □; **s'en foutre plein les poches** to rake it in; **se foutre par terre, se foutre la gueule par terre**[!!] to fall flat on one's face; **se foutre dedans** to screw up

(b) **se foutre de qch** not to give a shit about sth; **se foutre de qn** (être indifférent) not to give a damn or a shit about or Br a toss about sb; (se moquer) to make a fool of sb, Br to take the piss out of sb;

une montre en or! elle s'est pas foutue de toi! a gold watch! she didn't make a fool of you or Br take the piss out of you!

4[!!] nm spunk, come, cum
▸ see also **air, camp, gueule**

foutrement[!]   [futrəmã]   adv
damn(ed), Br bloody

foutu, -e [!] [futy] adj (a) (hors d'usage) **être foutu** to have had it, to be done, Br to be knackered or buggered

(b) (condamné à une mort certaine) **être foutu** to have had it, to be done for

(c) (dépréciatif) damn(ed), godawful, Br bloody; **elle a un foutu caractère** she's so damn(ed) or Br bloody difficult

(d) (fait) **être bien/mal foutu** to have/not to have a great bod; **elle est bien foutue, votre cuisine** your kitchen's really well designed □; **un roman bien foutu** a well-structured novel □

(e) **mal foutu** (souffrant) under the weather, Br off-colour, Am off-color

(f) (capable) **être foutu de faire qch** to be quite capable of doing sth □; **ne pas être foutu de faire qch** to be incapable of doing sth □
▸ see also **as**

fracasse [frakas], **fracassé, -e** [frakase] adj smashed, wrecked, wasted

fraîche [frɛʃ] nf (argent) cash, dough, Br dosh, Am bucks

frais¹ [frɛ] nm **mettre qn au frais** to put sb inside or away or behind bars

frais² nmpl **aux frais de la princesse** (aux frais de l'État) at the taxpayer's expense □; (aux frais d'une société) at the company's expense □

fraise [frɛz] nf **ramener sa fraise** (arriver) to turn up, to show (up), to show one's face; (intervenir inopportunément) to stick one's nose or oar in; **ramène ta fraise!** get over here!
▸ see also **sucrer**

franchouillard, -e [frãʃujar, -ard]
1 adj typically French

2 *nm,f* typical Frenchman, *f* French-woman □

This word, whilst not overly pejorative, describes the average French person complete with the stereotypical characteristics of narrow-mindedness and jingoism.

franco [frɑ̃ko] *adv* **vas-y franco!** *(pour encourager quelqu'un)* go for it!; **vas-y franco si tu veux que ça rentre** you'll have to hit/push/*etc* it hard for it to go in; **il y est allé franco avec le piment** he didn't hold back with the chilli; **elle lui a dit ce qu'elle pensait de lui et elle y est allé franco** she told him what she thought of him and she didn't mince her words

frangibus [frɑ̃ʒibys] *nm* brother □, bro

frangin [frɑ̃ʒɛ̃] *nm* brother □, bro

frangine [frɑ̃ʒin] *nf* **(a)** *(sœur)* sister □, sis **(b)** *(femme, fille)* chick, *Br* bird

frappadingue [frapadɛ̃g] *adj* crazy, bonkers, *Br* mental

frappe [frap] *nf* **une (petite) frappe** a (little) hoodlum *or Am* hood

frappé, -e [frape] *adj (fou)* crazy, loopy, touched

frapper [frape] **se frapper** *vpr* **ne pas se frapper** not to get worked up; **te frappe pas** take it easy!, chill out!

frérot [frero] *nm* brother □, bro

fric [frik] *nm* cash, dough, *Br* dosh, *Am* bucks

frichti [friʃti] *nm* cooked meal □

fricot [friko] *nm* food □, eats, chow, grub

fricoter [frikɔte] **1** *vt* **qu'est-ce qu'il fricote?** what's he up to?
2 *vi* **fricoter avec qn** *(avoir des relations sexuelles)* to have a thing going with sb; *(avoir des relations)* to have shady *or Br* dodgy dealings with sb

Fridolin [fridɔlɛ̃] *nm Offensive* Kraut

Depending on the context and the tone of voice used, this term may be either offensive or affectionately humorous. It is nonetheless inadvisable to use it unless one is quite sure of the reaction it will receive.

frigo [frigo] *nm (abbr* **frigidaire)** fridge

frime [frim] *nf* **(a)** *(fanfaronnade)* **les lunettes noires, c'est pour la frime** dark glasses are just for posing in; **bon, t'arrête ta frime?** will you stop showing off!; **tu l'aurais vu avec son nouveau cuir, la frime!** you should have seen him in his new leather jacket, what a poser! **(b)** *(comportement trompeur)* **c'est de la frime** it's all an act, it's all put on

frimer [frime] *vi* to show off

frimeur, -euse [frimœr, -øz] *nm,f* show-off

fringale [frɛ̃gal] *nf* hunger □; **avoir la fringale** to have the munchies

fringue [frɛ̃g] *nf* piece of clothing □; **j'ai plus une fringue à me mettre** I haven't a thing to wear; **des fringues** clothes □, threads, *Br* gear

fringuer [frɛ̃ge] **se fringuer** *vpr* to get dressed □; **être bien-/mal fringué** to be well-/badly-dressed □; **elle aime bien se fringuer pour sortir** she likes to get all dressed up to go out; **il sait pas se fringuer** he's got no dress sense; **elle se fringue très seventies** she wears really seventies clothes, she dresses really seventies

friqué, -e [frike] *adj* loaded, *Br* rolling in it, *Am* rolling in dough

Frisé [frize] *nm Offensive (Allemand)* Kraut

Depending on the context and the tone of voice used, this term may be either offensive or affectionately humorous. It is nonetheless inadvisable to use it unless one is quite sure of the reaction it will receive.

frisquet, -ette [friskɛ, -ɛt] *adj* chilly □, *Br* nippy, parky

frite [frit] *nf (énergie)* **avoir la frite** to be on top form, to have bags of energy

friter [frite] **1** *vt (battre)* **friter qn** to beat sb up, to kick sb's head in
2 se friter *vpr* to have a *Br* punch-up *or Am* fist fight

fritz [frits] *nm Offensive* Kraut

Depending on the context and the tone of voice used, this term may be either offensive or affectionately humorous. It is nonetheless inadvisable to use it unless one is quite sure of the reaction it will receive.

froc [frɔk] *nm (pantalon) Br* trousers □, keks, *Am* pants □; **faire dans son froc** *(déféquer, avoir peur)* to shit *or* crap oneself; **baisser son froc** to demean oneself □
▶ see also **chier, pisser**

fromage [frɔmaʒ] *nm* **il n'y a pas de quoi en faire tout un fromage** there's no need to make such a big deal *or* a song and dance about it, *Am* there's no need to make a federal case out of it

fromgi [frɔmʒi], **frometon** [frɔmtɔ̃] *nm* cheese □

frotteur [frɔtœr] *nm* = pervert who enjoys rubbing himself against women in crowded places

froussard, -e [frusar, -ard] *adj nm,f* chicken *(person)*

frousse [frus] *nf* **avoir la frousse** to be scared □; **foutre la frousse à qn** to scare the living daylights out of sb

frusques [frysk] *nfpl* clothes □, threads, *Br* gear

fumant, -e [fymã, -ãt] *adj* **un coup fumant** a masterstroke □

fumasse [fymas] *adj* fuming, livid

fumer [fyme] *vt* **(a)** *(battre)* to clobber, to thump **(b)** *(tuer)* to kill □, *Br* to do in

fumette [fymɛt] *nf* getting stoned; **c'est un habitué de la fumette** he gets stoned regularly; **il y a que la fumette qui l'intéresse** all he's interested in is getting stoned

fumier [!] [fymje] *nm* bastard, shit

fun [fœn] **1** *adj inv* fun □
2 *nm* fun □; **faire qch pour le fun** to do sth just for fun *or* for the fun of it

furax [fyraks], **furibard, -e** [fyribar, -ard] *adj* seething, livid

fusée [fyze] *nf* **lâcher une fusée** *(vomir)* to throw up, to puke, to chunder; *(faire un pet)* to fart, *Br* to let off

fusiller [fysije] *vt (briser)* to wreck, to bust, *Br* to knacker

futal [fytal], **fute** [fyt] *nm Br* trousers □, keks, *Am* pants □

fute-fute [fytfyt] *adj* **elle n'est pas fute-fute** she's not exactly bright, *Am* she's no rocket scientist

G

gadin [gadɛ̃] *nm* **prendre un gadin** to fall flat on one's face

gadji [gadʒi] *nf* chick, *Br* bird

gadjo [gadʒo] *nm* guy, *Br* bloke

gaffe [gaf] *nf* (**a**) *(bévue)* gaffe, blunder, *Br* boob, *Am* boo-boo; **faire une gaffe** to put one's foot in it, to boob, *Am* to make a boo-boo, to goof
(**b**) **fais gaffe, tu risques de glisser!** watch out, you might slip!; **faire gaffe à qch** *(y prendre garde)* to be careful of sth, to watch out for sth; **fais gaffe à toi!** *(prends soin de toi)* take care of yourself!; *(menace)* be careful!, watch it!; **fais gaffe à ce que tu dis!** be careful *or* watch what you say!

gaffer [gafe] *vi* to put one's foot in it, *Br* to boob, *Am* to make a boo-boo, to goof

gaffeur, -euse [gafœr, -øz] **1** *adj* **être gaffeur** to be always putting one's foot in it
2 *nm,f* **c'est un gaffeur** he's always putting his foot in it

gaga [gaga] *adj* gaga, *Br* away with the fairies

galère [galɛr] **1** *adj* **c'est galère** what a pain *or* hassle; **lui et ses plans galères!** him and his lousy ideas!
2 *nf* *(situation pénible)* pain, hassle; **c'est la galère!, quelle galère!** what a pain *or* hassle!; **se foutre dans une galère** to get oneself into a mess

galérer [galere] *vi* to have a hard time (of it); **tu vas galérer pour trouver à te garer dans le quartier** you're going to have a hard time *or* a lot of hassle finding a parking space in the area

galette [galɛt] *nf* *(argent)* cash, dough, *Br* dosh, *Am* bucks

galipote [galipɔt] *nf Can* **courir la galipote** to chase women, to be a skirtchaser

galoche [galɔʃ] *nf* French kiss; **rouler une galoche à qn** to French-kiss sb, *Br* to snog sb

galure [galyr], **galurin** [galyrɛ̃] *nm* hat □

gamberger [gɑ̃bɛrʒe] *vi* (**a**) *(réfléchir)* to think hard □ (**b**) *(ruminer)* to brood □

gambette [gɑ̃bɛt] *nf* leg □, pin
▶ *see also* **tricoter**

gamelle [gamɛl] *nf* (**a**) *(baiser)* French kiss; **rouler une gamelle à qn** to French-kiss sb, *Br* to snog sb (**b**) **prendre une gamelle** to fall flat on one's face

ganache [ganaʃ] *nf Br* divvy, wally, *Am* dork

gapette [gapɛt] *nf* cap □

garage [garaʒ] *nm Hum* **garage à bites** [!!] nympho; **c'est un vrai garage à bites** [!!] she's seen more ceilings than Michelangelo

garce [gars] *nf* bitch, *Br* cow

garde-à-vous [gardavu] *nm Hum* **être au garde-à-vous** *(avoir une érection)* to have a hard-on *or* boner

garetteci [garɛtsi] *nf* *(verlan* **cigarette**) *Br* fag, *Am* cig

garrocher [garɔʃe] *Can* **1** *vt* to chuck, to fling
2 se garrocher *vpr* to get a move on, to move it, *Am* to get it in gear

gaspard [gaspar] *nm* rat □

gâteau [gato] *nm* **c'est pas du gâteau**

(c'est pénible) it's no picnic, it's no walk in the park; *(ça demande un effort intellectuel)* it's no walkover, it's not as easy as it looks, *Am* it's no cakewalk

gâterie [gɑtri] *nf Hum* **faire une gâterie à qn** ⚠ *(fellation)* to go down on sb, to suck sb off; *(cunnilingus)* to go down on sb, to lick sb out

gauche [goʃ] *nf* **mettre de l'argent à gauche** to put some money aside or away □; **jusqu'à la gauche** totally □, completely □; **il s'est fait entuber jusqu'à la gauche** he got totally or completely conned
▸ see also **arme**

gaucho [goʃo] *nmf* leftie, lefty

gaule [gol] *nf* **avoir la gaule** ⚠⚠ to have a hard-on

gaulé, -e [gole] *adj* **être bien/mal gaulé** to have/not to have a great bod

gauler [gole] *vt (attraper)* to nab, *Br* to nick; **se faire gauler** to get nabbed or *Br* nicked

gaulois, -e [golwa, -az] *nm,f* = French person of native stock, as opposed to immigrants or their descendants

gaver [gave] *vt (importuner)* **gaver qn** to bug sb, *Br* to do sb's head in, to get up sh's nose, *Am* to give sb a pain (in the neck)

gay [gɛ] *adj & nm* gay □

gazer [gaze] *v imp* **ça gaze?** how's it going?, how's things?; **ça gaze** everything's fine

GDB [ʒedebe] *nf (abbr* **gueule de bois**) hangover □

géant, -e [ʒeɑ̃, -ɑ̃t] *adj (excellent)* wicked, cool, *Br* fab, *Am* awesome

gégène [ʒeʒɛn] **1** *adj* brilliant, great, terrific
2 *nf* **la gégène** = torture by electric shock

geler [ʒ(ə)le] **se geler** *vpr* to freeze to death; **se geler le cul** ⚠, **se les geler** ⚠ to freeze one's *Br* arse or *Am* ass off

gencives [ʒɑ̃siv] *nfpl* **qu'est-ce qu'il s'est pris dans les gencives!** he really got it in the neck!; **elle lui a envoyé dans les gencives que...** she told him straight to his face that...

génial, -e [ʒenjal] *adj (excellent)* great, brilliant, fantastic

genre [ʒɑ̃r] *nm* **(a)** *(environ)* **ça fait genre 200 francs** it's something like or somewhere around 200 francs **(b)** *(type)* **son copain c'est un mec genre hippie** her boyfriend's the hippy type

géo [ʒeo] *nf (abbr* **géographie**) geography □

gerbe [ʒɛrb] *nf (vomissement)* puke, vom, barf, **foutre la gerbe à qn** to make sb want to puke or barf; **avoir la gerbe** to want to puke or barf

gerber [ʒɛrbe] *vi* to puke, to throw up, to barf, to chunder

gicler [ʒikle] *vi* to be off, to push off, *Am* to split

giga [ʒiga] *adj* wicked, mega, *Br* fab, *Am* awesome

gigue [ʒig] *nf* **une grande gigue** a beanpole

girond, -e [ʒirɔ̃, -ɔ̃d] *adj* gorgeous, stunning, *Br* fit

givré, -e [ʒivre] *adj (fou)* crackers, crazy, *Br* bananas

glamour [glamur] *adj* glam

gland ⚠ [glɑ̃] *nm (imbécile)* dick, prick

glander [glɑ̃de] **1** *vt* **qu'est-ce que tu glandes?** what the hell are you doing?; **j'en ai rien à glander** I don't give a damn or *Br* a toss
2 *vi* to hang around, to bum around

glandes [glɑ̃d] *nfpl* **avoir les glandes** *(être énervé)* to be hacked off or cheesed off; *(être triste)* to be upset □; **foutre les glandes à qn** *(énerver)* to hack or cheese sb off; *(attrister)* to upset sb □

glandeur, -euse [glɑ̃dœr, -øz] *nm,f* layabout, *Am* goldbrick

glandouiller [glɑ̃duje] = **glander**

glandouilleur, -euse [glɑ̃dujœr, -øz] = **glandeur**

glandu [glɑ̃dy] *nm* halfwit, dope, *Br* plonker, *Am* flamer

glaouis [glawi] = **claouis**

glauque [glok] *adj* (personne, endroit) shady, *Br* dodgy; (ambiance) creepy

glaviot ! [glavjo] *nm* spit □, *Br* gob

glavioter ! [glavjɔte] *vi* to spit □, *Br* to gob

gnangnan [nɑ̃nɑ̃] *adj inv* (personne, air) twee; (film, livre) corny

gniac [njak] *nf* fighting spirit □, drive; **avoir la gniac, être plein de gniac** to have plenty of drive

gnognotte [nɔnɔt] *nf* **de la gnognotte** junk, trash, *Br* rubbish; **c'est pas de la gnognotte** it's quite something

gnole, gnôle [nol] *nf* firewater, *Am* alky

gnon [nɔ̃] *nm* thump, clout; **donner** *ou* **mettre un gnon à qn** to thump *or* clout sb

gnouf [nuf] *nm* glasshouse (prison)

go [go] *vi* **on y go?** shall we go?, shall we be off?

gober [gɔbe] **1** *vt* (croire) to swallow; **il gobe tout ce qu'on lui raconte** he swallows everything you tell him
2 se gober *vpr* to fancy oneself

godasse [gɔdas] *nf* shoe □

gode ! [gɔd] *nm* (abbr **godemiché**) dildo

godet [gɔdɛ] *nm* **prendre un godet** to have a drink □

godiche [gɔdiʃ] **1** *adj* (maladroit) ham-fisted, *Br* cack-handed; (niais) daft, *Am* dumb
2 *nf* **c'est une godiche** she's a ham-fisted *or Br* cack-handed idiot *or Am* klutz

godillot [gɔdijo] *nm* shoe □, clodhopper

gogo [gogo] *nm* sucker, *Br* mug, *Am* patsy

gogol [gɔgɔl] = **gol**

goguenots [gɔgno], **gogues** [gɔg] *nmpl Br* bog, *Am* john

goinfre [gwɛ̃fr] *nmf* pig, *Br* greedy-guts, gannet, *Am* hog

goinfrer [gwɛ̃fre] **se goinfrer** *vpr* to stuff oneself *or* one's face, to pig out

gol [gɔl] *nmf* (abbr **mongolien, -enne**) spaz, *Br* mong

> This term is used as a mild reproach to someone silly but because of its origins is extremely politically incorrect.

goldo [gɔldo] *nf* = Gauloise ® cigarette

gomme [gɔm] *nf* **mettre la gomme** (en voiture) to step on it, *Br* to put one's foot down, *Am* to step on the gas; **à la gomme** useless, pathetic

gommé [gɔme] *nm* (cocktail) = cocktail consisting of beer and lemon-flavoured syrup

gondoler [gɔ̃dɔle] **se gondoler** *vpr* (rire) to fall about laughing, to crack up

gonflant, -e [gɔ̃flɑ̃, -ɑ̃t] *adj* maddening; **être gonflant** to be a pain (in the neck)

gonflé, -e [gɔ̃fle] *adj* **être gonflé** to have a cheek *or* a nerve; **je le trouve gonflé de me demander de lui prêter ma caisse** I think he's got a cheek *or* a nerve asking me to lend him my car

gonfler [gɔ̃fle] *vt* (ennuyer) **gonfler qn** to bug sb, *Br* to get up sb's nose, to get on sb's wick, *Am* to tick sb off

gonflette [gɔ̃flɛt] *nf* pumping iron; **faire de la gonflette** to pump iron

gonze [gɔ̃z] *nm* guy, *Br* bloke

gonzesse [gɔ̃zɛs] *nf* chick, *Br* bird

gorgeon [gɔrʒɔ̃] *nm* drink □

gosse [gɔs] **1** *nmf* kid; **beau/belle gosse** good-looking guy/girl
2 *nm* **gosses** ! *Can* (testicules) balls, nuts, *Br* bollocks

gosser [gɔse] *vt Can* to whittle □

gouape [gwap] *nf* hoodlum, *Am* hood

goudou ⚠ [gudu] *nf Offensive* dyke, *Br* lezbo

gougnafier [guɲafje] *nm (individu grossier)* yokel, peasant, *Am* hick; *(bon à rien)* good-for-nothing, *Br* waster, *Am* slacker; *(mauvais ouvrier)* careless workman □, *Br* cowboy

gouine ⚠⚠ [gwin] *nf Offensive* dyke

goulot [gulo] *nm* mouth □, *Br* gob; **repousser** *ou* **refouler du goulot** to have rotten breath

goupiller [gupije] **1** *vt (arranger)* to cook up, to set up

 2 se goupiller *vpr (se passer)* to turn out, to work out

gourbi [gurbi] *nm* dump, hovel

gourdin ⚠⚠ [gurdɛ̃] *nm (pénis)* dick, prick, *Br* knob; **avoir le gourdin** to have a hard-on

gourer [gure] **se gourer** *vpr* (**a**) *(se tromper) Br* to boob, *Am* to goof (up) (**b**) *(se douter)* **je m'en gourais!** I thought as much!

gourmandise ⚠ [gurmɑ̃diz] *nf Hum (fellation)* blow-job; **faire une gourmandise à qn** to give sb a blow-job, to go down on sb

gousse ⚠⚠ [gus] *nf Offensive (lesbienne)* dyke

goutte [gut] *nf* **boire la goutte** to have a drop of brandy

grabuge [grabyʒ] *nm* trouble, *Br* aggro

graff [graf] *nm* graffiti □

graffeur [grafœr] *nm* graffiti artist □

graillaver [grɑjave] *vi* to eat □, to chow

graillé ⚠ [grɑje] *adj Can* well-hung

grailler ⚠ [grɑje] *vt & vi* to eat □

graillon [grɑjɔ̃] *nm* **sentir le graillon** to smell of burnt fat □; **avoir un goût de graillon** to taste of burnt fat □

graillonner [grɑjɔne] *vi* to clear one's throat noisily □

grain [grɛ̃] *nm* **avoir un grain** to be not all there, to be not right in the head, to have a screw loose

graine [grɛn] *nf* **casser la graine** to have a bite to eat; **de la graine de voyou** a future hooligan; **graine de con** ⚠ *Br* bloody *or Am* goddamn fool; **c'est de la mauvaise graine** he's a bad egg; **prends-en de la graine!** take note!, take a leaf out of his/her book!

grand-duc [grɑ̃dyk] *nm* **la tournée des grands-ducs** a big night out on the town; **faire la tournée des grands-ducs** to go for a big night out on the town

grand-mère [grɑ̃mɛr] *nf* **et ta grand-mère, elle fait du vélo?** mind your own business!

graph [graf] = **graff**

grapheur [grafœr] = **graffeur**

grappe [grap] *nf* **lâcher la grappe à qn** to get off sb's back *or* case

grappin [grapɛ̃] *nm* **mettre le grappin dessus à qn** *(arrêter)* to collar *or Br* lift *or* nick sb; *(accaparer)* to get one's hands on sb, to corner sb; **mettre le grappin sur qch** to get one's hands on sth

gratin [gratɛ̃] *nm (élite)* **le gratin** high society, *Br* the upper crust; **le gratin du monde du spectacle** the showbiz elite

gratiné, -e [gratine] *adj* over the top, *Br* OTT

gratos [gratos] *adv* free (of charge) □, for nothing □

gratte [grat] *nf* guitar □, *Br* axe, *Am* ax

gratter [grate] **1** *vt (devancer)* to overtake □

 2 *vi (travailler)* to work □

 3 se gratter *vpr* **tu peux toujours te gratter!** nothing doing!, no way!

grave [grav] **1** *adj (dérangé)* **il est grave** he's not all there, he's off his rocker *or Br* head

 2 *adv* seriously, in a bad way; **il me prend la tête grave** he seriously bugs me

Grecs [grɛk] *nmpl* **va te faire voir chez les Grecs!** go to hell!, *Br* sod off!, *Am* eat it!

greffier [grɛfje] *nm (chat)* puss, moggy

grelot [grəlo] *nm* **(a)** *(téléphone)* **un coup de grelot** a phone call □; **filer un coup de grelot à qn** to give sb a buzz *or Br* a bell **(b) grelots** [!] *(testicules)* balls, nuts, *Br* bollocks

greluche [grəlyʃ] *nf* chick, *Br* bird

greum [grœm] *adj (verlan* **maigre)** thin □

griller [grije] *vt* **(a) griller qn** *(devancer)* to leave sb standing, to leave sb for dead; *(compromettre)* to land sb in it **(b) en griller une** to have a smoke *or Br* a fag

grimpant [grɛ̃pɑ̃] *nm Br* trousers □, keks, *Am* pants □

grimper [!] [grɛ̃pe] *vt (posséder sexuellement)* to ride, to shaft, *Br* to shag

gringue [grɛ̃g] *nm* **faire du gringue à qn** to come on to sb, *Br* to chat sb up, *Am* to hit on sb

grisbi [grisbi] *nm* cash, dough, *Br* dosh, *Am* bucks

griveton [grivtɔ̃] *nm* private *(soldier)* □, *Br* squaddie, *Am* grunt

groggy [grɔgi] *adj inv (épuisé, sous l'effet de l'alcool)* out of it; *(étourdi)* dazed

grognasse [grɔɲas] *nf Pej (fille)* tart, *Br* slapper; *(copine)* girlfriend □, *(main)* squeeze, *Br* bird

grolle [grɔl] *nf* shoe □

gros-cul [groky] *nm (camion) Br* juggernaut, *Am* semi, eighteen-wheeler

grouiller [gruje] **se grouiller** *vpr* to get a move on, *Br* to shake a leg, *Am* to get it in gear

grue [gry] *nf* **(a)** *(fille facile) Br* tart, slapper, *Am* hooker **(b) faire le pied de grue** to hang about *or* around

guenon [gənɔ̃] *nf (femme laide)* dog, *Br* boot, *Am* beast

guêtres [gɛtr] *nfpl* **traîner ses guêtres quelque part** to wander about *or* around □

gueulante [gœlɑ̃t] *nf* **pousser une gueulante** to kick up a stink, to hit the *Br* roof *or Am* ceiling

gueulard, -e [gœlar, -ard] *nm,f* **(a)** *(personne qui parle fort)* **quel gueulard!** he's got a voice like a foghorn! **(b)** *(protestataire)* grouch, whinger

gueule [!] [gœl] *nf* **(a)** *(bouche)* mouth □, *Br* gob; **emporter** *ou* **arracher la gueule** to take the roof of one's mouth off; **puer de la gueule** to have rotten breath; **une grande gueule** a loudmouth; **être fort en gueule** to be a loudmouth, to have too much to say for oneself; **ta gueule!** shut your mouth *or* face!, shut it!; **pousser un coup de gueule** to kick up a stink, to hit the roof **(b)** *(visage)* face □, mug; **avoir une sale gueule** *(personne) (avoir l'air antipathique)* to look shady *or Br* dodgy; *(avoir l'air malade)* to look under the weather *or Br* off-colour *or Am* off-color; *(plat, aliment)* to look horrible; **il s'est fait arrêter pour délit de sale gueule** he got arrested just because they didn't like the look of him; **prendre un coup dans la gueule** *ou* **sur le coin de la gueule** to get hit in the face □; **il s'est pris le ballon en pleine gueule** the ball hit him right in the face □; **en mettre plein la gueule à qn** *(critiquer)* to give sb a mouthful; *(frapper)* to smash sb's face in; **en prendre plein la gueule (pour pas un rond)** *(se faire critiquer)* to get a real mouthful; *(se faire frapper)* to get one's face smashed in; **ça va me retomber sur la gueule** it's all going to come back on me, I'm going to get the blame for it all □; **se foutre sur la gueule** to go for each other; **foutre sur la gueule à qn** to sock sb in the face; **faire** *ou* **tirer la gueule** to be in a *or* the huff; **faire une gueule d'enterrement** to have a face like a wet weekend; **il en fait une gueule, qu'est-ce qu'il a?** he looks really down, what's wrong with him?; **faire la gueule à qn** to be in the huff with sb; **cracher à la gueule de qn** to spit in sb's face; **gueule de bois** hangover □; **avoir la gueule de bois** to have a hangover □, to be hungover □; **avoir de la gueule** (avoir du style) to have something; **cette bagnole a de la gueule** that's some car, that car's quite something, Br that's a car and a half; **gueule de con** Br arsehole, Am asshole; **gueule de raie** fishface

(**c**) (individu) **ma/ta/**etc **gueule** me/you/etc □; **se fiche** ou **se foutre** ! **de la gueule de qn** to make a fool of sb, Br to take the piss out of sb; **du coq au vin! elle s'est pas foutue de notre gueule!** ! coq au vin! she didn't make a fool of us or Br take the piss out of us; **c'est pour ma gueule** it's for me

▸ see also **arracher, bourrer, casser, crever, défoncer, éclater, enfarinée, fendre, fermer, flanquer, foutre, ouvrir, péter, soûler**

gueuler [gœle] vi (**a**) (crier) to yell (one's head off) (**b**) (protester) to kick up a fuss or stink

gueuleton [gœltɔ̃] nm blowout, feast, feed

gugus [gygys] = **gus**

guibolle [gibɔl] nf leg □, pin; **j'en ai plein les guibolles** my legs are killing me

guignard, -e [giɲar, -ard] nm,f unlucky person □, Am schmo

guigne [giɲ] nf rotten luck □; **avoir la guigne** to have a run of bad luck □

guignol [giɲɔl] nm (personne ridicule) clown, joker; **faire le guignol** to play the fool, to clown around

guimbarde [gɛ̃bard] nf (voiture) heap, rustbucket, Br banger

guincher [gɛ̃ʃe] vi to dance □, to bop

gus, gusse [gys] nm guy, Br bloke

H

H [aʃ] nm (haschisch) hash, Br blow

haine [ɛn] nf **avoir la haine** to be full of rage □

> This expression was brought to a wider audience by the 1995 film *La Haine* by Mathieu Kassovitz. Describing the lives of three teenagers of different backgrounds living in a deprived Paris suburb, it used a lot of slang vocabulary, and in particular **verlan** (see entry). See also the panel **l'argot des banlieues** (p. 133).

hallu [aly] nf (abbr **hallucination**) hallucination □; **je dois avoir des hallus!** I must be seeing things!

halluciner [alysine] vi **c'est pas vrai, j'hallucine!** I must be seeing things!

hardeux, -euse [ardø, -øz] nm,f (homme) rocker; (femme) rock chick

haricot [ariko] nm **courir sur le haricot à qn** Br to get on sb's wick or up sb's nose, Am to tick sb off; **c'est la fin des haricots** I've/we've/etc had it now; **des haricots!** not a chance!; **travailler pour des haricots** to work for peanuts

harponner [arpɔne] vt (retenir) to corner, to waylay

hasch [aʃ] nm (abbr **haschisch**) hash

haute [ot] nf **la haute** high society, Br the upper crust

hebdo [ɛbdo] nm (abbr **hebdomadaire**) weekly (magazine) □

herbe [ɛrb] nf (marijuana) grass, weed

héro [ero] nf (abbr **héroïne**) smack, scag, skag

hétéro [etero] adj & nmf (abbr **hétéro-**

sexuel, -elle) straight, hetero

hic [ik] nm **il y a un hic** there's a snag

histoire [istwar] nf **(a) qu'est-ce que c'est que cette histoire?** what the hell is going on? **(b) faire qch histoire de rigoler** to do sth just for a laugh; **je l'ai fait histoire de me changer les idées** I did it just to take my mind off things

homo [omo] (abbr **homosexuel, -elle**)
  1 adj gay □
  2 nmf gay □, homo

honte [ɔ̃t] nf **avoir la honte**, **se taper la honte** to be embarrassed □ or mortified; **(c'est) la honte!** the shame of it!

horreur [ɔrœr] nf **c'est l'horreur** it's the pits, it sucks, Am it bites

hosto [ɔsto] nm (abbr **hôpital**) hospital □

hotte [ɔt] nf **en avoir plein la hotte** to be bushed or Br knackered or Am beat

HP [aʃpe] nm (abbr **hôpital psychiatrique**) psychiatric hospital □

HS [aʃɛs] adj (abbr **hors service**) **(a)** (objet) bust, Br knackered **(b)** (personne) bushed, Br knackered, shattered, Am beat

hublots [yblo] nmpl specs

huile [ɥil] nf (personnage important) big shot, big cheese, big enchilada
  ▶ see also **pomme**

hyper [ipɛr] adv mega, Br dead, Am real, mondo; **on s'est hyper bien amusés** we had a blast, we had a great or wicked or Am awesome time

hypra [ipra] adv mega, Br dead, Am real, mondo

I

iech ⚠, **ièche** ⚠ [jɛʃ] vi (verlan **chier**) **faire iech qn** Br to piss sb off, to get on sb's tits, Am to break sb's balls; **se faire iech** to be bored shitless

illico [iliko] adv pronto

imbibé, -e [ɛ̃bibe] adj (ivre) tanked up, Br sozzled, legless

imbitable [ɛ̃bitabl] adj incomprehensible □; **il est imbitable son article** I can't make head or tail of his article

imbuvable [ɛ̃byvabl] adj (insupportable) unbearable □; **je le trouve imbu-**

Insultes

Abuse is perhaps the purest form of slang, and is certainly the most direct, as it is always meant to be rude. Some of the more typical patterns found in French insults are given below:

The simplest insult of all is a noun used as an exclamation (see the noun column below). This can itself be reinforced by a slang adjective (see column below). The table below shows this pattern with some of the most common words. Although some "mixing and matching" is possible, note that some combinations work better than others.

ADJECTIVE	NOUN	TAG
pauvre	andouille	de merde
sale	idiot(e)	
espèce de (sale)	con (conne) ⚠	
	connard (connasse) ⚠	
	salaud (salope) ⚠	
	enfoiré(e) ⚠⚠	
	pouffiasse ⚠⚠	
	enculé ⚠⚠	

Speakers of banlieue-type slang (see entry **l'argot des banlieues** on p.133) often use tags such as "de ta race" or "de ta mère" (eg: espèce d'enculé de ta mère *ou* de ta race!).

Many more colourful insults using a verbal construction begin with "va", eg

> va voir ailleurs si j'y suis!
> va te faire cuire un œuf!
> va te faire voir (chez les Grecs)! ⚠
> va te faire mettre! ⚠⚠
> va te faire foutre! ⚠⚠
> va te faire enculer! ⚠⚠

All of the above imperatives with the structure "va te faire" can be modified into "tu peux aller te faire... !"

vable, ce mec I can't stand (the sight of) that guy, I can't stomach or Br stick that guy

impasse [ɛ̃pas] nf (sujet non étudié) **faire une impasse** = to miss out part of a subject when revising

impayable [ɛ̃pɛjabl] adj (amusant) priceless

impec [ɛ̃pɛk] **1** adj (abbr **impeccable**) (très propre) spotless; (parfait) perfect □ **2** adv (abbr **impeccablement**) perfectly □; **tout s'est passé impec** everything went off like a dream; **ils nous ont reçus impec** they made us incredibly welcome; **c'est du travail de pro, il a fait ça impec** it's a really professional job, his work was faultless

in [in] adj inv in, trendy, hip

incendier [ɛ̃sɑ̃dje] vt **incendier qn** (le réprimander) to give sb hell, to haul sb over the coals

incruste [ɛ̃kryst] nf **si on l'invite, il va encore taper l'incruste** if we invite him, we'll never get rid of him; **il a tapé l'incruste à ma boum** he gatecrashed my party

incruster [ɛ̃kryste] **s'incruster** vpr **j'espère qu'il va pas s'incruster** I hope he doesn't stay all night or overstay his welcome □; **il s'est incrusté à ma boum** he gatecrashed my party

indic [ɛ̃dik] nm (abbr **indicateur**) squealer, Br grass, Am rat

infichu, -e [ɛ̃fiʃy] adj **être infichu de faire qch** to be incapable of doing sth □

info [ɛ̃fo] nf (abbr **information**) **(a) une info** a piece of info **(b) les infos** (les nouvelles) the news □

infoutu, -e [ɛ̃futy] adj **être infoutu de faire qch** to be incapable of doing sth □

inquiéter [ɛ̃kjete] **s'inquiéter** vpr **t'inquiète!** don't worry! □, take it easy!

instit [ɛ̃stit] nmf (abbr **instituteur, -trice**) (primary school) teacher □

intello [ɛ̃telo] (abbr **intellectuel, -elle**) **1** adj intellectual □, highbrow □ **2** nmf egghead

interpeller [ɛ̃tɛrpəle] vt **ça m'interpelle (quelque part)** I can relate to that

interro [ɛ̃tero] nf (abbr **interrogation**) test □ (at school)

intox [ɛ̃tɔks] nf (abbr **intoxication**) **de l'intox** brainwashing □

invite [ɛ̃vit] nf (abbr **invitation**) invite

iroquoise [irɔkwaz] nf (coupe de cheveux) mohican

J

jacasser [ʒakase] *vi* to chatter, to yap, *Br* to witter (on), to natter

Jacques [ʒak] *npr* **faire le Jacques** to play the fool, to clown around, *Am* to spaz out

jacter [ʒakte] *vi* to chatter, to yap, *Br* to witter (on), to natter

jaja [ʒaʒa] *nm* wine □, vino

jambe [ʒɑ̃b] *nf* (**a**) **tenir la jambe à qn** to drone on and on at sb (**b**) **faire une partie de jambes en l'air** *Br* to have a bonk, *Am* to get down (**c**) **ça me fait une belle jambe!** a fat lot of good that does me! (**d**) **en avoir plein les jambes** to be *Br* knackered *or* shattered *or* *Am* beat *or* pooped

jambonneau, -x [ʒɑ̃bɔno] *nm (cuisse)* thigh □

jap [ʒap] *Offensive* **1** *adj (abbr* **japonais, -e)** Jap
  2 *nmf* **Jap** *(abbr* **Japonais, -e)** Jap, Nip

jaquette [ʒakɛt] *nf Offensive* **la jaquette flottante** [!] *(les homosexuels)* *Br* poofs, *Am* fags; **être** *ou* **refiler de la jaquette (flottante)** [!] to be a *Br* poof *or Am* fag

jaspiner [ʒaspine] *vi* to chat, to yak, *Br* to natter

jaune [ʒon] *nm* (**a**) *(apéritif anisé)* pas-

tis □ (**b**) *(ouvrier non gréviste)* strike-breaker □, scab, *Br* blackleg

java [ʒava] *nf (fête)* party □, bash, do; **faire la java** to party

jean-foutre [!] [ʒɑ̃futr] *nm inv* loser, no-hoper, *Br* waster

je-m'en-foutisme [ʒmɑ̃futism] *nm* couldn't care less attitude

jeté, -e [ʒte] *adj (fou)* crazy, off one's rocker, *Br* barking (mad), *Am* loony-tunes

jeter [ʒ(ə)te] **1** *vt* (**a**) *(abandonner) (personne)* to chuck, to dump (**b**) *(chasser)* to throw *or* chuck out, *Am* to eighty-six; **se faire jeter** to get thrown *or* chucked out, *Am* to get eighty-sixed (**c**) **jeter du jus, en jeter** to be quite *or* really something, to be something else (**d**) **n'en jetez plus (la cour est pleine)!** give it a rest!, pack it in!
  2 **se jeter** *vpr* **s'en jeter un *(derrière la cravate)*** to have a drink □

jeton [ʒtɔ̃] *nm* (**a**) **être un faux jeton** to be two-faced (**b**) **avoir les jetons** to be scared □, to be spooked, *Br* to have the wind up; **foutre les jetons à qn** to give sb a fright □, to spook sb, *Br* to put the wind up sb

jeune [ʒœn] *adj (insuffisant)* **ça fait un**

Javanais

More a source of amusement for French schoolchildren than a true form of slang, "javanais" is formed by inserting the syllable "-av-", "-va-" or "-ag-" immediately after each consonant or group of consonants. "Chatte", for example, becomes "chagatte" and "pute" becomes "pavute". It is probably so called because the word "javanais" contains the syllable "av" and suggests an exotic, secret language.

peu jeune it's cutting it a bit fine, it's pushing it a bit

jeunot [ʒœno] *nm* lad, youngster

job [dʒɔb] *nm* job ⃞

jobard, -e [ʒɔbar, -ard] **1** *adj* gullible ⃞ **2** *nm,f* sucker, *Br* mug, *Am* schnook

joint [ʒwɛ̃] *nm* joint, spliff

jojo [ʒoʒo] **1** *adj inv* (*beau, correct*) **pas jojo** not very nice ⃞; **il est pas jojo son petit ami** her boyfriend's no oil painting; **c'est pas jojo ce qu'il a fait là** that wasn't a very nice thing for him to do **2** *nm* **un affreux jojo** a little horror *or* monster, a holy terror

jouasse [ʒwas] *adj* pleased ⃞, *Br* chuffed; **qu'est-ce que t'as, t'es pas jouasse?** got a problem?; **il avait pas l'air jouasse** he didn't look too pleased *or Br* chuffed

jouer [ʒwe] **1** *vt* **où t'as vu jouer ça?** are you mad?, have you got a screw loose?, are you off your rocker? **2 se jouer** *vpr* **se la jouer** to show off, to pose ▸ *see also* **caïd, touche-pipi, tripes**

joufflu [ʒufly] *nm Hum* (*postérieur*) butt, *Br* bum, *Am* fanny

jouir [ʒwir] *vi Ironic* (*souffrir*) to go through hell

jouissif, -ive [ʒwisif, -iv] *adj* (**a**) (*qui procure un grand plaisir*) orgasmic (**b**) *Ironic* (*douloureux*) *Br* bloody *or Am* goddamn painful; **s'écraser le petit orteil, c'est jouissif!** stubbing your little toe is a real barrel of laughs!

journaleux, -euse [ʒurnalø, -øz] *nm,f Pej* hack

joyeuses [ʒwajøz] *nfpl* (*testicules*) balls, nuts, *Br* bollocks

JT [ʒite] *nm* (*abbr* **journal télévisé**) TV news ⃞

juif, -ive [ʒɥif, -iv] *nm,f* (**a**) (*avare*) tightwad, skinflint (**b**) **le petit juif** the funny bone

This term as used in category (a), although not overtly racist, is nonetheless very politically incorrect and should be used with extreme caution.

Jules [ʒyl] *npr* boyfriend ⃞, man, (main) squeeze

Julie [ʒyli] *npr* girlfriend ⃞, (main) squeeze, *Br* bird

jus [ʒy] *nm* (**a**) (*eau*) **tomber au jus** to fall in (**b**) (*café*) coffee ⃞, *Am* java; **jus de chique** *ou* **de chaussette** dishwater (**c**) (*courant électrique*) juice; **prendre le jus** to get a shock; **être au jus** to know ⃞ ▸ *see also* **jeter**

jusque-là [ʒyskəla] *adv* (**a**) **s'en mettre jusque-là** to stuff oneself *or* one's face, to pig out, *Am* to munch out (**b**) **en avoir jusque-là** (**de**) to have had it up to here (with)

juter ‼ [ʒyte] *vi* (*éjaculer*) to come, to shoot one's load, to spurt

juteux¹ [ʒytø] *nm* (*adjudant*) *Br* ≃ warrant officer class II ⃞, *Am* ≃ warrant officer (junior grade) ⃞

juteux², -euse [ʒytø, -øz] *adj* (*fructueux*) lucrative ⃞; **une affaire juteuse** a goldmine, *Br* a nice little earner

kawa [kawa] *nm* coffee □, *Am* java

kebla [kəbla] *nmf* (*verlan* **black**) Black

kéblo [keblo] *adj* (*verlan* **bloqué**) hung-up, full of hang-ups

kébra [kebra] *vi* (*verlan* **braquer**) (*banque, bijouterie*) to hold up; **kébra qch à qn** to pinch *or Br* nick sth from sb

ken ! [kɛn] *vt* (*verlan* **niquer**) (**a**) (*posséder sexuellement*) to screw, to shaft, *Br* to have it off with, *Am* to slam (**b**) (*endommager*) to bust, *Br* to knacker, to bugger (**c**) (*duper*) to rip off, *Am* to rook (**d**) (*attraper*) to nab, to collar; **se faire ken** to get nabbed *or* collared

késako [kezako] = **quès aco**

keuf [kœf] *nm* (*verlan* **flic**) cop, *Am* flat-foot

keum [kœm] *nm* (*verlan* **mec**) guy, *Br* bloke

keupon [køpɔ̃] *nm* (*verlan* **punk**) punk

keusse [køs] *nm* (*verlan* **sac**) ten francs □

kif [kif] *nm* kif, kef

kiffer [kife] *vt* to like □

kif-kif [kifkif] *adv* **c'est kif-kif** it's six of one and half a dozen of the other, it's six and two threes

kiki [kiki] *nm* (**a**) (*cou*) neck □; (*gorge*) throat □; **serrer le kiki à qn** to wring sb's neck □ (**b**) (*type d'homosexuel*) = homosexual man who habitually wears jeans, a bomber jacket and baseball boots, and whose hair is either shaved or worn with a Tintin-style quiff (**c**) **c'est parti mon kiki** here we go!

kil [kil] *nm* **un kil de rouge** a bottle of red wine □

klébard [klebar], **klebs** [klɛps] *nm* mutt

kopeck [kɔpɛk] *nm* **pas un kopeck** not a bean *or Am* a cent; **il me reste plus un kopeck** I haven't a bean *or Am* a cent

kro [kro] *nf* Kronenbourg® beer □

kroumir [krumir] *nm* **(vieux) kroumir** old fogey, *Am* geezer

L

là [la] *adv* **il est un peu là, il se pose là** *(il est remarquable)* he makes his presence felt; **elle se pose là comme cuisinière** she's a mean cook, she's some cook; *Ironic* she's a mean cook...not!, she's a mean cook, I don't think!; **comme emmerdeur/menteur, il se pose là!** he's a total pain/liar!

labo [labo] *nm (abbr **laboratoire**)* lab

lâcher [laʃe] **1** *vt* (**a**) *(laisser tranquille)* **lâche-moi!** leave me alone!, get off my back *or* case!
(**b**) *(abandonner) (emploi)* to quit, *Br* to chuck *or* pack in; *(famille, associé)* to walk out on; *(amant)* to chuck, to dump
(**c**) **les lâcher** *(payer)* to cough up, to fork out; **il les lâche pas facilement** he's a real tightwad, he's really tight-fisted
(**d**) **en lâcher une** ⚠ to fart, *Br* to let off, *Am* to lay one
2 ⚠ *vi (émettre des gaz intestinaux)* to fart, *Br* to let off, *Am* to lay one
▶ see *also* **basket, caisse, fusée, grappe, louise, morceau, perle, perlouse, rampe**

lambin, -e [lɑ̃bɛ̃, -in] *nm,f Br* slowcoach, *Am* slowpoke

lambiner [lɑ̃bine] *vi* to dawdle

lampe [lɑ̃p] *nf* **s'en mettre** *ou* **s'en foutre** ⚠ **plein la lampe** to stuff oneself *or* one's face, to pig out

lance-pierres [lɑ̃spjɛr] *nm inv* **manger avec un lance-pierres** to wolf one's food down; **payer qn avec un lance-pierres** to pay sb peanuts *or Am* chump change

lancequiner ⚠ [lɑ̃skine] *vi* (**a**) *(pleuvoir)* **il lancequine** it's pissing down (**b**) *(uriner)* to pee, to piss, *Br* to have a slash

lapin [lapɛ̃] *nm* (**a**) **poser un lapin à qn** to stand sb up (**b**) **baiser comme des lapins** ⚠⚠ to fuck like rabbits
▶ see *also* **cage, chaud, pet¹, tirer**

lard [lar] *nm* **un gros lard** a big fat slob; **rentrer dans le lard à qn** to lay into sb, to set about sb, to go for sb; **faire du lard** to sit around and get fat

lardon [lardɔ̃] *nm (enfant)* kid

lardu [lardy] *nm* cop, *Am* flatfoot

larfeuil, larfeuille [larfœj] *nm Br* wallet ▫, *Am* billfold ▫

largeur [larʒœr] *nf* **dans les grandes largeurs** totally ▫, big time, in a big way; **ils se sont fait entubés dans les grandes largeurs** they got totally ripped off, they got ripped off big time *or* in a big way

---

Largonji

"Largonji" is a type of slang formed by replacing the initial consonant of a word with the letter "l" and moving the original consonant to the end of the word, where it is followed by a vowel to aid pronunciation. "À poil" thus becomes "à loilpé"; "en douce" becomes "en loucedé". The word "largonji" is itself the result of this procedure applied to the word "jargon".

largué, -e [large] adj **être largué** to be lost, not to have a clue

larguer [large] **1** vt (abandonner) (emploi) to quit, Br to chuck or pack in; (famille, associé) to walk out on; (amant) to chuck, to dump
  2 ! vi (émettre des gaz intestinaux) to fart, Br to let off, Am to lay one
  ▸ see also **caisse**

larmichette [larmiʃɛt] nf tiny drop

larve [larv] nf (personne faible) wimp, drip

latino [latino] (abbr **latino-américain, -e**) adj & nmf Latino

latte [lat] nf (chaussure) **un coup de latte** a kick □, a boot; **il m'a filé un coup de latte** he gave me a kick or a boot, he kicked or booted me; **ils lui ont défoncé la gueule à coups de lattes** they kicked or booted his head in

latter [late] vt to kick □, to boot, Br to put the boot into

lavasse [lavas] nf **de la lavasse** (café, bière) dishwater

lavette [lavɛt] nf (personne) wimp, drip

lèche [lɛʃ] nf **faire de la lèche** to be a bootlicker; **faire de la lèche à qn** to lick sb's boots

lèche-bottes [lɛʃbɔt] nmf inv bootlicker

lèche-cul !! [lɛʃky] nmf inv brownnose, Br arse-licker, Am ass-licker

lécheur, -euse [leʃœr, -øz] nm,f bootlicker

légitime [leʒitim] nf **ma légitime** my old lady, Br the missus, her indoors

lerche [lɛrʃ] adv **il y en a pas lerche** there isn't much/aren't many

lerga [lɛrga] nf (verlan **galère**) pain, hassle

lessivé, -e [lesive] adj (épuisé) washed out, wiped

lever [ləve] vt (a) (séduire) to pick up, Br to pull, to get off with (b) **lever le pied** (ralentir) to slow down □ (c) **lever le coude** (boire) to bend one's elbow

levrette [ləvrɛt] **en levrette** adv doggy-fashion

lézard [lezar] nm (difficulté) **il y a pas de lézards** no problem, no sweat, Br no probs

lézarder [lezarde] vi to soak up the sun, to catch some rays

ligne [liɲ] nf (a) (dose de cocaïne) line; **se faire une ligne** to do a line (b) **sur toute la ligne** from beginning to end

limace [limas] nf (chemise) shirt □

limer !! [lime] vt (posséder sexuellement) to hump, to screw, Br to shaft

limite [limit] adj inv **je me suis pas mis en colère, mais c'était limite** I didn't lose my temper, but it was a close thing; **question propreté, c'était limite** it certainly wasn't the cleanest place in the world; **ses blagues sont un peu limite** his jokes are a bit close to the bone

linge [lɛ̃ʒ] nm **du beau linge** high society, Br the upper crust

liquette [likɛt] nf shirt □; **mouiller sa liquette** to work up a sweat

liquider [likide] vt (a) (tuer) to bump off, to liquidate, to ice (b) (nourriture) to scoff, to guzzle; (boisson) to sink, to down, Am to inhale

litron [litrɔ̃] nm bottle of red wine □

locdu [lɔkdy] = **loquedu**

loilpé [lwalpe] **à loilpé** adv stark naked, in the buff, Br starkers

lolo [lolo] nm (a) (sein) boob (b) (lait) milk □

longe [lɔ̃ʒ] nf (année) year □

> This term is never used when referring to people's ages.

longuet, -ette [lɔ̃gɛ, -ɛt] adj longish, on the long side

look [luk] nm look, image; **avoir un look d'enfer** to look great or wicked or Br fab

looké, -e [luke] adj **être looké** punk/

grunge to have a punky/grungy look *or* image

lope [lɔp], **lopette** [lɔpɛt] *nf* (**a**) *Injurieux (homosexuel)* Br poof, poofter, Am fag, faggot (**b**) *(lâche)* wimp, Br big girl's blouse

loquedu [lɔkdy] *nm* (**a**) *(bon à rien)* good-for-nothing, loser, no-hoper, Br waster (**b**) *(individu méprisable)* scumbag, Br swine, Am stinker

loser [luzœr] *nm* loser

lot [lo] *nm (femme)* **un joli (petit) lot** a babe, a knockout, Br a smasher, a bit of all right

loub [lub] *nm (abbr* **loubard**) hood, hooligan, Br yob

loubard [lubar] *nm* hoodlum, hooligan, Br yob

loucedé [lusde] **en loucedé** *adv* on the quiet *or* sly

louche [luʃ] *nf (main)* hand ⁿ, mitt, paw; **serrer la louche à qn** to shake hands with sb ⁿ

loucher [luʃe] *vi* **loucher sur qch** to eye sth up, to have one's eye on sth

louf [luf], **loufedingue** [lufdɛ̃g] *adj* crazy, Br barking (mad), off one's head, Am loony-tunes

loufer [!] **louffer** [!] [lufe] *vi* to fart, Br to let off, Am to lay one

loufiat [lufja] *nm* waiter ⁿ *(in a café)*

louise [lwiz] *nf* fart; **lâcher une louise** to fart, Br to let off, Am to lay one

loulou, -oute [lulu, -ut] *nm,f* (**a**) *(personne)* hoodlum, hooligan (**b**) *(appellation affectueuse)* **mon loulou, ma louloute** sweetheart, honey, babe

louper [lupe] **1** *vt (examen)* to fail ⁿ, Am to flunk; *(train, cible)* to miss ⁿ

2 *vi* **j'étais sûr qu'il pleuverait, et ça n'a pas loupé!** I was sure that it would rain, and sure enough it did!

3 se louper *vpr* (**a**) *(échouer dans une tentative de suicide)* to bungle one's suicide attempt ⁿ; **il s'est coupé les**

cheveux tout seul et il s'est pas loupé! he cut his own hair and made some job of it!; **je me suis blessé avec l'ouvre-boîte – dis-donc, tu t'es pas loupé!** I've cut myself on the tin-opener – you certainly have!

(**b**) **vous vous êtes loupés de peu** you just missed each other ⁿ

▶ *see also* **une**

loupiot [lupjo] *nm* kid

loupiote [lupjɔt] *nf* lamp ⁿ, light ⁿ

lourd, -e [lur, lurd] **1** *adj (sans subtilité)* unsubtle ⁿ, in your face, Br OTT

2 *adv* **il en fiche pas lourd** he doesn't exactly overtax himself, he doesn't kill himself with overwork; **il en reste pas lourd** there's not that much/many left

lourde [lurd] *nf (porte)* door ⁿ

lourder [lurde] *vt* **lourder qn** to give sb the boot, to kick sb out

lourdingue [lurdɛ̃g] *adj* unsubtle ⁿ, in your face, Br OTT

loustic [lustik] *nm* (**a**) *(individu)* guy, Br bloke (**b**) *(farceur)* clown, joker; **c'est un sacré loustic** he's quite a character, he's a real case

loute [lut] *nf* chick, Br bird

LSD [!] [ɛlɛsde] *nf Hum (femme de petite taille)* shorty, squirt

This humorous but somewhat vulgar expression comes from a pun on LSD the drug and LSD, the initial letters of "elle (L) suce debout", meaning "she sucks standing up". The image is thus of a woman who is short enough to perform oral sex on a man while in a standing position.

luc [!] [lyk] *nm (verlan* **cul**) Br arse, Am ass

lune [lyn] *nf (derrière)* butt, Br bum, Am fanny; **se faire taper dans la lune** [!] to take it up the Br arse *or* Am ass, to get buggered

▶ *see also* **con**

luné, -e [lyne] *adj* **être bien/mal luné** to be in a good/bad mood ⁿ

M

maboul, -e [mabul] *adj* crazy, bananas, *Br* mental, *Am* wacko

mac [mak] *nm* (*abbr* **maquereau**) pimp, *Am* mack

macache [makaʃ] *exclam* **macache (bono)!** no way (José)!, no chance!, *Br* nothing doing!

macadam [makadam] *nm* **faire le macadam** to walk the streets, to be on the game, *Am* to hook

macaroni [makarɔni] *nm Offensive* (*Italien*) wop, Eyetie, *Am* guinea

Depending on the context and the tone of voice used, this term may be either offensive or affectionately humorous. It is nonetheless inadvisable to use it unless one is quite sure of the reaction it will receive.

macchabée [makabe] *nm* stiff (*corpse*)

machin, -e [maʃɛ̃, -in] **1** *nm* (*chose*) thing □, thingy (**b**) **espèce de vieux machin!** you old fool!
2 *npr* **Machin, Machine** (*personne*) thingy, what's-his-name, *f* what's-her-name

maganer [magane] *vt Can* (*personne*) to beat up; (*objet*) to damage □, to waste

magner [maɲe] **se magner** *vpr* **se magner (le train** *ou* **le popotin)** to get a move on, to get one's skates on, *Am* to get it in gear; **se magner le cul** !︎ to move or shift one's *Br* arse or *Am* ass

magnéto [maɲeto] *nm* (*abbr* **magnéto-phone**) tape recorder □, cassette player □

magot [mago] *nm* stash, hoard, pile

magouille [maguj] *nf* scheme; **ma-** gouilles électorales vote-rigging; **se livrer à des magouilles** to scheme, to do some wheeling and dealing

magouiller [maguje] *vi* to scheme, to do some wheeling and dealing

magouilleur, -euse [magujœr, -øz] *nm,f* schemer, wheeler-dealer

maigrichon, onne [megriʃɔ̃, -ɔn] *adj* skinny

maison [mezɔ̃] *adj inv* **une engueulade/une râclée maison** an almighty ticking-off/thrashing

mal [mal] *nm* **ça me ferait mal!, ça me ferait mal aux seins** !︎ it would kill me!; **ça te ferait mal de t'excuser?** it wouldn't hurt you to apologize!

malabar [malabar] *nm* hulk

malade [malad] **1** *adj* (*inconscient*) crazy, crackers, *Br* mental, *Am* gonzo
2 *nmf* (**a**) (*inconscient*) maniac, headcase, *Br* nutter, *Am* screwball; **il conduit comme un malade** he drives like a maniac; **bosser comme un malade** to work like crazy or like mad; **il a flippé comme un malade** he totally flipped or freaked out (**b**) (*fanatique*) nut, freak

malaise [malɛz] *nm* **il y a comme un malaise** there's a bit of a snag or a hitch

mal-baisée !!︎ [malbeze] *nf* **c'est une mal-baisée** she needs a good fuck

maldonne [maldɔn] *nf* **il y a maldonne** something's gone wrong somewhere

malle [mal] *nf* **se faire la malle** (*partir*) to beat it, *Br* to clear off, *Am* to book it; (*se détacher*) to fall off □

manche [mɑ̃ʃ] **1** *adj* (*maladroit*) hamfisted, *Br* cack-handed

2 nm (personne maladroite) Br cack-handed idiot, Am klutz, lug; (personne incapable) prat, Br pillock, Am lame
▸ see also **paire**

mandale [mɑ̃dal] nf clout, slap; **filer une mandale à qn** to clout or slap sb

manettes [manɛt] nfpl **à fond les manettes** at full speed, Br like the clappers, Am like sixty

manger [mɑ̃ʒe] **se manger** vpr **se manger qch** (percuter) to go head-first into sth

manif [manif] nf (abbr **manifestation**) demo

manip [manip] nf (abbr **manipulation**) process □

manitou [manitu] nm **un grand manitou** a big shot or cheese or enchilada

maous, -ousse [maus] adj ginormous, humongous, massive

maqué, -e [make] adj **être maqué** (homme) to have a woman; (femme) to have a man; **ils sont maqués** they're an item

maquer [make] **se maquer** vpr (se marier) to get hitched or spliced, to tie the knot; (s'établir en couple) to shack up together; **se maquer avec qn** (se marier avec) to get hitched or spliced to sb; (s'établir en couple avec) to shack up with sb

maquereau, -x [makro] nm (proxénète) pimp, Am mack

maquerelle [makʁɛl] nf **(mère) maquerelle** madam (in brothel)

marave[1] [maʁav] nf scuffle, Br punch-up, Am slugfest

marave[2]**, maraver** [maʁave] vt **(a)** (battre) **marave qn** to waste sb's face, Am to punch sb out **(b)** (tuer) to kill □, to waste, Am to snuff

marcel [maʁsɛl] nm Hum (maillot de corps sans manches) vest □

marcher [maʁʃe] vi **(a)** (croire naïvement quelque chose) to fall for it, to

swallow it; **faire marcher qn** to pull sb's leg, Br to wind sb up; **il a pas marché, il a couru** he fell for it or swallowed it hook, line and sinker **(b)** (accepter) **je marche** count me in; **je marche pas** count me out
▸ see also **radar**

margoulette [maʁɡulɛt] nf **casser la margoulette à qn** to smash sb's face in, to rearrange sb's features; **se casser la margoulette** to fall flat on one's face

margoulin [maʁɡulɛ̃] nm **(a)** (escroc) con man, crook, Am grifter **(b)** (incompétent) prat, Br pillock, Am lame

Marie-Chantal [maʁiʃɑ̃tal] npr inv Br ≃ Sloane (Ranger), Am ≃ preppy

Marie-couche-toi-là [maʁikuʃtwala] nf inv trollop, slut

marie-jeanne [maʁiʒan] nf inv (cannabis) Mary Jane, pot

mariole, mariolle [maʁjɔl] nmf clown, Am klutz; **faire le mariole** to act smart

marlou [maʁlu] nm (voyou) hoodlum, thug, hooligan; (proxénète) pimp, Am mack

marmaille [maʁmaj] nf brood, kids

marmot [maʁmo] nm kid

marner [maʁne] vi to slog, to sweat blood

maronner [maʁɔne] vi **(a)** (protester) to grumble, to grouch, to gripe **(b)** (attendre) to hang about or around

marrant, -e [maʁɑ̃, -ɑ̃t] **1** adj (amusant, bizarre) funny; **t'es pas marrant!** you're no fun! **2** nm,f **être un marrant** to be fun, to be a laugh or a riot; **son père, c'est pas un marrant** his dad's not much fun or not much of a laugh

marre [maʁ] adv **en avoir marre (de)** to be fed up (with) or hacked off (with) or sick and tired (of); **en avoir marre de faire qch** to be fed up with or hacked off with or sick and tired of doing sth; **c'est**

marre! that's enough!, that'll do!

marrer [mare] **se marrer** vpr to have a laugh; Ironic **alors là, je me marre!** that's a laugh!, don't make me laugh! **tu me fais marrer avec tes histoires de télépathie!** you make me laugh with all your stuff about telepathy!

marron [marɔ̃] **1** adj **(a)** (qui exerce clandestinement) unqualified ▫ **(b)** (dupé) **être marron** to have been taken in, to have been taken for a ride, Am to have been rooked; **faire qn marron** to take sb in, to take sb for a ride, Am to rook sb **2** nm (coup) belt, wallop; **coller un marron à qn** to belt or wallop sb one

marteau [marto] adj (fou) **être marteau** to be not all there, to have a screw or Br a slate loose

maso [mazo] (abbr **masochiste**) **1** adj masochistic ▫
2 nmf masochist ▫

masse [mas] nf **(a) être à la masse** to be off one's head, to be Br barking (mad) or Am wacko **(b) il y en a pas des masses** there isn't much/aren't many

mastard [mastar] nm hulk

mastoc [mastɔk] adj ginormous, humongous

mat' [mat] nm (abbr **matin**) **deux/trois heures du mat'** two/three a.m. or in the morning ▫

mater[1] [mate] vt to check out; (avec concupiscence) to eye up; **mate-moi ça!** check it out!, Br get a load of that!

mater[2] [matɛr], **maternelle** [maternɛl] nf old lady, Br old dear (mother)

mateur, -euse [matœr, -øz] nm,f **c'est un sacré mateur** he's always eyeing up women

maton, -onne [matɔ̃, -ɔn] nm,f screw (prison warder), Am hack, bull

matos [matos] nm stuff, gear

mauvaise [movɛz] adj **l'avoir mauvaise** to be hacked off or bummed

mauviette [movjɛt] nf wimp, Br big girl's blouse

max [maks] nm (abbr **maximum**) **un max de monde/de voitures** stacks or a ton of people/cars; **assurer un max** to do brilliantly; **sur scène ils assurent un max** they really kick ass on stage

maxi [maksi] adv (abbr **maximum**) **on sera vingt maxi** there'll be twenty of us max or tops; **ça prendra deux heures maxi** it'll take two hours max or tops

mec [mɛk] nm **(a)** (individu) guy, Br bloke; **salut les mecs!** hi, guys! **(b)** (compagnon) boyfriend ▫, man; **elle est venue sans son mec** she came without her man

meca [məka] nf (verlan came) drugs ▫, stuff, Br gear

méchamment [meʃamã] adv (très, beaucoup) really ▫, terribly, Am real

méchant, -e [meʃã, -ãt] adj (remarquable) amazing, terrific

mecton [mɛktɔ̃] nm guy, Br bloke

médoc [medɔk] nm medicine ▫

mégalo [megalo] (abbr **mégalomane**) **1** adj megalomaniac ▫, power-mad **2** nmf megalomaniac ▫, power maniac, control freak

mégoter [megote] vi to skimp (**sur** on); **arrête de mégoter, achète du vrai Champagne!** don't be stingy, buy real champagne!; **il a pas mégoté sur le piment** he didn't skimp on the chilli

meilleure [mejœr] nf **ça c'est la meilleure!** that just tops it all!

mélanger [melãʒe] **se mélanger** vpr Hum (avoir des rapports sexuels) to exchange bodily fluids

mêler [mele] **se mêler** vpr **de quoi je me mêle?** what's that got to do with you/him/etc?

mêle-tout [mɛltu] nmf inv busybody, Br nosey parker

mélo [melo] **1** adj (abbr **mélodramatique**) melodramatic ▫, over-the-top, Br OTT

2 *nm* (*abbr* **mélodrame**) melodrama □

melon [məlɔ̃] *nm Offensive* (*Maghrébin*) = racist term used to refer to a North African Arab

membré [mɑ̃bre] *adj* **être bien/mal membré** to be/not to be well-hung

mémère [memɛr] **1** *nf* (*femme d'un certain âge*) old biddy, *Br* old dear
2 *adj* frumpy, frumpish; **faire mémère** to look like an old woman
▶ *see also* **pousser**

méninges [menɛ̃ʒ] *nfpl* **se remuer les méninges** to rack *or Am* cudgel one's brains

menteuse [mɑ̃tøz] *nf* (*langue*) tongue □

merde [mɛrd] **1** *nf* (**a**) (*excrément*) shit, crap; **être dans la merde** to be in the shit, to be up shit creek (without a paddle); **traîner qn dans la merde** to drag sb's name through the mud; **ne pas se prendre pour de la merde** to think one's shit doesn't stink, *Br* to think the sun shines out of one's arse; **il a de la merde dans les yeux** he never sees a thing, he can't see what's going on right in front of him
(**b**) (*individu méprisable*) shit
(**c**) (*chose de mauvaise qualité*) **c'est une merde cet ordinateur** this computer's (a load of) shit; **de la merde** (a load of) shit; **c'est de la merde ce rasoir!** this razor's (a load of) shit!; **un boulot/un quartier de merde** a shit *or* shitty job/area; **tu vas l'éteindre, ta radio de merde, oui?** will you turn that *Br* bloody *or Am* goddamn radio off!
(**d**) (*désordre*) **semer** *ou* **foutre la merde** to create havoc; **c'est la merde dans le pays en ce moment** the country's a *Br* bloody *or Am* goddamn mess *or* shambles at the moment; **c'est la merde pour circuler dans Paris en ce moment** driving in Paris is a *Br* bloody *or Am* goddamn nightmare at the moment
(**e**) (*problème*) problem □; **et si il nous**

arrivait une merde? what if we ended up in the shit?; **il m'est arrivé une merde** something shit's happened
2 *exclam* (**a**) (*pour exprimer l'exaspération*) shit!; **dire merde à qn** to tell sb to piss off *or Br* bugger off; **alors, tu viens, oui ou merde?** are you coming or not, for Christ's sake?; **avoir un œil qui dit merde à l'autre** to have a squint □
(**b**) (*pour souhaiter bonne chance*) break a leg!
▶ *see also* **bordel, fouteur**

merder [mɛrde] **1** *vt* (*rater*) to screw up, *Br* to cock up, to balls up, *Am* to ball up
2 *vi* to screw up, *Br* to cock up

merdeux, -euse [mɛrdø, -øz] **1** *adj* (*coupable*) **se sentir merdeux** to feel shit *or* shitty
2 *nm,f* (**a**) (*personne méprisable*) shit (**b**) (*enfant*) kid

merdier [mɛrdje] *nm Br* bloody *or Am* goddamn mess *or* shambles

merdique [mɛrdik] *adj* shit, shitty

merdouille [mɛrduj] *nf* (**a**) (*situation déplaisante*) *Br* bloody *or Am* goddamn mess *or* shambles; **être dans la merdouille** to be in the shit (**b**) (*chose sans valeur*) **de la merdouille** (a load of) shit

merdouiller [mɛrduje], **merdoyer** [mɛrdwaje] *vi* to screw up, *Br* to cock up, to balls up, *Am* to ball up

mère [mɛr] *nf* **ta mère!** *Br* piss off!, *Am* take a hike!; **enculé de ta mère!** you fucking prick *or Br* arsehole *or* wanker *or Am* asshole!; **niquer sa mère à qn** to kick sb's fucking head in, *Am* to punch sb out; **flipper sa mère** to be scared stiff
▶ *see also* **maquerelle, niquer**

The word "mère", literally translated as "mother", appears in numerous slang expressions of the "banlieues" (see panel **l'argot des banlieues** on p.133) and functions as an intensifier. This usage almost indisputably has its origins in North African culture.

mérinos [merinos] *nm Hum* **laisser pisser le mérinos** to let things take their course ▫

merlan [mɛrlɑ̃] *nm* (**a**) *(coiffeur)* hairdresser ▫ (**b**) **regarder qn avec des yeux de merlan frit** *(sans comprendre)* to gaze blankly at sb, to gape at sb; *(amoureusement)* to make sheep's eyes at sb

métèque [metɛk] *nmf Offensive* = racist term used to refer to any dark-skinned foreigner living in France, especially one from the Mediterranean

métro [metro] *nm* (**a**) **il a toujours un métro de retard** he's always the last one to know what's going on (**b**) **métro, boulot, dodo** the daily grind, the nine-to-five routine

mettable ‼ [mɛtabl] *adj* fuckable, *Br* shaggable

mettre [mɛtr] **1** *vt* (**a**) ‼ *(posséder sexuellement)* to tuck, to screw, *Br* to shag; **va te faire mettre!** up yours!, fuck off!, go and fuck yourself!
(**b**) **les mettre, mettre les bouts** to make tracks, to hit the road, *Am* to book it
2 se mettre *vpr* (**a**) **son contrat, il peut se le mettre quelque part!** ‼ he can shove his contract up his *Br* arse or *Am* ass!
(**b**) **s'en mettre jusque-là** to stuff oneself or one's face, to pig out, *Am* to munch out; **qu'est-ce qu'on s'est mis!** we really stuffed ourselves or our faces!, we really pigged or *Am* munched out!
(**c**) **qu'est-ce qu'ils se sont mis!** *(dans une bagarre)* they really laid into each other!, they were going at it hammer and tongs!
▸ *see also* **coup, grappin, nez, paquet, veilleuse, vue**

meuf [mœf] *nf* (*verlan* **femme**) (**a**) *(fille)* chick, *Br* bird (**b**) *(compagne)* girlfriend ▫, woman, *Br* bird

meule [møl] *nf* (**a**) *(moto)* (motor)bike ▫ (**b**) **meules** *(postérieur)* butt, *Br* bum, *Am* fanny

mézigue [mezig] *pron* yours truly, *Br* muggins (here)

miches [miʃ] *nfpl* (**a**) *(postérieur)* butt, *Br* bum, *Am* buns, fanny (**b**) *(seins)* boobs, knockers

micheton [miʃtɔ̃] *nm Br* punter, *Am* john

mickey [mikɛ] *nm* nobody, non-entity

micmac [mikmak] *nm* muddle, shambles

millefeuille ‼ [milfœj] *nm (sexe de la femme)* muff, beaver, snatch

mimi [mimi] **1** *adj inv* cute ▫
2 *nm* (**a**) *(baiser)* kiss ▫ (**b**) *(chat)* pussy (cat) (**c**) ! *(sexe de la femme)* pussy, *Br* fanny

minable [minabl] **1** *adj* (**a**) *(mesquin, pauvre)* shabby, grotty (**b**) *(incompétent, insuffisant)* pathetic, lousy
2 *nmf* loser, no-hoper, dead loss

mince [mɛ̃s] *exclam (pour exprimer l'exaspération)* blast!, sugar!, *Am* shoot!; *(pour exprimer la surprise)* wow!, *Br* blimey!, strewth!, *Am* gee (whiz)!

minet, -ette [minɛ, -ɛt] **1** *nm* (**a**) *(chat)* pussy (cat) (**b**) ! *(sexe de la femme)* pussy, beaver, snatch
2 *nm,f (jeune personne à la mode)* trendy
3 ! *nf (sexe de la femme)* pussy, beaver, snatch; **faire minette (à qn)** to go down (on sb), to give (sb) head

minou [minu] *nm* (**a**) *(chat)* pussy (cat)
(**b**) ! *(sexe de la femme)* pussy, beaver, snatch

mioche [mjɔʃ] *nmf* kid

mirettes [mirɛt] *nfpl* eyes ▫

miro [miro] *adj* short-sighted ▫; **il est complètement miro** he's as blind as a bat

mitan [mitã] *nm* **le mitan** the underworld, gangland

mitard [mitar] *nm* disciplinary cell□, cooler; **se retrouver au mitard** to end up in solitary

miteux, -euse [mitø, -øz] *adj* shabby, grotty

mitraille [mitraj] *nf (petite monnaie)* small change□, *Br* coppers

mob [mɔb] *nf (abbr* **mobylette)** moped

moche [mɔʃ] *adj* **(a)** *(laid)* ugly□, hideous **(b)** *(moralement répréhensible)* rotten, lousy; **c'est moche ce qu'il a fait** that was a rotten *or* lousy thing he did **(c)** *(regrettable)* rotten; **c'est moche ce qui lui est arrivé** it was rotten *or* terrible what happened to him

mocheté [mɔʃte] *nf* **(a)** *(femme laide)* dog, hag, horror, *Br* boot, *Am* beast; *(homme laid)* horror **(b)** *(chose laide)* eyesore

moite-moite [mwatmwat] *adv* fifty-fifty, half-and-half

molard[!], **mollard**[!] [mɔlar] *nm* spit□, *Br* gob of spit

molarder[!], **mollarder**[!] [mɔlarde] *vi* to spit□, *Br* to gob

mollasson, -onne [mɔlasɔ̃, -ɔn] **1** *adj* slow□, sluggish□
2 *nm,f* lazy so-and-so

mollo [mɔlo] **1** *adv* **y aller mollo** to take it easy; **vas-y mollo avec la sauce** go easy on *or* take it easy with the sauce
2 *exclam* take it easy!

môme [mom] **1** *nmf (enfant)* kid
2 *nf* **(a)** *(fille)* chick, *Br* bird **(b)** *(compagne)* girlfriend□, *(main)* squeeze, *Br* bird

monaco [mɔnako] *nm* = cocktail consisting of beer, grenadine and lemonade

monnaie [mɔnɛ] *nf (argent)* cash, *Br* dosh, *Am* gelt, bucks

monstre [mɔ̃str] *adj* monstrous, ginormous, humongous

monté [mɔ̃te] *adj* **être bien monté** to be well-hung; **être monté comme un âne** *ou* **un bourricot** *ou* **un taureau**[!] to be hung like a horse *or Br* a donkey *or Am* a mule

montesquieu [mɔ̃tɛskjø] *nm (billet de deux cents francs)* two-hundred franc note□

The "montesquieu" is so called because a picture of the writer Charles Montesquieu features on the banknote.

morbac, morbaque [mɔrbak] *nm* **(a)**[!] *(pou du pubis)* crab **(b)** *(enfant)* kid

morceau, -x [mɔrso] *nm* **(a)** *(personne)* **un beau morceau** a babe, a knockout, *Br* a nice bit of stuff, a bit of all right; **un sacré morceau** a big bruiser
(b) casser *ou* **cracher** *ou* **lâcher** *ou* **manger le morceau** to spill the beans, to let the cat out of the bag
(c) casser le morceau à qn to give sb a piece of one's mind
(d) emporter *ou* **enlever le morceau** to get one's own way

mordicus [mɔrdikys] *adv* stubbornly□

mordu, -e [mɔrdy] **1** *adj (amoureux)* madly in love, completely smitten
2 *nm,f* fan, fanatic; **un mordu de football** a football fan *or* fanatic

morfale [mɔrfal] **1** *adj* greedy□
2 *nmf* pig, *Br* greedy-guts, gannet, *Am* hog

morfler [mɔrfle] **1** *vt* **(a)** *(recevoir)* to get; **il a morflé une claque dans la tronche** he got a slap in the face **(b)** *(se voir infliger une peine de)* to get, to cop
2 *vi* **(a)** *(être abîmé)* to get smashed up; *(être blessé)* to get injured□ **(b)** *(être sévèrement puni)* to catch it, *Br* to cop it

moricaud, -e [mɔriko, -od] **1** *adj* dark-skinned□, swarthy□
2 *nm,f* Offensive **(a)** *(personne de race noire)* nigger, *Br* wog **(b)** *(personne à la peau foncée)* dark-skinned *or* swarthy person□

morlingue [mɔrlɛ̃g] *nm (porte-monnaie) Br* purse□, *Am* change purse□; *(portefeuille) Br* wallet□, *Am* billfold□

mornifle [mɔrnifl] *nf* **(a)** *(argent)* bread, *Br* dosh, *Am* bucks, gelt **(b)** *(gifle)* slap, cuff

morpion [mɔrpjɔ̃] *nm* **(a)** *(pou du pubis)* crab **(b)** *(enfant)* kid

mort, -e [mɔr, mɔrt] **1** *adj* **(a)** *(hors d'usage)* **être mort** to be dead, to have had it, *Br* to be knackered **(b)** *(fatigué)* dead **(c)** **être mort de rire** to be killing oneself (laughing); **être mort de trouille** to be scared to death
2 **à mort** *adv* **freiner à mort** to slam on the brakes; **déconner à mort** [!] to talk complete crap *or* bull *or Br* bollocks; **bander à mort** [!!] to have a raging hard-on
▶ see also **rat**

mortel, -elle [mɔrtɛl] **1** *adj* **(a)** *(excellent)* wicked, *Br* fab, *Am* awesome, gnarly **(b)** *(très mauvais)* hellish, *Am* gnarly **(c)** *(ennuyeux)* deadly boring
2 *adv* **on s'est éclatés mortel!** we had a wicked *or Br* fab *or Am* awesome time!; **on s'est fait chier mortel** [!!] we were fucking bored to death
3 *exclam* wicked!, *Br* fab!, *Am* awesome!

mortibus [mɔrtibys] *adj* dead□

morue [!] [mɔry] *nf* **(a)** *(prostituée)* whore, hooker **(b)** *(femme)* tart, *Br* slapper

morveux, -euse [mɔrvø, -øz] **1** *adj* snotty-nosed
2 *nm,f* kid

motte [!!] [mɔt] *nf (sexe de la femme)* snatch, twat, pussy, *Br* minge; **s'astiquer la motte** to finger oneself, to play with oneself

motus [mɔtys] *exclam* **motus (et bouche cousue)!** not a word!, mum's the word!

mou [mu] **1** *adv (doucement)* **y aller mou** to go easy, to take it easy; **vas-y**

mou avec le piment go easy on *or* take it easy with the chilli
2 *nm* **(a)** **bourrer le mou à qn** to pull the wool over sb's eyes **(b)** **c'est du mou** *(c'est faux)* it's a load of garbage *or Br* rubbish **(c)** **rentrer dans le mou à qn** *(agresser qn)* to go for sb, to lay into sb, to set about sb
▶ see also **bourrage, chique**

mouchard, -e [muʃar, -ard] *nm,f* squealer, *Br* grass, *Am* rat; *(à l'école)* snitch, *Br* sneak, tell-tale, *Am* tattle-tale

moucharder [muʃarde] **1** *vt* to squeal on, *Br* to grass on, to shop, *Am* to rat on; *(à l'école)* to snitch on, *Br* to sneak on, to tell tales on
2 *vi* to squeal, *Br* to grass, *Am* to rat; *(à l'école)* to snitch, *Br* to sneak, to tell tales, *Am* to tattle

mouflet, -ette [muflɛ, -ɛt] *nm,f* kid

moufter [mufte] *vi* **ne pas moufter** to keep one's mouth shut, *Br* to keep schtum

mouille [!!] [muj] *nf (sécrétions vaginales)* lube, love juice; *(sexe de la femme)* pussy, twat, gash, *Br* minge

mouiller [muje] **1** *vt (compromettre)* to involve□, to drag in
2 *vi* **(a)** [!] *(avoir peur)* to wet oneself **(b)** [!!] *(être excitée sexuellement)* to be wet
3 **se mouiller** *vpr (se compromettre)* to stick one's neck out
▶ see also **liquette**

mouise [mwiz] *nf (misère)* poverty□; *(ennuis)* grief, hassle, *Br* aggro; **être dans la mouise** *(être dans la misère)* to be hard up *or* broke *or Br* skint; *(avoir des ennuis)* to be in a hole, *Am* to be behind the eightball

moule [!!] [mul] *nf (sexe de la femme)* pussy, snatch, twat, *Br* fanny, minge

moumoute [mumut] *nf* wig□, rug, *Br* syrup

mourir [murir] *vi* **plus débile/macho, tu meurs!** they don't come any more stupid/macho than that!

mouron [murɔ̃] *nm* **se faire du mouron** to worry oneself sick

mousse [mus] *nf* (**a**) *(bière)* beer □; **on se boit une mousse?** fancy a *Br* pint or *Am* brew? (**b**) **se faire de la mousse** to worry oneself sick

moutard [mutar] *nm* kid

muflée [myfle] *nf* **prendre une muflée** to get wrecked or wasted or *Br* legless or pissed; **il tenait une sacrée muflée** he was totally wrecked or wasted or *Br* legless or pissed

mule [myl] *nf (passeur de drogue)* mule

murge [myrʒ] *nf* **prendre une murge**

to get wrecked or wasted or *Br* legless or pissed; **il tenait une sacrée murge** he was totally wrecked or wasted or *Br* legless or pissed

muscu [mysky] *nf (abbr* **musculation**) body-building □; **faire de la muscu** to do body-building

musiciens [myzisjɛ̃] *nmpl (haricots)* beans □

musicos [myzikos] *nm* muso

must [mœst] *nm* must; **c'est un must** it's a must

mytho [mito] *nmf (abbr* **mythomane**) compulsive liar □

N

nager [naʒe] *vi (ne rien comprendre)* to be totally lost, not to have a clue

nana [nana] *nf (femme)* chick, *Br* bird; *(petite amie)* girlfriend □, (main) squeeze, *Br* bird

nanar [nanar] *nm* (**a**) *(marchandise sans valeur)* junk, trash, garbage (**b**) *(mauvais film)* lousy film, *Am* turkey

NAP [nap] *(abbr* **Neuilly-Auteuil-Passy**) **1** *adj Br* ≃ Sloany, *Am* ≃ preppy **2** *nmf Br* ≃ Sloane (Ranger), *Am* ≃ preppy

> Neuilly, Auteuil and Passy are areas in the west of Paris, and are among the wealthiest and most middle-class in the city, although strictly speaking Neuilly is not part of Paris, but in the adjoining département Hauts-de-Seine. A "NAP" is typically rich, expensively dressed, and politically to the right.

nase [naz] = **naze**

naseaux [nazo] *nmpl (narines)* nostrils □

navet [navɛ] *nm (mauvais film)* lousy film, *Am* turkey

naze [naz] *adj* (**a**) *(épuisé)* bushed, *Br* knackered, shattered, *Am* beat (**b**) *(hors d'usage)* kaput, bust, *Br* clapped-out (**c**) *(stupide)* thick, dense, *Am* dumb (**d**) *(de mauvaise qualité)* crap, crappy, lousy, *Am* rinky-dink

nèfles [nɛfl] *nfpl* **des nèfles!** no way!, no chance!

négatif [negatif] *exclam* no! □, nope!

negifran [nəʒifrɑ̃] *nf (verlan* **frangine**) chick, *Br* bird

négro [negro] *nm Offensive* Negro, nigger

neige [nɛʒ] *nf (cocaïne)* snow

nénés [nene] *nmpl* tits, knockers, jugs, *Am* hooters

nénette [nenɛt] *nf* (**a**) *(femme, fille)* chick, *Br* bird (**b**) *(tête)* **se casser la nénette (à faire qch)** to go to a lot of bother (to do sth); **te casse pas la nénette** don't worry about it, don't let it bother you

nerfs [nɛr] *nmpl* **avoir les nerfs** to be hacked off; **foutre les nerfs à qn** to hack sb off, to get sb's back up
▸ see also **paquet**

net, nette [nɛt] *adj* **pas net** *(louche)* shady, *Br* dodgy; *(ivre, drogué)* off one's face, wasted, wrecked; *(pas complètement sain d'esprit)* not all there, *Br* one sandwich short of a picnic

nettoyer [netwaje] *vt* (**a**) *(dépouiller)* to clean out, to take to the cleaners (**b**) *(tuer)* to bump off, *Am* to rub out, to off

neuneu [nønø] *adj* daft, *Am* dumb

nez [ne] *nm* (**a**) **avoir un coup dans le nez** to have had one too many (**b**) **elle m'a dans le nez** she can't stand or stomach or *Br* stick me, *Br* I get right up her nose (**c**) **mettre à qn le nez dans son caca** *ou* **dans sa merde** ‼ to call sb to order, to pull sb up
▸ see also **doigt, pendre, tirer**

niac [njak] *nmf Offensive* slant, *Am* gook

niacoué, -e [njakwe] *nm,f Offensive* slant, *Am* gook

niaiser [njɛze] *Can* **1** *vt* **niaiser qn** *(faire tourner en bourrique)* to drive sb crazy; *(se moquer de)* to laugh at sb, *Br* to wind sb up, *Am* to razz sb; *(raconter des* *histoires à)* to pull sb's leg, *Br* to wind sb up, to have sb on

2 *vi (ne rien faire)* to hang around doing nothing

niaiseux, -euse [njɛzø, -øz] *Can* **1** *adj* dense, *Am* dumb

2 *nm,f* moron, jerk, *Am* geek

nibard ⚠ [nibar] *nm* tit, knocker, jug

nichon [niʃɔ̃] *nm* boob, tit

nickel [nikɛl] **1** *adj (très propre)* spotless, gleaming

2 *adv* **faire qch nickel** to do sth really well □

nickelé [nikle] *adj* **avoir les pieds nickelés** *(être trop paresseux pour marcher)* to be too lazy to walk anywhere □; *(avoir de la chance)* to be lucky □ *or Br* jammy

niet [njɛt] *exclam* no way!, not a chance!

nipper [nipe] **se nipper** *vpr* to get dressed □; **il sait pas se nipper** he's got no dress sense

nippes [nip] *nfpl* clothes □, gear, *Br* threads

nique [nik] *nf* **faire la nique à qn** to thumb one's nose at sb

niquer ⚠⚠ [nike] **1** *vt* **(a)** *(posséder sexuellement)* to fuck, to screw, *Br* to shag, *Am* to ball; **va te faire niquer!, nique ta mère!** fuck off!, go and fuck yourself!

(b) *(endommager)* to bust, *Br* to knacker, to bugger; **il m'a niqué ma mob** he's bust *or Br* knackered *or* buggered my moped; **je vais lui niquer sa gueule!** I'm going to waste his fucking face!; **niquer sa mère à qn** to waste sb's face, *Br* to punch sb's lights out, *Am* to punch sb out

(c) *(attraper)* to nab, to collar; **il s'est fait niquer par les contrôleurs** he got nabbed *or* collared by the ticket collectors

(d) *(duper)* to shaft, to screw; **c'est un faux, tu t'es fait niquer!** it's a fake, you've been shafted *or* screwed!

2 *vi* to fuck, to screw, *Br* to shag, *Am* to ball

noce [nɔs] *nf* **(a)** **faire la noce** to live it up **(b)** **être à la noce** to have the time of one's life, to have a whale of a time; **on n'était pas à la noce** it was no picnic

nœud ⚠⚠ [nø] *nm (pénis)* cock, dick, prick; **à la mords-moi le nœud** lousy, crappy, *Br* poxy

▶ *see also* **tête**

nœud-pap [nøpap] *nm (abbr* **nœud papillon)** bow tie □

noiche [nwaʃ] *nmf (verlan* **chinois)** Chinese □

noir, -e [nwar] **1** *adj (ivre)* plastered, smashed, wasted

2 *nm* **un petit noir** a black coffee □

noircir [nwarsir] **se noircir** *vpr (s'enivrer)* to get plastered *or* smashed *or* wasted

noisettes ⚠ [nwazɛt] *nfpl (testicules)* balls, nuts, *Br* bollocks

noix [nwa] *nf* **à la noix (de coco)** lousy, *Br* poxy

nom [nɔ̃] **1** *nm* **nom à coucher dehors** mouthful; **il a un nom à coucher dehors** his name's a real mouthful; **petit nom** first name □

2 *exclam* **nom de nom!, nom d'un petit bonhomme!, nom d'une pipe!** for goodness' sake, *Br* blimey!, *Am* gee (whiz)!; **nom d'un chien!** hell!; **nom de Dieu!** for Christ's sake!, Christ (Almighty)!

nono, -ote [nono, nɔnɔt] *nm,f Can* jerk, *Br* pillock, plonker, *Am* schmuck

noraf [nɔraf], **nordaf** [nɔrdaf] *nm Offensive* = racist term used to refer to a North African Arab

nouba [nuba] *nf* party □; **faire la nouba** to party

nougats [nuga] *nmpl (pieds)* feet □, *Br* plates, *Am* dogs

nouille [nuj] *nf* **(a)** *(personne stupide)* dimwit, *Br* berk, divvy, *Am* meathead

(b) ⚠ *(pénis)* dick, tool, *Br* knob, *Am* schlong; **égoutter la nouille** to *Br* have or *Am* take a piss, *Br* to have a slash or a leak

nul, nulle [nyl] **1** *adj* crap, garbage, *Br* rubbish; *(personne)* useless, hopeless, clueless; **il est nul en anglais** he's crap or useless or hopeless at English; **c'est nul de pas l'avoir invité à ta boum** it was crap not to invite him to your party; **nul à chier** ⚠⚠ fucking awful
2 *nm,f* useless idiot, prat

nullard, -e [nylar, -ard] *nm,f* useless idiot, prat

nullité [nylite] *nf (personne)* useless idiot, prat

nullos [nylos] *nmf* **1** *adj* useless
2 *nmf* useless idiot, prat

numéro [nymero] *nm* **(a)** *(personne originale)* character, case; **quel numéro!** what a character or case!; **c'est un drôle de numéro!** he's a strange character!, *Br* he's a right one! **(b) avoir tiré le bon numéro** to have found Mr/Miss Right

nunuche [nynyʃ] *adj* daft, *Am* dumb

nympho [nɛ̃fo] *nf (abbr* **nymphomane**) nympho

o

occase [ɔkaz] *nf* (*abbr* **occasion**) chance□, opportunity□; **d'occase** second-hand□

occuper [ɔkype] **s'occuper** *vpr* **t'occupe!** mind your own business!, keep your nose out!, butt out!
► *see also* **oignon**

-oche [ɔʃ] *suffix* **baloche** local dance□; **cantoche** canteen□; **cinoche** *Br* pictures, *Am* movies; **fastoche** dead *or Am* real easy

This suffix is found at the end of many French slang nouns and adjectives and is used for either pejorative or humorous effect.

œil [œj] *nm* **mon œil!** my eye!, my foot!; **faire de l'œil à qn** to give sb the eye; **œil au beurre noir** black eye□, shiner; **à l'œil** free (of charge)□; **avoir qn à l'œil** to have one's eye on sb, to keep an eye on sb
► *see also* **battre, doigt, rincer, taper, tourner, yeux**

œuf [œf] *nm* (**a**) **va te faire cuire un œuf!** take a running jump, go and jump in the lake, *Am* take a hike! (**b**) *Hum* **œufs sur le plat** (*seins*) fried eggs
► *see also* **tête**

oigne ‼ [waɲ] *nm Br* arsehole, *Am* asshole; **l'avoir dans l'oigne** to have been shafted *or* screwed

oignon [ɔɲɔ̃] *nm* (**a**) ‼ (*anus*) *Br* arsehole, *Am* asshole; **l'avoir dans l'oignon** to have been shafted *or* screwed (**b**) **s'occuper de ses oignons** to mind one's own business; **c'est pas tes oignons!** it's none of your business! (**c**) **aux petits oignons** great, terrific
► *see also* **carrer**

oilpé [walpe] = **loilpé**

oinj [wɛ̃ʒ] *nm* (*verlan* **joint**) joint, spliff

oiseau, -x [wazo] *nm* **un drôle d'oiseau** an odd character, a funny old bird

ombre [ɔ̃br] *nf* (**a**) **être à l'ombre** (*en prison*) to be behind bars *or* inside; **mettre qn à l'ombre** to put sb behind bars *or* inside (**b**) **marche à l'ombre!** (*conseil*) keep a low profile!; (*menace*) stay out of my sight!

ordure [ɔrdyr] *nf* (*individu méprisable*) scumbag, *Br* rotter, *Am* stinker

orphelines ! [ɔrfəlin] *nfpl* (*testicules*) balls, nuts, *Br* bollocks

os [ɔs] *nm* (**a**) (*problème*) snag, hitch; **il y a un os** there's a snag *or* a hitch; **tomber sur un os** to hit a snag (**b**) **l'avoir dans l'os** ! to get screwed *or* shafted; **jusqu'à l'os** totally□, completely□
► *see also* **sac**

-os [ɔs] *suffix* **chicos** classy, smart; *Offensive* **portos** Dago (*from Portugal*); **nullos** useless idiot; **rapidos** pronto; **ringardos** uncool, unhip, square

This suffix is found at the end of many French nouns and adjectives and often indicates that the word is rather pejorative.

oseille [ozɛj] *nf* (*argent*) dough, *Br* dosh, *Am* bucks

ostrogoth [ostrogo] *nm* boor

ouais [wɛ] *exclam* yeah!

oublier [ublije] *vt* **oublie-moi!** get off my back *or* case!

ouf [uf] **1** *exclam* **il n'a pas eu le temps de dire ouf** he didn't even have time to catch his breath
2 *adj* (*verlan* **fou**) crazy, *Br* mental, barking, *Am* nutso

-ouille [uj] *suffix* **magouille** scheme; **merdouille** mess; *Pej* **pedzouille** yokel, peasant, *Am* hick

> This suffix is found at the end of many French nouns and adjectives and often indicates that the word is rather pejorative.

-ouse [uz] *suffix* **bagouse** ring □; **partouse** orgy; **perlouse** pearl □; **piquouse** shot, *Br* jab; *Offensive*

tantouse queer, *Br* poof, *Am* fag

> This suffix is found at the end of many French nouns and adjectives and often indicates that the word is rather pejorative.

outil [uti] *nm Hum* (*pénis*) tool
▶ *see also* **remballer**

outillé [utije] *adj Hum* **être bien outillé** to be well-hung

ouvrir [uvrir] *vt* **l'ouvrir, ouvrir sa gueule** [!] (*parler*) to open one's big mouth

-ouze [uz] = **-ouse**

P

pacson [paksɔ̃] nm **(a)** *(paquet)* parcel ◻, package ◻ **(b) toucher le pacson** *(dans une affaire)* to make a bundle *or Br* a packet; *(au jeu)* to win a bundle *or Br* a packet

paddock [padɔk] nm *(lit)* bed ◻, *Br* pit

paf [paf] **1** *adj* smashed, plastered, sozzled
  2 ⚠ nm *(pénis)* dick, knob, *Am* pecker

pagaïe, pagaille [pagaj] nf **(a)** *(désordre)* mess, shambles **(b) il y en a en pagaïe** there's loads *or* tons of it/them

page [paʒ], **pageot** [paʒo] nm *(lit)* bed ◻, *Br* pit

pager [paʒe], **pagnoter** [paɲɔte] **se pager, se pagnoter** vpr to hit the sack *or* the hay *or Am* the rack

paillasse [pajas] nf *(ventre)* stomach ◻, belly, guts; **trouer la paillasse à qn** to knife sb in the guts

paille [pɑj] nf **(a) être/finir sur la paille** to be/end up completely broke *or Br* on one's uppers *or Am* without a dime **(b)** *Ironic (petite somme)* **il a perdu vingt briques à la roulette – une paille!** he lost two hundred thousand francs at the roulette table – chickenfeed! *or* small change! *or* peanuts!

pain [pɛ̃] nm **(a)** *(coup)* belt, smack; **coller un pain à qn** to belt *or* smack sb **(b) ça mange pas de pain** it won't do any harm
  ► *see also* **planche**

paire [pɛr] nf **(a) se faire la paire** *(s'enfuir)* to take off, to make oneself scarce, *Br* to scarper; *(s'évader)* to break out ◻; *(faire une fugue)* to run away ◻, *Br* to do a bunk **(b) c'est une autre paire de**

manches that's a different kettle of fish, that's a whole different ball game **(c) en glisser une paire à qn** ⚠ to give sb one, *Br* to slip sb a length

paître [pɛtr] vi **envoyer qn paître** to tell sb where to go, *Br* to send sb packing

pâle [pɑl] adj **(a) se faire porter pâle** to call in sick *(when one is well enough to work)*, *Br* to take a sickie **(b) être pâle des genoux** to be *Br* knackered *or* shattered *or Am* beat

paletot [palto] nm **tomber sur le paletot à qn** to jump on sb, to go for sb; **mettre la main sur le paletot à qn** to nab *or Br* nick *or* lift sb

pâlichon, -onne [pɑliʃɔ̃, -ɔn] adj a bit pale ◻, on the pale side ◻

pallot ⚠ [palo] nm French kiss; **rouler un pallot à qn** to French-kiss sb, *Br* to snog sb

palmée [palme] adj *Hum* **les avoir palmées** to be bone idle *or* a complete layabout

palper [palpe] vi *(toucher de l'argent)* to get one's money ◻, to collect

palpitant [palpitɑ̃] nm *(cœur)* ticker

paluche [palyʃ] nf hand ◻, mitt, paw

palucher ⚠ [palyʃe] **1** vt to grope, to feel up, to touch up
  2 se palucher vpr to play with oneself, to touch oneself up

panade [panad] nf **être dans la panade** to be penniless ◻ *or Br* on one's uppers

panais ⚠⚠ [panɛ] nm **tremper son panais** to dip one's wick

Paname [panam] *npr* = nickname given to Paris

panard [panar] *nm* (**a**) *(pied)* foot □, *Br* plate, *Am* dog (**b**) *(plaisir intense)* **quel panard!** great!, cool!, *Br* fab!

panier [panje] *nm* (**a**) *(derrière)* **mettre la main au panier à qn** to goose sb (**b**) **panier à salade** *Br* Black Maria, *Am* paddy wagon

pantouflard, -e [pɑ̃tuflar, -ard] **1** *adj* **être pantouflard** to be a real stay-at-home *or* homebody
2 *nm,f* stay-at-home, homebody

papa [papa] **à la papa** *adv* leisurely □; **on va faire ça à la papa** we'll take it easy, we'll do it at our own pace

papelard [paplar] *nm* (**a**) *(papier)* paper □ (**b**) *(article de journal)* (newspaper) article □, piece (**c**) **papelards** *(papiers d'identité)* ID

papi [papi] *nm (homme âgé)* granddad

papier-cul, papier Q [papjeky] *nm Br* bog roll, *Am* TP

papillon [papijɔ̃] *nm (contravention)* (parking) ticket □

papoter [papɔte] *vi* to chat, to yak, *Br* to natter

papouilles [papuj] *nfpl* **faire des papouilles à qn** to stroke sb □, to caress sb □

pâquerette [pɑkrɛt] *nf* **voler au ras des pâquerettes** *(conversation, plaisanterie)* to be a bit on the basic side

paquet [pakɛ] *nm* (**a**) **mettre le paquet** to pull out all the stops, to go all out (**b**) **tout un paquet de** a pile *or* stack of (**c**) **un paquet de nerfs** a bag of nerves

parachuter [paraʃyte] *vt (faire venir de l'extérieur)* to draft in

parano [parano] **1** *adj (abbr* **paranoïaque**) paranoid □
2 *nmf (abbr* **paranoïaque**) paranoid person □
3 *nf (abbr* **paranoïa**) paranoia □

pardon [pardɔ̃] *exclam* **qu'est-ce qu'on a bien bouffé, alors là, pardon!** you should have seen how well we ate, it was something else!; **elle a une paire de lolos, pardon!** you should see the pair of boobs she's got on her!; **Ginger Spice, ah pardon! ça c'est une femme!** Ginger Spice, now that's what I call a woman!

pare-chocs [parʃɔk] *nmpl Hum (seins)* headlights, bumpers, knockers

parfum [parfœ̃] *nm* **être au parfum** to be in the know; **mettre qn au parfum** to fill sb in, to put sb in the picture

parigot, -e [parigo, -ɔt] **1** *adj* Parisian □
2 *nm f* **Parigot, Parigote** Parisian □

parler [parle] *vi* **tu parles!** *(absolument)* you're telling me!, absolutely!, *Br* too right!; *(absolument pas)* you must be joking!, are you kidding!; **tu parles d'une cuisinière! elle est pas fichue de faire cuire un œuf...** some cook she is, she can't even boil an egg!

parlote, parlotte [parlɔt] *nf* chat, chitchat

parole [parɔl] *exclam* cross my heart!, I swear to God!

parti, -e [parti] *adj (ivre)* wasted, plastered, *Br* legless, *Am* polluted, plowed

partie [parti] *nf* **partie fine** orgy; **partie carrée** foursome

partousard, -e, [partuzar, -ard] *nm,f* = person who takes part in an orgy

partouse [partuz] *nf* orgy

partouser [partuze] *vi* = to take part in an orgy

partouzard, -e [partuzar, -ard] = **partousard**

partouze [partuz] = **partouse**

partouzer [partuze] = **partouser**

pascal [paskal] *nm (billet de cinq cents francs)* five-hundred franc note □

The "pascal" is so called because a picture of the writer and philosopher Blaise Pascal features on the banknote.

passe [pas] *nf* (*d'une prostituée*) trick; **faire une passe** to turn a trick

passe-lacet [paslasε] *nm* **raide comme un passe-lacet** completely broke *or Br* skint *or* strapped (for cash)

passer [pase] *vi* (**a**) **y passer** to croak, *Br* to snuff it, *Am* to kick off, to cash in (**b**) *Hum* **il y a que le train qui lui soit pas passé dessus** she's the town bike, she's seen more ceilings than Michelangelo, they'll bury her in a Y-shaped coffin
▶ see *also* **arme, as, billard, casserole, pommade, savon, sentir, tabac**

passoire [paswar] *nf* (**a**) **transformer qn en passoire** to pump sb full of lead, to riddle sb with bullets (**b**) (*mauvais gardien de but*) **c'est une vraie passoire, ce gardien** this keeper lets everything in

pastaga [pastaga] *nm* (*pastis*) pastis □

patapouf [patapuf] *nm* **gros patapouf** fatso, fatty

pataquès [patakεs] *nm* mess, shambles; **faire un pataquès** to cause a stink, to set tongues wagging

patate [patat] *nf* (**a**) (*pomme de terre*) potato □, spud □ (**b**) (*coup*) thump, clout (**c**) (*dans les jeux de balle*) powerful shot □ (**d**) (*dix mille francs*) ten thousand francs □ (**e**) **en avoir gros sur la patate** to be down in the mouth (**f**) (*imbécile*) dork, *Br* divvy, wally, *Am* putz

patati [patati] *exclam* **et patati et patata** blah blah blah, and so on and so forth

patatras [patatra] *exclam* crash!

patauger [patoʒe] *vi* **patauger (dans la semoule)** to be totally lost

pâte [pat] *nf* **être bonne pâte** to be a good sort

pâtée [pate] *nf* thrashing, hammering; **foutre la pâtée à qn** (*correction, défaite*) to give sb a thrashing *or* a hammering

patelin [patlε̃] *nm* (*village*) village □; (*petite ville*) small town □

pater [patεr], **paternel** [patεrnεl] *nm* (*père*) old man

patin [patε̃] *nm* (**a**) [!] (*baiser*) French kiss; **rouler un patin à qn** to French-kiss sb, *Br* to snog sb (**b**) **donner** *ou* **filer un coup de patin** (*un coup de frein*) to slam on the brakes

patraque [patrak] *adj* out of sorts, under the weather, *Br* off-colour, *Am* off-color

patron, -onne [patrɔ̃, -ɔn] *nm,f* (*conjoint*) old man; (*conjointe*) old lady

patte [pat] *nf* (**a**) (*jambe*) leg □, pin; **tirer dans les pattes à qn** to cause trouble for sb; **retomber sur ses pattes** to land on one's feet (**b**) (*main*) hand □, mitt, paw; **tomber dans les pattes de qn** to fall into sb's clutches; **graisser la patte à qn** to grease sb's palm; **bas les pattes!** paws off!, keep your paws to yourself!
▶ see *also* **casser**

paturon [patyrɔ̃] *nm* foot □, *Br* plate, *Am* dog

paumé, -e [pome] **1** *adj* (**a**) (*reculé*) godforsaken (**b**) (*perdu, embrouillé*) lost **2** *nm,f* loser, dropout, *Br* waster, *Am* slacker

paumer [pome] **1** *vt* to lose □ **2 se paumer** *vpr* to get lost □

pavé [pave] *nm* (**a**) (*livre épais*) doorstop (**b**) (*dent*) tooth □

paveton [pavtɔ̃] *nm* (*pavé*) paving stone □

pavute [!] [pavyt] *nf* whore, hooker

paye [pεj] *nf* **ça fait une paye** it's been ages *or Br* yonks

payer [pεje] **se payer** *vpr* **il a brûlé un feu rouge et s'est payé un piéton** he went through a red light and hit a pedestrian □; **il s'est payé un arbre en moto** he crashed *or* smashed his motorbike into a tree □; **si il continue à m'énerver, celui-là, je vais me le payer!** if he carries on annoying me, I'm going to swing for him or thump him one!; **se payer la tête** ou **la tronche**[!] **de qn** Br to take the mick or mickey out of sb, to take the piss out of sb, Am to razz sb; **il s'est payé une crève carabinée** he came down with a stinking cold; **se payer du bon temps, s'en payer** to have a wicked or Br mental time, Am to have a blast

▶ see also **tranche**

peau, -x [po] nf **faire la peau à qn** to bump sb off, Br to do sb in; **trouer la peau à qn** to fill or pump sb full of lead; **avoir qn/qch dans la peau** to be mad or crazy about sb/sth; **avoir le rythme dans la peau** to have rhythm in one's blood; **il sait pas quoi faire de sa peau** he doesn't know what to do with himself; **coûter la peau des fesses** ou **du cul**[!] to cost an arm and a leg; **peau de balle** ou **de zébi!** no way!, no chance!, Br nothing doing!; **peau d'âne** diploma □; **peau de vache** (homme) Br swine, Am stinker; (femme) bitch, Br cow

pébroc, pébroque [pebrɔk] nm umbrella □, Br brolly

pêche [pɛʃ] nf **(a)** (coup) thump, wallop; **prendre une pêche** to get thumped or walloped **(b) avoir la pêche** to be on (top) form, to be full of go **(c) poser une pêche**[!] to Br have or Am take a dump, to drop a log

▶ see also **fendre**

pécho [peʃo] vt (verlan **choper**) **(a)** (saisir) to grab □ **(b)** (surprendre) to catch □, to nab; **se faire pécho** to get caught or nabbed **(c)** (maladie, coup de soleil) to catch □

pêchu, -e [pɛʃy] adj on (top) form, full of go

pécore [pekɔr] nmf Pej yokel, peasant, Am hick

pécos [pekos] nm bomber, cone (cannabis cigarette)

pécu [peky] nm Br bog roll, Am TP

pédale [pedal] nf **(a)** Offensive (homosexuel) queer, Br poof, Am fag; **être de la pédale** to be a queer or Br poof or Am fag **(b) perdre les pédales** to lose one's marbles, Br to lose the plot; **s'emmêler les pédales** to get all mixed up, to get hopelessly lost

pédaler [pedale] vi **pédaler dans la choucroute** ou **dans la semoule** ou **dans le yaourt** to get nowhere

pédé[!!] [pede] Offensive (abbr **pédéraste**) **1** adj queer, Br bent; **pédé comme un phoque** Br as bent as a nine bob note or as a three pound note, Am as queer as a three-dollar bill **2** nm queer, Br poof, Am fag

pédégé [pedeʒe] nm Hum Br MD, Am CEO

This expression comes from the humorous spelling of "P-DG", the abbreviation of "président-directeur général", as it is pronounced.

pédibus [pedibys] adv on foot □; **il y est allé pédibus** he went on foot □, he hoofed it

pedzouille [pɛdzuj] nmf Pej yokel, peasant, Am hick

peigne-cul [pɛɲky] nm (individu méprisable) jerk, Br tosser; (individu grossier) pig, boor, Am hog

peignée [peɲe] nf thrashing, hiding, hammering; **flanquer une peignée à qn** to give sb a thrashing or hiding or hammering; **recevoir une peignée** to get a thrashing or hiding or hammering

peinard, -e [pɛnar, -ard] **1** adj **(a)** (tranquille) **être peinard** to have it easy, to have an easy time of it; **ils sont peinards dans leur nouvelle baraque** they're nice and comfortable in their new place; **il a trouvé un coin peinard pour pioncer** he found a quiet corner

to crash out; **tiens-toi peinard!** keep your nose clean! (**b**) *(peu fatigant)* **un boulot peinard** a cushy job *or* number
2 *adv (tranquillement)* in peace □, peacefully □

pékin [pekɛ̃] *nm (individu)* guy, *Br* bloke

pelé [pəle] *nm* **il y avait trois pelés et un tondu** there was hardly a soul there

peler [pəle] **1** *vi* to be freezing (cold); **ça pèle** it's freezing (cold) *or Br* brass monkeys
2 se peler *vpr* **se (les) peler** to be freezing (cold)

pèlerin [pɛlrɛ̃] *nm (individu)* guy, *Br* bloke

pelle [pɛl] *nf* (**a**) ⚠️ *(baiser)* French kiss; **rouler une pelle à qn** to French-kiss sb, *Br* to snog sb (**b**) **à la pelle** in spades, by the bucketful
▸ *see also* **rond**

pelloche [pɛlɔʃ] *nf* film □ *(for camera)*

pélo [pelo] *nm (individu)* guy, *Br* bloke

peloter [plɔte] **1** *vt* to grope, to feel up, to touch up
2 se peloter *vpr* to grope each other, to feel *or* touch each other up

pelouse [pluz] *nf (marijuana)* grass, weed, herb

pelure [plyr] *nf (manteau)* coat □

pendouiller [pɑ̃duje] *vi* to dangle □, to hang down □

pendre [pɑ̃dr] *vi* **ça te pend au nez** you've got it coming to you; **être toujours pendu au téléphone** to be never off the phone, to spend one's life on the phone

péniches [peniʃ] *nfpl (grandes chaussures)* shoes □, clodhoppers

péno [peno] *nm (abbr* **penalty)** penalty □, *Br* pen *(in football)*

penser [pɑ̃se] *vt* **il peut se le mettre où je pense** he knows where he can stick it; **elle lui a fichu un coup de pied où je pense** she gave him a kick up the you-know-where

pépé [pepe] *nm (homme âgé)* granddad

pépée [pepe] *nf* chick, *Br* bird

pépère [pepɛr] **1** *adj (tranquille)* relaxing □ (**b**) *(peu fatigant)* **un boulot pépère** a cushy job *or* number
2 *nm* (**a**) *(homme âgé)* granddad (**b**) **un gros pépère** a big fatty *or* fatso
3 *adv* leisurely □; **on a fait ça pépère** we took it easy, we did it at our own pace

pépètes, pépettes [pepɛt] *nfpl* cash, dough, *Br* dosh, *Am* bucks

pépin [pepɛ̃] *nm* (**a**) *(problème)* hitch, snag; **avoir un pépin** to have a problem □ (**b**) *(parapluie)* umbrella □, *Br* brolly

péquenaud, -e [pekno, -od] *nm,f Pej* yokel, peasant, *Am* hick

péquenot [pekno] *nm Pej* yokel, peasant, *Am* hick

perche [pɛrʃ] *nf* (**a**) **grande perche** *(personne)* beanpole, *Am* stringbean (**b**) **tendre la perche à qn** to throw sb a line, to give sb a helping hand

percuter [pɛrkyte] *vi (comprendre)* to catch on

perdreau, -x [pɛrdro] *nm (policier)* cop

perfecto® [pɛrfɛkto] *nm* biker's jacket

périf, périph' [perif] *nm (abbr* **boulevard périphérique)** **le périf** = the ring road around Paris

perle ⚠️ [pɛrl] *nf (pet)* fart; **lâcher une perle** to fart, *Br* to let off, *Am* to lay one

perlouse, perlouze [pɛrluz] *nf* (**a**) *(perle)* pearl □ (**b**) ⚠️⚠️ *(pet)* fart; **lâcher une perlouse** to fart, *Br* to let off, *Am* to lay one

perm, perme [pɛrm] *nf (abbr* **permission)** leave □

Pérou [peru] *npr* **c'est pas le Pérou** it won't break the bank

perpète [pɛrpɛt] **à perpète** *adv (abbr* **à perpétuité)** (**a**) *(pour toujours)* **être condamné à perpète** to get life

(b) *(très loin)* miles away

perroquet [pɛrɔkɛ] *nm (cocktail)* = cocktail consisting of pastis and mint-flavoured syrup

perso [pɛrso] *adv (abbr* **personnellement)** **être** *ou* **jouer perso** to hog the ball

personne [pɛrsɔn] *pron* **quand il s'agit de faire la vaisselle/de payer, il n'y a plus personne** when it's time to do the dishes/to pay, you can't see anyone for dust

pervenche [pɛrvɑ̃ʃ] *nf (contractuelle)* *Br* (female) traffic warden[□], *Am* meter maid[□]

pèse [pɛz] = **pèze**

pet¹ [pɛ] *nm* **(a)** *(gaz intestinaux)* fart; **ça vaut pas un pet de lapin** it's not worth a monkey's fart **(b) faire le pet** *(faire le guet)* to keep watch *or* a lookout

pet² [pɛt] – **pète**

pétant, -e [petɑ̃, -ɑ̃t] *adj* **à cinq heures pétantes** at five sharp *or* on the dot

Pétaouchnock [petauʃnɔk] *npr* = imaginary distant place; **ils l'ont envoyé à Pétaouchnock** they sent him to some place in the back of beyond *or* to Timbuktu

pétard [petar] *nm* **(a)** *(cigarette de cannabis)* joint, spliff, reefer, number **(b) être en pétard** *(en colère)* to be fuming *or* livid; **se mettre en pétard** to go ballistic, to hit the roof *or Am* ceiling, to blow one's top *or Am* stack **(c)** *(pistolet)* shooter, *Am* piece **(d)** *(postérieur)* butt, *Br* bum, *Am* fanny **(e) faire du pétard** *(du bruit)* to make a racket *or* a din; *(du scandale)* to kick up a fuss, to cause a stink

pétasse [petas] *nf* **(a)** *(femme vulgaire)* slut, *Br* slapper, scrubber **(b)** *(prostituée)* whore, hooker

pète [pɛt] *nm (trace de coup)* dent[□], bash[□]

pété, -e [!] [pete] *adj (ivre)* shit-faced, *Br*
rat-arsed, pissed

pète-dans-le-sable [pɛtdɑ̃lsabl] *nmf* runt, squirt, shorty

péter [pete] **1** *vt* **(a)** *(briser)* to break[□]; *(mettre hors d'usage)* to bust, *Br* to knacker, to bugger; **péter la gueule à qn** to smash sb's face in, to waste sb's face
(b) péter le feu *ou* **des flammes** to be bursting with energy
(c) la péter *(avoir très faim)* to be starving *or* ravenous
(d) se la péter, péter sa frime to show off, to pose
2 *vi* **(a)** [!] *(émettre des gaz intestinaux)* to fart; **péter plus haut que son cul** to think one's shit doesn't stink, *Br* to think the sun shines out of one's arse; **péter dans la soie** to live in the lap of luxury; **envoyer qn péter** to tell sb where to go *or* where to get off
(b) *(casser)* to break[□], to bust
3 se péter *vpr* **(a)** *(se casser)* **se péter le poignet/la cheville** to break one's wrist/ankle[□]; **la poutre s'est pétée en deux** the beam broke in two[□]
(b) se péter la gueule *(tomber)* to fall flat on one's face; **se péter (la gueule)** [!!] *(s'enivrer)* to get shit-faced *or Br* rat-arsed *or* pissed
▸ see *also* **durite, plomb, sous-ventrière**

pète-sec [pɛtsɛk] **1** *adj inv* abrupt[□], snippy
2 *nmf inv* abrupt[□] *or* snippy person

péteux, -euse [petø, -øz] **1** *adj* **(a)** *(lâche)* chicken, yellow-bellied **(b)** *(prétentieux)* stuck-up, snooty **2** *nm,f* **(a)** *(lâche)* chicken **(b)** *(prétentieux)* upstart

pétochard, -e [petɔʃar, -ard] *adj & nm,f* chicken

pétoche [petɔʃ] *nf* fear[□]; **avoir la pétoche** to be scared stiff *or* witless

pétocher [petɔʃe] *vi* to be scared stiff *or* witless

pétoire [petwar] *nf Hum* old rifle □

peton [pətɔ̃] *nm* foot □, *Br* plate, *Am* dog

pétrin [petrɛ̃] *nm* **être/se mettre dans le pétrin** to be in/get into a fix *or* a mess

pétrolette [petrɔlɛt] *nf Hum (cyclomoteur)* moped □

peu [pø] *nm* **un peu (mon neveu)!** you bet!, sure thing!, *Br* too right!; **il est un peu bête, ce mec – un peu beaucoup!** the guy's a bit stupid – more than a bit!; **pas qu'un peu** more than a little

peuple [pœpl] *nm* **(a)** *(monde)* **il y avait du peuple** there were tons of people there **(b) que demande le peuple?** what more could you ask for?

peupons [pøpɔ̃] *nfpl (verlan* **pompes)** shoes □

pèze [pɛz] *nm* cash, dough, *Br* dosh, readies, *Am* bucks

philo [filo] *nf (abbr* **philosophie)** philosophy □

phosphorer [fɔsfɔre] *vi* to think hard

photo [foto] *nf* **tu veux ma photo?** what are YOU staring at?

piaf [pjaf] *nm (oiseau)* bird □; *(moineau)* sparrow □

piailler [pjaje] *vi (criailler)* to squawk, to screech

piane-piane [pjanpjan] *adv* slowly □; **vas-y piane-piane!** take your time!, there's no rush!

piano [pjano] **1** *adv* **piano (-piano)** *(doucement)* slowly □; **vas-y piano-piano!** take your time!, there's no rush!
  2 *nm* **piano du pauvre, piano à bretelles** squeezebox

piastre [pjastr] *nf Can* dollar □, buck

piaule [pjol] *nf* room □

picaillons [pikajɔ̃] *nmpl* dough, bread, *Br* dosh, *Am* bucks

pichtegorne [piʃtəgɔrn] *nm* wine □, vino, *Br* plonk

picole [pikɔl] *nf* boozing

picoler [pikɔle] **1** *vt* to knock back

  2 *vi* to booze, to knock it back

picoleur, -euse [pikɔlœr, -øz] *nm,f* boozer, alky, *Br* pisshead, *Am* boozehound

picrate [pikrat] *nm* wine □, vino, *Br* plonk

pièce [pjɛs] *nf* **(a) une belle pièce** *(femme)* a babe, *Br* a nice bit of stuff, a bit of all right **(b) on n'est pas aux pièces** we're not on piecework, there's no great hurry

pied [pje] *nm* **prendre son pied** *(atteindre l'orgasme)* to come, to get off; *(prendre du plaisir)* to get one's kicks; **c'est le pied** it's great *or* fantastic *or Br* fab *or Am* awesome; **il a fait ça comme un pied** he made a dog's breakfast *or Br* a pig's ear of it; **il chante/conduit comme un pied** he can't sing/drive to save his life; **être bête comme ses pieds** *Br* to be thick (as two short planks), to be as daft as a brush, *Am* to have rocks in one's head
  ▸ see also **grue, lever, nickelé**

piège [pjɛʒ] *nm* **piège à cons** con, scam

piercé, -e [pirse] *adj* pierced □ *(part of body)*

pierrot [pjɛro] *nm (moineau)* sparrow □

pieu, -x [pjø] *nm (lit)* bed □, *Br* pit; **se mettre au pieu** to hit the sack *or* the hay *or Am* the rack
  ▸ see also **affaire**

pieuter [pjøte] **1** *vi* to crash, to kip
  2 se pieuter *vpr* to hit the sack *or* the hay *or Am* the rack

pif [pif] *nm* **(a)** *(nez) Br* conk, hooter, *Am* schnozzle; **je l'ai dans le pif** I can't stand the sight of him, *Br* he gets right up my nose **(b)** *(abbr* **pifomètre) faire qch au pif** to do sth by guesswork

pifer, piffer [pife] *vt* **je ne peux pas le piffer** I can't stand *or* stomach *or Br* stick him, *Br* he gets right up my nose

pifomètre, piffomètre [pifɔmɛtr] *nm* **faire qch au piffomètre** to do sth by guesswork

pige [piʒ] *nf* year□

pigeon [piʒɔ̃] *nm (dupe)* sucker, *Br* mug, *Am* patsy

pigeonner [piʒɔne] *vt* **pigeonner qn** to take sb for a ride, to take sb in, *Am* to rook sb

piger [piʒe] *vt* to get it, to catch on

pignoler [piɲɔle] **se pignoler**[!] *vpr* to jerk off, to beat off, *Br* to toss oneself off

pignouf [piɲuf] *nm* slob, boor

pile [pil] **pile-poil!** *adv* wicked!, great!

This expression was popularized in *Les Guignols de l'Info*, a television programme in the form of a satirical puppet show.

piler [pile] *vi* to slam on the brakes

pillave [pijav], **pillaver** [pijave] *vi* to booze, to knock it back

pilule [pilyl] *nf* **dorer la pilule à qn** to *Br* sugar *or Am* sweeten the pill for sb; **se dorer la pilule** to catch some rays; **il a dit ça pour faire passer la pilule** he said it to *Br* sugar *or Am* sweeten the pill

pinailler [pinaje] *vi* to split hairs, to nitpick

pinard [pinar] *nm* wine□, vino, *Br* plonk

pince [pɛ̃s] *nf* **(a)** *(main)* hand□, mitt, paw; **serrer la pince à qn** to shake hands with sb□ **(b) aller à pinces** to go on foot□, to hoof it
▶ *see also* **chaud**

pinceaux [pɛ̃so] *nmpl (pieds)* feet□, *Br* plates, *Am* dogs; **s'emmêler les pinceaux** *(trébucher)* to trip up□, to stumble□; *(s'embrouiller)* to tie oneself in knots

pincer [pɛ̃se] **1** *vt* **(a)** *(arrêter)* to collar, to nab; **se faire pincer** to get collared *or* nabbed **(b) en pincer pour qn** to be crazy about sb, to have the hots for sb, *Br* to fancy sb like mad
2 *v imp* **ça pince** *(il fait froid)* it's chilly *or Br* nippy *or* parky

pincettes [pɛ̃sɛt] *nfpl* **ne pas être à prendre avec des pincettes** to be like a bear with a sore head

pine[!!] [pin] *nf* dick, prick, cock; **rentrer la pine sous le bras** to go home without getting laid *or Br* without getting one's oats

pinglot [pɛ̃glo] *nm* foot□, *Br* plate, *Am* dog

pinté, -e [pɛ̃te] *adj* smashed, sozzled, trashed

pinter [pɛ̃te] **se pinter** *vpr* to get smashed *or* sozzled *or* trashed

pion, pionne [pjɔ̃, pjɔn] *nm,f (surveillant)* supervisor□ *(student paid to supervise pupils outside class hours)*
▶ *see also* **damer**

pioncer [pjɔ̃se] *vi* to sleep□, to crash out

pipe [pip] *nf* **(a)**[!!] *(fellation)* blow-job; **tailler** *ou* **faire une pipe à qn** to give sb a blow-job, to suck sb off, to give sb head **(b) casser sa pipe** to croak, to kick the bucket, *Br* to snuff it, *Am* to check out
▶ *see also* **fendre, nom, tailleuse**

pipeau [pipo] *nm* **c'est du pipeau** it's a load of garbage *or Br* rubbish

pipeauter [pipote] *vi* to talk crap *or* bull

pipelette [piplɛt] *nf* chatterbox, gasbag

pipette [pipɛt] *nf Suisse* **ça ne vaut pas pipette** it's not worth a bean *or Am* a red cent

pipi [pipi] *nm* **(a)** *(urine)* pee; **faire pipi** to pee, to have a pee **(b) du pipi de chat** *(boisson insipide)* dishwater, gnat's piss

pipi-room [pipirum] *nm Br* loo, *Am* bathroom□

piqué, -e [pike] *adj* **(a)** *(fou)* crazy, loopy, *Br* bonkers, barking (mad) **(b) un film pas piqué des vers** *ou* **des hannetons** a heck of a good film; **un rhume pas piqué des vers** *ou* **des hannetons**

a stinking cold

piquer [pike] **1** vt **(a)** (voler) to pinch, Br to nick **(b)** (surprendre) to nab, Br to nick; **se faire piquer** to get nabbed or Br nicked **(c)** (faire) **piquer une colère** to go ballistic, to hit the roof or Am ceiling, to blow one's top or Am stack; **piquer un cent mètres** to sprint off; **piquer une tête** (plonger) to dive in; (se baigner) to have a dip

2 se piquer vpr (se droguer) to shoot up, to hit it up, to jack up

▶ see also **fard, ronflette, roupillon, ruche**

piquette [pikɛt] nf **(a)** (défaite) thrashing, pasting; **foutre la piquette à qn** to thrash or paste sb **(b)** (vin de mauvaise qualité) cheap wine □, Br plonk

piquouse, piquouze [pikuz] nf shot, Br jab

pisse [!] [pis] nf piss; **c'est de la pisse d'âne, ta bière!** your beer's like (gnat's) piss!

pisse-copie [piskɔpi] nmf inv hack

pisse-froid [pisfrwa] nmf inv cold fish

pissenlit [pisɑ̃li] nm **manger les pissenlits par la racine** (être mort) to be pushing up the daisies

pisser [pise] **1** vi **(a)** [!] (uriner) to piss; **c'est comme si je pissais dans un violon** it's a complete waste of time, it's like pissing in the wind; **laisse pisser!** forget it!, drop it!; **c'était à pisser de rire** it was an absolute scream; **pisser dans sa culotte** ou **son froc** to piss oneself or one's pants; **ils en pissaient dans leur culotte** ou **froc** they were pissing themselves (laughing); **envoyer pisser qn** to tell sb to piss off; **ça lui a pris comme une envie de pisser** the urge just came over him; **ça pisse pas loin** it's no great shakes, it's not up to much; **pisser à la raie à qn** [!!] not to give a shit about sb

(b) (fuir) to leak □

2 vt **(a)** **pisser du sang** [!] to piss blood;

pisser des lames de rasoir [!] (souffrir au cours de la miction) to piss razor blades

(b) **son bras pissait le sang** blood was pouring or gushing from his arm

▶ see also **mérinos, sentir**

pisseuse [pisøz] nf little girl □

pisseux, -euse [pisø, -øz] adj (couleur) washed-out

pissotière [pisɔtjɛr] nf (public) urinal □

pistoche [pistɔʃ] nf swimming pool □

pistolet [pistɔlɛ] nm **un drôle de pistolet** a shady or Br dodgy character

piston [pistɔ̃] nm (népotisme) string-pulling; **avoir du piston** to have friends in the right places

pistonner [pistɔne] vt **pistonner qn** to pull strings for sb; **il s'est fait pistonner** he got someone to pull strings for him

placard [plakar] nm (prison) slammer, clink, Br nick, Am pen; **mettre qn au placard** to put sb behind bars or inside or away

placer [plase] vt **ne pas pouvoir en placer une** to be unable to get a word in (edgeways)

placoter [plakɔte] vi Can to chat

plafond [plafɔ̃] nm **(a)** **être bas de plafond** to be a bit slow on the uptake **(b)** **avoir une araignée au plafond** to have bats in the belfry

plaire [plɛr] vi Ironic **il commence à me plaire, celui-là!** he's starting to bug me or Br do my head in or get up my nose or Am give me a pain (in the neck)!

plan [plɑ̃] nm **(a)** (projet) plan □; **lui et ses plans foireux!** him and his lousy plans!; **on se fait un plan ciné/resto?** shall we go to the Br cinema or Am movies/go out for a meal? **(b)** **laisser qn en plan** to leave sb in the lurch; **tout laisser en plan** to drop everything

planant, -e [planɑ̃, -ɑ̃t] adj (drogue) relaxing □; (musique) mellow

planche [plɑ̃ʃ] *nf* (**a**) **avoir du pain sur la planche** to have a lot on one's plate (**b**) **c'est une vraie planche à pain** *ou* **à repasser** *(elle a de petits seins)* she's as flat as a pancake *or* as an ironing-board

plancher[1] [plɑ̃ʃe] *nm* (**a**) **le plancher des vaches** dry land □, terra firma □ (**b**) **avoir un feu de plancher** = to be wearing trousers which are too short
▸ see also **débarrasser**

plancher[2] *vi* to be tested □, to have a test □ *(at school)*

planer [plane] *vi* (**a**) *(être sous l'influence d'une drogue)* to be flying, to be high (as a kite), to be spaced out (**b**) *(ne pas avoir le sens des réalités)* to always have one's head in the clouds, to be a space cadet; *(penser à autre chose)* to be miles away, to have one's head in the clouds

plan-plan [plɑ̃plɑ̃] *adj* routine □, humdrum □

planque [plɑ̃k] *nf* (**a**) *(cachette)* hiding place □, hidey-hole (**b**) *(surveillance)* stakeout; **ils étaient en planque autour de la maison** they were staking out the house (**c**) *(emploi tranquille)* cushy job *or* number

planqué, -e [plɑ̃ke] *nm,f* person with a cushy job *or* number

planquer [plɑ̃ke] **1** *vt* to hide □, to stash **2 se planquer** *vpr* (**a**) *(se cacher)* to hide □ (**b**) *(se protéger)* to take cover □

planter [plɑ̃te] **1** *vt* *(tuer à l'arme blanche)* to knife to death; *(blesser à l'arme blanche)* to knife, *Am* to shank, to shiv
2 se planter *vpr* (**a**) *(se tromper)* to get it wrong, to boob (**b**) *(avoir un accident de la route)* to have a crash □ (**c**) *(échouer)* to fail □, *Am* to flunk ; **il s'est planté à son examen** he failed □ *or Am* flunked his exam

plaque [plak] *nf* (**a**) **être à côté de la plaque** to be wide of the mark, to be off target, to be barking up the wrong tree

(**b**) *(dix mille francs)* ten thousand francs □

plaquer [plake] *vt* *(emploi)* to quit, *Br* to chuck *or* pack in; *(famille)* to walk out on; *(amant)* to chuck, to dump; **tout plaquer** *Br* to chuck *or* pack it all in, *Am* to chuck everything

plastoc, plastoque [plastɔk] *nm* plastic □

plat [pla] *nm* (**a**) **faire du plat à qn** *Br* to chat sb up, *Am* to hit on sb (**b**) **faire tout un plat de qch** to make a big song and dance *or* a big fuss about sth (**c**) **il en fait un plat** *(il fait très chaud)* it's a scorcher, *Br* it's roasting
▸ see also **œuf**

plâtrée [platre] *nf* huge helping; **une plâtrée de nouilles** a huge helping of noodles

plein, -e [plɛ̃, plɛn] *adj (ivre)* **être plein (comme une barrique)** to be plastered, to have had a skinful
▸ see also **as, botte, cul, dos, hotte, jambe**

pli [pli] *nm* **ça ne fait pas un pli** there's no doubt about it, it's bound to happen; **je me doutais qu'il se blesserait, et ça n'a pas fait un pli** I was just waiting for him to hurt himself, and sure enough he did

plié, -e [plije] *adj* **être plié (de rire)** to be doubled up *or* bent double (with laughter)

plier [plije] *vt (détruire)* to smash up, to wreck

plomb [plɔ̃] *nm* **péter les plombs** *(se mettre en colère)* to go ballistic, to hit the roof *or Am* ceiling, to blow one's top *or Am* stack
▸ see also **casquette**

plombe [plɔ̃b] *nf* hour □

plombé, -e [!] [plɔ̃be] *adj (atteint par une MST)* **être plombé** to have a dose

plomber [plɔ̃be] *vt* (**a**) *(tuer à l'aide d'une arme à feu)* to fill sb with lead, to pump sb full of lead (**b**) (*transmettre une MST à*) **plomber qn** 🔲 to give sb a dose

plonge [plɔ̃ʒ] *nf* **faire la plonge** to wash dishes ᵈ (*in a restaurant*), to be a washer-upper

plonger [plɔ̃ʒe] *vi* (**a**) (*être envoyé en prison*) to be put inside *or* away, *Br* to be sent down (**b**) (*prendre une décision importante*) to take the plunge, to go for it

plouc [pluk] *nmf* yokel, peasant, *Am* hick

pluie [plɥi] *nf* **pluie d'or** 🔲 (*pratique sexuelle*) golden showers

plumard [plymar], **plume¹** [plym] *nm* (*lit*) bed ᵈ, *Br* pit

plume² *nf* (**a**) ‼️ (*fellation*) blow-job; **tailler une plume à qn** to give sb a blow-job, to suck sb off, to go down on sb (**b**) (*cheveux*) **perdre ses plumes** to go thin on top (**c**) **il y a laissé des plumes** he didn't come out of it unscathed ᵈ (**d**) **voler dans les plumes à qn** to go for sb, to let fly at sb
▸ *see also* **tailleuse**

plumer [plyme] *vt* (*escroquer*) to fleece

pochard, -e [pɔʃar, -ard] *nm,f* alky, boozer, *Br* pisshead, *Am* boozehound

poche [pɔʃ] *nf* **c'est dans la poche** it's in the bag; **faire les poches à qn** to go through sb's pockets; **mets ça dans ta poche (et ton mouchoir par-dessus)!** put that in your pipe and smoke it!; **ne pas avoir les yeux dans sa poche** to have eyes in the back of one's head; **s'en mettre** *ou* **s'en foutre** 🔲 **plein les poches** to rake it in

pochetron [pɔʃtrɔ̃] *nm* alky, boozer, *Br* pisshead, *Am* boozehound

pochette-surprise [pɔʃɛtsyrpriz] *nf* **tu l'as eu dans une pochette-surprise, ton permis?** where did you get your licence - in a cornflakes packet *or* in a Christmas cracker?

pogne [pɔɲ] *nf* hand ᵈ, paw, mitt; **se faire une pogne** ‼️ to jerk off, to beat off, *Br* to have a wank

pogner [pɔɲe] **se pogner** ‼️ *vpr* to jerk off, to beat off, *Br* to have a wank

pognon [pɔɲɔ̃] *nm* cash, *Br* dosh, *Am* bucks

pogo [pɔgo] *nm* pogo (*dance*)

pogoter [pɔgɔte] *vi* to pogo

poignée [pwaɲe] *nf* **poignées d'amour** love handles

poil [pwal] *nm* **à poil** in the buff, *Br* starkers; **torse poil** (*homme*) bare-chested ᵈ; (*femme*) topless ᵈ; **être au (petit) poil** to be just the ticket; **tomber au poil** to arrive just at the right moment; **au (petit) poil!** great!, terrific!; **il a raté le train à un poil près** he missed the train by a hair's breadth *or* by a whisker; **son analyse est juste, à un poil près** his analysis is correct apart from one or two small details ᵈ; **avoir un poil dans la main** to be bone idle; **être de bon/mauvais poil** to be in a good/bad mood ᵈ; **rentrer dans qch au quart de poil** to fit into sth perfectly ᵈ; **démarrer au quart de poil** to start right away *or* first time ᵈ; **tomber sur le poil à qn** to jump on sb, to go for sb
▸ *see also* **tarte**

poilant, -e [pwalɑ̃, -ɑ̃t] *adj* hysterical, side-splitting

poiler [pwale] **se poiler** *vpr* (*rire*) to kill oneself (laughing), to laugh one's head off, to split one's sides; (*s'amuser*) to have a ball *or Am* a blast

pointer [pwɛ̃te] **se pointer** *vpr* to turn up, to show up

pointure [pwɛ̃tyr] *nf* (*personne remarquable en son genre*) **une (grosse) pointure** a big name

poire [pwar] *nf* (**a**) (*visage*) face ᵈ, mug, *Am* map; **il s'est pris le ballon en pleine poire** the ball hit him right in the face (**b**) (*personne facile à duper*) **une (bonne) poire** a sucker, *Br* a mug, *Am* a patsy
▸ *see also* **fendre**

poireau, -x [pwaro] *nm* (**a**) ‼ *(pénis)* dick, cock, prick; **souffler dans le poireau à qn** to give sb a blow-job, to suck sb off, to give sb head (**b**) **faire le poireau** to hang about *or* around

poireauter [pwarote] *vi* to hang about *or* around; **faire poireauter qn** to keep sb hanging about *or* around

poiscaille [pwaskaj] *nm (poisson)* fish □

poisse [pwas] *nf (malchance)* bad luck □; **avoir la poisse** to be unlucky □; **porter la poisse** to bring bad luck □

poisson [pwasɔ̃] *nm* **engueuler qn comme du poisson pourri** to bite sb's head off, to bawl sb out, to jump down sb's throat, to call sb every name under the sun

poivré, -e [pwavre] *adj (ivre)* wasted, trashed, *Br* legless, *Am* lushed

poivrer [pwavre] **se poivrer** *vpr* to get wasted *or* trashed *or Br* legless *or Am* lushed

poivrot, -ote [pwavro, -ɔt] *nm,f* alky, boozer, wino, lush

Polac, Polack [polak] *nmf Offensive* Polack

> Depending on the context and the tone of voice used, this term may be either offensive or affectionately humorous. It is nonetheless inadvisable to use it unless one is quite sure of the reaction it will receive.

polar [polar] *nm* whodunnit

polichinelle [poliʃinɛl] *nm* **avoir un polichinelle dans le tiroir** to have a bun in the oven, *Br* to be up the spout *or* the duff, *Am* to be knocked up

pommade [pomad] *nf* **passer de la pommade à qn** *(flatter)* to butter sb up

pomme [pom] *nf* (**a**) **tomber dans les pommes** to pass out □, to keel over (**b**) **aux pommes** *(excellent)* great, super, terrific (**c**) **pomme (à l'eau** *ou* **à l'huile)** *(personne naïve)* sucker, *Br* mug, *Am* patsy

(**d**) **ma pomme** *(moi)* yours truly; **ta/sa pomme** *(toi/lui ou elle)* you/him/her
▶ *see also* **sucer**

pompe [pɔ̃p] *nf* (**a**) **avoir un coup de pompe** to suddenly feel bushed *or Br* knackered *or* shattered *or Am* beat (**b**) *(chaussure)* shoe □; **un coup de pompe** a kick □; **être** *ou* **marcher à côté de ses pompes** to be screwed up (**c**) **à toute pompe** like lightning, *Am* like sixty (**d**) *(aide-mémoire) Br* crib, *Am* trot (**e**) **un soldat de deuxième pompe, un deuxième pompe** *Br* a squaddie, *Am* a grunt (**f**) *(seringue)* hypo, hype
▶ *see also* **cirer**

pompé, -e [pɔ̃pe] *adj (épuisé)* bushed, *Br* knackered, shattered, *Am* beat

pomper [pɔ̃pe] **1** *vt* (**a**) **pomper qn, pomper l'air à qn** *(l'importuner)* to get on sb's nerves, to bug sb, *Br* to get on sb's wick, *Am* to give sb a pain (**b**) *(copier)* to copy □, to crib; **il a pompé tout ça dans une encyclopédie** he copied *or* cribbed it all out of an encyclopedia (**c**) *(boire)* to knock back; **qu'est-ce qu'il pompe!** he can really knock it back! (**d**) *(épuiser)* to wear out, *Br* to knacker, to do in (**e**) **pomper qn** ‼, **pomper le dard à qn** ‼ *(lui faire une fellation)* to give sb a blow-job, to suck sb off, to go down on sb
2 *vi (copier)* to copy □, to crib; **pomper sur qn/dans qch** to copy *or* crib from sb/sth

pompette [pɔ̃pɛt] *adj* tipsy, merry

pompier ‼ [pɔ̃pje] *nm (fellation)* blow-job; **faire un pompier à qn** to give sb a blow-job, to suck sb off, to give sb head, to go down on sb

pompon [pɔ̃pɔ̃] *nm* **c'est le pompon!** that's the limit!; **avoir le pompon** to take the *Br* biscuit *or Am* cake

pondeuse [pɔ̃døz] *nf Hum (femme très féconde)* **c'est une sacrée pondeuse** she breeds like a rabbit, she's like a battery hen

pondre [pɔ̃dr] *vt* (**a**) *(mettre au monde)* to produce □, to drop (**b**) *(produire)* to produce □, to come up with; **il pond deux romans par an** he churns out two novels a year

Popaul ‼ [popol] *npr (pénis)* dick, prick, cock; **étrangler Popaul** to beat one's meat, to bang *or Br* bash the bishop

popof [popof] = **popov**

popote [popot] **1** *nf* cooking □; **faire la popote** to do the cooking □
2 *adj inv* overly houseproud □

popotin [popotɛ̃] *nm* butt, *Br* bum, *Am* fanny
▸ *see also* **magner**

popov [popof] **1** *adj inv* Russian □
2 *nmf inv* **Popov** Russki

poppers [popœrz] *nmpl* poppers

populo [popylo] *nm* (**a**) *(peuple)* **le populo** the plebs, the riff-raff, the rabble (**b**) *(monde)* crowd □; **il y avait un de ces populo en ville** the town was jam-packed *or Br* chock-a-block *or* heaving

porno [pɔrno] **1** *adj (abbr* **pornographique**) porn, porno
2 *nm (abbr* **pornographie**) porn

porte-poisse [pɔrtpwas] *nm inv* jinx □

portillon [pɔrtijɔ̃] *nm* **ça se bouscule au portillon** he/she/*etc* can't get his/her/*etc* words out

portos [pɔrtos] *nmf Offensive* Dago *(from Portugal)*

portrait [pɔrtrɛ] *nm (visage)* **abîmer le portrait à qn** to waste sb's face, to rearrange sb's features; **se faire tirer le portrait** to have one's photo taken □

portugaises [pɔrtygɛz] *nfpl (oreilles)* ears □; **avoir les portugaises ensablées** to be as deaf as a post

posse [pɔsi] *nf (bande)* posse

pot [po] *nm* (**a**) *(chance)* (good) luck □; **avoir du pot** to be lucky □; **manque de pot, la banque était fermée** as (bad) luck would have it, the bank was closed (**b**) *(postérieur)* butt, *Br* bum, *Am* fanny (**c**) **plein pot** *(à toute vitesse) Br* like the clappers, *Am* like sixty (**d**) **être sourd comme un pot** to be as deaf as a post (**e**) **être un vrai pot de peinture** *(très maquillée)* to wear make-up an inch thick, to put one's make-up on with a trowel

potable [pɔtabl] *adj (passable)* reasonable □, just about OK

potache [pɔtaʃ] *nm* schoolboy □, schoolkid

potage [pɔtaʒ] *nm* **être dans le potage** *(être évanoui)* to be out cold; *(être dans une situation pénible)* to be in the soup

potasser [pɔtase] **1** *vt Br* to swot up on , *Am* to bone up on
2 *vi Br* to swot, *Am* to bone up

pote [pɔt] **1** *adj* **être pote avec qn** to be pally with sb; **ils sont très potes** they're very pally
2 *nm* pal, *Br* mate, *Am* buddy; **salut mon pote!** hi pal *or Br* mate *or Am* buddy!

poteau, -x [pɔto] *nm* pal, *Br* mate, *Am* buddy

potin [pɔtɛ̃] *nm* racket, din

pou, -x [pu] *nm* **chercher des poux dans la tête à qn** to pick a quarrel with sb

poubelle [pubɛl] *nf (voiture)* heap, banger, rustbucket

pouce [pus] *nm Can* **faire du pouce** to thumb a *Br* lift *or Am* ride
▸ see *also* **tourner**

poudre [pudr] *nf (héroïne)* smack, skag, H; *(cocaïne)* coke, charlie, *Am* nose candy

pouffe [!!] [puf], **poufiasse** [!!], **pouffiasse** [!!] [pufjas] *nf* **(a)** *(prostituée)* whore, hooker **(b)** *(femme aux mœurs légères)* slut, tart, tramp, *Br* scrubber **(c)** *(femme désagréable)* bitch, *Br* cow

poulaille [pulaj] *nf* **la poulaille** the cops, *Br* the pigs, the fuzz

poule [pul] *nf* **(a)** *(prostituée)* whore, hooker **(b)** *(femme)* tart, *Br* slapper **(c)** *(terme d'affection)* sweetheart, honey, babe

poulet [pulɛ] *nm (policier, gendarme)* cop, plg

poulette [pulɛt] *nf* **(a)** *(fille, femme)* chick, *Br* bird **(b)** *(terme d'affection)* sweetheart, honey, babe

poumons [pumɔ̃] *nmpl Hum (seins)* knockers, jugs, *Am* hooters; **elle a des sacrés poumons** she's got a great pair of lungs on her

poupée [pupe] *nf (femme, fille)* babe, doll

poupoule [pupul] *nf* **ma poupoule** sweetheart, honey, babe

pourave [purav] *adj* crap, garbage, *Br* rubbish

pourliche [purliʃ] *nm* tip □ *(money)*

pourri, -e [puri] **1** *adj* **(a)** *(en mauvais état)* falling apart, *Br* knackered **(b)** *(mauvais)* rotten; **il a fait un temps pourri** the weather was rotten **(c)** *(de mauvaise qualité)* crappy, *Br* rubbish, *Am* rinky-dink **(d)** *(corrompu)* rotten to the core, *Br* bent
2 *nm,f (homme méprisable)* scumbag,

Br swine, *Am* stinker; *(femme méprisable)* bitch, *Br* cow
▸ see *also* **poisson**

pousse-au-crime [pusokrim] *nm inv* firewater, rotgut

pousser [puse] *vt* **(a) faut pas pousser (mémé** *ou* **mémère dans les orties)** that's pushing it a bit **(b) pousser la chansonnette, en pousser une** to sing a song □

P.Q. [peky] *nm Br* bog roll, *Am* TP

praline [pralin] *nf* **(a)** *(coup)* belt, wallop **(b)** *(balle d'arme à feu)* bullet □, slug **(c)** [!!] *(clitoris)* clit

précieuses [!] [presjøz] *nfpl Hum (testicules)* crown jewels, *Br* wedding tackle

première [prəmjɛr] **de première** *adj* first-class

prendre [prɑ̃dr] *vt* **(a) qu'est-ce qu'il a pris!** he really caught it! **(b) ça prend pas!** give me a break!, yeah right!, *Br* pull the other one!

pression [presjɔ̃] *nf* **mettre la pression à qn** to pressurize sb □, to put pressure on sb □

primo [primo] *adv* first of all □, for starters

privé [prive] *nm (abbr* **détective privé)** private eye, *Am* dick, shamus

pro [pro] *nmf (abbr* **professionnel, -elle)** pro

prof [prɔf] *nmf (abbr* **professeur)** teacher □

professionnelle [profɛsjɔnɛl] *nf* *(prostituée)* pro, streetwalker

projo [proʒo] *nm (abbr* **projecteur)** projector □

prolo [prolo] *(abbr* **prolétaire)** **1** *adj* plebby
2 *nmf* prole, pleb

promener [promne] **1** *vi* **envoyer promener qn** *(l'éconduire)* to send sb packing, to tell sb where to go; **tout envoyer promener** *Br* to chuck *or* pack it all in, *Am* to chuck everything

2 se promener *vpr (éprouver de la facilité)* **il se promène en anglais** he finds English a pushover

promo [promo] *nf (abbr* **promotion)** promotion □, promo

pronto [prɔ̃to] *adv* pronto

proprio [prɔprijo] *nmf (abbr* **propriétaire)** landlord, *f* landlady □

prose [proz] = **proze**

protal [prɔtal] *nm Br* headmaster □, head, *Am* principal □

prout [prut] *nm* **(a)** *(pet)* fart; **faire un prout** to fart, *Br* to let off, *Am* to lay one **(b) prout, ma chère!** *(pour singer un homosexuel)* ooh, ducky!

provo [provo] *nm Br* headmaster □, head, *Am* principal □

provoc [prɔvɔk] *nf (abbr* **provocation)** provocation □

proxo [prɔkso] *nm (abbr* **proxénète)** pimp, *Am* mack

proze ⚠ [proz], **prozinard** ⚠ [prɔzinar] *nm* butt, *Br* bum, *Am* fanny

prune [pryn] *nf* **(a)** *(coup de poing)* punch □, thump, clout **(b) pour des prunes** *(pour rien)* for nothing □ **(c)** *(contravention)* fine □

pruneau, -x [pryno] *nm (balle d'arme à feu)* bullet □, slug

psy [psi] *nmf (abbr* **psychanalyste)** shrink, *Am* bug doctor

puant, -e [pɥɑ̃, -ɑ̃t] **1** *adj (très vaniteux)* cocky

2 *nm (fromage)* smelly cheese □

puceau, -x [pyso] *nm* virgin □

pucelage [pyslaʒ] *nm* virginity □

pucelle [pysɛl] *nf* virgin □

pucier [pysje] *nm (lit)* bed □, *Br* pit

pue-la-sueur [pylasœr] *nm inv Pej* workman □

puissant, -e [pɥisɑ̃, -ɑ̃t] *adj (remarquable)* wicked, *Br* fab, *Am* awesome

punaise [pynɛz] *exclam* heck!, *Br* blast!, sugar!, *Am* shoot!

punkette [pœnkɛt] *nf* punkette

pur, -e [pyr] *adj (excellent)* wicked, cool, *Am* awesome

purée [pyre] **1** *nf* **balancer la purée** ‼ *(éjaculer)* to shoot one's load; **balancer la purée** ⚠ *(tirer avec une arme à feu)* to open fire □

2 *exclam* heck!, *Br* blast!, sugar!, *Am* shoot!

putain ⚠ [pytɛ̃] **1** *nf (prostituée)* whore, hooker; *(femme aux mœurs légères)* tart, slut, *Br* slapper, scrubber, slag; **faire la putain** *(chercher à plaire)* to prostitute oneself; **putain de bagnole/de temps!** fucking car/weather!

2 *exclam* fuck!, fucking hell!

pute ‼ [pyt] *nf (prostituée)* whore, hooker; *(femme facile)* tart, slut, *Br* slapper, scrubber, slag; **faire la pute** *(chercher à plaire)* to prostitute oneself; **fils de pute** son-of-a-bitch

Q

quadra [kadra] *nmf* (*abbr* **quadragénaire**) = person in his/her forties; **être quadra** to be in one's forties[□]; **c'est un quadra** he's in his forties[□]

quart [kar] *nm* **quart de brie** (*nez*) beak, *Br* conk, hooter, *Am* schnozzle
▶ *see also* **poil**

quatre [katr] *adj inv* **un de ces quatre (matins)** one of these days
▶ *see also* **fer**

quat'zyeux [katzjø] **entre quat'zyeux** *adv* in private[□]

quebri [kəbri] *nf* (*verlan* **brique**) ten thousand francs[□]

que dalle [kədal] *pron* zilch, sweet FA, *Br* bugger all, sod all; **j'y comprends que dalle** I don't understand a damn or *Br* bloody thing

quelque chose [kɛlkəʃoz] *pron* (**a**) **il s'est viandé, quelque chose de bien** he got smashed up something awful; **il lui a passé un savon, quelque chose de bien** he gave him an almighty telling-off; **il tenait quelque chose comme cuite!** he was totally plastered!; **il y a quelque chose comme vent dehors** there's a terrible wind outside (**b**) **mais c'est quelque chose!** that's a bit much!

quelque part [kɛlkəpar] *adv* **il lui a mis son pied quelque part** (*au derrière*) he gave him a kick up the you-know-what; **elle lui a foutu un coup de genou quelque part** (*dans les testicules*) she kneed him in the you-know-where or where it hurts most

quenotte [kənɔt] *nf* tooth[□]

que pouic [kəpwik] *pron* zilch, sweet FA, *Br* bugger all, sod all; **j'y com-** prends que pouic I don't underdstand a damn or *Br* bloody thing

quéquette [kekɛt] *nf* willy, *Am* peter, johnson

quès aco [kezako] *adv* what's that?[□]

question [kɛstjõ] *nf* **question soleil, on n'a pas été gâtés** we didn't see much in the way of sunshine; **question argent, j'ai pas à me plaindre** moneywise, I can't complain

que tchi [kətʃi] *pron* zilch, sweet FA, *Br* bugger all, sod all; **il y comprend que tchi** he doesn't understand a damn or *Br* bloody thing

qucude [kœd] = **que dalle**

queue [kø] *nf* (**a**) ‼ (*pénis*) dick, prick, cock; **se faire** *ou* **se taper une queue** to jerk off, *Br* to wank, to have a wank (**b**) **il y en avait pas la queue d'un/ d'une** there wasn't a single one, there wasn't one to be seen; **ne pas en avoir la queue d'un** to be broke or *Br* skint (**c**) **des queues!** ‼ no way!, no chance!
▶ *see also* **rond**

queutard ‼ [køtar] *nm* horny bastard

queuter ‼ [køte] *vt* to screw, to shaft

quillard [kijar] *nm* = soldier about to be discharged or nearing the end of his national service

quille [kij] *nf* (**a**) (*jambe*) leg[□], pin; **jouer des quilles** to beat it, to leg it (**b**) (*petite fille*) little girl[□] (**c**) (*fin de service militaire, démobilisation*) discharge[□], *Br* demob

quincaillerie [kɛ̃kajri] *nf* (**a**) (*armes à feu*) weapons (**b**) (*bijoux*) cheap costume *Br* jewellery or *Am* jewelry[□]

quiquette [kikɛt] = **quéquette**

R

rab [rab], **rabiot** [rabjo] nm (**a**) (excédent) leftovers □, extra □; **il y a du rab de poulet** there's some chicken left over; **qui veut du rab?** who wants seconds?; **t'aurais pas une clope en rab?** can I bum a smoke or Br fag?, have you got a spare smoke or Br fag?; **vous auriez pas un oreiller en rab?** do you have a spare pillow? (**b**) **faire du rab** (au travail) to put in a bit of overtime or a few extra hours; (à l'armée) to serve extra time □

rabioter [rabjɔte] **1** vt (obtenir en supplément) to wangle
2 vi to skimp; **rabioter sur qch** to skimp on sth

râble [rɑbl] nm **tomber sur le râble à qn** to lay into sb, to go for sb

raccrocher [rakrɔʃe] **1** vt **raccrocher le client** (prostituée) to solicit □, Am to hustle, to hook
2 vi (cesser une activité) to pack it in, Am to hang it up

race [ras] nf **ta race!** ⚠ Br piss off!, Am take a hike!; **enculé de ta race!** ⚠⚠ you fucking prick or Br arsehole or wanker or Am asshole!; **défoncer** ou **faire** ou **éclater sa race à qn** to waste sb's face, Br to punch sb's lights out, Am to punch sb out; **niquer sa race à qn** ⚠⚠ to beat the shit out of sb

> The word "race" appears in numerous slang expressions of the "banlieues" (see panel **l'argot des banlieues** on p.133) and functions as an intensifier. See also the entry for **mère**, which has a similar function.

racho [raʃo] (abbr **rachitique**) **1** adj (personne, arbre) weedy, scrawny; (portion) mean, stingy
2 nmf scrawny person

raclée [rakle] nf (correction, défaite) thrashing, hammering; **flanquer une raclée à qn** to give sb a thrashing or a hammering; **prendre une raclée** to Br get or Am take a thrashing or a hammering

racli [rakli] nf chick, Br bird

raclo [raklo] nm guy, Br bloke

raclure ⚠ [raklyr] nf (homme méprisable) bastard, Am son-of-a-bitch; (femme méprisable) bitch

raconter [rakɔ̃te] vt (**a**) **je te raconte pas!** you can't imagine!; **on s'est pris une de ces cuites, je te raconte pas...** you can't imagine how plastered we got (**b**) **se la raconter** to show off

radar [radar] nm **marcher au radar** (ne pas être bien réveillé) to be on automatic pilot

radasse ⚠⚠ [radas] nf (**a**) (prostituée) tart, hooker (**b**) Pej (femme) tart, Br slapper

rade[1] [rad] nm (café) bar, Br boozer

rade[2] **en rade** adv (**a**) (en panne) **être en rade** to have broken down □ or conked out; **tomber en rade** to break down □, to conk out (**b**) (abandonné) stranded; **laisser qn en rade** to leave sb stranded or in the lurch

radin, -e [radɛ̃, -in] **1** adj stingy, tightfisted
2 nm,f skinflint, tightwad

radiner [radine] **1** vi to turn up, to show up, to roll up; **alors, tu radines?** are you coming, then?

2 se radiner *vpr* to turn up, to show up, to roll up

radis [radi] *nm* (sou) **j'ai plus un radis** I haven't a bean *or Am* a red cent; **sans un radis** broke, *Br* skint

raffut [rafy] *nm* (**a**) *(bruit)* racket, din (**b**) *(scandale)* **faire du raffut** to cause a stink, to set tongues wagging

rafiot [rafjo] *nm* old tub *(boat)*

rageant, -e [raʒã, -ãt] *adj* infuriating □

ragnagnas [!] [raɲaɲa] *nmpl* **avoir ses ragnagnas** to have one's period □, to be on the rag

raide [rɛd] *adj* (**a**) *(drogué)* stoned, wasted, ripped; *(ivre)* plastered, *Br* off one's face, legless, *Am* shredded, tanked (**b**) *(sans argent)* broke, *Br* skint (**c**) **elle est raide, celle-là!** that's a bit far-fetched *or* hard to swallow!
▶ see also **passe-lacet**

raie [rɛ] *nf* **taper dans la raie à qn** [!!] *(sodomiser)* to fuck sb up the *Br* arse *or Am* ass
▶ see also **gueule, pisser**

rail [raj] *nm (de cocaïne)* line, **se faire un rail** to do a line

ralléger [raleʒe] *vi (venir)* to come □; *(revenir)* to come back □

ramasser [ramase] **1** *vt* (**a**) *(recevoir)* to get; **ramasser une gifle/un coup/un PV** to get a slap/a clout/a parking ticket (**b**) **se faire ramasser** *(se faire emmener par la police)* to get picked up *or Br* lifted *or* nicked; *(subir un échec)* to fail □, *Br* to come a cropper
2 *vi (recevoir une correction)* to get it, to catch it
3 se ramasser *vpr* (**a**) *(tomber)* to fall flat on one's face, to go flying (**b**) *(échouer)* to fail □, *Br* to come a cropper (**c**) *(recevoir)* **se ramasser une gifle/un coup/un PV** to get a slap/a clout/a parking ticket
▶ see also **bûche, cuiller**

rambo [rãbo] *nm* = security officer patrolling the Parisian railway network

or underground

ramdam [ramdam] *nm* racket, din; **faire du ramdam** to make a racket *or* a din

rame [ram], **ramée** [rame] *nf* **ne pas en fiche** *ou* **en foutre** [!] **une rame** *ou* **une ramée** to do zilch *or Br* bugger all *or* sod all

ramener [ramne] **1** *vt* **la ramener** *(intervenir de façon intempestive)* to stick one's oar in; *(se vanter)* to show off
2 se ramener *vpr* to turn up, to show up, to roll up
▶ see also **fraise**

ramer [rame] **1** *vt* **ne pas en ramer une** to do zilch *or Br* bugger all *or* sod all
2 *vi (éprouver des difficultés)* to have a hard time of it; **ramer pour faire qch** to sweat blood *or* to bust a gut to do sth

ramier [ramje] **1** *adj (fainéant)* lazy □
2 *nm (fainéant)* lazybones, lazy so-and-so

ramollo [ramolo] **1** *adj* washed out, wiped; **je me sens tout ramollo aujourd'hui** I feel like a wet rag today
2 *nmf* wet rag *(person)*

ramoner [!!] [ramone] *vt (posséder sexuellement)* to screw, to shaft, to hump, *Br* to shag

rampe [rãp] *nf* **lâcher la rampe** *(mourir)* to croak, to kick the bucket, *Br* to snuff it, *Am* to check out

ramponneau, -x [rãpono] *nm* clout, thump

rancard [rãkar] = **rencard**

rancarder [rãkarde] = **rencarder**

rancart [rãkar] *nm* **mettre** *ou* **jeter qn au rancart** to throw sb on the scrap heap; **mettre** *ou* **jeter qch au rancart** *(objet)* to chuck sth out; *(projet)* to scrap sth

ranger [rãʒe] **se ranger** *vpr* **se ranger des voitures** to settle down; *(criminel)* to go straight; **être rangé des voitures** to have settled down; *(criminel)* to have gone straight

raousse [raus] *exclam* (get) out!, *Br* on your bike!, *Am* take a hike!

> This term comes from the German "heraus", meaning "out". It entered the French language during the Second World War, when France was occupied by Germany.

râpe [rɑp] *nf* (guitare) guitar □, *Br* axe, *Am* ax

râpé [rɑpe] *adj* **c'est râpé** we've/you've/*etc* had it; **c'est râpé pour nos vacances en Australie!** bang goes our holiday in Australia!, that's our holiday in Australia out the window!

rapiat, -e [rapja, -at] **1** *adj* stingy, tight-fisted
2 *nm,f* skinflint, tightwad

rapido [rapido], **rapidos** [rapidos] *adv* quickly □; **boire un coup rapidos** to have a quick drink

raplapla [raplapla] *adj inv* washed out, wiped

rappliquer [raplike] *vi* (arriver) to turn up, to show up, to roll up; (revenir) to get back □

raquer [rake] **1** *vt* to cough up, to fork out; **combien t'as raqué pour ton blouson?** how much did your jacket set you back?
2 *vi* to pay up, to cough up

ras [rɑ] *adv* **en avoir ras le bol** *ou* **ras la casquette** *ou* **ras le cul** ! to have had it up to here, to be fed up (to the back teeth)
▸ see also **pâquerette**

rasant, -e [razɑ̃, -ɑ̃t] *adj* deadly dull; **c'était rasant** it was a real drag

rasdep ! [rasdɛp] *Offensive* (verlan **pédéraste**) **1** *adj* queer, *Br* bent
2 *nm* queer, *Br* poof, *Am* fag, faggot

rase-bitume [razbitym] *nmf inv* runt, squirt

raser [raze] **1** *vt* (ennuyer) **raser qn** to bore sb stiff *or* to tears

2 se raser *vpr* (s'ennuyer) to be bored stiff *or* to tears

raseur, -euse [razœr, -øz] *nm,f* bore; **quel raseur!** what a bore *or* drag!

rasibus [razibys] *adv* **(a)** (court) short □, very close □; **il s'est fait couper les cheveux rasibus** he's been scalped **(b)** (très près) very close □; **la balle est passée rasibus** the bullet whizzed past

rasoir [razwar] *adj* deadly dull; **ce qu'il peut être rasoir!** he's such a drag!
▸ see also **pisser**

rassis [rasi] *nm* **se taper un rassis** !! to jerk off, to beat off, *Br* to have a wank

rasta [rasta] *nmf* (abbr **rastafari**) rasta

rat [ra] **1** *adj* (avare) stingy, tight-fisted
2 *nm* **(a)** (avare) skinflint, tightwad **(b) s'emmerder** *ou* **se faire chier comme un rat mort** ! to be bored shitless
▸ see also **face**

rata [rata] *nm* food □, grub, chow; **ne pas s'endormir sur le rata** not to fall asleep on the job

ratatiner [ratatine] *vt* (vaincre) **ratatiner qn** to thrash sb, *Am* to kick sb's ass

rate [rat] *nf* **se dilater la rate** to be in stitches, to kill oneself (laughing), to split one's sides
▸ see also **fouler**

râtelier [ratəlje] *nm* **(a)** (dentier) dentures □ **(b) manger à tous les râteliers** to have a finger in every pie

ratiboiser [ratibwaze] *vt* **(a) ratiboiser qn** (au jeu) to clean sb out, to take sb to the cleaners; **ratiboiser qch à qn** (au jeu) to clean sb out of sth; (le lui voler) to pinch *or* *Br* nick sth from sb **(b) se faire ratiboiser (la colline)** (se faire couper les cheveux) to get scalped

ratiche [ratiʃ] *nf* tooth □

raton [ratɔ̃] *nm Offensive* = racist term used to refer to a North African Arab

ravagé, -e [ravaʒe] *adj* (fou) crazy, nuts, bonkers, *Br* barking, *Am* loony-tunes

227 rave ▶ reluquer

rave [reiv] *nf* rave

raymond [rɛmɔ̃] *adj & nm* square, straight

> This term comes from the first name "Raymond", which is nowadays considered rather unfashionable.

rayon [rɛjɔ̃] *nm* **c'est/c'est pas mon rayon** that's/that's not my department *or Am* turf; **en connaître un rayon** to know a thing or two, to be well clued-up

réac [reak] (*abbr* **réactionnaire**) *adj & nmf* reactionary □

rebelote [rəbəlɔt] *exclam* here we go again!, not again!

rebeu [rəbø] *nmf* (*verlan* **beur**) = person born and living in France of North African immigrant parents

> "Beur" is itself the verlan term for "Arabe". "Rebeu", then, is an example of a word which has been "verlanised" twice. See the panel at **verlan**.

récré [rekre] *nf* (*abbr* **récréation**) *Br* break time □, *Am* recess □

rectifier [rɛktifje] **1** *vt* (**a**) (*casser*) to break □ (**b**) (*tuer*) to bump off, *Br* to do in, *Am* to off (**c**) (*dépouiller*) to rob □, to mug, *Br* to do over
2 se rectifier *vpr* (*s'enivrer*) to have a skinful, to get wasted

recui [rəkɥi] *nm* (*verlan* **cuir**) leather jacket □

récup' [rekyp] *nf* (*abbr* **récupération**) (**a**) **de la récup'** (*matériaux*) scrap (**b**) (*récupération idéologique*) exploitation □

redescendre [rədesɑ̃dr] *vi* (*après une prise de drogue*) to come down

refaire [r(ə)fɛr] **1** *vt* (*duper*) to do, to have, to con; **j'ai été refait!** I've been done *or* had *or* conned!; **je me suis fait refaire de cinquante francs** I've been done out of fifty francs
2 se refaire *vpr* (*regagner une somme perdue*) to recoup one's losses □
▶ *see also* **devanture**

refiler [r(ə)file] *vt* (**a**) (*donner*) to give □; **il m'a refilé son vieux blouson** he gave me his old jacket (**b**) (*transmettre*) to give □; **le salaud, il m'a refilé son rhume!** [!] the bastard's given me his cold! (**c**) **refiler de la jaquette** [!] *ou* **de la dossière** [!!], **en refiler** [!!] to take it up the *Br* arse *or Am* ass
▶ *see also* **chouette**

refouler [!!] [r(ə)fule] *vi* (*sentir mauvais*) to stink □, *Br* to pong, to niff
▶ *see also* **goulot**

refroidir [r(ə)frwadir] *vt* (*tuer*) to ice, to bump off, to liquidate

regarder [r(ə)garde] *vt* **non mais tu m'as bien regardé?, tu m'as pas regardé?** what do you take me for?; **non mais tu t'es regardé?** who do you think you are?

réglo [reglo] **1** *adj* (*personne*) straight, on the level; (*opération, transaction*) legit, kosher
2 *adv* by the book, fair and square; **il a intérêt à jouer réglo** he'd better play fair; **on fait ça réglo, hein?** we'll do it by the book, OK?

régulière [regyljɛr] **1** *nf* (**a**) (*épouse*) old lady, *Br* missus (**b**) (*maîtresse*) mistress □, *Br* bit on the side
2 à la régulière *adv* fair and square

relax [rəlaks] **1** *adj* laid-back
2 *adv* **faire qch relax** to take it easy doing sth; **on a fait ça relax** we took it easy
3 *exclam* **relax, Max!** take it easy!, chill out!

relooker [r(ə)luke] **1** *vt* to revamp
2 se relooker *vpr* to change one's image □

reloquer [r(ə)lɔke] **se reloquer** *vpr* to put one's clothes back on □, *Br* to get one's kit back on

relou [rəlu] *adj* (*verlan* **lourd**) (*qui manque de subtilité*) unsubtle □, in your face, over the top, *Br* OTT

reluquer [r(ə)lyke] *vt* to eye up, to

check out, *Am* to scope (out)

remballer [rɑ̃bale] *vt Hum* **remballer ses outils** to put one's *Br* trousers □ *or* keks *or Am* pants □ back on

rembarrer [rɑ̃bare] *vt* **rembarrer qn** to tell sb where to go *or* where to get off, *Br* to knock sb back; **se faire rembarrer** to get told where to go *or* where to get off, *Br* to get knocked back

remettre [r(ə)mɛtr] *vt* (**a**) *(reconnaître)* to recognize □, to place; **tu me remets?** can you place me? (**b**) **remettre ça** *(recommencer)* to start again □; *(prendre un autre verre)* to have another one □
▶ see *also* **couvert**

rempiler [rɑ̃pile] *vi (se rengager)* to sign up again

remplumer [rɑ̃plyme] **se remplumer** *vpr* (**a**) *(reprendre du poids)* to put a bit of weight back on □ (**b**) *(améliorer sa situation financière)* to improve one's cash flow □, to get back on one's feet □

renauder [r(ə)node] *vi* to whinge, to gripe, to moan and groan

rencard [rɑ̃kar] *nm* (**a**) *(rendez-vous)* appointment □; *(amoureux)* date; **avoir un rencard avec qn** to have an appointment/a date with sb; **filer un rencard à qn** to fix an appointment/a date with sb (**b**) *(renseignement)* tip-off

rencarder [rɑ̃karde] **1** *vt* **rencarder qn** *(renseigner)* to tip sb off; *(donner rendez-vous à)* to arrange to meet sb
2 se rencarder *vpr (se renseigner)* to get information □

renifler [r(ə)nifle] *vi (sentir mauvais)* to stink, *Br* to pong, to niff

renoi [rənwa] *(verlan* **noir**) **1** *adj* black □
2 *nmf* Black

renps [rɑ̃p(s)] *nmpl (verlan* **parents**) folks, *Br* old dears, *Am* rents

rentre-dedans [rɑ̃tdədɑ̃] *nm* **faire du rentre-dedans à qn** to come on to sb, *Br* to chat sb up, *Am* to hit on sb

repasser [r(ə)pase] **1** *vt (escroquer)* to

do, to rip off
2 *vi* **tu repasseras!** no way!, no chance!, not on your life!; **il peut toujours repasser** he hasn't a hope, he's got another think coming
▶ see *also* **planche**

repiquer [r(ə)pike] **1** *vt (classe)* to repeat □
2 *vi* (**a**) *(redoubler une classe)* to repeat a *Br* year *or Am* grade (**b**) **repiquer au truc** *(reprendre une activité ou une habitude)* to be at it again

replonger [r(ə)plɔ̃ʒe] *vi* (**a**) *(retourner en prison)* to go back inside (**b**) *(reprendre une habitude)* to be at it again

répondant [repɔ̃dɑ̃] *nm* **avoir du répondant** *(avoir des économies)* to have plenty of cash stashed away

repousser [r(ə)puse] *vi (sentir mauvais)* to stink, *Br* to pong, to niff
▶ see *also* **goulot**

restau, resto [resto] *nm (abbr* **restaurant**) restaurant □; **restau-U** university cafeteria *or Br* canteen *or* refectory □

resucée [rəsyse] *nf* (**a**) *(quantité supplémentaire)* **une resucée** some more; **t'en prendras bien une petite resucée?** will you have some more? (**b**) *(copie)* rehash

résultat [rezylta] *nm* **résultat des courses,...** the upshot was..., as a result,...; **résultat des courses, on s'est retrouvés au poste** the whole thing ended up with us in the police station

rétamé, -e [retame] *adj* (**a**) *(ivre)* wasted, trashed, *Br* legless, *Am* fried (**b**) *(épuisé)* bushed, *Br* knackered, shattered, *Am* out of gas (**c**) *(hors d'usage)* wrecked, bust, *Br* knackered

rétamer [retame] **1** *vt* (**a**) *(rendre ivre)* **rétamer qn** to get sb wasted *or* trashed *or Br* legless *or Am* fried (**b**) *(épuiser)* to wear out, *Br* to knacker (**c**) *(mettre hors d'usage)* to wreck, to bust, *Br* to knacker
2 se rétamer *vpr (tomber)* to go flying, to take a tumble; *(échouer)* to fail □, *Am*

to flunk; **elle s'est rétamée à l'oral** she failed or Am flunked the oral

retape [rtap] nf **faire la retape** Br to be on the game, Am to hustle

retourne [rturn] nf **les avoir à la retourne** to be bone idle

rétro [retro] nm (abbr **rétroviseur**) rear-view mirror □

reuch [rœʃ] adj (verlan **cher**) expensive □, pricey

reum [rœm] nf (verlan **mère**) old lady, Br old dear

reunoi [rønwa] = **renoi**

reup [rœp] nm (verlan **père**) old man

reur [rør], **reureu** [rørø] nm (RER) = express rail network serving Paris and its suburbs

reuss [rœs] nf (verlan **sœur**) sister □, sis

reviens [rəvjɛ̃] nm **je te prête mon dico mais il s'appelle reviens** I'll lend you my dictionary but I'll need it back □

revoyure [rvwajyr] nf **à la revoyure!** see you!

revue [rvy] nf **être de la revue** to have to go without

ribambelle [ribɑ̃bɛl] nf **une ribambelle de** tons of, loads of

ricain, -e [rikɛ̃, -ɛn] (abbr **américain, -e**) **1** adj Yank, Br Yankee

2 nm,f **Ricain, Ricaine** Yank, Br Yankee

richard, -e [riʃar, -ard] nm,f moneybags, Br nob

ric-rac [rikrak] adv **c'était ric-rac** it was touch and go, it was a close thing

rideau [rido] exclam enough!, that'll do!

rien [rjɛ̃] adv (a) (très) very □, seriously, Br well, Am real; **elle est rien moche, sa copine** his girlfriend's a real dog or Am beast (b) **c'est rien de le dire** you can say that again, you said it
▸ see also **casser**

rififi [rififi] nm trouble, Br aggro; **il va y**

avoir du rififi there's going to be trouble or Br aggro

riflard [riflar] nm umbrella □, Br brolly

rigolade [rigɔlad] nf (a) (amusement) **quelle rigolade!** what a hoot or a scream!; **prendre qch à la rigolade** (avec humour) to see the funny side of sth, to treat sth as a joke; (avec légèreté) not to take sth too seriously □ (b) **c'est de la rigolade!** (facile) it's a piece of cake!, it's a walkover!; **c'est pas de la rigolade!** it's no picnic!

rigoler [rigɔle] vi to laugh □; **histoire de rigoler, pour rigoler** for a laugh, for fun; **fais ce que je te dis, je ne rigole pas!** do as you're told, I'm not kidding or joking!; **tu rigoles** are you kidding?, are you joking?; **ils rigolent pas avec la sécurité dans cet aéroport** they don't mess about or take any chances with security at this airport; Ironic **tu me fais rigoler, tiens!** you make me laugh!, don't make me laugh!

rigolo, -ote [rigɔlo, -ɔt] **1** adj funny □

2 nm,f (a) (personne amusante) hoot, scream (b) (personne peu sérieuse) clown, joker

rikiki [rikiki] = **riquiqui**

rincée [rɛ̃se] nf (averse) downpour □

rincer [rɛ̃se] **1** vt **se faire rincer** to get caught in a downpour

2 vi (offrir à boire) to buy the drinks □; **c'est moi qui rince!** I'm buying the drinks!, the drinks are on me!; **c'est le patron qui rince!** the drinks are on the house!

3 se rincer vpr **se rincer l'œil** to get an eyeful
▸ see also **dalle**

ringard, -e [rɛ̃gar, -ard] **1** adj tacky, Br naff

2 nm,f square, nerd, Br anorak

ringardise [rɛ̃gardiz] nf tackiness, Br naffness; **la déco était d'une ringardise, je te dis pas!** the decor was unbelievably tacky or Br naff!

ringardos [rɛ̃gardos] = **ringard**

ripatons [ripatɔ̃] nmpl feet□, Br plates, Am dogs

riper [ripe] vi to beat it, to push off, Am to beat feet, to book it

ripou, -x [ripu] nm (verlan **pourri**) Br bent or Am bad cop

> This expression was popularized by Claude Zidi's 1984 comedy film about corruption in the police force, Les Ripoux.

riquiqui [rikiki] adj inv teeny-weeny

rital, -e [rital] Offensive **1** adj wop, Eyetie
   2 nm (langue) Italian□
   3 nm,f **Rital, Ritale** wop, Eyetie

> Depending on the context and the tone of voice used, this term may be either offensive or affectionately humorous. It is nonetheless inadvisable to use it unless one is quite sure of the reaction it will receive.

roberts [rɔbɛr] nmpl (seins) tits, knockers, jugs

> This term comes from a once famous make of baby's bottle.

robineux [rɔbinø] nm Can tramp, Am hobo

rodéo [rɔdeo] nm (en voiture volée) joy-ride

rogne [rɔɲ] nf anger□, rage□; **être/se mettre en rogne** to be/go mad or crazy or ape

rognons [rɔɲɔ̃] nmpl (testicules) balls, nuts, Br bollocks

roi [rwa] nm **c'est le roi des cons**/**des poivrots** he's a complete prick/alky

romano [rɔmano] nmf Pej (abbr **romanichel, -elle**) gipsy□, gippo

rombière [rɔ̃bjɛr] nf (vieille) **rombière** stuck-up old cow

rond, -e [rɔ̃, rɔ̃d] **1** adj (ivre) wasted, loaded, Br pissed, Am fried; **rond comme une queue de pelle** ou **comme un boudin** Br as pissed as a newt, Am stewed to the gills
   2 nm (**a**) (argent) **ne pas avoir un rond** Br not to have a penny to one's name, Am not to have a red cent; **t'as des ronds sur toi?** got any cash on you? (**b**) **prendre** ou **filer du rond** to get fucked in the Br arse or Am ass
   3 adv **ne pas tourner rond** (machine) to be on the blink, Am to be on the fritz; (personne) to be not all there, to have a screw or Br a slate loose
   ▶ see also **flan, gueule**

rondelle [rɔ̃dɛl] nf (anus) ringpiece, Br arsehole, Am asshole; **défoncer** ou **casser la rondelle à qn** to fuck sb in the Br arse or Am ass

ronflette [rɔ̃flɛt] nf **piquer une ronflette** to have a nap or a snooze

roploplos [roploplo] nmpl tits, knockers, jugs

Rosbif [rɔsbif] nmf Offensive (Britannique) Brit

> This term originates in the stereotypical notion among the French that the British consume large quantities of roast beef. Depending on the context and the tone of voice used, this term may be either offensive or affectionately humorous.

rose [roz] nf (**a**) **ça sent pas la rose** it stinks a bit, Br it's a bit whiffy (**b**) **envoyer qn sur les roses** to send sb packing, to tell sb where to go or where to get off

roteuse [rɔtøz] nf (bouteille de Champagne) bottle of bubbly or Br champers

rotin [rɔtɛ̃] nm (sou) **ne pas avoir un rotin** to be totally broke or Br skint

rotoplots [rotoplo] = **roploplos**

rotule [rɔtyl] nf **être sur les rotules** to be wiped (out) or Br knackered; **mettre qn sur les rotules** to wipe sb out, Br to knacker sb

roubignoles, roubignolles [rubiɲɔl] = **roupettes**

rouflaquettes [ruflakɛt] *nfpl* sideburns □

rouge [ruʒ] *nm (vin rouge)* red wine □; **une bouteille de rouge** a bottle of red; **un coup de rouge** a glass of red wine □; **du gros rouge** cheap red wine □

roulée [rule] *adj* **bien roulée** curvy

rouler [rule] *vt* (**a**) **rouler les mécaniques** to walk with a swagger (**b**) **rouler une pelle** *ou* **une galoche** *ou* **un pallot** *ou* **un patin à qn** [!] to French-kiss sb, *Br* to snog sb

2 *vi (aller bien)* **ça roule** things are fine, everything's OK

3 se rouler *vpr* (**a**) **s'en rouler une** to roll a smoke *or Br* a fag (**b**) **se les rouler** to twiddle one's thumbs

▶ *see also* **bosse**

roulure [!] [rulyr] *nf* (**a**) *(prostituée)* hooker, whore (**b**) *(homme méprisable)* bastard, *Am* son-of-a-bitch; *(femme méprisable)* bitch

roupettes [!] [rupɛt], **roupignolles** [!] [rupiɲɔl] *nfpl* balls, nuts, *Br* bollocks

roupiller [rupije] *vi* to sleep, *Br* to kip

roupillon [rupijɔ̃] *nm* snooze, nap, *Br* kip; **piquer un roupillon** to have a snooze *or* a nap *or Br* a kip

rouquin [rukɛ̃] *nm (vin rouge)* red wine □

rouscailler [ruskaje] *vi* to gripe, to

whinge, to moan and groan

rouspétance [ruspetɑ̃s] *nf* **pas de rouspétance!** I don't want to hear any moaning and groaning *or* whinging *or* grumbling!

rouspéter [ruspete] *vi* to moan and groan, to whinge, to grumble

rouspéteur, -euse [ruspetœr, -øz] *nm,f* moan, whinge, grumbler

rousse [rus] *nf* **la rousse** *(la police)* the cops, the pigs

rouste [rust] *nf* thrashing, hammering; **flanquer une rouste à qn** to give sb a thrashing *or* a hammering

roustons [!] [rustɔ̃] *nmpl* balls, nuts, *Br* bollocks

R U [ry] *nm (abbr* **restaurant universitaire)** university cafeteria *or Br* canteen *or* refectory □

ruche [ryʃ] *nf* **se piquer la ruche** to get wasted *or* trashed *or Br* pissed

rupin, -e [rypɛ̃, -in] **1** *adj (personne)* loaded, *Br* rolling in it, *Am* rolling in dough; *(quartier)* plush, *Br* posh

2 *nm,f* moneybags

Ruskoff [ryskɔf] *nmf Offensive* Russki

Depending on the context and the tone of voice used, this term may be either offensive or affectionately humorous. It is nonetheless inadvisable to use it unless one is quite sure of the reaction it will receive.

S

sabrer [sɑbʀe] *vt* (**a**) *(couper) (texte)* to slash (**b**) *(noter sévèrement) (personne)* to slate (**c**) *(refuser) (candidat)* to fail □, *Am* to flunk (**d**) [!] *(posséder sexuellement)* to poke, *Br* to shaft

sac [sak] *nm* (**a**) *(dix francs)* ten francs □; **dix/vingt sacs** a hundred/two hundred francs (**b**) **sac d'os** *(personne maigre)* bag of bones

> In sense (a), "sac" is normally used in multiples of ten.

sacquer [sake] *vt* (**a**) *(congédier)* to fire, to sack (**b**) **je ne peux pas le sacquer** I can't stand *or Br* stick him

sacré, -e [sakʀe] *adj* **un sacré con** [!] a total *Br* arsehole *or Am* asshole; **un sacré fouteur de merde** [!] a hell of a shit-stirrer; **c'est un sacré numéro** he's quite a character *or* case!; **cette sacrée bagnole est encore en panne** the damn *or Br* bloody car's broken down again; **c'est un sacré veinard** he's a lucky *or Br* jammy devil

sacrément [sakʀemɑ̃] *adv* damn, *Br* bloody; **il s'est sacrément foutu de notre gueule** [!] he made a total damn *or Br* bloody fool of us; **il est sacrément radin celui-là!** he's so damn *or Br* bloody tight!; **il fait sacrément froid** it's damn *or Br* bloody cold

sado [sado] *nmf (abbr* **sadique***)* sadist □

sado-maso [sadomazo] *(abbr* **sado-masochiste***)* **1** *adj* SM, S & M
2 *nmf* sado-masochist □

sagouin, -e [sagwɛ̃, -in] *nm,f (personne malpropre)* filthy slob; **du travail de sagouin** sloppy work

saigner [seɲe] **1** *vt (tuer à l'arme blanche)* to stab to death □
2 *vi* **ça va saigner** there's going to be trouble

sainte-nitouche [sɛ̃tnituʃ] *nf* goody-two-shoes; **avec ses airs de sainte-nitouche** looking as though butter wouldn't melt in her mouth

> This term is a corruption of "sainte", meaning "saint", and "ne pas y toucher" meaning "not to touch" suggesting someone who avoids any activities of a sexual nature.

saint-frusquin [sɛ̃fʀyskɛ̃] *nm* **tout le saint-frusquin** the whole caboodle, *Br* the full monty, *Am* the whole megilla

Saint-Glinglin [sɛ̃glɛ̃glɛ̃] *nf* **attendre jusqu'à la Saint-Glinglin** to wait forever *or* until doomsday; **c'est maintenant qu'il faut le faire, pas à la Saint-Glinglin** it has to be done now, not whenever

salade [salad] *nf* (**a**) *(situation embrouillée)* muddle, mess; **quelle salade!** what a muddle *or* mess! (**b**) **vendre sa salade** to make a pitch □, to try to sell an idea □ (**c**) **raconter des salades** to tell fibs *or Br* porkies
▶ *see also* **panier**

salamalecs [salamalɛk] *nmpl* bowing and scraping

salaud [!] [salo] **1** *adj* **c'est salaud de faire/dire ça** that's a really shitty thing to do/say, that's a bastard of a thing to do/say; **il a été salaud avec elle** he's been a real bastard to her
2 *nm* bastard, *Am* son-of-a-bitch

sale [sal] *adj* **pas sale** pretty good, not bad

salé, -e [sale] *adj* (**a**) *(élevé) (note, addition)* steep (**b**) *(osé)* steamy, X-rated

salement [salmã] *adv (beaucoup)* badly$^\square$; *(très) Br* dead, *Am* real; **salement blessé** badly injured; **salement déçu** *Br* dead *or Am* real disappointed; **il a salement vieilli** he's really aged

saleté [salte] *nf* **saleté de bagnole/de temps!** this blasted *or Am* darn car/weather!

saligaud ⚠ [saligo] *nm (individu malpropre)* filthy pig; *(individu méprisable)* bastard, *Am* son-of-a-bitch

salingue ⚠ [salɛ̃g] **1** *adj* filthy
2 *nmf* filthy pig

salopard ⚠ [salɔpar] *nm* bastard, *Am* son-of-a-bitch

salope ⚠ [salɔp] **1** *nf* (**a**) *(femme méprisable)* bitch, *Br* cow; *(femme aux mœurs légères)* tart, slut, *Br* slapper (**b**) *(homme méprisable)* bastard, *Am* son-of-a-bitch

saloper [salɔpe] *vt* (**a**) *(salir)* to dirty$^\square$, to mess up (**b**) *(mal exécuter)* to make a dog's breakfast *or Br* a pig's ear of

saloperie [salɔpri] **1** *nf* (**a**) *(acte méprisable)* dirty trick; **faire une saloperie à qn** to play a dirty trick on sb, *Br* to do the dirty on sb, *Am* to do sb dirt
(**b**) *(marchandise de mauvaise qualité)* garbage, junk, *Br* rubbish; **saloperie de bagnole/d'ordinateur!** this blasted *or Am* darn car/computer!
(**c**) *(maladie, virus)* something nasty; **il a attrapé une saloperie en vacances** he caught something nasty on *Br* holiday *or Am* vacation; **c'est une vraie saloperie, ce nouveau virus** this new virus is really nasty
(**d**) *(homme méprisable)* bastard, *Am* son-of-a-bitch
2 saloperies *nfpl* (**a**) *(saletés)* crud, *Br* muck
(**b**) *(propos orduriers)* filthy language; **dire des saloperies** to use filthy language
(**c**) *(aliments malsains)* junk (food), garbage, *Br* rubbish; **il bouffe que des saloperies** he just eats garbage *or* junk *or Br* rubbish

sang [sã] *nm* **bon sang!** *(de surprise)* for Pete's sake!, *Br* blimey!, *Am* gee (whiz)!; *(de colère)* blast it!, hell!
▶ see *also* **pisser**

sans [sã] *prep* **sans un** broke, *Br* skint, strapped
▶ see *also* **dec, déconner**

santé [sãte] **1** *nf* **avoir de la santé** *(avoir de l'audace)* to have a nerve *or Br* a brass neck
2 *exclam* cheers!
▶ see *also* **voleuse**

santiags [sãtjag] *nfpl* cowboy boots$^\square$

saper [sape] **1** *vt* to dress$^\square$
2 se saper *vpr (s'habiller)* to get dressed$^\square$; *(s'habiller chic)* to get all dressed up$^\square$; **être bien/mal sapé** to be well-/badly-dressed$^\square$; **elle aime bien se saper pour sortir** she likes to get all dressed up to go out; **il sait pas se saper** he's got no dress sense; **elle se sape très seventies** she wears really seventies clothes, she dresses really seventies

sapes [sap] *nfpl* clothes$^\square$, threads, *Br* gear, clobber

sapeur [sapœr] *nm* = young, well-dressed African man

sapin [sapɛ̃] *nm Hum* **ça sent le sapin** he's/she's/*etc* on his/her/*etc* last legs; **une toux qui sent le sapin** a worryingly unhealthy cough$^\square$, a death-rattle of a cough

saquer [sake] = **sacquer**

saton [satɔ̃] *nm* **coup de saton** kick$^\square$, boot; **donner des coups de saton à qn/dans qch** to boot sb/sth, to give sb/sth a kicking

satonner [satɔne] *vt* **satonner qn/qch** to boot sb/sth, to give sb/sth a kicking

saturer [satyre] *vi* to have had enough, to have had as much as one can take

sauce [sos] *nf* (**a**) *(pluie)* rain□; **prendre la sauce** to get soaked *or* drenched□ (**b**) **mettre la sauce** to pull out all the stops, to go all out (**c**) **balancer la sauce** [!!] *(éjaculer)* to shoot one's load *or* wad

saucée [sose] *nf* downpour□

saucer [sose] *vt* **se faire saucer** to get soaked *or* drenched□

sauciflard [sosiflar] *nm* (dried) sausage□

saucisse [sosis] *nf* **grande saucisse** *(personne)* beanpole; **saucisse à pattes** sausage dog

saumâtre [somɑtr] *adj* **il l'a trouvée saumâtre** he didn't appreciate it at all□, he wasn't amused *or* impressed□

saute-au-paf [!] [sotopaf] *nf inv* nympho, *Br* goer

sauter [sote] **1** *vt* (**a**) [!!] *(posséder sexuellement)* to fuck, to screw, *Br* to shag (**b**) **la sauter** *(avoir faim)* to be starving *or* ravenous
  2 *vi* (**a**) **se faire sauter la cervelle** *ou* **le caisson** to blow one's brains out (**b**) **et que ça saute!** jump to it!, make it snappy! (**c**) *(perdre son emploi)* to get fired *or* *Br* sacked

sauterelle [sotrɛl] *nf* *(fille, femme)* chick, *Br* bird

sauterie [sotri] *nf* party□, do, get-together

savate [savat] *nf* (**a**) **il chante comme une savate** he can't sing to save his life, *Br* he can't sing for toffee (**b**) **traîner la savate** to be completely broke *or Br* on one's uppers *or Am* without a dime

savater [savate] *vt* to kick□, to boot

savon [savɔ̃] *nm* **passer un savon à qn** to give sb a roasting, to bawl sb out, to read sb the riot act, *Am* to chew sb out; **se faire passer** *ou* **prendre un savon** to get a roasting, to get bawled out *or Am* chewed out

savonnette [savɔnɛt] *nf* *(de cannabis)*

= 250-gramme block of hashish

scato [skato] *adj* *(abbr* **scatologique)** *(blague)* disgusting; **humour scato** toilet humour

schizo [skizo] *adj & nmf* *(abbr* **schizophrène)** schizo, *Am* schiz

schlass¹ [ʃlas] *nm* *(couteau)* knife□, blade, *Am* shiv

schlass², schlasse [ʃlas] *adj* *(ivre)* sozzled, trashed, wasted

schlinguer [ʃlɛ̃ge] = **chlinguer**

schlof [ʃlɔf] *nm* bed□, *Br* pit; **se mettre au schlof** to hit the sack *or* the hay *or Am* the rack

schmilblick [ʃmilblik] *nm* **faire avancer le schmilblick** to make progress□, to get somewhere; **tout ça, ça fait pas avancer le schmilblick** that's not getting us any further forward

This expression comes from a radio quiz show of the early 1970s, in which the contestants had to identify the mystery object (the "schmilblick") by asking the presenter a series of questions to which he could answer only yes or no. "Faire avancer le schmilblick" thus signified asking a question which gave the contestant additional clues to the object in question. The expression was popularized by the comedian Coluche, who performed a famous sketch based on this show.

schmitt [ʃmit] *nm* cop

schnock, schnoque [ʃnɔk] *nm* halfwit, dope, *Br* divvy, *Am* goober; **un vieux schnock** an old fogey, an old codger

schnouf, schnouffe [ʃnuf] = **chnouf**

schtarbé, -e [ʃtarbe] = **chtarbé**

schwartz [ʃwarts] *nm* (**a**) *(policier)* cop, *Am* flatfoot (**b**) *(Noir)* Black

scier [sje] *vt* *(surprendre)* to amaze□, to stagger, to flabbergast, *Am* to knock for a loop; **ça m'a scié d'apprendre que...** I was staggered or Br gobsmacked or Am knocked for a loop to find out that...

scoumoune [skumun] nf rotten luck; **avoir la scoumoune** to be jinxed

scratcher [skratʃe] **se scratcher** vpr to go off the road; **il s'est scratché avec la moto de son frère** he went off the road on his brother's motorbike

sec [sɛk] adv **(a)** (beaucoup) a lot▫; **il boit sec** he can really knock it back; **ils ont dérouillé sec pendant la guerre** they went through total hell during the war **(b)** **l'avoir sec** to be bummed (out) or Br gutted **(c)** **être à sec** to be broke or Br skint
▸ see also **cinq**

sèche [sɛʃ] nf (cigarette) smoke, Br fag, Am cig

sécher [seʃe] **1** vt (ne pas assister à) (cours) Br to bunk off, Am to skip
2 vi (ne pas aller en classe) Br to bunk off, Am to play hookey

sécot [seko] adj **(a)** (sec) dry▫ **(b)** (maigre) skinny, lanky

secoué, -e [skwe] adj (fou) off one's nut or rocker, Br crackers, Am nutso

secouer [s(ə)kwe] vt **(a)** **j'en ai rien à secouer** ⚠ I don't give a damn or Br a toss **(b)** **secouer les puces à qn** Br to tick sb off, Am to chew sb out

Sécu [seky] nf (abbr **Sécurité sociale**) Br ≃ Social Security▫, Am ≃ welfare▫

sensass [sɑ̃sas] adj (abbr **sensationnel**) sensational, terrific, Br smashing

sentiment [sɑ̃timɑ̃] nm **la faire au sentiment à qn** to get round sb

sentir [sɑ̃tir] **1** vt **(a)** **je ne peux pas la sentir** I can't stand or Br stick her; **je le sens pas bien, ce mec-là** there's something about that guy I don't like **(b)** **je l'ai senti passer!** (à propos d'une douleur, d'une facture, d'une réprimande) I knew all about it!
2 se sentir vpr Hum **ne plus se sentir**

(se comporter de façon étrange) to have taken leave of one's senses; **ne plus se sentir (pisser)** (être vaniteux) to be too big for one's Br boots or Am britches
▸ see also **rose, sapin**

sérieux [serjø] **1** nm (chope de bière) litre of beer▫
2 adv (sérieusement) seriously; **ils se sont foutus sur la gueule sérieux** they seriously went for each other; **sérieux?** seriously?

séropo [seropo] (abbr **séropositif, -ive**)
1 adj HIV-positive▫
2 nmf HIV-positive person▫

serre-patte [sɛrpat] nm sergeant▫

serrer [sere] vt (arrêter) Br to nick, to lift, Am to bust
▸ see also **kiki, louche, pince, vis**

service [sɛrvis] nm Hum **entrée de service** ⚠ (anus) back door, tradesman's entrance

sévère [sever] adv (gravement) severely, seriously; **il déjante sévère en ce moment** he's severely or seriously lost it at the moment; **on a morflé sévère** we went through total hell

SF [ɛsɛf] nf (abbr **science fiction**) sci-fi, SF

shit [ʃit] nm hash, shit, Br blow, draw

shoot [ʃut] nm (de drogue) fix, shot; **se faire un shoot** to shoot up, to jack up

shooté, -e [ʃute] **1** adj **(a)** (drogué) **être shooté** to be a druggy or a junkie **(b)** (fou) crazy, Br barking (mad), Am wacko
2 nm,f **(a)** (drogué) druggy, junkie **(b)** (fou) headcase, fruitcake, Br nutter, Am wacko

shooter [ʃute] **se shooter** vpr to shoot up, to jack up

shooteuse [ʃutøz] nf hype, hypo

sifflard [siflar] nm (dried) sausage▫

siffler [sifle] **1** vt (boire) to sink, to down, to knock back
2 se siffler vpr **il s'est sifflé un litre de rouge à lui tout seul** he sank or

downed *or* knocked back a whole litre of red wine on his own

sifflet [siflɛ] *nm* **couper le sifflet à qn** to leave sb speechless, to shut sb up

sinoque [sinɔk] = **cinoque**

siphonné, -e [sifɔne] *adj (fou)* crazy, bonkers, *Br* barking (mad)

six-quatre-deux [siskatdø] **à la six-quatre-deux** *adv* **faire qch à la six-quatre-deux** to do sth any old how

skeud [skœd] *nm (verlan* **disque)** record ⌐

skin [skin] *nm (abbr* **skinhead)** skin, skinhead

slibar [slibar] *nm Br* scants, *Am* shorts, skivvies

smack [smak] *nm* smack, scag, skag

smala, smalah [smala] *nf* family ⌐, tribe, clan

sniffer [snife] *vt* to sniff, *Am* to huff; *(cocaïne)* to snort, to sniff, *Am* to huff

snobinard, -e [snɔbinar, -ard] **1** *adj* stuck-up, snobby, lah-di-dah
  2 *nm,f* snob ⌐

socialo [sɔsjalo] *(abbr* **socialiste)** *adj &* *nmf* socialist ⌐, leftie, lefty

sœur [sœr] *nf* **(a)** *(femme)* chick, *Br* bird **(b) et ta sœur?** mind your own business!

soft [sɔft] *nm* soft porn

soif [swaf] *nf* **(a) jusqu'à plus soif** to one's heart's content **(b) il fait soif** I'd kill for a drink, *Br* I could murder a drink

soiffard, -e [swafar, -ard] *nm,f* alky, lush, boozer, *Br* pisshead, *Am* booze-hound

soigné, -e [swane] *adj (remarquable en son genre)* **une engueulade soignée** a hell of a telling-off, a telling-off and a half; **il lui a fichu une raclée, quelque chose de soigné!** he thrashed him to within an inch of his life!; **l'addition était soignée** the *Br* bill *or Am* check was exorbitant

soigner [swane] *vt* **faut te faire soigner!** you need your head examined!

soixante-neuf [swasãtnœf] *nm (position)* sixty-nine

sonné, -e [sɔne] *adj* **(a)** *(fou)* crazy, nuts, *Br* crackers, *Am* loony-tunes **(b)** *(étourdi)* groggy

sonner [sɔne] *vt* **(a)** *(assommer)* to knock out **(b) sonner les cloches à qn** to bawl sb out, to give sb what-for **(c) toi, on t'a pas sonné!** nobody asked you!

sono [sɔno] *nf (abbr* **sonorisation)** sound system ⌐

sortable [sɔrtabl] *adj* **il n'est pas sortable** you can't take him anywhere

sortir [sɔrtir] **1** *vt (dire)* to come out with; **ce qu'il peut sortir comme conneries!** [!] he can come out with some real crap *or* bullshit!
  2 *vi* **d'où tu sors?** where have you been?, what planet have you been on?

souffler [sufle] **1** *vt* **(a)** *(surprendre)* to amaze ⌐, to stagger, to flabbergast, *Am* to knock for a loop **(b)** *(dérober)* **souffler qch à qn** to pinch *or Br* nick sth from sb
  2 *vi* **souffler dans les bronches à qn** to bawl sb out, *Br* to give sb dog's abuse, *Am* to rank on sb
  ▶ *see also* **ballon, poireau**

souk [suk] *nm (désordre)* mess; **c'est le souk dans sa piaule!** his room's an absolute bombsite *or* pigsty!; **foutre le souk (dans)** *(mettre en désordre)* to make a mess (of); **il fout le souk en classe** he creates havoc in the classroom

soulager [sulaʒe] **1** *vt* **soulager qn de qch** *(lui voler quelque chose)* to relieve sb of sth
  2 se soulager *vpr* **(a)** *(uriner, déféquer)* to relieve oneself **(b)** *(se masturber)* to give oneself relief

soûlard, -e [sular, -ard] *nm,f* alky, lush, boozer, *Am* boozehound

soûler [sule] *vpr* **se soûler la gueule** [!]

Br to get pissed, *Am* to hang *or* tie one on

soûlot, -ote [sulo, -ɔt] *nm,f* alky, lush, boozer, *Am* boozehound

soupe [sup] *nf* (**a**) **par ici la bonne soupe!** that's the way to make money! (**b**) **faire la soupe à la grimace** to sulk ☐, to be in the huff (**c**) **à la soupe!** grub's up! (**d**) *(musique insipide)* supermarket *or* elevator music
▸ see *also* **cracher**

souper [supe] *vi* **en avoir soupé de qn/qch** to have had enough of sb/sth, to be fed up (to the back teeth) with sb/sth

sourdingue [surdɛ̃g] *adj* deaf ☐

souris [suri] *nf (femme)* chick, *Br* bird

sous-marin [sumarɛ̃] *nm* (**a**) *(véhicule de surveillance)* = converted van used for police surveillance (**b**) *(boisson)* = cocktail consisting of a pint of beer with a shot glass of tequila in the bottom of the beer glass, served with a straw

sous-merde [!] [sumɛrd] *nf* nobody, non-entity; **traiter qn comme une sous-merde** to treat sb like shit

sous-off [suzɔf] *nm* (*abbr* **sous-officier**) non-commissioned officer ☐

sous-ventrière [suvɑ̃trijɛr] *nf* **manger à s'en faire péter la sous-ventrière** to pig out, to stuff oneself *or* one's face, *Am* to munch out

soutif [sutif] *nm* bra ☐

speed [spid] **1** *adj (nerveux)* hyper
2 *nm (amphétamine)* speed

speedé, -e [spide] *adj* (**a**) *(nerveux)* hyper (**b**) *(drogué aux amphétamines)* **être speedé** to be speeding

speeder [spide] *vi* (**a**) *(être sous l'effet d'amphétamines)* to be speeding (**b**) *(se dépêcher)* to get a move on, *Am* to get it in gear

splif [splif] *nm* spliff, joint, number

sport [spɔr] *nm* (**a**) **il va y avoir du sport** now we're going to see some fun (**b**) *Hum* **sport en chambre** *(rapports sexuels)* bedroom sports

squatter [skwate] **1** *vt (monopoliser)* to take over, to hog; **il squatte toujours la télécommande quand on regarde un film** he always hogs the remote control when we're watching a film; **arrête de squatter le joint, fais tourner!** stop bogarting that joint, pass it round!
2 *vi* to squat; **ça fait trois semaines qu'il squatte chez moi** he's been squatting at mine for three weeks now

starsky [starski] *nm* cop, *Am* flatfoot

> This term comes from *Starsky and Hutch*, the popular 1970s American TV series about two policemen.

stick [stik] *nm* (thin) joint *or* spliff *or* number

stonba [stɔ̃ba] *nf* (*verlan* **baston**) scuffle, *Br* punch-up, *Am* slugfest

stone [ston], **stoned** [stond] *adj* stoned

stups [styp] *nmpl* **la Brigade des stups, les stups** the Drug Squad

suant, -e [sɥɑ̃, -ɑ̃t] *adj (fâcheux)* **être suant** to be a pain (in the neck)

subclaquant, -e [sybklakɑ̃, -ɑ̃t] *adj* **être subclaquant** to be on one's last legs, to have one foot in the grave

sucer [syse] *vt* (**a**) [!!] **sucer qn** *(pratiquer la fellation sur)* to go down on sb, to give sb head, to suck sb off; *(pratiquer le cunnilinctus sur)* to go down on sb, to give sb head, *Br* to lick sb out
(**b**) **sucer la pomme** *ou* **la couenne à qn** *Br* to snog sb, *Am* to make out with sb; **se sucer la pomme** *ou* **la couenne** *Br* to snog, *Am* to make out, to suck face
(**c**) **il suce pas que de la glace** he drinks like a fish

suceur [!] [sysœr] *nm (flatteur) Br* arse-licker, *Am* ass-licker

suceuse [!!] [sysøz] *nf (femme qui pratique la fellation)* **c'est une sacrée su-**

ceuse she gives a great blow-job, she gives great head

sucrer [sykre] **1** vt (**a**) (supprimer) (permis, licence) to take away; (permission, prime) to cancel; (argent de poche) to stop (**b**) **sucrer les fraises** to have shaky hands

 2 se sucrer vpr (s'octroyer un bénéfice) to line one's pockets

suer [sɥe] vi (**a**) **faire suer qn** (l'embêter) to bug sb, Br to get up sb's nose, to get on sb's wick, Am to tick sb off (**b**) **faire suer le burnous** to exploit one's workforce, to be a real slave-driver

suif [sɥif] nm **faire du suif** to kick up a fuss

sulfateuse [sylfatøz] nf (mitraillette) submachine gun

sup [syp] adj inv (abbr **supplémentaire**) **heures sup** overtime

super [sypɛr] **1** adj inv super, great, terrific

 2 adv Br dead, Am real; **un bouquin super chiant** a Br dead or Am real boring book; **on s'est super bien marrés** we had a Br fab or Am awesome time

This is by far the most common word used to describe the excellence of someone or something. "Super" and its accompanying term are often written as one word, eg "supernana", "superplan", "superchiant".

surgé [syrʒe] nmf (abbr **surveillant, -e général(e)**) head supervisor (in charge of school discipline)

surin [syrɛ̃] nm knife, blade, Am shiv, shank

suriner [syrine] vt (blesser avec un couteau) to knife, to cut, Am to shiv; (tuer avec un couteau) to stab to death

sympa [sɛ̃pa] adj (abbr **sympathique**) nice

syphilo [sifilo] nmf (abbr **syphilitique**) = person suffering from syphilis

système [sistɛm] nm (**a**) **taper sur le système à qn** Br to get on sb's wick, to get up sb's nose, to do sb's head in, Am to give sb a pain (in the neck), to tick sb off (**b**) **le système D** resourcefulness

T

tabac [taba] *nm* **(a) faire un tabac** to be a big hit **(b) passer qn à tabac** to beat sb up, to give sb a hammering; **passage à tabac** beating up, hammering **(c) c'est le même tabac** it's the same difference, it amounts to the same thing ► see *also* **blague**

tabasser [tabase] *vt* **tabasser qn** to beat sb up, to give sb a hammering; **se faire tabasser** to get beaten up, to *Br* get *or Am* take a hammering

table [tabl] *nf* **se mettre** *ou* **passer à table** *(faire des aveux)* to spill the beans

tablier [tablije] *nm Hum* **tablier de sapeur** *ou* **de forgeron**⟨!⟩ *(poils pubiens)* bush, pubes, beaver

tache [taʃ] *nf* **(a)** *(personne nulle)* non-entity, loser, no-hoper; **quelle tache ce mec-là!** what a total non-entity *or* loser *or* no-hoper that guy is! **(b) faire tache** *(jurer)* to stand *or* stick out like a sore thumb

tacot [tako] *nm* **(a)** *(vieille voiture)* heap, banger, rustbucket **(b)** *(taxi)* taxi □, cab, *Am* hack

taf [taf] *nm (travail)* work □; *(tâche, emploi)* job □

taffe [taf] *nf* drag, puff

tag [tag] *nm* tag *(piece of graffiti)*

tagger[1] [tage] *vt* to cover in graffiti □

tagger[2] [tagœr] *nm* graffiti artist □, tagger, *Am* writer

taguer [tage] = **tagger**[1]

taguer [tage] = **tagger**[2]

tailler [taje] **1** *vt* **(a) tailler une pipe** *ou* **une plume à qn**⟨!!⟩ to give sb a blow-job, to suck sb off, to give sb head **(b) tailler un costard à qn** *Br* to slag sb off, *Am* to bad-mouth sb **(c) tailler la route** *(parcourir beaucoup de chemin)* to eat up the miles; *(partir)* to beat it, *Br* to scarper, *Am* to book it
2 se tailler *vpr (partir)* to beat it, *Br* to scarper, *Am* to book it
► see *also* **bavette**

tailleuse [tajøz] *nf* **c'est une sacrée tailleuse de pipes** *ou* **de plumes**⟨!!⟩ she gives a great blow-job, she gives great head

taloche [talɔʃ] *nf* clout, cuff; **flanquer une taloche à qn** to clout *or* cuff sb

talocher [talɔʃe] *vt* to clout, to cuff

tambouille [tɑ̃buj] *nf* food □, grub, chow; **faire la tambouille** to do the cooking □

tamponner [tɑ̃pɔne] **se tamponner** *vpr* **s'en tamponner (le coquillard)** not to give a damn *or Br* a toss *or* a monkey's *or Am* a rap

tangente [tɑ̃ʒɑ̃t] *nf* **prendre la tangente** to slip off *or* away, to make oneself scarce

tango [tɑ̃go] *nm (boisson)* = cocktail consisting of beer and grenadine

tannée [tane] *nf (correction, défaite)* thrashing, hammering; **filer une tannée à qn** to thrash *or* hammer sb, to give sb a thrashing *or* a hammering; **prendre une tannée** to get thrashed *or* hammered

tanner [tane] *vt (importuner)* to pester, to badger, to bug
► see *also* **cuir**

tante [tɑ̃t], **tantouse, tantouze** [tɑ̃tuz] *nf Offensive (homosexuel)* fairy, queer, *Br* poof, *Am* fag

tapant, -e [tapã, -ãt] *adj* **à cinq heures tapantes** at five o'clock sharp *or* on the dot

tapé, -e [tape] *adj (fou)* nuts, *Br* crackers, *Am* loony-tunes

tapecul, tape-cul [tapky] *nm (véhicule)* boneshaker

tapée [tape] *nf* **(toute) une tapée de** loads of, tons of

taper [tape] *vt* **(a)** *(emprunter)* to bum, to cadge, *Br* to tap; **taper qch à qn, taper qn de qch** to bum *or* cadge sth off sb, to hit *or Br* tap sb for sth; **il m'a tapé dix francs** he bummed *or* cadged ten francs off me, he hit *or Br* tapped me for ten francs

(b) *(atteindre)* **taper le cent/le deux cents** to hit a hundred/two hundred (kilometres an hour)

(c) elle lui a tapé dans l'œil *(elle lui a plu)* he was really taken with her, he took quite a shine to her

2 se taper *vpr* **(a)** *(subir)* **on s'est tapé ses parents tout le week-end** we got stuck *or Br* landed *or* lumbered with his parents all weekend; **se taper le ménage/les courses** to get stuck *or Br* landed *or* lumbered with the housework/the shopping; **on s'est tapé de la pluie pendant trois semaines** we had rain every day for three weeks; **on s'est tapé deux heures d'embouteillages** we got stuck in traffic jams for two hours

(b) *(absorber) (nourriture)* to guzzle, to scoff; *(boisson)* to sink, to lower; **je me taperais bien une petite choucroute!** I'd kill for *or Br* I could murder a plate of sauerkraut!; **il a fallu que je me tape tout Proust pour l'examen** I had to devour the entire works of Proust for the exam

(c) !! *(posséder sexuellement)* **se taper qn** to screw *or Br* shag sb

(d) ! *(se désintéresser)* **je m'en tape** I don't give a shit *or Br* a toss *or Am* a rat's

ass

(e) à se taper le derrière *ou* **le cul** ! **par terre** hysterical, side-splitting

▸ *see also* **carton, cloche, colonne, honte, incruste, lune, queue, raie, rassis, système**

tapette [tapɛt] *nf Offensive (homosexuel)* queer, fairy, *Br* poof, *Am* fag

tapeur, -euse [tapœr, -øz] *nm,f* moocher, sponger, scrounger

tapin [tapɛ̃] *nm* **faire le tapin** to walk the streets, *Br* to be on the game, *Am* to hook

tapiner [tapine] *vi* to walk the streets, *Br* to be on the game, *Am* to hook

tapineur, -euse [tapinœr, -øz] *nm,f* streetwalker

taré, -e [tare] **1** *adj* crazy, off one's head *or* rocker, *Br* barking (mad)
2 *nm,f* nutcase, headcase, *Br* nutter

targettes [tarʒɛt] *nfpl* **(a)** *(pieds)* feet □, *Br* plates, *Am* dogs **(b)** *(chaussures)* shoes □

tarin [tarɛ̃] *nm Br* conk, hooter, *Am* schnozzle

tarpé [tarpe] *nm (verlan* **pétard)** joint, spliff, reefer, number

tarte [tart] **1** *adj* **(a)** *(ridicule)* ridiculous □, *Br* naff **(b)** *(stupide) Br* dim, thick, *Am* dumb
2 *nf* **(a)** *(coup)* clout, wallop; **flanquer une tarte à qn** to clout *or* wallop sb **(b) c'est pas de la tarte** *(c'est difficile)* it's no walkover, it's no picnic **(c) tarte aux poils** !! *(sexe de la femme)* bush, hairpie

Tartempion [tartãpjɔ̃] *npr* thingy, what's-his-name, *f* what's-her-name

tartignol, tartignolle [tartiɲɔl] *adj* ridiculous □, *Br* naff

tartine [tartin] *nf* **(a)** *(pied)* foot, *Br* plate, *Am* dog **(b)** *(chaussure)* shoe □ **(c)** *(texte long)* **en mettre une tartine** *ou* **des tartines** to write screeds, to waffle on

tartiner [tartine] **1** vt **(a)** (écrire) to churn out **(b)** (enduire en grande quantité) **tartiner qn/qch de qch** to cover sb/sth in sth □

2 se tartiner vpr **se tartiner de qch** to cover oneself in sth □

tartir [tartir] vi **se faire tartir**[!] to be bored shitless

tasse [tɑs] nf **(a) boire la tasse** (avaler de l'eau) to get a mouthful of water **(b) tasses** (urinoirs) street urinals □

tassé, -e [tɑse] adj **il a la cinquantaine bien tassée** he's fifty if he's a day, he's on the wrong side of fifty

tassepé[!] [taspe] nf (verlan **pétasse**) **(a)** (fille) slut, Br slapper, scrubber **(b)** (prostituée) whore, hooker

tata [tata] nf Offensive (homosexuel) queer, fairy, Br poof, Am fag

tatane [tatan] nf shoe □

taulard, -e [tolar, -ard] nm,f jailbird, con

taule [tol] nf **(a)** (prison) slammer, clink, Br nick, Am pen; **faire de la taule** to do time, to do a stretch **(b)** (lieu de travail) workplace □ **(c)** (chambre) room □

taulier, -ère [tolje, -ɛr] nm,f **(a)** (d'un hôtel) boss **(b)** (logeur) landlord, f landlady □

taupe [top] nf **avoir la taupe au bord du trou**[!!] to be dying for a shit

taxer [takse] vt **(a)** (emprunter) **taxer qch à qn** to scrounge or sponge or bum sth from sb **(b)** (voler) to pinch, Br to nick; **je me suis fait taxer mon cuir par une bande de skins** I got my leather jacket pinched or Br nicked by a bunch of skinheads

tchatche [tʃatʃ] nf **de la tchatche** the gift of the gab; **tout ça c'est de la tchatche** that's just a lot of talk

tchatcher [tʃatʃe] vi to chat

tchatcheur, -euse [tʃatʃœr, -øz] nm,f smooth talker

techi [tœʃi] nm (verlan **shit**) shit, hash, Br blow, draw

tehon [tœɔ̃] nf (verlan **honte**) **avoir** ou **se taper la tehon** to be embarrassed □ or mortified; **(c'est) la tehon!** the shame of it!

tèj [tɛʒ] vt (verlan **jeter**) (chasser) to throw or chuck out, Am to eighty-six; (abandonner) to chuck, to dump; **il s'est fait tèj par sa meuf** his woman chucked or dumped him

téléphoné, -e [telefɔne] adj **c'était téléphoné** you could see it coming (a mile off); **un gag téléphoné** a joke you can see coming (a mile off)

téloche [telɔʃ] nf TV, tube, Br telly

tenir [tanir] vt **tenir une bonne cuite** to be totally wrecked or wasted or Br legless or pissed; **qu'est-ce qu'il tient!** (il est vraiment stupide) what a jerk or Br tosser or Am klutz; (il est complètement ivre) he's totally wrecked or wasted or Br legless or pissed

▶ see also **bavarde, bout, chandelle, côte, couche, crachoir, dose, jambe**

têtard [tetar] nm (enfant) kid, brat

tête [tɛt] nf **être une tête** to be brainy, to have brains; **tête de con**[!], **tête de nœud**[!] dickhead; **quelle tête à claques ce mec!** he's got a face you want to slap!; **c'est quinze francs par tête de pipe** it's fifteen francs a head; **prendre la tête à qn** Br to get up sb's nose, to get on sb's wick, Am to tick sb off; **prise de tête** pain (in the neck); **tomber sur la tête** to go off one's rocker, to lose it, Br to lose the plot; **non mais t'es tombé sur la tête ou quoi?** were you dropped on the head or something?; **ça va pas la tête?** are you mad?; **avoir** ou **attraper la grosse tête** to have a big head, to be big-headed; **faire une (grosse) tête** ou **une tête au carré à qn** to smash sb's face in, Br to punch sb's lights out, Am to punch sb out; **avoir la tête dans le cul**[!] to be out of it

▶ see also **cul, payer, piquer, pou, yeux**

téter [tete] vi (boire avec excès) to knock it back, to drink like a fish

tétons [tetɔ̃] nmpl (seins) tits, boobs, knockers

teuch[1] [tœʃ] nm (verlan **shit**) shit, hash, Br blow, draw

teuch[2] [!!] nf (verlan **chatte**) pussy, snatch, Br minge

teuf [tœf] nf (verlan **fête**) party ▫

teup [!] [tœp] nf (verlan **pute**) (prostituée) whore, hooker; (femme facile) tart, slut, Br slapper, scrubber, slag

texto [tɛksto] adv (abbr **textuellement**) word for word

thon [tɔ̃] nm (femme laide) dog, Br boot, Am beast

thune [tyn] nf (a) (argent) cash, Br dosh, Am bucks (b) (pièce) **j'ai plus une thune** I haven't a bean or Am a cent

tiags [tjag] nfpl (abbr **santiags**) cowboy boots ▫

ticket [tikɛ] nm **avoir le ticket (avec qn)** to have made a hit (with sb)

tickson [tiksɔ̃] nm ticket ▫

tifs [tif] nmpl hair ▫; **il faut que j'aille me faire couper les tifs** I have to go and get my hair cut

tige [tiʒ] nf (a) (cigarette) Br fag, Am cig (b) [!!] (pénis) dick, prick, cock ▸ see also **brouter**

tignasse [tiɲas] nf (cheveux) mane, mop

tilt [tilt] nm **ça a fait tilt** the penny dropped, it clicked

timbré, -e [tɛ̃bre] adj (fou) nuts, crazy, Br barking, Am loco

tintin [tɛ̃tɛ̃] nm (a) **tintin!** no way (José)!, no chance!, nothing doing! (b) **faire tintin** to go without

tintouin [tɛ̃twɛ̃] nm (a) (vacarme) racket, din (b) (souci) grief, hassle; **elle me donne bien du tintouin** she's giving me so much trouble or hassle; **tous ces invités, ça fait du tintouin** all these guests is just a lot of hassle

tiquer [tike] vi to wince ▫; **il a pas tiqué** he didn't bat an eyelid or turn a hair; **ça l'a fait tiquer** it gave him a shake or a jolt

tire [tir] nf (voiture) car ▫, Br motor, Am ride

tire-au-cul [!] [tiroky], **tire-au-flanc** [tiroflã] nm inv Br skiver, Am goldbrick

tirée [tire] nf haul, trek; **ça fait une tirée d'ici à là-bas** it's a bit of a haul or trek from here

tire-jus [!] [tirʒy] nm snot-rag

tire-larigot [tirlarigo] **à tire-larigot** adv **boire à tire-larigot** to drink like a fish; **il y en a à tire-larigot** there's loads or tons of them

tirelire [tirlir] nf (a) (visage) face ▫, mug (b) (tête) head ▫, nut, Br bonce

tire-moelle [!] [tirmwal] nm inv snot-rag

tirer [tire] **1** vt (a) (voler) **tirer qch à qn** to pinch or Br nick sth from sb (b) (prendre pour cible) **ils tiraient les passants comme des lapins** they were picking off passers-by one by one (c) [!!] (posséder sexuellement) to fuck, to screw, to hump, Br to shag (d) [!!] **tirer un coup** to get laid, to have a fuck or a screw or Br a shag; **ça fait des semaines que j'ai pas tiré mon coup** I haven't got laid in weeks (e) (passer) **il est en train de tirer dix piges pour vol à main armée** he's doing a ten-year stretch for armed robbery; **encore deux mois à tirer avant les vacances** another two months to get through before the Br holidays or Am vacation (f) **tirer les vers du nez à qn** to worm or drag it out of sb

2 vi **tirer au flanc** ou **au cul** [!] to shirk, Br to skive

3 se tirer vpr (a) (partir) to hit the road,

to get going, to make tracks; *(se sauver)* to beat it, *Br* to clear off, *Am* to book it **(b) se tirer sur l'élastique** `!` to jerk off, to beat off, *Br* to wank, to have a wank

▸ see *also* **crampe, gueule, numéro, patte, portrait**

tiroir [tirwar] *nm (ventre)* stomach `▫`, belly

▸ see *also* **polichinelle**

tiser [tize] **1** *vt* to knock back
2 *vi* to booze, to knock it back

titi [titi] *nm* = Parisian street urchin

tocante [tɔkɑ̃t] *nf* watch `▫`

tocard, -e [tɔkar, -ard] **1** *nm,f (personne insignifiante)* non-entity, dead loss, loser
2 *nm (mauvais cheval de course)* rank outsider `▫`

toile [twal] *nf* **(a) se faire une toile** to go to the *Br* pictures *or Am* movies **(b) toiles** *(draps)* sheets `▫`; **se mettre dans les toiles** to hit the sack *or* the hay *or Am* the rack

tomate [tɔmat] *nf (cocktail)* = cocktail consisting of pastis and grenadine

tomber [tɔ̃be] **1** *vt* **(a)** *(séduire)* to pick up, *Br* to pull **(b)** *(enlever)* to take off `▫`; **il a tombé la veste** he took his jacket off **2** *vi* **(a)** *(être arrêté)* to get nabbed *or Br* lifted *or* nicked **(b)** *(pleuvoir)* to rain `▫`; **qu'est-ce qu'il est tombé hier soir!** it was raining cats and dogs *or Br* bucketing down *or* chucking it down last night! **(c) laisse tomber!** forget it!

▸ see *also* **carafe, cordes, jus, os, paletot, patte, poil, pomme, râble, rade, tête**

tombeur [tɔ̃bœr] *nm* **(a)** *(séducteur)* womanizer `▫`, *Am* mack **(b)** *(vainqueur)* **c'est lui le tombeur du champion du monde** he's the man who defeated the world champion `▫`

-ton [tɔ̃] *suffix* **biffeton** *(billet de banque)* note `▫`, *Am* greenback; *(de transport, de spectacle)* ticket `▫`; **cureton**

priest `▫`; **frometon** cheese `▫`; **mecton** guy, *Br* bloke

This suffix is found at the end of many French nouns and is used for either humorous or pejorative effect.

top [tɔp] **1** *adj* great, *Br* fab, *Am* awesome
2 *nm* **c'est le top (du top)** it's the best of stuff, *Br* it's the business!

topo [tɔpo] *nm* report `▫`; **faire un topo à qn sur qch** to give sb the lowdown on sth, *Am* to hip sb to sth; **tu vois (un peu) le topo** (you) see what I mean?; **c'est toujours le même topo** it's always the same old story

toqué, -e [tɔke] **1** *adj* crazy, nuts, *Br* mental, *Am* gonzo
2 *nm,f* headcase, *Br* nutter, *Am* wacko

torche-cul `!` [tɔrʃ(ə)ky] *nm (journal)* rag; *(texte)* trash, *Br* rubbish

torchée [tɔrʃe] *nf (correction)* thrashing, hammering; **filer une torchée à qn** to thrash *or* hammer sb

torcher [tɔrʃe] **1** *vt* **(a)** *(faire en vitesse)* to knock off, to dash off; **bien torché** well put-together **(b)** `!!` *(essuyer le derrière de)* **torcher (le cul de) qn** to wipe sb's *Br* arse *or Am* ass **2 se torcher** *vpr* **(a)** *(se battre)* to knock lumps out of each other, to have a *Br* punch-up *or Am* slugfest **(b)** `!!` *(s'essuyer)* **se torcher (le cul)** to wipe one's *Br* arse *or Am* ass; **je m'en torche!** I don't give a shit *or Am* a rat's ass! **(c)** `!` *(s'enivrer)* to get shit-faced *or Br* pissed *or* rat-arsed

torchon [tɔrʃɔ̃] *nm (mauvais journal)* rag; *(devoir mal présenté)* dog's breakfast *or* dinner

tordant, -e [tɔrdɑ̃, -ɑ̃t] *adj (amusant)* hysterical, side-splitting

tord-boyaux [tɔrbwajo] *nm* gutrot, rotgut, *Am* alky

tordre [tɔrdr] **se tordre** *vpr* **se tordre (de rire)** to be in stitches, to kill oneself (laughing), to be doubled up (with laughter)

tordu, -e [tɔrdy] *nm,f* nutcase, headcase, *Br* nutter, *Am* wacko

torgnole [tɔrɲɔl] *nf (gifle)* clout, wallop; **flanquer une torgnole à qn** to clout *or* wallop sb

torrieu [tɔrjø] *exclam Can* hell!

tortiller [tɔrtije] *vi* **y a pas à tortiller, y a pas à tortiller du cul pour chier droit**[!!] there's no getting away from it, there are no two ways about it

tos [tos] *nmf Offensive* Dago *(from Portugal)*

> Depending on the context and the tone of voice used, this term may be either offensive or affectionately humorous. It is nonetheless inadvisable to use it unless one is quite sure of the reaction it will receive.

tosser [tɔse] *vi* to get stoned

total [tɔtal] *adv* total, **j'ai perdu mon boulot/il a fallu que je recommence** the upshot is, I lost my job/I had to start again

totale [tɔtal] *nf* **quand il m'a demandée en mariage, il m'a fait la totale** when he proposed to me, he really went all out; **on a eu droit à la totale: verglas, embouteillages, barrages de routiers** black ice, traffic jams, lorry drivers' road blocks, you name it, we had it

> This expression originates from "la totale" meaning a hysterectomy. It is used to abbreviate a long list and may have either positive or negative connotations.

toto [toto] *nm* louse □, *Am* cootie

toubab [tubab] *nmf* = French person of native stock, as opposed to immigrants or their descendants

toubib [tubib] *nm* doctor □, doc

touche [tuʃ] *nf* **(a)** *(aspect)* look □; **il a**

une de ces touches avec sa veste à franges! he looks like something from another planet with that fringed jacket of his! **(b)** *(personne séduite)* conquest □; **faire une touche** to score, *Br* to pull

touche-pipi [tuʃpipi] *nm* **jouer à touche-pipi** to play at doctors and nurses

toucher [tuʃe] **1** *vi* **(a)** *(être doué)* to be brilliant **(en/à** at) **(b)** *(recevoir de l'argent)* to collect
2 se toucher *vpr* **(a)**[!!] *(se masturber)* to play with oneself, *Br* to touch oneself (up) **(b) se toucher (la nuit)** to fool oneself, to kid oneself on
▸ *see also* **bille, pacson**

touffe[!!] [tuf] *nf (toison pubienne)* bush, pubes; **une jupe ras la touffe** a micro mini-skirt □, *Br* a bum-freezer

touiller [tuje] *vt* to stir □

toupie [tupi] *nf* **une vieille toupie** an old crone *or* bag *or Am* goat

tournant [turnã] *nm* **attendre qn au tournant** to be waiting for a chance to get even with sb

tourner [turne] **1** *vi* **(a)** *(devenir)* **tourner homo/hippie** to become gay/a hippy **(b) tourner de l'œil** to pass out □, to keel over
2 se tourner *vpr* **se tourner les pouces, se les tourner** to twiddle one's thumbs
▸ *see also* **rond**

tournicoter [turnikɔte] *vi* to wander around aimlessly

toutim, toutime [tutim] *nm* **et tout le toutim** the works, the whole enchilada, *Br* the full monty

toutou [tutu] *nm* doggy, doggie

touzepar [tuzpar] *nf (verlan* **partouze)** orgy

toxico [tɔksiko] *nmf (abbr* **toxicomane)** addict, junkie, *Am* hophead

tracer [trase] *vi (aller vite)* to belt along, to bomb along; *(déguerpir)* to beat it, *Br* to clear off, *Am* to book it

traduc [tradyk] *nf* (*abbr* **traduction**) translation □

train [trɛ̃] *nm* (*postérieur*) backside, *Br* bum, *Am* fanny; **filer le train à qn** to shadow *or* tail sb
▶ see also **botter, magner**

traînailler [trɛnaje] *vi* (**a**) (*être lent*) to dawdle (**b**) (*perdre son temps*) to hang about, *Br* to faff about

traînard, -e [trɛnar, -ard] *nm,f Br* slowcoach, *Am* slowpoke

traîne [trɛn] *nf* **être à la traîne** to lag behind

traînée ⚠ [trɛne] *nf* (*femme*) tart, *Br* slapper, scrubber

traîner [trɛne] *vi* (*être posé*) to lie around, to hang around
▶ see also **guêtres, merde, savate**

traîne-savates [trɛnsavat] *nm inv* down-and-out, *Br* dosser, *Am* bum

traîneux [trɛnø] *nm Can* slob

traiter [trɛte] *vt* (*insulter*) *Br* to slag off, *Am* to bad-mouth

tralala [tralala] *nm* **et tout le tralala** the works, the whole enchilada, *Br* the full monty

tranche [trɑ̃ʃ] *nf* **s'en payer une tranche** to have a ball *or Am* a blast

transbahuter [trɑ̃sbayte] *vt* to shift, to hump, to lug

transfo [trɑ̃sfo] *nm* (*abbr* **transformateur**) transformer □

trapu, -e [trapy] *adj* (**a**) (*difficile*) tough, tricky (**b**) (*expert*) brainy, brilliant (**en/à** at)

travail [travaj] *nm* **et voilà le travail!** and that's all there is to it!, *Br* and Bob's your uncle!; **qu'est-ce que c'est que ce travail?** what's going on here?, what's the meaning of this?

travelo [travlo] *nm* drag queen, TV, *Br* tranny

traviole [travjɔl] **de traviole** *adv*

marcher de traviole to be staggering all over the place; **être de traviole** to be lop-sided *or* skew-whiff

trèfle [trɛfl] *nm* (*argent*) cash, dough, *Br* dosh, *Am* bucks

tremblement [trɑ̃bləmɑ̃] *nm* **et tout le tremblement** the works, the whole enchilada, *Br* the full monty

tremblote [trɑ̃blɔt] *nf* **avoir la tremblote** (*de peur*) to have the jitters; (*de froid, à cause de la fièvre*) to have the shivers; (*à cause d'une maladie*) to have the shakes; (*vieillard*) to be shaky

trempe [trɑ̃p] *nf* (*correction*) thrashing, pasting; **prendre une trempe** to get *or Am* take a thrashing *or* a pasting; **flanquer une trempe à qn** to give sb a thrashing *or* a pasting

tremper [trɑ̃pe] *vi* **tremper dans qch** to be mixed up in sth
▶ see also **biscuit, panais**

trempette [trɑ̃pɛt] *nf* **faire trempette** to have a dip

trente-six [trɑ̃tsis] *adj* **tous les trente-six du mois** once in a blue moon; **il y en a pas trente-six** there aren't that many of them; **des raisons, je pourrais t'en citer trente-six** I could give you umpteen reasons; **il y a pas trente-six solutions** there's no getting away from it, there are no two ways about it; **voir trente-six chandelles** to see stars

trente-sixième [trɑ̃tsizjɛm] *adj* **être au trente-sixième dessous** to be in a tight spot

trichlo [triklo] *nm* (*abbr* **trichloréthylène**) trichloroethylene □ (*used as a drug*)

tricoter [trikɔte] *vi* (*marcher vite*) **tricoter (des gambettes)** to leg it, to belt along

trifouiller [trifuje] **1** *vt* (**a**) (*fouiller*) to rummage through (**b**) (*toucher à*) to fiddle with, to tinker with
2 *vi* **trifouiller dans qch** to rummage

around in sth

Trifouillis-les-Oies [trifujilezwa] *npr* = fictional name for the archetypal isolated, dull village

trimarder [trimarde] *vi* to be on the road

trimardeur [trimardœr] *nm* tramp, *Am* hobo

trimballer [trɛ̃bale] **1** *vt* (**a**) *(transporter)* to hump, to schlep, to lug around; **il trimballe sa famille partout où il va** he has his family in tow everywhere he goes (**b**) **qu'est-ce qu'il trimballe!** what a total halfwit *or Br* tosser *or Am* klutz!

2 se trimballer *vpr* to schlep around, to trail around

trimer [trime] *vi* to slog away, to slave away; **faire trimer qn** to keep sb hard at it, to keep sb's nose to the grindstone

tringler ‼ [trɛ̃gle] *vt* to fuck, to screw, *Br* to shag

trinquer [trɛ̃ke] *vi* (*subir un désagrément*) to be the one who suffers, to pay the price

trip [trip] *nm* (**a**) *(centre d'intérêt)* kick; **il est en plein trip écolo en ce moment** he's on some environmental kick at the moment; **c'est vraiment pas mon trip, ce genre de truc** I'm not really into that kind of thing, it's not my scene, that kind of thing (**b**) *(produit par la drogue)* trip

tripaille [tripaj] *nf* innards, guts

triper [tripe] *vi* to trip *(after taking drugs)*

tripes [trip] *nfpl* (**a**) **jouer avec ses tripes** to give it one's all (**b**) **rendre** *ou* **vomir** *ou* **dégueuler tripes et boyaux** to be as sick as a dog, *Br* to spew one's guts up

tripette [tripɛt] *nf* **ça ne vaut pas tripette** it's a load of tripe *or* dross, *Am* it's not worth diddly

tripotée [tripɔte] *nf* (**a**) **une tripotée**

(de) tons (of), loads (of) (**b**) *(correction, défaite)* thrashing, hammering; **filer une tripotée à qn** to thrash *or* hammer sb, to give sb a thrashing *or* a hammering; **prendre une tripotée** to get thrashed *or* hammered

tripoter [tripɔte] **1** *vt* (**a**) *(toucher)* to fiddle with, to play with (**b**) *(se livrer à des attouchements sur)* to feel up, to grope, *Br* to touch up

2 se tripoter ! *vpr* to touch oneself up, to play with oneself

trique ‼ [trik] *nf* *(érection)* hard-on, boner; **avoir la trique** to have a hard-on *or* a boner

triquer ‼ [trike] *vi* to have a hard-on *or* a boner

trisser [trise] **1** *vi* to hightail it, to scoot, *Am* to split

2 se trisser *vpr* to hightail it, to scoot, *Am* to split

tristounet, -ette [tristunɛ, -ɛt] *adj* sad □

trogne [trɔɲ] *nf* *(visage)* face □, mug, *Am* map

trognon [trɔɲɔ̃] **1** *adj* *(mignon)* cute, sweet

2 *nm* **jusqu'au trognon** ! well and truly; **il s'est fait avoir jusqu'au trognon** ! he's been well and truly had

trom [trɔm], *nm* *(verlan* **métro***)* *Br* underground □, *Am* subway □

trombine [trɔ̃bin] *nf* face □, mug

trombiner ‼ [trɔ̃bine] *vt* *(posséder sexuellement)* to fuck, to screw, to shaft, *Br* to shag

tromé [trome] = **trom**

tronc [trɔ̃] *nm* **se casser le tronc** to worry □, *Br* to get one's knickers in a twist

tronche [trɔ̃ʃ] *nf* *(visage)* face □, mug; **il a une drôle de tronche** he looks really odd, he's really odd-looking; **faire la tronche** to sulk □, to be in a *or* the huff; **t'en fais une tronche, qu'est-ce qui**

t'arrive? you look really down, what's up? **(b)** *(personne intelligente)* brain, brainy person; **ce mec-là, c'est une tronche!** that guy's a real brain or so brainy!
▸ see also **payer**

troncher [tʁɔ̃ʃe] *vt* to fuck, to screw, to hump, *Br* to shag

trône [tʁon] *nm Hum* **être sur le trône** *(aux toilettes)* to be on the throne

trop [tʁo] **1** *adv (très)* **j'étais trop dégoûté** I was so bummed or *Br* gutted; **il est trop mortel, son plan** his plan's so or too brilliant; **j'étais trop mort de rire** I was absolutely killing myself
2 *adj inv (incroyable)* too much, unreal

troquet [tʁɔkɛ] *nm* bar □, *Br* boozer

trotte [tʁɔt] *nf* hike, stretch, schlep; **il y a** *ou* **ça fait une trotte d'ici à là-bas** it's quite a hike or stretch or schlep from here

trottoir [tʁɔtwaʁ] *nm* **faire le trottoir** to be on the game, *Am* to hook

trou [tʁu] *nm* **(a)** *(prison)* slammer, clink, *Br* nick, *Am* pen **(b)** *(endroit isolé)* hole; **il n'est jamais sorti de son trou** he's never been out of his own backyard **(c) boire comme un trou** to drink like a fish **(d) trou de balle**[!]**, trou du cul**[!!] *Br* arsehole, *Am* asshole
▸ see also **taupe, yeux**

trouduc[!] [tʁudyk]**, trou-du-cul**[!] [tʁudyky] *nm (imbécile) Br* arsehole, *Am* asshole

troufignon[!] [tʁufiɲɔ̃] *nm Br* arsehole, *Am* asshole

troufion [tʁufjɔ̃] *nm* **(a)** *(simple soldat) Br* squaddie, *Am* grunt **(b)**[!] *(postérieur) Br* arse, *Am* ass

trouillard, -e [tʁujaʁ, -aʁd] *nm,f* chicken *(person)*

trouille [tʁuj] *nf* fear □; **avoir la trouille** to be scared stiff; **foutre la trouille à qn** to scare the living daylights out of sb, to scare sb stiff

trouillomètre [tʁujɔmɛtʁ] *nm* **avoir le trouillomètre à zéro** to be scared stiff

trouilloter[!] [tʁujɔte] *vi* **(a)** *(avoir peur)* to be scared shitless, to be shitscared **(b)** *(sentir mauvais)* to stink, *Br* to pong

trousser[!] [tʁuse] *vt (posséder sexuellement)* to hump, *Br* to have it away or off with

truander [tʁyɑ̃de] **1** *vt* to swindle, to rip off, to con, *Am* to rook; **se faire truander** to get swindled or ripped off or conned or *Am* rooked
2 *vi (tricher)* to cheat □ **(à** in); *(resquiller)* to sneak in

truanderie [tʁyɑ̃dʁi] *nf* con, scam

truc [tʁyk] *nm* thing □; **c'est pas mon truc** it's not my scene or thing or bag or *Br* cup of tea; **c'est tout à fait son truc** it's just his sort of thing, *Br* it's right up his street

trucider [tʁyside] *vt* to bump off, to ice, to waste

Trucmuche [tʁykmyʃ] *npr* thingy, what's-his-name, *f* what's-her-name

truffe [tʁyf] *nf (imbécile) Br* divvy, dipstick, *Am* lamebrain, schmuck

trumeau, -x [tʁymo] *nm (femme laide)* dog, *Br* boot, *Am* beast

truster [tʁœste] *vt (monopoliser)* to monopolize □, to hog

tubard, -e [tybaʁ, -aʁd] **1** *adj* **être tubard** to have TB
2 *nm,f* TB sufferer

tuer [tɥe] *vt* **ça me tue!** it kills me!; **ça tue!** it's a killer!

tuile [tɥil] *nf (problème)* hassle; **il m'arrive une tuile** I'm in a bit of a mess

tune [tyn] = **thune**

turbin [tyʁbɛ̃] *nm* work □

turbine [tyʁbin] *nf* **turbine à chocolat**[!!] *Br* arsehole, dirtbox, *Am* asshole

turbiner [tyʁbine] *vi* **(a)** *(travailler)* to

slog *or* slave away (**b**) *(se livrer à la prostitution)* to turn tricks, *Br* to be on the game

turbo [tyrbo] *nm* **mettre le turbo** to get a move on, to get one's skates on, *Am* to get it in gear

turf [tyrf] *nm* (**a**) *(prostitution)* prostitution □; **faire le turf** to turn tricks, *Br* to be on the game (**b**) *(travail)* work □; *(lieu de travail)* workplace □

turista [turista] *nf* **la turista** Montezuma's revenge, Delhi belly, Spanish tummy

turlupiner [tyrlypine] *vt* to bother □, to bug

turlute [!] [tyrlyt] *nf* blow-job; **faire une turlute à qn** to give sb a blow-job, to go down on sb, to give sb head

turne [tyrn] *nf* room □

tuyau, -x [tɥijo] *nm* (**a**) *(conseil)* tip, hint, pointer; *(aux courses)* tip; *(renseignement)* tip-off; **un tuyau percé** a useless tip/tip-off (**b**) **la famille tuyau de poêle** = family whose members have an incestuous relationship

tuyauter [tɥijɔte] *vt (renseigner)* to tip off

tuyauterie [tɥijɔtri] *nf (organes de la digestion)* innards, guts; *(poumons)* lungs □

type [tip] *nm* guy, *Br* bloke; **un chic type** a nice guy, *Am* a mensch, a good Joe; **un sale type** a bad egg, a nasty piece of work; **un pauvre type** a sad individual

U, V

une [yn] *adj* **et d'une** for a start, for starters; **ne faire ni une ni deux** not to think twice; **il n'en loupe** *ou* **rate pas une** he's forever screwing up

unité [ynite] *nf (dix mille francs)* ten thousand francs □

urger [yrʒe] *vi* to be urgent □

usiner [yzine] *vi (travailler dur)* to slog *or* slave away, to be hard at it

vacciné, -e [vaksine] *adj* **être vacciné** to have learnt one's lesson; **être vacciné au vinaigre** to be in a foul mood; **être vacciné à la merde** [!] to be in a shit mood

vachard, -e [vaʃar, -ard] *adj* rotten, mean, nasty

vache [vaʃ] **1** (**a**) *adj (méchant)* rotten, mean, nasty; **ce qu'elle peut être vache!** she can be so bitchy *or* such a bitch!
(**b**) *(remarquable)* **il a un vache (de) coquard** he's got a hell of a black eye; **il a eu une vache d'idée** he had a hell of a good idea
2 *nf* (**a**) *(homme méchant)* Br swine, Am stinker; *(femme méchante)* bitch, Br cow; **elle lui a fait un coup en vache** she played a dirty trick on him, Br she did the dirty on him, Am she did him dirt; **elle a dit ça en vache** she just said that to be bitchy *or* a bitch
(**b**) **manger** *ou* **bouffer de la vache enragée** to have a hard *or* tough time of it
(**c**) **la vache!** *(de surprise)* God!, Br blimey!, Am gee (whiz)!; *(d'admiration)* wow!
(**d**) **mort aux vaches!** *(à bas la police)* kill the pigs!
▶ *see also* **peau, plancher**

vachement [vaʃmɑ̃] *adv* really □, Br dead, Am real; **on s'est vachement bien marrés** we had a really *or* Br dead *or* Am real good time; **il y a vachement de monde en ville** there are loads *or* tons of people in town

vacherie [vaʃri] *nf* (**a**) *(méchanceté)* meanness □, nastiness □ (**b**) *(action méchante)* dirty trick; **faire une vacherie à qn** to play a dirty trick on sb, Br to do the dirty on sb, Am to do sb dirt (**c**) *(parole blessante)* nasty remark □; **il m'a dit un tas de vacheries** he said loads of nasty things to me

vachté [vaʃte] *adv* really □, Br dead, Am real

va-comme-je-te-pousse [vakɔm- ʒtəpus] **à la va-comme-je-te-pousse** *adv* any old how

vadrouille [vadruj] *nf* wander; **être en vadrouille** to be wandering *or* roaming around; **il est rarement à son bureau, il est toujours en vadrouille** he's hardly ever at his desk, he's always wandering around somewhere

vadrouiller [vadruje] *vi* to wander *or* roam around

valda [valda] *nf (balle d'arme à feu)* bullet □, slug

This term comes from the name of a famous brand of throat pastilles, the shape of which is reminiscent of that of a bullet.

valdinguer [valdɛ̃ge] *vi* to go flying; **envoyer valdinguer qn/qch** to send sb/sth flying

valoche [valɔʃ] *nf* **(a)** *(valise)* suitcase □, case □ **(b) valoches** *(poches sous les yeux)* bags (under one's eyes)

valse [vals] *nf* **(a)** *(correction)* hammering, thrashing; **foutre une valse à qn** to give sb a hammering *or* a thrashing **(b)** *(cocktail)* = cocktail consisting of beer and mint-flavoured syrup

valser [valse] *vi* **(a)** *(perdre l'équilibre)* **il est allé valser contre la porte** he went flying into the door; **envoyer valser qch** to send sth flying; **envoyer valser qn** *(l'éconduire)* to send sb packing, to show sb the door; *(pousser)* to send sb flying **(b)** *(abandonner)* **j'ai envie de tout envoyer valser!** I feel like packing it all in *or Br* jacking it all in *or Am* chucking everything

valseur [valsœr] *nm (postérieur)* bum, *Am* fanny

valseuses [!] [valsøz] *nfpl (testicules)* balls, nuts, *Br* bollocks

This word became popular after the success of Bertrand Blier's 1972 film *Les Valseuses*, which told the story of two young dropouts, one of whom was played by Gérard Départdieu.

vanne [van] *nf* **(a)** *(remarque désobligeante)* snide remark □, dig, jibe, *Am* zinger; **envoyer des vannes à qn** to make digs at sb, *Am* to zing sb **(b)** *(plaisanterie)* joke □, crack

vanné, -e [vane] *adj* dead beat, bushed, *Br* knackered, *Am* pooped

vanner [vane] *vt (se moquer de)* to make digs at, *Am* to zing

vapes [vap] *nfpl* **être dans les vapes** to be out of it *or* in a daze *or Am* punchy; **tomber dans les vapes** to pass out □, to keel over

variétoche [varjetɔʃ] *nf* middle-of-the-road music

vaser [vaze] *v imp* to rain cats and dogs, *Br* to bucket down, to chuck it down

vaseux, -euse [vazø, -øz], **vasouillard, -e** [vazujar, -ard] *adj* **(a)** *(mauvais)* **plaisanterie/excuse vaseuse** feeble *or* pathetic joke/excuse; **raisonnement vaseux** woolly *or Br* dodgy reasoning **(b)** *(mal en point)* under the weather, out of sorts, *Br* off-colour, *Am* off-color

vautrer [votre] **se vautrer** *vpr (tomber)* to go flying

veau, -x [vo] *nm (véhicule poussif)* hairdrier on wheels

vécés [vese] *nmpl Br* loo, *Am* john

veilleuse [vɛjøz] *nf* **la mettre en veilleuse** to shut up, to put a sock in it

veinard, -e [vɛnar, -ard] **1** *adj* lucky □, *Br* jammy
2 *nm,f* lucky *or Br* jammy devil

veine [vɛn] *nf (chance)* luck □; **avoir de la veine** to be lucky □ *or Br* jammy
▸ *see also* **cocu**

vélo [velo] *nm* **avoir un petit vélo dans la tête** to be off one's rocker, to be not all there
▸ *see also* **grand-mère**

vénère [vener] **1** *adj (verlan énervé) Br* wound up, *Am* ticked off
2 *vt (verlan énerver)* **vénère qn** to bug sb, *Br* to wind sb up, *Am* to tick sb off

vent [vã] *nm* **(a)** **avoir du vent dans les voiles** to be three sheets to the wind **(b)** **du vent!** clear off!, buzz off!, get lost!

verni, -e [vɛrni] *adj (qui a de la chance)* lucky □, *Br* jammy

vérole [verɔl] *nf* **(a)** *(syphilis)* **la vérole** the pox **(b)** **quelle vérole!** what a pain!

vesse [vɛs] *nf* silent but deadly fart

veste [vɛst] *nf* **(se) prendre une veste** *(échouer)* to come unstuck; *(être rejeté)* to get turned down □, *Br* to get a knock-back

véto [veto] *nm (abbr vétérinaire)* vet □

veuve [vœv] *nf Hum* **la veuve Poignet** masturbation □; **fréquenter la veuve**

Poignet to bang *or Br* bash the bishop, to beat one's meat

viande [vjɑ̃d] *nf (corps humain)* **amène** *ou* **aboule ta viande!** get your butt *or* carcass over here!; **il y a de la viande soûle dans les rues** the streets are full of drunken bodies; **de la viande froide** *(un cadavre)* a stiff; *(des cadavres)* stiffs

viander [vjɑ̃de] **se viander** *vpr* to get smashed up

vicelard, -e [vislar, -ard] **1** *adj* **(a)** *(retors)* crafty, sneaky **(b)** *(lubrique)* kinky, *Br* pervy

2 *nm,f* **(a)** *(personne retorse)* crafty *or* sneaky person **(b)** *(personne lubrique)* perv; **un vieux vicelard** a dirty old man

vidé, -e [vide] *adj (épuisé)* wiped, dead beat, *Br* done in, *Am* pooped, out of gas

vider [vide] *vt* **(a)** *(expulser, licencier)* **vider qn** to throw sb out (on his ear), *Br* to turf sb out, *Am* to eighty-six sb **(b)** *(épuiser)* to drain, to wipe out
  ▶ see also **burettes, burnes**

videur [vidœr] *nm* bouncer

vieille [vjɛj] *nf (mère)* old lady, *Br* old dear

vieux [vjø] *nm* **(a)** *(père)* old man; **mes** *ou* **les vieux** *Br* my old dears, *Am* my rents **(b)** *(terme d'adresse)* pal, *Br* mate, *Am* buddy; **comment ça va, vieux?** how are you doing, pal *or Br* mate *or Am* buddy?

vinaigre [vinɛgr] *nm* **(a)** **faire vinaigre** to get a move on, to get one's skates on, *Am* to get it in gear **(b)** **tourner au vinaigre** *(discussion, relation)* to turn sour; *(opération, expédition)* to go wrong □, to screw up, *Br* to cock up
  ▶ see also **vacciné**

vinasse [vinas] *nf* cheap wine □, *Br* plonk

vingt-deux [vɛ̃ddø] *exclam (attention)* watch out!, watch it!

vioc [vjɔk] = **vioque**

violon [vjɔlɔ̃] *nm (prison)* slammer, clink, *Br* nick, *Am* pokey; **il s'est retrouvé au violon** he wound up in the slammer *or* clink *or Br* nick *or Am* pokey
  ▶ see also **pisser**

vioque [vjɔk] **1** *adj* old □

Verlan

"Verlan" is the most frequently used form of slang among young French people, particularly in the impoverished areas of large cities. It is formed by inverting the syllables of the word and making any spelling changes necessary to aid pronunciation. The word "verlan" is itself the inverted form of "l'envers" meaning "the other way round".

Some verlan terms have passed into spoken French generally and are used or understood by a great many speakers, eg "laisse béton" (laisse tomber) – popularized by the singer Renaud – "ripou" (pourri) and "meuf" (femme). It is, however, an extremely generative form of slang and any word can, in theory, be "verlanised". Some examples: "pétard" becomes "tarpé", "bizarre" becomes "zarbi", and "pute" becomes "teupu" which is then shortened to "teup".

Monosyllabic words can also be "verlanised", eg "chaud" becomes "auch"; an "e" is frequently added to aid pronunciation, eg "flic" becomes "keufli" which is shortened to "keuf"; "mère" becomes "reumè", which is in turn shortened to "reum". A term may be "verlanised" twice – the term "rebeu", for example, comes from the verlan for "Arabe" – "beur" – which is then "re-verlanised" to give "rebeu".

See also the panel at **l'argot des banlieues** on p. 133.

2 *nmf* old fossil, *Br* wrinkly, *Am* geezer; **mes** *ou* **les vioques** *Br* my old dears, *Am* my rents

virer [vire] **1** *vt (congédier)* to chuck out, to kick out

2 *vi (devenir)* **virer homo** to become gay; **virer voyou** to become *or* turn into a thug

▸ *see also* **cuti**

virolo [viʀɔlo] *nm* bend □ *(in road)*

vis [vis] *nf* **serrer la vis à qn** *(sévir)* to crack down on sb, to tighten the screws on sb; *(être strict)* to be hard on sb

viser [vize] *vt (regarder)* to check out, *Am* to scope

vissé, -e [vise] *adj* **être bien vissé** *(de bonne humeur)* to be in a good mood; **être mal vissé** *(de mauvaise humeur)* to be in a foul mood

vite [vit] *adv* **vite fait** quickly □; **boire un coup vite fait** to have a quick drink; **faire qch vite fait bien fait** to do sth in next to no time

voile [vwal] *nf* **être** *ou* **marcher à voile et à vapeur** to be AC/DC, to swing both ways

▸ *see also* **vent**

voir [vwaʀ] *vt* **(a) va te faire voir (chez les Grecs)!** [!] go to hell!, *Br* bugger off!, piss off!

(b) en voir (de toutes les couleurs) to go through hell, to have a hellish time of it; **en faire voir (de toutes les couleurs) à qn** to make sb's life a misery, to put sb through hell

(c) j'en ai jamais vu la couleur I haven't seen hide nor hair of it

vol [vɔl] *nm* *Hum* **elle a pas mal d'heures de vol** she's no spring chicken

volée [vɔle] *nf (correction)* thrashing, hammering; **flanquer une volée à qn** to thrash *or* hammer sb; **recevoir une volée** to get thrashed *or* hammered

voleuse [vɔløz] *nf* *Hum* **voleuse de santé** nympho, *Br* goer

vouloir [vulwaʀ] *vt* **(a) en vouloir** *(être ambitieux)* to want to make it **(b) je veux!** absolutely!, you bet!, *Br* too right!

voyage [vwajaʒ] *nm* **(a) être en voyage** *(être en prison)* to be inside *or* behind bars **(b)** *Ironic* **si il vient se plaindre à moi, il va pas être déçu du voyage!** if he comes complaining to me, he'll wish he hadn't bothered!

vu [vy] *adj* **vu?, c'est vu?** OK?, all right?, got it?

▸ *see also* **embrouiller**

vue [vy] *nf* **en mettre plein la vue à qn** to knock sb dead, to blow sb away

▸ *see also* **air**

vulgos [vylgos] *adj* vulgar □, coarse □

W, X, Y

WW [dubləvedubləve] *adj inv* brand new □

In France new cars are given temporary registration plates marked with the letters WW until full registration has taken place.

X [iks, ɛks] *nf (ecstasy)* X, E

yaourt [jaurt] *nm (charabia)* = type of gibberish which imitates English sounds without forming actual words, used by people who want to sound as if they are talking or singing in English
► *see also* **pédaler**

yeux [jø] *nmpl* **avoir les yeux qui se croisent les bras** to be cross-eyed □; **coûter les yeux de la tête** to cost a fortune *or* a bundle *or Br* a packet; **il n'a pas les yeux en face des trous** *(il est mal réveillé)* he hasn't come to yet, his brain isn't in gear yet; *(il n'est pas observateur)* he's as blind as a bat, he never sees what's going on right in front of him; **il a une petite amie/une bagnole, attention les yeux!** you should see his girlfriend/car!, his girlfriend/car is an absolute *Br* cracker *or Am* cracker-jack!; **il n'a pas froid aux yeux** he's got plenty of nerve, he's not backward

in coming forward; **il/ça me sort par les yeux** I can't stand *or Br* stick him/it
► *see also* **œil, merde, merlan, poche**

yo [jo] *exclam* yeah!

youde [jud] *Offensive* **1** *adj* Jewish □, yid
2 *nmf* yid, kike, *Am* hebe

yougo [jugo] *Offensive* **1** *adj (abbr* **yougoslave)** Yugoslav □
2 *nmf* **Yougo** *(abbr* **Yougoslave)** Yugoslav □

Depending on the context and the tone of voice used, this term may be either offensive or affectionately humorous. It is nonetheless inadvisable to use it unless one is quite sure of the reaction it will receive.

youpin, -e [jupɛ̃, -in] *Offensive* **1** *adj* Jewish □, yid
2 *nm,f* yid, kike, *Am* hebe

youtre [jutr] *Offensive* **1** *adj* Jewish □
2 *nmf* yid, kike, *Am* hebe

youve [juv], **youvoi** [juvwa] *nm (verlan* **voyou)** hood, hooligan, *Br* yob

yoyoter [jojote] *vi* **(a)** *(mal fonctionner)* to be on the blink, *Am* to be on the fritz **(b)** *(déraisonner)* to have a screw *or Br* a slate loose, to be off one's trolley

zapper [zape] **1** vt (supprimer) to scrap, to scratch

2 vi (changer de chaîne) to channel-surf, to channel-hop

zappette [zapɛt] nf remote control▫, zapper

zarbi [zarbi] adj (verlan **bizarre**) strange▫, weird▫, odd▫

zarma [zarma] exclam wow!, God!, Br blimey!, Am gee (whiz)!

zeph [zɛf] nm (abbr **zéphyr**) wind▫

zéro [zero] **1** nm (**a**) (individu nul) non-entity, nobody, zero (**b**) **les avoir à zéro** to be scared stiff or witless

2 adv **il est bien gentil, mais pour le travail, zéro!** he's nice enough, but when it comes to work he's a dead loss
▶ see also **boule, trouillomètre**

zgueg ⚠ [zgɛg] nm dick, willy, Am peter

zicmu [zikmy] nf (verlan **musique**) music▫, sounds, tunes

zieuter [zjøte] vt to check out, to eyeball, Am to scope

zig [zig] nm guy, Br bloke

zigomar [zigɔmar], **zigoto** [zigɔto] nm crackpot, crank, Am kook; **faire le zigoto** to act the fool, to clown around

zigouigoui [zigwigwi] nm Hum (**a**) (pénis) willy, Am peter (**b**) (sexe de la femme) pussy, Br fanny (**c**) (objet) thingy, whatsit

zigouiller [ziguje] vt to bump off, to liquidate, to ice

zigue [zig] = **zig**

zig-zig [zigzig] nm **faire zig-zig** to have a bit of nookie or Br rumpy-pumpy

zinc [zɛ̃k] nm (**a**) (comptoir de café) bar▫ (**b**) (avion) plane

zinzin [zɛ̃zɛ̃] adj loopy, Br hatstand, Am loony-tunes

zizi [zizi] nm (**a**) (pénis) willy, Am peter (**b**) (sexe de la femme) pussy, Br fanny

zizique [zizik] nf music▫, sounds, tunes

zob ⚠ [zɔb] nm dick, knob

zomblou [zɔ̃blu] nm (verlan **blouson**) jacket▫

zonard, -e [zonar, -ard] nm,f (marginal) dropout

zone [zon] **1** adj (sans intérêt, de mauvaise qualité) crap, lousy

2 nf (**a**) **la zone** (banlieue misérable) slum area▫, rough area▫; (endroit pauvre) dump, hole, dive; (endroit sale) tip, pigsty, bombsite (**b**) **c'est la zone!** it sucks!, it's the pits!, Am it bites!

zoner [zone] **1** vi (**a**) (traîner) to hang around, to bum around (**b**) (faire) **qu'est-ce que tu zones?** what are you up to?

2 se zoner vpr to hit the sack or the hay or Am the rack

zonga [zɔ̃ga] nm (verlan **gazon**) (marijuana) grass, weed, herb

zonzon [zɔ̃zɔ̃] nf slammer, clink, Br nick, Am pen

zoulou [zulu] nm (jeune noir) = young black man

zyeuter [zjøte] = **zieuter**